PENAL CODE

2002
CALIFORNIA
ABRIDGED
EDITION

LawTech Publishing Co., Ltd.

ABOUT THIS BOOK

This book consists primarily of the enforcement statutes from the 2002 Penal Code and an appendix of related penal provisions from other California Codes.

General and permanent laws are enacted currently in California as additions to or amendments of the Codes. The code section numbers, as well as Title, Division, Part, Chapter, and Article headings, where appropriate, are included in the laws as enacted. However, section titles for LawTech's Codes are prepared by the LawTech editorial staff.

LEGEND

Section Numbers: Section numbers appear in **bold** type at the left margin on the line directly above the beginning of the text of each section. **Section Titles:** Section titles appear in **bold** type on the same line as Section Numbers. **Amended Sections:** Text added to sections by 2002 Legislation is <u>underlined</u>. Text deleted from sections by 2002 Legislation appears as three (3) asterisks ***. **Repealed or Renumbered Sections:** Sections repealed or renumbered by 2002 Legislation are represented by the section number, title and the word "Repealed"or "Renumbered"and the new section number. Sometimes the Legislature repeals a section and then adds it back in the same legislative session. The section they add back is typically the same subject matter, but with some changes. In these cases, the section has basically been amended. Therefore, we show the section with asterisks and underlining (as we do other amended sections) as a matter of convenience for the reader. If a section has been repealed and then added back as an entirely new subject , it will be shown as a newly added section... without underlining. **Legislative Histories:** Each section that has been affected by legislation is followed by the last year that it was affected, and the type of action that affected that section. For example: *(AM '01)*. **Table of Sections Affected:** A table of sections affected by 2002 Legislation follows this page.

Legal Advice

The publisher is not engaged in the business of providing legal advice or interpretations of law. For legal advice or interpretations of law, we recommend contacting a licensed law practitioner.

Section Titles, Table of Contents, Index, and Cover Design:
Copyright © 2002 by *LawTech Publishing Co., Ltd.*
QWIK-CODE is a trademark of *LawTech Publishing Co., Ltd.*

Comments and suggestions are welcome.

LawTech Publishing Co., Ltd.
1060 Calle Cordillera, Ste. 105
San Clemente, CA 92673
(949) 498-4815
Fax: (949) 498-4858
Web site: www.lawtech.cc

FREE Emergency Legislation Notification: If you wish to receive free information regarding emergency legislation pertaining to this book, call or write LawTech and indicate the title of your book, and that you wish to be added to the "emergency legislation"notification list. Emergency legislation is that which, due to the urgency thereof, becomes operative immediately instead of the following year.
[NOTE: Emergency Legislative Updates are only for titles that contain the current year's date.]

408 Pgs.

ISBN: 1-930466-35-8

3

TABLE OF CONTENTS
CALIFORNIA PENAL CODE

SELECTED PENAL PROVISIONS
FROM OTHER CALIFORNIA CODES

PRELIMINARY PROVISIONS
PERSONS RESPONSIBLE FOR CRIME
PARTIES TO CRIME

15. Definition of Crime or Public Offense

A crime or public offense is an act committed or omitted in violation of a law forbidding or commanding it, and to which is annexed, upon conviction, either of the following punishments:

1. Death;
2. Imprisonment;
3. Fine;
4. Removal from office; or,
5. Disqualification to hold and enjoy any office of honor, trust or profit in this State.

16. Kinds and Degrees of Crime

Crimes and public offenses include:

1. Felonies;
2. Misdemeanors; and
3. Infractions.

17. Felony and Misdemeanor Defined

(a) A felony is a crime which is punishable with death or by imprisonment in the state prison. Every other crime or public offense is a misdemeanor except those offenses that are classified as infractions.

(b) When a crime is punishable, in the discretion of the court, by imprisonment in the state prison or by fine or imprisonment in the county jail, it is a misdemeanor for all purposes under the following circumstances:

(1) After a judgment imposing a punishment other than imprisonment in the state prison.

(2) When the court, upon committing the defendant to the Youth Authority, designates the offense to be a misdemeanor.

(3) When the court grants probation to a defendant without imposition of sentence and at the time of granting probation, or on application of the defendant or probation officer thereafter, the court declares the offense to be a misdemeanor.

(4) When the prosecuting attorney files in a court having jurisdiction over misdemeanor offenses a complaint specifying that the offense is a misdemeanor, unless the defendant at the time of his or her arraignment or plea objects to the offense being made a misdemeanor, in which event the complaint shall be amended to charge the felony and the case shall proceed on the felony complaint.

(5) When, at or before the preliminary examination or prior to filing an order pursuant to Section 872, the magistrate determines that the offense is a misdemeanor, in which event the case shall proceed as if the defendant had been arraigned on a misdemeanor complaint.

(c) When a defendant is committed to the Youth Authority for a crime punishable, in the discretion of the court, by imprisonment in the state prison or by fine or imprisonment in the county jail, the offense shall, upon the discharge of the defendant from the Youth Authority, thereafter be deemed a misdemeanor for all purposes.

(d) A violation of any code section listed in Section 19.8 is an infraction subject to the procedures described in Sections 19.6 and 19.7 when:

(1) The prosecutor files a complaint charging the offense as an infraction unless the defendant, at the time he or she is arraigned, after being informed of his or her rights, elects to have the case proceed as a misdemeanor, or;

(2) The court, with the consent of the defendant, determines that the offense is an infraction in which event the case shall proceed as if the defendant had been arraigned on an infraction complaint.

(e) Nothing in this section authorizes a judge to relieve a defendant of the duty to register as a sex offender pursuant to Section 290 if the defendant is charged with an offense for which registration as a sex offender is required pursuant to Section 290, and for which the trier of fact has found the defendant guilty. *(AM '98)*

18. Punishment for Felony

Except in cases where a different punishment is prescribed by any law of this state, every offense declared to be a felony, or to be punishable by imprisonment in a state prison, is punishable by imprisonment in any of the state prisons for 16 months, or two or three years; provided, however, every offense which is prescribed by any law of the state to be a felony punishable by imprisonment in any of the state prisons or by a fine, but without an alternate sentence to the county jail, may be punishable by imprisonment in the county jail not exceeding one year or by a fine, or by both.

19. Punishment for Misdemeanor

Except in cases where a different punishment is prescribed by any law of this state, every offense declared to be a misdemeanor is punishable by imprisonment in the county jail not exceeding six months, or by fine not exceeding one thousand dollars ($1,000), or by both.

19.2. Confinement in County Jail Not to Exceed One Year

In no case shall any person sentenced to confinement in a county or city jail, or in a county or joint county penal farm, road camp, work camp, or other county adult detention facility, or committed to the sheriff for placement in any county adult detention facility, on conviction of a misdemeanor, or as a condition of probation upon conviction of either a felony or a misdemeanor, or upon commitment for civil contempt, or upon default in the payment of a fine upon conviction of either a felony or a misdemeanor, or for any reason except upon conviction of more than one offense when consecutive sentences have been imposed, be committed for a period in excess of one year; provided, however, that the time allowed on parole shall not be considered as a part of the period of confinement.

19.4. Public Offense With No Prescribed Penalty is Misdemeanor

When an act or omission is declared by a statute to be a public offense and no penalty for the offense is prescribed in any statute, the act or omission is punishable as a misdemeanor.

19.6. Infractions Not Punishable by Imprisonment

An infraction is not punishable by imprisonment. A person charged with an infraction shall not be entitled to a trial by . A person charged with an infraction shall not be entitled to have the public defender or other counsel appointed at public expense to represent him or her unless he or she is arrested and not released on his or her written promise to appear, his or her own recognizance, or a deposit of bail.

19.7. Application of Misdemeanor Laws to Infractions

Except as otherwise provided by law, all provisions of law relating to misdemeanors shall apply to infractions including, but not limited to, powers of peace officers, jurisdiction of courts, periods for commencing action and for bringing a case to trial and burden of proof.

19.8. Offenses Subject to Provisions of Penal Code Section 17

The following offenses are subject to subdivision (d) of Section 17: Sections 193.8, 330, 415, 485, 555, 652, and 853.7, of this code; subdivision (m) of Section 602 of this code; subdivision (b) of Section 25658 and Sections 21672, 25658.5, 25661, and 25662 of the Business and Professions Code; Section 27204 of the Government Code; subdivision (c) of Section 23109 and Sections 12500, 14601.1, 27150.1, 40508, and 42005 of the Vehicle Code, and any other offense which the Legislature makes subject to subdivision (d) of Section 17. Except where a lesser maximum fine is expressly provided for violation of any of those sections, any violation which is an infraction is punishable by a fine not exceeding two hundred fifty dollars ($250).

Except for the violations enumerated in subdivision (d) of Section 13202.5 of the Vehicle Code, and Section 14601.1 of the Vehicle Code based upon failure to appear, a conviction for any offense made an infraction under subdivision (d) of Section 17 is not grounds for the suspension, revocation, or denial of any license, or for the revocation of probation or parole of the person convicted.

This section shall remain in effect only until January 1, 2005, and as of that date is repealed, unless a later enacted statute, that is enacted before January 1, 2005, deletes or extends that date.

19.8. Offenses Subject to Provisions of Penal Code Section 17 [Effective 1-1-2005]

The following offenses are subject to subdivision (d) of Section 17: Sections 193.8, 330, 415, 485, 555, and 853.7, of this code; subdivision (m) of Section 602 of this code; subdivision (b) of Section 25658 and Sections 21672, 25658.5, 25661, and 25662 of the Business and Professions Code; Section 27204 of the Government Code; subdivision (c) of Section 23109 and Sections 12500, 14601.1, 27150.1, 40508, and 42005 of the Vehicle Code, and any other offense which the Legislature makes subject to subdivision (d) of Section 17. Except where a lesser maximum fine is expressly provided for violation of any of those sections, any violation which is an infraction is punishable by a fine not exceeding two hundred fifty dollars ($250).

Except for the violations enumerated in subdivision (d) of Section 13202.5 of the Vehicle Code, and Section 14601.1 of the Vehicle Code based upon failure to appear, a conviction for any offense made an infraction under subdivision (d) of Section 17 is not grounds for the suspension, revocation, or denial of any license, or for the revocation of probation or parole of the person convicted.

This section shall become operative on January 1, 2005.

20. Unity of Act and Intent or Negligence

In every crime or public offense there must exist a union, or joint operation of act and intent, or criminal negligence.

21. Intent Manifested by Circumstances

(a) The intent or intention is manifested by the circumstances connected with the offense.

(b) In the guilt phase of a criminal action or a juvenile adjudication hearing, evidence that the accused lacked the capacity or ability to control his conduct for any reason shall not be admissible on the issue of whether the accused actually had any mental state with respect to the commission of any crime. This subdivision is not applicable to Section 26.

21a. Elements of Attempt

An attempt to commit a crime consists of two elements: a specific intent to commit the crime, and a direct but ineffectual act done toward its commission.

30. Parties to Crimes Classified

The parties to crimes are classified as:

1. Principals; and,
2. Accessories.

31. Principals

All persons concerned in the commission of a crime, whether it be felony or misdemeanor, and whether they directly commit the act constituting the offense, or aid and abet in its commission, or not being present, have advised and encouraged its commission, and all persons counseling, advising or encouraging children under the age of fourteen years, lunatics or idiots, to commit any crime, or who, by fraud, contrivance or force, occasion the drunkenness of another for the purpose of causing him to commit any crime, or who, by threats, menaces, command or coercion, compel another to commit any crime, are principals in any crime so committed.

32. Accessories

Every person who, after a felony has been committed, harbors, conceals or aids a principal in such felony, with the intent that said principal may avoid or escape from arrest, trial, conviction or punishment, having knowledge that said principal has committed such felony or has been charged with such felony or convicted thereof, is an accessory to such felony.

33. Punishment of Accessories

Except in cases where a different punishment is prescribed, an accessory is punishable by a fine not exceeding five thousand dollars ($5,000), or by imprisonment in the state prison, or in a county jail not exceeding one year, or by both such fine and imprisonment.

CRIMES BY OR AGAINST THE EXECUTIVE POWER

67. Bribing Executive Officer

Every person who gives or offers any bribe to any executive officer in this state, with intent to influence him in respect to any act, decision, vote, opinion, or other proceeding as such officer is punishable by imprisonment in the state prison for two, three or four years, and is disqualified from holding any office in this state.

67.5. Bribing Ministerial Officer

(a) Every person who gives or offers as a bribe to any ministerial officer, employee, or appointee of the State of California, county or city therein, or political subdivision thereof, any thing the theft of which would he petty theft is guilty of a misdemeanor.

(b) If the theft of the thing given or offered would be grand theft the offense is a felony.

68. Officer Asking or Receiving Bribes

(a) Every executive or ministerial officer, employee or appointee of the State of California, county or city therein or political subdivision thereof, who asks, receives, or agrees to receive, any bribe, upon any agreement or understanding that his or her vote, opinion, or action upon any matter then pending, or *** that may be brought before him or her in his or her official capacity, shall be influenced thereby, is punishable by imprisonment in the state prison for two, three ***, or four years and, in cases where no bribe has been actually received, by a restitution fine of not less than two thousand dollars ($2,000) or not more than ten thousand dollars ($10,000) or, in cases where a bribe was actually received, by a restitution fine of at least the actual amount of the bribe received or two thousand dollars ($2,000), whichever is greater, or any larger amount of not more than double the amount of any bribe received or ten thousand dollars ($10,000), whichever is greater, and, in addition thereto, forfeits his or her office, employment, or appointment, and is forever disqualified from holding any office ***, employment, or appointment, in this state.

(b) In imposing a restitution fine under this section, the court shall consider the defendant's ability to pay the fine. *(AM '01)*

69. Resisting or Deterring Officer

Every person who attempts, by means of any threat or violence, to deter or prevent an executive officer from performing any duty imposed upon such officer by law, or who knowingly resists, by the use of force or violence, such officer, in the performance of his duty, is punishable by a fine not exceeding ten thousand dollars ($10,000), or by imprisonment in the state prison, or in a county jail not exceeding one year, or by both such fine and imprisonment.

71. Threat of Injury Made to Officer in Performance of His Duties

Every person who, with intent to cause, attempts to cause, or causes, any officer or employee of any public or private educational institution or any public officer or employee to do, or refrain from doing, any act in the performance of his duties, by means of a threat, directly communicated to such person, to inflict an unlawful injury upon any person or property, and it reasonably appears to the recipient of the threat that such threat could be carried out, is guilty of a public offense punishable as follows:

(1) Upon a first conviction, such person is punishable by a fine not exceeding ten thousand dollars ($10,000), or by imprisonment in the state prison, or in a county jail not exceeding one year, or by both such fine and imprisonment.

(2) If such person has been previously convicted of a violation of this section, such previous conviction shall be charged in the accusatory pleading, and if such previous conviction is found to be true by the jury, upon a jury trial, or by the court, upon a court trial, or is admitted by the defendant, he is punishable by imprisonment in the state prison.

As used in this section, "directly communicated"includes, but is not limited to, a communication to the recipient of the threat by telephone, telegraph, or letter.

76. Threaten Life of Government Official

(a) Every person who knowingly and willingly threatens the life of, or threatens serious bodily harm to, any elected public official, county public defender, county clerk, exempt appointee of the Governor, judge, or Deputy Commissioner of the Board of Prison Terms, or the staff or immediate family of any elected public official, county public defender, county clerk, exempt appointee of the Governor, judge, or Deputy Commissioner of the Board of Prison Terms, with the specific intent that the statement is to be taken as a threat, and the apparent ability to carry out that threat by any means, is guilty of a public offense, punishable as follows:

(1) Upon a first conviction, the offense is punishable by a fine not exceeding five thousand dollars ($5,000), or by imprisonment in the state prison, or in a county jail not exceeding one year, or by both that fine and imprisonment.

(2) If the person has been convicted previously of violating this section, the previous conviction shall be charged in the accusatory pleading, and if the previous conviction is found to be true by the jury upon a jury trial, or by the court upon a court trial, or is admitted by the defendant, the offense is punishable by imprisonment in the state prison.

(b) Any law enforcement agency that has knowledge of a violation of this section involving a constitutional officer of the state, a Member of the Legislature, or a member of the judiciary shall immediately report that information to the Department of the California Highway Patrol.

(c) For purposes of this section, the following definitions shall apply:

(1) "Apparent ability to carry out that threat"includes the ability to fulfill the threat at some future date when the person making the threat is an incarcerated prisoner with a stated release date.

(2) "Serious bodily harm"includes serious physical injury or serious traumatic condition.

(3) "Immediate family"means a spouse, parent, or child, or anyone who has regularly resided in the household for the past six months.

(4) "Staff of a judge"means court officers and employees, including commissioners, referees, and retired judges sitting on assignment.

(5) "Threat"means a verbal or written threat or a threat implied by a pattern of conduct or a combination of verbal or written statements and conduct made with the intent and the apparent ability to carry out the threat so as to cause the person who is the target of the threat to reasonably fear for his or her safety or the safety of his or her immediate family.

(d) As for threats against staff, the threat must relate directly to the official duties of the staff of the elected public official, county public defender, county clerk, exempt appointee of the Governor, judge, or Deputy Commissioner of the Board of Prison Terms in order to constitute a public offense under this section.

(e) A threat must relate directly to the official duties of a Deputy Commissioner of the Board of Prison Terms in order to constitute a public offense under this section. *(AM '98, '00)*

CRIMES AGAINST PUBLIC JUSTICE

95. Influencing Jurors, Referees or Umpires

Every person who corruptly attempts to influence a juror, or any person summoned or drawn as a juror, or chosen as an arbitrator, or umpire, or appointed a referee, in respect to his verdict in, or decision of any cause, or proceeding, pending, or about to be brought before him or her is punishable by fine not exceeding ten thousand dollars ($10,000) or by imprisonment in the state prison, if it is by means of any of the following:

(a) Any communication, oral or written, had with him except in the regular course of proceedings;

(b) Any book, paper, or instrument exhibited, otherwise than in the regular course of proceedings;

(c) Any threat, intimidation, persuasion, or entreaty; or,

(d) Any promise, or assurance of any pecuniary or other advantage.

95.1. Threatening Jurors Following Verdict in Criminal Proceeding

Every person who threatens a juror with respect to a criminal proceeding in which a verdict has been rendered and who has the intent and apparent ability to carry out the threat so as to cause the target of the threat to reasonably fear for his or her safety or the safety of his or her immediate family, is guilty of a public offense and shall be punished by imprisonment in a county jail for not more than one year, or by imprisonment in the state prison, or by a fine not exceeding ten thousand dollars ($10,000), or both that imprisonment and fine.

102. Retaking of Property From Officer

Every person who willfully injures or destroys, or takes or attempts to take, or assists any person in taking or attempting to take, from the custody of any officer or person, any personal property which such officer or person has in charge under any process of law, is guilty of a misdemeanor.

107. Escape From Hospital or Reformatory

Every prisoner charged with or convicted of a felony who is an inmate of any public training school or reformatory or county hospital who escapes or attempts to escape from such public training school or reformatory or county hospital is guilty of a felony and is punishable by imprisonment in the state prison, or by a fine not exceeding ten thousand dollars ($10,000), or by both such fine and imprisonment.

109. Assisting Escape From Reformatory

Any person who willfully assists any inmate of any public training school or reformatory to escape, or in an attempt to escape from such public training school or reformatory is punishable by imprisonment in the state prison, and fine not exceeding ten thousand dollars ($10,000).

110. Supplying Material to Aid Escape From Reformatory

Every person who carries or sends into a public training school, or reformatory, anything useful to aid a prisoner or inmate in making his escape, with intent thereby to facilitate the escape of any prisoner or inmate confined therein, is guilty of a felony.

112. Mfg. or Sell False Government Document to Conceal Citizenship, etc. [Renumbered from §113]

(a) Any person who manufactures, distributes or sells false documents or sells any false government document with the intent to conceal the true citizenship or resident alien status of another person is guilty of a felony, misdemeanor and shall be punished by imprisonment in the state prison for five years or by a fine of seventy-five thousand dollars ($75,000). a county jail for one year. Every false government document that is manufactured or sold in violation of this section may be charged and prosecuted as a separate and distinct violation, and consecutive sentences may be imposed for each violation.

(b) A prosecuting attorney shall have discretion to charge a defendant with a violation of this section or any other law that applies.

(c) As used in this section, "government document" means any document issued by the United States government or any state or local government, including, but not limited to, any passport, immigration visa, employment authorization card, birth certificate, driver's license, identification card, or social security card. *(AM/RN '01)*

113. Mfg. or Sell False Government Document to Conceal Citizenship, etc.

(a) Any person who manufactures or sells any false government document with the intent to conceal the true citizenship or resident alien status of another person is guilty of a misdemeanor and shall be punished by imprisonment in a county jail for one year. Every false government document that is manufactured or sold in violation of this section may be charged and prosecuted as a separate and distinct violation, and consecutive sentences may be imposed for each violation.

(b) A prosecuting attorney shall have discretion to charge a defendant with a violation of this section or any other law that applies.

(c) As used in this section, "government document" means any document issued by the United States government or any state or local government, including, but not limited to, any passport, immigration visa, employment authorization card, birth certificate, driver's license, identification card, or social security card.

[Editor's Note: §113 unaffected by legislation and remains operative.]

114. Use of False Citizenship or Resident Alien Documents

Any person who uses false documents to conceal his or her true citizenship or resident alien status is guilty of a felony, and shall be punished by imprisonment in the state prison for five years or by a fine of twenty-five thousand dollars ($25,000).

115. Attempt to Record False or Forged Instrument

(a) Every person who knowingly procures or offers any false or forged instrument to be filed, registered, or recorded in any public office within this state, which instrument, if genuine, might be filed, registered, or recorded under any law of this state or of the United States, is guilty of a felony.

(b) Each instrument which is procured or offered to be filed, registered, or recorded in violation of subdivision (a) shall constitute a separate violation of this section.

(c) Except in unusual cases where the interests of justice would best be served if probation is granted, probation shall not be granted to, nor shall the execution or imposition of sentence be suspended for, any of the following persons:

(1) Any person with a prior conviction under this section who is again convicted of a violation of this section in a separate proceeding.

(2) Any person who is convicted of more than one violation of this section in a single proceeding, with intent to defraud another, and where the violations resulted in a cumulative financial loss exceeding one hundred thousand dollars ($100,000).

(d) For purposes of prosecution under this section, each act of procurement or of offering a false or forged instrument to be filed, registered, or recorded shall be considered a separately punishable offense.

118. Perjury

(a) Every person who, having taken an oath that he or she will testify, declare, depose, or certify truly before any competent tribunal, officer, or person, in any of the cases in which the oath may by law of the State of California be administered, willfully and contrary to the oath, states as true any material matter which he or she knows to be false, and every person who testifies, declares, deposes, or certifies under penalty of perjury in any of the cases in which the testimony, declarations, depositions, or certification is permitted by law of the State of California under penalty of perjury and willfully states as true any material matter which he or she knows to be false, is guilty of perjury.

This subdivision is applicable whether the statement, or the testimony, declaration, deposition, or certification is made or subscribed within or without the State of California.

(b) No person shall be convicted of perjury where proof of falsity rests solely upon contradiction by testimony of a single person other than the defendant. Proof of falsity may be established by direct or indirect evidence.

118a. False Affidavit

Any person who, in any affidavit taken before any person authorized to administer oaths, swears, affirms, declares, deposes, or certifies that he will testify, declare, depose, or certify before any competent tribunal, officer, or person, in any case then pending or thereafter to be instituted, in any particular manner, or to any particular fact, and in such affidavit willfully and contrary to such oath states as true any material matter which he knows to be false, is guilty of perjury. In any prosecution under this section, the subsequent testimony of such person, in any action involving the matters in such affidavit contained, which is contrary to any of the matters in such affidavit contained, shall be prima facie evidence that the matters in such affidavit were false.

118.1. False Report by Peace Officer

Every peace officer who files any report with the agency which employs him or her regarding the commission of any crime or any investigation of any crime, if he or she knowingly and intentionally makes any statement regarding any material matter in the report which the officer knows to be false, whether or not the statement is certified or otherwise expressly reported as true, is guilty of filing a false report punishable by imprisonment in the county jail for up to one year, or in the state prison for one, two, or three years. This section shall not apply to the contents of any statement which the peace officer attributes in the report to any other person.

132.5. Crime Witness Selling Information

(a) The Legislature supports and affirms the constitutional right of every person to communicate on any subject. This section is intended to preserve the right of every accused person to a fair trial, the right of the people to due process of law, and the integrity of judicial proceedings. This section is not intended to prevent any person from disseminating any information or opinion.

The Legislature hereby finds and declares that the disclosure for valuable consideration of information relating to crimes by prospective witnesses can cause the loss of credible evidence in criminal trials and threatens to erode the reliability of verdicts.

The Legislature further finds and declares that the disclosure for valuable consideration of information relating to crimes by prospective witnesses creates an appearance of injustice that is destructive of public confidence.

(b) A person who is a witness to an event or occurrence that he or she knows is a crime or who has personal knowledge of facts that he or she knows or reasonably should know may require that person to be called as a witness in a criminal prosecution shall not accept or receive, directly or indirectly, any money or its equivalent in consideration for providing information obtained as result of witnessing the event or occurrence or having personal knowledge of the facts.

(c) Any person who is a witness to an event or occurrence that he or she reasonably should know is a crime shall not accept or receive, directly or indirectly, any money or its equivalent in consideration for providing information obtained as a result of his or her witnessing the event or occurrence.

(d) The Attorney General or the district attorney of the county in which an alleged violation of subdivision (c) occurs may institute a civil proceeding. Where a final judgment is rendered in the civil proceeding, the defendant shall be punished for the violation of subdivision (c) by a fine equal to 150 percent of the amount received or contracted for by the person.

(e) A violation of subdivision (b) is a misdemeanor punishable by imprisonment for a term not exceeding six months in a county jail, a fine not exceeding three times the amount of compensation requested, accepted, or received, or both the imprisonment and fine.

(f) This section does not apply if more than one year has elapsed from the date of any criminal act related to the information that is provided under subdivision (b) or (c) unless prosecution has commenced for that criminal act. If prosecution has commenced, this section shall remain applicable until the final judgment in the action.

(g) This section does not apply to any of the following circumstances:

(1) Lawful compensation paid to expert witnesses, investigators, employees, or agents by a prosecutor, law enforcement agency, or an attorney employed to represent a person in a criminal matter.

(2) Lawful compensation provided to an informant by a prosecutor or law enforcement agency.

(3) Compensation paid to a publisher, editor, reporter, writer, or other person connected with or employed by a newspaper, magazine, or other publication or a television or radio news reporter or other person connected with a television or radio station, for disclosing information obtained in the ordinary course of business.

(4) Statutorily authorized rewards offered by governmental agencies or private reward programs offered by victims of crimes for information leading to the arrest and conviction of specified offenders.

(h) For purposes of this section, "information" does not include a photograph, videotape, audiotape, or any other direct recording of an event or occurrence.

(i) For purposes of this section, "victims of crimes" shall be construed in a manner consistent with Section 28 of Article I of the California Constitution, and shall include victims, as defined in subdivision (3) of Section 136.

135. Destroying or Concealing Documentary Evidence

Every person who, knowing that any book, paper, record, instrument in writing, or other matter or thing, is about to be produced in evidence upon any trial, inquiry, or investigation whatever, authorized by law, willfully destroys or conceals the same, with intent thereby to prevent it from being produced, is guilty of a misdemeanor.

136.1. Preventing or Dissuading Victim or Witness From Attending or Giving Testimony

(a) Except as provided in subdivision (c), any person who does any of the following is guilty of a public offense and shall be punished by imprisonment in a county jail for not more than one year or in the state prison:

(1) Knowingly and maliciously prevents or dissuades any witness or victim from attending or giving testimony at any trial, proceeding, or inquiry authorized by law.

(2) Knowingly and maliciously attempts to prevent or dissuade any witness or victim from attending or giving testimony at any trial, proceeding, or inquiry authorized by law.

(3) For purposes of this section, evidence that the defendant was a family member who interceded in an effort to protect the witness or victim shall create a presumption that the act was without malice.

(b) Except as provided in subdivision (c), every person who attempts to prevent or dissuade another person who has been the victim of a crime or who is witness to a crime from doing any of the following is guilty of a public offense and shall be punished by imprisonment in a county jail for not more than one year or in the state prison:

(1) Making any report of that victimization to any peace officer or state or local law enforcement officer or probation or parole or correctional officer or prosecuting agency or to any judge.

(2) Causing a complaint, indictment, information, probation or parole violation to be sought and prosecuted, and assisting in the prosecution thereof.

(3) Arresting or causing or seeking the arrest of any person in connection with that victimization.

(c) Every person doing any of the acts described in subdivision (a) or (b) knowingly and maliciously under any one or more of the following circumstances, is guilty of a felony punishable by imprisonment in the state prison for two, three, or four years under any of the following circumstances:

(1) Where the act is accompanied by force or by an express or implied threat of force or violence, upon a witness or victim or any third person or the property of any victim, witness, or any third person.

(2) Where the act is in furtherance of a conspiracy.

(3) Where the act is committed by any person who has been convicted of any violation of this section, any predecessor law hereto or any federal statute or statute of any other state which, if the act prosecuted was committed in this state, would be a violation of this section.

(4) Where the act is committed by any person for pecuniary gain or for any other consideration acting upon the request of any other person. All parties to such a transaction are guilty of a felony.

(d) Every person attempting the commission of any act described in subdivisions (a), (b), and (c) is guilty of the offense attempted without regard to success or failure of the attempt. The fact that no person was injured physically, or in fact intimidated, shall be no defense against any prosecution under this section.

(e) Nothing in this section precludes the imposition of an enhancement for great bodily injury where the injury inflicted is significant or substantial.

(f) The use of force during the commission of any offense described in subdivision (c) shall be considered a circumstance in aggravation of the crime in imposing a term of imprisonment under subdivision (b) of Section 1170.

136.5. Carrying a Deadly Weapon to Prevent a Witness From Testifying

Any person who has upon his person a deadly weapon with the intent to use such weapon to commit a violation of Section 136.1 is guilty of an offense punishable by imprisonment in the county jail for not more than one year, or in the state prison.

137. Bribery of Witness to Induce False Testimony

(a) Every person who gives or offers, or promises to give, to any witness, person about to be called as a witness, or person about to give material information pertaining to a crime to a law enforcement official, any bribe, upon any understanding or agreement that the testimony of such witness or information given by such person shall be thereby influenced is guilty of a felony.

(b) Every person who attempts by force or threat of force or by the use of fraud to induce any person to give false testimony or withhold true testimony or to give false material information pertaining to a crime to, or withhold true material information pertaining to a crime from, a law enforcement official is guilty of a felony, punishable by imprisonment in the state prison for two, three, or four years.

As used in this subdivision, "threat of force" means a credible threat of unlawful injury to any person or damage to the property of another which is communicated to a person for the purpose of inducing him to give false testimony or withhold true testimony or to give false material information pertaining to a crime to, or to withhold true material information pertaining to a crime from, a law enforcement official.

(c) Every person who knowingly induces another person to give false testimony or withhold true testimony not privileged by law or to give false material information pertaining to a crime to, or to withhold true material information pertaining to a crime from, a law enforcement official is guilty of a misdemeanor.

(d) At the arraignment, on a showing of cause to believe this section may be violated, the court, on motion of a party, shall admonish the person who there is cause to believe may violate this section and shall announce the penalties and other provisions of this section.

(e) As used in this section "law enforcement official" includes any district attorney, deputy district attorney, city attorney, deputy city attorney, the Attorney General or any deputy attorney general, or any peace officer included in Chapter 4.5 (commencing with Section 830) of Title 3 of Part 2.

(f) The provisions of subdivision (c) shall not apply to an attorney advising a client or to a person advising a member of his or her family.

138. Witnesses: Bribing or Receiving Bribe Not to Attend Trial

(a) Every person who gives or offers or promises to give to any witness or person about to be called as a witness, any bribe upon any understanding or agreement that the person shall not attend upon any trial or other judicial proceeding, or every person who attempts by means of any offer of a bribe to dissuade any person from attending upon any trial or other judicial proceeding, is guilty of a felony.

(b) Every person who is a witness, or is about to be called as such, who receives, or offers to receive, any bribe, upon any understanding that his or her testimony shall be influenced thereby, or that he or she will absent himself or herself from the trial or proceeding upon which his or her testimony is required, is guilty of a felony.

139. Threatening Witnesses

(a) Except as provided in Sections 71 and 136.1, any person who has been convicted of any felony offense specified in Section 12021.1 who willfully and maliciously communicates to a witness to, or a victim of, the crime for which the person was convicted, a credible threat to use force or violence upon that person or that person's immediate family, shall be punished by imprisonment in the county jail not exceeding one year or by imprisonment in the state prison for two, three, or four years.

(b) Any person who is convicted of violating subdivision (a) who subsequently is convicted of making a credible threat, as defined in subdivision (c), which constitutes a threat against the life of, or a threat to cause great bodily injury to, a person described in subdivision (a), shall be sentenced to consecutive terms of imprisonment as prescribed in Section 1170.13.

(c) As used in this section, "a credible threat" is a threat made with the intent and the apparent ability to carry out the threat so as to cause the target of the threat to reasonably fear for his or her safety or the safety of his or her immediate family.

(d) The present incarceration of the person making the threat shall not be a bar to prosecution under this section.

(e) As used in this section, "malice,""witness,"and "victim"have the meanings given in Section 136.

140. Threat of Force or Violence Because of Assistance in Prosecution

(a) Except as provided in Section 139, every person who willfully uses force or threatens to use force or violence upon the person of a witness to, or a victim of, a crime or any other person, or to take, damage, or destroy any property of any witness, victim, or any other person, because the witness, victim, or other person has provided any assistance or information to a law enforcement officer, or to a public prosecutor in a criminal proceeding or juvenile court proceeding, shall be punished by imprisonment in the county jail not exceeding one year, or by imprisonment in the state prison for two, three, or four years.

(b) A person who is punished under another provision of law for an act described in subdivision (a) shall not receive an additional term of imprisonment under this section. *(AM '98)*

141. Tampering with Physical Evidence

(a) Except as provided in subdivision (b), any person who knowingly, willfully, and intentionally alters, modifies, plants, places, manufactures, conceals, or moves any physical matter, with specific intent that the action will result in a person being charged with a crime or with the specific intent that the physical matter will be wrongfully produced as genuine or true upon any trial, proceeding, or inquiry whatever, is guilty of a misdemeanor.

(b) Any peace officer who knowingly, willfully, and intentionally alters, modifies, plants, places, manufactures, conceals, or moves any physical matter, with specific intent that the action will result in a person being charged with a crime or with the specific intent that the physical matter will be wrongfully produced as genuine or true upon any trial, proceeding, or inquiry whatever, is guilty of a felony punishable by two, three, or five years in the state prison.

(c) Nothing in this section shall preclude prosecution under both this section and any other provision of law. *(AD '00)*

142. Officer Refusing to Receive or Arrest Criminal

(a) Any peace officer who has the authority to receive or arrest a person charged with a criminal offense and willfully refuses to receive or arrest such person shall be punished by a fine not exceeding ten thousand dollars ($10,000), or by imprisonment in the state prison, or in a county jail not exceeding one year, or by both such fine and imprisonment.

(b) Notwithstanding subdivision (a), the sheriff may determine whether any jail, institution, or facility under his direction shall be designated as a reception, holding, or confinement facility, or shall be used for several of such purposes, and may designate the class of prisoners for which such facility shall be used.

146. Officer Acting Without Regular Process or Lawful Authority

Every public officer, or person pretending to be a public officer, who, under the pretense or color of any process or other legal authority, does any of the following, without a regular process or other lawful authority, is guilty of a misdemeanor:

(a) Arrests any person or detains that person against his or her will.

(b) Seizes or levies upon any property.

(c) Dispossesses any one of any lands or tenements.

146a. Impersonate Officer and Commit Specified Crimes

Any person who falsely represents himself or herself to be a deputy or clerk in any state department and who, in that assumed character, does any of the following is guilty of a misdemeanor punishable by imprisonment in a county jail, not exceeding six months, or by a fine, not exceeding two thousand five hundred dollars ($2,500), or by both the fine and imprisonment:

(1) Arrests, detains, or threatens to arrest or detain any person.

(2) Otherwise intimidates any person.

(3) Searches any person, building, or other property of any person.

(4) Obtains money, or property, or other thing of value.

(b) Any person who falsely represents himself or herself to be a police officer, investigator, or inspector in any state department and who, in that assumed character, does any of the following shall be punished by imprisonment in a county jail not exceeding one year, by a fine not to exceed two thousand five hundred dollars ($2,500), or by both that fine and imprisonment, or by imprisonment in the state prison:

(1) Arrests, detains, or threatens to arrest or detain any person.

(2) Otherwise intimidates any person.

(3) Searches any person, building, or other property of any person.

(4) Obtains money, or property, or other thing of value.

146e. Disclosure of Residence Address or Telephone Number of Peace Officer or Relative

(a) Every person who maliciously, and with the intent to obstruct justice or the due administration of the laws, publishes, disseminates, or otherwise discloses the residence address or telephone number of any peace officer, nonsworn police dispatcher, or employee of a city police department or county sheriff's office, or that of the spouse or children of these persons, whether living with them or not, while designating the peace officer or nonsworn police dispatcher or relative of these persons as such, without the authorization of the employing agency, is guilty of a misdemeanor.

(b) A violation of subdivision (a) with regard to any peace officer, employee of a city police department or county sheriff's office, or the spouse or children of these persons that results in bodily injury to the peace officer, employee of the city police department or county sheriff's office, or the spouse or children of these persons is a felony.

147. Inhumane or Oppressive Treatment of Prisoner

Every officer who is guilty of willful inhumanity or oppression toward any prisoner under his care or in his custody, is punishable by fine not exceeding four thousand dollars ($4,000), and by removal from office.

148. Resisting or Obstructing Public Officer, Etc.; Removal of Officer's Firearm

(a)(1) Every person who willfully resists, delays, or obstructs any public officer, peace officer, or an emergency medical technician, as defined in Division 2.5 (commencing with Section 1797) of the Health and Safety Code, in the discharge or attempt to discharge any duty of his or her office or employment, when no other punishment is prescribed, shall be punished by a fine not exceeding one thousand dollars ($1,000), or by imprisonment in a county jail not to exceed one year, or by both that fine and imprisonment.

(2) Except as provided by subdivision (d) of Section 653t, every person who knowingly and maliciously interrupts, disrupts, impedes, or otherwise interferes with the transmission of a communication over a public safety radio frequency shall be punished by a fine not exceeding one thousand dollars ($1,000), imprisonment in a county jail not exceeding one year, or by both that fine and imprisonment.

(b) Every person who, during the commission of any offense described in subdivision (a), removes or takes any weapon, other than a firearm, from the person of, or immediate presence of, a public officer or peace officer shall be punished by imprisonment in a county jail not to exceed one year or in the state prison.

(c) Every person who, during the commission of any offense described in subdivision (a), removes or takes a firearm from the person of, or immediate presence of, a public officer or peace officer shall be punished by imprisonment in the state prison.

(d) Except as provided in subdivision (c) and notwithstanding subdivision (a) of Section 489, every person who removes or takes without intent to permanently deprive, or who attempts to remove or take a firearm from the person of, or immediate presence of, a public officer or peace officer, while the officer is engaged in the performance of his or her lawful duties, shall be punished by imprisonment in a county jail not to exceed one year or in the state prison.

In order to prove a violation of this subdivision, the prosecution shall establish that the defendant had the specific intent to remove or take the firearm by demonstrating that any of the following direct, but ineffectual, acts occurred:

(1) The officer's holster strap was unfastened by the defendant.

(2) The firearm was partially removed from the officer's holster by the defendant.

(3) The firearm safety was released by the defendant.

(4) An independent witness corroborates that the defendant stated that he or she intended to remove the firearm and the defendant actually touched the firearm.

(5) An independent witness corroborates that the defendant actually had his or her hand on the firearm and tried to take the firearm away from the officer who was holding it.

(6) The defendant's fingerprint was found on the firearm or holster.

(7) Physical evidence authenticated by a scientifically verifiable procedure established that the defendant touched the firearm.

(8) In the course of any struggle, the officer's firearm fell and the defendant attempted to pick it up.

(e) A person shall not be convicted of a violation of subdivision (a) in addition to a conviction of a violation of subdivision (b), (c), or (d) when the resistance, delay, or obstruction, and the removal or taking of the weapon or firearm or attempt thereof, was committed against the same public officer, peace officer, or emergency medical technician. A person may be convicted of multiple violations of this section if more than one public officer, peace officer, or emergency medical technician are victims.

(f) This section shall not apply if the public officer, peace officer, or emergency medical technician is disarmed while engaged in a criminal act. *(AM '99)*

148.1. Falsely Reporting Planting of Bomb

(a) Any person who reports to any peace officer listed in Section 830.1 or 830.2, or subdivision (a) of Section 830.33, employee of a fire department or fire service, district attorney, newspaper, radio station, television station, deputy district attorney, employees of the Department of Justice, employees of an airline, employees of an airport, employees of a railroad or busline, an employee of a telephone company, occupants of a building or a news reporter in the employ of a newspaper or radio or television station, that a bomb or other explosive has been or will be placed or secreted in any public or private place, knowing that the report is false, is guilty of a crime punishable by imprisonment in the state prison, or imprisonment in the county jail not to exceed one year.

(b) Any person who reports to any other peace officer defined in Chapter 4.5 (commencing with Section 830) of Title 3 of Part 2 that a bomb or other explosive has been or will be placed or secreted in any public or private place, knowing that the report is false, is guilty of a crime punishable by imprisonment in the state prison or in the county jail not to exceed one year if (1) the false information is given while the peace officer is engaged in the performance of his or her duties as a peace officer and (2) the person providing the false information knows or should have known that the person receiving the information is a peace officer.

(c) Any person who maliciously informs any other person that a bomb or other explosive has been or will be placed or secreted in any public or private place, knowing that the information is false, is guilty of a crime punishable by imprisonment in the state prison, or imprisonment in the county jail not to exceed one year.

(d) Any person who maliciously gives, mails, sends, or causes to be sent any false or facsimile bomb to another person, or places, causes to be placed, or maliciously possesses any false or facsimile bomb, with the intent to cause another to fear for his or her personal safety or the safety of others, is guilty of a crime punishable by imprisonment in the state prison, or imprisonment in the county jail not to exceed one year. *(AM '98)*

148.2. Interfering With Discharge of Duty by Fireman or Emergency Rescue Personnel

Every person who willfully commits any of the following acts at the burning of a building or at any other time and place where any fireman or firemen or emergency rescue personnel are discharging or attempting to discharge an official duty, is guilty of a misdemeanor:

1. Resists or interferes with the lawful efforts of any fireman or firemen or emergency rescue personnel in the discharge or attempt to discharge an official duty.

2. Disobeys the lawful orders of any fireman or public officer.

3. Engages in any disorderly conduct which delays or prevents a fire from being timely extinguished.

4. Forbids or prevents others from assisting in extinguishing a fire or exhorts another person, as to whom he has no legal right or obligation to protect or control, from assisting in extinguishing a fire.

148.3. Falsely Reporting Emergency

(a) Any individual who reports, or causes any report to be made, to any city, county, city and county, or state department, district, agency, division, commission, or board, that an "emergency" exists, knowing that such report is false, is guilty of a misdemeanor and, upon conviction thereof, shall be punishable by imprisonment in the county jail, not exceeding one year, or by a fine, not exceeding one thousand dollars ($1,000), or by both such fine and imprisonment.

(b) Any individual who reports, or causes any report to be made, to any city, county, city and county, or state department, district, agency, division, commission, or board, that an "emergency" exists, knowing that such report is false, and great bodily injury or death is sustained by any person as a result of such false report, is guilty of a felony and upon conviction thereof shall be punishable by imprisonment in the state prison, or by a fine of not more than ten thousand dollars ($10,000), or by both such fine and imprisonment.

(c) "Emergency" as used in this section means any condition which results in, or which could result in, the response of a public official in an authorized emergency vehicle, or any condition which jeopardizes or could jeopardize public safety and results in, or could result in, the evacuation of any area, building, structure, vehicle or of any other place which any individual may enter.

148.4. Tampering With Fire Alarm

(a) Any person who does any of the following is guilty of a misdemeanor and upon conviction is punishable by imprisonment in a county jail, not exceeding one year, or by a fine, not exceeding one thousand dollars ($1,000), or by both that fine and imprisonment:

(1) Willfully and maliciously tampers with, molests, injures, or breaks any fire protection equipment, fire protection installation, fire alarm apparatus, wire, or signal.

(2) Way and maliciously sends, gives, transmits, or sounds any false alarm of fire, by means of any fire alarm system or signal or by any other means or methods.

(b) Any person who willfully and maliciously sends, gives, transmits, or sounds any false alarm of fire, by means of any fire alarm system or signal, or by any other means or methods, is guilty of a felony and upon conviction is punishable by imprisonment in the state prison or by a fine of not less thank five hundred dollars ($500) nor more than ten thousand dollars ($10,000), or by both that fine and imprisonment, if any person sustains as a result thereof, any of the following:

(1) Great bodily injury.

(2) Death.

148.5. Falsely Reporting Crime

(a) Every person who reports to any peace officer listed in Section 830.1 or 830.2, or subdivision (a) of Section 830.33, district attorney, or deputy district attorney that a felony or misdemeanor has been committed, knowing the report to be false, is guilty of a misdemeanor.

(b) Every person who reports to any other peace officer, as defined in Chapter 4.5 (commencing with Section 830) of Title 3 of Part 2, that a felony or misdemeanor has been committed, knowing the report to be false, is guilty of a misdemeanor if (1) the false information is given while the peace officer is engaged in the performance of his or her duties as a peace officer and (2) the person providing the false information knows or should have known that the person receiving the information is a peace officer.

(c) Except as provided in subdivisions (a) and (b), every person who reports to any employee who is assigned to accept reports from citizens, either directly or by telephone, and who is employed by a state or local agency which is designated in Section 830.1, 830.2, subdivision (e) of Section 830.3, Section 830.31, 830.32, 830.33, 830.34, 830.35, 830.36, 830.37, or 830.4, that a felony or misdemeanor has been committed, knowing the report to be false, is guilty of a misdemeanor if (1) the false information is given while the employee is engaged in the performance of his or her duties as an agency employee and (2) the person providing the false information knows or should have known that the person receiving the information is an agency employee engaged in the performance of the duties described in this subdivision.

(d) Every person who makes a report to a grand jury that a felony or misdemeanor has been committed, knowing the report to be false, is guilty of a misdemeanor. This subdivision shall not be construed as prohibiting or precluding a charge of perjury or contempt for any report made under oath in an investigation or proceeding before a grand jury.

(e) This section does not apply to reports made by persons who are required by statute to report known or suspected instances of child abuse, dependent adult abuse, or elder abuse. *(AM '98)*

148.6. Peace Officer Misconduct, False Report of

(a)(1) Every person who files any allegation of misconduct against any peace officer, as defined in Chapter 4.5 (commencing with Section 830) of Title 3 of Part 2, knowing the allegation to be false, is guilty of a misdemeanor.

(2) Any law enforcement agency accepting an allegation of misconduct against a peace officer shall require the complainant to read and sign the following advisory, all in boldface type: YOU HAVE THE RIGHT TO MAKE A COMPLAINT AGAINST A POLICE OFFICER FOR ANY IMPROPER POLICE CONDUCT. CALIFORNIA LAW REQUIRES THIS AGENCY TO HAVE A PROCEDURE TO INVESTIGATE CITIZENS' COMPLAINTS. YOU HAVE A RIGHT TO A WRITTEN DESCRIPTION OF THIS PROCEDURE. THIS AGENCY MAY FIND AFTER INVESTIGATION THAT THERE IS NOT ENOUGH EVIDENCE TO WARRANT ACTION ON YOUR COMPLAINT; EVEN IF THAT IS THE CASE, YOU HAVE THE RIGHT TO MAKE THE COMPLAINT AND HAVE IT INVESTIGATED IF YOU BELIEVE AN OFFICER BEHAVED IMPROPERLY. CITIZEN COMPLAINTS AND ANY REPORTS OR FINDINGS RELATING TO COMPLAINTS MUST BE RETAINED BY THIS AGENCY FOR AT LEAST FIVE YEARS. IT IS AGAINST THE LAW TO MAKE A COMPLAINT THAT YOU KNOW TO BE FALSE. IF YOU MAKE A COMPLAINT AGAINST AN OFFICER KNOWING THAT IT IS FALSE, YOU CAN BE PROSECUTED ON A MISDEMEANOR CHARGE.

I have read and understood the above statement.

_____ Complainant

(3) The advisory shall be available in multiple languages.

(b) Every person who files a civil claim against a peace officer or a lien against his or her property, knowing the claim or lien to be false and with the intent to harass or dissuade the officer from carrying out his or her official duties, is guilty of a misdemeanor. This section applies only to claims pertaining to actions that arise in the course and scope of the peace officer's duties. *(AM '00)*

148.7. Serving Sentence of Another; False Representations

Every person who, for the purpose of serving in any county or city jail, industrial farm or road camp, or other local correctional institution any part or all of the sentence of another person, or any part or all of a term of confinement that is required to be served by another person as a condition of probation, represents to any public officer or employee that he is such other person, is guilty of a misdemeanor.

148.9. Giving False Identification

(a) Any person who falsely represents or identifies himself or herself as another person or as a fictitious person to any peace officer listed in Section 830.1 or 830.2, or subdivision (a) of Section 830.33, upon a lawful detention or arrest of the person, either to evade the process of the court, or to evade the proper identification of the person by the investigating officer is guilty of a misdemeanor.

(b) Any person who falsely represents or identifies himself or herself as another person or as a fictitious person to any other peace officer defined in Chapter 4.5 (commencing with Section 830) of Title 3 of Part 2, upon lawful detention or arrest of the person, either to evade the process of the court, or to evade the proper identification of the person by the arresting officer is guilty of a misdemeanor if (1) the false information is given while the peace officer is engaged in the performance of his or her duties as a peace officer and (2) the person providing the false information knows or should have known that the person receiving the information is a peace officer. *(AM '98)*

148.10. Resisting Peace Officer - Death or Serious Bodily Injury

(a) Every person who willfully resists a peace officer in the discharge or attempt to discharge any duty of his or her office or employment and whose willful resistance proximately causes death or serious bodily injury to a peace officer shall be punished by imprisonment in the state prison for two, three, or four years, or by a fine of not less than one thousand dollars ($1,000) or more than ten thousand dollars ($10,000), or by both that fine and imprisonment, or by imprisonment in a county jail for not more than one year, or by a fine of not more than one thousand dollars ($1,000), or by both that fine and imprisonment.

(b) For purposes of subdivision (a), the following facts shall be found by the trier of fact:

(1) That the peace officer's action was reasonable based on the facts or circumstances confronting the officer at the time.

(2) That the detention and arrest was lawful and there existed probable cause or reasonable cause to detain.

(3) That the person who willfully resisted any peace officer knew or reasonably should have known that the other person was a peace officer engaged in the performance of his or her duties.

(c) This section does not apply to conduct that occurs during labor picketing, demonstrations, or disturbing the peace.

(d) For purposes of this section, "serious bodily injury"is defined in paragraph (4) of subdivision (f) of Section 243. *(AM '99)*

149. Assault and Battery by Officer - Third Degree

Every public officer who, under color of authority, without lawful necessity, assaults or beats any person, is punishable by a fine not exceeding ten thousand dollars ($10,000), or by imprisonment in the state prison, or in a county jail not exceeding one year, or by both such fine and imprisonment.

150. Refusal to Aid Posse or Assist in Making Arrest

Every able-bodied person above 18 years of age who neglects or refuses to join the posse comitatus or power of the county, by neglecting or refusing to aid and assist in taking or arresting any person against whom there may be issued any process, or by neglecting to aid and assist in retaking any person who, after being arrested or confined, may have escaped from arrest or imprisonment, or by neglecting or refusing to aid and assist in preventing any breach of the peace, or the commission of any criminal offense, being thereto lawfully required by any uniformed peace officer, or by any peace officer described in Section 830.1, subdivision (a), (b), (c), (d), (e), or (f) of Section 830.2, or subdivision (a) of Section 830.33, who identifies himself or herself with a badge or identification card issued by the officer's employing agency, or by any judge, is punishable by a fine of not less than fifty dollars ($50) nor more than one thousand dollars ($1,000). *(AM '98)*

151. Advocating Injury or Death of Peace Officer

(a) Any person who advocates the willful and unlawful killing or injuring of a peace officer, with the specific intent to cause the willful and unlawful killing or injuring of a peace officer, and such advocacy is done at a time, place, and under circumstances in which the advocacy is likely to cause the imminent willful and unlawful killing or injuring of a peace officer is guilty of (1) a misdemeanor if such advocacy does not cause the unlawful and willful killing or injuring of a peace officer, or (2) a felony if such advocacy causes the unlawful and willful killing or injuring of a peace officer.

(b) As used in this section, "advocacy"means the direct incitement of others to cause the imminent willful and unlawful killing or injuring of a peace officer, and not the mere abstract teaching of a doctrine.

152. Concealment of Accidental Death

(a) Every person who, having knowledge of an accidental death, actively conceals or attempts to conceal that death, shall be guilty of a misdemeanor punishable by imprisonment in a county jail for not more than one year, or by a fine of not less than one thousand dollars ($1,000) nor more than ten thousand dollars ($10,000), or by both that fine and imprisonment.

(b) For purposes of this section, "to actively conceal an accidental death"means any of the following:

(1) To perform an overt act that conceals the body or directly impedes the ability of authorities or family members to discover the body.

(2) To directly destroy or suppress evidence of the actual physical body of the deceased, including, but not limited to, bodily fluids or tissues.

(3) To destroy or suppress the actual physical instrumentality of death. *(AD '99)*

152.3. Mandatory Reporting of Certain Crimes Where Victim is Under the Age of 14

(a) Any person who reasonably believes that he or she has observed the commission of any of the following offenses where the victim is a child under the age of 14 years shall notify a peace officer, as defined in Chapter 4.5 (commencing with Section 830) of Title 3 of Part 2:

(1) Murder.

(2) Rape.

(3) A violation of paragraph (1) of subdivision (b) of Section 288 of the Penal Code.

(b) This section shall not be construed to affect privileged relationships as provided by law.

(c) The duty to notify a peace officer imposed pursuant to subdivision (a) is satisfied if the notification or an attempt to provide notice is made by telephone or any other means.

(d) Failure to notify as required pursuant to subdivision (a) is a misdemeanor and is punishable by a fine of not more than one thousand five hundred dollars ($1,500), by imprisonment in a county jail for not more than six months, or by both that fine and imprisonment.

(e) The requirements of this section shall not apply to the following:

(1) A person who is related to either the victim or the offender, including a husband, wife, parent, child, brother, sister, grandparent, grandchild, or other person related by consanguinity or affinity.

(2) A person who fails to report based on a reasonable mistake of fact.

(3) A person who fails to report based on a reasonable fear for his or her own safety or for the safety of his or her family. *(AD '00)*

153. Compounding or Concealing Crime

Every person who, having knowledge of the actual commission of a crime, takes money or property of another, or any gratuity or reward, or any engagement, or promise thereof, upon any agreement or understanding to compound or conceal such crime, or to abstain from any prosecution thereof, or to withhold any evidence thereof, except in the cases provided for by law, in which crimes may be compromised by leave of court, is punishable as follows:

1. By imprisonment in the state prison, or in a county jail not exceeding one year, where the crime was punishable by death or imprisonment in the state prison for life;

2. By imprisonment in the state prison, or in the county jail not exceeding six months, where the crime was punishable by imprisonment in the state prison for any other term than for life;

3. By imprisonment in the county jail not exceeding six months, or by fine not exceeding one thousand dollars ($1,000), where the crime was a misdemeanor.

154. Defrauding Creditors by Selling or Concealing Property

(a) Every debtor who fraudulently removes his or her property or effects out of this state, or who fraudulently sells, conveys, assigns or conceals his or her property with intent to defraud, hinder or delay his or her creditors of their rights, claims, or demands, is punishable by imprisonment in the county jail not exceeding one year, or by fine not exceeding one thousand dollars($1,000), or by both that fine and imprisonment.

(b) Where the property so removed, sold, conveyed, assigned, or concealed consists of a stock in trade, or a part thereof, of a value exceeding one hundred dollars ($100), the offense shall be a felony and punishable as such.

165. Giving or Offering Bribe to Councilman or Supervisor

Every person who gives or offers a bribe to any member of any common council, board of supervisors, or board of trustees of any county, city and county, city, or public corporation, with intent to corruptly influence such member in his action on any matter or subject pending before, or which is afterward to be considered by, the body of which he is a member, and every member of any of the bodies mentioned in this section who receives, or offers or agrees to receive any bribe upon any understanding that his official vote, opinion, judgment, or action shall be influenced thereby, or shall be given in any particular manner or upon any particular side of any question or matter, upon which he may be required to act in his official capacity, is punishable by imprisonment in the state prison for two, three or four years, and upon conviction thereof shall, in addition to said punishment, forfeit his office, and forever be disfranchised and disqualified from holding any public office or trust.

166. Contempt of Court

(a) Except as provided in subdivisions (b), (c), and (d), every person guilty of any contempt of court, of any of the following kinds, is guilty of a misdemeanor:

(1) Disorderly, contemptuous, or insolent behavior committed during the sitting of any court of justice, in immediate view and presence of the court, and directly tending to interrupt its proceedings or to impair the respect due to its authority.

(2) Behavior as specified in paragraph (1) committed in the presence of any referee, while actually engaged in any trial or hearing, pursuant to the order of any court, or in the presence of any jury while actually sitting for the trial of a cause, or upon any inquest or other proceedings authorized by law.

(3) Any breach of the peace, noise, or other disturbance directly tending to interrupt the proceedings of any court.

(4) Willful disobedience of the terms as written of any process or court order or out-of-state court order, lawfully issued by any court, including orders pending trial.

(5) Resistance willfully offered by any person to the lawful order or process of any court.

(6) The contumacious and unlawful refusal of any person to be sworn as a witness; or, when so sworn, the like refusal to answer any material question.

(7) The publication of a false or grossly inaccurate report of the proceedings of any court.

(8) Presenting to any court having power to pass sentence upon any prisoner under conviction, or to any member of the court, any affidavit or testimony or representation of any kind, verbal or written, in aggravation or mitigation of the punishment to be imposed upon the prisoner, except as provided in this code.

(b)(1) Any person who is guilty of contempt of court under paragraph (4) of subdivision (a) by willfully contacting a victim by phone, mail, or directly and who has been previously convicted of a violation of Section 646.9 shall be punished by imprisonment in a county jail for not more than one year, by a fine of five thousand dollars ($5,000), or by both that fine and imprisonment.

(2) For the purposes of sentencing under this subdivision, each contact shall constitute a separate violation of this subdivision.

(3) The present incarceration of a person who makes contact with a victim in violation of paragraph (1) is not a defense to a violation of this subdivision.

(c)(1) Notwithstanding paragraph (4) of subdivision (a), any willful and knowing violation of any protective order or stay away court order issued pursuant to Section 136.2, in a pending criminal proceeding involving domestic violence, as defined in Section 13700, or issued as a condition of probation after a conviction in a criminal proceeding involving domestic violence, as defined in Section 13700, which is an order described in paragraph (3), shall constitute contempt of court, a misdemeanor, punishable by imprisonment in a county jail for not more than one year, by a fine of not more than one thousand dollars ($1,000), or by both that imprisonment and fine.

(2) If a violation of paragraph (1) results in a physical injury, the person shall be imprisoned in a county jail for at least 48 hours, whether a fine or imprisonment is imposed, or the sentence is suspended.

(3) Paragraphs (1) and (2) shall apply to the following court orders:

(A) Any order issued pursuant to Section 6320 or 6389 of the Family Code.

(B) An order excluding one party from the family dwelling or from the dwelling of the other.

(C) An order enjoining a party from specified behavior that the court determined was necessary to effectuate the orders described in paragraph (1).

(4) A second or subsequent conviction for a violation of any order described in paragraph (1) occurring within seven years of a prior conviction for a violation of any of those orders and involving an act of violence or "a credible threat"of violence, as provided in subdivisions (c) and (d) of Section 139, is punishable by imprisonment in a county jail not to exceed one year, or in the state prison for 16 months or two or three years.

(5) The prosecuting agency of each county shall have the primary responsibility for the enforcement of the orders described in paragraph (1).

(d)(1) Every person who owns, possesses, purchases, or receives a firearm knowing he or she is prohibited from doing so by the provisions of a protective order as defined in Section 136.2 of this code, Section 6218 of the Family Code, or Sections 527.6 or 527.8 of the Code of Civil Procedure, shall be punished under the provisions of subdivision (g) of Section 12021.

(2) Every person subject to a protective order described in paragraph (1) shall not be prosecuted under this section for owning, possessing, purchasing, or receiving a firearm to the extent that firearm is granted an exemption pursuant to subdivision (h) of Section 6389 of the Family Code.

(e)(1) If probation is granted upon conviction of a violation of subdivision (c), the court shall impose probation consistent with the provisions of Section 1203.097 of the Penal Code.

(2) If probation is granted upon conviction of a violation of subdivision (c), the conditions of probation may include, in lieu of a fine, one or both of the following requirements:

(A) That the defendant make payments to a battered women's shelter, up to a maximum of one thousand dollars ($1,000).

(B) That the defendant provide restitution to reimburse the victim for reasonable costs of counseling and other reasonable expenses that the court finds are the direct result of the defendant's offense.

(3) For any order to pay a fine, make payments to a battered women's shelter, or pay restitution as a condition of probation under this subdivision or subdivision (c), the court shall make a determination of the defendant's ability to pay. In no event shall any order to make payments to a battered women's shelter be made if it would impair the ability of the defendant to pay direct restitution to the victim or court-ordered child support.

(4) Where the injury to a married person is caused in whole or in part by the criminal acts of his or her spouse in violation of subdivision (c), the community property may not be used to discharge the liability of the offending spouse for restitution to the injured spouse, required by Section 1203.04, as operative on or before August 2, 1995, or Section 1202.4, or to a shelter for costs with regard to the injured spouse and dependents, required by this subdivision, until all separate property of the offending spouse is exhausted.

(5) Any person violating any order described in subdivision (c), may be punished for any substantive offenses described under Section 136.1 or 646.9. No finding of contempt shall be a bar to prosecution for a violation of Section 136.1 or 646.9. However, any person held in contempt for a violation of subdivision (c) shall be entitled to credit for any punishment imposed as a result of that violation against any sentence imposed upon conviction of an offense described in Section 136.1 or 646.9. Any conviction or acquittal for any substantive offense under Section 136.1 or 646.9 shall be a bar to a subsequent punishment for contempt arising out of the same act. *(AM '99)*

168. Disclosing Warrant Prior to Execution

(a) Every district attorney, clerk, judge or peace officer who, except by issuing or in executing a search warrant or warrant of arrest for a felony, willfully discloses the fact of the warrant prior to execution for the purpose of preventing the search or seizure of property or the arrest of any person shall be punished by imprisonment in the state prison or in a county jail for not exceeding one year.

(b) This section shall not prohibit the following:

(1) A disclosure made by a district attorney or the Attorney General for the sole purpose of securing voluntary compliance with the warrant.

(2) Upon the return of an indictment and the issuance of an arrest warrant, a disclosure of the existence of the indictment and arrest warrant by a district attorney or the Attorney General to assist in the apprehension of a defendant.

171. Communication With Inmate of Reformatory

Every person, not authorized by law, who, without the permission of the officer in charge of any reformatory in this State, communicates with any person detained therein, or brings therein or takes therefrom any letter, writing, literature, or reading matter to or from any person confined therein, is guilty of a misdemeanor.

171b. Bringing Firearm or Other Specified Weapons Into State or Local Public Bldg. or Meeting Required to be Open to the Public

(a) Any person who brings or possesses within any state or local public building or at any meeting required to be open to the public pursuant to Chapter 9 (commencing with Section 54950) of Part 1 of Division 2 of Title 5 of, or Article 9 (commencing with Section 11120) of Chapter 1 of Part 1 of Division 3 of Title 2 of, the Government Code, any of the following is guilty of a public offense punishable by imprisonment in a county jail for not more than one year, or in the state prison:

(1) Any firearm.

(2) Any deadly weapon described in Section 653k or 12020.

(3) Any knife with a blade length in excess of four inches, the blade of which is fixed or is capable of being fixed in an unguarded position by the use of one or two hands.

(4) Any unauthorized tear gas weapon.

(5) Any taser or stun gun, as defined in Section 244.5.

(6) Any instrument that expels a metallic projectile, such as a BB or pellet, through the force of air pressure, CO_2 pressure, or spring action, or any spot marker gun or paint gun.

(b) Subdivision (a) shall not apply to, or affect, any of the following:

(1) A person who possesses weapons in, or transports weapons into, a court of law to be used as evidence.

(2)(A) A duly appointed peace officer as defined in Chapter 4.5 (commencing with Section 830) of Title 3 of Part 2, a retired peace officer with authorization to carry concealed weapons as described in subdivision (a) of Section 12027, a full-time paid peace officer of another state or the federal government who is carrying out official duties while in California, or any person summoned by any of these officers to assist in making arrests or preserving the peace while he or she is actually engaged in assisting the officer.

(B) Notwithstanding subparagraph (A), subdivision (a) shall apply to any person who brings or possesses any weapon specified therein within any courtroom if he or she is a party to an action pending before the court.

(3) A person holding a valid license to carry the firearm pursuant to Article 3 (commencing with Section 12050) of Chapter 1 of Title 2 of Part 4.

(4) A person who has permission to possess that weapon granted in writing by a duly authorized official who is in charge of the security of the state or local government building.

(5) A person who lawfully resides in, lawfully owns, or is in lawful possession of, that building with respect to those portions of the building that are not owned or leased by the state or local government.

(6) A person licensed or registered in accordance with, and acting within the course and scope of, Chapter 11.5 (commencing with Section 7512) or Chapter 11.6 (commencing with Section 7590) of Division 3 of the Business and Professions Code who has been hired by the owner or manager of the building if the person has permission pursuant to paragraph (5).

(7)(A) A person who, for the purpose of sale or trade, brings any weapon that may otherwise be lawfully transferred, into a gun show conducted pursuant to Sections 12071.1 and 12071.4.

(B) A person who, for purposes of an authorized public exhibition, brings any weapon that may otherwise be lawfully possessed, into a gun show conducted pursuant to Sections 12071.1 and 12071.4.

(c) As used in this section, "state or local public building" means a building that meets all of the following criteria:

(1) It is a building or part of a building owned or leased by the state or local government, if state or local public employees are regularly present for the purposes of performing their official duties. A state or local public building includes, but is not limited to, a building that contains a courtroom.

(2) It is not a building or facility, or a part thereof, that is referred to in Section 171c, 171d, 626.9, 626.95, or 626.10 of this code, or in Section 18544 of the Elections Code.

(3) It is a building not regularly used, and not intended to be used, by state or local employees as a place of residence. *(AM '99)*

171c. Bringing Loaded Firearm Into State Office, State Capitol Grounds or Public School Grounds

Any person, except a duly appointed peace officer as defined in Chapter 4.5 of Title 3 of Part 2, a full-time paid peace officer of another state or the federal government who is carrying out official duties while in California, any person summoned by any such officer to assist in making arrests or preserving the peace while he is actually engaged in assisting such officer, a member of the military forces of this state or the United States engaged in the performance of his duties, or a person holding a valid license to carry the firearm pursuant to Article 3 of Chapter 1 of Title 2 of Part 4, who brings a loaded firearm into, or possesses a loaded firearm within, the State Capitol, any legislative office, any office of the Governor or other constitutional officer, or any hearing room in which any committee of the Senate or Assembly is conducting a hearing, or upon the grounds of the State Capitol, which is bounded by 10th, L, 15th, and N Streets in the City of Sacramento, shall be punished by imprisonment in the county jail for a period of not more than one year, a fine of not more than one thousand dollars ($1,000), or both such imprisonment and fine, or by imprisonment in the state prison.

171e. When Firearm Deemed Loaded

A firearm shall be deemed loaded for the purposes of Sections 171c and 171d whenever both the firearm and unexpended ammunition capable of being discharged from such firearm are in the immediate possession of the same person.

In order to determine whether or not a firearm is loaded for the purpose of enforcing Section 171c or 171d, peace officers are authorized to examine any firearm carried by anyone on his person or in a vehicle while in any place or on the grounds of any place in or on which the possession of a loaded firearm is prohibited by Section 171c or 171d. Refusal to allow a peace officer to inspect a firearm pursuant to the provisions of this section constitutes probable cause for arrest for violation of Section 171c or 171d.

182. Conspiracy Defined

(a) If two or more persons conspire:

(1) To commit any crime.

(2) *** <u>Falsify</u> and maliciously to indict another for any crime, or to procure another to be charged or arrested for any crime.

(3) Falsely to move or maintain any suit, action, or proceeding.

(4) To cheat and defraud any person of any property, by any means which are in themselves criminal, or to obtain money or property by false pretenses or by false promises with fraudulent intent not to perform *** <u>those</u> promises.

(5) To commit any act injurious to the public health, to public morals, or to pervert or obstruct justice, or the due administration of the laws.

(6) To commit any crime against the person of the President or Vice President of the United States, the *** <u>Governor</u> of any state or territory, any United States justice or judge, or the secretary of any of the executive departments of the United States.

They are punishable as follows:***

When they conspire to commit any crime against the person of any official specified in paragraph (6), they are guilty of a felony and are punishable by imprisonment in the state prison for five, seven, or nine years.

When they conspire to commit any other felony, they shall be punishable in the same manner and to the same extent as is provided for the punishment of *** that felony. If the felony is one for which different punishments are prescribed for different degrees, the jury or court which finds the defendant guilty thereof shall determine the degree of the felony the defendant conspired to commit. If the degree is not so determined, the punishment for conspiracy to commit the felony shall be that prescribed for the lesser degree, except in the case of conspiracy to commit murder, in which case the punishment shall be that prescribed for murder in the first degree.

If the felony is conspiracy to commit two or more felonies which have different punishments and the commission of those felonies constitute but one offense of conspiracy, the penalty shall be that prescribed for the felony which has the greater maximum term.

When they conspire to do an act described in paragraph (4), they shall be punishable by imprisonment in the state prison, or by imprisonment in the county jail for not more than one year, or by a fine not exceeding ten thousand dollars ($10,000), or *** by both that imprisonment and fine.

When they conspire to do any of the other acts described in this section, they shall be punishable by imprisonment in the county jail for not more than one year, or in the state prison, or by a fine not exceeding ten thousand dollars ($10,000) ***, or by both that imprisonment and fine.

All cases of conspiracy may be prosecuted and tried in the superior court of any county in which any overt act tending to effect *** the conspiracy shall be done.

(b) Upon a trial for conspiracy, in a case where an overt act is necessary to constitute the offense, the defendant cannot be convicted unless one or more overt acts are expressly alleged in the indictment or information, nor unless one of the acts alleged is proved; but other overt acts not alleged may be given in evidence. *(AM '01)*

[Editor's Note: (a)(2) should probably read "Falsely"not "Falsify."The wording was changed in the section during amendment in the Assembly.]

182.5. Participation in Criminal Street Gang; Conspiracy to Commit a Felony

Notwithstanding subdivisions (a) or (b) of Section 182, any person who actively participates in any criminal street gang, as defined in subdivision (f) of Section 186.22, with knowledge that its members engage in or have engaged in a pattern of criminal gang activity, as defined in subdivision (e) of Section 186.22, and who willfully promotes, furthers, assists, or benefits from any felonious criminal conduct by members of that gang is guilty of conspiracy to commit that felony and may be punished as specified in subdivision (a) of Section 182. *(Added by Prop. 21, 3-7-2000 Election)*

184. Acts Effectuating Conspiracy

No agreement amounts to a conspiracy, unless some act, besides such agreement, be done within this State to effect the object thereof, by one or more of the parties to such agreement and the trial of cases of conspiracy may be had in any county in which any such act be done.

185. Wearing Mask or Disguise

It shall be unlawful for any person to wear any mask, false whiskers, or any personal disguise (whether complete or partial) for the purpose of:

One - Evading or escaping discovery, recognition, or identification in the commission of any public offense.

Two - Concealment, flight, or escape when charged with, arrested for, or convicted of, any public offense. Any person violating any of the provisions of this section shall be deemed guilty of a misdemeanor.

186.22. Criminal Street Gang Activity

(a) Any person who actively participates in any criminal street gang with knowledge that its members engage in or have engaged in a pattern of criminal gang activity, and who willfully promotes, furthers, or assists in any felonious criminal conduct by members of that gang, shall be punished by imprisonment in a county jail for a period not to exceed one year, or by imprisonment in the state prison for 16 months, or two or three years.

(b)(1) Except as provided in *** <u>paragraphs</u> (4) and (5), any person who is convicted of a felony committed for the benefit of, at the direction of, or in association with any criminal street gang, with the specific intent to promote, further, or assist in any criminal conduct by gang members, shall, upon conviction of that felony, in addition and consecutive to the punishment prescribed for the felony or attempted felony of which he or she has been convicted, <u>be punished as follows:</u>

<u>(A) Except as provided in subparagraphs (B) and (C), the person shall</u> be punished by an additional term of two, three, or four years at the court's discretion***.

<u>(B)</u> <u>If</u> the felony is a serious felony, as defined in subdivision (c) of Section 1192.7, the person shall be punished by an additional term of five years.

<u>(C)</u> If the felony is a violent felony, as defined in subdivision (c) of Section 667.5, the person shall be punished by an additional term of 10 years.

(2) If the underlying felony described in paragraph (1) is committed on the grounds of, or within 1,000 feet of, a public or private elementary, vocational, junior high, or high school, during hours in which the facility is open for classes or school-related programs or when minors are using the facility that fact shall be a circumstance in aggravation of the crime in imposing a term under paragraph (1).

(3) The court shall order the imposition of the middle term of the sentence enhancement, unless there are circumstances in aggravation or mitigation. The court shall state the reasons for its choice of *** <u>sentencing</u> enhancements on the record at the time of the sentencing.

(4) Any person who is convicted of a felony enumerated in this paragraph committed for the benefit of, at the direction of, or in association with any criminal street gang, with the specific intent to promote, further, or assist in any criminal conduct by gang members, shall, upon conviction of that felony, be sentenced to an indeterminate term of life imprisonment with a minimum term of the indeterminate sentence calculated as the greater of:

(A) The term determined by the court pursuant to Section 1170 for the underlying conviction, including any enhancement applicable under Chapter 4.5 (commencing with Section 1170) of Title 7 of Part 2, or any period prescribed by Section 3046, if the felony is any of the offenses enumerated in subparagraphs (B) or (C) of this paragraph.

(B) Imprisonment in the state prison for 15 years, if the felony is a home invasion robbery, in violation of subparagraph (A) of paragraph (1) of subdivision (a) of Section 213; carjacking, as defined in Section 215; a felony violation of Section 246; or a violation of Section 12022.55.

(C) Imprisonment in the state prison for seven years, if the felony is extortion, as defined in Section 519; or threats to victims and witnesses, as defined in Section 136.1.

(5) Except as provided in paragraph (4), any person who violates this subdivision in the commission of a felony punishable by imprisonment in the state prison for life, shall not be paroled until a minimum of 15 calendar years have been served.

(c) If the court grants probation or suspends the execution of sentence imposed upon the defendant for a violation of subdivision (a), or in cases involving a true finding of the enhancement enumerated in subdivision (b), the court shall require that the defendant serve a minimum of 180 days in a county jail as a condition thereof.

(d) Any person who is convicted of a public offense punishable as a felony or a misdemeanor, which is committed for the benefit of, at the direction of or in association with, any criminal street gang with the specific intent to promote, further, or assist in any criminal conduct by gang members, shall be punished by imprisonment in the county jail not to exceed one year, or by imprisonment in the state prison for one, two, or three years, provided that any person sentenced to imprisonment in the county jail shall be imprisoned for a period not to exceed one year, but not less than 180 days, and shall not be eligible for release upon completion of sentence, parole, or any other basis, until he or she has served 180 days. If the court grants probation or suspends the execution of sentence imposed upon the defendant, it shall require as a condition thereof that the defendant serve 180 days in a county jail.

(e) As used in this chapter, "pattern of criminal gang activity" means the commission of, attempted commission of, conspiracy to commit, or solicitation of, sustained juvenile petition for, or conviction of two or more of the following offenses, provided at least one of these offenses occurred after the effective date of this chapter and the last of those offenses occurred within three years after a prior offense, and the offenses were committed on separate occasions, or by two or more persons:

(1) Assault with a deadly weapon or by means of force likely to produce great bodily injury, as defined in Section 245.

(2) Robbery, as defined in Chapter 4 (commencing with Section 211) of Title 8 of Part 1.

(3) Unlawful homicide or manslaughter, as defined in Chapter 1 (commencing with Section 187) of Title 8 of Part 1.

(4) The sale, possession for sale, transportation, manufacture, offer for sale, or offer to manufacture controlled substances as defined in Sections 11054, 11055, 11056, 11057, and 11058 of the Health and Safety Code.

(5) Shooting at an inhabited dwelling or occupied motor vehicle, as defined in Section 246.

(6) Discharging or permitting the discharge of a firearm from a motor vehicle, as defined in subdivisions (a) and (b) of Section 12034.

(7) Arson, as defined in Chapter 1 (commencing with Section 450) of Title 13.

(8) The intimidation of witnesses and victims, as defined in Section 136.1.

(9) Grand theft, as defined in *** subdivision (a) or (c) of Section 487***.

(10) Grand theft of any firearm, vehicle, trailer, or vessel.

(11) Burglary, as defined in Section 459.

(12) Rape, as defined in Section 261.

(13) Looting, as defined in Section 463.

(14) Money laundering, as defined in Section 186.10.

(15) Kidnapping, as defined in Section 207.

(16) Mayhem, as defined in Section 203.

(17) Aggravated mayhem, as defined in Section 205.

(18) Torture, as defined in Section 206.

(19) Felony extortion, as defined in Sections 518 and 520.

(20) Felony vandalism, as defined in paragraph (1) of subdivision (b) of Section 594.

(21) Carjacking, as defined in Section 215.

(22) The sale, delivery, or transfer of a firearm, as defined in Section 12072.

(23) Possession of a pistol, revolver, or other firearm capable of being concealed upon the person in violation of paragraph (1) of subdivision (a) of Section 12101.

(24) Threats to commit crimes resulting in death or great bodily injury, as defined in Section 422.

(25) Theft and unlawful taking or driving of a vehicle, as defined in Section 10851 of the Vehicle Code.

(f) As used in this chapter, "criminal street gang" means any ongoing organization, association, or group of three or more persons, whether formal or informal, having as one of its primary activities the commission of one or more of the criminal acts enumerated in paragraphs (1) to (25), inclusive, of subdivision (e), having a common name or common identifying sign or symbol, and whose members individually or collectively engage in or have engaged in a pattern of criminal gang activity.

(g) Notwithstanding any other law, the court may strike the additional punishment for the enhancements provided in this section or refuse to impose the minimum jail sentence for misdemeanors in an unusual case where the interests of justice would best be served, if the court specifies on the record and enters into the minutes the circumstances indicating that the interests of justice would best be served by that disposition.

(h) Notwithstanding any other provision of law, for each person committed to the Youth Authority for a conviction pursuant to subdivision (a) or (b) of this section, the offense shall be deemed one for which the state shall pay the rate of 100 percent of the per capita institutional cost of the Department of Youth Authority, pursuant to Section 912.5 of the Welfare and Institutions Code.

(i) In order to secure a conviction, or sustain a juvenile petition, pursuant to subdivision (a), it is not necessary for the prosecution to prove that the person devotes all, or a substantial part of his or her time or efforts to the criminal street gang, nor is it necessary to prove that the person is a member of the criminal street gang. Active participation in the criminal street gang is all that is required. *(AM '01)*

186.22a. Building or Place Used by Street Gangs Declared a Nuisance

(a) Every building or place used by members of a criminal street gang for the purpose of the commission of the offenses listed in subdivision (e) of Section 186.22 or any offense involving dangerous or deadly weapons, burglary, or rape, and every building or place wherein or upon which that criminal conduct by gang members takes place, is a nuisance which shall be enjoined, abated, and prevented, and for which damages may be recovered, whether it is a public or private nuisance.

(b) Any action for injunction or abatement filed pursuant to subdivision (a), including an action filed by the Attorney General, shall proceed according to the provisions of Article 3 (commencing with Section 11570) of Chapter 10 of Division 10 of the Health and Safety Code, except that all of the following shall apply:

(1) The court shall not assess a civil penalty against any person unless that person knew or should have known of the unlawful acts.

(2) No order of eviction or closure may be entered.

(3) All injunctions issued shall be limited to those necessary to protect the health and safety of the residents or the public or those necessary to prevent further criminal activity.

(4) Suit may not be filed until 30-day notice of the unlawful use or criminal conduct has been provided to the owner by mail, return receipt requested, postage prepaid, to the last known address.

(c) Whenever an injunction is issued pursuant to subdivision (a), or Section 3479 of the Civil Code, to abate gang activity constituting a nuisance, the Attorney General may maintain an action for money damages on behalf of the community or neighborhood injured by that nuisance. Any money damages awarded shall be paid by or collected from assets of the criminal street gang or its members that were derived from the criminal activity being abated or enjoined. Only persons who knew or should have known of the unlawful acts shall be personally liable for the payment of the damages awarded. In a civil action for damages brought pursuant to this subdivision, the Attorney General may use, but is not limited to the use of, the testimony of experts to establish damages suffered by the community or neighborhood injured by the nuisance. The damages recovered pursuant to this subdivision shall be deposited into a separate segregated fund for payment to the governing body of the city or county in whose political subdivision the community or neighborhood is located, and that governing body shall use those assets solely for the benefit of the community or neighborhood that has been injured by the nuisance.

(d) No nonprofit or charitable organization which is conducting its affairs with ordinary care or skill, and no governmental entity, shall be abated pursuant to subdivisions (a) and (b).

(e) Nothing in this chapter shall preclude any aggrieved person from seeking any other remedy provided by law.

(f)(1) Any firearm, ammunition which may be used with the firearm, or any deadly or dangerous weapon which is owned or possessed by a member of a criminal street gang for the purpose of the commission of any of the offenses listed in subdivision (e) of Section 186.22, or the commission of any burglary or rape, may be confiscated by any law enforcement agency or peace officer.

(2) In those cases where a law enforcement agency believes that the return of the firearm, ammunition, or deadly weapon confiscated pursuant to this subdivision, is or will be used in criminal street gang activity or that the return of the item would be likely to result in endangering the safety of others, the law enforcement agency shall initiate a petition in the superior court to determine if the item confiscated should be returned or declared a nuisance.

(3) No firearm, ammunition, or deadly weapon shall be sold or destroyed unless reasonable notice is given to its lawful owner if his or her identity and address can be reasonably ascertained. The law enforcement agency shall inform the lawful owner, at that person's last known address by registered mail, that he or she has 30 days from the date of receipt of the notice to respond to the court clerk to confirm his or her desire for a hearing and that the failure to respond shall result in a default order forfeiting the confiscated firearm, ammunition, or deadly weapon as a nuisance.

(4) If the person requests a hearing, the court clerk shall set a hearing no later than 30 days from receipt of that request. The court clerk shall notify the person, the law enforcement agency involved, and the district attorney of the date, time, and place of the hearing.

(5) At the hearing, the burden of proof is upon the law enforcement agency or peace officer to show by a preponderance of the evidence that the seized item is or will be used in criminal street gang activity or that return of the item would be likely to result in endangering the safety of others. All returns of firearms shall be subject to subdivision (d) of Section 12072.

(6) If the person does not request a hearing within 30 days of the notice or the lawful owner cannot be ascertained, the law enforcement agency may file a petition that the confiscated firearm, ammunition, or deadly weapon be declared a nuisance. If the items are declared to be a nuisance, the law enforcement agency shall dispose of the items as provided in Section 12028. *(AM '98)*

186.26. Solicit or Recruit Another to Actively Participate in Criminal Street Gang; Same, Threaten or Use Physical Violence [Added by Initiative Measure]

(a) Any person who solicits or recruits another to actively participate in a criminal street gang, as defined in subdivision (f) of Section 186.22, with the intent that the person solicited or recruited participate in a pattern of criminal street gang activity, as defined in subdivision (e) of Section 186.22, or with the intent that the person solicited or recruited promote, further, or assist in any felonious conduct by members of the criminal street gang, shall be punished by imprisonment in the state prison for 16 months, or two or three years.

(b) Any person who threatens another person with physical violence on two or more separate occasions within any 30-day period with the intent to coerce, induce, or solicit any person to actively participate in a criminal street gang, as defined in subdivision (f) of Section 186.22, shall be punished by imprisonment in the state prison for two, three, or four years.

(c) Any person who uses physical violence to coerce, induce, or solicit another person to actively participate in any criminal street gang, as defined in subdivision (f) of Section 186.22, or to prevent the person from leaving a criminal street gang, shall be punished by imprisonment in the state prison for three, four, or five years.

(d) If the person solicited, recruited, coerced, or threatened pursuant to subdivision (a), (b), or (c) is a minor, an additional term of three years shall be imposed in addition and consecutive to the penalty prescribed for a violation of any of these subdivisions.

(e) Nothing in this section shall be construed to limit prosecution under any other provision of law. *(AM '01)*

186.28. Prohibited Transfer of Firearm

(a) Any person, corporation, or firm who shall knowingly supply, sell or give possession or control of any firearm to another shall be punished by imprisonment in the state prison, or in a county jail for a term not exceeding one year, or by a fine not exceeding one thousand dollars ($1,000), or by both that fine and imprisonment if all of the following apply:

(1) The person, corporation, or firm has actual knowledge that the person will use the firearm to commit a felony described in subdivision (e) of Section 186.22, while actively participating in any criminal street gang, as defined in subdivision (f) of Section 186.22, the members of which engage in a pattern of criminal activity, as defined in subdivision (e) of Section 186.22.

(2) The firearm is used to commit the felony.

(3) A conviction for the felony violation under subdivision (e) of Section 186.22 has first been obtained of the person to whom the firearm was supplied, sold, or given possession or control pursuant to this section.

(b) This section shall only be applicable where the person is not convicted as a principal to the felony offense committed by the person to whom the firearm was supplied, sold, or given possession or control pursuant to this section.

186.30. Criminal Street Gang – Registration Required [Added by Initiative Measure]

(a) Any person described in subdivision (b) shall register with the chief of police of the city in which he or she resides, or the sheriff of the county if he or she resides in an unincorporated area, within 10 days of release from custody or within 10 days of his or her arrival in any city, county, or city and county to reside there, whichever occurs first.

(b) Subdivision (a) shall apply to any person convicted in a criminal court or who has had a petition sustained in a juvenile court in this state for any of the following offenses:

(1) Subdivision (a) of Section 186.22.

(2) Any crime where the enhancement specified in subdivision (b) of Section 186.22 is found to be true.

(3) Any crime that the court finds is gang related at the time of sentencing or disposition. *(AD '00)*

186.33. Criminal Street Gang Registration – Violation of Provisions [Added by Initiative Measure]

(a) Any person required to register pursuant to Section 186.30 who knowingly violates any of its provisions is guilty of a misdemeanor.

(b)(1) Any person who knowingly fails to register pursuant to Section 186.30 and is subsequently convicted of, or any person for whom a petition is subsequently sustained for a violation of, any of the offenses specified in Section 186.30, shall be punished by an additional term of imprisonment in the state prison for 16 months, or 2, or 3 years. The court shall order imposition of the middle term unless there are circumstances in aggravation or mitigation. The court shall state its reasons for the enhancement choice on the record at the time of sentencing.

(2) The existence of any fact bringing a person under this subdivision shall be alleged in the information, indictment, or petition, and be either admitted by the defendant or minor in open court, or found to be true or not true by the trier of fact. *(AD '00)*

CRIMES AGAINST THE PERSON

187. Murder

(a) Murder is the unlawful killing of a human being, or a fetus, with malice aforethought.

(b) This section shall not apply to any person who commits an act which results in the death of a fetus if any of the following apply:

(1) The act complied with the Therapeutic Abortion Act, Article 2 (commencing with Section 123400) of Chapter 2 of Part 2 of Division 106 of the Health and Safety Code.

(2) The act was committed by a holder of a physician's and surgeon's certificate, as defined in the Business and Professions Code, in a case where, to a medical certainty, the result of childbirth would be death of the mother of the fetus or where her death from childbirth, although not medically certain, would be substantially certain or more likely than not.

(3) The act was solicited, aided, abetted, or consented to by the mother of the fetus.

(c) Subdivision (b) shall not be construed to prohibit the prosecution of any person under any other provision of law.

189. Murder - Degrees

All murder which is perpetrated by means of a destructive device or explosive, knowing use of ammunition designed primarily to penetrate metal or armor, poison, lying in wait, torture, or by any other kind of willful, deliberate, and premeditated killing, or which is committed in the perpetration of, or attempt to perpetrate, arson, rape, carjacking, robbery, burglary, mayhem, kidnapping, train wrecking, or any act punishable under Section 206, 286, 288, 288a, or 289, or any murder which is perpetrated by means of discharging a firearm from a motor vehicle, intentionally at another person outside of the vehicle with the intent to inflict death, is murder of the first degree. All other kinds of murders are of the second degree.

As used in this section, "destructive device"means any destructive device as defined in Section 12301, and "explosive"means any explosive as defined in Section 12000 of the Health and Safety Code.

To prove the killing was "deliberate and premeditated," it shall not be necessary to prove the defendant maturely and meaningfully reflected upon the gravity of his or her act. *(AM '99)*

190.03. First Degree Murder Penalty When Killing Due to Victim's Disability, Gender or Sexual Orientation

(a) A person who commits first-degree murder shall be punished by imprisonment in the state prison for life without the possibility of parole, if the defendant intentionally killed the victim because of the victim's disability, gender, or sexual orientation or because of the defendant's perception of the victim's disability, gender, or sexual orientation.

(b) The term authorized by subdivision (a) shall not apply unless the allegation is charged in the accusatory pleading and admitted by the defendant or found true by the trier of fact. The court shall not strike the allegation, except in the interest of justice, in which case the court shall state its reasons in writing for striking the allegation.

(c) For the purpose of this section, "because of" means the bias motivation must be a cause in fact of the offense, whether or not other causes also exist. When multiple concurrent motives exist, the prohibited bias must be a substantial factor in bringing about the particular result. This subdivision does not constitute a change in, but is declaratory of, existing law as set forth in In Re M.S. (1995) 10 Cal.4th 698, 716-720 and People v. Superior Court of San Diego County (Aishman)(1995) 10 Cal.4th 735.

(d) Nothing in this section shall be construed to prevent punishment instead pursuant to any other provision of law that imposes a greater or more severe punishment. *(AD '99)*

191.5. Gross Vehicular Manslaughter While Intoxicated

(a) Gross vehicular manslaughter while intoxicated is the unlawful killing of a human being without malice aforethought, in the driving of a vehicle, where the driving was in violation of Section 23140, 23152, or 23153 of the Vehicle Code, and the killing was either the proximate result of the commission of an unlawful act, not amounting to a felony, and with gross negligence, or the proximate result of the commission of a lawful act which might produce death, in an unlawful manner, and with gross negligence.

(b) Gross vehicular manslaughter while intoxicated also includes operating a vessel in violation of subdivision (b), (c), (d), (e), or (f) of Section 655 of the Harbors and Navigation Code, and in the commission of an unlawful act, not amounting to felony, and with gross negligence; or operating a vessel in violation of subdivision (b), (c), (d), (e), or (f) of Section 655 of the Harbors and Navigation Code, and in the commission of a lawful act which might produce death, in an unlawful manner, and with gross negligence.

(c) Gross vehicular manslaughter while intoxicated is punishable by imprisonment in the state prison for 4, 6, or 10 years.

(d) Any person convicted of violating this section who has one or more prior convictions of this section or of paragraph (1) or (3) of subdivision (c) of Section 192, subdivision (a) or (c) of Section 192.5 of this code, or of violating Section 23152 punishable under Sections 23540, 23542, 23546, 23548, 23550, or 23552 of, or convicted of Section 23153 of, the Vehicle Code, shall be punished by imprisonment in the state prison for a term of 15 years to life. Article 2.5 (commencing with Section 2930) of Chapter 7 of Title 1 of Part 3 shall apply to reduce the term imposed pursuant to this subdivision.

(e) This section shall not be construed as prohibiting or precluding a charge of murder under Section 188 upon facts exhibiting wantonness and a conscious disregard for life to support a finding of implied malice, or upon facts showing malice consistent with the holding of the California Supreme Court in People v. Watson, 30 Cal. 3d 290.

(f) This section shall not be construed as making any homicide in the driving of a vehicle or the operation of a vessel punishable which is not a proximate result of the commission of an unlawful act, not amounting to felony, or of the commission of a lawful act which might produce death, in an unlawful manner. *(AM '98)*

192. Manslaughter

Manslaughter is the unlawful killing of a human being without malice. It is of three kinds:

(a) Voluntary—upon a sudden quarrel or heat of passion.

(b) Involuntary—in the commission of an unlawful act, not amounting to felony; or in the commission of a lawful act which might produce death, in an unlawful manner, or without due caution and circumspection. This subdivision shall not apply to acts committed in the driving of a vehicle.

(c) Vehicular

(1) Except as provided in Section 191.5, driving a vehicle in the commission of an unlawful act, not amounting to felony, and with gross negligence; or driving a vehicle in the commission of a lawful act which might produce death, in an unlawful manner, and with gross negligence.

(2) Except as provided in paragraph (3), driving a vehicle in the commission of an unlawful act, not amounting to felony, but without gross negligence; or driving a vehicle in the commission of a lawful act which might produce death, in an unlawful manner, but without gross negligence.

(3) Driving a vehicle in violation of Section 23140, 23152, or 23153 of the Vehicle Code and in the commission of an unlawful act, not amounting to felony, but without gross negligence; or driving a vehicle in violation of Section 23140, 23152, or 23153 of the Vehicle Code and in the commission of a lawful act which might produce death, in an unlawful manner, but without gross negligence.

(4) Driving a vehicle in connection with a violation of paragraph (3) of subdivision (a) of Section 550, where the vehicular collision or vehicular accident was knowingly caused for financial gain and proximately resulted in the death of any person. This provision shall not be construed to prevent prosecution of a defendant for the crime of murder.

This section shall not be construed as making any homicide in the driving of a vehicle punishable which is not a proximate result of the commission of an unlawful act, not amounting to felony, or of the commission of a lawful act which might produce death, in an unlawful manner.

"Gross negligence," as used in this section, shall not be construed as prohibiting or precluding a charge of murder under Section 188 upon facts exhibiting wantonness and a conscious disregard for life to support a finding of implied malice, or upon facts showing malice, consistent with the holding of the California Supreme Court in People v. Watson, 30 Cal. 3d 290. *(AM '98)*

192.5. Vehicular Manslaughter Involving Vessel

Vehicular manslaughter pursuant to subdivision (c) of Section 192 includes:

(a) Except as provided in subdivision (b) of Section 191.5, operating a vessel in the commission of an unlawful act, not amounting to felony, and with gross negligence; or operating a vessel in the commission of a lawful act which might produce death, in an unlawful manner, and with gross negligence.

(b) Except as provided in subdivision (c), operating a vessel in the commission of an unlawful act, not amounting to felony, but without gross negligence; or operating a vessel in the commission of a lawful act which might produce death, in an unlawful manner, but without gross negligence.

(c) Operating a vessel in violation of subdivisions (b) to (e), inclusive, of Section 655 of the Harbors and Navigation Code, and in the commission of an unlawful act, not amounting to felony, but without gross negligence; or operating a vessel in violation of subdivisions (b) to (e), inclusive, of Section 655 of the Harbors and Navigation Code, and in the commission of a lawful act which might produce death, in an unlawful manner, but without gross negligence.

(d) This section shall become operative on January 1, 1992.

193. Manslaughter - Punishment

(a) Voluntary manslaughter is punishable by imprisonment in the state prison for three, six, or eleven years.

(b) Involuntary manslaughter is punishable by imprisonment in the state prison for two, three, or four years.

(c) Vehicular manslaughter is punishable as follows:

(1) A violation of paragraph (1) of subdivision (c) of Section 192 is punishable either by imprisonment in the county jail for not more than one year or by imprisonment in the state prison for two, four, or six years.

(2) A violation of paragraph (2) of subdivision (c) of Section 192 is punishable by imprisonment in the county jail for not more than one year.

(3) A violation of paragraph (3) of subdivision (c) of Section 192 is punishable either by imprisonment in the county jail for not more than one year or by imprisonment in the state prison for 16 months or two or four years.

(4) A violation of paragraph (4) of subdivision (c) of Section 192 is punishable by imprisonment in the state prison for 4, 6, or 10 years. *(AM '98)*

193.8. Relinquishing Motor Vehicle to Minor Prohibited

(a) It is unlawful for any adult who is the registered owner of a motor vehicle or in possession of a motor vehicle to relinquish possession of the vehicle to a minor for the purpose of driving if the following conditions exist:

(1) The adult owner or person in possession of the vehicle knew or reasonably should have known that the minor was intoxicated at the time possession was relinquished.

(2) A petition was sustained or the minor was convicted of a violation of Section 23103 as specified in Section 23103.5, 23140, 23152, or 23153 of the Vehicle Code or a violation of Section 191.5 or paragraph (3) of subdivision (c) of Section 192.

(3) The minor does not otherwise have a lawful right to possession of the vehicle.

(b) The offense described in subdivision (a) shall not apply to commercial bailments, motor vehicle leases, or parking arrangements, whether or not for compensation, provided by hotels, motels, or food facilities for customers, guests, or other invitees thereof. For purposes of this subdivision, hotel and motel shall have the same meaning as in subdivision (b) of Section 25503.16 of the Business and Professions Code and food facility shall have the same meaning as in Section 113785 of the Health and Safety Code.

(c) If any adult is convicted of the offense described in subdivision (a), that person shall be punished by a fine not exceeding one thousand dollars ($1,000), or by imprisonment in a county jail not exceeding six months, or by both the fine and imprisonment. Any adult convicted of the offense described in subdivision (a) shall not be subject to driver's license suspension or revocation or attendance at a licensed alcohol or drug education and counseling program for persons who drive under the influence.

195. Accidental and Excusable Homicide

Homicide is excusable in the following cases:

1. When committed by accident and misfortune, or in doing any other lawful act by lawful means, with usual and ordinary caution, and without any unlawful intent.

2. When committed by accident and misfortune, in the heat of passion, upon any sudden and sufficient provocation, or upon a sudden combat, when no undue advantage is taken, nor any dangerous weapon used, and when the killing is not done in a cruel or unusual manner.

196. Justifiable Homicide by Public Officer

Homicide is justifiable when committed by public officers and those acting by their command in their aid and assistance, either —

1. In obedience to any judgment of a competent Court; or,

2. When necessarily committed in overcoming actual resistance to the execution of some legal process, or in the discharge of any other legal duty; or,

3. When necessarily committed in retaking felons who have been rescued or have escaped, or when necessarily committed in arresting persons charged with felony, and who are fleeing from justice or resisting such arrest.

197. Killing in Defense of Self or Property, in Arresting Fugitive or Quelling Riot

Homicide is also justifiable when committed by any person in any of the following cases:

1. When resisting any attempt to murder any person, or to commit a felony, or to do some great bodily injury upon any person; or,

2. When committed in defense of habitation, property, or person, against one who manifestly intends or endeavors, by violence or surprise, to commit a felony, or against one who manifestly intends and endeavors, in a violent, riotous or tumultuous manner, to enter the habitation of another for the purpose of offering violence to any person therein; or,

3. When committed in the lawful defense of such person, or of a wife or husband, parent, child, master, mistress, or servant of such person, when there is reasonable ground to apprehend a design to commit a felony or to do some great bodily injury, and imminent danger of such design being accomplished; but such person, or the person in whose behalf the defense was made, if he was the assailant or engaged in mutual combat, must really and in good faith have endeavored to decline any further struggle before the homicide was committed; or,

4. When necessarily committed in attempting, by lawful ways and means, to apprehend any person for any felony committed, or in lawfully suppressing any riot, or in lawfully keeping and preserving the peace.

203. Mayhem Defined

Every person who unlawfully and maliciously deprives a human being of a member of his body, or disables, disfigures, or renders it useless, or cuts or disables the tongue, or puts out an eye, or slits the nose, ear, or lip, is guilty of mayhem.

205. Aggravated Mayhem

A person is guilty of aggravated mayhem when he or she unlawfully, under circumstances manifesting extreme indifference to the physical or psychological well-being of another person, intentionally causes permanent disability or disfigurement of another human being or deprives a human being of a limb, organ, or member of his or her body. For purposes of this section, it is not necessary to prove an intent to kill. Aggravated mayhem is a felony punishable by imprisonment in the state prison for life with the possibility of parole.

206. Torture

Every person who, with the intent to cause cruel or extreme pain and suffering for the purpose of revenge, extortion, persuasion, or for any sadistic purpose, inflicts great bodily injury as defined in Section 12022.7 upon the person of another, is guilty of torture.

The crime of torture does not require any proof that the victim suffered pain.

207. Kidnapping Defined

(a) Every person who forcibly, or by any other means of instilling fear, steals or takes, or holds, detains, or arrests any person in this state, and carries the person into another country, state, or county, or into another part of the same county, is guilty of kidnapping.

(b) Every person, who for the purpose of committing any act defined in Section 288, hires, persuades, entices, decoys, or seduces by false promises, misrepresentations, or the like, any child under the age of 14 years to go out of this country, state, or county, or into another part of the same county, is guilty of kidnapping.

(c) Every person who forcibly, or by any other means of instilling fear, takes or holds, detains, or arrests any person, with a design to take the person out of this state, without having established a claim, according to the laws of the United States, or of this state, or who hires, persuades, entices, decoys, or seduces by false promises, misrepresentations, or the like, any person to go out of this state, or to be taken or removed therefrom, for the purpose and with the intent to sell that person into slavery or involuntary servitude, or otherwise to employ that person for his or her own use, or to the use of another, without the free will and consent of that persuaded person, is guilty of kidnapping.

(d) Every person who, being out of this state, abducts or takes by force or fraud any person contrary to the law of the place where that act is committed, and brings, sends, or conveys that person within the limits of this state, and is afterwards found within the limits thereof, is guilty of kidnapping.

(e) Subdivisions (a) to (d), inclusive, do not apply to any of the following:

(1) To any person who steals, takes, entices away, detains, conceals, or harbors any child under the age of 14 years, if that act is taken to protect the child from danger of imminent harm.

(2) To any person acting under Section 834 or 837.

209. Kidnapping for Ransom or Extortion

(a) Any person who seizes, confines, inveigles, entices, decoys, abducts, conceals, kidnaps or carries away another person by any means whatsoever with intent to hold or detain, or who holds or detains, that person for ransom, reward or to commit extortion or to exact from another person any money or valuable thing, or any person who aids or abets any such act, is guilty of a felony, and upon conviction thereof, shall be punished by imprisonment in the state prison for life without possibility of parole in cases in which any person subjected to any such act suffers death or bodily harm, or is intentionally confined in a manner which exposes that person to a substantial likelihood of death, or shall be punished by imprisonment in the state prison for life with the possibility of parole in cases where no such person suffers death or bodily harm.

(b)(1) Any person who kidnaps or carries away any individual to commit robbery, rape, spousal rape, oral copulation, sodomy, or sexual penetration in violation of Section 289, shall be punished by imprisonment in the state prison for life with possibility of parole.

(2) This subdivision shall only apply if the movement of the victim is beyond that merely incidental to the commission of, and increases the risk of harm to the victim over and above that necessarily present in, the intended underlying offense.

(c) In all cases in which probation is granted, the court shall, except in unusual cases where the interests of justice would best be served by a lesser penalty, require as a condition of the probation that the person be confined in the county jail for 12 months. If the court grants probation without requiring the defendant to be confined in the county jail for 12 months, it shall specify its reason or reasons for imposing a lesser penalty.

(d) Subdivision (b) shall not be construed to supersede or affect Section 667.61. A person may be charged with a violation of subdivision (b) and Section 667.61. However, a person may not be punished under subdivision (b) and Section 667.61 for the same act that constitutes a violation of both subdivision (b) and Section 667.61. *(AM '00)*

209.5 Kidnapping Pursuant to Carjacking

(a) Any person who, during the commission of a carjacking and in order to facilitate the commission of the carjacking, kidnaps another person who is not a principal in the commission of the carjacking shall be punished by imprisonment in the state prison for life with the possibility of parole.

(b) This section shall only apply if the movement of the victim is beyond that merely incidental to the commission of the carjacking, the victim is moved a substantial distance from the vicinity of the carjacking, and movement of the victim increases the risk of harm to the victim over and above that necessarily present in the crime of carjacking itself.

(c) In all cases in which probation is granted, the court shall, except in unusual cases where the interests of justice would best be served by a lessor penalty, require as a condition of the probation that the person be confined in the county jail for 12 months. If the court grants probation without requiring the defendant to be confined in the county jail for 12 months, it shall specify its reason or reasons for imposing a lessor penalty.

210. Posing as Kidnapper, Etc.

Every person who for the purpose of obtaining any ransom or reward, or to extort or exact from any person any money or thing of value, poses as, or in any manner represents himself to be a person who has seized, confined, inveigled, enticed, decoyed, abducted, concealed, kidnapped or carried away any person, or who poses as, or in any manner represents himself to be a person who holds or detains such person, or who poses as, or in any manner represents himself to be a person who has aided or abetted any such act, or who poses as or in any manner represents himself to be a person who has the influence, power, or ability, to obtain the release of such person so seized, confined, inveigled, enticed, decoyed, abducted, concealed, kidnapped or carried away, is guilty of a felony and upon conviction thereof shall be punished by imprisonment for two, three or four years.

Nothing in this section prohibits any person who, in good faith believes that he can rescue any person who has been seized, confined, inveigled, enticed, decoyed, abducted, concealed, kidnapped or carried away, and who has had no part in, or connection with, such confinement, inveigling, decoying, abducting, concealing, kidnapping, or carrying away, from offering to rescue or obtain the release of such person for a monetary consideration or other thing of value.

210.5. Taking Hostages

Every person who commits the offense of false imprisonment, as defined in Section 236, against a person for purposes of protection from arrest, which substantially increases the risk of harm to the victim, or for purposes of using the person as a shield is punishable by imprisonment in the state prison for three, five, or eight years.

211. Robbery Defined

Robbery is the felonious taking of personal property in the possession of another, from his person or immediate presence, and against his will, accomplished by means of force or fear.

212. Fear Defined

The fear mentioned in Section 211 may be either:

1.   The fear of an unlawful injury to the person or property of the person robbed, or of any relative of his or member of his family; or,

2.   The fear of an immediate and unlawful injury to the person or property of anyone in the company of the person robbed at the time of the robbery.

212.5. First and Second Degree Robbery

(a) Every robbery of any person who is performing his or her duties as an operator of any bus, taxicab, cable car, streetcar, trackless trolley, or other vehicle, including a vehicle operated on stationary rails or on a track or rail suspended in the air, and used for the transportation of persons for hire, every robbery of any passenger which is perpetrated on any of these vehicles, and every robbery which is perpetrated in an inhabited dwelling house, a vessel as defined in Section 21 of the Harbors and Navigation Code which is inhabited and designed for habitation, an inhabited floating home as defined in subdivision (d) of Section 18075.55 of the Health and Safety Code, a trailer coach as defined in the Vehicle Code which is inhabited, or the inhabited portion of any other building is robbery of the first degree.

(b) Every robbery of any person while using an automated teller machine or immediately after the person has used an automated teller machine and is in the vicinity of the automated teller machine is robbery of the first degree.

(c) All kinds of robbery other than those listed in subdivisions (a) and (b) are of the second degree.

214. Train Robbery

Every person who goes upon or boards any railroad train, car or engine, with the intention of robbing any passenger or other person on such train, car or engine, of any personal property thereon in the possession or care or under the control of any such passenger or other person, or who interferes in any manner with any switch, rail, sleeper, viaduct, culvert, embankment, structure or appliance pertaining to or connected with any railroad, or places any dynamite or other explosive substance or material upon or near the tract of any railroad, or who sets fire to any railroad bridge or trestle, or who shows, masks, extinguishes, or alters any light or other signal, or exhibits or compels any other person to exhibit any false light or signal, or who stops any such train, car or engine, or slackens the speed thereof, or who compels or attempts to compel any person in charge or control thereof to stop any such train, car or engine, or slacken the speed thereof, with the intention of robbing any passenger or other person on such train, car or engine, of any personal property thereon in the possession or charge or under the control of any such passenger or other person, is guilty of a felony.

215. Carjacking

(a) "Carjacking"is the felonious taking of a motor vehicle in the possession of another, from his or her person or immediate presence, or from the person or immediate presence of a passenger of the motor vehicle, against his or her will and with the intent to either permanently or temporarily deprive the person in possession of the motor vehicle of his or her possession, accomplished by means of force or fear.

(b) Carjacking is punishable by imprisonment in the state prison for a term of three, five, or nine years.

(c) This section shall not be construed to supersede or affect Section 211. A person may be charged with a violation of this section and Section 211. However, no defendant may be punished under this section and Section 211 for the same act which constitutes a violation of both this section and Section 211.

217.1. Assault on President or Other Governmental Official

(a) Except as provided in subdivision (b), every person who commits any assault upon the President or Vice President of the United States, the Governor of any state or territory, any justice, judge, or former judge of any local, state, or federal court of record, any commissioner, referee, or other subordinate judicial officer of any court of record, the secretary or director of any executive agency or department of the United States or any state or territory, or any other official of the United States or any state or territory holding elective office, any mayor, city council member, county supervisor, sheriff, district attorney, prosecutor or assistant prosecutor of any local, state, or federal prosecutor's office, a former prosecutor or assistant prosecutor of any local, state, or federal prosecutor's office, public defender or assistant public defender of any local, state, or federal public defender's office, a former public defender or assistant public defender of any local, state, or federal public defender's office, the chief of police of any municipal police department, any peace officer, any juror in any local, state, or federal court of record, or the immediate family of any of these officials, in retaliation for or to prevent the performance of the victim's official duties, shall be punished by imprisonment in the county jail not exceeding one year or by imprisonment in the state prison.

(b) Notwithstanding subdivision (a), every person who attempts to commit murder against any person listed in subdivision (a) in retaliation for or to prevent the performance of the victim's official duties, shall be confined in the state prison for a term of 15 years to life. The provisions of Article 2.5 (commencing with Section 2930) of Chapter 7 of Title 1 of Part 3 shall apply to reduce any minimum term of 15 years in a state prison imposed pursuant to this section, but that person shall not otherwise be released on parole prior to such time.

(c) For the purposes of this section, the following words have the following meanings:

(1) "Immediate family" means spouse, child, stepchild, brother, stepbrother, sister, stepsister, mother, stepmother, father, or stepfather.

(2) "Peace officer" means any person specified in subdivision (a) of Section 830.1 or Section 830.5. *(AM '99)*

218. Derailing or Wrecking Train

Every person who unlawfully throws out a switch, removes a rail, or places any obstruction on any railroad with the intention of derailing any passenger, freight or other train, car or engine, or who unlawfully places any dynamite or other explosive material or any other obstruction upon or near the track of any railroad with the intention of blowing up or derailing any such train, car or engine, or who unlawfully sets fire to any railroad bridge or trestle, over which any such train, car or engine must pass with the intention of wrecking such train, car or engine, is guilty of a felony, and shall be punished by imprisonment in the State prison for life without possibility of parole.

219. Penalty for Wrecking Train or Firing Bridge

Every person who unlawfully throws out a switch, removes a rail, or places any obstruction on any railroad with the intention of derailing any passenger, freight or other train, car or engine and thus derails the same, or who unlawfully places any dynamite or other explosive material or any other obstruction upon or near the track of any railroad with the intention of blowing up or derailing any such train, car or engine and thus blows up or derails the same, or who unlawfully sets fire to any railroad bridge or trestle over which any such train, car or engine must pass with the intention of wrecking such train, car or engine, and thus wrecks the same, is guilty of a felony and punishable with death or imprisonment in the state prison for life without possibility of parole in cases where any person suffers death as a proximate result thereof, or imprisonment in the state prison for life with the possibility of parole, in cases where no person suffers death as a proximate result thereof. The penalty shall be determined pursuant to Section 190.3 and 190.4.

219.1. Throwing Missile at Vehicle of Common Carrier

Every person who unlawfully throws, hurls or projects at a vehicle operated by a common carrier, while such vehicle is either in motion or stationary, any rock, stone, brick, bottle, piece of wood or metal or any other missile of any kind or character, or does any unlawful act, with the intention of wrecking such vehicle and doing bodily harm, and thus wrecks the same and causes bodily harm, is guilty of a felony and punishable by imprisonment in the state prison for two, four, or six years.

219.2. Throwing Missile or Shooting at Trains, Streetcars, or Vessels

Every person who willfully throws, hurls, or projects a stone or other hard substance, or shoots a missile, at a train, locomotive, railway car, caboose, cable railway car, street railway car, or bus or at a steam vessel or watercraft used for carrying passengers or freight on any of the waters within or bordering on this state, is punishable by imprisonment in the county jail not exceeding one year, or in a state prison, or by fine not exceeding two thousand dollars ($2,000), or by both such fine and imprisonment.

219.3. Throwing Missile From Toll Bridge

Any person who willfully drops or throws any object or missile from any toll bridge is guilty of a misdemeanor.

220. Assault With Intent to Commit Mayhem, Rape, Sodomy, Oral Copulation

Every person who assaults another with intent to commit mayhem, rape, sodomy, oral copulation, or any violation of Section 264.1, 288 or 289 is punishable by imprisonment in the state prison for two, four, or six years.

222. Administering Controlled Substances or Anesthetic to Aid Felony

Every person guilty of administering to another any chloroform, ether, laudanum, or any controlled substance, anesthetic, or intoxicating agent, with intent thereby to enable or assist himself or herself or any other person to commit a felony, is guilty of a felony.

236. False Imprisonment

False imprisonment is the unlawful violation of the personal liberty of another.

237. False Imprisonment, Penalty

(a) False imprisonment is punishable by a fine not exceeding one thousand dollars ($1,000), or by imprisonment in the county jail for not more than one year, or by both that fine and imprisonment. If the false imprisonment be effected by violence, menace, fraud, or deceit, it shall be punishable by imprisonment in the state prison.

(b) False imprisonment of an elder or dependent adult by use of violence, menace, fraud, or deceit shall be punishable as described in subdivision (f) of Section 368. *(AM '99)*

240. Assault Defined

An assault is an unlawful attempt, coupled with a present ability, to commit a violent injury on the person of another.

241. Assault; Assault Against Peace Officer or Other Specified Persons Engaged in Performance of Duties

(a) An assault is punishable by a fine not exceeding one thousand dollars ($1,000), or by imprisonment in the county jail not exceeding six months, or by both the fine and imprisonment.

(b) When an assault is committed against the person of a peace officer, firefighter, emergency medical technician, mobile intensive care paramedic, lifeguard, process server, traffic officer, or animal control officer engaged in the performance of his or her duties, or a physician or nurse engaged in rendering emergency medical care outside a hospital, clinic, or other health care facility, and the person committing the offense knows or reasonably should know that the victim is a peace officer, firefighter, emergency medical technician, mobile intensive care paramedic, lifeguard, process server, traffic officer, or animal control officer engaged in the performance of his or her duties, or a physician or nurse engaged in rendering emergency medical care, the assault is punishable by a fine not exceeding two thousand dollars ($2,000), or by imprisonment in the county jail not exceeding one year, or by both the fine and imprisonment.

(c) As used in this section, the following definitions apply:

(1) Peace officer means any person defined in Chapter 4.5 of Title 3 of Part 2.

(2) "Emergency medical technician" means a person possessing a valid course completion certificate from a program approved by the State Department of Health Services for the medical training and education of ambulance personnel-and who meets the standards of Division 2.5 of the Health and Safety Code.

(3) "Mobile intensive care paramedic" refers to those persons who meet the standards set forth in Division 2.5 of the Health and Safety Code.

(4) "Nurse" means a person who meets the standards of Division 2.5 of the Health and Safety Code.

(5) "Lifeguard" means a person who is:

(A) Employed as a lifeguard by the state, a county, or a city, and is designated by local ordinance as a public officer who has a duty and responsibility to enforce local ordinances and misdemeanors through the issuance of citations.

(B) Wearing distinctive clothing which includes written identification of the person s status as a lifeguard and which clearly identifies the employing organization.

(6) "Process server" means any person who meets the standards or is expressly exempt from the standards set forth in Section 22350 of the Business and Professions Code.

(7) "Traffic officer" means any person employed by a county or city to monitor and enforce state laws and local ordinances relating to parking and the operation of vehicles.

(8) "Animal control officer" means any person employed by a county or city for purposes of enforcing animal control laws or regulations.

241.1. Assault on Custodial Officer

When an assault is committed against the person of a custodial officer as defined in Section 831 or 831.5, and the person committing the offense knows or reasonably should know that such victim is such a custodial officer engaged in the performance of his duties, the offense shall be punished by imprisonment in the county jail not exceeding one year or by imprisonment in the state prison.

241.2. Assault on Any Person on School or Park Property

(a)(1) When an assault is committed on school or park property against any person, the assault is punishable by a fine not exceeding two thousand dollars ($2,000), or by imprisonment in the county jail not exceeding one year, or by both *** that fine and imprisonment.

(2) When a violation of this section is committed by a minor on school property, the court may, in addition to any other fine, sentence, or as a condition of probation, order the minor to attend counseling as deemed appropriate by the court at the expense of the minor's parents. The court shall take into consideration the ability of the minor's parents to pay, however, no minor shall be relieved of attending counseling because of the minor's parents' inability to pay for the counseling imposed by this section.

(b) "School," as used in this section, means any elementary school, junior high school, four-year high school, senior high school, adult school or any branch thereof, opportunity school, continuation high school, regional occupational center, evening high school, technical school, or community college.

(c) "Park," as used in this section, means any publicly maintained or operated park. It does not include any facility when used for professional sports or commercial events. *(AM '01)*

241.3. Assault Committed Against Public Transit Employee or Passenger

(a) When an assault is committed against any person on the property of, or on a motor vehicle of, a public transportation provider, the offense shall be punished by a fine not to exceed two thousand dollars ($2,000), or by imprisonment in a county jail not to exceed one year, or by both the fine and imprisonment.

(b) As used in this section, "public transportation provider" means a publicly or privately owned entity that operates, for the transportation of persons for hire, a bus, taxicab, streetcar, cable car, trackless trolley, or other motor vehicle, including a vehicle operated on stationary rails or on a track or rail suspended in air, or that operates a schoolbus.

(c) As used in this section, "on the property of"means the entire station where public transportation is available, including the parking lot reserved for the public who utilize the transportation system.

241.4. Assault on School Police Department Member

An assault is punishable by fine not exceeding one thousand dollars ($1,000), or by imprisonment in the county jail not exceeding six months, or by both. When the assault is committed against the person of a peace officer engaged in the performance of his or her duties as a member of a police department of a school district pursuant to Section 39670 of the Education Code, and the person committing the offense knows or reasonably should know that the victim is a peace officer engaged in the performance of his or her duties, the offense shall be punished by imprisonment in the county jail not exceeding one year or by imprisonment in the state prison.

241.6. Assault on School Employee

When an assault is committed against a school employee engaged in the performance of his or her duties, or in retaliation for an act performed in the course of his or her duties, whether on or off campus, during the schoolday or at any other time, and the person committing the offense knows or reasonably should know the victim is a school employee, the assault is punishable by imprisonment in the county jail not exceeding one year, or by a fine not exceeding two thousand dollars ($2,000), or by both the fine and imprisonment.

For purposes of this section, "school employee"has the same meaning as defined in subdivision (d) of Section 245.5.

This section shall not apply to conduct arising during the course of an otherwise lawful labor dispute.

241.7. Assault on Juror

Any person who is a party to a civil or criminal action in which a jury has been selected to try the case and who, while the legal action is pending or after the conclusion of the trial, commits an assault against any juror or alternate juror who was selected and sworn in that legal action, shall be punished by a fine not to exceed two thousand dollars ($2,000), or by imprisonment in the county jail not exceeding one year, or by both such fine and imprisonment, or by imprisonment in the state prison.

242. Battery Defined

A battery is any willful and unlawful use of force or violence upon the person of another.

243. Battery: Punishment

(a) A battery is punishable by a fine not exceeding two thousand dollars ($2,000), or by imprisonment in a county jail not exceeding six months, or by both that fine and imprisonment.

(b) When a battery is committed against the person of a peace officer, custodial officer, firefighter, emergency medical technician, lifeguard, process server, traffic officer, or animal control officer engaged in the performance of his or her duties, whether on or off duty, including when the peace officer is in a police uniform and is concurrently performing the duties required of him or her as a peace officer while also employed in a private capacity as a part-time or casual private security guard or patrolman, or a nonsworn employee of a probation department engaged in the performance of his or her duties, whether on or off duty, or a physician or nurse engaged in rendering emergency medical care outside a hospital, clinic, or other health care facility, and the person committing the offense knows or reasonably should know that the victim is a peace officer, custodial officer, firefighter, emergency medical technician, lifeguard, process server, traffic officer, or animal control officer engaged in the performance of his or her duties, nonsworn employee of a probation department, or a physician or nurse engaged in rendering emergency medical care, the battery is punishable by a fine not exceeding two thousand dollars ($2,000), or by imprisonment in a county jail not exceeding one year, or by both that fine and imprisonment.

(c)(1) When a battery is committed against a custodial officer, firefighter, emergency medical technician, lifeguard, process server, traffic officer, or animal control officer engaged in the performance of his or her duties, whether on or off duty, or a nonsworn employee of a probation department engaged in the performance of his or her duties, whether on or off duty, or a physician or nurse engaged in rendering emergency medical care outside a hospital, clinic, or other health care facility, and the person committing the offense knows or reasonably should know that the victim is a nonsworn employee of a probation department, custodial officer, firefighter, emergency medical technician, lifeguard, process server, traffic officer, or animal control officer engaged in the performance of his or her duties, or a physician or nurse engaged in rendering emergency medical care, and an injury is inflicted on that victim, the battery is punishable by a fine of not more than two thousand dollars ($2,000), by imprisonment in a county jail not exceeding one year, or by both that fine and imprisonment, or by imprisonment in the state prison for 16 months, or two or three years.

(2) When the battery specified in paragraph (1) is committed against a peace officer engaged in the performance of his or her duties, whether on or off duty, including when the peace officer is in a police uniform and is concurrently performing the duties required of him or her as a peace officer while also employed in a private capacity as a part-time or casual private security guard or patrolman and the person committing the offense knows or reasonably should know that the victim is a peace officer engaged in the performance of his or her duties, the battery is punishable by a fine of not more than ten thousand dollars ($10,000), or by imprisonment in a county jail not exceeding one year or in the state prison for 16 months, or two or three years, or by both that fine and imprisonment.

(d) When a battery is committed against any person and serious bodily injury is inflicted on the person, the battery is punishable by imprisonment in a county jail not exceeding one year or imprisonment in the state prison for two, three, or four years.

(e)(1) When a battery is committed against a spouse, a person with whom the defendant is cohabiting, a person who is the parent of the defendant's child, former spouse, fiance, or fiancee, or a person with whom the defendant currently has, or has previously had, a dating or engagement relationship, the battery is punishable by a fine not exceeding two thousand dollars ($2,000), or by imprisonment in a county jail for a period of not more than one year, or by both that fine and imprisonment. If probation is granted, or the execution or imposition of the sentence is suspended, it shall be a condition thereof that the defendant participate in, for no less than one year, and successfully complete, a batterer's treatment program, as defined in Section 1203.097, or if none is available, another appropriate counseling program designated by the court. However, this provision shall not be construed as requiring a city, a county, or a city and county to provide a new program or higher level of service as contemplated by Section 6 of Article XIIIB of the California Constitution.

(2) Upon conviction of a violation of this subdivision, if probation is granted, the conditions of probation may include, in lieu of a fine, one or both of the following requirements:

(A) That the defendant make payments to a battered women's shelter, up to a maximum of five thousand dollars ($5,000).

(B) That the defendant reimburse the victim for reasonable costs of counseling and other reasonable expenses that the court finds are the direct result of the defendant's offense.

For any order to pay a fine, make payments to a battered women's shelter, or pay restitution as a condition of probation under this subdivision, the court shall make a determination of the defendant's ability to pay. In no event shall any order to make payments to a battered women's shelter be made if it would impair the ability of the defendant to pay direct restitution to the victim or court-ordered child support. Where the injury to a married person is caused in whole or in part by the criminal acts of his or her spouse in violation of this section, the community property may not be used to discharge the liability of the offending spouse for restitution to the injured spouse, required by Section 1203.04, as operative on or before August 2, 1995, or Section 1202.4, or to a shelter for costs with regard to the injured spouse and dependents, required by this section, until all separate property of the offending spouse is exhausted.

(3) Upon conviction of a violation of this subdivision, if probation is granted or the execution or imposition of the sentence is suspended and the person has been previously convicted of a violation of this subdivision and sentenced under paragraph (1), the person shall be imprisoned for not less than 48 hours in addition to the conditions in paragraph (1). However, the court, upon a showing of good cause, may elect

not to impose the mandatory minimum imprisonment as required by this subdivision and may, under these circumstances, grant probation or order the suspension of the execution or imposition of the sentence.

(4) The Legislature finds and declares that these specified crimes merit special consideration when imposing a sentence so as to display society's condemnation for these crimes of violence upon victims with whom a close relationship has been formed.

(f) As used in this section:

(1) "Peace officer" means any person defined in Chapter 4.5 (commencing with Section 830) of Title 3 of Part 2.

(2) "Emergency medical technician" means a person who is either an EMT-I, EMT-II, or EMT-P (paramedic), and possesses a valid certificate or license in accordance with the standards of Division 2.5 (commencing with Section 1797) of the Health and Safety Code.

(3) "Nurse" means a person who meets the standards of Division 2.5 (commencing with Section 1797) of the Health and Safety Code.

(4) "Serious bodily injury" means a serious impairment of physical condition, including, but not limited to, the following: loss of consciousness; concussion; bone fracture; protracted loss or impairment of function of any bodily member or organ; a wound requiring extensive suturing; and serious disfigurement.

(5) "Injury" means any physical injury which requires professional medical treatment.

(6) "Custodial officer" means any person who has the responsibilities and duties described in Section 831 and who is employed by a law enforcement agency of any city or county or who performs those duties as a volunteer.

(7) "Lifeguard" means a person defined in paragraph (5) of subdivision (c) of Section 241.

(8) "Traffic officer" means any person employed by a city, county, or city and county to monitor and enforce state laws and local ordinances relating to parking and the operation of vehicles.

(9) "Animal control officer" means any person employed by a city, county, or city and county for purposes of enforcing animal control laws or regulations.

(10) "Dating relationship" means frequent, intimate associations primarily characterized by the expectation of affectional or sexual involvement independent of financial considerations.

(g) It is the intent of the Legislature by amendments to this section at the 1981-82 and 1983-84 Regular Sessions to abrogate the holdings in cases such as People v. Corey, 21 Cal. 3d 738, and Cervantez v. J.C. Penney Co., 24 Cal. 3d 579, and to reinstate prior judicial interpretations of this section as they relate to criminal sanctions for battery on peace officers who are employed, on a part-time or casual basis, while wearing a police uniform as private security guards or patrolmen and to allow the exercise of peace officer powers concurrently with that employment. *(AM '99, '00)*

243.1. Battery Against Custodial Officer

When a battery is committed against the person of a custodial officer as defined in Section 831 of the Penal Code, and the person committing the offense knows or reasonably should know that *** the victim is a custodial officer engaged in the performance of his or her duties, and *** the custodial officer is engaged in the performance of his or her duties, the offense shall be punished by imprisonment in the state prison. *(AM '01)*

243.2. Battery Committed on Any Person on School or Park Property

(a)(1) Except as otherwise provided in Section 243.6, when a battery is committed on school property, park property, or the grounds of a public or private hospital, against any person, the battery is punishable by a fine not exceeding two thousand dollars ($2,000), or by imprisonment in the county jail not exceeding one year, or by both the fine and imprisonment.

(2) When a violation of this section is committed by a minor on school property, the court may, in addition to any other fine, sentence, or as a condition of probation, order the minor to attend counseling as deemed appropriate by the court at the expense of the minor's parents. The court shall take into consideration the ability of the minor's parents to pay, however, no minor shall be relieved of attending counseling because of the minor's parents' inability to pay for the counseling imposed by this section.

(b) For the purposes of this section, the following terms have the following meanings:

(1) "Hospital"means a facility for the diagnosis, care, and treatment of human illness that is subject to, or specifically exempted from, the licensure requirements of Chapter 2 (commencing with Section 1250) of Division 2 of the Health and Safety Code.

(2) "Park"means any publicly maintained or operated park. It does not include any facility when used for professional sports or commercial events.

(3) "School" means any elementary school, junior high school, four-year high school, senior high school, adult school or any branch thereof, opportunity school, continuation high school, regional occupational center, evening high school, technical school, or community college.

(c) This section shall not apply to conduct arising during the course of an otherwise lawful labor dispute. *(AM '01)*

243.3. Battery Committed Against Public Transit Employee or Passenger

When a battery is committed against the person of an operator, driver, or passenger on a bus, taxicab, streetcar, cable car, trackless trolley, or other motor vehicle, including a vehicle operated on stationary rails or on a track or rail suspended in the air, used for the transportation of persons for hire, or against a schoolbus driver, or against the person of a station agent or ticket agent for the entity providing the transportation, and the person who commits the offense knows or reasonably should know that the victim, in the case of an operator, driver, or agent, is engaged in the performance of his or her duties, or is a passenger the offense shall be punished by a fine not exceeding ten thousand dollars ($10,000), or by imprisonment in a county jail not exceeding one year, or by both that fine and imprisonment. If an injury is inflicted on that victim, the offense shall be punished by a fine not exceeding ten thousand dollars ($10,000), or by imprisonment in a county jail not exceeding one year or in the state prison for 16 months, or two or three years, or by both that fine and imprisonment.

243.35. Battery Committed Against Public Transit Employee or Passenger: Punishment

(a) Except as provided in Section 243.3, when a battery is committed against any person on the property of, or in a motor vehicle of, a public transportation provider, the offense shall be punished by a fine not to exceed two thousand dollars ($2,000), or by imprisonment in a county jail not to exceed one year, or by both the fine and imprisonment.

(b) As used in this section, "public transportation provider"means a publicly or privately owned entity that operates, for the transportation of persons for hire, a bus, taxicab, streetcar, cable car, trackless trolley, or other motor vehicle, including a vehicle operated on stationary rails or on a track or rail suspended in air, or that operates a schoolbus.

(c) As used in this section, "on the property of"means the entire station where public transportation is available, including the parking lot reserved for the public who utilize the transportation system.

243.4. Sexual Battery

(a) Any person who touches an intimate part of another person while that person is unlawfully restrained by the accused or an accomplice, and if the touching is against the will of the person touched and is for the purpose of sexual arousal, sexual gratification, or sexual abuse, is guilty of sexual battery. A violation of this subdivision is punishable by imprisonment in a county jail for not more than one year, and by a fine not exceeding two thousand dollars ($2,000); or by imprisonment in the state prison for two, three, or four years, and by a fine not exceeding ten thousand dollars ($10,000).

(b) Any person who touches an intimate part of another person who is institutionalized for medical treatment and who is seriously disabled or medically incapacitated, if the touching is against the will of the person touched, and if the touching is for the purpose of sexual arousal, sexual gratification, or sexual abuse, is guilty of sexual battery. A violation of this subdivision is punishable by imprisonment in a county jail for not more than one year, and by a fine not exceeding two thousand dollars ($2,000); or by imprisonment in the state prison for two, three, or four years, and by a fine not exceeding ten thousand dollars ($10,000).

(c) Any person who, for the purpose of sexual arousal, sexual gratification, or sexual abuse, causes another, against that person's will while that person is unlawfully restrained either by the accused or an accomplice, or is institutionalized for medical treatment and is seriously disabled or medically incapacitated, to masturbate or touch an intimate part of either of those persons or a third person, is guilty of sexual battery. A violation of this subdivision is punishable by imprisonment in a county jail for not more than one year, and by a fine not exceeding two thousand dollars ($2,000); or by imprisonment in the state prison for two, three, or four years, and by a fine not exceeding ten thousand dollars ($10,000).

(d)(1) Any person who touches an intimate part of another person, if the touching is against the will of the person touched, and is for the specific purpose of sexual arousal, sexual gratification, or sexual abuse, is guilty of misdemeanor sexual battery, punishable by a fine not exceeding two thousand dollars ($2,000), or by imprisonment in a county jail not exceeding six months, or by both that fine and imprisonment. However, if the defendant was an employer and the victim was an employee of the defendant, the misdemeanor sexual battery shall be punishable by a fine not exceeding three thousand dollars ($3,000), by imprisonment in a county jail not exceeding six months, or by both that fine and imprisonment. Notwithstanding any other provision of law, any amount of a fine above two thousand dollars ($2,000) which is collected from a defendant for a violation of this subdivision shall be transmitted to the State Treasury and, upon appropriation by the Legislature, distributed to the Department of Fair Employment and Housing for the purpose of enforcement of the California Fair Employment and Housing Act (Part 2.8 (commencing with Section 12900) of Division 3 of Title 2 of the Government Code), including, but not limited to, laws that proscribe sexual harassment in places of employment. However, in no event shall an amount over two thousand dollars ($2,000) be transmitted to the State Treasury until all fines, including any restitution fines that may have been imposed upon the defendant, have been paid in full.

(2) As used in this subdivision, "touches" means physical contact with another person, whether accomplished directly, through the clothing of the person committing the offense, or through the clothing of the victim.

(e) As used in subdivisions (a), (b), and (c), "touches" means physical contact with the skin of another person whether accomplished directly or through the clothing of the person committing the offense.

(f) As used in this section, the following terms have the following meanings:

(1) "Intimate part" means the sexual organ, anus, groin, or buttocks of any person, and the breast of a female.

(2) "Sexual battery" does not include the crimes defined in Section 261 or 289.

(3) "Seriously disabled" means a person with severe physical or sensory disabilities.

(4) "Medically incapacitated" means a person who is incapacitated as a result of prescribed sedatives, anesthesia, or other medication.

(5) "Institutionalized" means a person who is located voluntarily or involuntarily in a hospital, medical treatment facility, nursing home, acute care facility, or mental hospital.

(6) "Minor" means a person under 18 years of age.

(g) This section shall not be construed to limit or prevent prosecution under any other law which also proscribes a course of conduct that also is proscribed by this section.

(h) In the case of a felony conviction for a violation of this section, the fact that the defendant was an employer and the victim was an employee of the defendant shall be a factor in aggravation in sentencing.

(i) A person who commits a violation of subdivision (a), (b), or (c) against a minor when the person has a prior felony conviction for a violation of this section shall be guilty of a felony, punishable by imprisonment in the state prison for two, three, or four years and a fine not exceeding ten thousand dollars ($10,000).

243.5. Assault or Battery on School Property; When a Peace Officer May Arrest Without a Warrant

(a) When a person commits an assault or battery on school property during hours when school activities are being conducted, a peace officer may, without a warrant, notwithstanding paragraph (2) or (3) of subdivision (a) of Section 836, arrest the person who commits the assault or battery:

(1) Whenever the person has committed the assault or battery, although not in the peace officer's presence.

(2) Whenever the peace officer has reasonable cause to believe that the person to be arrested has committed the assault or battery, whether or not it has in fact been committed.

(b) "School,"as used in this section, means any elementary school, junior high school, four-year high school, senior high school, adult school or any branch thereof, opportunity school, continuation high school, regional occupational center, evening high school, technical school, or community college.

243.6. Battery Committed Against School Employee

When a battery is committed against a school employee engaged in the performance of his or her duties, or in retaliation for an act performed in the course of his or her duties, whether on or off campus, during the schoolday or at any other time, and the person committing the offense knows or reasonably should know that the victim is a school employee, the battery is punishable by imprisonment in the county jail not exceeding one year, or by a fine not exceeding two thousand dollars ($2,000), or by both the fine and imprisonment. However, if an injury is inflicted on the victim, the battery shall be punishable by imprisonment in the county jail for not more than one year, or by a fine of not more than two thousand dollars ($2,000), or by imprisonment in the state prison for 16 months, or two or three years.

For purposes of this section, "school employee"has the same meaning as defined in subdivision (d) of Section 245.5.

This section shall not apply to conduct arising during the course of an otherwise lawful labor dispute.

243.7. Battery Committed Against Juror

Any person who is a party to a civil or criminal action in which a jury has been selected to try the case and who, while the legal action is pending or after the conclusion of the trial commits a battery against any juror or alternate juror who was selected and sworn in that legal action shall be punished b a fine not to exceed five thousand dollars ($5,000), or by imprisonment in the county jail not exceeding one year, or by both such fine and imprisonment, or by the imprisonment in the state prison for 16 months, or for two or three years.

243.8. Battery Committed Against Sports Official

(a) When a battery is committed against a sports official immediately prior to, during, or immediately following an interscholastic, intercollegiate, or any other organized amateur or professional athletic contest in which the sports official is participating, and the person who commits the offense knows or reasonably should know that the victim is engaged in the performance of his or her duties, the offense shall be punishable by a fine not exceeding two thousand dollars ($2,000), or by imprisonment in the county jail not exceeding one year, or by both that fine and imprisonment.

(b) For purposes of this section, "sports official"means any individual who serves as a referee, umpire, linesman, or who serves in a similar capacity but may be known by a different title or name and is duly registered by, or a member of, a local, state, regional, or national organization engaged in part in providing education and training to sports officials.

243.9. Battery by Gassing Upon any Peace Officer in Local Detention Facility

(a) Every person confined in any local detention facility who commits a battery by gassing upon the person of any peace officer, as defined in Chapter 4.5 (commencing with Section 830) of Title 3 of Part 2, or employee of the local detention facility is guilty of aggravated battery and shall be punished by imprisonment in a county jail or by imprisonment in the state prison for two, three, or four years.

(b) For purposes of this section, "gassing"means intentionally placing or throwing, or causing to be placed or thrown, upon the person of another, any human excrement or other bodily fluids or bodily substances or any mixture containing human excrement or other bodily fluids or bodily substances that results in actual contact with the person's skin or membranes.

(c) The person in charge of the local detention facility shall use every available means to immediately investigate all reported or suspected violations of subdivision (a), including, but not limited to, the use of forensically acceptable means of preserving and testing the suspected gassing substance to confirm the presence of human excrement or other bodily fluids or bodily substances. If there is probable cause to believe that the inmate has violated subdivision (a), the chief medical officer of the local detention facility, or his or her designee, may, when he or she deems it medically necessary to protect the health of an officer or employee who may have been subject to a violation of this section, order the inmate to receive an examination or test for hepatitis or tuberculosis or both hepatitis and tuberculosis on either a voluntary or involuntary basis immediately after the event, and periodically thereafter as determined to be necessary by the medical officer in order to ensure that further hepatitis or tuberculosis transmission does not occur. These decisions shall be consistent with an occupational exposure as defined by the Center for Disease Control and Prevention. The results of any examination or test shall be provided to the officer or employee who has been subject to a reported or suspected violation of this section. Nothing in this subdivision shall be construed to otherwise supersede the operation of Title 8 (commencing with Section 7500). Any person performing tests, transmitting test results, or disclosing information pursuant to this section shall be immune from civil liability for any action taken in accordance with this section.

(d) The person in charge of the local detention facility shall refer all reports for which there is probable cause to believe that the inmate has violated subdivision (a) to the local district attorney for prosecution.

(e) Nothing in this section shall preclude prosecution under both this section and any other provision of law. *(AD '00)*

244. Throwing Acid With Intent to Disfigure or Burn

Any person who willfully and maliciously places or throws, or causes to be placed or thrown, upon the person of another, any vitriol, corrosive acid, flammable substance, or caustic chemical of any nature, with the intent to injure the flesh or disfigure the body of that person, is punishable by imprisonment in the state prison for two, three or four years.

As used in this section, "flammable substance"means gasoline, petroleum products, or flammable liquids with a flashpoint of 150 degrees Fahrenheit or less.

244.5. Assault With Stun Gun or Taser

(a) As used in this section, "stun gun"means any item, except a taser, used or intended to be used as either an offensive or defensive weapon that is capable of temporarily immobilizing a person by the infliction of an electrical charge.

(b) Every person who commits an assault upon the person of another with a stun gun or taser shall be punished by imprisonment in a county jail for a term not exceeding one year, or by imprisonment in the state prison for 16 months, two, or three years.

(c) Every person who commits an assault upon the person of a peace officer or firefighter with a stun gun or taser, who knows or reasonably should know that the person is a peace officer or firefighter engaged in the performance of his or her duties, when the peace officer or firefighter is engaged in the performance of his or her duties, shall be punished by imprisonment in the county jail for a term not exceeding one year, or by imprisonment in the state prison for two, three, or four years.

(d) This section shall not be construed to preclude or in any way limit the applicability of Section 245 in any criminal prosecution.

245. Assault With Deadly Weapon, Firearm, Assault Weapon, or Machine gun

(a)(1) Any person who commits an assault upon the person of another with a deadly weapon or instrument other than a firearm or by any means of force likely to produce great bodily injury shall be punished by imprisonment in the state prison for two, three, or four years, or in a county jail for not exceeding one year, or by a fine not exceeding ten thousand dollars ($10,000), or by both the fine and imprisonment.

(2) Any person who commits an assault upon the person of another with a firearm shall be punished by imprisonment in the state prison for two, three, or four years, or in a county jail for not less than six months and not exceeding one year, or by both a fine not exceeding ten thousand dollars ($10,000) and imprisonment.

(3) Any person who commits an assault upon the person of another with a machinegun, as defined in Section 12200, or an assault weapon, as defined in Section 12276 or 12276.1, shall be punished by imprisonment in the state prison for 4, 8, or 12 years.

(b) Any person who commits an assault upon the person of another with a semiautomatic firearm shall be punished by imprisonment in the state prison for three, six, or nine years.

(c) Any person who commits an assault with a deadly weapon or instrument, other than a firearm, or by any means likely to produce great bodily injury upon the person of a peace officer or firefighter, and who knows or reasonably should know that the victim is a peace officer or firefighter engaged in the performance of his or her duties, when the peace officer or firefighter is engaged in the performance of his or her duties, shall be punished by imprisonment in the state prison for three, four, or five years.

(d)(1) Any person who commits an assault with a firearm upon the person of a peace officer or firefighter, and who knows or reasonably should know that the victim is a peace officer or firefighter engaged in the performance of his or her duties, when the peace officer or firefighter is engaged in the performance of his or her duties, shall be punished by imprisonment in the state prison for four, six, or eight years.

(2) Any person who commits an assault upon the person of a peace officer or firefighter with a semiautomatic firearm and who knows or reasonably should know that the victim is a peace officer or firefighter engaged in the performance of his or her duties, when the peace officer or firefighter is engaged in the performance of his or her duties, shall be punished by imprisonment in the state prison for five, seven, or nine years.

(3) Any person who commits an assault with a machinegun, as defined in Section 12200, or an assault weapon, as defined in Section 12276 or 12276.1, upon the person of a peace officer or firefighter, and who knows or reasonably should know that the victim is a peace officer or firefighter engaged in the performance of his or her duties, shall be punished by imprisonment in the state prison for 6, 9, or 12 years.

(e) When a person is convicted of a violation of this section in a case involving use of a deadly weapon or instrument or firearm, and the weapon or instrument or firearm is owned by that person, the court shall order that the weapon or instrument or firearm be deemed a nuisance, and it shall be confiscated and disposed of in the manner provided by Section 12028.

(f) As used in this section, "peace officer" refers to any person designated as a peace officer in Chapter 4.5 (commencing with Section 830) of Title 3 of Part 2. *(AM '99)*

245.2. Assault with Deadly Weapon Committed Against Public Transit Employee

Every person who commits an assault with a deadly weapon or instrument or by any means of force likely to produce great bodily injury upon the person of an operator, driver, or passenger on a bus, taxicab, streetcar, cable car, trackless trolley, or other motor vehicle, including a vehicle operated on stationary rails or on a track or rail suspended in the air, used for the transportation of persons for hire, or upon the person of a station agent or ticket agent for the entity providing such transportation, when the driver, operator, or agent is engaged in the performance of his or her duties, and where the person who commits the assault knows or reasonably should know that the victim is engaged in the performance of his or her duties, or is a passenger, shall be punished by imprisonment in the state prison for three, four, or five years.

245.3. Assault With Deadly Weapon on Custodial Officer

Every person who commits an assault with a deadly weapon or instrument or by any means likely to produce great bodily injury upon the person of a custodial officer as defined in Section 831 or 831.5, and who knows or reasonably should know that such victim is such a custodial officer engaged in the performance of his duties, shall be punished by imprisonment in the state prison for three, four, or five years.

When a person is convicted of a violation of this section in a case involving use of a deadly weapon or instrument, and such weapon or instrument is owned by such person, the court may, in its discretion, order that the weapon or instrument be deemed a nuisance and shall be confiscated and destroyed in the manner provided by Section 12028.

245.5. Assault With Deadly Weapon on School Employee

(a) Every person who commits an assault with a deadly weapon or instrument, other than a firearm, or by any means likely to produce great bodily injury upon the person of a school employee, and who knows or reasonably should know that the victim is a school employee engaged in the performance of his or her duties, when that school employee is engaged in the performance of his or her duties, shall be punished by imprisonment in the state prison for three, four, or five years, or in a county jail not exceeding one year.

(b) Every person who commits an assault with a firearm upon the person of a school employee, and who knows or reasonably should know that the victim is a school employee engaged in the performance of his or her duties, when the school employee is engaged in the performance of his or her duties, shall be punished by imprisonment in the state prison for four, six, or eight years, or in a county jail for a term of not less than six months and not exceeding one year.

(c) Every person who commits an assault upon the person of a school employee with a stun gun or taser, and who knows or reasonably should know that the person is a school employee engaged in the performance of his or her duties, when the school employee is engaged in the performance of his or her duties, shall be punished by imprisonment in a county jail for a term not exceeding one year or by imprisonment in the state prison for two, three, or four years.

This subdivision shall not be construed to preclude or in any way limit the applicability of Section 245 in any criminal prosecution.

(d) As used in the section, "school employee"means any person employed as a permanent or probationary certificated or classified employee of a school district on a part-time or full-time basis, including a substitute teacher. "School employee,"as used in this section, also includes a student teacher, or a school board member. "School,"as used in this section, has the same meaning as that term is defined in Section 626.

246. Discharge of Firearms at Inhabited Dwelling, Vehicle, or Aircraft

Any person who shall maliciously and willfully discharge a firearm at an inhabited dwelling house, occupied building, occupied motor vehicle, occupied aircraft, inhabited housecar, as defined in Section 362 of the Vehicle Code, or inhabited camper, as defined in Section 243 of the Vehicle Code, is guilty of a felony, and upon conviction shall be punished by imprisonment in the state prison for three, five, or seven years, or by imprisonment in the county jail for a term of not less than six months and not exceeding one year. As used in this section, "inhabited"means currently being used for dwelling purposes, whether occupied or not.

246.3. Discharge of Firearm in Grossly Negligent Manner That Could Result in Injury or Death of a Person

Except as otherwise authorized by law, any person who willfully discharges a firearm in a grossly negligent manner which could result in injury or death to a person is guilty of a public offense and shall be punished by imprisonment in the county jail not exceeding one year, or by imprisonment in the state prison.

247. Discharging Firearm at Unoccupied Aircraft or Motor Vehicle or Uninhabited Building or Dwelling House

(a) Any person who willfully and maliciously discharges a firearm at an unoccupied aircraft is guilty of a felony.

(b) Any person who discharges a firearm at an unoccupied motor vehicle or an uninhabited building or dwelling house is guilty of a public offense punishable by imprisonment in the county jail for not more than one year or in the state prison. This subdivision does not apply to shooting at an abandoned vehicle, unoccupied vehicle, uninhabited building, or dwelling house with the permission of the owner.

As used in this section and Section 246 "aircraft"means any contrivance intended for and capable of transporting persons through the airspace.

247.5. Discharging Laser at Aircraft

Any person who willfully and maliciously discharges a laser at an aircraft, whether in motion or in flight, while occupied, is guilty of a violation of this section, which shall be punishable as either a misdemeanor by imprisonment in the county jail for not more than one year or by a fine of one thousand dollars ($1,000), or a felony by imprisonment in the state prison for 16 months, two years, or three years, or by a fine of two thousand dollars ($2,000). This section does not apply to the conduct of laser development activity by or on behalf of the United States Armed Forces.

As used in this section, "aircraft"means any contrivance intended for and capable of transporting persons through the airspace.

As used in this section, "laser"means a device that utilizes the natural oscillations of atoms or molecules between energy levels for generating coherent electromagnetic radiation in the ultraviolet, visible, or infrared region of the spectrum, and when discharged exceeds one milliwatt continuous wave.

248. Interfere with Aircraft Operation - Light or Bright Device

Any person who, with the intent to interfere with the operation of an aircraft, willfully shines a light or other bright device, of an intensity capable of impairing the operation of an aircraft, at an aircraft, shall be punished by a fine not exceeding one thousand dollars ($1,000), or by imprisonment in a county jail not exceeding one year, or by both that fine and imprisonment. *(AM '98)*

CRIMES AGAINST THE PERSON, PUBLIC DECENCY & MORALS

261. Rape

(a) Rape is an act of sexual intercourse accomplished with a person not the spouse of the perpetrator, under any of the following circumstances:

(1) Where a person is incapable, because of a mental disorder or developmental or physical disability, of giving legal consent, and this is known or reasonably should be known to the person committing the act. Notwithstanding the existence of a conservatorship pursuant to the provisions of the Lanterman-Petris-Short Act (Part 1 (commencing with Section 5000) of Division 5 of the Welfare and Institutions Code), the prosecuting attorney shall prove, as an element of the crime, that a mental disorder or developmental or physical disability rendered the alleged victim incapable of giving consent.

(2) Where it is accomplished against a person's will by means of force, violence, duress, menace, or fear of immediate and unlawful bodily injury on the person or another.

(3) Where a person is prevented from resisting by any intoxicating or anesthetic substance, or any controlled substance, and this condition was known, or reasonably should have been known by the accused.

(4) Where a person is at the time unconscious of the nature of the act, and this is known to the accused. As used in this paragraph, "unconscious of the nature of the act"means incapable of resisting because the victim meets one of the following conditions:

(A) Was unconscious or asleep.

(B) Was not aware, knowing, perceiving, or cognizant that the act occurred.

(C) Was not aware, knowing, perceiving, or cognizant of the essential characteristics of the act due to the perpetrator's fraud in fact.

(5) Where a person submits under the belief that the person committing the act is the victim's spouse, and this belief is induced by any artifice, pretense, or concealment practiced by the accused, with intent to induce the belief.

(6) Where the act is accomplished against the victim's will by threatening to retaliate in the future against the victim or any other person, and there is a reasonable possibility that the perpetrator will execute the threat. As used in this paragraph, "threatening to retaliate"means a threat to kidnap or falsely imprison, or to inflict extreme pain, serious bodily injury, or death.

(7) Where the act is accomplished against the victim's will by threatening to use the authority of a public official to incarcerate, arrest, or deport the victim or another, and the victim has a reasonable belief that the perpetrator is a public official. As used in this paragraph, "public official"means a person employed by a governmental agency who has the authority, as part of that position, to incarcerate, arrest, or deport another. The perpetrator does not actually have to be a public official.

(b) As used in this section, "duress"means a direct or implied threat of force, violence, danger, or retribution sufficient to coerce a reasonable person of ordinary susceptibilities to perform an act which otherwise would not have been performed, or acquiesce in an act to which one otherwise would not have submitted. The total circumstances, including the age of the victim, and his or her relationship to the defendant, are factors to consider in appraising the existence of duress.

(c) As used in this section, "menace"means any threat, declaration, or act which shows an intention to inflict an injury upon another.

261.5. Unlawful Sexual Intercourse With Person Under 18 yrs.

(a) Unlawful sexual intercourse is an act of sexual intercourse accomplished with a person who is not the spouse of the perpetrator, if the person is a minor. For the purposes of this section, a "minor"is a person under the age of 18 years and an "adult"is a person who is at least 18 years of age.

(b) Any person who engages in an act of unlawful sexual intercourse with a minor who is not more than three years older or three years younger than the perpetrator, is guilty of a misdemeanor.

(c) Any person who engages in an act of unlawful sexual intercourse with a minor who is more than three years younger than the perpetrator is guilty of either a misdemeanor or a felony, and shall be punished by imprisonment in a county jail not exceeding one year, or by imprisonment in the state prison.

(d) Any person 21 years of age or older who engages in an act of unlawful sexual intercourse with a minor who is under 16 years of age is guilty of either a misdemeanor or a felony, and shall be punished by imprisonment in a county jail not exceeding one year, or by imprisonment in the state prison for two, three, or four years.

(e)(1) Notwithstanding any other provision of this section, an adult who engages in an act of sexual intercourse with a minor in violation of this section may be liable for civil penalties in the following amounts:

(A) An adult who engages in an act of unlawful sexual intercourse with a minor less than two years younger than the adult is liable for a civil penalty not to exceed two thousand dollars ($2,000).

(B) An adult who engages in an act of unlawful sexual intercourse with a minor at least two years younger than the adult is liable for a civil penalty not to exceed five thousand dollars ($5,000).

(C) An adult who engages in an act of unlawful sexual intercourse with a minor at least three years younger than the adult is liable for a civil penalty not to exceed ten thousand dollars ($10,000).

(D) An adult over the age of 21 years who engages in an act of unlawful sexual intercourse with a minor under 16 years of age is liable for a civil penalty not to exceed twenty-five thousand dollars ($25,000).

(2) The district attorney may bring actions to recover civil penalties pursuant to this subdivision. From the amounts collected for each case, an amount equal to the costs of pursuing the action shall be deposited with the treasurer of the county in which the judgment was entered, and the remainder shall be deposited in the Underage Pregnancy Prevention Fund, which is hereby created in the State Treasury. Amounts deposited in the Underage Pregnancy Prevention Fund may be used only for the purpose of preventing underage pregnancy upon appropriation by the Legislature.

(3) In addition to any punishment imposed under this section, the judge may assess a fine not to exceed seventy dollars ($70) against any person who violates this section with the proceeds of this fine to be used in accordance with Section 1463.23. The court shall, however, take into consideration the defendant's ability to pay, and no defendant shall be denied probation because of his or her inability to pay the fine permitted under this subdivision. *(AM '99)*

261.6. Consent Defined

In prosecutions under Section 261, 262, 286, 288a, or 289, in which consent is at issue, "consent"shall be defined to mean positive cooperation in act or attitude pursuant to an exercise of free will. The person must act freely and voluntarily and have knowledge of the nature of the act or transaction involved. A current or previous dating or marital relationship shall not be sufficient to constitute consent where consent is at issue in a prosecution under Section 261, 262, 286, 288a, or 289. Nothing in this section shall affect the admissibility of evidence or the burden of proof on the issue of consent. *(AM '98)*

261.7. Sex Crime Victim; Request for Condom, Other Birth Control Device Not Sufficient to Constitute Consent

In prosecutions under Section 261, 262, 286, 288a, or 289, in which consent is at issue, evidence that the victim suggested, requested, or otherwise communicated to the defendant that the defendant use a condom or other birth control device, without additional evidence of consent, is not sufficient to constitute consent.

262. Rape of Person Who Is Spouse of Perpetrator

(a) Rape of a person who is the spouse of the perpetrator is an act of sexual intercourse accomplished under any of the following circumstances:

(1) Where it is accomplished against a person's will by means of force, violence, duress, menace, or fear of immediate and unlawful bodily injury on the person or another.

(2) Where a person is prevented from resisting by any intoxicating or anesthetic substance, or any controlled substance, and this condition was known, or reasonably should have been known, by the accused.

(3) Where a person is at the time unconscious of the nature of the act, and this is known to the accused. As used in this paragraph, "unconscious of the nature of the act"means incapable of resisting because the victim meets one of the following conditions:

(A) Was unconscious or asleep.

(B) Was not aware, knowing, perceiving, or cognizant that the act occurred.

(C) Was not aware, knowing, perceiving, or cognizant of the essential characteristics of the act due to the perpetrator's fraud in fact.

(4) Where the act is accomplished against the victim's will by threatening to retaliate in the future against the victim or any other person, and there is a reasonable possibility that the perpetrator will execute the threat. As used in this subdivision "threatening to retaliate"means a threat to kidnap or falsely imprison, or to inflict extreme pain, serious bodily injury, or death.

(5) Where the act is accomplished against the victim's will by threatening to use the authority of a public official to incarcerate, arrest, or deport the victim or another, and the victim has a reasonable belief that the perpetrator is a public official. As used in this paragraph, "public official"means a person employed by a governmental agency who has the authority, as part of that position, to incarcerate, arrest, or deport another. The perpetrator does not actually have to be a public official.

(b) Section 800 shall apply to this section. However, no prosecution shall be commenced under this section unless the violation was reported to medical personnel, a member of the clergy, an attorney, a shelter representative, a counselor, a judicial officer, a rape crisis agency, a prosecuting agency, a law enforcement officer, or a firefighter within one year after the date of the violation. The reporting requirement shall not apply if the victim's allegation of the offense is corroborated by independent evidence that would otherwise be admissible during trial.

(c) As used in this section, "duress"means a direct or implied threat of force, violence, danger, or retribution sufficient to coerce a reasonable person of ordinary susceptibilities to perform an act which one otherwise would not have been performed, or acquiesce in an act to which otherwise would not have submitted. The total circumstances, including the age of the victim, and his or her relationship to the defendant, are factors to consider in apprising the existence of duress.

(d) As used in this section, "menace"means any threat, declaration, or act that shows an intention to inflict an injury upon another.

(e) If probation is granted upon conviction of a violation of this section, the conditions of probation may include, in lieu of a fine, one or both of the following requirements:

(1) That the defendant make payments to a battered women's shelter, up to a maximum of one thousand dollars ($1,000).

(2) That the defendant reimburse the victim for reasonable costs of counseling and other reasonable expenses that the court finds are the direct result of the defendant's offense.

For any order to pay a fine, make payments to a battered women's shelter, or pay restitution as a condition of probation under this subdivision, the court shall make a determination of the defendant's ability to pay. In no event shall any order to make payments to a battered women's shelter be make if it would impair the ability of the defendant to pay direct restitution to the victim or court ordered child support. Where the injury to a married person is caused in whole or in part by the criminal acts of his or her spouse in violation of this section, the community property may not be used to discharge the liability of the offending spouse for restitution to the injured spouse, required by Section 1203.04, or to a shelter for costs with regard to the injured spouse and dependents, required by this section, until all separate property of the offending spouse is exhausted.

263. Essential Elements of Rape; Penetration

The essential guilt of rape consists in the outrage to the person and feelings of the victim of the rape. Any sexual penetration, however slight, is sufficient to complete the crime.

264.1. Punishment When Defendant Acted in Concert With Another Person to Commit Rape

The provisions of Section 264 notwithstanding, in any case in which the defendant, voluntarily acting in concert with another person, by force or violence and against the will of the victim, committed an act described in Section 261, 262, or 289, either personally or by aiding and abetting the other person, that fact shall be charged in the indictment or information and if found to be true by the jury, upon a jury trial, or if found to be true by the court, upon a court trial, or if admitted by the defendant, the defendant shall suffer confinement in the state prison for five, seven, or nine years.

264.2. Police Officer Duty to Provide "Victim of Domestic Violence" Card

(a) Whenever there is an alleged violation or violations of subdivision (e) of Section 243, or Section 261, 261.5, 262, 273.5, 286, 288a, or 289, the law enforcement officer assigned to the case shall immediately provide the victim of the crime with the "Victims of Domestic Violence"card, as specified in subparagraph (G) of paragraph (9) of subdivision (c) of Section 13701 of the Penal Code.

(b)(1) The law enforcement officer, or his or her agency, shall immediately notify the local rape victim counseling center, whenever a victim of an alleged violation of Section 261, 261.5, 262, 286, 288a, or 289 is transported to a hospital for any medical evidentiary or physical examination. The victim shall have the right to have a sexual assault victim counselor, as defined in Section 1035.2 of the Evidence Code, and a support person of the victim's choosing present at any medical evidentiary or physical examination.

(2) Prior to the commencement of any initial medical evidentiary or physical examination arising out of a sexual assault, a victim shall be notified orally or in writing by the medical provider that the victim has the right to have present a sexual assault victim counselor and at least one other support person of the victim's choosing.

(3) The hospital may verify with the law enforcement officer, or his or her agency, whether the local rape victim counseling center has been notified, upon the approval of the victim.

(4) A support person may be excluded from a medical evidentiary or physical examination if the law enforcement officer or medical provider determines that the presence of that individual would be detrimental to the purpose of the examination. *(AM '98)*

265. Abduction to Force Marriage or Defilement

Every person who takes any woman unlawfully, against her will, and by force, menace or duress, compels her to marry him, or to marry any other person, or to be defiled, is punishable by imprisonment in the state prison.

266. Procuring, Assignation and Seduction

Every person who inveigles or entices any unmarried female, of previous chaste character, under the age of 18 years, into any house of ill fame, or of assignation, or elsewhere, for the purpose of prostitution, or to have illicit carnal connection with any man; and every person who aids or assists in such inveiglement or enticement; and every person who, by any false pretenses, false representation, or other fraudulent means, procures any female to have illicit carnal connection with any man, is punishable by imprisonment in the state prison, or by imprisonment in a county jail not exceeding one year, or by a fine not exceeding two thousand dollars ($2,000), or by both such fine and imprisonment.

266a. Procuring Person by Force or False Inducement

Every person who, within this state, takes any person against his or her will and without his or her consent, or with his or her consent procured by fraudulent inducement or misrepresentation, for the purpose of prostitution, as defined in subdivision (b) of Section 647, is punishable by imprisonment in the state prison, and a fine not exceeding two thousand dollars ($2,000).

266c. Inducing Commission of Sexual Act Through False Representation Creating Fear

Every person who induces any other person to engage in sexual intercourse, sexual penetration, oral copulation, or sodomy when his or her consent is procured by false or fraudulent representation or pretense that is made with the intent to create fear, and which does induce fear, and that would cause a reasonable person in like circumstances to act contrary to the person's free will, and does cause the victim to so act, is punishable by imprisonment in a county jail for not more than one year or in the state prison for two, three, or four years.

As used in this section, "fear"means the fear of physical injury or death to the person or to any relative of the person or member of the person's family. *(AM '00)*

266h. Pimping

(a) Except as provided in subdivision (b), any person who, knowing another person is a prostitute, lives or derives support or maintenance in whole or in part from the earnings or proceeds of the person's prostitution, or from money loaned or advanced to or charged against that person by any keeper or manager or inmate of a house or other place where prostitution is practiced or allowed, or who solicits or receives compensation for soliciting for the person, is guilty of pimping, a felony, and shall be punished by imprisonment in the state prison for three, four, or six years.

(b) If the person engaged in prostitution is a minor over the age of 16 years, the offense is punishable by imprisonment in the state prison for three, four, or six years. If the person engaged in prostitution is under 16 years of age, the offense is punishable by imprisonment in the state prison for three, six, or eight years.

266i. Pandering

(a) Except as provided in subdivision (b), any person who does any of the following is guilty of pandering, a felony, and shall be punished by imprisonment in the state prison for three, four, or six years:

(1) Procures another person for the purpose of prostitution.

(2) By promises, threats, violence, or by any device or scheme, causes, induces, persuades or encourages another person to become a prostitute.

(3) Procures for another person a place as an inmate in a house of prostitution or as an inmate of any place in which prostitution is encouraged or allowed within this state.

(4) By promises, threats, violence or by any device or scheme, causes, induces, persuades or encourages an inmate of a house of prostitution, or any other place in which prostitution is encouraged or allowed, to remain therein as an inmate.

(5) By fraud or artifice, or by duress of person or goods, or by abuse of any position of confidence or authority, procures another person for the purpose of prostitution, or to enter any place in which prostitution is encouraged or allowed within this state, or to come into this state or leave this state for the purpose of prostitution.

(6) Receives or gives, or agrees to receive or give, any money or thing of value for procuring, or attempting to procure, another person for the purpose of prostitution, or to come into this state or leave this state for the purpose of prostitution.

(b) If the other person is a minor over the age of 16 years, the offense is punishable by imprisonment in the state prison for three, four, or six years. Where the other person is under 16 years of age, the offense is punishable by imprisonment in the state prison for three, six, or eight years.

266j. Providing or Transporting Child Under 16 for Purpose of Lewd or Lascivious Act

Any person who intentionally gives, transports, provides, or makes available, or who offers to give, transport, provide, or make available to another person, a child under the age of 16 for the purpose of any lewd or lascivious act as defined in Section 288, or who causes, induces, or persuades a child under the age of 16 to engage in such an act with another person, is guilty of a felony and shall be imprisoned in the state prison for a term of three, six, or eight years, and by a fine not to exceed fifteen thousand dollars ($15,000).

267 Abduction for Prostitution

Every person who takes away any other person under the age of 18 years from the father, mother, guardian, or other person having the legal charge of the other person, without their consent, for the purpose of prostitution, is punishable by imprisonment in the state prison, and a fine not exceeding two thousand dollars ($2,000).

269. Assault on Child Under Age 14 Years

(a) Any person who commits any of the following acts upon a child who is under 14 years of age and 10 or more years younger than the person is guilty of aggravated sexual assault of a child:

(1) A violation of paragraph (2) of subdivision (a) of Section 261.

(2) A violation of Section 264.1.

(3) Sodomy, in violation of Section 286, when committed by force, violence, duress, menace, or fear of immediate and unlawful bodily injury on the victim or another person.

(4) Oral copulation, in violation of Section 288a, when committed by force, violence, duress, menace, or fear of immediate and unlawful bodily injury on the victim or another person.

(5) A violation of subdivision (a) of Section 289.

(b) Any person who violates this section is guilty of a felony and shall be punished by imprisonment in the state prison for 15 years to life.

270. Child Neglect - Liability of Person Adjudicated as Parent

If a parent of a minor child willfully omits, without lawful excuse, to furnish necessary clothing, food, shelter or medical attendance, or other remedial care for his or her child, he or she is guilty of a misdemeanor punishable by a fine not exceeding two thousand dollars ($2,000), or by imprisonment in a county jail not exceeding one year, or by both such fine and imprisonment. If a court of competent jurisdiction has made a final adjudication in either a civil or a criminal action that a person is the parent of a minor child and the person has notice of such adjudication and he or she then willfully omits, without lawful excuse, to furnish necessary clothing, food, shelter, medical attendance or other remedial care for his or her child, this conduct is punishable by imprisonment in the county jail not exceeding one year or in a state prison for a determinate term of one year and one day, or by a fine not exceeding two thousand dollars ($2,000), or by both such fine and imprisonment. This statute shall not be construed so as to relieve such parent from the criminal liability defined herein for such omission merely because the other parent of such child is legally entitled to the custody of such child nor because the other parent of such child or any other person or organization voluntarily or involuntarily furnishes such necessary food, clothing, shelter or medical attendance or other remedial care for such child or undertakes to do so. Proof of abandonment or desertion of a child by such parent, or the omission by such parent to furnish necessary food, clothing, shelter or medical attendance or other remedial care for his or her child is prima facie evidence that such abandonment or desertion or omission to furnish necessary food, clothing, shelter or medical attendance or other remedial care is willful and without lawful excuse. The court, in determining the ability of the parent to support his or her child, shall consider all income, including social insurance benefits and gifts. The provisions of this section are applicable whether the parents of such child are or were ever married or divorced, and regardless of any decree made in any divorce action relative to alimony or to the support of the child. A child conceived but not yet born is to be deemed an existing person insofar as this section is concerned. The husband of a woman who bears a child as a result of artificial insemination shall be considered the father of that child for the purpose of this section, if he consented in writing to the artificial insemination.

If a parent provides a minor with treatment by spiritual means through prayer alone in accordance with the tenets and practices of a recognized church or religious denomination, by a duly accredited practitioner thereof, such treatment shall constitute "other remedial care", as used in this section.

270a. Unjustified Abandonment of Destitute Spouse

Every individual who has sufficient ability to provide for his or her spouse's support, or who is able to earn the means of such spouse's support, who willfully abandons and leaves his or her spouse in a destitute condition, or who refuses or neglects to provide such spouse with necessary food, clothing, shelter, or medical attendance, unless by such spouse's conduct the individual was justified in abandoning such spouse, is guilty of a misdemeanor.

270c. Neglect of Indigent Parent

Except as provided in Chapter 2 (commencing with Section 4410) of Part 4 of Division 9 of the Family Code, every adult child who, having the ability so to do, fails to provide necessary food, clothing, shelter, or medical attendance for an indigent parent, is guilty of a misdemeanor.

270.5. Refusing to Accept Minor Child Into Home

(a) Every parent who refuses, without lawful excuse, to accept his or her minor child into the parent's home, or, failing to do so, to provide alternative shelter, upon being requested to do so by a child protective agency and after being informed of the duty imposed by this statute to do so, is guilty of a misdemeanor and shall be punished by a fine of not more than five hundred dollars ($500).

(b) For purposes of this section, "child protective agency" means a police or sheriff's department, a county probation department, or a county welfare department.

(c) For purposes of this section, "lawful excuse" shall include, but not be limited to, a reasonable fear that the minor child's presence in the home will endanger the safety of the parent or other persons residing in the home.

271. Abandonment of Child Under 14 Years of Age

Every parent of any child under the age of 14 years, and every person to whom any such child has been confided for nurture, or education, who deserts such child in any place whatever with intent to abandon it, is punishable by imprisonment in the state prison or in the county jail not exceeding one year or by fine not exceeding one thousand dollars ($1,000) or by both.

271a. Failure to Provide For Child Under 14 Years of Age

Every person who knowingly and willfully abandons, or who, having ability so to do, fails or refuses to maintain his or her minor child under the age of 14 years, or who falsely, knowing the same to be false, represents to any manager, officer or agent of any orphan asylum or charitable institution for the care of orphans, that any child for whose admission into such asylum or institution application has been made is an orphan, is punishable by imprisonment in the state prison, or in the county jail not exceeding one year, or by fine not exceeding one thousand dollars ($1,000), or by both.

271.5. No Prosecution if Physical Custody Surrendered

(a) No parent or other person having lawful custody of a minor child 72 hours old or younger may be prosecuted for a violation of Section 270, 270.5, 271, or 271a if he or she voluntarily surrenders physical custody of the child to any employee, designated pursuant to this section, on duty at a public or private hospital emergency room or any additional location designated by the county board of supervisors by resolution. Each such hospital or other designated entity shall designate the classes of employees required to take custody of these children.

(b) This section shall be repealed on January 1, 2006, unless a later enacted statute extends or deletes that date. *(AD '00)*

272. Contributing to Delinquency of Minor

(a)(1) Every person who commits any act or omits the performance of any duty, which act or omission causes or tends to cause or encourage any person under the age of 18 years to come within the provisions of Section 300, 601, or 602 of the Welfare and Institutions Code or which act or omission contributes thereto, or any person who, by any act or omission, or by threats, commands, or persuasion, induces or endeavors to induce any person under the age of 18 years or any ward or dependent child of the juvenile court to fail or refuse to conform to a lawful order of the juvenile court, or to do or to perform any act or to follow any course of conduct or to so live as would cause or manifestly tend to cause *** <u>that</u> person to become or to remain a person within the provisions of Section 300, 601, or 602 of the Welfare and Institutions Code, is guilty of a misdemeanor and upon conviction thereof shall be punished by a fine not exceeding two thousand five hundred dollars ($2,500), or by imprisonment in the county jail for not more than one year, or by both *** fine and imprisonment in a county jail, or may be released on probation for a period not exceeding five years.

(2) For purposes of this subdivision, a parent or legal guardian to any person under the age of 18 years shall have the duty to exercise reasonable care, supervision, protection, and control over their minor child.

(b)(1) An adult stranger who is 21 years of age or older, who knowingly contacts or communicates with a minor who is 12 years of age or younger, who knew or reasonably should have known that the minor is 12 years of age or younger, for the purpose of persuading and luring, or transporting, or attempting to persuade and lure, or transport, that minor away from the minor's home or from any location known by the minor's parent, legal guardian, or custodian, to be a place where the minor is located, for any purpose, without the express consent of the minor's parent or legal guardian, and with the intent to avoid the consent of the minor's parent or legal guardian, is guilty of an infraction or a misdemeanor.

(2) This subdivision shall not apply in an emergency situation.

(3) As used in this subdivision, the following terms are defined to mean:

(A) "Emergency situation" means a situation where the minor is threatened with imminent bodily harm, emotional harm, or psychological harm.

(B) "Contact" or "communication" includes, but is not limited to, the use of a telephone or the Internet, as defined in Section 17538 of the Business and Professions Code.

(C) "Stranger" means a person of casual acquaintance with whom no substantial relationship exists, or an individual with whom a relationship has been established or promoted for the primary purpose of victimization, as defined in subdivision (e) of Section 6600 of the Welfare and Institutions Code.

(D) "Express consent" means oral or written permission that is positive, direct, and unequivocal, requiring no inference or implication to supply its meaning.

***(4) This section shall not be interpreted to criminalize acts of persons contacting minors within the scope and course of their employment, or status as a volunteer of a recognized civic or charitable organization.

***(5) This section is intended to protect minors and to help parents and legal guardians exercise reasonable care, supervision, protection, and control over minor children. *(AM '01)*

273. Paying Parent for Adoption of Child

(a) It is a misdemeanor for any person or agency to pay, offer to pay, or to receive money or anything of value for the placement for adoption or for the consent to an adoption of a child. This subdivision shall not apply to any fee paid for adoption services provided by the State Department of Social Services, a licensed adoption agency, adoption services providers, as defined in Section 8502 of the Family Code, or an attorney providing adoption legal services.

(b) This section shall not make it unlawful to pay or receive the maternity-connected medical or hospital and necessary living expenses of the mother preceding and during confinement as an act of charity, as long as the payment is not contingent upon placement of the child for adoption, consent to the adoption, or cooperation in the completion of the adoption.

(c) It is a misdemeanor punishable by imprisonment in a county jail not exceeding one year or by a fine not exceeding two thousand five hundred dollars ($2,500) for any parent to obtain the financial benefits set forth in subdivision (b) with the intent to receive those financial benefits where there is an intent to do either of the following:

(1) Not complete the adoption.

(2) Not consent to the adoption.

(d) It is a misdemeanor punishable by imprisonment in a county jail not exceeding one year or by a fine not exceeding two thousand five hundred dollars ($2,500) for any parent to obtain the financial benefits set forth in subdivision (b) from two or more prospective adopting families or persons, if either parent does both of the following:

(1) Knowingly fails to disclose to those families or persons that there are other prospective adopting families or persons interested in adopting the child, with knowledge that there is an obligation to disclose that information.

(2) Knowingly accepts the financial benefits set forth in subdivision (b) if the aggregate amount exceeds the reasonable maternity-connected medical or hospital and necessary living expenses of the mother preceding and during the pregnancy.

(e) Any person who has been convicted previously of an offense described in subdivision (c) or (d), who is separately tried and convicted of a subsequent violation of subdivision (c) or (d), is guilty of a public offense punishable by imprisonment in a county jail or in the state prison.

(f) Nothing in this section shall be construed to prohibit the prosecution of any person for a misdemeanor or felony pursuant to Section 487 or any other provision of law in lieu of prosecution pursuant to this section.

273a. Harm, Injure or Endanger Child

(a) Any person who, under circumstances or conditions likely to produce great bodily harm or death, willfully causes or permits any child to suffer, or inflicts thereon unjustifiable physical pain or mental suffering, or having the care or custody of any child, willfully causes or permits the person or health of that child to be injured, or willfully causes or permits that child to be placed in a situation where his or her person or health is endangered, shall be punished by imprisonment in a county jail not exceeding one year, or in the state prison for two, four, or six years.

(b) Any person who, under circumstances or conditions other than those likely to produce great bodily harm or death, willfully causes or permits any child to suffer, or inflicts thereon unjustifiable physical pain or mental suffering, or having the care or custody of any child, willfully causes or permits the person or health of that child to be injured, or willfully causes or permits that child to be placed in a situation where his or her person or health may be endangered, is guilty of a misdemeanor.

(c) If a person is convicted of violating this section and probation is granted, the court shall require the following minimum conditions of probation:

(1) A mandatory minimum period of probation of 48 months.

(2) A criminal court protective order protecting the victim from further acts of violence or threats, and, if appropriate, residence exclusion or stay-away conditions.

(3)(A) Successful completion of no less than one year of a child abuser's treatment counseling program approved by the probation department. The defendant shall be ordered to begin participation in the program immediately upon the grant of probation. The counseling program shall meet the criteria specified in Section 273.1. The defendant shall produce documentation of program enrollment to the court within 30 days of enrollment, along with quarterly progress reports.

(B) The terms of probation for offenders shall not be lifted until all reasonable fees due to the counseling program have been paid in full, but in no case shall probation be extended beyond the term provided in subdivision (a) of Section 1203.1. If the court finds that the defendant does not have the ability to pay the fees based on the defendant's changed circumstances, the court may reduce or waive the fees.

(4) If the offense was committed while the defendant was under the influence of drugs or alcohol, the defendant shall abstain from the use of drugs or alcohol during the period of probation and shall be subject to random drug testing by his or her probation officer.

(5) The court may waive any of the above minimum conditions of probation upon a finding that the condition would not be in the best interests of justice. The court shall state on the record its reasons for any waiver.

273ab. Assault on Child Under 8 years; Force Likely to Produce Great Bodily Injury or Death

Any person who, having the care or custody of a child who is under eight years of age, assaults the child by means of force that to a reasonable person would be likely to produce great bodily injury, resulting in the child's death, shall be punished by imprisonment in the state prison for 25 years to life. Nothing in this section shall be construed as affecting the applicability of subdivision (a) of Section 187 or Section 189.

273b. Imprisoning Child Under 16 Years of Age

No child under the age of 16 years shall be placed in any courtroom, or in any vehicle for transportation to any place, in company with adults charged with or convicted of crime, except in the presence of a proper official.

273d. Inflicting Corporal Injury Upon Child

(a) Any person who willfully inflicts upon a child any cruel or inhuman corporal punishment or an injury resulting in a traumatic condition is guilty of a felony and shall be punished by imprisonment in the state prison for two, four, or six years, or in a county jail for not more than one year, by a fine of up to six thousand dollars ($6,000), or by both that imprisonment and fine.

(b) Any person who is found guilty of violating subdivision (a) shall receive a four-year enhancement for a prior conviction of that offense provided that no additional term shall be imposed under this subdivision for any prison term served prior to a period of 10 years in which the defendant remained free of both prison custody and the commission of an offense that results in a felony conviction.

(c) If a person is convicted of violating this section and probation is granted, the court shall require the following minimum conditions of probation:

(1) A mandatory minimum period of probation of 36 months.

(2) A criminal court protective order protecting the victim from further acts of violence or threats, and, if appropriate, residence exclusion or stay-away conditions.

(3)(A) Successful completion of no less than one year of a child abuser's treatment counseling program approved by the probation department. The defendant shall be ordered to begin participation in the program immediately upon the grant of probation. The counseling program shall meet the criteria specified in Section 273.1. The defendant shall produce documentation of program enrollment to the court within 30 days of enrollment, along with quarterly progress reports.

(B) The terms of probation for offenders shall not be lifted until all reasonable fees due to the counseling program have been paid in full, but in no case shall probation be extended beyond the term provided in subdivision (a) of Section 1203.1. If the court finds that the defendant does not have the ability to pay the fees based on the defendant's changed circumstances, the court may reduce or waive the fees.

(4) If the offense was committed while the defendant was under the influence of drugs or alcohol, the defendant shall abstain from the use of drugs or alcohol during the period of probation and shall be subject to random drug testing by his or her probation officer.

(5) The court may waive any of the above minimum conditions of probation upon a finding that the condition would not be in the best interests of justice. The court shall state on the record its reasons for any waiver. *(AM '99)*

273g. Lewdness and Drunkenness in Presence of Child

Any person who in the presence of any child indulges in any degrading, lewd, immoral or vicious habits or practices, or who is habitually drunk in the presence of any child in his care, custody or control, is guilty of a misdemeanor.

273.4. Female Genital Mutilation

(a) If the act constituting a felony violation of subdivision (a) of Section 273a was female genital mutilation, as defined in subdivision (b), the defendant shall be punished by an additional term of imprisonment in the state prison for one year, in addition and consecutive to the punishment prescribed by Section 273a.

(b) "Female genital mutilation" means the excision or infibulation of the labia majora, labia minora, clitoris, or vulva, performed for nonmedical purposes.

(c) Nothing in this section shall preclude prosecution under Section 203, 205, or 206 or any other provision of law.

273.5. Infliction of Corporal Injury on Spouse, Cohabitant, Etc.

(a) Any person who willfully inflicts upon a person who is his or her spouse, former spouse, cohabitant, former cohabitant, or the mother or father of his or her child, corporal injury resulting in a traumatic condition, is guilty of a felony, and upon conviction thereof shall be punished by imprisonment in the state prison for two, three, or four years, or in a county jail for not more than one year, or by a fine of up to six thousand dollars ($6,000) or by both that fine and imprisonment.

(b) Holding oneself out to be the husband or wife of the person with whom one is cohabiting is not necessary to constitute cohabitation as the term is used in this section.

(c) As used in this section, "traumatic condition" means a condition of the body, such as a wound or external or internal injury, whether of a minor or serious nature, caused by a physical force.

(d) For the purpose of this section, a person shall be considered the father or mother of another person's child if the alleged male parent is presumed the natural father under Sections 7611 and 7612 of the Family Code.

(e) Any person convicted of violating this section for acts occurring within seven years of a previous conviction under subdivision (a), or subdivision (d) of Section 243, or Section 243.4, 244, 244.5, or 245, shall be punished by imprisonment in a county jail for not more than one year, or by imprisonment in the state prison for two, four, or five years, or by both imprisonment and a fine of up to ten thousand dollars ($10,000).

(f) If probation is granted to any person convicted under subdivision (a), the court shall impose probation consistent with the provisions of Section 1203.097.

(g) If probation is granted, or the execution or imposition of a sentence is suspended, for any defendant convicted under subdivision (a) who has been convicted of any prior offense specified in subdivision (e), the court shall impose one of the following conditions of probation:

(1) If the defendant has suffered one prior conviction within the previous seven years for a violation of any offense specified in subdivision (e), it shall be a condition thereof, in addition to the provisions contained in Section 1203.097, that he or she be imprisoned in a county jail for not less than 15 days.

(2) If the defendant has suffered two or more prior convictions within the previous seven years for a violation of any offense specified in subdivision (e), it shall be a condition of probation, in addition to the provisions contained in Section 1203.097, that he or she be imprisoned in a county jail for not less than 60 days.

(3) The court, upon a showing of good cause, may find that the mandatory imprisonment required by this subdivision shall not be imposed and shall state on the record its reasons for finding good cause.

(h) If probation is granted upon conviction of a violation of subdivision (a), the conditions of probation may include, consistent with the terms of probation imposed pursuant to Section 1203.097, in lieu of a fine, one or both of the following requirements:

(1) That the defendant make payments to a battered women's shelter, up to a maximum of five thousand dollars ($5,000), pursuant to Section 1203.097.

(2) That the defendant reimburse the victim for reasonable costs of counseling and other reasonable expenses that the court finds are the direct result of the defendant's offense.

For any order to pay a fine, make payments to a battered women's shelter, or pay restitution as a condition of probation under this subdivision, the court shall make a determination of the defendant's ability to pay. In no event shall any order to make payments to a battered women's shelter be made if it would impair the ability of the defendant to pay direct restitution to the victim or court-ordered child support. Where the injury to a married person is caused in whole or in part by the criminal acts of his or her spouse in violation of this section, the community property may not be used to discharge the liability of the offending spouse for restitution to the injured spouse, required by Section 1203.04, as operative on or before August 2, 1995, or Section 1202.4, or to a shelter for costs with regard to the injured spouse and dependents, required by this section, until all separate property of the offending spouse is exhausted. *(AM '99, '00)*

273.6. Court Order Violations; Civil Code and Code of Civil Procedure

(a) Any intentional and knowing violation of a protective order, as defined in Section 6218 of the Family Code, or of an order issued pursuant to Section 527.6 or 527.8 of the Code of Civil Procedure, or Section 15657.03 of the Welfare and Institutions Code, is a misdemeanor punishable by a fine of not more than one thousand dollars ($1,000), or by imprisonment in a county jail for not more than one year, or by both that fine and imprisonment.

(b) In the event of a violation of subdivision (a) which results in physical injury, the person shall be punished by a fine of not more than two thousand dollars ($2,000), or by imprisonment in a county jail for not less than 30 days nor more than one year, or by both that fine and imprisonment. However, if the person is imprisoned in a county jail for at least 48 hours, the court may, in the interest of justice and for reasons stated on the record, reduce or eliminate the 30-day minimum imprisonment required by this subdivision. In determining whether to reduce or eliminate the minimum imprisonment pursuant to this subdivision, the court shall consider the seriousness of the facts before the court, whether there are additional allegations of a violation of the order during the pendency of the case before the court, the probability of future violations, the safety of the victim, and whether the defendant has successfully completed or is making progress with counseling.

(c) Subdivisions (a) and (b) shall apply to the following court orders:

(1) Any order issued pursuant to Section 6320 or 6389 of the Family Code.

(2) An order excluding one party from the family dwelling or from the dwelling of the other.

(3) An order enjoining a party from specified behavior which the court determined was necessary to effectuate the order described in subdivision (a).

(4) Any order issued by another state that is recognized under *** Part 5 (commencing with Section 6400) of Division 10 of the Family Code.

(d) A subsequent conviction for a violation of an order described in subdivision (a), occurring within seven years of a prior conviction for a violation of an order described in subdivision (a) and involving an act of violence or "a credible threat"of violence, as defined in subdivision (c) of Section 139, is punishable by imprisonment in a county jail not to exceed one year, or in the state prison.

(e) In the event of a subsequent conviction for a violation of an order described in subdivision (a) for an act occurring within one year of a prior conviction for a violation of an order described in subdivision (a) that results in physical injury to a victim, the person shall be punished by a fine of not more than two thousand dollars ($2,000), or by imprisonment in a county jail for not less than six months nor more than one year, by both that fine and imprisonment, or by imprisonment in the state prison. However, if the person is imprisoned in a county jail for at least 30 days, the court may, in the interest of justice and for reasons stated in the record, reduce or eliminate the six-month minimum imprisonment required by this subdivision. In determining whether to reduce or eliminate the minimum imprisonment pursuant to this subdivision, the court shall consider the seriousness of the facts before the court, whether there are additional allegations of a violation of the order during the pendency of the case before the court, the probability of future violations, the safety of the victim, and whether the defendant has successfully completed or is making progress with counseling.

(f) The prosecuting agency of each county shall have the primary responsibility for the enforcement of orders described in subdivisions (a), (b), (d), and (e).

(g)(1) Every person who owns, possesses, purchases, or receives a firearm knowing he or she is prohibited from doing so by the provisions of a protective order as defined in Section 136.2 of this code, Section 6218 of the Family Code, or *** Section 527.6 or 527.8 of the Code of Civil Procedure, shall be punished under the provisions of subdivision (g) of Section 12021.

(2) Every person subject to a protective order described in paragraph (1) shall not be prosecuted under this section for owning, possessing, purchasing, or receiving a firearm to the extent that firearm is granted an exemption pursuant to subdivision (h) of Section 6389 of the Family Code.

(h) If probation is granted upon conviction of a violation of subdivision (a), (b), (c), (d), or (e), the court shall impose probation consistent with the provisions of Section 1203.097, and the conditions of probation may include, in lieu of a fine, one or both of the following requirements:

(1) That the defendant make payments to a battered women's shelter*** or to a shelter for abused elder persons or dependent adults, up to a maximum of five thousand dollars ($5,000), pursuant to Section 1203.097.

(2) That the defendant reimburse the victim for reasonable costs of counseling and other reasonable expenses that the court finds are the direct result of the defendant's offense.

(i) For any order to pay a fine, make payments to a battered women's shelter, or pay restitution as a condition of probation under subdivision (e), the court shall make a determination of the defendant's ability to pay. In no event shall any order to make payments to a battered women's shelter be made if it would impair the ability of the defendant to pay direct restitution to the victim or court-ordered child support. Where the injury to a married person is caused in whole or in part by the criminal acts of his or her spouse in violation of this section, the community property may not be used to discharge the liability of the offending spouse for restitution to the injured spouse, required by Section 1203.04, as operative on or before August 2, 1995, or Section 1202.4, or to a shelter for costs with regard to the injured spouse and dependents, required by this section, until all separate property of the offending spouse is exhausted. *(AM '01)*

273.7. Disclosing Location of Domestic Violence Shelter

(a) Any person who maliciously publishes, disseminates, or otherwise discloses the location of any domestic violence shelter or any place designated as a domestic violence shelter, without the authorization of that domestic violence shelter, is guilty of a misdemeanor.

(b)(1) For purposes of this section, "domestic violence shelter" means a confidential location which provides emergency housing on a 24-hour basis for victims of sexual assault, spousal abuse, or both, and their families.

(2) Sexual assault, spousal abuse, or both, includes but is not limited to, those crimes described in Sections 240, 242, 243.4, 261, 261.5, 262, 264.1, 266, 266a, 266b, 266c, 266f, 273.5, 273.6, 285, 288, and 289.

(c) Nothing in this section shall apply to confidential communications between an attorney and his or her client.

274. Abortion - Definition, Punishment and Exception

Every person who provides, supplies, or administers to any woman, or procures any woman to take any medicine, drug, or substance, or uses or employs any instrument or other means whatever, with intent thereby to procure the miscarriage of the woman, except as provided in the Therapeutic Abortion Act, Article 2 (commencing with Section 123400) of Chapter 2 of Part 2 of Division 106 of the Health and Safety Code, is punishable by imprisonment in the state prison.

275. Woman Soliciting and Submitting to Abortion - Exception

Every woman who solicits of any person any medicine, drug, or substance whatever, and takes the same, or who submits to any operation, or to the use of any means whatever, with intent thereby to procure a miscarriage, except as provided in the Therapeutic Abortion Act, Article 2 (commencing with Section 123400) of Chapter 2 of Part 2 of Division 106 of the Health and Safety Code, is punishable by imprisonment in the state prison.

276. Solicitation of Woman to Submit to or Procure Abortion - Exception

Every person who solicits any woman to submit to any operation, or to the use of any means whatever, to procure a miscarriage, except as provided in the Therapeutic Abortion Act, Article 2 (commencing with Section 123400) of Chapter 2 of Part 2 of Division 106 of the Health and Safety Code, is punishable by imprisonment in the county jail not longer than one year or in the state prison, or by a fine of not more than ten thousand dollars ($10,000). This offense must be proved by the testimony of two witnesses, or of one witness and corroborating circumstances.

277. Taking Minor From Person or Public Agency

In the absence of a court order determining rights of custody or visitation to a minor child, every person having a right of custody of the child who maliciously takes, detains, conceals, or entices away that child within or without the state, without good cause, and with the intent to deprive the custody right of another person or a public agency also having a custody right to that child, shall be punished by imprisonment in the county jail for a period of not more than one year, a fine of one thousand dollars ($1,000), or both, or by imprisonment in the state prison for 16 months, or two or three years, a fine of not more than ten thousand dollars ($10,000), or both.

A subsequently obtained court order for custody or visitation shall not affect the application of this section.

As used in this section, "good cause"means a good faith and reasonable belief that the taking, detaining, concealing, or enticing away of the child is necessary to protect the child from immediate bodily injury or emotional harm. "Good cause"also includes the good faith and reasonable belief by a person with a right of custody of the child who has been the victim of domestic violence by another person with a right of custody of the child, that the child, if left with the other person, will suffer immediate bodily injury or emotional harm. The person who takes, detains, or conceals the child shall file a report with the district attorney's office of his or her action, and shall file a request for custody, within a reasonable time in the jurisdiction where the child had been living, setting forth the basis for the immediate bodily injury or emotional harm to the child. The address of the parent, or a person who has been granted access to the minor child by a court order, who takes, detains, or conceals the child, with good cause, shall remain confidential until released by court order.

As used in this section:

(a) "Domestic violence"means abuse perpetrated against any of the following persons:

(1) A spouse, former spouse, cohabitant, former cohabitant, any other adult person related by consanguinity or affinity within the second degree, or a person with whom the respondent has had a dating or engagement relationship.

(2) A person who is the parent of a child and the presumption applies that the male parent is the father of any child of the female parent to the Uniform Parentage Act (Part 7 (commencing with Section 7000 of Division 4 of the Civil Code).

(b) "Emotional Harm includes having a parent who has committed domestic violence against the parent who is taking and concealing the child.

278. Person Without Custody Rights Take, Conceal, etc. Child From Custodian

Every person, not having a right of custody, who maliciously takes, detains, conceals, or entices away, any minor child with intent to detain or conceal that child from a person, guardian, or public agency having the lawful charge of the child shall be punished by imprisonment in the state prison for two, three or four years, a fine of not more than ten thousand dollars ($10,000), or both, or imprisonment in a county jail for a period of not more than one year, a fine of not more than one thousand dollars ($1,000), or both.

278.5. Violation of Custody Order; Take, Conceal, etc. Child

Every person who has a right to physical custody of or visitation with a child pursuant to an order, judgment, or decree of any court which grants another person, guardian, or public agency right to physical custody of or visitation with that child, and who within or without the state detains, conceals, takes, or entices away that child with the intent to deprive the other person of that right to custody or visitation shall be punished by imprisonment in the state prison for 16 months, or two or three years, a fine of not more than ten thousand dollars ($10,000), or both; or by imprisonment in a county jail for a period of not more than one year, a fine of not more than one thousand dollars ($1,000), or both.

278.7. Exceptions: Requirements

(a) Section 278.5 does not apply to a person with a right to custody of a child who, with a good faith and reasonable belief that the child, if left with the other person, will suffer immediate bodily injury or emotional harm, takes, entices away, keeps, withholds, or conceals that child.

(b) Section 278.5 does not apply to a person with a right to custody of a child who has been a victim of domestic violence who, with a good faith and reasonable belief that the child, if left with the other person, will suffer immediate bodily injury or emotional harm, takes, entices away, keeps, withholds, or conceals that child. "Emotional harm"includes having a parent who has committed domestic violence against the parent who is taking, enticing away, keeping, withholding, or concealing the child.

(c) The person who takes, entices away, keeps, withholds, or conceals a child shall do all of the following:

(1) Within a reasonable time from the taking, enticing away, keeping, withholding, or concealing, make a report to the office of the district attorney of the county where the child resided before the action. The report shall include the name of the person, the current address and telephone number of the child and the person, and the reasons the child was taken, enticed away, kept, withheld, or concealed.

(2) Within a reasonable time from the taking, enticing away, keeping, withholding, or concealing, commence a custody proceeding in a court of competent jurisdiction consistent with the federal Parental Kidnapping Prevention Act (Section 1738A, Title 28, United States Code) or the Uniform Child Custody Jurisdiction Act (Part 3 (commencing with Section 3400) of Division 8 of the Family Code).

(3) Inform the district attorney's office of any change of address or telephone number of the person and the child.

(d) For the purposes of this article, a reasonable time within which to make a report to the district attorney's office is at least 10 days and a reasonable time to commence a custody proceeding is at least 30 days. This section shall not preclude a person from making a report to the district attorney's office or commencing a custody proceeding earlier than those specified times.

(e) The address and telephone number of the person and the child provided pursuant to this section shall remain confidential unless released pursuant to state law or by a court order that contains appropriate safeguards to ensure the safety of the person and the child.

279. Protective Custody of Minor Child During Investigation; Return of Child, Etc.

(a) A peace officer investigating a report of a violation of Section 277, 278, or 278.5 may take a minor child into protective custody if it reasonably appears to the officer that any person unlawfully will flee the jurisdictional territory with the minor child.

(b) A child who has been detained or concealed shall be returned to the person, guardian, or public agency having lawful charge of the child, or to the court in which a custody proceeding is pending, or to the probation department of the juvenile court in the county in which the victim resides. Notwithstanding any other provision of law, when a person is arrested for an alleged violation of Section 277, 278, or 278.5 the court shall, at the time of the arraignment, impose the condition that the child shall be returned to the person or public agency having lawful charge of the child, and the court shall specify the date by which the child shall be returned. If conflicting custodial orders exist within this state, or between this state and a foreign state, the court shall set a hearing within five court days to determine which court has jurisdiction under the laws of this state, if the conflicting custodial orders are within this state, or if the conflict exists between this state and a foreign state, the court shall determine which state has subject matter jurisdiction to issue a custodial order under the laws of this state, the Uniform Child Custody Jurisdiction Act (Part 3(commencing with Section 3400) of Division 8 of the Family Code), or federal law, if applicable. At the conclusion of the hearing, the court shall enter an order as to which custody order is valid and is to be enforced. If the child has not been returned at the conclusion of the hearing, the court shall set a date within a reasonable time by which the child shall be returned to the person or agency having lawful charge of the child, and order the defendant to comply by this date, or to show cause on that date why he or she has not returned the child as directed. The court shall only enforce its order, or any subsequent orders for the return of the child, under subdivision (a) of Section 1219 of the Code of Civil Procedure, to ensure that the child is promptly placed with the person or agency having lawful charge of the child. An order adverse to either the prosecution or defense is reviewable by a writ of mandate or prohibition addressed to the appropriate court.

(c) The offenses enumerated in Sections 277, 278, and 278.5 are continuous in nature, and continue for so long as the minor child is concealed or detained.

(d) Any expenses incurred in returning the child shall be reimbursed as provided in Section 3134 of the Family Code. Those expenses, and costs reasonably incurred by the victim, shall be assessed against any defendant convicted of a violation of Section 277, 278, or 278.5.

(e) Pursuant to Sections 27 and 778, violation of Section 277, 278, or 278.5 is punishable in California, whether the intent to commit the offense is formed within or without the state, if the child was a resident of California or present in California at the time of the taking, if the child thereafter is found in California, or if one of the parents, or a person granted access to the minor child by a court order, is a resident of California at the time of the alleged violation of Section 277, 278, or 278.5 by a person who was not a resident of or present in California at the time of the alleged offense.

(f) For purposes of Sections 277, 278, and 278.5:

(1) "A person having a right of custody" means the legal guardian of the child, a person who has a parent and child relationship with the child pursuant to Section 3010 of the Family Code, or a person or an agency that has been granted custody of the child pursuant to a court order.

(2) A "right of custody" means the right to physical custody of the child. In the absence of a court order to the contrary, a parent loses his or her right of custody of the child to the other parent if the parent having the right of custody is dead, is unable or refuses to take the custody has abandoned his or her family.

279.6. When Law Enforcement Officer May Take Child into Protective Custody

(a) A law enforcement officer may take a child into protective custody under any of the following circumstances:

(1) It reasonably appears to the officer that a person is likely to conceal the child, flee the jurisdiction with the child, or, by flight or concealment, evade the authority of the court.

(2) There is no lawful custodian available to take custody of the child.

(3) There are conflicting custody orders or conflicting claims to custody and the parties cannot agree which party should take custody of the child.

(4) The child is an abducted child.

(b) When a law enforcement officer takes a child into protective custody pursuant to this section, the officer shall do one of the following:

(1) Release the child to the lawful custodian of the child, unless it reasonably appears that the release would cause the child to be endangered, abducted, or removed from the jurisdiction.

(2) Obtain an emergency protective order pursuant to Part 3 (commencing with Section 6240) of Division 10 of the Family Code ordering placement of the child with an interim custodian who agrees in writing to accept interim custody.

(3) Release the child to the social services agency responsible for arranging shelter or foster care.

(4) Return the child as ordered by a court of competent jurisdiction.

(c) Upon the arrest of a person for a violation of Section 278 or 278.5, a law enforcement officer shall take possession of an abducted child who is found in the company of, or under the control of, the arrested person and deliver the child as directed in subdivision (b).

(d) Notwithstanding any other law, when a person is arrested for an alleged violation of Section 278 or 278.5, the court shall, at the time of the arraignment or thereafter, order that the child shall be returned to the lawful custodian by or on a specific date, or that the person show cause on that date why the child has not been returned as ordered. If conflicting custodial orders exist within this state, or between this state and a foreign state, the court shall set a hearing within five court days to determine which court has jurisdiction under the laws of this state and determine which state has subject matter jurisdiction to issue a custodial order under the laws of this state, the Uniform Child Custody Jurisdiction Act (Part 3 (commencing with Section 3400) of Division 8 of the Family Code), or federal law, if applicable. At the conclusion of the hearing, or if the child has not been returned as ordered by the court at the time of arraignment, the court shall enter an order as to which custody order is valid and is to be enforced. If the child has not been returned at the conclusion of the hearing, the court shall set a date within a reasonable time by which the child shall be returned to the lawful custodian, and order the defendant to comply by this date, or to show cause on that date why he or she has not returned the child as directed. The court shall only enforce its order, or any subsequent orders for the return of the child, under subdivision (a) of Section 1219 of the Code of Civil Procedure, to ensure that the child is promptly placed with the lawful custodian. An order adverse to either the prosecution or defense is reviewable by a writ of mandate or prohibition addressed to the appropriate court.

281. Bigamy

(a) Every person having a husband or wife living, who marries any other person, except in the cases specified in Section 282, is guilty of bigamy.

(b) Upon a trial for bigamy, it is not necessary to prove either of the marriages by the register, certificate, or other record evidence thereof, but the marriages may be proved by evidence which is admissible to prove a marriage in other cases; and when the second marriage took place out of this state, proof of that fact, accompanied with proof of cohabitation thereafter in this state, is sufficient to sustain the charge.

282. Bigamy, Exceptions; Effect of Five Years Absence or Dissolution of Marriage

Section 281 does not extend to any of the following:

(a) To any person by reason of any former marriage whose husband or wife by such marriage has been absent for five successive years without being known to such person within that time to be living.

(b) To any person by reason of any former marriage which has been pronounced void, annulled, or dissolved by the judgment of a competent court.

284. Marrying Spouse of Another

Every person who knowingly and willfully marries the husband or wife of another, in any case in which such husband or wife would be punishable under the provisions of this chapter, is punishable by fine not less than five thousand dollars ($5,000), or by imprisonment in the state prison.

285. Incest

Persons being within the degrees of consanguinity within which marriages are declared by law to be incestuous and void, who intermarry with each other, or who commit fornication or adultery with each other, are punishable by imprisonment in the state prison.

286. Sodomy

(a) Sodomy is sexual conduct consisting of contact between the penis of one person and the anus of another person. Any sexual penetration, however slight, is sufficient to complete the crime of sodomy.

(b)(1) Except as provided in Section 288, any person who participates in an act of sodomy with another person who is under 18 years of age shall be punished by imprisonment in the state prison, or in a county jail for not more than one year.

(2) Except as provided in Section 288, any person over the age of 21 years who participates in an act of sodomy with another person who is under 16 years of age shall be guilty of a felony.

(c)(1) Any person who participates in an act of sodomy with another person who is under 14 years of age and more than 10 years younger than he or she shall be punished by imprisonment in the state prison for three, six, or eight years.

(2) Any person who commits an act of sodomy when the act is accomplished against the victim's will by means of force, violence, duress, menace, or fear of immediate and unlawful bodily injury on the victim or another person shall be punished by imprisonment in the state prison for three, six, or eight years.

(3) Any person whom commits an act of sodomy where the act is accomplished against the victim's will by threatening to retaliate in the future against the victim or any other person, and there is a reasonable possibility that the perpetrator will execute the threat shall be punished by imprisonment in the state prison for three, six, or eight years.

(d) Any person who, while voluntarily acting in concert with another person, either personally or aiding and abetting that other person, commits an act of sodomy when the act is accomplished against the victim's will by means of force or fear of immediate and unlawful bodily injury on the victim or another person or where the act is accomplished against the victim's will by threatening to retaliate in the future against the victim or any other person, and there is a reasonable possibility that the perpetrator will execute the threat shall be punished by imprisonment in the state prison for five, seven, or nine years.

(e) Any person who participates in an act of sodomy with any person of any age while confined in any state prison, as defined in Section 4504, or in any local detention facility, as defined in Section 6031.4, shall be punished by imprisonment in the state prison, or in a county jail for not more than one year.

(f) Any person who commits an act of sodomy, and the victim is at the time unconscious of the nature of the act and this is known to the person committing the act, shall be punished by imprisonment in the state prison for three, six, or eight years. As used in this subdivision, "unconscious of the nature of the act" means incapable of resisting because the victim meets one of the following conditions:

(1) Was unconscious or asleep.

(2) Was not aware, knowing, perceiving, or cognizant that the act occurred.

(3) Was not aware, knowing, perceiving, or cognizant of the essential characteristics of the act due to the perpetrator's fraud in fact.

(g) Except as provided in subdivision (h), a person who commits an act of sodomy, and the victim is at the time incapable, because of a mental disorder or developmental or physical disability, of giving legal consent, and this is known or reasonably should be known to the person committing the act, shall be punished by imprisonment in the state prison for three, six, or eight years. Notwithstanding the existence of a conservatorship pursuant to the Lanterman-Petris-Short Act (Part 1 (commencing with Section 5000) of Division 5 of the Welfare and Institutions Code), the prosecuting attorney shall prove, as an element of the crime, that a mental disorder or developmental or physical disability rendered the alleged victim incapable of giving consent.

(h) Any person who commits an act of sodomy, and the victim is at the time incapable, because of a mental disorder or developmental or physical disability, of giving legal consent, and this is known or reasonably should be known to the person committing the act, and both the defendant and the victim are at the time confined in a state hospital for the care and treatment of the mentally disordered or in any other public or private facility for the care and treatment of the mentally disordered approved by a county mental health director, shall be punished by imprisonment in the state prison, or in a county jail for not more than one year. Notwithstanding the existence of a conservatorship pursuant to the Lanterman-Petris-Short Act (Part 1 (commencing with Section 5000) of Division 5 of the Welfare and Institutions Code), the prosecuting attorney shall prove, as an element of the crime, that a mental disorder or developmental or physical disability rendered the alleged victim incapable of giving legal consent.

(i) Any person who commits an act of sodomy, where the victim is prevented from resisting by an intoxicating or anesthetic substance, or any controlled substance, and this condition was known, or reasonably should have been known by the accused, shall be punished by imprisonment in the state prison for three, six, or eight years.

(j) Any person who commits an act of sodomy, where the victim submits under the belief that the person committing the act is the victim's spouse, and this belief is induced by any artifice, pretense, or concealment practiced by the accused, with intent to induce the belief, shall be punished by imprisonment in the state prison for three, six, or eight years.

(k) Any person who commits an act of sodomy, where the act is accomplished against the victim's will by threatening to use the authority of a public official to incarcerate, arrest, or deport the victim or another, and the victim has a reasonable belief that the perpetrator is a public official, shall be punished by imprisonment in the state prison for three, six, or eight years.

As used in this subdivision, "public official" means a person employed by a governmental agency who has the authority, as part of that position, to incarcerate, arrest, or deport another. The perpetrator does not actually have to be a public official.

(l) As used in subdivisions (c) and (d), "threatening to retaliate" means a threat to kidnap or falsely imprison, or inflict extreme pain, serious bodily injury, or death.

(m) In addition to any punishment imposed under this section, the judge may assess a fine not to exceed seventy dollars ($70) against any person who violates this section, with the proceeds of this fine to be used in accordance with Section 1463.23. The court, however, shall take into consideration the defendant's ability to pay, and no defendant shall be denied probation because of his or her inability to pay the fine permitted under this subdivision. *(AM '98)*

286.5. Sexually Assaulting Animals

Any person who sexually assaults any animal protected by Section 597f for the purpose of arousing or gratifying the sexual desire of the person is guilty of a misdemeanor.

288. Lewd Act on Child

(a) Any person who willfully and lewdly commits any lewd or lascivious act, including any of the acts constituting other crimes provided for in Part 1, upon or with the body, or any part or member thereof, of a child who is under the age of 14 years, with the intent of arousing, appealing to, or gratifying the lust, passions, or sexual desires of that person or the child, is guilty of a felony and shall be punished by imprisonment in the state prison for three, six, or eight years.

(b)(1) Any person who commits an act described in subdivision (a) by use of force, violence, duress, menace, or fear of immediate and unlawful bodily injury on the victim or another person, is guilty of a felony and shall be punished by imprisonment in the state prison for three, six, or eight years.

(2) Any person who is a caretaker and commits an act described in subdivision (a) upon a dependent adult by use of force, violence, duress, menace, or fear of immediate and unlawful bodily injury on the victim or another person, with the intent described in subdivision (a), is guilty of a felony and shall be punished by imprisonment in the state prison for three, six, or eight years.

(c)(1) Any person who commits an act described in subdivision (a) with the intent described in that subdivision, and the victim is a child of 14 or 15 years, and that person is at least 10 years older than the child, is guilty of a public offense and shall be punished by imprisonment in the state prison for one, two, or three years, or by imprisonment in a county jail for not more than one year. In determining whether the person is at least 10 years older than the child, the difference in age shall be measured from the birth date of the person to the birth date of the child.

(2) Any person who is a caretaker and commits an act described in subdivision (a) upon a dependent adult, with the intent described in subdivision (a), is guilty of a public offense and shall be punished by imprisonment in the state prison for one, two, or three years, or by imprisonment in a county jail for not more than one year.

(d) In any arrest or prosecution under this section or Section 288.5, the peace officer, district attorney, and the court shall consider the needs of the child victim and shall do whatever is necessary, within existing budgetary resources, and constitutionally permissible to prevent psychological harm to the child victim or to prevent psychological harm to the dependent adult victim resulting from participation in the court process.

(e) Upon the conviction of any person for a violation of subdivision (a) or (b), the court may, in addition to any other penalty or fine imposed, order the defendant to pay an additional fine not to exceed ten thousand dollars ($10,000). In setting the amount of the fine, the court shall consider any relevant factors, including, but not limited to, the seriousness and gravity of the offense, the circumstances of its commission, whether the defendant derived any economic gain as a result of the crime, and the extent to which the victim suffered economic losses as a result of the crime. Every fine imposed and collected under this section shall be deposited in the Victim-Witness Assistance Fund to be available for appropriation to fund child sexual exploitation and child sexual abuse victim counseling centers and prevention programs pursuant to Section 13837.

If the court orders a fine imposed pursuant to this subdivision, the actual administrative cost of collecting that fine, not to exceed 2 percent of the total amount paid, may be paid into the general fund of the county treasury for the use and benefit of the county.

(f) For purposes of paragraph (2) of subdivision (b) and paragraph (2) of subdivision (c), the following definitions apply:

(1) "Caretaker"means an owner, operator, administrator, employee, independent contractor, agent, or volunteer of any of the following public or private facilities when the facilities provide care for elder or dependent adults:

(A) Twenty-four hour health facilities, as defined in Sections 1250, 1250.2, and 1250.3 of the Health and Safety Code.

(B) Clinics.

(C) Home health agencies.

(D) Adult day health care centers.

(E) Secondary schools that serve dependent adults ages 18 to 22 years and postsecondary educational institutions that serve dependent adults or elders.

(F) Sheltered workshops.

(G) Camps.

(H) Community care facilities, as defined by Section 1402 of the Health and Safety Code, and residential care facilities for the elderly, as defined in Section 1569.2 of the Health and Safety Code.

(I) Respite care facilities.

(J) Foster homes.

(K) Regional centers for persons with developmental disabilities.

(L) A home health agency licensed in accordance with Chapter 8 (commencing with Section 1725) of Division 2 of the Health and Safety Code.

(M) An agency that supplies in-home supportive services.

(N) Board and care facilities.

(O) Any other protective or public assistance agency that provides health services or social services to elder or dependent adults, including, but not limited to, in-home supportive services, as defined in Section 14005.14 of the Welfare and Institutions Code.

(P) Private residences.

(2) "Board and care facilities"means licensed or unlicensed facilities that provide assistance with one or more of the following activities:

(A) Bathing.

(B) Dressing.

(C) Grooming.

(D) Medication storage.

(E) Medical dispensation.

(F) Money management.

(3) "Dependent adult"means any person 18 years of age or older who has a mental disability or disorder that restricts his or her ability to carry out normal activities or to protect his or her rights, including, but not limited to, persons who have developmental disabilities, persons whose mental abilities have significantly diminished because of age.

(g) Paragraph (2) of subdivision (b) and paragraph (2) of subdivision (c) apply to the owners, operators, administrators, employees, independent contractors, agents, or volunteers working at these public or private facilities and only to the extent that the individuals personally commit, conspire, aid, abet, or facilitate any act prohibited by paragraph (2) of subdivision (b) and paragraph (2) of subdivision (c).

(h) Paragraph (2) of subdivision (b) and paragraph (2) of subdivision (c) do not apply to a caretaker who is a spouse of, or who is in an equivalent domestic relationship with, the dependent adult under care. *(AM '98)*

288a.　Oral Copulation

(a) Oral copulation is the act of copulating the mouth of one person with the sexual organ or anus of another person.

(b)(1) Except as provided in Section 288, any person who participates in an act of oral copulation with another person who is under 18 years of age shall be punished by imprisonment in the state prison, or in a county jail for a period of not more than one year.

(2) Except as provided in Section 288, any person over the age of 21 years who participates in an act of oral copulation with another person who is under 16 years of age is guilty of a felony.

(c)(1) Any person who participates in an act of oral copulation with another person who is under 14 years of age and more than 10 years younger than he or she shall be punished by imprisonment in the state prison for three, six, or eight years.

(2) Any person who commits an act of oral copulation when the act is accomplished against the victim's will by means of force, violence, duress, menace, or fear of immediate and unlawful bodily injury on the victim or another person shall be punished by imprisonment in the state prison for three, six, or eight years.

(3) Any person who commits an act of oral copulation where the act is accomplished against the victim's will by threatening to retaliate in the future against the victim or any other person, and there is a reasonable possibility that the perpetrator will execute the threat shall be punished by imprisonment in the state prison for three, six, or eight years.

(d) Any person who, while voluntarily acting in concert with another person, either personally or by aiding and abetting that other person, commits an act of oral copulation (1) when the act is accomplished against the victim's will by means of force or fear of immediate and unlawful bodily injury on the victim or another person, or (2) where the act is accomplished against the victim's will by threatening to retaliate in the future against the victim or any other person, and there is a reasonable possibility that the perpetrator will execute the threat, or (3) where the victim is at the time incapable, because of a mental disorder or developmental or physical disability, of giving legal consent, and this is known or reasonably should be known to the person committing the act shall be punished by imprisonment in the state prison for five, seven, or nine years. Notwithstanding the appointment of a conservator with respect to the victim pursuant to the provisions of the Lanterman-Petris-Short Act (Part 1 (commencing with Section 5000) of Division 5 of the Welfare and Institutions Code), the prosecuting attorney shall prove, as an element of the crime described under paragraph (3), that a mental disorder or developmental or physical disability rendered the alleged victim incapable of giving legal consent.

(e) Any person who participates in an act of oral copulation while confined in any state prison, as defined in Section 4504 or in any local detention facility as defined in Section 6031.4, shall be punished by imprisonment in the state prison, or in a county jail for a period of not more than one year.

(f) Any person who commits an act of oral copulation, and the victim is at the time unconscious of the nature of the act and this is known to the person committing the act, shall be punished by imprisonment in the state prison for a period of three, six, or eight years. As used in this subdivision, "unconscious of the nature of the act" means incapable of resisting because the victim meets one of the following conditions:

(1) Was unconscious or asleep.

(2) Was not aware, knowing, perceiving, or cognizant that the act occurred.

(3) Was not aware, knowing, perceiving, or cognizant of the essential characteristics of the act due to the perpetrator's fraud in fact.

(g) Except as provided in subdivision (h), any person who commits an act of oral copulation, and the victim is at the time incapable, because of a mental disorder or developmental or physical disability, of giving legal consent, and this is known or reasonably should be known to the person committing the act, shall be punished by imprisonment in the state prison, for three, six, or eight years. Notwithstanding the existence of a conservatorship pursuant to the provisions of the Lanterman-Petris-Short Act (Part 1 (commencing with Section 5000) of Division 5 of the Welfare and Institutions Code), the prosecuting attorney shall prove, as an element of the crime, that a mental disorder or developmental or physical disability rendered the alleged victim incapable of giving consent.

(h) Any person who commits an act of oral copulation, and the victim is at the time incapable, because of a mental disorder or developmental or physical disability, of giving legal consent, and this is known or reasonably should be known to the person committing the act, and both the defendant and the victim are at the time confined in a state hospital for the care and treatment of the mentally disordered or in any other public or private facility for the care and treatment of the mentally disordered approved by a county mental health director, shall be punished by imprisonment in the state prison, or in a county jail for a period of not more than one year. Notwithstanding the existence of a conservatorship pursuant to the provisions of the Lanterman-Petris-Short Act (Part 1 (commencing with Section 5000) of Division 5 of the Welfare and Institutions Code), the prosecuting attorney shall prove, as an element of the crime, that a mental disorder or developmental or physical disability rendered the alleged victim incapable of giving legal consent.

(i) Any person who commits an act of oral copulation, where the victim is prevented from resisting by any intoxicating or anesthetic substance, or any controlled substance, and this condition was known, or reasonably should have been known by the accused, shall be punished by imprisonment in the state prison for a period of three, six, or eight years.

(j) Any person who commits an act of oral copulation, where the victim submits under the belief that the person committing the act is the victim's spouse, and this belief is induced by any artifice, pretense, or concealment practiced by the accused, with intent to induce the belief, shall be punished by imprisonment in the state prison for a period of three, six, or eight years.

(k) Any person who commits an act of oral copulation, where the act is accomplished against the victim's will by threatening to use the authority of a public official to incarcerate, arrest, or deport the victim or another, and the victim has a reasonable belief that the perpetrator is a public official, shall be punished by imprisonment in the state prison for a period of three, six, or eight years.

As used in this subdivision, "public official" means a person employed by a governmental agency who has the authority, as part of that position, to incarcerate, arrest, or deport another. The perpetrator does not actually have to be a public official.

(l) As used in subdivisions (c) and (d), "threatening to retaliate" means a threat to kidnap or falsely imprison, or to inflict extreme pain, serious bodily injury, or death.

(m) In addition to any punishment imposed under this section, the judge may assess a fine not to exceed seventy dollars ($70) against any person who violates this section, with the proceeds of this fine to be used in accordance with Section 1463.23. The court shall, however, take into consideration the defendant's ability to pay, and no defendant shall be denied probation because of his or her inability to pay the fine permitted under this subdivision. *(AM '98)*

288.2. Distribution or Exhibition of Lewd Material to Minor

(a) Every person who, with knowledge that a person is a minor, or who fails to exercise reasonable care in ascertaining the true age of a minor, knowingly distributes, sends, causes to be sent, exhibits, or offers to distribute or exhibit by any means, including, but not limited to, live or recorded telephone messages, any harmful matter, as defined in Section 313, to a minor with the intent of arousing, appealing to, or gratifying the lust or passions or sexual desires of that person or of a minor, and with the intent or for the purpose of seducing a minor, is guilty of a public offense and shall be punished by imprisonment in the state prison or in a county jail.

A person convicted of a second and any subsequent conviction for a violation of this section is guilty of a felony.

(b) Every person who, with knowledge that a person is a minor, knowingly distributes, sends, causes to be sent, exhibits, or offers to distribute or exhibit by electronic mail, the Internet, as defined in Section 17538 of the Business and Professions Code, or a commercial online service, any harmful matter, as defined in Section 313, to a minor with the intent of arousing, appealing to, or gratifying the lust or passions or sexual desires of that person or of a minor, and with the intent, or for the purpose of seducing a minor, is guilty of a public offense and shall be punished by imprisonment in the state prison or in a county jail.

A person convicted of a second and any subsequent conviction for a violation of this section is guilty of a felony.

(c) It shall be a defense to any prosecution under this section that a parent or guardian committed the act charged in aid of legitimate sex education.

(d) It shall be a defense in any prosecution under this section that the act charged was committed in aid of legitimate scientific or educational purposes.

(e) It does not constitute a violation of this section for a telephone corporation, as defined in Section 234 of the Public Utilities Code, a cable television company franchised pursuant to Section 53066 of the

Government Code, or any of its affiliates, an Internet service provider, or commercial online service provider, to carry, broadcast, or transmit messages described in this section or perform related activities in providing telephone, cable television, Internet, or commercial online services. *(AM '97)*

288.5. Engaging in Three or More Acts of Substantial Sexual Conduct With a Child Under Age 14

(a) Any person who either resides in the same home with the minor child or has recurring access to the child, who over a period of time, not less than three months in duration, engages in three or more acts of substantial sexual conduct with a child under the age of 14 years at the time of the commission of the offense, as defined in subdivision (b) of Section 1203.066, or three or more acts of lewd or lascivious conduct under Section 288, with a child under the age of 14 years at the time of the commission of the offense is guilty of the offense of continuous sexual abuse of a child and shall be punished by imprisonment in the state prison for a term of 6, 12, or 16 years.

(b) To convict under this section the trier of fact, if a jury, need unanimously agree only that the requisite number of acts occurred not on which acts constitute the requisite number.

(c) No other felony sex offense involving the same victim may be charged in the same proceeding with a charge under this section unless the other charged offense occurred outside the time period charged under this section or the other offense is charged in the alternative. A defendant may be charged with only one count under this section unless more than one victim is involved in which case a separate count may be charged for each victim.

289. Sexual Penetration by Foreign Object For Sexual Purpose

(a)(1) Any person who commits an act of sexual penetration when the act is accomplished against the victim's will by means of force, violence, duress, menace, or fear of immediate and unlawful bodily injury on the victim or another person shall be punished by imprisonment in the state prison for three, six, or eight years.

(2) Any person who commits an act of sexual penetration when the act is accomplished against the victim's will by threatening to retaliate in the future against the victim or any other person, and there is a reasonable possibility that the perpetrator will execute the threat, shall be punished by imprisonment in the state prison for three, six, or eight years.

(b) Except as provided in subdivision (c), any person who commits an act of sexual penetration, and the victim is at the time incapable, because of a mental disorder or developmental or physical disability, of giving legal consent, and this is known or reasonably should be known to the person committing the act or causing the act to be committed, shall be punished by imprisonment in the state prison for three, six, or eight years. Notwithstanding the appointment of a conservator with respect to the victim pursuant to the provisions of the Lanterman-Petris-Short Act (Part 1 (commencing with Section 5000) of Division 5 of the Welfare and Institutions Code), the prosecuting attorney shall prove, as an element of the crime, that a mental disorder or developmental or physical disability rendered the alleged victim incapable of giving legal consent.

(c) Any person who commits an act of sexual penetration, and the victim is at the time incapable, because of a mental disorder or developmental or physical disability, of giving legal consent, and this is known or reasonably should be known to the person committing the act or causing the act to be committed and both the defendant and the victim are at the time confined in a state hospital for the care and treatment of the mentally disordered or in any other public or private facility for the care and treatment of the mentally disordered approved by a county mental health director, shall be punished by imprisonment in the state prison, or in a county jail for a period of not more than one year. Notwithstanding the existence of a conservatorship pursuant to the provisions of the Lanterman-Petris-Short Act (Part 1 (commencing with Section 5000) of Division 5 of the Welfare and Institutions Code), the prosecuting attorney shall prove, as an element of the crime, that a mental disorder or developmental or physical disability rendered the alleged victim incapable of giving legal consent.

(d) Any person who commits an act of sexual penetration, and the victim is at the time unconscious of the nature of the act and this is known to the person committing the act or causing the act to be committed, shall be punished by imprisonment in the state prison for three, six, or eight years. As used in this subdivision, "unconscious of the nature of the act"means incapable of resisting because the victim meets one of the following conditions:

(1) Was unconscious or asleep.

(2) Was not aware, knowing, perceiving, or cognizant that the act occurred.

(3) Was not aware, knowing, perceiving, or cognizant of the essential characteristics of the act due to the perpetrator's fraud in fact.

(e) Any person who commits an act of sexual penetration when the victim is prevented from resisting by any intoxicating or anesthetic substance, or any controlled substance, and this condition was known, or reasonably should have been known by the accused, shall be punished by imprisonment in the state prison for a period of three, six, or eight years.

(f) Any person who commits an act of sexual penetration when the victim submits under the belief that the person committing the act or causing the act to be committed is the victim's spouse, and this belief is induced by any artifice, pretense, or concealment practiced by the accused, with intent to induce the belief, shall be punished by imprisonment in the state prison for a period of three, six, or eight years.

(g) Any person who commits an act of sexual penetration when the act is accomplished against the victim's will by threatening to use the authority of a public official to incarcerate, arrest, or deport the victim or another, and the victim has a reasonable belief that the perpetrator is a public official, shall be punished by imprisonment in the state prison for a period of three, six, or eight years.

As used in this subdivision, "public official"means a person employed by a governmental agency who has the authority, as part of that position, to incarcerate, arrest, or deport another. The perpetrator does not actually have to be a public official.

(h) Except as provided in Section 288, any person who participates in an act of sexual penetration with another person who is under 18 years of age shall be punished by imprisonment in the state prison or in the county jail for a period of not more than one year.

(i) Except as provided in Section 288, any person over the age of 21 years who participates in an act of sexual penetration with another person who is under 16 years of age shall be guilty of a felony.

(j) Any person who participates in an act of sexual penetration with another person who is under 14 years of age and who is more than 10 years younger than he or she shall be punished by imprisonment in the state prison for three, six, or eight years.

(k) As used in this section:

(1) "Sexual penetration"is the act of causing the penetration, however slight, of the genital or anal openings of any person or causing another person to so penetrate the defendant's or another person's genital or anal openings for the purpose of sexual arousal, gratification, or abuse by any foreign object, substance, instrument, or device, or by any unknown object.

(2) "Foreign object, substance, instrument, or device"shall include any part of the body, except a sexual organ.

(3) "Unknown object"shall include any foreign object, substance, instrument, or device, or any part of the body, including a penis, when it is not known whether penetration was by a penis or by a foreign object, substance, instrument, or device, or by any other part of the body.

(l) As used in subdivision (a), "threatening to retaliate"means a threat to kidnap or falsely imprison, or inflict extreme pain, serious bodily injury or death.

(m) As used in this section, "victim"includes any person who the defendant causes to penetrate the genital or anal openings of the defendant or another person or whose genital or anal openings are caused to be penetrated by the defendant or another person and who otherwise qualifies as a victim under the requirements of this section. *(AM '99)*

289.5. Entry Into California to Avoid Prosecution for Offense Requiring 290 PC Registration

(a) Every person who flees to this state with the intent to avoid prosecution for an offense which, if committed or attempted in this state, would have been punishable as one or more of the offenses described in subparagraph (A) of paragraph (2) of subdivision (a) of Section 290, and who has been charged with that offense under the laws of the jurisdiction from which the person fled, is guilty of a misdemeanor.

(b) Every person who flees to this state with the intent to avoid custody or confinement imposed for conviction of an offense under the laws of the jurisdiction from which the person fled, which offense, if committed or attempted in this state, would have been punishable as one or more of the offenses described in subparagraph (A) of paragraph (2) of subdivision (a) of Section 290, is guilty of a misdemeanor.

(c) No person shall be charged and prosecuted for an offense under this section unless the prosecutor has requested the other jurisdiction to extradite the person and the other jurisdiction has refused to do so.

(d) Any person who is convicted of any felony sex offense described in subparagraph (A) of paragraph (2) of subdivision (a) of Section 290, that is committed after fleeing to this state under the circumstances described in subdivision (a) or (b) of this section, shall, in addition and consecutive to the punishment for that conviction, receive an additional term of two years' imprisonment.

289.6. Sex With Inmate

(a)(1) An employee or officer of a public entity health facility, or an employee, officer, or agent of a private person or entity that provides a health facility or staff for a health facility under contract with a public entity, who engages in sexual activity with a consenting adult who is confined in a health facility is guilty of a public offense. As used in this paragraph, "health facility" means a health facility as defined in subdivisions (b), (e), (g), (h), and (j), and subparagraph (C) of paragraph (2) of subdivision (i) of Section 1250 of the Health and Safety Code, in which the victim has been confined involuntarily.

(2) An employee or officer of a public entity detention facility, or an employee, officer, or agent of a private person or entity that provides a detention facility or staff for a detention facility, or person or agent of a public or private entity under contract with a detention facility, or a volunteer of a private or public entity detention facility, who engages in sexual activity with a consenting adult who is confined in a detention facility, is guilty of a public offense.

(3) An employee with a department, board, or authority under the Youth and Adult Correctional Agency or a facility under contract with a department, board, or authority under the Youth and Adult Correctional Agency, who, during the course of his or her employment directly provides treatment, care, control, or supervision of inmates, wards, or parolees, and who engages in sexual activity with a consenting adult who is an inmate, ward, or parolee, is guilty of a public offense.

(b) As used in this section, the term "public entity" means the state, federal government, a city, a county, a city and county, a joint county jail district, or any entity created as a result of a joint powers agreement between two or more public entities.

(c) As used in this section, the term "detention facility" means:

(1) A prison, jail, camp, or other correctional facility used for the confinement of adults or both adults and minors.

(2) A building or facility used for the confinement of adults or adults and minors pursuant to a contract with a public entity.

(3) A room that is used for holding persons for interviews, interrogations, or investigations and that is separate from a jail or located in the administrative area of a law enforcement facility.

(4) A vehicle used to transport confined persons during their period of confinement.

(5) A court holding facility located within or adjacent to a court building that is used for the confinement of persons for the purpose of court appearances.

(d) As used in this section, "sexual activity" means:

(1) Sexual intercourse.

(2) Sodomy, as defined in subdivision (a) of Section 286.

(3) Oral copulation, as defined in subdivision (a) of Section 288a.

(4) Sexual penetration, as defined in subdivision (k) of Section 289.

(5) The rubbing or touching of the breasts or sexual organs of another, or of oneself in the presence of and with knowledge of another, with the intent of arousing, appealing to, or gratifying the lust, passions, or sexual desires of oneself or another.

(e) Consent by a confined person or parolee to sexual activity proscribed by this section is not a defense to a criminal prosecution for violation of this section.

(f) This section does not apply to sexual activity between consenting adults that occurs during an overnight conjugal visit that takes place pursuant to a court order or with the written approval of an authorized representative of the public entity that operates or contracts for the operation of the detention facility where the conjugal visit takes place, to physical contact or penetration made pursuant to a lawful search, or bona fide medical examinations or treatments, including clinical treatments.

(g) Any violation of paragraph (1) of subdivision (a), or a violation of paragraph (2) or (3) of subdivision (a) as described in paragraph (5) of subdivision (d), is a misdemeanor.

(h) Any violation of paragraph (2) or (3) of subdivision (a), as described in paragraph (1), (2), (3), or (4) of subdivision (d), shall be punished by imprisonment in a county jail not exceeding one year, or in the state prison, or by a fine of not more than ten thousand dollars ($10,000) or by both that fine and imprisonment.

(i) Any person previously convicted of a violation of this section shall, upon a subsequent violation, be guilty of a felony.

(j) Anyone who is convicted of a felony violation of this section who is employed by a department, board, or authority within the Youth and Adult Correctional Agency shall be terminated in accordance with the State Civil Service Act (Part 2 (commencing with Section 18500) of Title 2 of Division 5 of the Government Code). Anyone who has been convicted of a felony violation of this section shall not be eligible to be hired or reinstated by a department, board, or authority within the Youth and Adult Correctional Agency. *(AM '99, '00)*

290. Sex Offender Registration

(a)(1)(A) Every person described in paragraph (2), for the rest of his or her life while residing in, or, if he or she has no residence, while located within California, or while attending school or working in California, as described in subparagraph (G), shall be required to register with the chief of police of the city in which he or she is residing, or if he or she has no residence, is located, or the sheriff of the county if he or she is residing, or if he or she has no residence, is located, in an unincorporated area or city that has no police department, and, additionally, with the chief of police of a campus of the University of California, the California State University, or community college if he or she is residing, or if he or she has no residence, is located upon the campus or in any of its facilities, within five working days of coming into, or changing his or her residence or location within, any city, county, or city and county, or campus in which he or she temporarily resides, or, if he or she has no residence, is located.

(B) If the person who is registering has more than one residence address or location at which he or she regularly resides or is located, he or she shall register in accordance with subparagraph (A) in each of the jurisdictions in which he or she regularly resides or is located. If all of the addresses or locations are within the same jurisdiction, the person shall provide the registering authority with all of the addresses or locations where he or she regularly resides or is located.

(C) If the person who is registering has no residence address, he or she shall update his or her registration no less than once every *** 60 days in addition to the requirement in subparagraph (A), on a form as may be required by the Department of Justice, with the entity or entities described in subparagraph (A) in whose jurisdiction he or she is located at the time he or she is updating the registration. It is the intent of the Legislature that efforts be made with respect to persons who are subject to this subparagraph who are on probation or parole to engage them in treatment.

(D) Beginning on his or her first birthday following registration or change of address, the person shall be required to register annually, within five working days of his or her birthday, to update his or her registration with the entities described in subparagraph (A)***. At the annual update, the person shall provide current information as required on the Department of Justice annual update form, including the information described in subparagraphs (A) to (C), inclusive, of paragraph (2) of subdivision (e).

(E) In addition, every person who has ever been adjudicated a sexually violent predator, as defined in Section 6600 of the Welfare and Institutions Code, shall, after his or her release from custody, verify his or her address no less than once every 90 days and place of employment, including the name and address of the employer, in a manner established by the Department of Justice.

(F) No entity shall require a person to pay a fee to register or update his or her registration pursuant to this section. The registering agency shall submit registrations, including annual updates or changes of address, directly into the Department of Justice Violent Crime Information Network (VCIN).

(G) Persons required to register in their state of residence who are out-of-state residents employed, or carrying on a vocation in California on a full-time or part-time basis, with or without compensation, for more than 14 days, or for an aggregate period exceeding 30 days in a calendar year, shall register in accordance with subparagraph (A). Persons described in paragraph (2) who are out-of-state residents enrolled in any educational institution in California, as defined in Section 22129 of the Education Code, on a full-time or part-time basis, shall register in accordance with subparagraph (A). The place where the out-of-state resident is located, for purposes of registration, shall be the place where the person is employed, carrying on a vocation, or attending school. The out-of-state resident subject to this subparagraph shall, in addition to the information required pursuant to subdivision (e), provide the registering authority with the name of his or her place of employment or the name of the school attended in California, and his or her address or location in his or her state of residence. The registration requirement for persons subject to this subparagraph shall become operative on November 25, 2000. The terms "employed or carries on a vocation"include employment whether or not financially compensated, volunteered, or performed for government or educational benefit.

(2) The following persons shall be required to register pursuant to paragraph (1):

(A) Any person who, since July 1, 1944, has been or is hereafter convicted in any court in this state or in any federal or military court of a violation of Section 207 or 209 committed with intent to violate Section 261, 286, 288, 288a, or 289, Section 220, except assault to commit mayhem, Section 243.4, paragraph (1), (2), (3), (4), or (6) of subdivision (a) of Section 261, or paragraph (1) of subdivision (a) of Section 262 involving the use of force or violence for which the person is sentenced to the state prison, Section 264.1, 266, 266c, subdivision (b) of Section 266h, subdivision (b) of Section 266i, 266j, 267, 269, 285, 286, 288, 288a, 288.5, or 289, subdivision (b), (c), or (d) of Section 311.2, Section 311.3, 311.4, 311.10, 311.11, or 647.6, former Section 647a, subdivision (c) of Section 653f, subdivision 1 or 2 of Section 314, any offense involving lewd or lascivious conduct under Section 272, or any felony violation of Section 288.2; or any person who since that date has been or is hereafter convicted of the attempt to commit any of the above-mentioned offenses.

(B) Any person who, since July 1, 1944, has been or hereafter is released, discharged, or paroled from a penal institution where he or she was confined because of the commission or attempted commission of one of the offenses described in subparagraph (A).

(C) Any person who, since July 1, 1944, has been or hereafter is determined to be a mentally disordered sex offender under Article 1 (commencing with Section 6300) of Chapter 2 of Part 2 of Division 6 of the Welfare and Institutions Code or any person who has been found guilty in the guilt phase of a trial for an offense for which registration is required by this section but who has been found not guilty by reason of insanity in the sanity phase of the trial.

(D) Any person who, since July 1, 1944, has been, or is hereafter convicted in any other court, including any state, federal, or military court, of any offense *** that, if committed or attempted in this state, would have been punishable as one or more of the offenses described in subparagraph (A) or any person ordered by any other court, including any state, federal, or military court, to register as a sex offender for any offense, if the court found at the time of conviction or sentencing that the person committed the offense as a result of sexual compulsion or for purposes of sexual gratification.

(E) Any person ordered by any court to register pursuant to this section for any offense not included specifically in this section if the court finds at the time of conviction or sentencing that the person committed the offense as a result of sexual compulsion or for purposes of sexual gratification. The court shall state on the record the reasons for its findings and the reasons for requiring registration.

(F)(i) Notwithstanding any other subdivision, a person who was convicted before January 1, 1976, under subdivision (a) of Section 286, or Section 288a, shall not be required to register pursuant to this section for that conviction if the conviction was for conduct between consenting adults that was decriminalized by Chapter 71 of the Statutes of 1975 or Chapter 1139 of the Statutes of 1976. The Department of Justice shall remove that person from the Sex Offender Registry, and the person is discharged from his or her duty to register pursuant to the following procedure:

(I) The person submits to the Department of Justice official documentary evidence, including court records or police reports, *** that demonstrate that the person's conviction pursuant to either of those sections was for conduct between consenting adults that was decriminalized; or

(II) The person submits to the department a declaration stating that the person's conviction pursuant to either of those sections was for consensual conduct between adults that has been decriminalized. The declaration shall be confidential and not a public record, and shall include the person's name, address, telephone number, date of birth, and a summary of the circumstances leading to the conviction, including the date of the conviction and county of the occurrence.

(III) The department shall determine whether the person's conviction was for conduct between consensual adults that has been decriminalized. If the conviction was for consensual conduct between adults that has been decriminalized, and the person has no other offenses for which he or she is required to register pursuant to this section, the department shall, within 60 days of receipt of those documents, notify the person that he or she is relieved of the duty to register, and shall notify the local law enforcement agency with which the person is registered that he or she has been relieved of the duty to register. The local law enforcement agency shall remove the person's registration from its files within 30 days of receipt of notification. If the documentary or other evidence submitted is insufficient to establish the person's claim, the department shall, within 60 days of receipt of those documents, notify the person that his or her claim cannot be established, and that the person shall continue to register pursuant to this section. The department shall provide, upon the person's request, any information relied upon by the department in making its determination that the person shall continue to register pursuant to this section. Any person whose claim has been denied by the department pursuant to this clause may petition the court to appeal the department's denial of the person's claim.

(ii) On or before July 1, 1998, the department shall make a report to the Legislature concerning the status of persons who may come under the provisions of this subparagraph, including the number of persons who were convicted before January 1, 1976, under subdivision (a) of Section 286 or Section 288a and are required to register under this section, the average age of these persons, the number of these persons who have any subsequent convictions for a registerable sex offense, and the number of these persons who have sought successfully or unsuccessfully to be relieved of their duty to register under this section.

(b)(1) Any person who is released, discharged, or paroled from a jail, state or federal prison, school, road camp, or other institution where he or she was confined because of the commission or attempted commission of one of the offenses specified in subdivision (a) or is released from a state hospital to which he or she was committed as a mentally disordered sex offender under Article 1 (commencing with Section 6300) of Chapter 2 of Part 2 of Division 6 of the Welfare and Institutions Code, shall, prior to discharge, parole, or release, be informed of his or her duty to register under this section by the official in charge of the place of confinement or hospital, and the official shall require the person to read and sign any form that may be required by the Department of Justice, stating that the duty of the person to register under this section has been explained to the person. The official in charge of the place of confinement or hospital shall obtain the address where the person expects to reside upon his or her discharge, parole, or release and shall report the address to the Department of Justice. The official shall at the same time forward a current photograph of the person to the Department of Justice.

(2) The official in charge of the place of confinement or hospital shall give one copy of the form to the person and shall send one copy to the Department of Justice and one copy to the appropriate law enforcement agency or agencies having jurisdiction over the place the person expects to reside upon discharge, parole, or release. If the conviction that makes the person subject to this section is a felony conviction, the

official in charge shall, not later than 45 days prior to the scheduled release of the person, send one copy to the appropriate law enforcement agency or agencies having local jurisdiction where the person expects to reside upon discharge, parole, or release; one copy to the prosecuting agency that prosecuted the person; and one copy to the Department of Justice. The official in charge of the place of confinement or hospital shall retain one copy.

(c)(1) Any person who is convicted in this state of the commission or attempted commission of any of the offenses specified in subdivision (a) and who is released on probation, *** shall, prior to release or discharge, be informed of the duty to register under this section by the probation department, and a probation officer shall require the person to read and sign any form that may be required by the Department of Justice, stating that the duty of the person to register under this section has been explained to him or her. The probation officer shall obtain the address where the person expects to reside upon release or discharge and shall report within three days the address to the Department of Justice. The probation officer shall give one copy of the form to the person, send one copy to the Department of Justice, and forward one copy to the appropriate law enforcement agency or agencies having local jurisdiction where the person expects to reside upon his or her discharge, parole, or release.

(2) Any person who is convicted in this state of the commission or attempted commission of any of the offenses specified in subdivision (a) and who is granted conditional release without supervised probation, or discharged upon payment of a fine, shall, prior to release or discharge, be informed of the duty to register under this section in open court by the court in which the person has been convicted, and the court shall require the person to read and sign any form that may be required by the Department of Justice, stating that the duty of the person to register under this section has been explained to him or her. If the court finds that it is in the interest of the efficiency of the court, the court may assign the bailiff to require the person to read and sign forms under this section. The court shall obtain the address where the person expects to reside upon release or discharge and shall report within three days the address to the Department of Justice. The court shall give one copy of the form to the person, send one copy to the Department of Justice, and forward one copy to the appropriate law enforcement agency or agencies having local jurisdiction where the person expects to reside upon his or her discharge, parole, or release.

(d)(1) Any person who, on or after January 1, 1986, is discharged or paroled from the Department of the Youth Authority to the custody of which he or she was committed after having been adjudicated a ward of the juvenile court pursuant to Section 602 of the Welfare and Institutions Code because of the commission or attempted commission of any offense described in paragraph (3) shall be subject to registration under the procedures of this section.

(2) Any person who is discharged or paroled from a facility in another state that is equivalent to the Department of the Youth Authority, to the custody of which he or she was committed because of an offense which, if committed or attempted in this state, would have been punishable as one or more of the offenses described in paragraph (3), shall be subject to registration under the procedures of this section.

(3) Any person described in this subdivision who committed an offense in violation of any of the following provisions shall be required to register pursuant to this section:

(A) Assault with intent to commit rape, sodomy, oral copulation, or any violation of Section 264.1, 288, or 289 under Section 220.

(B) Any offense defined in paragraph (1), (2), (3), (4), or (6) of subdivision (a) of Section 261, Section 264.1, 266c, or 267, paragraph (1) of subdivision (b) of, or subdivision (c) or (d) of, Section 286, Section 288 or 288.5, paragraph (1) of subdivision (b) of, or subdivision (c) or (d) of, Section 288a, subdivision (a) of Section 289, or Section 647.6.

(C) A violation of Section 207 or 209 committed with the intent to violate Section 261, 286, 288, 288a, or 289.

(4) Prior to discharge or parole from the Department of the Youth Authority, any person who is subject to registration under this subdivision shall be informed of the duty to register under the procedures set forth in this section. Department of the Youth Authority officials shall transmit the required forms and information to the Department of Justice.

(5) All records specifically relating to the registration in the custody of the Department of Justice, law enforcement agencies, and other agencies or public officials shall be destroyed when the person who is required to register has his or her records sealed under the procedures set forth in Section 781 of the Welfare and Institutions Code. This subdivision shall not be construed as requiring the destruction of other criminal offender or juvenile records relating to the case that are maintained by the Department of Justice, law enforcement agencies, the juvenile court, or other agencies and public officials unless ordered by a court under Section 781 of the Welfare and Institutions Code.

(e)(1) On or after January 1, 1998, upon incarceration, placement, or commitment, or prior to release on probation, any person who is required to register under this section shall preregister. The preregistering official shall be the admitting officer at the place of incarceration, placement, or commitment, or the probation officer if the person is to be released on probation. The preregistration shall consist of both of the following:

(A) A preregistration statement in writing, signed by the person, giving information that shall be required by the Department of Justice.

(B) The fingerprints and a current photograph of the person.

(C) Any person who is preregistered pursuant to this subdivision is required to be preregistered only once.

(2) A person described in paragraph (2) of subdivision (a) shall register, or reregister if the person has previously registered, upon release from incarceration, placement, or commitment, pursuant to paragraph (1) of subdivision (a). The registration shall consist of all of the following:

(A) A statement in writing signed by the person, giving information as shall be required by the Department of Justice and giving the name and address of the person's employer, and the address of the person's place of employment if that is different from the employer's main address.

(B) The fingerprints and a current photograph of the person taken by the registering official.

(C) The license plate number of any vehicle owned by, regularly driven by, or registered in the name of the person.

(D) Notice to the person that, in addition to the requirements of paragraph (4), he or she may have a duty to register in any other state where he or she may relocate.

(E) Copies of adequate proof of residence, which shall be limited to a California driver's license, California identification card, recent rent or utility receipt, printed personalized checks or other recent banking documents showing that person's name and address, or any other information that the registering official believes is reliable. If the person has no residence and no reasonable expectation of obtaining a residence in the foreseeable future, the person shall so advise the registering official and shall sign a statement provided by the registering official stating that fact. Upon presentation of proof of residence to the registering official or a signed statement that the person has no residence, the person shall be allowed to register. If the person claims that he or she has a residence but does not have any proof of residence, he or she shall be allowed to register but shall furnish proof of residence within 30 days of the day he or she is allowed to register.

(3) Within three days thereafter, the preregistering official or the registering law enforcement agency or agencies shall forward the statement, fingerprints, photograph, and vehicle license plate number, if any, to the Department of Justice.

(f)(1) If any person who is required to register pursuant to this section changes his or her residence address or location, whether within the jurisdiction in which he or she is currently registered or to a new jurisdiction inside or outside the state, the person shall inform, in writing within five working days, the law enforcement agency or agencies with which he or she last registered of the new address or location. The law enforcement agency or agencies shall, within three days after receipt of this information, forward a copy of the change of address or location information to the Department of Justice. The Department of Justice shall forward appropriate registration data to the law enforcement agency or agencies having local jurisdiction of the new place of residence or location.

(2) If the person's new address is in a Department of the Youth Authority facility or a state prison or state mental institution, an official of the place of incarceration, placement, or commitment shall, within 90 days of receipt of the person, forward the registrant's change of address information to the Department of Justice. The agency need not provide a physical address for the registrant but shall indicate that he or she is serving a period of incarceration or commitment in a facility under the agency's jurisdiction. This paragraph shall apply to persons received in a Department of the Youth Authority facility or a state prison or state mental institution on or after January 1, 1999. The Department of Justice shall forward the change of address information to the agency with which the person last registered.

(3) If any person who is required to register pursuant to this section changes his or her name, the person shall inform, in person, the law enforcement agency or agencies with which he or she is currently registered within five working days. The law enforcement agency or agencies shall forward a copy of this information to the Department of Justice within three days of its receipt.

(g)(1) Any person who is required to register under this section based on a misdemeanor conviction or juvenile adjudication who willfully violates any requirement of this section is guilty of a misdemeanor punishable by imprisonment in a county jail not exceeding one year.

(2) Except as provided in paragraphs (5) and (7), any person who is required to register under this section based on a felony conviction or juvenile adjudication who willfully violates any requirement of this section or who has a prior conviction or juvenile adjudication for the offense of failing to register under this section and who subsequently and willfully violates any requirement of this section is guilty of a felony and shall be punished by imprisonment in the state prison for 16 months, or two or three years.

If probation is granted or if the imposition or execution of sentence is suspended, it shall be a condition of the probation or suspension that the person serve at least 90 days in a county jail. The penalty described in this paragraph shall apply whether or not the person has been released on parole or has been discharged from parole.

(3) Any person determined to be a mentally disordered sex offender or who has been found guilty in the guilt phase of trial for an offense for which registration is required under this section, but who has been found not guilty by reason of insanity in the sanity phase of the trial, or who has had a petition sustained in a juvenile adjudication for an offense for which registration is required under this section pursuant to subdivision (d), but who has been found not guilty by reason of insanity, who willfully violates any requirement of this section is guilty of a misdemeanor and shall be punished by imprisonment in a county jail not exceeding one year. For any second or subsequent willful violation of any requirement of this section, the person is guilty of a felony and shall be punished by imprisonment in the state prison for 16 months, or two or three years.

(4) If, after discharge from parole, the person is convicted of a felony or suffers a juvenile adjudication as specified in this subdivision, he or she shall be required to complete parole of at least one year, in addition to any other punishment imposed under this subdivision. A person convicted of a felony as specified in this subdivision may be granted probation only in the unusual case where the interests of justice would best be served. When probation is granted under this paragraph, the court shall specify on the record and shall enter into the minutes the circumstances indicating that the interests of justice would best be served by the disposition.

(5) Any person who has ever been adjudicated a sexually violent predator, as defined in Section 6600 of the Welfare and Institutions Code, and who fails to verify his or her registration every 90 days as required pursuant to subparagraph (E) of paragraph (1) of subdivision (a), shall be punished by imprisonment in the state prison, or in a county jail not exceeding one year.

(6) Except as otherwise provided in paragraph (5), and in addition to any other penalty imposed under this subdivision, any person who is required pursuant to subparagraph (C) of paragraph (1) of subdivision (a) to update his or her registration every *** 60 days and willfully fails to update his or her registration is guilty of a misdemeanor and shall be punished by imprisonment in a county jail not exceeding six months. Any subsequent violation of this requirement that persons described in subparagraph (C) of paragraph (1)

of subdivision (a) shall update their registration every *** 60 days is also a misdemeanor and shall be punished by imprisonment in a county jail not exceeding six months.

(7) Any person who fails to provide proof of residence as required by subparagraph (E) of paragraph (2) of subdivision (e), regardless of the offense upon which the duty to register is based, is guilty of a misdemeanor punishable by imprisonment in a county jail not exceeding six months.

(8) Any person who is required to register under this section who willfully violates any requirement of this section is guilty of a continuing offense.

(h) Whenever any person is released on parole or probation and is required to register under this section but fails to do so within the time prescribed, the parole authority, the Youthful Offender Parole Board, or the court, as the case may be, shall order the parole or probation of the person revoked. For purposes of this subdivision, "parole authority" has the same meaning as described in Section 3000.

(i) Except as provided in subdivisions (m) and (n) and Section 290.4, the statements, photographs, and fingerprints required by this section shall not be open to inspection by the public or by any person other than a regularly employed peace officer or other law enforcement officer.

(j) In any case in which a person who would be required to register pursuant to this section for a felony conviction is to be temporarily sent outside the institution where he or she is confined on any assignment within a city or county including firefighting, disaster control, or of whatever nature the assignment may be, the local law enforcement agency having jurisdiction over the place or places where the assignment shall occur shall be notified within a reasonable time prior to removal from the institution. This subdivision shall not apply to any person who is temporarily released under guard from the institution where he or she is confined.

(k) As used in this section, "mentally disordered sex offender" includes any person who has been determined to be a sexual psychopath or a mentally disordered sex offender under any provision which, on or before January 1, 1976, was contained in Division 6 (commencing with Section 6000) of the Welfare and Institutions Code.

(l)(1) Every person who, prior to January 1, 1997, is required to register under this section, shall be notified whenever he or she next reregisters of the reduction of the registration period from 14 to five working days. This notice shall be provided in writing by the registering agency or agencies. Failure to receive this notification shall be a defense against the penalties prescribed by subdivision (g) if the person did register within 14 days.

(2) Every person who, as a sexually violent predator, as defined in Section 6600 of the Welfare and Institutions Code, is required to verify his or her registration every 90 days, shall be notified wherever he or she next registers of his or her increased registration obligations. This notice shall be provided in writing by the registering agency or agencies. Failure to receive this notice shall be a defense against the penalties prescribed by paragraph (5) of subdivision (g).

(m)(1) When a peace officer reasonably suspects, based on information that has come to his or her attention through information provided by any peace officer or member of the public, that a child or other person may be at risk from a sex offender convicted of a crime listed in paragraph (1) of subdivision (a) of Section 290.4, a law enforcement agency may, notwithstanding any other provision of law, provide any of the information specified in paragraph (4) of this subdivision about that registered sex offender that the agency deems relevant and necessary to protect the public, to the following persons, agencies, or organizations the offender is likely to encounter, including, but not limited to, the following:

(A) Public and private educational institutions, day care establishments, and establishments and organizations that primarily serve individuals likely to be victimized by the offender.

(B) Other community members at risk.

(2) The law enforcement agency may authorize persons and entities who receive the information pursuant to paragraph (1) to disclose information to additional persons only if the agency does the following:

(A) Determines that all conditions set forth in paragraph (1) have been satisfied regarding disclosure to the additional persons.

(B) Identifies the appropriate scope of further disclosure.

(3) Persons notified pursuant to paragraph (1) may disclose the information provided by the law enforcement agency in the manner and to the extent authorized by the law enforcement agency.

(4) The information that may be disclosed pursuant to this section includes the following:

(A) The offender's full name.

(B) The offender's known aliases.

(C) The offender's gender.

(D) The offender's race.

(E) The offender's physical description.

(F) The offender's photograph.

(G) The offender's date of birth.

(H) Crimes resulting in registration under this section.

(I) The offender's address, which must be verified prior to publication.

(J) Description and license plate number of offender's vehicles or vehicles the offender is known to drive.

(K) Type of victim targeted by the offender.

(L) Relevant parole or probation conditions, such as one prohibiting contact with children.

(M) Dates of crimes resulting in classification under this section.

(N) Date of release from confinement.

(O) The offender's enrollment, employment, or vocational status with any university, college, community college, or other institution of higher learning.

However, information disclosed pursuant to this subdivision shall not include information that would identify the victim.

(5) If a law enforcement agency discloses information pursuant to this subdivision, it shall include, with the disclosure, a statement that the purpose of the release of the information is to allow members of the public to protect themselves and their children from sex offenders.

(6) For purposes of this section, "likely to encounter" means both of the following:

(A) That the agencies, organizations, or other community members are in a location or in close proximity to a location where the offender lives or is employed, or that the offender visits or is likely to visit on a regular basis.

(B) The types of interaction that ordinarily occur at that location and other circumstances indicate that contact with the offender is reasonably probable.

(7) For purposes of this section, "reasonably suspects" means that it is objectively reasonable for a peace officer to entertain a suspicion, based upon facts that could cause a reasonable person in a like position, drawing when appropriate on his or her training and experience, to suspect that a child or other person is at risk.

(8) For purposes of this section, "at risk" means a person is or may be exposed to a risk of becoming a victim of a sex offense committed by the offender.

(9) A law enforcement agency may continue to disclose information on an offender under this subdivision for as long as the offender is included in Section 290.4.

(n) In addition to the procedures set forth elsewhere in this section, a designated law enforcement entity may advise the public of the presence of high-risk sex offenders in its community pursuant to this subdivision.

(1) For purposes of this subdivision:

(A) A high-risk sex offender is a person who has been convicted of an offense specified in paragraph (1) of subdivision (a) of Section 290.4, and also meets one of the following criteria:

(i) Has been convicted of three or more violent sex offenses, at least two of which were brought and tried separately.

(ii) Has been convicted of two violent sex offenses and one or more violent nonsex offenses, at least two of which were brought and tried separately.

(iii) Has been convicted of one violent sex offense and two or more violent nonsex offenses, at least two of which were brought and tried separately.

(iv) Has been convicted of either two violent sex offenses or one violent sex offense and one violent nonsex offense, at least two of which were brought and tried separately, and has been arrested on separate occasions for three or more violent sex offenses, violent nonsex offenses, or associated offenses.

(v) Has been adjudicated a sexually violent predator pursuant to Article 4 (commencing with Section 6600) of Chapter 2 of Part 2 of Division 6 of the Welfare and Institutions Code.

(B) A violent sex offense means any offense defined in Section 220, except attempt to commit mayhem, or Section 261, 264.1, 286, 288, 288a, 288.5, 289, or 647.6, or infliction of great bodily injury during the commission of a sex offense, as provided in Section 12022.8.

(C) A violent nonsex offense means any offense defined in Section 187, subdivision (a) of Section 192, or Section 203, 206, 207, or 236, provided that the offense is a felony, subdivision (a) of Section 273a, Section 273d or 451, or attempted murder, as defined in Sections 187 and 664.

(D) An associated offense means any offense defined in Section 243.4, provided that the offense is a felony, Section 311.1, 311.2, 311.3, 311.4, 311.5, 311.6, 311.7, or 314, Section 459, provided the offense is of the first degree, Section 597 or 646.9, subdivision (d), (h), or (i) of Section 647, Section 653m, or infliction of great bodily injury during the commission of a felony, as defined in Section 12022.7.

(E) For purposes of subparagraphs (B) to (D), inclusive, an arrest or conviction for the statutory predecessor of any of the enumerated offenses, or an arrest or conviction in any other jurisdiction for any offense that, if committed or attempted in this state, would have been punishable as one or more of the offenses described in those subparagraphs, is to be considered in determining whether an offender is a high-risk sex offender.

(F) For purposes of subparagraphs (B) to (D), inclusive, an arrest as a juvenile or an adjudication as a ward of the juvenile court within the meaning of Section 602 of the Welfare and Institutions Code for any of the offenses described in those subparagraphs is to be considered in determining whether an offender is a high-risk sex offender.

(G) Notwithstanding subparagraphs (A) to (D), inclusive, an offender shall not be considered to be a high-risk sex offender if either of the following apply:

(i) The offender's most recent conviction or arrest for an offense described in subparagraphs (B) to (D), inclusive, occurred more than five years prior to the high-risk assessment by the Department of Justice, excluding periods of confinement.

(ii) The offender notifies the Department of Justice, on a form approved by the department and available at any sheriff's office, that he or she has not been convicted in the preceding 15 years, excluding periods of confinement, of an offense for which registration is required under paragraph (2) of subdivision (a), and the department is able, upon exercise of reasonable diligence, to verify the information provided in paragraph (2).

(H) "Confinement" means confinement in a jail, prison, school, road camp, or other penal institution, confinement in a state hospital to which the offender was committed as a mentally disordered sex offender under Article 1 (commencing with Section 6300) of Chapter 2 of Part 2 of Division 6 of the Welfare and Institutions Code, or confinement in a facility designated by the Director of Mental Health to which the offender was committed as a sexually violent predator under Article 4 (commencing with Section 6600) of Chapter 2 of Part 2 of Division 6 of the Welfare and Institutions Code.

(I) "Designated law enforcement entity" means any of the following: municipal police department; sheriff's department; district attorney's office; county probation department; Department of Justice; Department of Corrections; Department of the Youth Authority; Department of the California Highway Patrol; or the police department of any campus of the University of California, California State University, or community college.

(2) The Department of Justice shall continually search the records provided to it pursuant to subdivision (b) and identify, on the basis of those records, high-risk sex offenders. Four times each year, the department shall provide to each chief of police and sheriff in the state, and to any other designated law enforcement entity upon request, the following information regarding each identified high-risk sex of-

fender: full name; known aliases; gender; race; physical description; photograph; date of birth; and crimes resulting in classification under this section.

(3) The Department of Justice and any designated law enforcement entity to which notice has been given pursuant to paragraph (2) may cause to be made public, by whatever means the agency deems necessary to ensure the public safety, based upon information available to the agency concerning a specific person, including, but not limited to, the information described in paragraph (2); the offender's address, which shall be verified prior to publication; description and license plate number of the offender's vehicles or vehicles the offender is known to drive; type of victim targeted by the offender; relevant parole or probation conditions, such as one prohibiting contact with children; dates of crimes resulting in classification under this section; and date of release from confinement; but excluding information that would identify the victim.

(4) Notwithstanding any other provision of law, any person described in paragraph (2) of subdivision (p) who receives information from a designated law enforcement entity pursuant to paragraph (3) *** may disclose that information in the manner and to the extent authorized by the law enforcement entity.

(5) The law enforcement agency may authorize persons and entities who receive the information pursuant to paragraph (3) to disclose information to additional persons only if the agency does the following:

(A) Determines that all conditions set forth in this subdivision have been satisfied regarding disclosure to the additional persons.

(B) Identifies the appropriate scope of further disclosure.

(o) Agencies disseminating information to the public pursuant to Section 290.4 shall maintain records of those persons requesting to view the CD-ROM or other electronic media for a minimum of five years. Agencies disseminating information to the public pursuant to subdivision (n) shall maintain records of the means and dates of dissemination for a minimum of five years.

(p)(1) Any law enforcement agency and employees of any law enforcement agency shall be immune from liability for good faith conduct under this section. For the purposes of this section, "law enforcement agency" means the Attorney General of California, every district attorney, the Department of Corrections, the Department of the Youth Authority, and every state or local agency expressly authorized by statute to investigate or prosecute law violators.

(2) Any public or private educational institution, day care facility, or any child care custodian described in Section 11165.7, or any employee of a public or private educational institution or day care facility which in good faith disseminates information as authorized pursuant to paragraph (3) of subdivision (m) or paragraph (4) of subdivision (n) that is provided by a law enforcement agency or an employee of a law enforcement agency shall be immune from civil liability.

(q)(1) Any person who uses information disclosed pursuant to this section to commit a felony shall be punished, in addition and consecutive to any other punishment, by a five-year term of imprisonment in the state prison.

(2) Any person who uses information disclosed pursuant to this section to commit a misdemeanor shall be subject to, in addition to any other penalty or fine imposed, a fine of not less than five hundred dollars ($500) and not more than one thousand dollars ($1,000).

(r) The registration and public notification provisions of this section are applicable to every person described in this section, without regard to when his or her crimes were committed or his or her duty to register pursuant to this section arose, and to every offense described in this section, regardless of when it was committed. *(AM '01)*

290.1. Sex Offender; Section 290 Registrant

Notwithstanding Section 1203.4 and except as provided in Section 290.5, a person who is convicted of a sex offense for which registration is required under Section 290 shall not be relieved from the duty to register under that section.

302. Disorderly Conduct at Church Service

(a) Every person who intentionally disturbs or disquiets any assemblage of people met for religious worship at a tax-exempt place of worship, by profane discourse, rude or indecent behavior, or by any unnecessary noise, either within the place where the meeting is held, or so near it as to disturb the order and solemnity of the meeting, is guilty of a misdemeanor punishable by a fine not exceeding one thousand dollars ($1,000), or by imprisonment in a county jail for a period not exceeding one year, or by both that fine and imprisonment.

(b) A court may require performance of community service of not less than 50 hours and not exceeding 80 hours as an alternative to imprisonment or a fine.

(c) In addition to the penalty set forth in subdivision (a), a person who has suffered a previous conviction of a violation of this section or Section 403, shall be required to perform community service of not less than 120 hours and not exceeding 160 hours.

(d) The existence of any fact which would bring a person under subdivision (c) or (d) shall be alleged in the complaint, information, or indictment and either:

(1) Admitted by the defendant in open court.

(2) Found to be true by a jury trying the issue of guilt.

(3) Found to be true by the court where guilt is established by a plea of guilty or nolo contendere.

(4) Found to be true by trial by the court sitting without a jury.

(e) Upon conviction of any person under this section for disturbances of religious worship, the court may, in accordance with the performance of community service imposed under this section, consistent with public safety interests and with the victim's consent, order the defendant to perform a portion of, or all of, the required community service at the place where the disturbance of religious worship occurred.

(f) The court may waive the mandatory minimum requirements for community service whenever it is in the interest of justice to do so. When a waiver is granted, the court shall state on the record all reasons supporting the waiver.

303. Encouraging Sale of Alcoholic Beverages

It shall be unlawful for any person engaged in the sale of alcoholic beverages, other than in the original package, to employ upon the premises where the alcoholic beverages are sold any person for the purpose of procuring or encouraging the purchase or sale of such beverages, or to pay any person a percentage or commission on the sale of such beverages for procuring or encouraging such purchase or sale. Violation of this section shall be a misdemeanor.

303a. Soliciting Purchase of Alcoholic Beverages

It shall be unlawful, in any place of business where alcoholic beverages are sold to be consumed upon the premises, for any person to loiter in or about said premises for the purpose of begging or soliciting any patron or customer of, or visitor in, such premises to purchase any alcoholic beverage for the one begging or soliciting. Violation of this section shall be a misdemeanor.

307. Sell, Give Away or Furnish Confection Containing Alcohol to Minor

Every person, firm, or corporation which sells or gives or in any way furnishes to another person, who is in fact under the age of 21 years, any candy, cake, cookie, or chewing gum which contains alcohol in excess of 1/2 of 1 percent by weight, is guilty of a misdemeanor.

308. Selling Cigarettes or Tobacco to Minor

(a) Every person, firm, or corporation which knowingly <u>or under circumstances in which it has knowledge, or should otherwise have grounds for knowledge,</u> sells, gives, or in any way furnishes to another person who is under the age of 18 years any tobacco, cigarette, or cigarette papers, or any other preparation of tobacco, or any other instrument or paraphernalia that is designed for the smoking or ingestion of tobacco, products prepared from tobacco, or any controlled substance, is subject to either a criminal action for a misdemeanor or to a civil action brought by a city attorney, a county counsel, or a district attorney, punishable by a fine of two hundred dollars ($200) for the first offense, five hundred dollars ($500) for the second offense, and one thousand dollars ($1,000) for the third offense.

Notwithstanding Section 1464 or any other provision of law, 25 percent of each civil and criminal penalty collected pursuant to this subdivision shall be paid to the office of the city attorney, county counsel, or district attorney, whoever is responsible for bringing the successful action, and 25 percent of each civil and criminal penalty collected pursuant to this subdivision shall be paid to the city or county for the administration and cost of the community service work component provided in subdivision (b).

Proof that a defendant, or his or her employee or agent, demanded, was shown, and reasonably relied upon evidence of majority shall be defense to any action brought pursuant to this subdivision. Evidence of majority of a person is a facsimile of or a reasonable likeness of a document issued by a federal, state, county, or municipal government, or subdivision or agency thereof, including, but not limited to, a motor vehicle operator's license, a registration certificate issued under the Federal Selective Service Act, or an identification card issued to a member of the *** Armed Forces.

For purposes of this section, the person liable for selling or furnishing tobacco products to minors by a tobacco vending machine shall be the person authorizing the installation or placement of the tobacco vending machine upon premises he or she manages or otherwise controls and under circumstances in which he or she has knowledge, or should otherwise have grounds for knowledge, that the tobacco vending machine will be utilized by minors.

(b) Every person under the age of 18 years who purchases, receives, or possesses any tobacco, cigarette, or cigarette papers, or any other preparation of tobacco, or any other instrument or paraphernalia that is designed for the smoking of tobacco, products prepared from tobacco, or any controlled substance shall, upon conviction, be punished by a fine of seventy-five dollars ($75) or 30 hours of community service work.

(c) Every person, firm, or corporation which sells, or deals in tobacco or any preparation thereof, shall post conspicuously and keep so posted in his, her, or their place of business at each point of purchase the notice required pursuant to subdivision (b) of Section 22952 of the Business and Professions Code, and any person failing to do so shall upon conviction be punished by a fine of ten dollars ($10) for the first offense and fifty dollars ($50) for each succeeding violation of this provision, or by imprisonment for not more than 30 days.

(d) For purposes of determining the liability of persons, firms, or corporations controlling franchises or business operations in multiple locations for the second and subsequent violations of this section, each individual franchise or business location shall be deemed a separate entity.

(e) It is the Legislature's intent to regulate the subject matter of this section. As a result, no city, county, or city and county shall adopt any ordinance or regulation inconsistent with this section.

(f) Notwithstanding any other provision of this section, the Director of Corrections may sell or supply tobacco and tobacco products, including cigarettes and cigarette papers, to any person confined in any institution or facility under his*** or her*** jurisdiction who has attained the age of 16 years, if the parent or guardian of the person consents thereto, and may permit smoking by *** the person in any *** institution or facility. No officer or employee of the Department of Corrections shall be considered to have violated this section by any act authorized by this subdivision. *(AM '01)*

308b.   Delivery of Unsolicited Tobacco Products Prohibited

(a) Except as provided in subdivision (b), every person who knowingly delivers or causes to be delivered to any residence in this state any tobacco products unsolicited by any person residing therein is guilty of a misdemeanor.

(b) It is a defense to a violation of this section that the recipient of the tobacco products is personally known to the defendant at the time of the delivery.

(c) The distribution of unsolicited tobacco products to residences in violation of this section is a nuisance within the meaning of Section 3479 of the Civil Code.

(d) Nothing in this section shall be construed to impose any liability on any employee of the United States Postal Service for actions performed in the scope of his employment by the United States Postal Service.

308.2.   Cigarettes: Sale when Not Sealed and Properly Packaged

(a) Every person who sells one or more cigarettes, other than in a sealed and properly labeled package, is guilty of an infraction.

(b) "A sealed and properly labeled package,"as used in this section, means the original packaging or sanitary wrapping of the manufacturer or importer which conforms to federal labeling requirements, including the federal warning label.

308.5. Paid Tobacco or Alcohol Advertisements in Video Games

(a) No person or business shall sell, lease, rent, or provide, or offer to sell, lease, rent, or otherwise offer to the public or to public establishments in this state, any video game intended for either private use or for use in a public establishment and intended primarily for use by any person under the age of 18 years, which contains, in its design and in the on-screen presentation of the video game, any paid commercial advertisement of alcoholic beverage or tobacco product containers or other forms of consumer packaging, particular brand names, trademarks, or copyrighted slogans of alcoholic beverages or tobacco products.

(b) As used in this section, "video game"means any electronic amusement device that utilizes a computer, microprocessor, or similar electronic circuitry and its own cathode ray tube, or is designed to be used with a television set or a monitor, that interacts with the user of the device.

(c) A violation of this section is a misdemeanor.

309. Admitting or Keeping Minor in House of Prostitution

Any proprietor, keeper, manager, conductor, or person having the control of any house of prostitution, or any house or room resorted to for the purpose of prostitution, who shall admit or keep any minor of either sex therein; or any parent or guardian of any such minor, who shall admit or keep such minor, or sanction, or connive at the admission or keeping thereof, into, or in any such house, or room, shall be guilty of a misdemeanor.

310. Attendance of Minor at Prizefight or Cockfight

Any minor under the age of 16 years who visits or attends any prizefight, cockfight, or place where any prizefight, or cockfight, is advertised to take place, and any owner, lessee, or proprietor, or the agent of any owner, lessee, or proprietor of any place where any prizefight or cockfight is advertised or represented to take place who admits any minor to a place where any prizefight or cockfight is advertised or represented to take place or who admits, sells or gives to any such minor a ticket or other paper by which such minor may be admitted to a place where a prizefight or cockfight is advertised to take place, is guilty of a misdemeanor, and is punishable by a fine of not exceeding one hundred dollars ($100) or by imprisonment in the county jail for not more than 25 days.

310.5. Child Agreements With Perpetrator of Sex Act Upon The Child

(a) Any parent or guardian of a child who enters into an agreement on behalf of that child which is in violation of Section 1669.5 of the Civil Code, and any alleged perpetrator of an unlawful sex act upon that child who enters into such an agreement, is guilty of a misdemeanor.

(b) Every person convicted of a violation of subdivision (a) shall be punished by a fine of not less than one hundred dollars ($100) nor more than one thousand dollars ($1,000), by imprisonment in the county jail for not less than 30 days nor more than six months, or by both such a fine and imprisonment, at the discretion of the court.

(c) For purposes of this section, "unlawful sex act,"means a felony sex offense committed against a minor.

311. Obscene Matter - Definitions

As used in this chapter, the following definitions apply:

(a) "Obscene matter"means matter, taken as a whole, that to the average person, applying contemporary statewide standards, appeals to the prurient interest, that, taken as a whole, depicts or describes sexual conduct in a patently offensive way, and that, taken as a whole, lacks serious literary, artistic, political, or scientific value.

(1) If it appears from the nature of the matter or the circumstances of its dissemination, distribution, or exhibition that it is designed for clearly defined deviant sexual groups, the appeal of the matter shall be judged with reference to its intended recipient group.

(2) In prosecutions under this chapter, if circumstances of production, presentation, sale, dissemination, distribution, or publicity indicate that matter is being commercially exploited by the defendant for the sake of its prurient appeal, this evidence is probative with respect to the nature of the matter and may justify the conclusion that the matter lacks serious literary, artistic, political, or scientific value.

(3) In determining whether the matter taken as a whole lacks serious literary, artistic, political, or scientific value in description or representation of those matters, the fact that the defendant knew that the matter depicts persons under the age of 16 years engaged in sexual conduct, as defined in subdivision (c) of Section 311.4, is a factor that may be considered in making that determination.

(b) "Matter" means any book, magazine, newspaper, or other printed or written material, or any picture, drawing, photograph, motion picture, or other pictorial representation, or any statue or other figure, or any recording, transcription, or mechanical, chemical, or electrical reproduction, or any other article, equipment, machine, or material. "Matter" also means live or recorded telephone messages if transmitted, disseminated, or distributed as part of a commercial transaction.

(c) "Person" means any individual, partnership, firm, association, corporation, limited liability company, or other legal entity.

(d) "Distribute" means transfer possession of, whether with or without consideration.

(e) "Knowingly" means being aware of the character of the matter or live conduct.

(f) "Exhibit" means show.

(g) "Obscene live conduct" means any physical human body activity, whether performed or engaged in alone or with other persons, including but not limited to singing, speaking, dancing, acting, simulating, or pantomiming, taken as a whole, that to the average person, applying contemporary statewide standards, appeals to the prurient interest and is conduct that, taken as a whole, depicts or describes sexual conduct in a patently offensive way and that, taken as a whole, lacks serious literary, artistic, political, or scientific value.

(1) If it appears from the nature of the conduct or the circumstances of its production, presentation, or exhibition that it is designed for clearly defined deviant sexual groups, the appeal of the conduct shall be judged with reference to its intended recipient group.

(2) In prosecutions under this chapter, if circumstances of production, presentation, advertising, or exhibition indicate that live conduct is being commercially exploited by the defendant for the sake of its prurient appeal, that evidence is probative with respect to the nature of the conduct and may justify the conclusion that the conduct lacks serious literary, artistic, political, or scientific value.

(3) In determining whether the live conduct taken as a whole lacks serious literary, artistic, political, or scientific value in description or representation of those matters, the fact that the defendant knew that the live conduct depicts persons under the age of 16 years engaged in sexual conduct, as defined in subdivision (c) of Section 311.4, is a factor that may be considered in making that determination.

(h) The Legislature expresses its approval of the holding of People v. Cantrell, 7 Cal. App. 4th 523, that, for the purposes of this chapter, matter that "depicts a person under the age of 18 years personally engaging in or personally simulating sexual conduct" is limited to visual works that depict that conduct.

311.1. Import Matter Depicting Person Under 18 years Engaging In Sexual Conduct

(a) Every person who knowingly sends or causes to be sent, or brings or causes to be brought, into this state for sale or distribution, or in this state possesses, prepares, publishes, produces, develops, duplicates, or prints any representation of information, data, or image, including, but not limited to, any film, filmstrip, photograph, negative, slide, photocopy, videotape, video laser disc, computer hardware, computer software, computer floppy disc, data storage media, CD-ROM, or computer-generated equipment or any other computer-generated image that contains or incorporates in any manner, any film or filmstrip, with intent to distribute or to exhibit to, or to exchange with, others, or who offers to distribute, distributes, or exhibits to, or exchanges with, others, any obscene matter, knowing that the matter depicts a person under the age of 18 years personally engaging in or personally simulating sexual conduct, as defined in Section 311.4, shall be punished either by imprisonment in the county jail for up to one year, by a fine not to exceed one thousand dollars ($1,000), or by both the fine and imprisonment, or by imprisonment in the state prison, by a fine not to exceed ten thousand dollars ($10,000), or by the fine and imprisonment.

(b) This section does not apply to the activities of law enforcement and prosecuting agencies in the investigation and prosecution of criminal offenses or to legitimate medical, scientific, or educational activities, or to lawful conduct between spouses.

(c) This section does not apply to matter which depicts a child under the age of 18, which child is legally emancipated, including lawful conduct between spouses when one or both are under the age of 18.

(d) It does not constitute a violation of this section for a telephone corporation, as defined by Section 234 of the Public Utilities Code, to carry or transmit messages described in this chapter or perform related activities in providing telephone services.

311.2. Bringing Obscene Matter Into or Distributing Within State

(a) Every person who knowingly sends or causes to be sent, or brings or causes to be brought, into this state for sale or distribution, or in this state possesses, prepares, publishes, produces, or prints, with intent to distribute or to exhibit to others, or who offers to distribute, distributes, or exhibits to others, any obscene matter is for a first offense, guilty of a misdemeanor. If the person has previously been convicted of any violation of this section, the court may, in addition to the punishment authorized in Section 311.9, impose a fine not exceeding fifty thousand dollars ($50,000).

(b) Every person who knowingly sends or causes to be sent, or brings or causes to be brought, into this state for sale or distribution, or in this state possesses, prepares, publishes, produces, develops, duplicates, or prints any representation of information, data, or image, including, but not limited to, any film, filmstrip, photograph, negative, slide, photocopy, videotape, video laser disc, computer hardware, computer software, computer floppy disc, data storage media, CD-ROM, or computer-generated equipment or any other computer-generated image that contains or incorporates in any manner, any film or filmstrip, with intent to distribute or to exhibit to, or to exchange with, others for commercial consideration, or who offers to distribute, distributes, or exhibits to, or exchanges with, others for commercial consideration, any obscene matter, knowing that the matter depicts a person under the age of 18 years personally engaging in or personally simulating sexual conduct, as defined in Section 311.4, is guilty of a felony and shall be punished by imprisonment in the state prison for two, three, or six years, or by a fine not exceeding one hundred thousand dollars ($100,000), in the absence of a finding that the defendant would be incapable of paying such a fine, or by both that fine and imprisonment.

(c) Every person who knowingly sends or causes to be sent, or brings or causes to be brought, into this state for sale or distribution, or in this state possesses, prepares, publishes, produces, develops, duplicates, or prints any representation of information, data, or image, including, but not limited to, any film, filmstrip, photograph, negative, slide, photocopy, videotape, video laser disc, computer hardware, computer software, computer floppy disc, data storage media, CD-ROM, or computer-generated equipment or any other computer-generated image that contains or incorporates in any manner, any film or filmstrip, with intent to distribute or exhibit to, or to exchange with, a person 18 years of age or older, or who offers to distribute, distributes, or exhibits to, or exchanges with, a person 18 years of age or older any matter, knowing that the matter depicts a person under the age of 18 years personally engaging in or personally simulating sexual conduct, as defined in Section 311.4, is guilty of a misdemeanor and shall be punished by imprisonment in the county jail for up to one year, or by a fine not exceeding two thousand dollars ($2,000), or by both that fine and imprisonment. It is not necessary to prove commercial consideration or that the matter is obscene in order to establish a violation of this subdivision. If a person has been previously convicted of a violation of this subdivision, he or she is guilty of a felony.

(d) Every person who knowingly sends or causes to be sent, or brings or causes to be brought, into this state for sale or distribution, or in this state possesses, prepares, publishes, produces, develops, duplicates, or prints any representation of information, data, or image, including, but not limited to, any film, filmstrip, photograph, negative, slide, photocopy, videotape, video laser disc, computer hardware, computer software, computer floppy disc, data storage media, CD-ROM, or computer-generated equipment or any other computer-generated image that contains or incorporates in any manner, any film or filmstrip, with intent to distribute or exhibit to, or to exchange with, a person under 18 years of age, or who offers to distribute, distributes, or exhibits to, or exchanges with, a person under 18 years of age any matter, knowing that the matter depicts a person under the age of 18 years personally engaging in or personally simulating sexual conduct, as defined in Section 311.4, is guilty of a felony. It is not necessary to prove commercial consideration or that the matter is obscene in order to establish a violation of this subdivision.

(e) Subdivisions (a) to (d), inclusive, do not apply to the activities of law enforcement and prosecuting agencies in the investigation and prosecution of criminal offenses, to legitimate medical, scientific, or educational activities, or to lawful conduct between spouses.

(f) This section does not apply to matter that depicts a legally emancipated child under the age of 18 years or to lawful conduct between spouses when one or both are under the age of 18 years.

(g) It does not constitute a violation of this section for a telephone corporation, as defined by Section 234 of the Public Utilities Code, to carry or transmit messages described in this chapter or to perform related activities in providing telephone services.

311.3. Development and Duplication of Obscene Matter

(a) A person is guilty of sexual exploitation of a child if he or she knowingly develops, duplicates, prints, or exchanges any representation of information, data, or image, including, but not limited to, any film, filmstrip, photograph, negative, slide, photocopy, videotape, video laser disc, computer hardware, computer software, computer floppy disc, data storage media, CD-ROM, or computer-generated equipment or any other computer-generated image that contains or incorporates in any manner, any film or filmstrip that depicts a person under the age of 18 years engaged in an act of sexual conduct.

(b) As used in this section, "sexual conduct" means any of the following:

(1) Sexual intercourse, including genital-genital, oral-genital, anal-genital, or oral-anal, whether between persons of the same or opposite sex or between humans and animals.

(2) Penetration of the vagina or rectum by any object.

(3) Masturbation for the purpose of sexual stimulation of the viewer.

(4) Sadomasochistic abuse for the purpose of sexual stimulation of the viewer.

(5) Exhibition of the genitals or the pubic or rectal area of any person for the purpose of sexual stimulation of the viewer.

(6) Defecation or urination for the purpose of sexual stimulation of the viewer.

(c) Subdivision (a) does not apply to the activities of law enforcement and prosecution agencies in the investigation and prosecution of criminal offenses or to legitimate medical, scientific, or educational activities, or to lawful conduct between spouses.

(d) Every person who violates subdivision (a) shall be punished by a fine of not more than two thousand dollars ($2,000) or by imprisonment in a county jail for not more than one year, or by both that fine and imprisonment. If the person has been previously convicted of a violation of subdivision (a) or any section of this chapter, he or she shall be punished by imprisonment in the state prison.

(e) The provisions of this section do not apply to an employee of a commercial film developer who is acting within the scope of his or her employment and in accordance with the instructions of his or her employer, provided that the employee has no financial interest in the commercial developer by which he or she is employed.

(f) Subdivision (a) does not apply to matter that is unsolicited and is received without knowledge or consent through a facility, system, or network over which the person or entity has no control.

311.4. Using Minor to Assist in Distribution of Obscene Matter; Posing or Modeling Involving Sexual Conduct

(a) Every person who, with knowledge that a person is a minor, or who, while in possession of any facts on the basis of which he or she should reasonably know that the person is a minor, hires, employs, or uses the minor to do or assist in doing any of the acts described in Section 311.2, is, for a first offense, guilty of a misdemeanor. If the person has previously been convicted of any violation of this section, the court may, in addition to the punishment authorized in Section 311.9, impose a fine not exceeding fifty thousand dollars ($50,000).

(b) Every person who, with knowledge that a person is a minor under the age of 18 years, or who, while in possession of any facts on the basis of which he or she should reasonably know that the person is a minor under the age of 18 years, knowingly promotes, employs, uses, persuades, induces, or coerces a minor under the age of 18 years, or any parent or guardian of a minor under the age of 18 years under his or her control who knowingly permits the minor, to engage in or assist others to engage in either posing or modeling alone or with others for purposes of preparing any representation of information, data, or image, including, but not limited to, any film, filmstrip, photograph, negative, slide, photocopy, videotape, video laser disc, computer hardware, computer software, computer floppy disc, data storage media, CD-ROM, or computer-generated equipment or any other computer-generated image that contains or incorporates in any manner, any film, filmstrip, or a live performance involving, sexual conduct by a minor under the age of 18 years alone or with other persons or animals, for commercial purposes, is guilty of a felony and shall be punished by imprisonment in the state prison for three, six, or eight years.

(c) Every person who, with knowledge that a person is a minor under the age of 18 years, or who, while in possession of any facts on the basis of which he or she should reasonably know that the person is a minor under the age of 18 years, knowingly promotes, employs, uses, persuades, induces, or coerces a minor under the age of 18 years, or any parent or guardian of a minor under the age of 18 years under his or her control who knowingly permits the minor, to engage in or assist others to engage in either posing or modeling alone or with others for purposes of preparing any representation of information, data, or image, including, but not limited to, any film, filmstrip, photograph, negative, slide, photocopy, videotape, video laser disc, computer hardware, computer software, computer floppy disc, data storage media, CD-ROM, or computer-generated equipment or any other computer-generated image that contains or incorporates in any manner, any film, filmstrip, or a live performance involving, sexual conduct by a minor under the age of 18 years alone or with other persons or animals, is guilty of a felony. It is not necessary to prove commercial purposes in order to establish a violation of this subdivision.

(d)(1) As used in subdivisions (b) and (c), "sexual conduct"means any of the following, whether actual or simulated: sexual intercourse, oral copulation, anal intercourse, anal oral copulation, masturbation, bestiality, sexual sadism, sexual masochism, penetration of the vagina or rectum by any object in a lewd or lascivious manner, exhibition of the genitals or pubic or rectal area for the purpose of sexual stimulation of the viewer, any lewd or lascivious sexual act as defined in Section 288, or excretory functions performed in a lewd or lascivious manner, whether or not any of the above conduct is performed alone or between members of the same or opposite sex or between humans and animals. An act is simulated when it gives the appearance of being sexual conduct.

(2) As used in subdivisions (b) and (c), "matter"means any film, filmstrip, photograph, negative, slide, photocopy, videotape, video laser disc, computer hardware, computer software, computer floppy disc, or any other computer-related equipment or computer-generated image that contains or incorporates in any manner, any film, filmstrip, photograph, negative, slide, photocopy, videotape, or video laser disc.

(e) This section does not apply to a legally emancipated minor or to lawful conduct between spouses if one or both are under the age of 18.

(f) In every prosecution under this section involving a minor under the age of 14 years at the time of the offense, the age of the victim shall be pled and proven for the purpose of the enhanced penalty provided in Section 647.6. Failure to plead and prove that the victim was under the age of 14 years at the time of the offense is not a bar to prosecution under this section if it is proven that the victim was under the age of 18 years at the time of the offense.

311.5. Advertising Obscene Matter

Every person who writes, creates, or solicits the publication or distribution of advertising or other promotional material, or who in any manner promotes, the sale, distribution, or exhibition of matter represented or held out by him to be obscene, is guilty of a misdemeanor.

311.6. Engaging in Obscene Live Conduct

Every person who knowingly engages or participates in, manages, produces, sponsors, presents or exhibits obscene live conduct to or before an assembly or audience consisting of at least one person or spectator in any public place or in any place exposed to public view, or in any place open to the public or to a segment thereof, whether or not an admission fee is charged, or whether or not attendance is conditioned upon the presentation of a membership card or other token, is guilty of a misdemeanor.

311.7. Requiring Acceptance of Obscene Matter as Condition for Receiving Other Merchandise

Every person who, knowingly, as a condition to a sale, allocation, consignment, or delivery for resale of any paper, magazine, book, periodical, publication or other merchandise, requires that the purchaser or consignee receive any obscene matter or who denies or threatens to deny a franchise, revokes or threatens to revoke, or imposes any penalty, financial or otherwise, by reason of the failure of any person to accept obscene matter, or by reason of the return of such obscene matter, is guilty of a misdemeanor.

311.10. Distributors of Obscene Matter Depicting Person Under Age 18

(a) Any person who advertises for sale or distribution any obscene matter knowing that it depicts a person under the age of 18 years personally engaging in or personally simulating sexual conduct, as defined in Section 311.4, is guilty of a felony and is punishable by imprisonment in the state prison for two, three, or four years, or in a county jail not exceeding one year, or by a fine not exceeding fifty thousand dollars ($50,000), or by both such fine and imprisonment.

(b) Subdivision (a) shall not apply to the activities of law enforcement and prosecution agencies in the investigation and prosecution of criminal offenses.

311.11. Possession or Control of Matter Depicting Sexual Conduct of Person Under Age 18

(a) Every person who knowingly possesses or controls any matter, representation of information, data, or image, including, but not limited to, any film, filmstrip, photograph, negative, slide, photocopy, videotape, video laser disc, computer hardware, computer software, computer floppy disc, data storage media, CD-ROM, or computer-generated equipment or any other computer-generated image that contains or incorporates in any manner, any film or filmstrip, the production of which involves the use of a person under the age of 18 years, knowing that the matter depicts a person under the age of 18 years personally engaging in or simulating sexual conduct, as defined in subdivision (d) of Section 311.4, is guilty of a public offense and shall be punished by imprisonment in the county jail for up to one year, or by a fine not exceeding two thousand five hundred dollars ($2,500), or by both the fine and imprisonment.

(b) If a person has been previously convicted of a violation of this section, or of a violation of subdivision (b) of Section 311.2, or subdivision (b) of Section 311.4, he or she is guilty of a felony and shall be punished by imprisonment for two, four, or six years.

(c) It is not necessary to prove that the matter is obscene in order to establish a violation of this section.

(d) This section does not apply to drawings, figurines, statues, or any film rated by the Motion Picture Association of America, nor does it apply to live or recorded telephone messages when transmitted, disseminated, or distributed as part of a commercial transaction. *(AM '01)*

313. Harmful Matter - Definitions

As used in this chapter:

(a) "Harmful matter"means matter, taken as a whole, which to the average person, applying contemporary statewide standards, appeals to the prurient interest, and is matter which, taken as a whole, depicts or describes in a patently offensive way sexual conduct and which, taken as a whole, lacks serious literary, artistic, political, or scientific value for minors.

(1) When it appears from the nature of the matter or the circumstances of its dissemination, distribution or exhibition that it is designed for clearly defined deviant sexual groups, the appeal of the matter shall be judged with reference to its intended recipient group.

(2) In prosecutions under this chapter, where circumstances of production, presentation, sale, dissemination, distribution, or publicity indicate that matter is being commercially exploited by the defendant for the sake of its prurient appeal, that evidence is probative with respect to the nature of the matter and can justify the conclusion that the matter lacks serious literary, artistic, political, or scientific value for minors.

(b) "Matter"means any book, magazine, newspaper, video recording, or other printed or written material or any picture, drawing, photograph, motion picture, or other pictorial representation or any statue or other figure, or any recording, transcription, or mechanical, chemical, or electrical reproduction or any other articles, equipment, machines, or materials. "Matter"also includes live or recorded telephone messages when transmitted, disseminated, or distributed as part of a commercial transaction.

(c) "Person"means any individual, partnership, firm, association, corporation, limited liability company, or other legal entity.

(d) "Distribute"means to transfer possession of, whether with or without consideration.

(e) "Knowingly"means being aware of the character of the matter.

(f) "Exhibit"means to show.

(g) "Minor"means any natural person under 18 years of age.

313.1. Distribution to Minors; Local Ordinance Restricting Display, Sale, or Rental of Video Recordings; Transmission of Telephone Messages

(a) Every person who, with knowledge that a person is a minor, or who fails to exercise reasonable care in ascertaining the true age of a minor, knowingly sells, rents, distributes, sends, causes to be sent, exhibits, or offers to distribute or exhibit by any means, including, but not limited to, live or recorded telephone messages, any harmful matter to the minor shall be punished as specified in Section 313.4.

It does not constitute a violation of this section for a telephone corporation, as defined by Section 234 of the Public Utilities Code, to carry or transmit messages described in this chapter or to perform related activities in providing telephone services.

(b) Every person who misrepresents himself or herself to be the parent or guardian of a minor and thereby causes the minor to be admitted to an exhibition of any harmful matter shall be punished as specified in Section 313.4.

(c)(1) Any person who knowingly displays, sells, or offers to sell in any coin-operated or slug-operated vending machine or mechanically or electronically controlled vending machine that is located in a public place, other than a public place from which minors are excluded, any harmful matter displaying to the public view photographs or pictorial representations of the commission of any of the following acts shall be punished as specified in Section 313.4: sodomy, oral copulation, sexual intercourse, masturbation, bestiality, or a photograph of an exposed penis in an erect and turgid state.

(2) Any person who knowingly displays, sells, or offers to sell in any coin-operated vending machine that is not supervised by an adult and that is located in a public place, other than a public place from which minors are excluded, any harmful matter, as defined in subdivision (a) of Section 313, shall be punished as specified in Section 313.4.

(d) Nothing in this section invalidates or prohibits the adoption of an ordinance by a city, county, or city and county that restricts the display of material that is harmful to minors, as defined in this chapter, in a public place, other than a public place from which minors are excluded, by requiring the placement of devices commonly known as blinder racks in front of the material, so that the lower two-thirds of the material is not exposed to view.

(e) Any person who sells or rents video recordings of harmful matter shall create an area within his or her business establishment for the placement of video recordings of harmful matter and for any material that advertises the sale or rental of these video recordings. This area shall be labeled "adults only."The failure to create and label the area is an infraction, punishable by a fine not to exceed one hundred dollars ($100). The failure to place a video recording or advertisement, regardless of its content, in this area shall not constitute an infraction. Any person who sells or distributes video recordings of harmful matter to others for resale purposes shall inform the purchaser of the requirements of this section. This subdivision shall not apply to public libraries as defined in Section 18710 of the Education Code.

(f) Any person who rents a video recording and alters the video recording by adding harmful material, and who then returns the video recording to a video rental store, shall be guilty of a misdemeanor. It shall be a defense in any prosecution for a violation of this subdivision that the video rental store failed to post a sign, reasonably visible to all customers, delineating the provisions of this subdivision.

(g) It shall be a defense in any prosecution for a violation of subdivision (a) by a person who knowingly distributed any harmful matter by the use of telephones or telephone facilities to any person under the age of 18 years that the defendant has taken either of the following measures to restrict access to the harmful matter by persons under 18 years of age:

(1) Required the person receiving the harmful matter to use an authorized access or identification code, as provided by the information provider, before transmission of the harmful matter begins, where the defendant previously has issued the code by mailing it to the applicant after taking reasonable measures to ascertain that the applicant was 18 years of age or older and has established a procedure to immediately cancel the code of any person after receiving notice, in writing or by telephone, that the code has been lost, stolen, or used by persons under the age of 18 years or that the code is no longer desired.

(2) Required payment by credit card before transmission of the matter.

(h) It shall be a defense in any prosecution for a violation of paragraph (2) of subdivision (c) that the defendant has taken either of the following measures to restrict access to the harmful matter by persons under 18 years of age:

(1) Required the person receiving the harmful matter to use an authorized access or identification card to the vending machine after taking reasonable measures to ascertain that the applicant was 18 years of age or older and has established a procedure to immediately cancel the card of any person after receiving notice, in writing or by telephone, that the code has been lost, stolen, or used by persons under the age of 18 years or that the card is no longer desired.

(2) Required the person receiving the harmful matter to use a token in order to utilize the vending machine after taking reasonable measures to ascertain that the person was 18 years of age or older.

(i) Any list of applicants or recipients compiled or maintained by an information-access service provider for purposes of compliance with paragraph (1) of subdivision (g) is confidential and shall not be sold or otherwise disseminated except upon order of the court.

313.2. Exception of Parents From Act

(a) Nothing in this chapter shall prohibit any parent or guardian from distributing any harmful matter to his child or ward or permitting his child or ward to attend an exhibition of any harmful matter if the child or ward is accompanied by him.

(b) Nothing in this chapter shall prohibit any person from exhibiting any harmful matter to any of the following:

(1) A minor who is accompanied by his parent or guardian.

(2) A minor who is accompanied by an adult who represents himself to be the parent or guardian of the minor and whom the person, by the exercise of reasonable care, does not have reason to know is not the parent or guardian of the minor.

314. Indecent Exposure

Every person who willfully and lewdly, either:

1. Exposes his person, or the private parts thereof, in any public place, or in any place where there are present other persons to be offended or annoyed thereby; or,

2. Procures, counsels, or assists any person so to expose himself or take part in any model artist exhibition, or to make any other exhibition of himself to public view, or the view of any number of persons such as is offensive to decency, or is adapted to excite to vicious or lewd thoughts or acts, is guilty of a misdemeanor.

Every person who violates subdivision 1 of this section after having entered, without consent, an inhabited dwelling house, or trailer coach as defined in Section 635 of the Vehicle Code, or the inhabited portion of any other building, is punishable by imprisonment in the state prison, or in the county jail not exceeding one year.

Upon the second and each subsequent conviction under subdivision 1 of this section, or upon a first conviction under subdivision 1 of this section after a previous conviction under Section 288, every person so convicted is guilty of a felony, and is punishable by imprisonment in state prison.

315. Keeping or Living in House of Prostitution

Every person who keeps a house of ill-fame in this state, resorted to for the purposes of prostitution or lewdness, or who willfully resides in such house, is guilty of a misdemeanor; and in all prosecutions for keeping or resorting to such a house common repute may be received as competent evidence of the character of the house, the purpose for which it is kept or used, and the character of the women inhabiting or resorting to it.

316. Keeping Disorderly or Assignation House

Every person who keeps any disorderly house, or any house for the purpose of assignation or prostitution, or any house of public resort, by which the peace, comfort, or decency of the immediate neighborhood is habitually disturbed, or who keeps any inn in a disorderly manner; and every person who lets any apartment or tenement, knowing that it is to be used for the purpose of assignation or prostitution is guilty of a misdemeanor.

318. Pimping, Capping or Soliciting Patrons

Whoever, through invitation or device, prevails upon any person to visit any room, building, or other places kept for the purpose of illegal gambling or prostitution, is guilty of a misdemeanor, and, upon conviction thereof, shall be confined in the county jail not exceeding six months, or fined not exceeding five hundred dollars ($500), or be punished by both such fine and imprisonment.

LOTTERIES

319. Lottery - Defined

A lottery is any scheme for the disposal or distribution of property by chance, among persons who have paid or promised to pay any valuable consideration for the chance of obtaining such property or a portion of it, or for any share or any interest in such property, upon any agreement, understanding, or expectation that it is to be distributed or disposed of by lot or chance, whether called a lottery, raffle, or gift enterprise, or by whatever name the same may be known.

320. Lottery - Contriving, Proposing, or Drawing

Every person who contrives, prepares, sets up, proposes, or draws any lottery, is guilty of a misdemeanor.

321. Lottery - Selling Chances, Shares, or Tickets

Every person who sells, gives, or in any manner whatever, furnishes or transfers to or for any other person any ticket, chance, share, or interest, or any paper, certificate, or instrument purporting or understood to be or to represent any ticket, chance, share, or interest in, or depending upon the event of any lottery, is guilty of a misdemeanor.

322. Assisting Lottery by Printing or Advertising

Every person who aids or assists, either by printing, writing, advertising, publishing, or otherwise in setting up, managing, or drawing any lottery, or in selling or disposing of any ticket, chance, or share therein, is guilty of a misdemeanor.

326.5. Bingo Games

(a) Neither this chapter nor Chapter 10 (commencing with Section 330) applies to any bingo game that is conducted in a city, county, or city and county pursuant to an ordinance enacted under Section 19 of Article IV of the State Constitution, if the ordinance allows games to be conducted only by organizations exempted from the payment of the bank and corporation tax by Sections 23701a, 23701b, 23701d, 23701e, 23701f, 23701g, and 23701l of the Revenue and Taxation Code and by mobilehome park associations and senior citizens organizations; and if the receipts of those games are used only for charitable purposes.

(b) It is a misdemeanor for any person to receive or pay a profit, wage, or salary from any bingo game authorized by Section 19 of Article IV of the State Constitution. Security personnel employed by the organization conducting the bingo game may be paid from the revenues of bingo games, as provided in subdivisions (j) and (k).

(c) A violation of subdivision (b) shall be punishable by a fine not to exceed ten thousand dollars ($10,000), which fine is deposited in the general fund of the city, county, or city and county that enacted the ordinance authorizing the bingo game. A violation of any provision of this section, other than subdivision (b), is a misdemeanor.

(d) The city, county, or city and county that enacted the ordinance authorizing the bingo game may bring an action to enjoin a violation of this section.

(e) No minors shall be allowed to participate in any bingo game.

(f) An organization authorized to conduct bingo games pursuant to subdivision (a) shall conduct a bingo game only on property owned or leased by it, or property whose use is donated to the organization, and which property is used by that organization for an office or for performance of the purposes for which the organization is organized. Nothing in this subdivision shall be construed to require that the property owned or leased by, or whose use is donated to, the organization be used or leased exclusively by, or donated exclusively to, that organization.

(g) All bingo games shall be open to the public, not just to the members of the authorized organization.

(h) A bingo game shall be operated and staffed only by members of the authorized organization that organized it. Those members shall not receive a profit, wage, or salary from any bingo game. Only the organization authorized to conduct a bingo game shall operate such a game, or participate in the promotion, supervision, or any other phase of a bingo game. This subdivision does not preclude the employment of security personnel who are not members of the authorized organization at a bingo game by the organization conducting the game.

(i) No individual, corporation, partnership, or other legal entity, except the organization authorized to conduct a bingo game, shall hold a financial interest in the conduct of a bingo game.

(j) With respect to organizations exempt from payment of the bank and corporation tax by Section 23701d of the Revenue and Taxation Code, all profits derived from a bingo game shall be kept in a special fund or account and shall not be commingled with any other fund or account. Those profits shall be used only for charitable purposes.

(k) With respect to other organizations authorized to conduct bingo games pursuant to this section, all proceeds derived from a bingo game shall be kept in a special fund or account and shall not be commingled with any other fund or account. Proceeds are the receipts of bingo games conducted by organizations not within subdivision (j). Those proceeds shall be used only for charitable purposes, except as follows:

(1) The proceeds may be used for prizes.

(2) A portion of the proceeds, not to exceed 20 percent of the proceeds before the deduction for prizes, or two thousand dollars ($2,000) per month, whichever is less, may be used for the rental of property and for overhead, including the purchase of bingo equipment, administrative expenses, security equipment, and security personnel.

(3) The proceeds may be used to pay license fees.

(4) A city, county, or city and county that enacts an ordinance permitting bingo games may specify in the ordinance that if the monthly gross receipts from bingo games of an organization within this subdivision exceed five thousand dollars ($5,000), a minimum percentage of the proceeds shall be used only for charitable purposes not relating to the conducting of bingo games and that the balance shall be used for prizes, rental of property, overhead, administrative expenses, and payment of license fees. The amount of proceeds used for rental of property, overhead, and administrative expenses is subject to the limitations specified in paragraph (2).

(l)(1) A city, county, or city and county may impose a license fee on each organization that it authorizes to conduct bingo games. The fee, whether for the initial license or renewal, shall not exceed fifty dollars ($50) annually, except as provided in paragraph (2). If an application for a license is denied, one-half of any license fee paid shall be refunded to the organization.

(2) In lieu of the license fee permitted under paragraph (1), a city, county, or city and county may impose a license fee of fifty dollars ($50) paid upon application. If an application for a license is denied, one-half of the application fee shall be refunded to the organization. An additional fee for law enforcement and pub-

lic safety costs incurred by the city, county, or city and county that are directly related to bingo activities may be imposed and shall be collected monthly by the city, county, or city and county issuing the license; however, the fee shall not exceed the actual costs incurred in providing the service.

(m) No person shall be allowed to participate in a bingo game, unless the person is physically present at the time and place where the bingo game is being conducted.

(n) The total value of prizes awarded during the conduct of any bingo games shall not exceed two hundred fifty dollars ($250) in cash or kind, or both, for each separate game which is held.

(o) As used in this section, "bingo"means a game of chance in which prizes are awarded on the basis of designated numbers or symbols on a card that conform to numbers or symbols selected at random. Notwithstanding Section 330c, as used in this section, the game of bingo includes cards having numbers or symbols that are concealed and preprinted in a manner providing for distribution of prizes. The winning cards shall not be known prior to the game by any person participating in the playing or operation of the bingo game. All preprinted cards shall bear the legend, "for sale or use only in a bingo game authorized under California law and pursuant to local ordinance."It is the intention of the Legislature that bingo as defined in this subdivision applies exclusively to this section and shall not be applied in the construction or enforcement of any other provision of law.

327. Endless Chain Schemes

Every person who contrives, prepares, sets up, proposes, or operates any endless chain is guilty of a public offense, and is punishable by imprisonment in the county jail not exceeding one year or in state prison for 16 months, two, or three years.

As used in this section, an "endless chain"means any scheme for the disposal or distribution of property whereby a participant pays a valuable consideration for the chance to receive compensation for introducing one or more additional persons into participation in the scheme or for the chance to receive compensation when a person introduced by the participant introduces a new participant. Compensation, as used in this section, does not mean or include payment based upon sales made to persons who are not participants in the scheme and who are not purchasing in order to participate in the scheme.

GAMING

330. Gaming Defined

Every person who deals, plays, or carries on, opens, or causes to be opened, or who conducts, either as owner or employee, whether for hire or not, any game of faro, monte, roulette, lansquenet, rouge-et-noire, rondo, tan, fan-tan, seven-and-a-half, twenty-one, hokeypokey, or any banking or percentage game played with cards, dice, or any device, for money, checks, credit, or other representative of value, and every person who plays or bets at or against any of those prohibited games, is guilty of a misdemeanor, and shall be punishable by a fine not less than one hundred dollars ($100) nor more than one thousand dollars ($1,000), or by imprisonment in the county jail not exceeding six months, or by both such fine and imprisonment.

330a. Slot Machines, Card and Dice Games

Every person, who has in his possession or under his control, either as owner, lessee, agent, employee, mortgagee, or otherwise, or who permits to be placed, maintained or kept, in any room, space, inclosure or building owned, leased or occupied by him, or under his management or control, any slot or card machine, contrivance, appliance or mechanical device, upon the result of action of which money or other valuable thing is staked or hazarded, and which is operated, or played, by placing or depositing therein any coins, checks, slugs, balls, or other articles or device, or in any other manner and by means whereof, or as a result of the operation of which any merchandise, money, representative or articles of value, checks, or tokens, redeemable in, or exchangeable for money or any other thing of value, is won or lost, or taken from or obtained from such machine, when the result of action or operation of such machine, contrivance, appliance, or mechanical device is dependent upon hazard or chance, and every person, who has in his possession or under his control, either as owner, lessee, agent, employee, mortgagee, or otherwise, or who permits to be placed, maintained or kept, in any room, space, inclosure or building, owned, leased or occupied by him, or under his management or control, any card dice, or any dice having more than six faces or bases each, upon the result of action of which any money or other valuable thing is staked or hazarded, or as a result of the operation of which any merchandise, money, representative or article of value, check or token, redeemable in or exchangeable for money or any other thing of value, is won or lost or taken, when the result of action or operation of such dice is dependent upon hazard or chance, is guilty of a misdemeanor, and shall be punishable by a fine not less than one hundred dollars ($100) nor more than one thousand dollars ($1,000), or by imprisonment in the county jail not exceeding six months, or by both such fine and imprisonment. *(AM '83)*

330b. Slot Machines - Possession or Keeping of

(1) It is unlawful for any person to manufacture, repair, own, store, possess, sell, rent, lease, let on shares, lend or give away, transport, or expose for sale or lease, or to offer to repair, sell, rent, lease, let on shares, lend or give away, or to permit the operation of, or for any person to permit to be placed, maintained or kept in any place, room, space or building owned, leased or occupied by him or under his management or control, any slot machine or device as hereinafter defined, or to make or to permit to be made with any person any agreement with reference to any slot machine or device, as hereinafter defined, pursuant to which the user thereof, as a result of any element of hazard or chance or other outcome unpredictable by him, may become entitled to receive any money, credit, allowance, or thing of value or additional chance or right to use such slot machine or device, or to receive any check, slug, token or memorandum entitling the holder to receive any money, credit, allowance or thing of value; provided, however, that this section, insofar as it relates to owning, storing, possessing, or transporting any slot machine or device as hereinafter defined, shall not apply to any slot machine or device as hereinafter defined, located upon or being transported by any vessel regularly operated and engaged in interstate or foreign commerce, so long as such slot machine or device is located in a locked compartment of the vessel, is not accessible for use and is not used or operated within the territorial jurisdiction of this State.

(2) Any machine, apparatus or device is a slot machine or device within the provisions of this section if it is one that is adapted, or may readily be converted into one that is adapted, for use in such a way that, as a result of the insertion of any piece of money or coin or other object, or by any other means, such machine or device is caused to operate or may be operated, and by reason of any element of hazard or chance or of other outcome of such operation unpredictable by him, the user may receive or become entitled to receive any piece of money, credit, allowance or thing of value or additional chance or right to use such slot machine or device, or any check, slug, token or memorandum, whether of value or otherwise, which may be exchanged for any money, credit, allowance or thing of value, or which may be given in trade, irrespective of whether it may, apart from any element of hazard or chance or unpredictable outcome of such operation, also sell, deliver or present some merchandise, indication of weight, entertainment or other thing of value.

(3) Every person who violates this section is guilty of a misdemeanor.

(4) It is expressly provided that with respect to the provisions of Section 330b only of this code, pin ball, and other amusement machines or devices which are predominantly games of skill, whether affording the opportunity of additional chances or free plays or not, are not intended to be and are not included within the term slot machine or device as defined in said Section 330b of this code.

330c. Punchboard Is Slot Machine

A punchboard as hereinafter defined is hereby declared to be a slot machine or device within the meaning of Section 330b of this code and shall be subject to the provisions thereof. For the purposes of this section, a punchboard is any card, board or other device which may be played or operated by pulling, pressing, punching out or otherwise removing any slip, tab, paper or other substance therefrom to disclose any concealed number, name or symbol.

330.1. Slot Machines Forbidden

Every person who manufactures, owns, stores, keeps, possesses, sells, rents, leases, lets on shares, lends or gives away, transports or exposes for sale or lease or offers to sell, rent, lease, let on shares, lend or give away or who permits the operation of or permits to be placed, maintained, used or kept in any room, space or building owned, leased or occupied by him or under his management or control, any slot machine or device as hereinafter defined, and every person who makes or permits to be made with any person any agreement with reference to any slot machine or device as hereinafter defined, pursuant to which agreement the user thereof, as a result of any element of hazard or chance, may become entitled to receive anything of value or additional chance or right to use such slot machine or device, or to receive any check, slug, token or memorandum, whether of value or otherwise, entitling the holder to receive anything of value, is guilty of a misdemeanor and shall be punishable by a fine of not more than one thousand dollars ($1,000) or by imprisonment in the county jail not exceeding six months or by both such fine and imprisonment. A slot machine or device within the meaning of Sections 330.1 to 330.5, inclusive, of this code is one that is, or may be, used or operated in such a way that, as a result of the insertion of any piece of money or coin or other object such machine or device is caused to operate or may be operated or played, mechanically, electrically, automatically or manually, and by reason of any element of hazard or chance, the user may receive or become entitled to receive anything of value or any check, slug, token or memorandum, whether of value or otherwise, which may be given in trade, or the user may secure additional chances or rights to use such machine or device, irrespective of whether it may, apart from any element of hazard or chance also sell, deliver or present some merchandise, indication of weight, entertainment or other thing of value. *(AM '83)*

330.3. Seizure and Disposal of Slot Machine

In addition to any other remedy provided by law any slot machine or device may be seized by any of the officers designated by Sections 335 and 335a of the Penal Code, and in such cases shall be disposed of, together with any and all money seized in or in connection with such machine or device, as provided in Section 335a of the Penal Code.

330.4. Mere Possession of Slot Machine Prohibited

It is specifically declared that the mere possession or control, either as owner, lessee, agent, employee, mortgagor, or otherwise of any slot machine or device, as defined in Section 330.1 of this code, is prohibited and penalized by the provisions of Sections 330.1 to 330.5, inclusive, of this code.

It is specifically declared that every person who permits to be placed, maintained or kept in any room, space, enclosure, or building owned, leased or occupied by him, or under his management or control, whether for use or operation or for storage, bailment, safekeeping or deposit only, any slot machine or device, as defined in Section 330.1 of this code, is guilty of a misdemeanor and punishable as provided in Section 330.1 of this code.

It is further declared that the provisions of this section specifically render any slot machine or device as defined in Section 330.1 of this code subject to confiscation as provided in Section 335a of this code.

330.5. Possession of Slot Machines - Exception

It is further expressly provided that Sections 330.1 to 330.4, inclusive, of this code shall not apply to music machines, weighing machines and machines which vend cigarettes, candy, ice cream, food, confections or other merchandise, in which there is deposited an exact consideration and from which in every case the customer obtains that which he purchases; and it is further expressly provided that with respect to the provisions of Sections 330.1 to 330.4, inclusive, only, of this code, pin ball, and other amusement machines or devices which are predominantly games of skill, whether affording the opportunity of additional chances or free plays or not, are not intended to be and are not included within the term slot machine or device as defined within Sections 330.1 to 330.4, inclusive, of this code.

330.6. Exception As to Machines On Board Ship

The provisions of Sections 330.1 to 330.5, inclusive, of this code, with respect to owning, storing, keeping, possessing, or transporting any slot machine or device as therein defined, shall not apply to any slot machine or device as therein defined, located upon or being transported by any vessel regularly operated and engaged in interstate or foreign commerce, so long as such slot machine or device is located in a locked compartment of the vessel, is not accessible for use and is not used or operated within the territorial jurisdiction of this State.

330.7. Antique Slot Machines

(a) It shall be a defense to any prosecution under this chapter relating to slot machines, as defined in subdivision (2) of Section 330b, if the defendant shows that the slot machine is an antique slot machine and was not operated for gambling purposes while in the defendant's possession. For the purposes of this section, the term "antique slot machine" means a slot machine that is over 25 years of age.

(b) Notwithstanding Section 335a, whenever the defense provided by subdivision (a) is offered, no slot machine seized from any defendant shall be destroyed or otherwise altered until after a final court determination that such defense is not applicable. If the defense is applicable, the machine shall be returned pursuant to provisions of law providing for the return of property.

(c) It is the purpose of this section to protect the collection and restoration of antique slot machines not presently utilized for gambling purposes because of their aesthetic interest and importance in California history. *(AM '85, '93)*

330.8. Sale, Transportation, etc. of Gambling Devices; When Permitted

Notwithstanding Sections 330a, 330b, and 330.1 to 330.5, inclusive, the sale, transportation, storage, and manufacture of gambling devices, as defined in Section 330.1, including the acquisition of essential parts therefor and the assembly of such parts, is permitted, provided those devices are sold, transported, stored, and manufactured only for subsequent transportation in interstate or foreign commerce when that transportation is not prohibited by any applicable federal law. Those activities may be conducted only by persons who have registered with the United States government pursuant to Chapter 24 (commencing with Section 1171) of Title 15 of the United States Code, as amended. Those gambling devices shall not be displayed to the general public or sold for use in California regardless of where purchased, nor held nor manufactured in violation of any applicable federal law. A violation of this section is a misdemeanor. *(AD '79; AM '87)*

330.9. Transportation or Possession of Slot Machine for Display at Trade Show, etc.

(a) Notwithstanding Sections 330a, 330b, 330.1 to 330.5, inclusive, or any other provision of law, it shall be lawful for any person to transport and possess any slot machine or device for display at a trade show, conference, or convention being held within this state.

(b) Subdivision (a) shall apply only if the slot machine or device is adjusted to render the machine or device inoperable.

(c) This section is intended to constitute a state exemption as provided in Section 1172 of Title 15 of the United States Code.

(d) For purposes of this section, "slot machine or device" has the same meaning as "slot machine or device" as defined in Section 330.1, or "gambling device" as defined in paragraph (1) of subsection (a) of Section 1171 of Title 15 of the United States Code. *(AD '99)*

335. Duty to Enforce Gaming Laws

Every district attorney, sheriff, or police officer must inform against and diligently prosecute persons whom they have reasonable cause to believe offenders against the provisions of this chapter, and every officer refusing or neglecting so to do, is guilty of a misdemeanor.

336. Permitting Minors to Play Games Where Liquor Sold

Every owner, lessee, or keeper of any house used in whole, or in part, as a saloon or drinking place, who knowingly permits any person under 18 years of age to play at any game of chance therein, is guilty of a misdemeanor.

337. Receiving Protection-Money or Granting Privileges

Every state, county, city, city and county, town, or judicial district officer, or other person who shall ask for, receive, or collect any money, or other valuable consideration, either for his own or the public use, for and with the understanding that he will aid, exempt, or otherwise assist any person from arrest or conviction for a violation of Section 330 of the Penal Code; or who shall issue, deliver, or cause to be given or delivered to any person or persons, any license, permit, or other privilege, giving, or pretending to give, any authority or right to any person or persons to carry on, conduct, open, or cause to be opened, any game or games which are forbidden or prohibited by Section 330 of said code; and any of such officer or officers who shall vote for the passage of any ordinance or by-law, giving, granting, or pretending to give or grant to any person or persons any authority or privilege to open, carry on, conduct, or cause to be opened, carried on, or conducted, any game or games prohibited by said Section 330 of the Penal Code, is guilty of a felony.

337a. Pool Selling, Bookmaking or Wagering

Every person,

1. Who engages in pool selling or bookmaking, with or without writing, at any time or place; or

2. Who, whether for gain, hire, reward, or gratuitously, or otherwise, keeps or occupies, for any period of time whatsoever, any room, shed, tenement, tent, booth, building, float, vessel, place, stand or enclosure, of any kind, or any part thereof, with a book or books, paper or papers, apparatus, device or paraphernalia, for the purpose of recording or registering any bet or bets, or any purported bet or bets, or wager or wagers, or any purported wager or wagers, or of selling pools, or purported pools, upon the result, or purported result, of any trial, or purported trial, or contest, or purported contest, of skill, speed or power of endurance of man or beast, or between men, beasts, or mechanical apparatus, or upon the result, or purported result, of any lot, chance, casualty, unknown or contingent event whatsoever; or

3. Who, whether for gain, hire, reward, or gratuitously, or otherwise, receives, holds, or forwards, or purports or pretends to receive, hold, or forward, in any manner whatsoever, any money, thing or consideration of value, or the equivalent or memorandum thereof, staked, pledged, bet or wagered, or to be staked, pledged, bet or wagered, or offered for the purpose of being staked, pledged, bet or wagered, upon the result, or purported result, of any trial, or purported trial, or contest, or purported contest, of skill, speed or power of endurance of man or beast, or between men, beasts, or mechanical apparatus, or upon the result, or purported result, of any lot, chance, casualty, unknown or contingent event whatsoever; or

4. Who, whether for gain, hire, reward, or gratuitously, or otherwise, at any time or place, records, or registers any bet or bets, wager or wagers, upon the result, or purported result, of any trial, or purported trial, or contest, or purported contest, of skill, speed or power of endurance of man or beast, or between men, beasts, or mechanical apparatus, or upon the result, or purported result, of any lot, chance, casualty, unknown or contingent event whatsoever; or

5. Who, being the owner, lessee or occupant of any room, shed, tenement, tent, booth, building, float, vessel, place, stand, enclosure or grounds, or any part thereof, whether for gain, hire, reward, or gratuitously, or otherwise, permits the same to be used or occupied for any purpose, or in any manner prohibited by subdivision 1, 2, 3 or 4 of this section; or 6. Who lays, makes, offers or accepts any bet or bets, or wager or wagers, upon the result, or purported result, of any trial, or purported trial, or contest, or purported contest, of skill, speed or power of endurance of man or beast, or between men, beasts, or mechanical apparatus, is punishable by imprisonment in the county jail for a period of not more than one year or in the state prison.

(a) In any accusatory pleading charging a violation of this section, if the defendant has been once previously convicted of a violation of any subdivision of this section, the previous conviction shall be charged in the accusatory pleading, and, if the previous conviction is found to be true by the jury, upon a jury trial, or by the court, upon a court trial, or is admitted by the defendant, the defendant shall, if he is not imprisoned in the state prison, be imprisoned in the county jail for a period of not more than one year or pay a fine of not less than five hundred dollars ($500) nor more than five thousand dollars ($5,000), or be punished by both such fine and imprisonment. Nothing in this paragraph shall prohibit a court from placing such a person on probation, provided, however, that such person shall be required to pay a fine of not less than five hundred dollars ($500) nor more than five thousand dollars ($5,000) or to be imprisoned in the county jail for a period of not more than one year as a condition thereof. In no event does the court have the power to absolve a person convicted hereunder from either being imprisoned or from paying a fine of not less than five hundred dollars ($500).

(b) In any accusatory pleading charging a violation of this section, if the defendant has been previously convicted two or more times of a violation of any subdivision of this section, each such previous conviction shall be charged in the accusatory pleadings; and if two or more of such previous convictions are found to be true by the jury, upon a jury trial, or by the court, upon a court trial, or are admitted by the defendant, the defendant shall, if he is not imprisoned in the state prison, be imprisoned in the county jail for a period of not more than one year or pay a fine of not less than one thousand dollars ($1,000) nor more than five thousand dollars ($5,000), or be punished by both such fine and imprisonment. Nothing in this paragraph shall prohibit a court from placing such a person on probation, provided, however, that such person shall be required to pay a fine of not less than one thousand dollars ($1,000) nor more than five thousand dollars ($5,000) or to be imprisoned in the county jail for a period of not more than one year as a condition thereof. In no event does the court have the power to absolve a person convicted hereunder from either being imprisoned or from paying a fine of not less than one thousand dollars ($1,000).

Except where the existence of a previous conviction of any subdivision of this section was not admitted or not found to be true pursuant to this section, or the court finds that a prior conviction was invalid, the court shall not strike or dismiss any prior convictions alleged in the information or indictment.

This section shall apply not only to persons who may commit any of the acts designated in subdivisions 1 to 6 inclusive of this section, as a business or occupation, but shall also apply to every person or persons who may do in a single instance any one of the acts specified in said subdivisions 1 to 6 inclusive.

337j. Prohibited Games

(a) It is unlawful for any person, as owner, lessee, or employee, whether for hire or not, either solely or in conjunction with others, to do any of the following without having first procured and thereafter maintained in effect all federal, state, and local licenses required by law:

(1) To deal, operate, carry on, conduct, maintain, or expose for play in this state any controlled game.

(2) To receive, directly or indirectly, any compensation or reward or any percentage or share of the revenue, for keeping, running, or carrying on any controlled game.

(3) To manufacture, distribute, or repair any gambling equipment within the boundaries of this state, or to receive, directly or indirectly, any compensation or reward for the manufacture, distribution, or repair of any gambling equipment within the boundaries of this state.

(b) It is unlawful for any person to knowingly permit any controlled game to be conducted, operated, dealt, or carried on in any house or building or other premises that he or she owns or leases, in whole or in part, if that activity is undertaken by a person who is not licensed as required by state law, or by an employee of that person.

(c) It is unlawful for any person to knowingly permit any gambling equipment to be manufactured, stored, or repaired in any house or building or other premises that the person owns or leases, in whole or in part, if that activity is undertaken by a person who is not licensed as required by state law, or by an employee of that person.

(d) Any person who violates, attempts to violate, or conspires to violate this section shall be punished by imprisonment in a county jail for not more than one year, or by a fine of not more than five thousand dollars ($5,000), or by both that imprisonment and fine.

(e)(1) As used in this section, "controlled game"means any game of chance, including any gambling device, played for currency, check, credit, or any other thing of value that is not prohibited and made unlawful by statute or local ordinance.

(2) As used in this section, "controlled game"does not include any of the following:

(A) The game of bingo conducted pursuant to Section 326.5.

(B) Parimutuel racing on horse races regulated by the California Horse Racing Board.

(C) Any lottery game conducted by the California State Lottery.

(D) Games played with cards in private homes or residences, in which no person makes money for operating the game, except as a player.

(f) This subdivision is intended to be dispositive of the law relating to the collection of player fees in gambling establishments. No fee may be calculated as a portion of wagers made or from winnings earned.

Fees charged for all wagers shall be determined and collected prior to the start of play of any hand or round. Ample notice shall be provided to the patrons of gambling establishments relating to the assessment of fees. Flat fees on each wager may be assessed at different collection rates, but no more than three collection rates may be established per table. This legislation codifies the holding in Sullivan v. Fox (1987) 189 Cal.App.3d 673, as to the collection of player fees in licensed gambling establishments, that no fee shall be calculated as a portion of wagers made or winnings earned, exclusive of charges or fees for the use of space and facilities.

(1) In the same manner as fees were collected in the establishment as of January 1, 1997, if the method of fee collection is permitted by ordinance, resolution, letter, or other written authorization of the local governmental entity having regulatory jurisdiction or law enforcement authority over the gambling establishment.

(2) In the same manner as fees were collected in the establishment as of January 1, 1997, if all of the following are true:

(A) The amount of the fee is fixed in advance of the game.

(B) There is no minimum wager in any game, round, or hand.

(C) No fee is deducted from the amount wagered.

(D) In any game or round, the same fixed fee is collected from all players at the table.

(E) The method of fee collection has not been challenged by, and is not prohibited by any ordinance or resolution of, the local governmental entity having regulatory jurisdiction or law enforcement authority over the gambling establishment. *(AM '98)*

337.1. False Persuasion in Betting - Touting

Any person, who knowingly and designedly by false representation attempts to, or does persuade, procure or cause another person to wager on a horse in a race to be run in this state or elsewhere, and upon which money is wagered in this state, and who asks or demands compensation as a reward for information or purported information given in such case is a tout, and is guilty of touting.

346. Ticket Scalping

Any person who, without the written permission of the owner or operator of the property on which an entertainment event is to be held or is being held, sells a ticket of admission to the entertainment event, which was obtained for the purpose of resale, at any price which is in excess of the price that is printed or endorsed upon the ticket, while on the grounds of or in the stadium, arena, theater, or other place where an event for which admission tickets are sold is to be held or is being held, is guilty of a misdemeanor.

347. Mingling Harmful Substance With Food or Drink

(a)(1) Every person who willfully mingles any poison or harmful substance with any food, drink, medicine, or pharmaceutical product or who willfully places any poison or harmful substance in any spring, well, reservoir, or public water supply, where the person knows or should have known that the same would be taken by any human being to his or her injury, is guilty of a felony punishable by imprisonment in the state prison for two, four, or five years.

(2) Any violation of paragraph (1) involving the use of a poison or harmful substance that may cause death if ingested or that causes the infliction of great bodily injury on any person shall be punished by an additional term of three years.

(b) Any person who maliciously informs any other person that a poison or other harmful substance has been or will be placed in any food, drink, medicine, pharmaceutical product, or public water supply, knowing that such report is false, is guilty of a crime punishable by imprisonment in the state prison, or by imprisonment in the county jail not to exceed one year.

(c) The court may impose the maximum fine for each item tampered with in violation of subdivision (a). *(AM '00)*

365.5. Equal Access for Handicapped Persons With Specially Trained Dogs

(a) Any blind person, deaf person, or disabled person who is a passenger on any common carrier, airplane, motor vehicle, railway train, motorbus, streetcar, boat, or any other public conveyance or mode of transportation operating within this state, shall be entitled to have with him or her a specially trained guide dog, signal dog, or service dog.

(b) No blind person, deaf person, or disabled person and his or her specially trained guide dog, signal dog, or service dog shall be denied admittance to hotels, restaurants, lodging places, places of public accommodation, amusement, or resort or other places to which the general public is invited within this state because of that guide dog, signal dog, or service dog.

(c) Any person, firm, association, or corporation, or the agent of any person, firm, association, or corporation, who prevents a disabled person from exercising, or interferes with a disabled person in the exercise of, the rights specified in this section is guilty of a misdemeanor punishable by a fine not exceeding two thousand five hundred dollars ($2,500).

(d) As used in this section, "guide dog" means any guide dog or Seeing Eye dog which was trained by a person licensed under Chapter 9.5 (commencing with Section 7200) of Division 3 of the Business and Professions Code or which meets the definition criteria under federal regulations adopted to implement Title III of the Americans with Disabilities Act of 1990 (Public Law 101-336).

(e) As used in this section, "signal dog" means any dog trained to alert a deaf person, or a person whose hearing is impaired, to intruders or sounds.

(f) As used in this section "service dog" means any dog individually trained to do work or perform tasks for the benefit of an individual with a disability, including, but not limited to, minimal protection work, rescue work, pulling a wheelchair, or fetching dropped items.

(g) Nothing in this section is intended to affect any civil remedies available for a violation of this section.

(h) The exercise of rights specified in subdivisions (a) and (b) by any person may not be conditioned upon payment of any extra charge, provided that the person shall be liable for any provable damage done to the premises or facilities by his or her dog.

(i) Any trainer or individual with a disability may take dogs in any of the places specified in subdivisions (a) and (b) for the purpose of training the dogs as guide dogs, signal dogs, or service dogs. However, the person shall be liable for any provable damage done to the premises or facilities by his or her dog.

365.6 Interfere, Harass, or Obstruct Guide Dog or Guide Dog User

(a) Any person who, with no legal justification, intentionally interferes with the use of a guide dog by harassing or obstructing the guide dog user or his or her guide dog, is guilty of a misdemeanor, punishable by imprisonment in the county jail not exceeding six months, or by a fine of not less than one thousand five hundred dollars ($1,500) nor more than two thousand five hundred dollars ($2,500), or both.

(b) As used in this section, "guide dog" means any guide dog or seeing-eye dog which was trained by a person licensed under Chapter 9.5 (commencing with Section 7200) of Division 3 of the Business and Professions Code or as defined in the regulations implementing Title III of the Americans with Disabilities Act of 1990 (Public Law 101-336), or trained by a school recognized in another state to train guide or seeing-eye dogs.

(c) Nothing in this section is intended to affect any civil remedies available for a violation of this section.

367f. Sale of Human Organs for Purposes of Transplantation and Valuable Consideration

(a) Except as provided in subdivisions (d) and (e), it shall be unlawful for any person to knowingly acquire, receive, sell, promote the transfer of, or otherwise transfer any human organ, for purposes of transplantation, for valuable consideration.

(b) Except as provided in subdivisions (d), (e), and (f), it shall be unlawful to remove or transplant any human organ with the knowledge that the organ has been acquired or will be transferred or sold for valuable consideration in violation of subdivision (a).

(c) For purposes of this section, the following definitions apply:

(1) "Human organ" includes, but is not limited to, a human kidney, liver, heart, lung, pancreas, or any other human organ or nonrenewable or nonregenerative tissue except plasma and sperm.

(2) "Valuable consideration" means financial gain or advantage, but does not include the reasonable costs associated with the removal, storage, transportation, and transplantation of a human organ, or re-

imbursement for those services, or the expenses of travel, housing, and lost wages incurred by the donor of a human organ in connection with the donation of the organ.

(d) No act respecting the nonsale donation of organs or other nonsale conduct pursuant to or In the furtherance of the purposes of the Uniform Anatomical Gift Act, Chapter 3.5 Part 1 of Division 7 of the Health and Safety Code, including acts pursuant to anatomical gifts offered under Section 12811 of the Vehicle Code, shall be made unlawful by this section.

(e) This section shall not apply to the person from whom the organ is removed, nor to the person who receives the transplant, or those persons' next-of-kin who assisted in obtaining the organ for purposes of transplantation's.

(f) A licensed physician and surgeon who transplants a human organ in violation of subdivision (b) shall not be criminally liable under that subdivision if the act is performed under emergency and life-threatening conditions.

(g) Any person who violates subdivision (a) or (b) shall be punished by a fine not to exceed fifty thousand dollars ($50,000), or by imprisonment in the state prison for three, four, or five years, or both.

368. Elder or Dependent Adult Abuse; Theft or Embezzlement by Caretaker

(a) The Legislature finds and declares that crimes against elders and dependent adults are deserving of special consideration and protection, not unlike the special protections provided for minor children, because elders and dependent adults may be confused, on various medications, mentally or physically impaired, or incompetent, and therefore less able to protect themselves, to understand or report criminal conduct, or to testify in court proceedings on their own behalf.

(b)(1) Any person who, under circumstances or conditions likely to produce great bodily harm or death, willfully causes or permits any elder or dependent adult, with knowledge that he or she is an elder or a dependent adult, to suffer, or inflicts thereon unjustifiable physical pain or mental suffering, or having the care or custody of any elder or dependent adult, willfully causes or permits the person or health of the elder or dependent adult to be injured, or willfully causes or permits the elder or dependent adult to be placed in a situation in which his or her person or health is endangered, is punishable by imprisonment in a county jail not exceeding one year, or by a fine not to exceed six thousand dollars ($6,000), or by both that fine and imprisonment, or in the state prison for two, three, or four years.

(2) If in the commission of an offense described in paragraph (1), the victim suffers great bodily injury, as defined in *** Section 12022.7, the defendant shall receive an additional term in the state prison as follows:

(A) Three years if the victim is under 70 years of age.

(B) Five years if the victim is 70 years of age or older.

(3) If in the commission of an offense described in paragraph (1), the defendant proximately causes the death of the victim, the defendant shall receive an additional term in the state prison as follows:

(A) Five years if the victim is under 70 years of age.

(B) Seven years if the victim is 70 years of age or older.

(c) Any person who, under circumstances or conditions other than those likely to produce great bodily harm or death, willfully causes or permits any elder or dependent adult, with knowledge that he or she is an elder or a dependent adult, to suffer, or inflicts thereon unjustifiable physical pain or mental suffering, or having the care or custody of any elder or dependent adult, willfully causes or permits the person or health of the elder or dependent adult to be injured or willfully causes or permits the elder or dependent adult to be placed in a situation in which his or her person or health may be endangered, is guilty of a misdemeanor.

(d) Any person who is not a caretaker who violates any provision of law proscribing theft or embezzlement, with respect to the property of an elder or dependent adult, and who knows or reasonably should know that the victim is an elder or dependent adult, is punishable by imprisonment in a county jail not exceeding one year, or in the state prison for two, three, or four years, when the money, labor, or real or personal property taken is of a value exceeding four hundred dollars ($400); and by a fine not exceeding one thousand dollars ($1,000), by imprisonment in a county jail not exceeding one year, or by both that fine and imprisonment, when the money, labor, or real or personal property taken is of a value not exceeding four hundred dollars ($400).

(e) Any caretaker of an elder or a dependent adult who violates any provision of law proscribing theft or embezzlement, with respect to the property of that elder or dependent adult, is punishable by imprisonment in a county jail not exceeding one year, or in the state prison for two, three, or four years when the money, labor, or real or personal property taken is of a value exceeding four hundred dollars ($400), and by a fine not exceeding one thousand dollars ($1,000), by imprisonment in a county jail not exceeding one year, or by both that fine and imprisonment, when the money, labor, or real or personal property taken is of a value not exceeding four hundred dollars ($400).

(f) Any person who commits the false imprisonment of an elder or dependent adult by the use of violence, menace, fraud, or deceit is punishable by imprisonment in the state prison for two, three, or four years.

(g) As used in this section, "elder" means any person who is 65 years of age or older.

(h) As used in this section, "dependent adult" means any person who is between the ages of 18 and 64, who has physical or mental limitations which restrict his or her ability to carry out normal activities or to protect his or her rights, including, but not limited to, persons who have physical or developmental disabilities or whose physical or mental abilities have diminished because of age. "Dependent adult" includes any person between the ages of 18 and 64 who is admitted as an inpatient to a 24-hour health facility, as defined in Sections 1250, 1250.2, and 1250.3 of the Health and Safety Code.

(i) As used in this section, "caretaker" means any person who has the care, custody, or control of, or who stands in a position of trust with, an elder or a dependent adult.

(j) Nothing in this section shall preclude prosecution under both this section and Section 187 or 12022.7 or any other provision of law. However, a person shall not receive an additional term of imprisonment under both paragraphs (2) and (3) of subdivision (b) for any single offense, nor shall a person receive an additional term of imprisonment under both Section 12022.7 and paragraph (2) or (3) of subdivision (b) for any single offense. *(AM '01)*

CRIMES AGAINST PUBLIC HEALTH & SAFETY

369g. Trespass on Railroad Track

(a) Any person who rides, drives, or propels any vehicle upon and along the track of any railroad, through or over its private right of way, without the authorization of its superintendent or officer in charge thereof, is guilty of a misdemeanor.

(b) Any Person who rides, drives, or propels any vehicle upon and along the track of any railline owned or operated by a county transportation commission or transportation authority without the authorization of the commission or authority is guilty of a misdemeanor.

369i. Trespass on Railroad Property

Any person who enters or remains upon the property of any railroad without the permission of the owner of such land, his agent or the person in lawful possession and whose entry or presence or conduct upon such property interferes with, interrupts, or hinders, or which, if allowed to continue, would interfere with, interrupt, or hinder the safe and efficient operation of any locomotive, railway car or train is guilty of a misdemeanor.

As used in this section, "property of any railroad" means any land owned, leased, or possessed by a railroad upon which is placed a railroad track and the land immediately adjacent thereto, to the distance of 20 feet on either side of the track, which is owned, leased or possessed by a railroad.

This section does not prohibit picketing in such immediately adjacent area or any lawful activity by which the public is informed of the existence of an alleged labor dispute.

370. Public Nuisance Defined

Anything which is injurious to health, or is indecent, or offensive to the senses, or an obstruction to the free use of property, so as to interfere with the comfortable enjoyment of life or property by an entire community or neighborhood, or by any considerable number of persons, or unlawfully obstructs the free passage or use, In the customary manner, of any navigable lake, or river, bay, stream, canal, or basin, or any public park, square, street, or highway, is a public nuisance.

372. Maintaining Public Nuisance

Every person who maintains or commits any public nuisance, the punishment for which is not otherwise prescribed, or who willfully omits to perform any legal duty relating to the removal of a public nuisance, is guilty of a misdemeanor.

374. "Littering" and "Waste Matter" Defined

(a) Littering means the willful or negligent throwing, dropping, placing, depositing, or sweeping, or causing any such acts, of any waste matter on land or water in other than appropriate storage containers or areas designated for such purposes.

(b) Waste matter means discarded, used, or leftover substance including, but not limited to, a lighted or nonlighted cigarette, cigar, match, or any flaming or glowing material, or any garbage, trash, refuse, paper, container, packaging or construction material, carcass of a dead animal, any nauseous or offensive matter of any kind, or any object likely to injure any person or create a traffic hazard.

374c. Discharging Firearms on a Public Highway

Every person who shoots any firearm from or upon a public road or highway is guilty of a misdemeanor.

374.2. Unlawful Discharge of Materials Into Public Sewers

(a) It is unlawful for any person to maliciously discharge, dump, release, place, drop, pour, or otherwise deposit, or to maliciously cause to be discharged, dumped, released, placed, dropped, poured, or otherwise deposited, any substance capable of causing substantial damage or harm to the operation of a public sewer sanitary facility, or to deposit in commercial quantities any other substance, into a manhole, cleanout, or other sanitary sewer facility, not intended for use as a point of deposit for sewage, which is connected to a public sanitary sewer system, without possessing a written authorization therefor granted by the public entity which is charged with the administration of the use of the affected public sanitary sewer system or the affected portion of the public sanitary sewer system. As used in this section, "maliciously"means an intent to do a wrongful act.

(b) For the purposes of this section "person"means an individual, trust, firm, partnership, joint stock company, limited liability company, or corporation, and "deposited in commercial quantities"refers to any substance deposited or otherwise discharged in any amount greater than for normal domestic sewer use.

(c) Lack of specific knowledge that the facility into which the prohibited discharge or release occurred is connected to a public sanitary sewer system shall not constitute a defense to a violation charged under this section.

(d) Any person who violates this section shall be punished by imprisonment in the county jail for not more than one year, or by a fine of up to twenty-five thousand dollars ($25,000), or by both a fine and imprisonment. If the conviction is for a second or subsequent violation, the person shall be punished by imprisonment in the county jail for not more than one year, or imprisonment in the state prison for 16, 20, or 24 months, and by a fine of not less than five thousand dollars ($5,000) or more than twenty-five thousand dollars ($25,000).

374.3. Dumping Refuse on Public or Private Roads or Property

(a) It is unlawful to dump or cause to be dumped any waste matter in or upon any public or private highway or road, including any portion of the right-of-way thereof, or in or upon any private property into or upon which the public is admitted by easement or license, or upon any private property without the consent of the owner, or in or upon any public park or other public property other than property designated or set aside for that purpose by the governing board or body having charge of that property.

(b) It is unlawful to place, deposit, or dump, or cause to be placed, deposited, or dumped, any rocks or dirt in or upon any private highway or road, including any portion of the right-of-way thereof, or any private property, without the consent of the owner, or in or upon any public park or other public property, without the consent of the state or local agency having jurisdiction over the highway, road, or property.

(c) Any person violating this section is guilty of an infraction. Each day that waste placed, deposited, or dumped in violation of this section remains is a separate violation.

(d) This section does not restrict a private owner in the use of his or her own private property, unless the placing, depositing, or dumping of the waste matter on the property creates a public health and safety hazard, a public nuisance, or a fire hazard, as determined by a local health department, local fire department or district providing fire protection services, or the Department of Forestry and Fire Protection, in which case this section applies.

(e) A person convicted of a violation of this section shall be punished by a mandatory fine of not less than two hundred fifty dollars ($250) nor more than one thousand dollars ($1,000) upon a first conviction, by a mandatory fine of not less than five hundred dollars ($500) nor more than one thousand dollars ($1,000) upon a second conviction, and by a mandatory fine of not less than seven hundred fifty dollars ($750) nor more than two thousand five hundred dollars ($2,500) upon a third or subsequent conviction. If the court finds that the waste matter placed, deposited, or dumped was used tires, the fine prescribed in this subdivision shall be doubled.

(f) The court may require, in addition to any fine imposed upon a conviction, that, as a condition of probation and in addition to any other condition of probation, a person convicted under this section remove, or pay the cost of removing, any waste matter which the convicted person dumped or caused to be dumped upon public or private property.

(g) Except when the court requires the convicted person to remove waste matter which he or she is responsible for dumping as a condition of probation, the court may, in addition to the fine imposed upon a conviction, require as a condition of probation, in addition to any other condition of probation, that any person convicted of a violation of this section pick up waste matter at a time and place within the jurisdiction of the court for not less than 12 hours.

(h)(1) Any person who places, deposits, or dumps, or causes to be placed, deposited, or dumped, waste matter in violation of this section in commercial quantities shall be guilty of a misdemeanor punishable by imprisonment in a county jail for not more than six months and by a fine. The fine is mandatory and shall amount to not less than five hundred dollars ($500) nor more than one thousand five hundred dollars ($1,500) upon a first conviction, not less than one thousand five hundred dollars ($1,500) nor more than three thousand dollars ($3,000) upon a second conviction, and not less than two thousand seven hundred fifty dollars ($2,750) nor more than four thousand dollars ($4,000) upon a third or subsequent conviction.

(2) "Commercial quantities" means an amount of waste matter generated in the course of a trade, business, profession, or occupation, or an amount equal to or in excess of one cubic yard. This subdivision does not apply to the dumping of household waste at a person's residence.

(i) For purposes of this section, "person" means an individual, trust, firm, partnership, joint stock company, joint venture, or corporation.

(j) Except in unusual cases where the interests of justice would be best served by waiving or reducing a fine, the minimum fines provided by this section shall not be waived or reduced. *(AM '98)*

374.4. Littering on Public or Private Property

(a) It is unlawful to litter or cause to be littered in or upon any public or private property. Any person, firm, or corporation violating this section is guilty of an infraction.

(b) This section does not restrict a private owner in the use of his or her own property, unless the littering of waste matter on the property creates a public health and safety hazard, a public nuisance, or a fire hazard, as determined by a local health department, local fire department or district providing fire protection services, or the Department of Forestry and Fire Protection, in which case this section applies.

(c) As used in this section, "litter" means the discarding, dropping, or scattering of small quantities of waste matter ordinarily carried on or about the person, including, but not limited to, beverage containers and closures, packaging, wrappers, wastepaper, newspapers, and magazines, in a place other than a place or container for the proper disposal thereof, and including waste matter which escapes or is allowed to escape from a container, receptacle, or package.

(d) A person, firm, or corporation convicted of a violation of this section shall be punished by a mandatory fine of not less than one hundred dollars ($100) nor more than one thousand dollars ($1,000) upon a first conviction, by a mandatory fine of not less than five hundred dollars ($500) nor more than one thousand dollars ($1,000) upon a second conviction, and by a mandatory fine of not less than seven hundred fifty dollars ($750) nor more than one thousand dollars ($1,000) upon a third or subsequent conviction.

(e) The court may, in addition to the fine imposed upon a conviction, require as a condition of probation, in addition to any other condition of probation, that any person convicted of a violation of this section pick up litter at a time and place within the jurisdiction of the court for not less than eight hours.

374.7. Littering Waters or Shore

(a) Every person who litters or causes to be littered, or dumps or causes to be dumped, any waste matter into any bay, lagoon, channel, river, creek, slough, canal, lake, or reservoir, or other stream or body of water, or upon a bank, beach, or shore within 150 feet of the high water mark of any stream or body of water, is guilty of a misdemeanor.

(b) Every person convicted of a violation of subdivision (a) shall be punished by a mandatory fine of not less than one hundred dollars ($100) nor more than one thousand dollars ($1,000) upon a first conviction, by a mandatory fine of not less than five hundred dollars ($500) nor more than one thousand dollars ($1,000) upon a second conviction, and by a mandatory fine of not less than seven hundred fifty dollars ($750) nor more than one thousand dollars ($1,000) upon a third or subsequent conviction.

(c) The court may, in addition to the fine imposed upon a conviction, require as a condition of probation, in addition to any other condition of probation, that any person convicted of a violation of subdivision (a) pick up litter at a time and place within the jurisdiction of the court for not less than eight hours.

374.8. Dumping Hazardous Material

(a) In any prosecution under this section, proof of the elements of the offense shall not be dependent upon the requirements of Title 22 of the California Code of Regulations.

(b) Any person who knowingly causes any hazardous substance to be deposited into or upon any road, street, highway, alley, or railroad right-of-way, or upon the land of another, without the permission of the owner, or into the waters of this state is punishable by imprisonment in the county jail for not more than one year or by imprisonment in the state prison for a term of 16 months, 2, or 3 years, or by a fine of not less than fifty dollars ($50) nor more than ten thousand dollars ($10,000), or by both the fine and imprisonment, unless the deposit occurred as a result of an emergency that the person promptly reported to the appropriate regulatory authority.

(c) For purposes of this section, "hazardous substance" means either of the following:

(1) Any material that, because of its quantity, concentration, or physical or chemical characteristics, poses a significant present or potential hazard to human health and safety or to the environment if released into the environment, including, but not limited to, hazardous waste and any material that the administering agency or a handler as defined in Chapter 6.91 (commencing with Section 25410) of division 20 of the Health and Safety Code, has a reasonable basis for believing would be injurious to the health and safety of persons or harmful to the environment if released into the environment.

(2) Any substance or chemical product for which one of the following applies.

(A) The manufacturer of producer is required to prepare a MSDS, as defined in Section 6374 of the Labor Code, for the substance or product pursuant to the Hazardous Substances Information Act (Chapter 2.5 (commencing with Section 6360) of Part 1 of Division 5 of the Labor Code) or pursuant to any applicable federal law or regulation.

(B) The substance is described as a radioactive material in Chapter 1 of Title 10 of the Code of Federal Regulations maintained and updated by the nuclear Regulatory Commission.

(C) The substance is designated by the Secretary of Transportation in Chapter 27 (commencing with Section 1801) of the appendix to Title 49 of the US Code and taxed as a radioactive substance or material.

(D) The materials listed in subdivision (b) of Section 6382 of the Labor Code.

375. Use of Offensive Substance in Place of Public Assembly; Manufacture of Offensive Substance

(a) It shall be unlawful to throw, drop, pour, deposit, release, discharge or expose, or to attempt to throw, drop, pour, deposit, release, discharge or expose in, upon or about any theater, restaurant, place of business, place of amusement or any place of public assemblage, any liquid, gaseous or solid substance or matter of any kind which is injurious to person or property, or is nauseous, sickening, irritating or offensive to any of the senses.

(b) It shall be unlawful to manufacture or prepare, or to possess any liquid, gaseous, or solid substance or matter of any kind which is injurious to person or property, or is nauseous, sickening, irritating or offensive, to any of the senses with intent to throw, drop, pour, deposit, release, discharge or expose the same in, upon or about any theater, restaurant, place of business, place of amusement, or any other place of public assemblage.

(c) Any person violating any of the provisions hereof shall be punished by imprisonment in the county jail for not less than three months and not more than one year, or by a fine of not less than five hundred dollars ($500) and not more than two thousand dollars ($2,000), or by both such fine and imprisonment.

(d) Any person who, in violating any of the provisions of subdivision (a), willfully employs or uses any liquid, gaseous or solid substance which may produce serious illness or permanent injury through being vaporized or otherwise dispersed in the air or who, in violating any of the provisions of subdivision (a), willfully employs or uses any tear gas, mustard gas or any of the combinations or compounds thereof, or willfully employs or uses acid or explosives, shall be guilty of a felony and shall be punished by imprisonment in the state prison.

377. False Representation to Procure Drug

Every person who, in order to obtain for himself or another any drug that can be lawfully dispensed by a pharmacist only on prescription, falsely represents himself to be a physician or other person who can lawfully prescribe such drug, or falsely represents that he is acting on behalf of a person who can lawfully prescribe such drug, in a telephone communication with a pharmacist, is guilty of a misdemeanor.

380. Sale or Distribution of Toluene to Persons Under 18 Years

(a) Every person who sells, dispenses or distributes toluene, or any substance or material containing toluene, to any person who is less than 18 years of age shall be guilty of a misdemeanor, and upon conviction shall ice fined in a sum of not less that one thousand dollars ($1,000), nor more than two thousand five hundred dollars ($2,500), or by imprisonment for not less than six months nor more than one year.

(b) The court shall order the suspension of the business license, for a period of one year, of a person who knowingly violates any of the provisions of this section after having been previously convicted of a violation of this section unless the owner of such business license can demonstrate a good faith attempt to prevent illegal sales or deliveries by employees. The provisions of this subdivision shall become operative on July 1, 1980.

(c) The provisions of this section shall apply to, but are not limited to, the sale or distribution of glue, cement, dope, paint thinners, paint, and any combination of hydrocarbons either alone or in combination with any substance or material including, but not limited to, paint, paint thinners, shellac thinners, and solvents which, when inhaled, ingested or breathed, can cause a person to be under the influence of, or intoxicated from, any such combination of hydrocarbons.

This section shall not prohibit the sale of gasoline or other motor vehicle fuels to persons less than 18 years of age.

(d) This section shall not apply to any glue or cement which has been certified by the State Department of Health Services as containing a substance which makes such glue or cement malodorous or causes such glue or cement to induce sneezing, nor shall this section apply where the glue or cement is sold, delivered, or given away simultaneously with or as part of a kit used for the construction of model airplanes, model boats, model automobiles, model trains, or other similar models or used for the assembly or creation of hobby craft items using such components as beads, tiles, tiffany glass, ceramics, clay, or other craft-related components.

381. Possessing Toluene or Similar Substance With Intent to Inhale and Become Intoxicated

(a) Any person who possesses toluene or any substance or material containing toluene, including, but not limited to, glue, cement, dope, paint thinner, paint and any combination of hydrocarbons, either alone or in combination with any substance or material including but not limited to paint, paint thinner, shellac thinner, and solvents, with the intent to breathe, inhale or ingest for the purpose of causing a condition of intoxication, elation, euphoria, dizziness, stupefaction, or dulling of the senses or for the purpose of, in any manner, changing, distorting or disturbing the audio, visual, or mental processes, or who knowingly and with the intent to do so is under the influence of toluene or any material containing toluene, or any combination of hydrocarbons is guilty of a misdemeanor.

(b) Any person who possesses any substance or material, which the State Department of Health Services has determined by regulations adopted pursuant to the Administrative Procedures Act (Chapter 3.5 of Part 1 of Division 3 of Title 2 of the Government Code) has toxic qualities similar to toluene, with the intent to breathe, inhale, or ingest for the purpose of causing a condition of intoxication, elation, euphoria, dizziness, excitement, irrational behavior, exhilaration, satisfaction, stupefaction, or dulling of the senses or for the purpose of, in any manner, changing, distorting or disturbing the audio, visual, or mental processes, or who is under the influence of such substance or material is guilty of a misdemeanor.

381b. Nitrous Oxide

Any person who possesses nitrous oxide or any substance containing nitrous oxide, with the intent to breathe, inhale, or ingest for the purpose of causing a condition of intoxication, elation, euphoria, dizziness, stupefaction, or dulling of the senses or for the purpose of, in any manner, changing, distorting, or disturbing the audio, visual, or mental processes, or who knowingly and with the intent to do so is under the influence of nitrous oxide or any material containing nitrous oxide is guilty of a misdemeanor. This section shall not apply to any person who is under the influence of nitrous oxide or any material containing nitrous oxide pursuant to an administration for the purpose of medical, surgical, or dental care by a person duly licensed to administer such an agent.

384a. Cutting or Destroying Shrubs

Every person who within the State of California willfully or negligently cuts, destroys, mutilates, or removes any tree or shrub, or fern or herb or bulb or cactus or flower, or huckleberry or redwood greens, or portion of any tree or shrub, or fern or herb or bulb or cactus or flower, or huckleberry or redwood greens, growing upon state or county highway rights-of-way, or who removes leaf mold thereon; provided, however, that the provisions of this section shall not be construed to apply to any employee of the state or of any political subdivision thereof engaged in work upon any state, county, or public road or highway while performing work under the supervision of the state or of any political subdivision thereof, and every person who willfully or negligently cuts, destroys, mutilates, or removes any tree or shrub, or fern or herb or bulb or cactus or flower, or huckleberry or redwood greens, or portions of any tree or shrub, or fern or herb or bulb or cactus or flower, or huckleberry or redwood greens, growing upon public land or upon land not his or her own, or leaf mold on the surface of public land, or upon land not his or her own, without a written permit from the owner of the land signed by the owner or the owner's authorized agent, and every person who knowingly sells, offers, or exposes for sale, or transports for sale, any tree or shrub, or fern or herb or bulb or cactus or flower, or huckleberry or redwood greens, or portion of any tree or shrub, or fern or herb or bulb or cactus or flower, or huckleberry or redwood greens, or leaf mold, so cut or removed from state or county highway rights-of-way, or removed from public land or from land not owned by the person who cut or removed the same without the written permit from the owner of the land, signed by the owner or the owner's authorized agent, is guilty of a misdemeanor and upon conviction thereof shall be punished by a fine of not more than one thousand dollars ($1,000) or by imprisonment in a county jail for not more than six months or by both fine and imprisonment.

The written permit required under this section shall be signed by the landowner, or the landowner's authorized agent, and acknowledged before a notary public, or other person authorized by law to take acknowledgments. The permit shall contain the number and species of trees and amount of shrubs or ferns or herbs or bulbs or cacti or flowers, or huckleberry or redwood greens, or portions of any tree or shrub and shall contain the legal description of the real property as usually found in deeds and conveyances of the land on which cutting or removal, or both, shall take place. One copy of the permit shall be filed in the office of the sheriff of the county in which the land described in the permit is located. The permit shall be filed prior to commencement of cutting of the trees or shrub or fern or herb or bulb or cactus or flower or huckleberry or redwood green or portions of any tree or shrub authorized by the permit. The permit required by this section need not be notarized or filed with the office of the sheriff of the county where trees are to he removed when five or less trees or five or less pounds of shrubs or boughs are to be cut or removed.

Any county or state fire warden, or personnel of the Department of Forestry as designated by the Director of Forestry, and personnel of the United States Forest Service as designated by the Regional Forester, Region 5, of the United States Forest Service, or any peace officer of the State of California, may enforce the provisions hereof and may confiscate any and all such shrubs, trees, ferns or herbs or bulbs or cacti or flowers, or huckleberry or redwood greens or leaf mold, or parts thereof unlawfully cut or removed or knowingly sold, offered, or exposed or transported for sale as provided in this section.

The provisions of this section do not apply to any tree or shrub, or fern or herb or bulb or cactus or flower, or greens declared by law to be a public nuisance.

The provisions of this section do not apply to the necessary cutting or trimming of any trees, shrubs, or ferns or herbs or bulbs or cacti or flowers, or greens if done for the purpose of protecting or maintaining an electric powerline telephone line, or other property of a public utility.

The provisions of this section do not apply to persons engaged in logging operations, or in suppressing fires.

384c. Transportation Tags for Trees or Shrubs

Persons purchasing trees, shrubs, or boughs from harvesters thereof shall not transport more than five trees or more than five pounds of shrubs or boughs on the public roads or highways without obtaining from the seller of the trees, shrubs, or boughs and having validated as provided in Section 384d a transportation tag for each load of the trees, shrubs, or boughs. Unless a valid transportation tag issued in California for a tree, shrub, or bough has already been obtained, persons who harvest trees, shrubs, or boughs from their own land or the land of another or who are in possession of trees, shrubs, or boughs shall, before transporting on the public roads or highways or selling or consigning for removal and transportation over the public roads and highways more than five trees or more than five pounds of other shrubs or boughs, file with the sheriff of each county in which the trees, shrubs, or boughs are to be harvested an application for transportation tags and obtain a supply of these transportation tags sufficient to provide one tag for each load of trees, shrubs, or boughs to be so transported or sold. No person shall knowingly make any false statement on any application for the transportation tags and the application shall contain, but is not limited to, the following information:

(a) The name and address of the applicant.

(b) The amount and species of trees, shrubs, or boughs to be transported.

(c) The name of the county from which the trees, shrubs, or boughs are to be removed.

(d) A legal description of the real property from which the trees, shrubs, or boughs are to be removed.

(e) The name or names of the owner of the real property from which the trees, shrubs, or boughs are to be removed.

(f) The applicant's timber operator permit number, if the harvesting of the trees, shrubs, or boughs is subject to the Z'berg-Nejedly Forest Practice Act of 1973 (Chapter 8 (commencing with Section 4511) of Part 2 of Division 4 of the Public Resources Code).

(g) The destination of the trees, shrubs, or boughs.

(h) The proposed date or dates of the transportation. Every applicant shall, at the time of application, show to the sheriff his or her permit or proof of ownership of the trees, shrubs, or boughs. The application forms and transportation tags shall be printed and distributed by the sheriff of each county.

384h. Killing or Injuring Domestic Animal While Hunting

Every person who willfully or negligently, while hunting upon the inclosed lands of another, kills, maims, or wounds an animal, the property of another, is guilty of a misdemeanor.

386. Inoperable or Impaired Fire-Protection System

(a) Any person who willfully or maliciously constructs or maintains a fire-protection system in any structure with the intent to install a fire protection system which is known to be inoperable or to impair the effective operation of a system, so as to threaten the safety of any occupant or user of the structure in the event of a fire, shall be subject to imprisonment in the state prison for two, three, or four years.

(b) A violation of subdivision (a) which proximately results in great bodily injury or death is a felony punishable by imprisonment in the state prison for five, six, or seven years.

(c) As used in this section, "fire-protection system" includes, but is not limited to, an automatic fire sprinkler system, standpipe system, automatic fixed fire extinguishing system, and fire alarm system.

(d) For purposes of this section, the following definitions shall control:

(1) "Automatic fire sprinkler system" means an integrated system of underground and overhead piping designed in accordance with fire protection engineering standards. The portion of the sprinkler system above ground is a network of specially sized or hydraulically designed piping installed in a building, structure, or area, generally overhead, and to which sprinklers are attached in a systematic pattern. The valve controlling each system riser is located in the system riser or its supply piping. Each sprinkler system riser includes a device for activating an alarm when the system is in operation. The system is normally activated by heat from a fire, and it discharges water over the fire area.

(2) "Standpipe system" means an arrangement of piping, valves, and hose connectors and allied equipment installed in a building or structure with the hose connectors located in a manner that water can be discharged in streams or spray patterns through attached hose and nozzles. The purpose of the system is to extinguish a fire, thereby protecting a building or structure and its contents and occupants. This system relies upon connections to water supply systems or pumps, tanks, and other equipment necessary to provide an adequate supply of water to the hose connectors.

(3) "Automatic fixed fire extinguishing system" means either of the following:

(A) An engineered fixed extinguishing system which is custom designed for a particular hazard, using components which are approved or listed only for their broad performance characteristics. Components may be arranged into a variety of configurations. These systems shall include, but not be limited to, dry chemical systems, carbon dioxide systems, halogenated agent systems, steam systems, high expansion foam systems, foam extinguishing systems, and liquid agent systems.

(B) A pre-engineered fixed extinguishing system is a system where the number of components and their configurations are included in the description of the system's approval and listing. These systems include, but are not limited to, dry chemical systems, carbon dioxide systems, halogenated agent systems, and liquid agent systems.

(4) "Fire alarm system" means a control unit and a combination of electrical interconnected devices designed and intended to cause an alarm or warning of fire in a building or structure by either manual or automatic activation, or by both, and includes the systems installed throughout any building or portion thereof.

(5) "Structure" means any building, whether private, commercial, or public, or any bridge, tunnel, or powerplant.

396. Price Gouging During State of Emergency

(a) The Legislature hereby finds that during emergencies and major disasters, including, but not limited to, earthquakes, fires, floods, or civil disturbances, some merchants have taken unfair advantage of consumers by greatly increasing prices for essential consumer goods and services. While the pricing of consumer goods and services is generally best left to the marketplace under ordinary conditions, when a declared state of emergency results in abnormal disruptions of the market, the public interest requires that excessive and unjustified increases in the prices of essential consumer goods and services be prohibited. It is the intent of the Legislature in enacting this act to protect citizens from excessive and unjustified increases in the prices charged during or shortly after a declared state of emergency for goods and services that are vital and necessary for the health, safety, and welfare of consumers. Further it is the intent of the Legislature that this section be liberally construed so that its beneficial purposes may be served.

(b) Upon the proclamation of a state of emergency resulting from an earthquake, flood, fire, riot, storm, or natural or manmade disaster declared by the President of the United States or the Governor, or upon the declaration of a local emergency resulting from an earthquake, flood, fire, riot, storm, or natural or manmade disaster by the executive officer of any county, city, or city and county, and for a period of 30 days following that declaration, it is unlawful for any person, contractor, business, or other entity to sell or offer to sell any consumer food items or goods, goods or services used for emergency cleanup, emergency supplies, medical supplies, home heating oil, building materials, housing, transportation, freight, and storage services, or gasoline or other motor fuels for a price of more than 10 percent above the price charged by that person for those goods or services immediately prior to the proclamation of emergency. However, a greater price increase shall not be unlawful if that person can prove that the increase in price was directly attributable to additional costs imposed on it by the supplier of the goods, or directly attributable to additional costs for labor or materials used to provide the services, provided that in those situations where the increase in price is attributable to additional costs imposed by the seller's supplier or additional costs of providing the good or service during the state of emergency, the price represents no more than 10 percent above the total of the cost to the seller plus the markup customarily applied by the seller for that good or service in the usual course of business immediately prior to the onset of the state of emergency.

(c) Upon the proclamation of a state of emergency resulting from an earthquake, flood, fire, riot, or storm declared by the President of the United States or the Governor, or upon the declaration of a local emergency resulting from an earthquake, flood, fire, riot, or storm by the executive officer of any county, city, or city and county, and for a period of 180 days following that declaration, it is unlawful for any contractor to sell or offer to sell any repair or reconstruction services or any services used in emergency cleanup for a price of more than 10 percent above the price charged by that person for those services immediately prior to the proclamation of emergency. However, a greater price increase shall not be unlawful if that person can prove that the increase in price was directly attributable to additional costs imposed on it by the supplier of the goods, or directly attributable to additional costs for labor or materials used to provide the services, provided that in those situations where the increase in price is attributable to the additional costs imposed by the contractor's supplier or additional costs of providing the service during the state of emergency, the price represents no more than 10 percent above the total of the cost to the contractor plus the markup customarily applied by the contractor for that good or service in the usual course of business immediately prior to the onset of the state of emergency.

(d) The provisions of this section may be extended for additional 30-day periods by a local legislative body or the California Legislature if deemed necessary to protect the lives, property, or welfare of the citizens.

(e) A violation of this section is a misdemeanor punishable by imprisonment in a county jail for a period not exceeding one year, or by a fine of not more than ten thousand dollars ($10,000), or by both that fine and imprisonment.

(f) A violation of this section shall constitute an unlawful business practice and an act of unfair competition within the meaning of Section 17200 of the Business and Professions Code. The remedies and penalties provided by this section are cumulative to each other, the remedies under Section 17200 of the Business and Professions Code, and the remedies or penalties available under all other laws of this state.

(g) For the purposes of this section:

(i) "State of emergency" means a natural or manmade disaster or emergency resulting from an earthquake, flood, fire, riot, or storm for which a state of emergency has been declared by the President of the United States or the Governor of California.

(2) "Local emergency" means a natural or manmade disaster or emergency resulting from an earthquake, flood, fire, riot, or storm for which a local emergency has been declared by the executive officer or governing body of any city or county in California.

(3) "Consumer food item" means any article that is used or intended for use for food, drink, confection, or condiment by a person or animal.

(4) "Repair or reconstruction services" means services performed by any person who is required to be licensed under the Contractors'State License Law (Chapter 9 (commencing with Section 7000) of Division 3 of the Business and Professions Code), for repairs to residential or commercial property of any type that is damaged as a result of a disaster.

(5) "Emergency supplies" includes, but is not limited to, water, flashlights, radios, batteries, candles, blankets, soaps, diapers, temporary shelters, tape, toiletries, plywood, nails, and hammers.

(6) "Medical supplies" includes, but is not limited to, prescription and nonprescription medications, bandages, gauze, isopropyl alcohol, and antibacterial products.

(7) "Building materials" means lumber, construction tools, windows, and anything else used in the building or rebuilding of property.

(8) "Gasoline" means any fuel used to power any motor vehicle or power tool.

(9) "Transportation, freight, and storage services" means any service that is performed by any company that contracts to move, store, or transport personal or business property or rents equipment for those purposes.

(10) "Housing" means any rental housing leased on a month-to-month term.

(11) "Goods" has the same meaning as defined in subdivision (c) of Section 1689.5 of the Civil Code.

(h) Nothing in this section shall preempt any local ordinance prohibiting the same or similar conduct or imposing a more severe penalty for the same conduct prohibited by this section.

(i) Any business offering an item for sale at a reduced price immediately prior to the proclamation of the emergency may use the price at which they usually sell the item to calculate the price pursuant to subdivision (b) or (c).

396.5. Food Stamps; Furnishing Unauthorized Goods and Services

It shall be unlawful for any retail food store or wholesale food concern, as defined in Section 3(k) of the federal Food Stamp Act of 1977 (Public Law 95-113) (7 U.S.C Sec. 2012(k)), or any person, to sell, furnish or give away any goods or services, other than those items authorized by the Food Stamp Act of 1964, as amended (Public Law 88-525) (Chapter 51 (commencing with Section 2011) of Title 7 of the United States Code), in exchange for food stamps issued pursuant to Chapter 10 (commencing with Section 18900), Part 6, Division 9 of the Welfare and Institutions Code.

Any violator of this section is guilty of a misdemeanor and shall be punished by a fine of not more than five thousand dollars ($5,000) or by imprisonment in the county jail not exceeding 90 days, or by both that fine and imprisonment.

397. Selling Intoxicants to Common Drunkards or Incompetents

Every person who sells or furnishes, or causes to be sold or furnished, intoxicating liquors to any habitual or common drunkard, or to any person who has been adjudged legally incompetent or insane by any court of this State and has not been restored to legal capacity, knowing such person to have been so adjudged, is guilty of a misdemeanor.

399. Allowing Vicious Animals at Large

(a) If *** any person owning or having custody or control of a mischievous animal, knowing its propensities, willfully suffers it to go at large, or keeps it without ordinary care, and *** the animal, while so at large, or while not kept with ordinary care, kills any human being who has taken all the precautions *** that the circumstances permitted, or which a reasonable person would ordinarily take in the same situation, is guilty of a felony.

(b) If any person owning or having custody or control of a mischievous animal, knowing its propensities, willfully suffers it to go at large, or keeps it without ordinary care, and the animal, while so at large, or while not kept with ordinary care, causes serious bodily injury to any human being who has taken all the precautions that the circumstances permitted, or which a reasonable person would ordinarily take in the same situation, is guilty of a misdemeanor or a felony. *(AM '01)*

399.5. Owner's Failure to Exercise Ordinary Care With Certain Dogs

(a) Any person owning or having custody or control of a dog trained to fight, attack, or kill is guilty of a felony or a misdemeanor, punishable by imprisonment in the state prison for two, three, or four years, or in a county jail not to exceed one year, or by a fine not exceeding ten thousand dollars ($10,000), or by both the fine and imprisonment, if, as a result of that person's failure to exercise ordinary care, the dog bites a human being, on two separate occasions or on one occasion causing substantial physical injury. No person shall be criminally liable under this section, however, unless he or she knew or reasonably should have known of the vicious or dangerous nature of the dog, or if the victim failed to take all the precautions that a reasonable person would ordinarily take in the same situation.

(b) Following the conviction of an individual for a violation of this section, the court shall hold a hearing to determine whether conditions of the treatment or confinement of the dog or other circumstances existing at the time of the bite or bites have changed so as to remove the danger to other persons presented by the animal. The court, after hearing, may make any order it deems appropriate to prevent the recurrence of such an incident, including, but not limited to, the removal of the animal from the area or its destruction if necessary.

(c) Nothing in this section shall authorize the bringing of an action pursuant to subdivision (a) based on a bite or bites inflicted upon a trespasser, upon a person who has provoked the dog or contributed to his or her own injuries, or by a dog used in military or police work if the bite or bites occurred while the dog was actually performing in that capacity. As used in this subdivision, "provocation"includes, but is not limited to, situations where a dog held on a leash by its owner or custodian reacts in a protective manner to a person or persons who approach the owner or custodian in a threatening manner.

(d) Nothing in this section shall be construed to affect the liability of the owner of a dog under Section 399 or any other provision of law.

(e) This section shall not apply to a veterinarian or an on-duty animal control officer while in the performance of his or her duties, or to a peace officer, as defined in Chapter 4.5 (commencing with Section 830) of Title 3 of Part 2, if he or she is assigned to a canine unit.,1 *(AM '99)*

401. Advising or Encouraging Suicide

Every person who deliberately aids, or advises, or encourages another to commit suicide, is guilty of a felony.

402. Sightseeing at Scene of Emergency

(a) Every person who goes to the scene of an emergency, or stops at the scene of an emergency, for the purpose of viewing the scene or the activities of police officers, firefighters, emergency medical, or other emergency personnel, or military personnel coping with the emergency in the course of their duties during the time it is necessary for emergency vehicles or those personnel to be at the scene of the emergency or to be moving to or from the scene of the emergency for the purpose of protecting lives or property, unless it is part of the duties of that person's employment to view that scene or activities, and thereby impedes police officers, firefighters, emergency medical, or other emergency personnel or military personnel, in the performance of their duties in coping with the emergency, is guilty of a misdemeanor.

(b) Every person who knowingly resists or interferes with the lawful efforts of a lifeguard in the discharge or attempted discharge of an official duty in an emergency situation, when the person knows or reasonably should know that the lifeguard is engaged in the performance of his or her official duty, is guilty of a misdemeanor.

(c) For the purposes of this section, an emergency includes a condition or situation involving injury to persons, damage to property, or peril to the safety of persons or property, which results from a fire, an explosion, an airplane crash, flooding, windstorm damage, a railroad accident, a traffic accident, a power plant accident, a toxic chemical or biological spill, or any other natural or human-caused event.

402b. Abandoning Refrigerator or Other Appliances

Any person who discards or abandons or leaves in any place accessible to children any refrigerator, icebox, deep-freeze locker, clothes dryer, washing machine, or other appliance, having a capacity of one and one-half cubic feet or more, which is no longer in use, and which has not had the door removed or the hinges and such portion of the latch mechanism removed to prevent latching or locking of the door, is guilty of a misdemeanor. Any owner, lessee, or manager who knowingly permits such a refrigerator, icebox, deep-freeze locker, clothes dryer, washing machine, or other appliance to remain on premises under his control without having the door removed or the hinges and such portion of the latch mechanism removed to prevent latching or locking of the door, is guilty of a misdemeanor. Guilt of a violation of this section shall not, in itself, render one guilty of manslaughter, battery or other crime against a person who may suffer death or injury from entrapment in such a refrigerator, icebox, deep-freeze locker, clothes dryer, washing machine, or other appliance.

The provisions of this section shall not apply to any vendor or seller of refrigerators, iceboxes, deep-freeze lockers, clothes dryers, washing machines, or other appliances, who keeps or stores them for sale purposes, if the vendor or seller takes reasonable precautions to effectively secure the door of any such refrigerator, icebox, deep-freeze locker, clothes dryer, washing machine, or other appliance so as to prevent entrance by children small enough to fit therein.

402c. Integral Lock Necessary for Refrigerator, Icebox or Deep-Freeze Locker

On and after January 1, 1970, any person who sells a new refrigerator, icebox or deep-freeze locker not equipped with an integral lock in this state, having a capacity of two cubic feet or more, which cannot be opened from the inside by the exertion of 15 pounds of force against the latch edge of the closed door is guilty of a misdemeanor.

CRIMES AGAINST PUBLIC PEACE

403. Disturbing an Assembly

Every person who, without authority of law, willfully disturbs or breaks up any assembly or meeting, not unlawful in its character, other than such as is mentioned in Section 302 of the Penal Code and Section 29440 of the Elections Code, is guilty of a misdemeanor.

404. Riot - Defined

(a) Any use of force or violence, disturbing the public peace, or any threat to use such force or violence, if accompanied by immediate power of execution, by two or more persons acting together, and without authority of law, is a riot.

(b) As used in this section, disturbing the public peace may occur in any place of confinement. Place of confinement means any state prison, county jail, industrial farm, or road camp, or any city jail, industrial farm, or road camp, or any juvenile hall, juvenile camp, juvenile ranch, or juvenile forestry camp.

404.6. Incite to Riot, Arson, or Vandalism

(a) Every person who with the intent to cause a riot does an act or engages in conduct that urges a riot, or urges others to commit acts of force or violence, or the burning or destroying of property, and at a time and place and under circumstances that produce a clear and present and immediate danger of acts of force or violence or the burning or destroying of property, is guilty of incitement to riot.

(b) Incitement to riot is punishable by a fine not exceeding one thousand dollars ($1,000), or by imprisonment in a county jail not exceeding one year, or by both that fine and imprisonment.

(c) Every person who incites any riot in the state prison or a county jail that results in serious bodily injury, shall be punished by either imprisonment in a county jail for not more than one year, or imprisonment in the state prison.

(d) The existence of any fact that would bring a person under subdivision (c) shall be alleged in the complaint, information, or indictment and either admitted by the defendant in open court, or found to be true by the jury trying the issue of guilt, by the court where guilt is established by a plea of guilty or nolo contendere, or by trial by the court sitting without a jury. *(AM '98)*

405a. Lynching Defined

The taking by means of a riot of any person from the lawful custody of any peace officer is a lynching.

406. Rout Defined

Whenever two or more persons, assembled and acting together, make any attempt or advance toward the commission of an act which would be a riot if actually committed, such an assembly is a rout.

407. Unlawful Assembly

Whenever two or more persons assemble together to do an unlawful act, or do a lawful act in a violent, boisterous, or tumultuous manner, such assembly is an unlawful assembly.

408. Participating in Rout or Unlawful Assembly

Every person who participates in any rout or unlawful assembly is guilty of a misdemeanor.

409. Refusal to Disperse When Ordered

Every person remaining present at the place of any riot, rout, or unlawful assembly, after the same has been lawfully warned to disperse, except public officers and persons assisting them in attempting to disperse the same, is guilty of a misdemeanor.

409.5. Closing Areas in Emergencies

(a) Whenever a menace to the public health or safety is created by a calamity including a flood, storm, fire, earthquake, explosion, accident, or other disaster, officers of the Department of the California Highway Patrol, police departments, marshal's office or sheriff's office, any officer or employee of the Department of Forestry and Fire Protection designated a peace officer by subdivision (g) of Section 830.2, any officer or employee of the Department of Parks and Recreation designated a peace officer by subdivision (f) of Section 830.2, any officer or employee of the Department of Fish and Game designated a peace officer under subdivision (e) of Section 830.2, and any publicly employed full-time lifeguard or publicly employed full-time marine safety officer while acting in a supervisory position in the performance of his or her official duties, may close the area where the menace exists for the duration thereof by means of ropes, markers, or guards to any and all persons not authorized by the lifeguard or officer to enter or remain within the enclosed area. If the calamity creates an immediate menace to the public health, the local health officer may close the area where the menace exists pursuant to the conditions set forth in this section.

(b) Officers of the Department of the California Highway Patrol, police departments, marshal's office or sheriff's office, officers of the Department of Fish and Game designated as peace officers by subdivision (e) of Section 830.2, or officers of the Department of Forestry and Fire Protection designated as peace officers by subdivision (g) of Section 830.2 may close the immediate area surrounding any emergency field command post or any other command post activated for the purpose of abating any calamity enumerated in this section or any riot or other civil disturbance to any and all unauthorized persons pursuant to the conditions set forth in this section whether or not the field command post or other command post is located near to the actual calamity or riot or other civil disturbance.

(c) Any unauthorized person who willfully and knowingly enters an area closed pursuant to subdivision (a) or (b) and who willfully remains within the area after receiving notice to evacuate or leave shall be guilty of a misdemeanor.

(d) Nothing in this section shall prevent a duly authorized representative of any news service, newspaper, or radio or television station or network from entering the areas closed pursuant to this section.

409.6. Closing Areas in Disasters - Avalanche

(a) Whenever a menace to the public health or safety is created by an avalanche, officers of the Department of the California Highway Patrol, police departments, or sheriff's offices, any officer or employee of the Department of Forestry and Fire Protection designated a peace officer by subdivision (g) of Section

830.2, and any officer or employee of the Department of Parks and Recreation designated a peace officer by subdivision (f) of Section 830.2, may close the area where the menace exists for the duration thereof by means of ropes, markers, or guards to any and all persons not authorized by that officer to enter or remain within the closed area. If an avalanche creates an immediate menace to the public health, the local health officer may close the area where the menace exists pursuant to the conditions which are set forth above in this section.

(b) Officers of the Department of the California Highway Patrol, police departments, or sheriff's offices, or officers of the Department of Forestry and Fire Protection designated as peace officers by subdivision (g) of Section 830.2, may close the immediate area surrounding any emergency field command post or any other command post activated for the purpose of abating hazardous conditions created by an avalanche to any and all unauthorized persons pursuant to the conditions which are set forth in this section whether or not that field command post or other command post is located near the avalanche.

(c) Any unauthorized person who willfully and knowingly enters an area closed pursuant to subdivision (a) or (b) and who willfully remains within that area, or any unauthorized person who willfully remains within an area closed pursuant to subdivision (a) or (b), after receiving notice to evacuate or leave from a peace officer named in subdivision (a) or (b), shall be guilty of a misdemeanor. If necessary, a peace officer named in subdivision (a) or (b) may use reasonable force to remove from the closed area any unauthorized person who willfully remains within that area after receiving notice to evacuate or leave.

(d) Nothing in this section shall prevent a duly authorized representative of any news service, newspaper, or radio or television station or network from entering the areas closed pursuant to this section.

410. Duty to Suppress Riot or Rout

If a magistrate or officer, having notice of an unlawful or riotous assembly, mentioned in this chapter, neglects to proceed to the place of assembly, or as near thereto as he can with safety, and to exercise the authority with which he is invested for suppressing the same and arresting the offenders, he is guilty of a misdemeanor.

415. Fighting, Causing Loud Noise, or Using Offensive Words in Public Place

Any of the following persons shall be punished by imprisonment in the county jail for a period of not more than 90 days, a fine of not more than four hundred dollars ($400), or both such imprisonment and fine:

(1) Any person who unlawfully fights in a public place or challenges another person in a public place to fight.

(2) Any person who maliciously and willfully disturbs another person by loud and unreasonable noise.

(3) Any person who uses offensive words in a public place which are inherently likely to provoke an immediate violent reaction.

415.5. Unlawful Acts Committed in Buildings or Grounds of College or University

(a) Any person who (1) unlawfully fights within any building or upon the grounds of any school, community college, university, or state university or challenges another person within any building or upon the grounds to fight, or (2) maliciously and willfully disturbs another person within any of these buildings or upon the grounds by loud and unreasonable noise, or (3) uses offensive words within any of these buildings or upon the grounds which are inherently likely to provoke an immediate violent reaction is guilty of a misdemeanor punishable by a fine not exceeding four hundred dollars ($400) or by imprisonment in the county jail for a period of not more than 90 days, or both.

(b) If the defendant has been previously convicted once of a violation of this section or of any offense defined in Chapter 1 (commencing with Section 626) of Title 15 of Part 1, the defendant shall be sentenced to imprisonment in the county jail for a period of not less than 10 days or more than six months, or by both that imprisonment and a fine of not exceeding one thousand dollars ($1,000), and shall not be released on probation, parole, or any other basis until not less than 10 days of imprisonment has been served.

(c) If the defendant has been previously convicted two or more times of a violation of this section or of any offense defined in Chapter 1 of Title 15 of Part 1, the defendant shall be sentenced to imprisonment in the county jail for a period of not less than 90 days or more than six months, or by both that imprisonment and a fine of not exceeding one thousand dollars ($1,000), and shall not be released on probation, parole, or any other basis until not less than 90 days of imprisonment has been served.

(d) For the purpose of determining the penalty to be imposed pursuant to this section, the court may consider a written report from the Department of Justice containing information from its records showing prior convictions; and the communication is prima facie evidence of such convictions, if the defendant admits them, regardless of whether or not the complaint commencing the proceedings has alleged prior convictions.

(e) As used in this section "state university," "university," "community college," and "school" have the same meaning as these terms are given in Section 626.

(f) This section shall not apply to any person who is a registered student of the school, or to any person who is engaged in any otherwise lawful employee concerted activity.

416. Duty of Crowds to Disperse When Ordered; Restitution for Property Damage

(a) If two or more persons assemble for the purpose of disturbing the public peace, or committing any unlawful act, and do not disperse on being desired or commanded so to do by a public officer, the persons so offending are severally guilty of a misdemeanor.

(b) Any person who, as a result of violating subdivision (a), personally causes damage to real or personal property, which is either publicly or privately owned, shall make restitution for the damage he or she caused, including, but not limited to, the costs of cleaning up, repairing, replacing, or restoring the property. Any restitution required to be paid pursuant to this subdivision shall be paid directly to the victim. If the court determines that the defendant is unable to pay restitution, the court shall order the defendant to perform community service, as the court deems appropriate, in lieu of the direct restitution payment.

(c) This section shall not preclude the court from imposing restitution in the form of a penalty assessment pursuant to Section 1464 if the court, in its discretion, deems that additional restitution appropriate.

(d) The burden of proof on the issue of whether any defendant or caused any property damage shall rest with the prosecuting agency or claimant. In no event shall the burden of proof on this issue shift to the defendant or any of several defendants to prove that he or she was not responsible for the property damage.

417. Drawing or Exhibiting Weapon in a Rude or Threatening Manner

(a)(1) Every person who, except in self-defense, in the presence of any other person, draws or exhibits any deadly weapon whatsoever, other than a firearm, in a rude, angry, or threatening manner, or who in any manner, unlawfully uses a deadly weapon other than a firearm in any fight or quarrel is guilty of a misdemeanor, punishable by imprisonment in a county jail for not less than 30 days. (2) Every person who, except in self-defense, in the presence of any other person, draws or exhibits any firearm, whether loaded or unloaded, in a rude, angry, or threatening manner, or who in any manner, unlawfully uses a firearm in any fight or quarrel is punishable as follows:

(A) If the violation occurs in a public place and the firearm is a pistol, revolver, or other firearm capable of being concealed upon the person, by imprisonment in a county jail for not less than three months and not more than one year, by a fine not to exceed one thousand dollars ($1,000), or by both that fine and imprisonment.

(B) In all cases other than that set forth in subparagraph (A), a misdemeanor, punishable by imprisonment in a county jail for not less than three months.

(b) Every person who, except in self-defense, in the presence of any other person, draws or exhibits any loaded firearm in a rude, angry, or threatening manner, or who, in any manner, unlawfully uses any loaded firearm in any fight or quarrel upon the grounds of any day care center, as defined in Section 1596.76 of the Health and Safety Code, or any facility where programs, including day care programs or recreational programs, are being conducted for persons under 18 years of age, including programs conducted by a nonprofit organization, during the hours in which the center or facility is open for use, shall be punished by imprisonment in the state prison for 16 months, or two or three years, or by imprisonment in a county jail for not less than three months, nor more than one year.

(c) Every person who, in the immediate presence of a peace officer, draws or exhibits any firearm, whether loaded or unloaded, in a rude, angry, or threatening manner, and who knows, or reasonably should know, by the officer's uniformed appearance or other action of identification by the officer, that he or she is a peace officer engaged in the performance of his or her duties, and that peace officer is engaged in the performance of his or her duties, shall be punished by imprisonment in a county jail for not less than nine months and not to exceed one year, or in the state prison.

(d) Except where a different penalty applies, every person who violates this section when the other person is in the process of cleaning up graffiti or vandalism is guilty of a misdemeanor, punishable by imprisonment in a county jail for not less than three months nor more than one year.

(e) As used in this section, "peace officer" means any person designated as a peace officer pursuant to Chapter 4.5 (commencing with Section 830) of Title 3 of Part 2.

(f) As used in this section, "public place" means any of the following:

(1) A public place in an incorporated city.

(2) A public street in an incorporated city.

(3) A public street in an unincorporated area. *(AM '98, '00)*

417.2. Drawing or Exhibiting Replica of Firearm; Sale, Etc., of Imitation Firearm

(a) Any person who, for commercial purposes, purchases, sells, manufactures, ships, transports, distributes, or receives, by mail order or in any other manner, an imitation firearm except as permitted by this section shall be liable for a civil fine in an action brought by the city attorney of the city or the district attorney of the county of not more than ten thousand dollars ($10,000) for each violation.

(b) The manufacture, purchase, sale, shipping, transport, distribution, or receipt, by mail or in any other manner, of imitation firearms is permitted if the device is manufactured, purchased, sold, shipped, transported, distributed, or received for any of the following purposes:

(1) Solely for export in interstate or foreign commerce.

(2) Solely for lawful use in theatrical productions, including motion picture, television, and stage productions.

(3) For use in a certified or regulated athletic event or competition.

(4) For use in military or civil defense activities.

(5) For public displays authorized by public or private schools.

(c) As used in this section, "imitation firearm" means a replica of a firearm that is so substantially similar in physical properties to an existing firearm as to lead a reasonable person to conclude that the replica is a firearm.

(d) As used in this section, "imitation firearm" does not include any of the following:

(1) A nonfiring collector's replica of an antique firearm that was designed prior to 1898, is historically significant, and is offered for sale in conjunction with a wall plaque or presentation case.

(2) A nonfiring collector's replica of a firearm that was designed after 1898, is historically significant, was issued as a commemorative by a nonprofit organization, and is offered for sale in conjunction with a wall plaque or presentation case.

(3) A device, as defined in subdivision (g) of Section 12001.

(4) An imitation firearm where the coloration of the entire exterior surface of the device is bright orange or bright green, either singly or in combination.

(5) An instrument that expels a metallic projectile, such as a BB or pellet, through the force of air pressure, CO_2 pressure, or spring action, or a spot marker gun. *(AM '01)*

417.25. Point or Aim Laser Scope

(a) Every person who, except in self-defense, aims or points a laser scope, as defined in subdivision (b), or a laser pointer, as defined in subdivision (c), at another person in a threatening manner with the specific intent to cause a reasonable person fear of bodily harm is guilty of a misdemeanor, punishable by imprisonment in a county jail for up to 30 days. For purposes of this section, the laser scope need not be attached to a firearm.

(b) As used in this section, "laser scope"means a portable battery-powered device capable of being attached to a firearm and capable of projecting a laser light on objects at a distance.

(c) As used in this section, "laser pointer"means any hand held laser beam device or demonstration laser product that emits a single point of light amplified by the stimulated emission of radiation that is visible to the human eye. *(AM '99)*

417.26. Aim Laser Scope at Peace Officer to Cause Apprehension or Fear of Bodily Harm

(a) Any person who aims or points a laser scope as defined in subdivision (b) of Section 417.25, or a laser pointer, as defined in subdivision (c) of that section, at a peace officer with the specific intent to cause the officer apprehension or fear of bodily harm and who knows or reasonably should know that the person at whom he or she is aiming or pointing is a peace officer, is guilty of a misdemeanor punishable by imprisonment in a county jail for a term not exceeding six months.

(b) Any person who commits a second or subsequent violation of subdivision (a) shall be punished by imprisonment in a county jail for not more than one year. *(AD '99)*

417.27. Sale of Laser Pointer to Minor Prohibited

(a) No person, corporation, firm, or business entity of any kind shall knowingly sell a laser pointer to a person 17 years of age or younger, unless he or she is accompanied and supervised by a parent, legal guardian, or any other adult 18 years of age or older.

(b) No student shall possess a laser pointer on any elementary or secondary school premises unless possession of a laser pointer on the elementary or secondary school premises is for a valid instructional or other school-related purpose, including employment.

(c) No person shall direct the beam from a laser pointer directly or indirectly into the eye or eyes of another person or into a moving vehicle with the intent to harass or annoy the other person or the occupants of the moving vehicle.

(d) No person shall direct the beam from a laser pointer directly or indirectly into the eye or eyes of a guide dog, signal dog, service dog, or dog being used by a peace officer with the intent to harass or annoy the animal.

(e) A violation of subdivision (a), (b), (c), or (d) shall be an infraction that is punished by either a fine of fifty dollars ($50) or four hours of community service, and a second or subsequent violation of any of these subdivisions shall be an infraction that is punished by either a fine of one hundred dollars ($100) or eight hours of community service.

(f) As used in this section, "laser pointer"has the same meaning as set forth in subdivision (c) of Section 417.25.

(g) As used in this section, "guide dog,""signal dog,"and "service dog,"respectively, have the same meaning as set forth in subdivisions (d), (e), and (f) of Section 365.5. *(AD '99)*

417.3. Drawing or Exhibiting Firearm to Person in Motor Vehicle

Every person who, except in self-defense, in the presence of any other person who is an occupant of a motor vehicle proceeding on a public street or highway, draws or exhibits any firearm, whether loaded or unloaded, in a threatening manner against another person in such a way as to cause a reasonable person apprehension or fear of bodily harm is guilty of a felony punishable by imprisonment in the state prison for 16 months or two or three years or by imprisonment for 16 months or two or three years and a three thousand dollar ($3,000) fine.

Nothing in this section shall preclude or prohibit prosecution under any other statute.

417.4. Brandishing of Imitation Firearm

Every person who, except in self-defense, draws or exhibits an imitation firearm in a threatening manner against another in such a way as to cause a reasonable person apprehension or fear of bodily harm is guilty of a misdemeanor punishable by imprisonment in a county jail for a term of not less than 30 days. For purposes of this section, an imitation firearm means a replica of a firearm that is so substantially similar in physical properties to an existing firearm as to lead a reasonable person to conclude that the replica is a firearm.

417.6. Drawing or Exhibiting Weapon - Intentional Infliction of Great Bodily Injury

(a) If, in the commission of a violation of Section 417 or 417.8, serious bodily injury is intentionally inflicted by the person drawing or exhibiting the firearm or deadly weapon, the offense shall be punished by imprisonment in the county jail not exceeding one year or by imprisonment in the state prison.

(b) As used in this section, "serious bodily injury"means a serious impairment of physical condition, including, but not limited to, the following: loss of consciousness; concussion; bone fracture; protracted loss or impairment of function of any bodily member or organ; a wound requiring extensive suturing; and serious disfigurement.

(c) When a person is convicted of a violation of Section 417 or 417.8 and the deadly weapon or firearm used by the person is owned by that person, the court shall order that the weapon or firearm be deemed a nuisance and disposed of in the manner provided by Section 12028. *(AM '00)*

417.8. Drawing or Exhibiting Weapon at Peace Officer

Every person who draws or exhibits any firearm, whether loaded or unloaded, or other deadly weapon, with the intent to resist or prevent the arrest or detention of himself or another by a peace officer shall be imprisoned in the state prison for two, three, or four years.

418. Forcible Entry or Detainer of Land

Every person using or procuring, encouraging or assisting another to use, any force or violence in entering upon or detaining any lands or other possessions of another. except in cases and in the manner allowed by law, is guilty of a misdemeanor.

419. Repossession of Land After Legal Ouster

Every person who has been removed from any lands by process of law, or who has removed from any lands pursuant to the lawful adjudication or direction of any Court, tribunal, or officer, and who afterwards unlawfully returns to settle, reside upon, or take possession of such lands, is guilty of a misdemeanor.

420. Obstructing Entry on Government Lands

Every person who unlawfully prevents, hinders, or obstructs any person from peacefully entering upon or establishing a settlement or residence on any tract of public land of the United States within the State of California, subject to settlement or entry under any of the public land laws of the United States; or who unlawfully hinders, prevents, or obstructs free passage over or through the public lands of the United States within the State of California, for the purpose of entry, settlement, or residence as aforesaid, is guilty of a misdemeanor.

420.1. Prevent, Hinder or Obstruct Entering or Leaving Private Property

Anyone who willfully and knowingly prevents, hinders, or obstructs any person from entering, passing over, or leaving land in which that person enjoys, either personally or as an agent, guest, licensee, successor-in-interest, or contractor, a right to enter, use, cross, or inspect the property pursuant to an easement, covenant, license, profit, or other interest in the land, is guilty of an infraction punishable by a fine not to exceed five hundred dollars ($500), provided that the interest to be exercised has been duly recorded with the county recorder's office. This section shall not apply to the following persons: (1) any person engaged in lawful labor union activities that are permitted to be carried out by state or federal law; or (2) any person who is engaging in activities protected by the California Constitution or the United States Constitution. *(AD '98)*

TERRORIST THREATS

422. Threats to Commit Crime Resulting in Death or Great Bodily Injury

Any person who willfully threatens to commit a crime which will result in death or great bodily injury to another person, with the specific intent that the statement, made verbally, in writing, or by means of an electronic communication device, is to be taken as a threat, even if there is no intent of actually carrying it out, which, on its face and under the circumstances in which it is made, is so unequivocal, unconditional, immediate, and specific as to convey to the person threatened, a gravity of purpose and an immediate prospect of execution of the threat, and thereby causes that person reasonably to be in sustained fear for his or her own safety or for his or her immediate family's safety, shall be punished by imprisonment in the county jail not to exceed one year, or by imprisonment in the state prison.

For the purposes of this section, "immediate family" means any spouse, whether by marriage or not, parent, child, any person related by consanguinity or affinity within the second degree, or any other person who regularly resides in the household, or who, within the prior six months, regularly resided in the household.

"Electronic communication device" includes, but is not limited to, telephones, cellular telephones, computers, video recorders, fax machines, or pagers. "Electronic communication" has the same meaning as the term defined in Subsection 12 of Section 2510 of Title 18 of the United States Code. *(AM '98)*

CIVIL RIGHTS

422.6. Civil Rights; Interfere With, Property Damage or Speech

(a) No person, whether or not acting under color of law, shall by force or threat of force, willfully injure, intimidate, interfere with, oppress, or threaten any other person in the free exercise or enjoyment of any right or privilege secured to him or her by the Constitution or laws of this state or by the Constitution or laws of the United States because of the other person's race, color, religion, ancestry, national origin, disability, gender, or sexual orientation, or because he or she perceives that the other person has one or more of those characteristics.

(b) No person, whether or not acting under color of law, shall knowingly deface, damage, or destroy the real or personal property of any other person for the purpose of intimidating or interfering with the free exercise or enjoyment of any right or privilege secured to the other person by the Constitution or laws of this state or by the Constitution or laws of the United States, because of the other person's race, color, religion, ancestry, national origin, disability, gender, or sexual orientation, or because he or she perceives that the other person has one or more of those characteristics.

(c) Any person convicted of violating subdivision (a) or (b) shall be punished by imprisonment in a county jail not to exceed one year, or by a fine not to exceed five thousand dollars ($5,000), or by both that imprisonment and fine, and the court shall order the defendant to perform a minimum of community service, not to exceed 400 hours, to be performed over a period not to exceed 350 days, during a time other than his or her hours of employment or school attendance. However, no person shall be convicted of violating subdivision (a) based upon speech alone, except upon a showing that the speech itself threatened violence against a specific person or group of persons and that the defendant had the apparent ability to carry out the threat. *(AM '98)*

CRIMES AGAINST PROPERTY

450. Definition of Terms - Arson Related Crimes

In this chapter, the following terms have the following meanings:

(a) "Structure" means any building, or commercial or public tent, bridge, tunnel, or power-plant.

(b) "Forest land" means any brush covered land, cut-over land, forest, grasslands, or woods.

(c) "Property" means real property or personal property, other than a structure or forest land.

(d) "Inhabited" means currently being used for dwelling purposes whether occupied or not. "Inhabited structure" and "inhabited property" do not include the real property on which an inhabited structure or an inhabited property is located.

(e) "Maliciously"imports a wish to vex, defraud, annoy, or injure another person, or an intent to do a wrongful act, established either by proof or presumption of law.

(f) "Recklessly"means a person is aware of and consciously disregards a substantial and unjustifiable risk that his or her act will set fire to, burn, or cause to burn a structure, forest land, or property. The risk shall be of such nature and degree that disregard thereof constitutes a gross deviation from the standard of conduct that a reasonable person would observe in the situation. A person who creates such a risk but is unaware thereof solely by reason of voluntary intoxication also acts recklessly with respect thereto.

451. Arson

A person is guilty of arson when he or she willfully and maliciously sets fire to or burns or causes to be burned or who aids, counsels, or procures the burning of, any structure, forest land, or property.

(a) Arson that causes great bodily injury is a felony punishable by imprisonment in the state prison for five, seven, or nine years.

(b) Arson that causes an inhabited structure or inhabited property to burn is a felony punishable by imprisonment in the state prison for three, five, or eight years.

(c) Arson of a structure or forest land is a felony punishable by imprisonment in the state prison for two, four, or six years.

(d) Arson of property is a felony punishable by imprisonment in the state prison for 16 months, two, or three years. For purposes of this paragraph, arson of property does not include one burning or causing to be burned his or her own personal property unless there is an intent to defraud or there is injury to another person or another person's structure, forest land, or property.

(e) In the case of any person convicted of violating this section while confined in a state prison, prison road camp, prison forestry camp, or other prison camp or prison farm, or while confined in a county jail while serving a term of imprisonment for a felony or misdemeanor conviction, any sentence imposed shall be consecutive to the sentence for which the person was then confined.

451.5 Aggravated Arson

(a) Any person who willfully, maliciously, deliberately, with premeditation, and with intent to cause injury to one or more persons or to cause damage to property under circumstances likely to produce injury to one or more persons or to cause damage to one or more structures or inhabited dwellings, sets fire to, burns, or causes to be burned, or aids, counsels, or procures the burning of any residence, structure, forest land, or property is guilty of aggravated arson if one or more of the following aggravating factors exists:

(1) The defendant has been previously convicted of arson on one or more occasions within the past 10 years.

(2)(A) The fire caused property damage and other losses in excess of five million dollars ($5,000,000).

(B) In calculating the total amount of property damage and other losses under subparagraph (A), the court shall consider the cost of fire suppression. It is the intent of the Legislature that this paragraph be reviewed within five years to consider the effects of inflation on the dollar amount stated herein. For that reason, this paragraph shall remain in effect only until January 1, 2005, and as of that date is repealed, unless a later enacted statute, which is enacted before January 1, 2005, deletes or extends that date.

(3) The fire caused damage to, or the destruction of, five or more inhabited structures.

(b) Any person who is convicted under subdivision (a) shall be punished by imprisonment in the state prison for 10 years to life.

(c) Any person who is sentenced under subdivision (b) shall not be eligible for release on parole until 10 calendar years have elapsed. *(AM '99)*

452. Unlawfully Causing a Fire

A person is guilty of unlawfully causing a fire when he recklessly sets fire to or burns or causes to be burned, any structure, forest land or property.

(a) Unlawfully causing a fire that causes great bodily injury is a felony punishable by imprisonment in the state prison for two, four or six years, or by imprisonment in the county jail for not more than one year, or by a fine, or by both such imprisonment and fine.

(b) Unlawfully causing a fire that causes an inhabited structure or inhabited property to burn is a felony punishable by imprisonment in the state prison for two, three or four years, or by imprisonment in the county jail for not more than one year, or by a fine, or by both such imprisonment and fine.

(c) Unlawfully causing a fire of a structure or forest land is a felony punishable by imprisonment in the state prison for 16 months, two or three years, or by imprisonment in the county jail for not more than six months, or by a fine, or by both such imprisonment and fine.

(d) Unlawfully causing a fire of property is a misdemeanor. For purposes of this paragraph, unlawfully causing a fire of property does not include one burning or causing to be burned his own personal property unless there is injury to another person or to another person's structure, forest land or property.

(e) In the case of any person convicted of violating this section while confined in a state prison, prison road camp, prison forestry camp, or other prison camp or prison farm, or while confined in a county jail while serving a term of imprisonment for a felony or misdemeanor conviction, any sentence imposed shall be consecutive to the sentence for which the person was then confined.

453. Possession or Manufacture of Combustible or Explosive Material or Fire Bomb

(a) Every person who possesses, manufactures, or disposes of any flammable, or combustible material or substance, or any incendiary device in an arrangement or preparation, with intent to willfully and maliciously use this material, substance, or device to set fire to or burn any structure, forest land, or property, shall be punished by imprisonment in the state prison, or in a county jail, not exceeding one year.

(b) For the purposes of this section:

(1) "Disposes of" means to give, give away, loan, offer, offer for sale, sell, or transfer.

(2) "Incendiary device" means a device that is constructed or designed to start an incendiary fire by remote, delayed, or instant means, but no device commercially manufactured primarily for the purpose of illumination shall be deemed to be an incendiary device for the purposes of this section.

(3) "Incendiary fire" means a fire that is deliberately ignited under circumstances in which a person knows that the fire should not be ignited.

(c) Subdivision (a) does not prohibit the authorized use or possession of any material, substance or device described therein by a member of the armed forces of the United States or by firemen, police officers, peace officers, or law enforcement officers authorized by the properly constituted authorities; nor does that subdivision prohibit the use or possession of any material, substance or device described therein when used solely for scientific research or educational purposes, or for disposal of brush under permit as provided for in Section 4494 of the Public Resources Code, or for any other lawful burning. Subdivision (a) does not prohibit the manufacture or disposal of an incendiary device for the parties or purposes described in this subdivision.

454. Arson or Unlawful Burning Within Area of Insurrection or Emergency

(a) Every person who violates Section 451 or 452 during and within an area of any of the following, when proclaimed by the Governor, shall be punished by imprisonment in the state prison, as specified in subdivision (b):

(1) A state of insurrection pursuant to Section 143 of the Military and Veterans Code.

(2) A state of emergency pursuant to Section 8625 of the Government Code.

(b) Any person who is described in subdivision (a) and who violates subdivision (a), (b), or (c) of Section 451 shall be punished by imprisonment in the state prison for five, seven, or nine years. All other persons who are described in subdivision (a) shall be punished by imprisonment in the state prison for three, five, or seven years.

(c) Probation shall not be granted to any person who is convicted of violating this section, except in unusual cases where the interest of justice would best be served.

452. Unlawfully Causing a Fire

A person is guilty of unlawfully causing a fire when he recklessly sets fire to or burns or causes to be burned, any structure, forest land or property.

(a) Unlawfully causing a fire that causes great bodily injury is a felony punishable by imprisonment in the state prison for two, four or six years, or by imprisonment in the county jail for not more than one year, or by a fine, or by both such imprisonment and fine.

(b) Unlawfully causing a fire that causes an inhabited structure or inhabited property to burn is a felony punishable by imprisonment in the state prison for two, three or four years, or by imprisonment in the county jail for not more than one year, or by a fine, or by both such imprisonment and fine.

(c) Unlawfully causing a fire of a structure or forest land is a felony punishable by imprisonment in the state prison for 16 months, two or three years, or by imprisonment in the county jail for not more than six months, or by a fine, or by both such imprisonment and fine.

(d) Unlawfully causing a fire of property is a misdemeanor. For purposes of this paragraph, unlawfully causing a fire of property does not include one burning or causing to be burned his own personal property unless there is injury to another person or to another person's structure, forest land or property.

(e) In the case of any person convicted of violating this section while confined in a state prison, prison road camp, prison forestry camp, or other prison camp or prison farm, or while confined in a county jail while serving a term of imprisonment for a felony or misdemeanor conviction, any sentence imposed shall be consecutive to the sentence for which the person was then confined.

455. Attempts to Burn

Any person who willfully and maliciously attempts to set fire to or attempts to burn or to aid, counsel or procure the burning of any structure, forest land or property, or who commits any act preliminary thereto, or if furtherance thereof, is punishable by imprisonment in the state prison for 16 months, two or three years.

The placing or distributing of any flammable, explosive or combustible material or substance, or any device in or about any structure, forest land or property in an arrangement or preparation with intent to eventually willfully and maliciously set fire to or burn same, or to procure the setting fire to or burning of the same shall, for the purposes of this act constitute an attempt to burn such structure, forest land or property.

457.1. Arson; Registration Required

(a) As used in this section, "arson"means a violation of Section 451, 451.5, or 453, and attempted arson, which includes, but is not limited to, a violation of Section 455.

(b)(1) Every person described in paragraph (2), (3), and (4), for the periods specified therein, shall, while residing in, or if the person has no residence, while located in California, be required to, within 14 days of coming into, or changing the person's residence or location within any city, county, city and county, or campus wherein the person temporarily resides, or if the person has no residence, is located:

(A) Register with the chief of police of the city where the person is residing, or if the person has no residence, where the person is located.

(B) Register with the sheriff of the county where the person is residing, or if the person has no residence, where the person is located in an unincorporated area or city that has no police department.

(C) In addition to (A) or (B) above, register with the chief of police of a campus of the University of California , the California State University, or community college where the person is residing, or if the person has no residence, where the person is located upon the campus or any of its facilities.

(2) Any person who, on or after November 30, 1994, is convicted in any court in this state of arson or attempted arson shall be required to register, in accordance with the provisions of this section, for the rest of his or her life.

(3) Any person who, having committed the offense of arson or attempted arson, and after having been adjudicated a ward of the juvenile court on or after January 1, 1993, is discharged or paroled from the Department of the Youth Authority shall be required to register, in accordance with the provisions of this section, until that person attains the age of 25 years, or until the person has his or her records sealed pursuant to Section 781 of the Welfare and Institutions Code, whichever comes first.

(4) Any person convicted of the offense of arson or attempted arson on or after January 1, 1985, through November 29, 1994, inclusive, in any court of this state, shall be required to register, in accor-

dance with the provisions of this section, for a period of five years commencing, in the case where the person was confined for the offense, from the date of their release from confinement, or in the case where the person was not confined for the offense, from the date of sentencing or discharge, if that person was ordered by the court at the time that person was sentenced to register as an arson offender. The law enforcement agencies shall make registration information available to the chief fire official of a legally organized fire department or fire protection district having local jurisdiction where the person resides.

(c) Any person required to register pursuant to this section who is discharged or paroled from a jail, prison, school, road camp, or other penal institution, or from the Department of the Youth Authority where he or she was confined because of the commission or attempted commission of arson, shall, prior to the discharge, parole, or release, be informed of his or her duty to register under this section by the official in charge of the place of confinement. The official shall require the person to read and sign the form as may be required by the Department of Justice, stating that the duty of the person to register under this section has been explained to him or her. The official in charge of the place of confinement shall obtain the address where the person expects to reside upon his or her discharge, parole, or release and shall report the address to the Department of Justice. The official in charge of the place of confinement shall give one copy of the form to the person, and shall, not later than 45 days prior to the scheduled release of the person, send one copy to the appropriate law enforcement agency having local jurisdiction where the person expects to reside upon his or her discharge, parole, or release; one copy to the prosecuting agency that prosecuted the person; one copy to the chief fire official of a legally organized fire department or fire protection district having local jurisdiction where the person expects to reside upon his or her discharge, parole, or release; and one copy to the Department of Justice. The official in charge of the place of confinement shall retain one copy. All forms shall be transmitted in time so as to be received by the local law enforcement agency and prosecuting agency 30 days prior to the discharge, parole, or release of the person.

(d) All records relating specifically to the registration in the custody of the Department of Justice, law enforcement agencies, and other agencies or public officials shall be destroyed when the person required to register under this subdivision for offenses adjudicated by a juvenile court attains the age of 25 years or has his or her records sealed under the procedures set forth in Section 781 of the Welfare and Institutions Code, whichever event occurs first. This subdivision shall not be construed to require the destruction of other criminal offender or juvenile records relating to the case that are maintained by the Department of Justice, law enforcement agencies, the juvenile court, or other agencies and public officials unless ordered by the court under Section 781 of the Welfare and Institutions Code.

(e) Any person who is required to register pursuant to this section who is released on probation or discharged upon payment of a fine shall, prior to the release or discharge, be informed of his or her duty to register under this section by the probation department of the county in which he or she has been convicted, and the probation officer shall require the person to read and sign the form as may be required by the Department of Justice, stating that the duty of the person to register under this section has been explained to him or her. The probation officer shall obtain the address where the person expects to reside upon his or her release or discharge and shall report within three days the address to the Department of Justice. The probation officer shall give one copy of the form to the person, and shall send one copy to the appropriate law enforcement agency having local jurisdiction where the person expects to reside upon his or her discharge or release, one copy to the prosecuting agency that prosecuted the person, one copy to the chief fire official of a legally organized fire department or fire protection district having local jurisdiction where the person expects to reside upon his or her discharge or release, and one copy to the Department of Justice. The probation officer shall also retain one copy.

(f) The registration shall consist of (1) a statement in writing signed by the person, giving the information as may be required by the Department of Justice, and (2) the fingerprints and photograph of the person. Within three days thereafter, the registering law enforcement agency shall electronically forward the statement, fingerprints, and photograph to the Department of Justice.

(g) If any person required to register by this section changes his or her residence address, he or she shall inform, in writing within 10 days, the law enforcement agency with whom he or she last registered of his or her new address. The law enforcement agency shall, within three days after receipt of the information, electronically forward it to the Department of Justice. The Department of Justice shall forward appropriate registration data to the law enforcement agency having local jurisdiction of the new place of residence.

(h) Any person required to register under this section who violates any of the provisions thereof is guilty of a misdemeanor. Any person who has been convicted of arson or attempted arson and who is required to register under this section who willfully violates any of the provisions thereof is guilty of a misdemeanor and shall be sentenced to serve a term of not less than 90 days nor more than one year in a county jail. In no event does the court have the power to absolve a person who willfully violates this section from the obligation of spending at least 90 days of confinement in a county jail and of completing probation of at least one year.

(i) Whenever any person is released on parole or probation and is required to register under this section but fails to do so within the time prescribed, the Board of Prison Terms, the Department of the Youth Authority, or the court, as the case may be, shall order the parole or probation of that person revoked.

(j) The statements, photographs, and fingerprints required by this section shall not be open to inspection by the public or by any person other than a regularly employed peace officer or other law enforcement officer.

(k) In any case in which a person who would be required to register pursuant to this section is to be temporarily sent outside the institution where he or she is confined on any assignment within a city or county, including, but not limited to, firefighting or disaster control, the local law enforcement agency having jurisdiction over the place or places where that assignment shall occur shall be notified within a reasonable time prior to removal from the institution. This subdivision shall not apply to any person temporarily released under guard from the institution where he or she is confined.

(l) Nothing in this section shall be construed to conflict with Section 1203.4 concerning termination of probation and release from penalties and disabilities of probation.

A person required to register under this section may initiate a proceeding under Chapter 3.5 (commencing with Section 4852.01) of Title 6 of Part 3 and, upon obtaining a certificate of rehabilitation, shall be relieved of any further duty to register under this section. This certificate shall not relieve the petitioner of the duty to register under this section for any offense subject to this section of which he or she is convicted in the future.

Any person who is required to register under this section due to a misdemeanor conviction shall be relieved of the requirement to register if that person is granted relief pursuant to Section 1203.4. *(AM '99)*

459. Burglary; "Inhabited" Defined

Every person who enters any house, room, apartment, tenement, shop, warehouse, store, mill, barn, stable, outhouse or other building, tent, vessel, as defined in Section 21 of the Harbors and Navigation Code, floating home, as defined in subdivision (d) of Section 18075.55 of the Health and Safety Code, railroad car, locked or sealed cargo container, whether or not mounted on a vehicle, trailer coach, as defined in Section 635 of the Vehicle Code, any house car, as defined in Section 362 of the Vehicle Code, inhabited camper, as defined in Section 243 of the Vehicle Code, vehicle as defined by the Vehicle Code, when the doors are locked, aircraft as defined by Section 21012 of the Public Utilities Code, or mine or any underground portion thereof, with intent to commit grand or petit larceny or any felony is guilty of burglary. As used in this chapter, "inhabited" means currently being used for dwelling purposes, whether occupied or not. A house, trailer, vessel designed for habitation, or portion of a building is currently being used for dwelling purposes if, at the time of the burglary, it was not occupied solely because a natural or other disaster caused the occupants to leave the premises.

460. Degrees of Burglary

(a) Every burglary of an inhabited dwelling house, vessel, as defined in the Harbors and Navigation Code, which is inhabited and designed for habitation, floating home, as defined in subdivision (d) of Section 18075.55 of the Health and Safety Code, or trailer coach as defined by the Vehicle Code, or the inhabited portion of any other building, is burglary of the first degree.

(b) All other kinds of burglary are of the second degree.

(c) This section shall not be construed to supersede or affect Section 464 of the Penal Code.

463. Burglary During State of Emergency

(a) Every person who violates Section 459, punishable as a second-degree burglary pursuant to subdivision 2 of Section 461, during and within an affected county in a "state of emergency"or a "local emergency"resulting from an earthquake, fire, flood, riot, or other natural or manmade disaster shall be guilty of the crime of looting, punishable by imprisonment in a county jail for one year or in the state prison. Any person convicted under this subdivision who is eligible for probation and who is granted probation shall, as a condition thereof, be confined in a county jail for at least 180 days, except that the court may, in the case where the interest of justice would best be served, reduce or eliminate that mandatory jail sentence, if the court specifies on the record and enters into the minutes the circumstances indicating that the interest of justice would best be served by that disposition. In addition to whatever custody is ordered, the court, in its discretion, may require any person granted probation following conviction under this subdivision to serve up to 240 hours of community service in any program deemed appropriate by the court, including any program created to rebuild the community.

For purposes of this section, the fact that the structure entered has been damaged by the earthquake, fire, flood, or other natural or manmade disaster shall not, in and of itself, preclude conviction.

(b) Every person who commits the crime of grand theft, as defined in Section 487, except grand theft of a firearm, during and within an affected county in a "state of emergency"or a "local emergency"resulting from an earthquake, fire, flood, riot, or other natural or unnatural disaster shall be guilty of the crime of looting, punishable by imprisonment in a county jail for one year or in the state prison. Every person who commits the crime of grand theft of a firearm, as defined in Section 487, during and within an affected county in a "state of emergency"or a "local emergency"resulting from an earthquake, fire, flood, riot, or other natural or unnatural disaster shall be guilty of the crime of looting, punishable by imprisonment in the state prison, as set forth in subdivision (a) of Section 489. Any person convicted under this subdivision who is eligible for probation and who is granted probation shall, as a condition thereof, be confined in a county jail for at least 180 days, except that the court may, in the case where the interest of justice would best be served, reduce or eliminate that mandatory jail sentence, if the court specifies on the record and enters into the minutes the circumstances indicating that the interest of justice would best be served by that disposition. In addition to whatever custody is ordered, the court, in its discretion, may require any person granted probation following conviction under this subdivision to serve up to 160 hours of community service in any program deemed appropriate by the court, including any program created to rebuild the community.

(c) Every person who commits the crime of petty theft, as defined in Section 488, during and within an affected county in a "state of emergency"or a "local emergency"resulting from an earthquake, fire, flood, riot, or other natural or manmade disaster shall be guilty of a misdemeanor, punishable by imprisonment in a county jail for six months. Any person convicted under this subdivision who is eligible for probation and who is granted probation shall, as a condition thereof, be confined in a county jail for at least 90 days, except that the court may, in the case where the interest of justice would best be served, reduce or eliminate that mandatory minimum jail sentence, if the court specifies on the record and enters into the minutes the circumstances indicating that the interest of justice would best be served by that disposition. In addition to whatever custody is ordered, the court, in its discretion, may require any person granted probation following conviction under this subdivision to serve up to 80 hours of community service in any program deemed appropriate by the court, including any program created to rebuild the community.

(d)(1) For purposes of this section, "state of emergency"means conditions which, by reason of their magnitude, are, or are likely to be, beyond the control of the services, personnel, equipment, and facilities of any single county, city and county, or city and require the combined forces of a mutual aid region or regions to combat.

(2) For purposes of this section, "local emergency"means conditions which, by reason of their magnitude, are, or are likely to be, beyond the control of the services, personnel, equipment, and facilities of any

single county, city and county, or city and require the combined forces of a mutual aid region or regions to combat.

(3) For purposes of this section, a "state of emergency"shall exist from the time of the proclamation of the condition of the emergency until terminated pursuant to Section 8629 of the Government Code. For purposes of this section only, a "local emergency"shall exist from the time of the proclamation of the condition of the emergency by the local governing body until terminated pursuant to Section 8630 of the Government Code.

(4) Consensual entry into a commercial structure with the intent to commit a violation of Section 470, 476, 476a, 484f, or 484g of the Penal Code, shall not be charged as a violation under this section.

464. Burglary by Acetylene Torch or Explosive

Any person who, with intent to commit crime, enters, either by day or by night, any building, whether inhabited or not, and opens or attempts to open any vault, safe, or other secure place by use of acetylene torch or electric arc, burning bar, thermal lance, oxygen lance, or any other similar device capable of burning through steel, concrete, or any other solid substance, or by use of nitroglycerine, dynamite, gunpowder, or any other explosive, is guilty of a felony and, upon conviction, shall be punished by imprisonment in the state prison for a term of three, five, or seven years.

466. Possession of Burglar Tools

Every person having upon him or her in his or her possession a picklock, crow, *** keybit, crowbar, screwdriver, *** vise grip pliers, water-pump pliers, *** slidehammer, slim jim, tension bar, lock pick gun, tubular lock pick, floor-safe door puller, master key, or other instrument or tool with intent feloniously to break or enter into any building, railroad car, aircraft, or vessel, trailer coach, or vehicle as defined in the Vehicle Code, or who shall knowingly make or alter, or shall attempt to make or alter, any key or other instrument named above *** so that the same will fit or open the lock of a building, railroad car, aircraft, *** vessel, trailer coach, or vehicle as defined in the Vehicle Code, without being requested *** to do so by some person having the right to open the same, or who shall make, alter, or repair any instrument or thing, knowing or having reason to believe that it is intended to be used in committing a misdemeanor or felony, is guilty of a misdemeanor. Any of the structures mentioned in Section 459 shall be deemed to be a building within the meaning of this section. *(AM '01)*

466.3. Vending Machine Theft - Possession of Tools to Open, Etc.

(a) Whoever possesses a key, tool, instrument, explosive, or device, or a drawing, print, or mold of a key, tool, instrument, explosive, or device, designed to open, break into, tamper with, or damage a coin-operated machine as defined in subdivision (b), with intent to commit a theft from such machine, is punishable by imprisonment in the county jail for not more than one year, or by fine of not more than one thousand dollars ($1,000), or by both.

(b) As used in this section, the term "coin-operated machine"shall include any automatic vending machine or any part thereof, parking meter, coin telephone, coin laundry machine, coin dry cleaning machine, amusement machine, music machine, vending machine dispensing goods or services, or moneychanger.

466.5. Motor Vehicle Master Key - Motor Vehicle Wheel Lock Master Key

(a) Every person who, with the intent to use it in the commission of an unlawful act, possesses a motor vehicle master key or a motor vehicle wheel lock master key is guilty of a misdemeanor.

(b) Every person who, with the intent to use it in the commission of an unlawful act, uses a motor vehicle master key to open a lock or operate the ignition switch of any motor vehicle or uses a motor vehicle wheel lock master key to open a wheel lock on any motor vehicle is guilty of a misdemeanor.

(c) Every person who knowingly manufactures for sale, advertises for sale, offers for sale, or sells a motor vehicle master key or a motor vehicle wheel lock master key, except to persons who use such keys in their lawful occupations or businesses, is guilty of a misdemeanor.

(d) As used in this section:

(1) "Motor vehicle master key"means a key which will operate all the locks or ignition switches, or both the locks and ignition switches, in a given group of motor vehicle locks or motor vehicle ignition switches,

or both motor vehicle locks and motor vehicle ignition switches, each of which can be operated by a key which will not operate one or more of the other locks or ignition switches in such group.

(2) "Motor vehicle wheel lock"means a device attached to a motor vehicle wheel for theft protection purposes which can be removed only by a key unit unique to the wheel lock attached to a particular motor vehicle.

(3) "Motor vehicle wheel lock master key"means a key unit which will operate all the wheel locks in a given group of motor vehicle wheel locks, each of which can be operated by a key unit which will not operate any of the other wheel locks in the group.

466.6. Motor Vehicle Ignition Key Made Other Than by Duplication of Existing Key

(a) Any person who makes a key capable of operating the ignition of a motor vehicle or personal property registered under the Vehicle Code for another by any method other than by the duplication of an existing key, whether or not for compensation, shall obtain the name, address, telephone number, if any, date of birth, and driver's license number or identification number of the person requesting or purchasing the key; and the registration or identification number, license number, year, make, model, color, and vehicle identification number of the vehicle or personal property registered under the Vehicle Code for which the key is to be made. Such information, together with the date the key was made and the signature of the person for whom the key was made, shall be set forth on a work order. A copy of each such work order shall be retained for two years, shall include the name and permit number of the locksmith performing the service, and shall be open to inspection by any peace officer or by the Bureau of Collection and Investigative Services during business hours or submitted to the bureau upon request.

Any person who violates any provision of this subdivision is guilty of a misdemeanor.

(b) The provisions of this section shall include, but are not limited to, the making of a key from key codes or impressions.

(c) Nothing contained in this section shall be construed to prohibit the duplication of any key for a motor vehicle from another key.

466.7. Unlawful Possession of Key Made Other Than by Duplication

Every person who, with the intent to use it in the commission of an unlawful act, possesses a motor vehicle key with knowledge that such key was made without the consent of either the registered or legal owner of the motor vehicle or of a person who is in lawful possession of the motor vehicle, is guilty of a misdemeanor.

466.9. Possession of Code Grabbing Device

(a) Every person who possesses a code grabbing device, with the intent to use it in the commission of an unlawful act, is guilty of a misdemeanor.

(b) Every person who uses a code grabbing device to disarm the security alarm system of a motor vehicle, with the intent to use the device in the commission of an unlawful act, is guilty of a misdemeanor.

(c) As used in this section, "code grabbing device"means a device that can receive and record the coded signal sent by the transmitter of a motor vehicle security alarm system and can play back the signal to disarm that system.

468. Possession, Etc., of Sniperscope

Any person who knowingly buys, sells, receives, disposes of, conceals, or has in his possession a sniperscope shall be guilty of a misdemeanor, punishable by a fine not to exceed one thousand dollars ($1,000) or by imprisonment in the county jail for not more than one year, or by both such fine and imprisonment.

As used in this section, sniperscope means any attachment, device or similar contrivance designed for or adaptable to use on a firearm which, through the use of a projected infrared light source and electronic telescope, enables the operator thereof to visually determine and locate the presence of objects during the nighttime.

This section shall not prohibit the authorized use or possession of such sniperscope by a member of the armed forces of the United States or by police officers, peace officers, or law enforcement officers authorized by properly constituted authorities for the enforcement of law or ordinances; nor shall this section prohibit the use or possession of such sniperscope when used solely for scientific research or educational purposes.

470. Forgery

(a) Every person who, with the intent to defraud, knowing that he or she has no authority to do so, signs the name of another person or of a fictitious person to any of the items listed in subdivision (d) is guilty of forgery.

(b) Every person who, with the intent to defraud, counterfeits or forges the seal or handwriting of another is guilty of forgery.

(c) Every person who, with the intent to defraud, alters, corrupts, or falsifies any record of any will, codicil, conveyance, or other instrument, the record of which is by law evidence, or any record of any judgment of a court or the return of any officer to any process of any court, is guilty of forgery.

(d) Every person who, with the intent to defraud, falsely makes, alters, forges, or counterfeits, utters, publishes, passes or attempts or offers to pass, as true and genuine, any of the following items, knowing the same to be false, altered, forged, or counterfeited, is guilty of forgery: any check, bond, bank bill, or note, cashier's check, traveler's check, money order, post note, draft, any controller's warrant for the payment of money at the treasury, county order or warrant, or request for the payment of money, receipt for money or goods, bill of exchange, promissory note, order, or any assignment of any bond, writing obligatory, or other contract for money or other property, contract, due bill for payment of money or property, receipt for money or property, passage ticket, lottery ticket or share purporting to be issued under the California State Lottery Act of 1984, trading stamp, power of attorney, certificate of ownership or other document evidencing ownership of a vehicle or undocumented vessel, or any certificate of any share, right, or interest in the stock of any corporation or association, or the delivery of goods or chattels of any kind, or for the delivery of any instrument of writing, or acquittance, release or discharge of any debt, account, suit, action, demand, or any other thing, real or personal, or any transfer or assurance of money, certificate of shares of stock, goods, chattels, or other property whatever, or any letter of attorney, or other power to receive money, or to receive or transfer certificates of shares of stock or annuities, or to let, lease, dispose of, alien, or convey any goods, chattels, lands, or tenements, or other estate, real or personal; or any matter described in subdivision (b).

(e) Upon a trial for forging any bill or note purporting to be the bill or note of an incorporated company or bank, or for passing, or attempting to pass, or having in possession with intent to pass, any forged bill or note, it is not necessary to prove the incorporation of the bank or company by the charter or act of incorporation, but it may be proved by general reputation; and persons of skill are competent witnesses to prove that the bill or note is forged or counterfeited. *(RP, AD '98)*

470a. Forging Driver's License or Identification Card

Every person who alters, falsifies, forges, duplicates or in any manner reproduces or counterfeits any driver's license or identification card issued by a governmental agency with the intent that such driver's license or identification card be used to facilitate the commission of any forgery, is punishable by imprisonment in the state prison, or by imprisonment in the county jail for not more than one year.

470b. Possessing Forged Driver's License or Identification Card

Every person who displays or causes or permits to be displayed or has in his possession any driver's license or identification card of the type enumerated in Section 470a with the intent that such driver's license or identification card be used to facilitate the commission of any forgery, is punishable by imprisonment in the state prison, or by imprisonment in the county jail for not more than one year.

475. Possessing, Receiving or Uttering Forged Notes, Etc.

(a) Every person who possesses or receives, with the intent to pass or facilitate the passage or utterance of any forged, altered, or counterfeit items, or completed items contained in subdivision (d) of Section 470 with intent to defraud, knowing the same to be forged, altered, or counterfeit, is guilty of forgery.

(b) Every person who possesses any blank or unfinished check, note, bank bill, money order, or traveler's check, whether real or fictitious, with the intention of completing the same or the intention of facilitating the completion of the same, in order to defraud any person, is guilty of forgery.

(c) Every person who possesses any completed check, money order, traveler's check, warrant or county order, whether real or fictitious, with the intent to utter or pass or facilitate the utterance or passage of the same, in order to defraud any person, is guilty of forgery. *(RP, AD '98)*

475a. Possession or Passing Check, Money Order, or Warrant to Defraud [Repealed '98]

476. Making, Passing or Possessing Fictitious Bill, Note or Check

Every person who makes, passes, utters, or publishes, with intent to defraud any other person, or who, with the like intent, attempts to pass, utter, or publish, or who has in his or her possession, with like intent to utter, pass, or publish, any fictitious or altered bill, note, or check, purporting to be the bill, note, or check, or other instrument in writing for the payment of money or property of any real or fictitious financial institution as defined in Section 186.9 is guilty of forgery. *(RP, AD '98)*

476a. Making, Drawing or Passing Worthless Check, Draft or Order

(a) Any person who for himself or as the agent or representative of another or as an officer of a corporation, willfully, with intent to defraud, makes or draws or utters or delivers any check, or draft or order upon any bank or depositary, or person, or firm, or corporation, for the payment of money, knowing at the time of such making, drawing, uttering or delivering that the maker or drawer or the corporation has not sufficient funds in, or credit with said bank or depositary, or person, or firm, or corporation, for the payment of such check, draft, or order and all other checks, drafts, or orders upon such funds then outstanding, in full upon its presentation, although no express representation is made with reference thereto, is punishable by imprisonment in the county jail for not more than one year, or in the state prison.

(b) However, if the total amount of all such checks, drafts, or orders that the defendant is charged with and convicted of making, drawing, or uttering does not exceed two hundred dollars ($200), the offense is punishable only by imprisonment in the county jail for not more than one year, except that this subdivision shall not be applicable if the defendant has previously been convicted of a violation of Section 470, 475, or 476, or of this section, or of the crime of petty theft in a case in which defendant's offense was a violation also of Section 470, 475, or 476 or of this section or if the defendant has previously been convicted of any offense under the laws of any other state or of the United States which, if committed in this state, would have been punishable as a violation of Section 470, 475 or 476 or of this section or if he has been so convicted of the crime of petty theft in a case in which, if defendant's offense had been committed in this state, it would have been a violation also of Section 470, 475, or 476, or of this section.

(c) Where such check, draft, or order is protested, on the ground of insufficiency of funds or credit, the notice of protest thereof shall be admissible as proof of presentation, nonpayment and protest and shall be presumptive evidence of knowledge of insufficiency of funds or credit with such bank or depositary, or person, or firm, or corporation.

(d) In any prosecution under this section involving two or more checks, drafts, or orders, it shall constitute prima facie evidence of the identity of the drawer of a check, draft, or order if:

(1) At the time of the acceptance of such check, draft or order from the drawer by the payee there is obtained from the drawer the following information: name and residence of the drawer, business or mailing address, either a valid driver's license number or Department of Motor Vehicles identification card number, and the drawer's home or work phone number or place of employment. Such information may be recorded on the check, draft, or order itself or may be retained on file by the payee and referred to on the check, draft, or order by identifying number or other similar means; and

(2) The person receiving the check, draft, or order witnesses the drawer's signature or endorsement, and, as evidence of that, initials the check, draft, or order at the time of receipt.

(e) The word "credit" as used herein shall be construed to mean an arrangement or understanding with the bank or depositary or person or firm or corporation for the payment of such check, draft or order.

(f) If any of the preceding paragraphs, or parts thereof, shall be found unconstitutional or invalid, the remainder of this section shall not thereby be invalidated, but shall remain in full force and effect.

(g) A sheriff's department, police department, or other law enforcement agency may collect a fee from the defendant for investigation, collection, and processing of checks referred to their agency for investigation of alleged violations of this section or Section 476.

The amount of the fee shall not exceed twenty-five dollars ($25) for each bad check in addition to the amount of any bank charges incurred by the victim as a result of the alleged offense. If the sheriff's department, police department, or other law enforcement agency collects any fee for the bank charges incurred by the victim pursuant to this section, that fee shall be paid to the victim for any bank fees the victim may have been assessed. In no event shall reimbursement of the bank charge to the victim pursuant to this section exceed ten dollars ($10) per check.

481.1. Counterfeiting or Altering Public Transportation Fare Media

(a) Every person who counterfeits, forges, or alters any fare media designed to entitle the holder to a ride on vehicles of a public transportation system, as defined by Section 99211 of the Public Utilities Code, or on vehicles operated by entities subsidized by the Department of Transportation is punishable by imprisonment in *** a county jail, not exceeding one year, or in the state prison.

(b) Every person who knowingly possesses any counterfeit, forged, or altered fare media designed to entitle the holder to a ride on vehicles of a public transportation system, as defined by Section 99211 of the Public Utilities Code, or on vehicles operated by entities subsidized by the Department of Transportation, or who utters, publishes, or puts into circulation any fare media with intent to defraud is punishable by imprisonment in *** a county jail not exceeding one year, or by a fine not exceeding one thousand dollars ($1,000), or by both that imprisonment and fine. *(AM '01)*

483.5. Deceptive Identification Document - Manufacture, Sale, etc.

(a) No deceptive identification document shall be manufactured, sold, offered for sale, furnished, offered to be furnished, transported, offered to be transported, or imported or offered to be imported into this state unless there is diagonally across the face of the document, in not less than 14-point type and printed conspicuously on the document in permanent ink, the following statement: NOT A GOVERNMENT DOCUMENT and, also printed conspicuously on the document, the name of the manufacturer.

(b) As used in this section, "deceptive identification document" means any document not issued by a governmental agency of this state, another state, or the federal government, which purports to be, or which might deceive an ordinary reasonable person into believing that it is, a document issued by such an agency, including, but not limited to, a driver's license, identification card, birth certificate, passport, or social security card.

(c) Any person who violates or proposes to violate this section may be enjoined by any court of competent jurisdiction. Actions for injunction under this section may be prosecuted by the Attorney General or any district attorney in this state in the name of the people of the State of California upon their own complaint or upon the complaint of any person.

(d) Any person who violates the provisions of subdivision (a) who knows or reasonably should know that the deceptive identification document will be used for fraudulent purposes is guilty of a crime, and upon conviction therefor, shall be punished by imprisonment in the county jail not to exceed one year, or by imprisonment in the state prison.

484. Theft Defined

(a) Every person who shall feloniously steal, take, carry, lead, or drive away the personal property of another, or who shall fraudulently appropriate property which has been entrusted to him or her, or who shall knowingly and designedly, by any false or fraudulent representation or pretense, defraud any other person of money, labor or real or personal property, or who causes or procures others to report falsely of his or her wealth or mercantile character and by thus imposing upon any person, obtains credit and thereby fraudulently gets or obtains possession of money, or property or obtains the labor or service of another, is guilty of theft. In determining the value of the property obtained, for the purposes of this section, the reasonable and fair market value shall be the test, and in determining the value of services received the contract price shall be the test. If there be no contract price, the reasonable and going wage for the service rendered shall govern. For the purposes of this section, any false or fraudulent representation or pretense made shall be treated as continuing, so as to cover any money, property or service received as a result thereof, and the complaint, information or indictment may charge that the crime was committed on any date during the particular period in question. The hiring of any additional employee or employees without advising each of them of every labor claim due and unpaid and every judgment that the employer has been unable to meet shall be prima facie evidence of intent to defraud.

(b)(1) Except as provided in Section 10855 of the Vehicle Code, where a person has leased or rented the personal property of another person pursuant to a written contract, and that property has a value greater than one thousand dollars ($1,000) and is not a commonly used household item, intent to commit theft by fraud shall be rebuttably presumed if the person fails to return the personal property to its owner within 10 days after the owner has made written demand by certified or registered mail following the expiration of the lease or rental agreement for return of the property so leased or rented.

(2) Except as provided in Section 10855 of the Vehicle Code, where a person has leased or rented the personal property of another person pursuant to a written contract, and where the property has a value no greater than one thousand dollars ($1,000), or where the property is a commonly used household item, intent to commit theft by fraud shall be rebuttably presumed if the person fails to return the personal property to its owner within 20 days after the owner has made written demand by certified or registered mail following the expiration of the lease or rental agreement for return of the property so leased or rented.

(c) Notwithstanding the provisions of subdivision (b), if one presents with criminal intent identification which bears a false or fictitious name or address for the purpose of obtaining the lease or rental of the personal property of another, the presumption created herein shall apply upon the failure of the lessee to return the rental property at the expiration of the lease or rental agreement, and no written demand for the return of the leased or rented property shall be required.

(d) The presumptions created by subdivisions (b) and (c) are presumptions affecting the burden of producing evidence.

(e) Within 30 days after the lease or rental agreement has expired, the owner shall make written demand for return of the property so leased or rented. Notice addressed and mailed to the lessee or renter at the address given at the time of the making of the lease or rental agreement and to any other known address shall constitute proper demand. Where the owner fails to make such written demand the presumption created by subdivision (b) shall not apply. *(AM '00)*

484b. Diversion of Construction Funds

Any person who receives money for the purpose of obtaining or paying for services, labor, materials or equipment and willfully fails to apply such money for such purpose by either willfully failing to complete the improvements for which funds were provided or willfully failing to pay for services, labor, materials or equipment provided incident to such construction, and wrongfully diverts the funds to a use other than that for which the funds were received, shall be guilty of a public offense and shall be punishable by a fine not exceeding ten thousand dollars ($10,000), or by imprisonment in the state prison, or in the county jail not exceeding one year, or by both such fine and such imprisonment if the amount diverted is in excess of one thousand dollars ($1,000). If the amount diverted is less than one thousand dollars ($1,000), the person shall be guilty of a misdemeanor.

484c. Obtaining Construction Funds by False Voucher is Embezzlement

Any person who submits a false voucher to obtain construction loan funds and does not use the funds for the purpose for which the claim was submitted is guilty of embezzlement.

484d. Access Cards - Definition of Terms

As used in this section and Sections 484e to 484j, inclusive:

(1) "Cardholder"means any person to whom an access card is issued or any person who. has agreed with the card issuer to pay obligations arising from the issuance of an access card to another person.

(2) "Access card"means any card, plate, code, account number, or other means of account access that can be used, alone or in conjunction with another access card, to obtain money, goods, services, or any other thing of value, or that can be used to initiate a transfer of funds, other than a transfer originated solely by a paper instrument.

(3) "Expired access card"means an access card which shows on its face it has elapsed.

(4) "Card issuer"means any person who issues an access card or the agent of that person with respect to that card.

(5) "Retailer"means every person who is authorized by an issuer to furnish money, goods, services, or anything else of value upon presentation of an access card by a cardholder.

(6) An access card is "incomplete"if part of the matter other than the signature of the cardholder which an issuer requires to appear on the access card before it can be used by a cardholder has not been stamped, embossed, imprinted, or written on it.

(7) "Revoked access card"means an access card which is no longer authorized for use by the issuer, that authorization having been suspended or terminated and written notice thereof having been given to the cardholder.

(8) "Counterfeit access card"means any access card that is counterfeit, fictitious, altered, or forged, or any false representation or depiction of an access card or a component thereof.

(9) "Traffic"means to transfer or otherwise dispose of property to another, or to obtain control of property with intent to transfer or dispose of it to another.

(10) "Card making equipment"means any equipment, machine, plate, mechanism, impression, or other device designed, used, or intended to be used to produce an access card.

484e. Acquiring Access Cards Without Cardholder's or Issuer's Consent

(a) Every person who, with intent to defraud, sells, transfers, or conveys, an access card, without the cardholder's or issuer's consent, is guilty of grand theft.

(b) Every person, other than the issuer, who within any consecutive 12-month period, acquires access cards issued in the names of four or more persons which he or she has reason to know were taken or retained under circumstances which constitute a violation of subdivision (a), (c), or (d) is guilty of grand theft.

(c) Every person who, with the intent to defraud, acquires or retains possession of an access card without the cardholder's or issuer's consent, with intent to use, sell, or transfer it to a person other than the cardholder or issuer is guilty of petty theft.

(d) Every person who acquires or retains possession of access card account information with respect to an access card validly issued to another person, without the cardholder's or issuer's consent, with the intent to use it fraudulently, is guilty of grand theft. *(RP, AD '98)*

484f. Forging Access Card or Cardholder's Signature

(a) Every person who, with the intent to defraud, designs, makes, alters, or embosses a counterfeit access card or utters or otherwise attempts to use a counterfeit access card is guilty of forgery.

(b) A person other than the cardholder or a person authorized by him or her who, with the intent to defraud, signs the name of another or of a fictitious person to an access card, sales slip, sales draft, or instrument for the payment of money which evidences an access card transaction, is guilty of forgery. *(RP, AD '98)*

484g. Using Access Card Obtained Without Consent of Cardholder or Issuer

Every person who, with the intent to defraud, (a) uses, for the purpose of obtaining money, goods, services, or anything else of value, an access card or access card account information that has been altered, obtained, or retained in violation of Section 484e or 484f, or an access card which he or she knows is forged, expired, or revoked, or (b) obtains money, goods, services, or anything else of value by representing without the consent of the cardholder that he or she is the holder of an access card and the card has not in fact been issued, is guilty of theft. If the value of all money, goods, services, and other things of value obtained in violation of this section exceeds four hundred dollars ($400) in any consecutive six-month period, then the same shall constitute grand theft. *(RP, AD '98)*

484h. Access Cards - Offenses by Merchant

Every retailer or other person who, with intent to defraud:

(a) Furnishes money, goods, services or anything else of value upon presentation of an access card obtained or retained in violation of Section 484e or an access card which he or she knows is a counterfeit access card or is forged, expired, or revoked, and who receives any payment therefor, is guilty of theft. If the payment received by the retailer or other person for all money, goods, services, and other things of value furnished in violation of this section exceeds four hundred dollars ($400) in any consecutive six-month period, then the same shall constitute grand theft.

(b) Presents for payment a sales slip or other evidence of an access card transaction, and receives payment therefor, without furnishing in the transaction money, goods, services, or anything else of value that is equal in value to the amount of the sales slip or other evidence of an access card transaction, is guilty of theft. If the difference between the value of all money, goods, services, and anything else of value actually furnished and the payment or payments received by the retailer or other person therefor upon presentation of a sales slip or other evidence of an access card transaction exceeds four hundred dollars ($400) in any consecutive six-month period, then the same shall constitute grand theft.

484i. Access Cards - Counterfeiting

(a) Every person who possesses an incomplete access card, with intent to complete it without the consent of the issuer, is guilty of a misdemeanor.

(b) Every person who, with the intent to defraud, makes, alters, varies, changes, or modifies access card account information on any part of an access card, including information encoded in a magnetic stripe or other medium on the access card not directly readable by the human eye, or who authorizes or consents to alteration, variance, change, or modification of access card account information by another, in a manner that causes transactions initiated by that access card to be charged or billed to a person other than the cardholder to whom the access card was issued, is guilty of forgery.

(c) Every person who designs, makes, possesses, or traffics in card making equipment or incomplete access cards with the intent that the equipment or cards be used to make counterfeit access cards, is punishable by imprisonment in a county jail for not more than one year, or by imprisonment in the state prison.
(RP, AD '98)

484j. Publishing Access Card Number or Code with Intent to Defraud

Any person who publishes the number or code of an existing, canceled, revoked, expired or nonexistent access card, personal identification number, computer password, access code, debit card number, bank account number, or the numbering or coding which is employed in the issuance of access cards, with the intent that it be used or with knowledge or reason to believe that it will be used to avoid the payment of any lawful charge, or with intent to defraud or aid another in defrauding, is guilty of a misdemeanor. As used in this section, "publishes" means the communication of information to any one or more persons, either orally, in person or by telephone, radio or television, or on a computer network or computer bulletin board, or in a writing of any kind, including without limitation a letter or memorandum, circular or handbill, newspaper or magazine article, or book.

484.1. Providing False Identity Information to Pawnbroker or Secondhand Dealer

(a) Any person who knowingly gives false information or provides false verification as to the person's true identity or as to the person's ownership interest in property or the person's authority to sell property in order to receive money or other valuable consideration from a pawnbroker or secondhand dealer and who receives money or other valuable consideration from the pawnbroker or secondhand dealer is guilty of theft.

(b) Upon conviction of the offense described in subdivision (a), the court may require, in addition to any sentence or fine imposed, that the defendant make restitution to the pawnbroker or secondhand dealer in an amount not exceeding the actual losses sustained pursuant to the provisions of subdivision (c) of Section 13967 of the Government Code, as operative on or before September 28, 1994, if the defendant is denied probation, or Section 1203.04, as operative on or before August 2, 1995, if the defendant is granted probation or Section 1202.4.

(c) Upon the setting of a court hearing date for sentencing of any person convicted under this section, the probation officer, if one is assigned, shall notify the pawnbroker or secondhand dealer or coin dealer of the time and place of the hearing.

485. Lost Property - Locate Owner

One who finds lost property under circumstances which give him knowledge of or means of inquiry as to the true owner, and who appropriates such property to his own use, or to the use of another person not entitled thereto, without first making reasonable and just efforts to find the owner and to restore the property to him, is guilty of theft.

487. Grand Theft

Grand theft is theft committed in any of the following cases:

(a) When the money, labor, or real or personal property taken is of a value exceeding four hundred dollars ($400), except as provided in subdivision (b).

(b) Notwithstanding subdivision (a), grand theft is committed in any of the following cases:

(1)(A) When domestic fowls, avocados, olives, citrus or deciduous fruits, other fruits, vegetables, nuts, artichokes, or other farm crops are taken of a value exceeding one hundred dollars ($100).

(B) For the purposes of establishing that the value of avocados or citrus fruit under this paragraph exceeds one hundred dollars ($100), that value may be shown by the presentation of credible evidence which establishes that on the day of the theft avocados or citrus fruit of the same variety and weight exceeded one hundred dollars ($100) in wholesale value.

(2) When fish, shellfish, mollusks, crustaceans, kelp, algae, or other aquacultural products are taken from a commercial or research operation which is producing that product, of a value exceeding one hundred dollars ($100).

(3) Where the money, labor, or real or personal property is taken by a servant, agent, or employee from his or her principal or employer and aggregates four hundred dollars ($400) or more in any 12 consecutive month period.

(c) When the property is taken from the person of another.

(d) When the property taken is an automobile, firearm, horse, mare, gelding, any bovine animal, any caprine animal, mule, jack, jenny, sheep, lamb, hog, sow, boar, gilt, barrow, or pig.

(e) This section shall become operative on January 1, 1997.

487a. Theft of Animal Carcass

(a) Every person who shall feloniously steal, take, transport or carry the carcass of any bovine, caprine, equine, ovine, or swine animal or of any mule, jack or jenny, which is the personal property of another, or who shall fraudulently appropriate such property which has been entrusted to him, is guilty of grand theft.

(b) Every person who shall feloniously steal, take, transport, or carry any portion of the carcass of any bovine, caprine, equine, ovine or swine animal or of any mule, jack, or jenny, which has been killed without the consent of the owner thereof, is guilty of grand theft.

487b. Conversion of Real Property by Severance - $100 or More

Every person who converts real estate of the value of one hundred dollars ($100) or more into personal property by severance from the realty of another, and with felonious intent to do so, steals, takes, and carries away such property is guilty of grand theft and is punishable by imprisonment in the state prison.

487c.   Conversion of Real Property by Severance - Less Than $100

Every person who converts real estate of the value of less than one hundred dollars ($100) into personal property by severance from the realty of another, and with felonious intent to do so steals, takes, and carries away such property is guilty of petty theft and is punishable by imprisonment in the county jail for not more than one year, or by a fine not exceeding one thousand dollars ($1,000), or by both such fine and imprisonment. *(AM '00)*

487d.   Theft of Gold Dust, Amalgam or Quicksilver

Every person who feloniously steals, takes, and carries away, or attempts to take, steal, and carry from any mining claim, tunnel, sluice, undercurrent, riffle box, or sulfurate machine, another's gold dust, amalgam, or quicksilver is guilty of grand theft and is punishable by imprisonment in the state prison.

487e.   Theft of Dogs - Value of $400 or More

Every person who feloniously steals, takes, or carries away a dog of another which is of a value exceeding four hundred dollars ($400) is guilty of grand theft.

487f.   Theft of Dogs - Value of $400 or Less

Every person who feloniously steals, takes, or carries away a dog of another which is of a value not exceeding four hundred dollars ($400) is guilty of petty theft.

487g.   Theft of Dogs for Research or Commercial Uses

Every person who steals or maliciously takes or carries away any animal of another for purposes of sale, medical research, slaughter, or other commercial use, or who knowingly, by any false representation or pretense, defrauds another person of any animal for purposes of sale, medical research, slaughter, or other commercial use is guilty of a public offense punishable by imprisonment in a county jail not exceeding one year or in the state prison.

488.   Petty Theft Defined

Theft in other cases is petty theft.

490.5.   Petty Theft of Merchandise From Merchant or Library Facility; Detention of Suspect

(a) Upon a first conviction for petty theft involving merchandise taken from a merchant's premises or a book or other library materials taken from a library facility, a person shall be punished by a mandatory fine of not less than fifty dollars ($50) and not more than one thousand dollars ($1,000) for each such violation; and may also be punished by imprisonment in the county jail, not exceeding six months, or both such fine and imprisonment.

(b) When an unemancipated minor's willful conduct would constitute petty theft involving merchandise taken from a merchant's premises or a book or other library materials taken from a library facility, any merchant or library facility who has been injured by that conduct may bring a civil action against the parent or legal guardian having control and custody of the minor. For the purposes of those actions the misconduct of the unemancipated minor shall be imputed to the parent or legal guardian having control and custody of the minor. The parent or legal guardian having control or custody of an unemancipated minor whose conduct violates this subdivision shall be jointly and severally liable with the minor to a merchant or to a library facility for damages of not less than fifty dollars ($50) nor more than five hundred dollars ($500), plus costs. In addition to the foregoing damages, the parent or legal guardian shall be jointly and severally liable with the minor to the merchant for the retail value of the merchandise if it is not recovered in merchantable condition or to a library facility for the fair market value of its book or other library materials. Recovery of these damages may be had in addition to, and is not limited by, any other provision of law which limits the liability of a parent or legal guardian for the tortious conduct of a minor. An action for recovery of damages, pursuant to this subdivision, may be brought in small claims court if the total damages do not exceed the jurisdictional limit of that court, or in any other appropriate court; however, total damages, including the value of the merchandise or book or other library materials, shall not exceed five hundred dollars ($500) for each action brought under this section.

The provisions of this subdivision are in addition to other civil remedies and do not limit merchants or other persons to elect to pursue other civil remedies, except that the provisions of Section 1714.1 of the Civil Code shall not apply herein.

(c) When an adult or emancipated minor has unlawfully taken merchandise from a merchant's premises, or a book or other library materials from a library facility, the adult or emancipated minor shall be liable to the merchant or library facility for damages of not less than fifty dollars ($50) nor more than five hundred dollars ($500), plus costs. In addition to the foregoing damages, the adult or emancipated minor shall be liable to the merchant for the retail value of the merchandise if it is not recovered in merchantable condition, or to a library facility for the fair market value of its book or other library materials. An action for recovery of damages, pursuant to this subdivision, may be brought in small claims court if the total damages do not exceed the jurisdictional limit of such court, or in any other appropriate court. The provisions of this subdivision are in addition to other civil remedies and do not limit merchants or other persons to elect to pursue other civil remedies.

(d) In lieu of the fines prescribed by subdivision (a), any person may be required to perform public services designated by the court, provided that in no event shall any such person be required to perform less than the number of hours of such public service necessary to satisfy the fine assessed by the court as provided by subdivision (a) at the minimum wage prevailing in the state at the time of sentencing.

(e) All fines collected under this section shall be collected and distributed in accordance with Sections 1463 and 1463.1 of the Penal Code; provided, however, that a county may, by a majority vote of the members of its board of supervisors, allocate any amount up to, but not exceeding 50 percent of such fines to the county superintendent of schools for allocation to local school districts. The fines allocated shall be administered by the county superintendent of schools to finance public school programs, which provide counseling or other educational services designed to discourage shoplifting, theft, and burglary. Subject to rules and regulations as may be adopted by the Superintendent of Public Instruction, each county superintendent of schools shall allocate such funds to school districts within the county which submit project applications designed to further the educational purposes of this section. The costs of administration of this section by each county superintendent of schools shall be paid from the funds allocated to the county superintendent of schools.

(f)(1) A merchant may detain a person for a reasonable time for the purpose of conducting an investigation in a reasonable manner whenever the merchant has probable cause to believe the person to be detained is attempting to unlawfully take or has unlawfully taken merchandise from the merchant's premises.

A person employed by a library facility may detain a person for a reasonable time for the purpose of conducting an investigation in a reasonable manner whenever the person employed by a library facility has probable cause to believe the person to be detained is attempting to unlawfully remove or has unlawfully removed books or library materials from the premises of the library facility.

(2) In making the detention a merchant or a person employed by a library facility may use a reasonable amount of nondeadly force necessary to protect himself or herself and to prevent escape of the person detained or the loss of property.

(3) During the period of detention any items which a merchant or any items which a person employed by a library facility has probable cause to believe are unlawfully taken from the premises of the merchant or library facility and which are in plain view may be examined by the merchant or person employed by a library facility for the purposes of ascertaining the ownership thereof.

(4) A merchant, a person employed by a library facility, or an agent thereof, having probable cause to believe the person detained was attempting to unlawfully take or has taken any item from the premises, may request the person detained to voluntarily surrender the item. Should the person detained refuse to surrender the item of which there is probable cause to believe has been unlawfully taken from the premises, or attempted to be unlawfully taken from the premises, a limited and reasonable search may be conducted by those authorized to make the detention in order to recover the item. Only packages, shopping bags, handbags or other property in the immediate possession of the person detained, but not including any clothing worn by the person, may be searched pursuant to this subdivision. Upon surrender or discovery of the item,

the person detained may also be requested, but may not be required, to provide adequate proof of his or her true identity.

(5) A peace officer who accepts custody of a person arrested for an offense contained in this section may, subsequent to the arrest, search the person arrested and his or her immediate possessions for any item or items alleged to have been taken.

(6) In any civil action brought by any person resulting from a detention or arrest by a merchant, it shall be a defense to such action that the merchant detaining or arresting such person had probable cause to believe that the person had stolen or attempted to steal merchandise and that the merchant acted reasonably under all the circumstances.

In any civil action brought by any person resulting from a detention or arrest by a person employed by a library facility, it shall be a defense to such action that the person employed by a library facility detaining or arresting such person had probable cause to believe that the person had stolen or attempted to steal books or library materials and that the person employed by a library facility acted reasonably under all the circumstances.

(g) As used in this section:

(1) "Merchandise" means any personal property, capable of manual delivery, displayed, held or offered for retail sale by a merchant.

(2) "Merchant" means an owner or operator, and the agent, consignee, employee, lessee, or officer of an owner or operator, of any premises used for the retail purchase or sale of any personal property capable of manual delivery.

(3) The terms "book or other library materials" include any book, plate, picture, photograph, engraving, painting, drawing, map, newspaper, magazine, pamphlet, broadside, manuscript, document, letter, public record, microform, sound recording, audiovisual material in any format, magnetic or other tape, electronic data-processing record, artifact, or other documentary, written or printed material regardless of physical form or characteristics, or any part thereof, belonging to, on loan to, or otherwise in the custody of a library facility.

(4) The term "library facility" includes any public library; any library of an educational, historical or eleemosynary institution, organization or society; any museum; any repository of public records.

(h) Any library facility shall post at its entrance and exit a conspicuous sign to read as follows:

"IN ORDER TO PREVENT THE THEFT OF BOOKS AND LIBRARY MATERIALS, STATE LAW AUTHORIZES THE DETENTION FOR A REASONABLE PERIOD OF ANY PERSON USING THESE FACILITIES SUSPECTED OF COMMITTING "LIBRARY THEFT" (PENAL CODE Section 490.5)."

491. Nature and Value of Dogs

Dogs are personal property, and their value is to be ascertained in the same manner as the value of other property.

496. Receiving Stolen Property

(a) Every person who buys or receives any property that has been stolen or that has been obtained in any manner constituting theft or extortion, knowing the property to be so stolen or obtained, or who conceals, sells, withholds, or aids in concealing, selling, or withholding any property from the owner, knowing the property to be so stolen or obtained, shall be punished by imprisonment in a state prison, or in a county jail for not more than one year. However, if the district attorney or the grand jury determines that this action would be in the interests of justice, the district attorney or the grand jury, as the case may be, may, if the value of the property does not exceed four hundred dollars ($400), specify in the accusatory pleading that the offense shall be a misdemeanor, punishable only by imprisonment in a county jail not exceeding one year.

A principal in the actual theft of the property may be convicted pursuant to this section. However, no person may be convicted both pursuant to this section and of the theft of the same property.

(b) Every swap meet vendor, as defined in Section 21661 of the Business and Professions Code, and every person whose principal business is dealing in, or collecting, merchandise or personal property, and every agent, employee, or representative of that person, who buys or receives any property of a value in excess of four hundred dollars ($400) that has been stolen or obtained in any manner constituting theft or extortion, under circumstances that should cause the person, agent, employee, or representative to make reasonable inquiry to ascertain that the person from whom the property was bought or received had the legal right to sell or deliver it, without making a reasonable inquiry, shall be punished by imprisonment in a state prison, or in a county jail for not more than one year.

Every swap meet vendor, as defined in Section 21661 of the Business and Professions Code, and every person whose principal business is dealing in, or collecting, merchandise or personal property, and every agent, employee, or representative of that person, who buys or receives any property of a value of four hundred dollars ($400) or less that has been stolen or obtained in any manner constituting theft or extortion, under circumstances that should cause the person, agent, employee, or representative to make reasonable inquiry to ascertain that the person from whom the property was bought or received had the legal right to sell or deliver it, without making a reasonable inquiry, shall be guilty of a misdemeanor.

(c) Any person who has been injured by a violation of subdivision (a) or (b) may bring an action for three times the amount of actual damages, if any, sustained by the plaintiff, costs of suit, and reasonable attorney's fees.

(d) Notwithstanding Section 664, any attempt to commit any act prohibited by this section, except an offense specified in the accusatory pleading as a misdemeanor, is punishable by imprisonment in the state prison, or in a county jail for not more than one year.

497. Bringing Goods Stolen in Another State into California

Every person who, in another state or country steals or embezzles the property of another, or receives such property knowing it to have been stolen or embezzled, and brings the same into this state, may be convicted and punished in the same manner as if such larceny, or embezzlement, or receiving, had been committed in this state.

498. Utility Services - Unauthorized Diversion, Tampering, Connection, Reconnection, or Use

(a) The following definitions govern the construction of this section:

(1) "Person"means any individual, or any partnership, firm, association, corporation, limited liability company, or other legal entity.

(2) "Utility"means any electrical, gas, or water corporation as those terms are defined in the Public Utilities Code, and electrical, gas, or water systems operated by any political subdivision.

(3) "Customer"means the person in whose name utility service is provided.

(4) "Utility service"means the provision of electricity, gas, water, or any other service provided by the utility for compensation.

(5) "Divert"means to change the intended course or path of electricity, gas, or water without the authorization or consent of the utility.

(6) "Tamper"means to rearrange, injure, alter, interfere with, or otherwise prevent from performing a normal or customary function.

(7) "Reconnection"means the reconnection of utility service by a customer or other person after service has been lawfully disconnected by the utility.

(b) Any person who, with intent to obtain for himself or herself utility services without paying the full lawful charge therefor, or with intent to enable another person to do so, or with intent to deprive any utility of any part of the full lawful charge for utility services it provides, commits, authorizes, solicits, aids, or abets any of the following shall be guilty of a misdemeanor:

(1) Diverts or causes to be diverted utility services, by any means whatsoever.

(2) Prevents any utility meter, or other device used in determining the charge for utility services, from accurately performing its measuring function by tampering or by any other means.

(3) Tampers with any property owned by or used by the utility to provide utility services.

(4) Makes or causes to be made any connection with or reconnection with property owned or used by the utility to provide utility services without the authorization or consent of the utility.

(5) Uses or receives the direct benefit of all or a portion of utility services with knowledge or reason to believe that the diversion, tampering, or unauthorized connection existed at the time of that use, or that the use or receipt was otherwise without the authorization or consent of the utility.

(c) In any prosecution under this section, the presence of any of the following objects, circumstances, or conditions on premises controlled by the customer or by the person using or receiving the direct benefit of all or a portion of utility services obtained in violation of this section shall permit an inference that the customer or person intended to and did violate this section:

(1) Any instrument, apparatus, or device primarily designed to be used to obtain utility services without paying the full lawful charge therefor.

(2) Any meter that has been altered, tampered with, or bypassed so as to cause no measurement or inaccurate measurement of utility services.

(d) If the value of all utility services obtained in violation of this section totals more than four hundred dollars ($400) or if the defendant has previously been convicted of an offense under this section or any former section which would be an offense under this section, or of an offense under the laws of another state or of the United States which would have been an offense under this section if committed in this state, then the violation is punishable by imprisonment in the county jail for not more than one year, or in the state prison.

(e) This section shall not be construed to preclude the applicability of any other provision of the criminal law of this state.

499b. Temporarily Taking Bicycle, Motorboat or Vessel

Any person who shall, without the permission of the owner thereof, take any bicycle or motorboat or vessel, for the purpose of temporarily using or operating the same, shall be deemed guilty of a misdemeanor, and upon conviction thereof, shall be punished by a fine not exceeding four hundred dollars ($400), or by imprisonment not exceeding three months, or by both that fine and imprisonment.

499c. Theft of Trade Secrets

(a) As used in this section:

(1) "Access" means to approach, a way or means of approaching, nearing, admittance to, including to instruct, communicate with, store information in, or retrieve information from a computer system or computer network.

(2) "Article" means any object, material, device, or substance or copy thereof, including any writing, record, recording, drawing, sample, specimen, prototype, model, photograph, micro-organism, blueprint, map, or tangible representation of a computer program or information, including both human and computer readable information and information while in transit.

(3) "Benefit" means gain or advantage, or anything regarded by the beneficiary as gain or advantage, including benefit to any other person or entity in whose welfare he or she is interested.

(4) "Computer system" means a machine or collection of machines, one or more of which contain computer programs and information, that performs functions, including, but not limited to, logic, arithmetic, information storage and retrieval, communications, and control.

(5) "Computer network" means an interconnection of two or more computer systems.

(6) "Computer program" means an ordered set of instructions or statements, and related information that, when automatically executed in actual or modified form in a computer system, causes it to perform specified functions.

(7) "Copy" means any facsimile, replica, photograph or other reproduction of an article, and any note, drawing or sketch made of or from an article.

(8) "Representing" means describing, depicting, containing, constituting, reflecting or recording.

(9) "Trade secret" means information, including a formula, pattern, compilation, program, device, method, technique, or process, that:

(A) Derives independent economic value, actual or potential, from not being generally known to the public or to other persons who can obtain economic value from its disclosure or use; and

(B) Is the subject of efforts that are reasonable under the circumstances to maintain its secrecy.

(b) Every person is guilty of theft who, with intent to deprive or withhold the control of a trade secret from its owner, or with an intent to appropriate a trade secret to his or her own use or to the use of another, does any of the following:

(1) Steals, takes, carries away, or uses without authorization, a trade secret.

(2) Fraudulently appropriates any article representing a trade secret entrusted to him or her.

(3) Having unlawfully obtained access to the article, without authority makes or causes to be made a copy of any article representing a trade secret.

(4) Having obtained access to the article through a relationship of trust and confidence, without authority and in breach of the obligations created by that relationship, makes or causes to be made, directly from and in the presence of the article, a copy of any article representing a trade secret.

(c) Every person who promises, offers or gives, or conspires to promise or offer to give, to any present or former agent, employee or servant of another, a benefit as an inducement, bribe or reward for conveying, delivering or otherwise making available an article representing a trade secret owned by his or her present or former principal, employer or master, to any person not authorized by the owner to receive or acquire the trade secret and every present or former agent, employee, or servant, who solicits, accepts, receives or takes a benefit as an inducement, bribe or reward for conveying, delivering or otherwise making available an article representing a trade secret owned by his or her present or former principal, employer or master, to any person not authorized by the owner to receive or acquire the trade secret, shall be punished by imprisonment in the state prison, or in a county jail not exceeding one year, or by a fine not exceeding five thousand dollars ($5,000), or by both that fine and imprisonment.

(d) In a prosecution for a violation of this section, it shall be no defense that the person returned or intended to return the article.

499d. Taking or Operating Aircraft Without Consent of Owner

Any person who operates or takes an aircraft not his own, without the consent of the owner thereof, and with intent to either permanently or temporarily deprive the owner thereof of his title to or possession of such vehicle, whether with or without intent to steal the same, or any person who is a party or accessory to or an accomplice in any operation or unauthorized taking or stealing is guilty of a felony, and upon conviction thereof shall be punished by imprisonment in the state prison, or in the county jail for not more than one year or by a fine of not more than ten thousand dollars ($10,000) or by both such fine and imprisonment.

502. Computer Related Crimes

(a) It is the intent of the Legislature in enacting this section to expand the degree of protection afforded to individuals, businesses, and governmental agencies from tampering, interference, damage, and unauthorized access to lawfully created computer data and computer systems. The Legislature finds and declares that the proliferation of computer technology has resulted in a concomitant proliferation of computer crime and other forms of unauthorized access to computers, computer systems, and computer data.

The Legislature further finds and declares that protection of the integrity of all types and forms of lawfully created computers, computer systems, and computer data is vital to the protection of the privacy of individuals as well as to the well-being of financial institutions, business concerns, governmental agencies, and others within this state that lawfully utilize those computers, computer systems, and data.

(b) For the purposes of this section, the following terms have the following meanings:

(1) "Access"means to gain entry to, instruct, or communicate with the logical, arithmetical, or memory function resources of a computer, computer system, or computer network.

(2) "Computer network"means any system that provides communications between one or more computer systems and input/output devices including, but not limited to, display terminals and printers connected by telecommunication facilities.

(3) "Computer program or software"means a set of instructions or statements, and related data, that when executed in actual or modified form, cause a computer, computer system, or computer network to perform specified functions.

(4) "Computer services"includes, but is not limited to, computer time, data processing, or storage functions, or other uses of a computer, computer system, or computer network.

(5) "Computer system"means a device or collection of devices, including support devices and excluding calculators that are not programmable and capable of being used in conjunction with external files, one or more of which contain computer programs, electronic instructions, input data, and output data, that performs functions including, but not limited to, logic, arithmetic, data storage and retrieval, communication, and control.

(6) "Data" means a representation of information, knowledge, facts, concepts, computer software, computer programs or instructions. Data may be in any form, in storage media, or as stored in the memory of the computer or in transit or presented on a display device.

(7) "Supporting documentation"includes, but is not limited to, all information, in any form, pertaining to the design, construction, classification, implementation, use, or modification of a computer, computer system, computer network, computer program, or computer software, which information is not generally available to the public and is necessary for the operation of a computer, computer system, computer network, computer program, or computer software.

(8) "Injury"means any alteration, deletion, damage, or destruction of a computer system, computer network, computer program, or data caused by the access, or the denial of access to legitimate users of a computer system, network, or program.

(9) "Victim expenditure"means any expenditure reasonably and necessarily incurred by the owner or lessee to verify that a computer system, computer network, computer program, or data was or was not altered, deleted, damaged, or destroyed by the access.

(10) "Computer contaminant" means any set of computer instructions that are designed to modify, damage, destroy, record, or transmit information within a computer, computer system, or computer network without the intent or permission of the owner of the information. They include, but are not limited to, a group of computer instructions commonly called viruses or worms, that are self-replicating or self-propagating and are designed to contaminate other computer programs or computer data, consume computer resources, modify, destroy, record, or transmit data, or in some other fashion usurp the normal operation of the computer, computer system, or computer network.

(11) "Internet domain name"means a globally unique, hierarchical reference to an Internet host or service, assigned through centralized Internet naming authorities, comprising a series of character strings separated by periods, with the rightmost character string specifying the top of the hierarchy.

(c) Except as provided in subdivision (h), any person who commits any of the following acts is guilty of a public offense:

(1) Knowingly accesses and without permission alters, damages, deletes, destroys, or otherwise uses any data, computer, computer system, or computer network in order to either (A) devise or execute any scheme or artifice to defraud, deceive, or extort, or (B) wrongfully control or obtain money, property, or data.

(2) Knowingly accesses and without permission takes, copies, or makes use of any data from a computer, computer system, or computer network, or takes or copies any supporting documentation, whether existing or residing internal or external to a computer, computer system, or computer network.

(3) Knowingly and without permission uses or causes to be used computer services.

(4) Knowingly accesses and without permission adds, alters, damages, deletes, or destroys any data, computer software, or computer programs which reside or exist internal or external to a computer, computer system, or computer network.

(5) Knowingly and without permission disrupts or causes the disruption of computer services or denies or causes the denial of computer services to an authorized user of a computer, computer system, or computer network.

(6) Knowingly and without permission provides or assists in providing a means of accessing a computer, computer system, or computer network in violation of this section.

(7) Knowingly and without permission accesses or causes to be accessed any computer, computer system, or computer network.

(8) Knowingly introduces any computer contaminant into any computer, computer system, or computer network.

(9) Knowingly and without permission uses the Internet domain name of another individual, corporation, or entity in connection with the sending of one or more electronic mail messages, and thereby damages or causes damage to a computer, computer system, or computer network.

(d)(1) Any person who violates any of the provisions of paragraph (1), (2), (4), or (5) of subdivision (c) is punishable by a fine not exceeding ten thousand dollars ($10,000), or by imprisonment in the state prison for 16 months, or two or three years, or by both that fine and imprisonment, or by a fine not exceeding five thousand dollars ($5,000), or by imprisonment in a county jail not exceeding one year, or by both that fine and imprisonment.

(2) Any person who violates paragraph (3) of subdivision (c) is punishable as follows:

(A) For the first violation that does not result in injury, and where the value of the computer services used does not exceed four hundred dollars ($400), by a fine not exceeding five thousand dollars ($5,000), or by imprisonment in a county jail not exceeding one year, or by both that fine and imprisonment.

(B) For any violation that results in a victim expenditure in an amount greater than five thousand dollars ($5,000) or in an injury, or if the value of the computer services used exceeds four hundred dollars ($400), or for any second or subsequent violation, by a fine not exceeding ten thousand dollars ($10,000), or by imprisonment in the state prison for 16 months, or two or three years, or by both that fine and imprisonment, or by a fine not exceeding five thousand dollars ($5,000), or by imprisonment in a county jail not exceeding one year, or by both that fine and imprisonment.

(3) Any person who violates paragraph (6) or (7) of subdivision (c) is punishable as follows:

(A) For a first violation that does not result in injury, an infraction punishable by a fine not exceeding one thousand dollars ($1,000).

(B) For any violation that results in a victim expenditure in an amount not greater than five thousand dollars ($5,000), or for a second or subsequent violation, by a fine not exceeding five thousand dollars ($5,000), or by imprisonment in a county jail not exceeding one year, or by both that fine and imprisonment.

(C) For any violation that results in a victim expenditure in an amount greater than five thousand dollars ($5,000), by a fine not exceeding ten thousand dollars ($10,000), or by imprisonment in the state prison for 16 months, or two or three years, or by both that fine and imprisonment, or by a fine not exceeding five thousand dollars ($5,000), or by imprisonment in a county jail not exceeding one year, or by both that fine and imprisonment.

(4) Any person who violates paragraph (8) of subdivision (c) is punishable as follows:

(A) For a first violation that does not result in injury, a misdemeanor punishable by a fine not exceeding five thousand dollars ($5,000), or by imprisonment in a county jail not exceeding one year, or by both that fine and imprisonment.

(B) For any violation that results in injury, or for a second or subsequent violation, by a fine not exceeding ten thousand dollars ($10,000), or by imprisonment in a county jail not exceeding one year, or in the state prison, or by both that fine and imprisonment.

(5) Any person who violates paragraph (9) of subdivision (c) is punishable as follows:

(A) For a first violation that does not result in injury, an infraction punishable by a fine not one thousand dollars.

(B) For any violation that results in injury, or for a second or subsequent violation, by a fine not exceeding five thousand dollars ($5,000), or by imprisonment in a county jail not exceeding one year, or by both that fine and imprisonment.

(e)(1) In addition to any other civil remedy available, the owner or lessee of the computer, computer system, computer network, computer program, or data who suffers damage or loss by reason of a violation of any of the provisions of subdivision (c) may bring a civil action against the violator for compensatory damages and injunctive relief or other equitable relief. Compensatory damages shall include any expenditure reasonably and necessarily incurred by the owner or lessee to verify that a computer system, computer network, computer program, or data was or was not altered, damaged, or deleted by the access. For the purposes of actions authorized by this subdivision, the conduct of an unemancipated minor shall be imputed to the parent or legal guardian having control or custody of the minor, pursuant to the provisions of Section 1714.1 of the Civil Code.

(2) In any action brought pursuant to this subdivision the court may award reasonable attorney's fees.

(3) A community college, state university, or academic institution accredited in this state is required to include computer-related crimes as a specific violation of college or university student conduct policies and regulations that may subject a student to disciplinary sanctions up to and including dismissal from the academic institution. This paragraph shall not apply to the University of California unless the Board of Regents adopts a resolution to that effect.

(4) In any action brought pursuant to this subdivision for a willful violation of the provisions of subdivision (c), where it is proved by clear and convincing evidence that a defendant has been guilty of oppression, fraud, or malice as defined in subdivision (c) of Section 3294 of the Civil Code, the court may additionally award punitive or exemplary damages.

(5) No action may be brought pursuant to this subdivision unless it is initiated within three years of the date of the act complained of, or the date of the discovery of the damage, whichever is later.

(f) This section shall not be construed to preclude the applicability of any other provision of the criminal law of this state which applies or may apply to any transaction, nor shall it make illegal any employee labor relations activities that are within the scope and protection of state or federal labor laws.

(g) Any computer, computer system, computer network, or any software or data, owned by the defendant, that is used during the commission of any public offense described in subdivision (c) or any computer, owned by the defendant, which is used as a repository for the storage of software or data illegally obtained in violation of subdivision (c) shall be subject to forfeiture, as specified in Section 502.01.

(h)(1) Subdivision (c) does not apply to punish any acts which are committed by a person within the scope of his or her lawful employment. For purposes of this section, a person acts within the scope of his or her employment when he or she performs acts which are reasonably necessary to the performance of his or her work assignment.

(2) Paragraph (3) of subdivision (c) does not apply to penalize any acts committed by a person acting outside of his or her lawful employment, provided that the employee's activities do not cause an injury, as defined in paragraph (8) of subdivision (b), to the employer or another, or provided that the value of supplies or computer services, as defined in paragraph (4) of subdivision (b), which are used does not exceed an accumulated total of one hundred dollars ($100).

(i) No activity exempted from prosecution under paragraph (2) of subdivision (h) which incidentally violates paragraph (2), (4), or (7) of subdivision (c) shall be prosecuted under those paragraphs.

(j) For purposes of bringing a civil or a criminal action under this section, a person who causes, by any means, the access of a computer, computer system, or computer network in one jurisdiction from another jurisdiction is deemed to have personally accessed the computer, computer system, or computer network in each jurisdiction.

(k) In determining the terms and conditions applicable to a person convicted of a violation of this section the court shall consider the following:

(1) The court shall consider prohibitions on access to and use of computers.

(2) Except as otherwise required by law, the court shall consider alternate sentencing, including community service, if the defendant shows remorse and recognition of the wrongdoing, and an inclination not to repeat the offense. *(AM '99, '00)*

502.7. Obtaining Telephone and Telegraph Service by Fraud

(a) Any person who, knowingly, willfully, and with intent to defraud a person providing telephone or telegraph service, avoids or attempts to avoid, or aids, abets or causes another to avoid the lawful charge, in whole or in part, for telephone or telegraph service by any of the following means is guilty of a misdemeanor or a felony, except as provided in subdivision (g):

(1) By charging the service to an existing telephone number or credit card number without the authority of the subscriber thereto or the lawful holder thereof.

(2) By charging the service to a nonexistent telephone number or credit card number, or to a number associated with telephone service which is suspended or terminated, or to a revoked or canceled (as distinguished from expired) credit card number, notice of the suspension, termination, revocation, or cancellation of the telephone service or credit card having been given to the subscriber thereto or the holder thereof.

(3) By use of a code, prearranged scheme, or other similar stratagem or device whereby the person, in effect, sends or receives information.

(4) By rearranging, tampering with, or making connection with telephone or telegraph facilities or equipment, whether physically, electrically, acoustically, inductively, or otherwise, or by using telephone or telegraph service with knowledge or reason to believe that the rearrangement, tampering, or connection existed at the time of the use.

(5) By using any other deception, false pretense, trick, scheme, device, conspiracy, or means, including the fraudulent use of false, altered, or stolen identification.

(b) Any person who does either of the following is guilty of a misdemeanor or a felony, except as provided in subdivision (g):

(1) Makes, possesses, sells, gives, or otherwise transfers to another, or offers or advertises any instrument, apparatus, or device with intent to use it or with knowledge or reason to believe it is intended to be used to avoid any lawful telephone or telegraph toll charge or to conceal the existence or place of origin or destination of any telephone or telegraph message.

(2) Sells, gives, or otherwise transfers to another or offers, or advertises plans or instructions for making or assembling any instrument, apparatus, or device described in paragraph (1) of this subdivision with knowledge or reason to believe that they may be used to make or assemble the instrument, apparatus, or device.

(c) Any person who publishes the number or code of an existing, canceled, revoked, expired, or nonexistent credit card, or the numbering or coding which is employed in the issuance of credit cards, with the intent that it be used or with knowledge or reason to believe that it will be used to avoid the payment of any lawful telephone or telegraph toll charge is guilty of a misdemeanor. Subdivision (g) shall not apply to this subdivision. As used in this section, "publishes" means the communication of information to any one or more persons, either orally, in person or by telephone, radio, or television, or electronic means, including, but not limited to, a bulletin board system, or in a writing of any kind, including without limitation a letter or memorandum, circular or handbill, newspaper, or magazine article, or book.

(d) Any person who is the issuee of a calling card, credit card, calling code, or other means or device for the legal use of telecommunications services and who receives anything of value for knowingly allowing another person to use the means or device in order to fraudulently obtain telecommunications services is guilty of a misdemeanor or a felony, except as provided in subdivision (g).

(e) Subdivision (a) applies when the telephone or telegraph communication involved either originates or terminates, or both originates and terminates, in this state, or when the charges for service would have been billable, in normal course, by a person providing telephone or telegraph service in this state, but for the fact that the charge for service was avoided, or attempted to be avoided, by one or more of the means set forth in subdivision (a).

(f) Jurisdiction of an offense under this section is in the jurisdictional territory where the telephone call or telegram involved in the offense originates or where it terminates, or the jurisdictional territory to which the bill for the service is sent or would have been sent but for the fact that the service was obtained or attempted to be obtained by one or more of the means set forth in subdivision (a).

(g) Theft of any telephone or telegraph services under this section by a person who has prior misdemeanor or felony conviction for theft of services under this section within the past five years, is a felony.

(h) Any person or telephone company defrauded by any acts prohibited under this section shall be entitled to restitution for the entire amount of the charges avoided from any person or persons convicted under this section.

(i) Any instrument, apparatus, device, plans, instructions, or written publication described in subdivision (b) or (c) may be seized under warrant or incident to a lawful arrest, and, upon the conviction of a person for a violation of subdivision (a), (b), or (c) the instrument, apparatus, device, plans, instructions, or written publication may be destroyed as contraband by the sheriff of the county in which the person was convicted or turned over to the person providing telephone or telegraph service in the territory in which it was seized.

(j) Any computer, computer system, computer network, or any software or data, owned by the defendant, which is used during the commission of any public offense described in this section or any computer, owned by the defendant, which is used as a repository for the storage of software or data illegally obtained in violation of this section shall be subject to forfeiture.

502.8. Use of Telecommunications Device to Avoid Payment of Charges; Possession of Device with Intent to Avoid Lawful Charges; Penalties

(a) Any person who knowingly advertises illegal telecommunications equipment is guilty of a misdemeanor.

(b) Any person who possesses or uses illegal telecommunications equipment intending to avoid the payment of any lawful charge for telecommunications service or to facilitate other criminal conduct is guilty of a misdemeanor.

(c) Any person found guilty of violating subdivision (b), who has previously been convicted of the same offense, shall be guilty of a felony, punishable by imprisonment in state prison, a fine of up to fifty thousand dollars ($50,000), or both.

(d) Any person who possesses illegal telecommunications equipment with intent to sell, transfer, or furnish or offer to sell, transfer, or furnish the equipment to another, intending to avoid the payment of any lawful charge for telecommunications service or to facilitate other criminal conduct is guilty of a misdemeanor punishable by one year in a county jail or imprisonment in state prison or a fine of up to ten thousand dollars ($10,000), or both.

(e) Any person who possesses 10 or more items of illegal telecommunications equipment with intent to sell or offer to sell the equipment to another, intending to avoid payment of any lawful charge for telecommunications service or to facilitate other criminal conduct, is guilty of a felony, punishable by imprisonment in state prison, a fine of up to fifty thousand dollars ($50,000), or both.

(f) Any person who manufactures 10 or more items of illegal telecommunications equipment with intent to sell or offer to sell the equipment to another, intending to avoid the payment of any lawful charge for telecommunications service or to facilitate other criminal conduct is guilty of a felony punishable by imprisonment in state prison or a fine of up to fifty thousand dollars ($50,000), or both.

(g) For purposes of this section, "illegal telecommunications equipment" means equipment that operates to evade the lawful charges for any telecommunications service; surreptitiously intercept electronic serial numbers or mobile identification numbers; alter electronic serial numbers; circumvent efforts to confirm legitimate access to a telecommunications account; conceal from any telecommunications service provider or lawful authority the existence, place of origin, or destination of any telecommunication; or otherwise facilitate any other criminal conduct. "Illegal telecommunications equipment" includes, but is not limited to, any unauthorized electronic serial number or mobile identification number, whether incorporated into a wireless telephone or other device or otherwise. Items specified in this paragraph shall be considered illegal telecommunications equipment notwithstanding any statement or disclaimer that the items are intended for educational, instructional, or similar purposes.

(h)(1) In the event that a person violates the provisions of this section with the intent to avoid the payment of any lawful charge for telecommunications service to a telecommunications service provider, the court shall order the person to pay restitution to the telecommunications service provider in an amount that is the greater of the following:

(A) Five thousand dollars ($5,000).

(B) Three times the amount of actual damages, if any, sustained by the telecommunications service provider, plus reasonable attorney fees.

(2) It is not a necessary prerequisite to an order of restitution under this section that the telecommunications service provider has suffered, or be threatened with, actual damages. *(AD '93; AM '97)*

503. Embezzlement Defined

Embezzlement is the fraudulent appropriation of property by a person to whom it has been intrusted.

518. Extortion Defined

Extortion is the obtaining of property from another, with his consent, or the obtaining of an official act of a public officer, induced by a wrongful use of force or fear, or under color of official right.

519. Fear Induced by Threat

Fear, such as will constitute extortion, may be induced by a threat, either:

1. To do an unlawful injury to the person or property of the individual threatened or of a third person; or,

2. To accuse the individual threatened, or any relative of his, or member of his family, of any crime; or,

3. To expose, or to impute to him or them any deformity, disgrace or crime; or,

4. To expose any secret affecting him or them.

523. Extortion - Written Threat Made

Every person who, with intent to extort any money or other property from another, sends or delivers to any person any letter or other writing, whether subscribed or not, expressing or implying, or adapted to imply, any threat such as is specified in section 519, is punishable in the same manner as if such money or property were actually obtained by means of such threat.

524. Extortion - Attempt or Threat

Every person who attempts, by means of any threat, such as is specified in Section 519 of this code, to extort money or other property from another is punishable by imprisonment in the county jail not longer than one year or in the state prison or by fine not exceeding ten thousand dollars ($10,000), or by both such fine and imprisonment.

529. Acts in Assumed Character

Every person who falsely personates another in either his private or official capacity, and in such assumed character either:

1. Becomes bail or surety for any party in any proceeding whatever, before any court or officer authorized to take such bail or surety;

2. Verifies, publishes, acknowledges, or proves, in the name of another person, any written instrument, with intent that the same may be recorded, delivered, or used as true; or,

3. Does any other act whereby, if done by the person falsely personated, he might, in any event, become liable to any suit or prosecution, or to pay any sum of money, or to incur any charge, forfeiture, or penalty, or whereby any benefit might accrue to the party personating, or to any other person; Is punishable by a fine not exceeding ten thousand dollars ($10,000), or by imprisonment in the state prison, or in a county jail not exceeding one year, or by both such fine and imprisonment.

529a. Manufacture, Sale, or Possession of False Birth or Baptismal Certificate

Every person who manufactures, produces, sells, offers, or transfers to another any document purporting to be either a certificate of birth or certificate of baptism, knowing such document to be false or counterfeit and with the intent to deceive, is guilty of a crime, and upon conviction therefor, shall be punished by imprisonment in the county jail not to exceed one year, or by imprisonment in the state prison. Every person who offers, displays, or has in his or her possession any false or counterfeit certificate of birth or certificate of baptism, or any genuine certificate of birth which describes a person then living or deceased, with intent to represent himself or herself as another or to conceal his or her true identity, is guilty of a crime, and upon conviction therefor, shall be punished by imprisonment in the county jail not to exceed one year.

529.5. Manufacture, Sale, or Transfer of Documents Purporting to Be Government Issued Identification Card or Driver's License.

(a) Every person who manufactures, sells, offers for sale, or transfers any document, not amounting to counterfeit, purporting to be a government-issued identification card or driver's license, which by virtue of the wording or appearance thereon could reasonably deceive an ordinary person into believing that it is issued by a government agency, and who knows that the document is not a government-issued document, is guilty of a misdemeanor, punishable by imprisonment in a county jail not exceeding one year, or by a fine not exceeding one thousand dollars ($1,000), or by both the fine and imprisonment.

(b) Any person who, having been convicted of a violation of subdivision (a), is subsequently convicted of a violation of subdivision (a), is punishable for the subsequent conviction by imprisonment in a county jail not exceeding one year, or by a fine not exceeding five thousand dollars ($5,000), or by both the fine and imprisonment.

(c) Any person who possesses a document described in subdivision (a) and who knows that the document is not a government-issued document is guilty of a misdemeanor punishable by a fine of not less than one thousand dollars ($1,000) and not more than two thousand five hundred dollars ($2,500). The misdemeanor fine shall be imposed except in unusual cases where the interests of justice would be served. The court may allow an offender to work off the fine by doing community service. If community service work is not available, the misdemeanor shall be punishable by a fine of up to one thousand dollars ($1,000), based on the person's ability to pay.

(d) If an offense specified in this section is committed by a person when he or she is under 21 years of age, but is 13 years of age or older, the court also may suspend the person's driving privilege for one year, pursuant to Section 13202.5 of the Vehicle Code.

530. Receiving Property in Assumed Character

Every person who falsely personates another, in either his private or official capacity, and in such assumed character receives any money or property, knowing that it is intended to be delivered to the individual so personated, with intent to convert the same to his own use, or to that of another person, or to deprive the true owner thereof, is punishable in the same manner and to the same extent as for larceny of the money or property so received.

530.5. Obtain or Use Personal Identifying Information without Authorization, Etc.

(a) Every person who willfully obtains personal identifying information, as defined in subdivision (b), of another person ***, and uses that information for any unlawful purpose, including to obtain, or attempt to obtain, credit, goods, services, or medical information in the name of the other person without the consent of that person, is guilty of a public offense, and upon conviction therefor, shall be punished either by imprisonment in a county jail not to exceed one year, a fine not to exceed one thousand dollars ($1,000), or both that imprisonment and fine, or by imprisonment in the state prison, a fine not to exceed ten thousand dollars ($10,000), or both that imprisonment and fine.

(b) "Personal identifying information,"as used in this section, means the name, address, telephone number, driver's license number, social security number, place of employment, employee identification number, mother's maiden name, demand deposit account number, savings account number, or credit card number of an individual person.

(c) In any case in which a person willfully obtains personal identifying information of another person without the authorization of that person, and uses that information to commit a crime in addition to a violation of subdivision (a), and is convicted of that crime, the court records shall reflect that the person whose identity was falsely used to commit the crime did not commit the crime. *(AM '01)*

532. Obtaining Property, Labor or Services by False Pretenses

(a) Every person who knowingly and designedly, by any false or fraudulent representation or pretense, defrauds any other person of money, labor, or property, whether real or personal, or who causes or procures others to report falsely of his wealth or mercantile character and by thus imposing upon any person obtains credit, and thereby fraudulently gets possession of money or property, or obtains the labor or service of another, is punishable in the same manner and to the same extent as for larceny of the money or property so obtained.

(b) Upon a trial for having, with an intent to cheat or defraud another designedly, by any false pretense, obtained the signature of any person to a written instrument, or having obtained from any person any labor, money, or property, whether real or personal, or valuable thing, the defendant cannot be convicted if the false pretense was expressed in language unaccompanied by a false token or writing, unless the pretense, or some note or memorandum thereof is in writing, subscribed by or in the handwriting of the defendant, or unless the pretense is proven by the testimony of two witnesses, or that of one witness and corroborating circumstances. This section does not apply to a prosecution for falsely representing or personating another, and, in that assumed character, marrying, or receiving any money or property.

537. Defrauding Innkeeper, Etc.

(a) Any person who obtains any food, fuel, services, or accommodations at a hotel, inn, restaurant, boardinghouse, lodginghouse, apartment house, bungalow court, motel, marina, marine facility, autocamp, ski area, or public or private campground, without paying therefor, with intent to defraud the proprietor or manager thereof, or who obtains credit at an hotel, inn, restaurant, boardinghouse, lodginghouse, apartment house, bungalow court, motel, marina, marine facility, autocamp, or public or private campground by the use of any false pretense, or who, after obtaining credit, food, fuel, services, or accommodations, at an hotel, inn, restaurant, boardinghouse, lodginghouse, apartment house, bungalow court, motel, marina, marine facility, autocamp, or public or private campground, absconds, or surreptitiously, or by force, menace, or threats, removes any part of his or her baggage therefrom with the intent not to pay for his or her food or accommodations is guilty of a public offense punishable as follows:

(1) If the value of the credit, food, fuel, services, or accommodations is four hundred dollars ($400) or less, by a fine not exceeding one thousand dollars ($1,000) or by imprisonment in the county jail for a term not exceeding six months, or both.

(2) If the value of the credit, food, fuel, services, or accommodations is greater than four hundred dollars ($400), by imprisonment in the county jail for a term of not more than one year, or in the state prison.

(b) Any person who uses or attempts to use ski area facilities for which payment is required without paying as required, or who resells a ski lift ticket to another when the resale is not authorized by the proprietor, is guilty of an infraction.

(c) Evidence that a person left the premises of such an hotel, inn, restaurant, boardinghouse, lodginghouse, apartment house, bungalow court, motel, marina, marine facility, autocamp, ski area, or public or private campground, without paying or offering to pay for such food, fuel, services, use of facilities, or accommodation, or that the person, without authorization from the proprietor, resold his or her ski lift ticket to another person after making use of such facilities, shall be prima facie evidence of the following:

(1) That the person obtained such food, fuel, services, use of facilities or accommodations with intent to defraud the proprietor or manager.

(2) That, if, after obtaining the credit, food, fuel, services, or accommodations, the person absconded, or surreptitiously, or by force, menace, or threats, removed part of his or her baggage therefrom, the person did so with the intent not to pay for the credit, food, fuel, services, or accommodations.

537b. Livery stables; Defrauding Proprietors or Abusing of Hired Animals

Any person who obtains any livery hire or other accommodation at any livery or feed stable, kept for profit, in this state, without paying therefor, with intent to defraud the proprietor or manager thereof; or who obtains credit at any such livery or feed stable by the use of any false pretense; or who after obtaining a horse, vehicle, or other property at such livery or feed stable, willfully or maliciously abuses the same by beating, goading, overdriving or other willful or malicious conduct, or who after obtaining such horse, vehicle, or other property, shall, with intent to defraud the owner, manager or proprietor of such livery or feed stable, keep the same for a longer period, or take the same to a greater distance than contracted for; or allow a feed bill or other charges to accumulate against such property, without paying therefor; or abandon or leave the same, is guilty of a misdemeanor.

537c. Livery stables; Unauthorized Use of Animals or Equipment

Every owner, manager, proprietor, or other person, having the management, charge or control of any livery stable, feed or boarding stable, and every person pasturing stock, who shall receive and take into his possession, charge, care or control, any horse, mare, or other animal, or any buggy, or other vehicle, belonging to any other person, to be by him kept, fed, or cared for, and who, while said horse, mare or other animal or buggy or other vehicle, is thus in his possession, charge, care or under his control, as aforesaid, shall drive, ride or use, or knowingly permit or allow any person other than the owner or other person entitled so to do, to drive, ride, or otherwise use the same, without the consent or permission of the owner thereof, or other person charged with the care, control or possession of such property, shall be guilty of a misdemeanor.

537e. Possession of Articles From Which Name Plates Removed

(a) Any person who knowingly buys, sells, receives, disposes of, conceals, or has in his or her possession any personal property from which the manufacturer's serial number, identification number, electronic serial number, or any other distinguishing number or identification mark has been removed, defaced, covered, altered, or destroyed, is guilty of a public offense, punishable as follows:

(1) If the value of the property does not exceed four hundred dollars ($400), by imprisonment in a county jail not exceeding six months.

(2) If the value of the property exceeds four hundred dollars ($400), by imprisonment in a county jail not exceeding one year.

(3) If the property is an integrated computer chip or panel of a value of four hundred dollars ($400) or more, by imprisonment in the state prison for 16 months, or 2 or 3 years or by imprisonment in a county jail not exceeding one year.

For purposes of this subdivision, "personal property" includes, but is not limited to, the following:

(1) Any television, radio, recorder, phonograph, telephone, piano, or any other musical instrument or sound equipment.

(2) Any washing machine, sewing machine, vacuum cleaner, or other household appliance or furnishings.

(3) Any typewriter, adding machine, dictaphone, or any other office equipment or furnishings.

(4) Any computer, printed circuit, integrated chip or panel, or other part of a computer.

(5) Any tool or similar device, including any technical or scientific equipment.

(6) Any bicycle, exercise equipment, or any other entertainment or recreational equipment.

(7) Any electrical or mechanical equipment, contrivance, material, or piece of apparatus or equipment.

(8) Any clock, watch, watch case, or watch movement.

(9) Any vehicle or vessel, or any component part thereof.

(b) When property described in subdivision (a) comes into the custody of a peace officer it shall become subject to the provision of Chapter 12 (commencing with Section 1407) of Title 10 of Part 2, relating to the disposal of stolen or embezzled property. Property subject to this section shall be considered stolen or embezzled property for the purposes of that chapter, and prior to being disposed of, shall have an identification mark imbedded or engraved in, or permanently affixed to it.

(c) This section does not apply to those cases or instances where any of the changes or alterations enumerated in subdivision (a) have been customarily made or done as an established practice in the ordinary and regular conduct of business, by the original manufacturer, or by his or her duly appointed direct representative, or under specific authorization from the original manufacturer.

537g. Alteration or Destruction of Owner Identification Number

(a) Unless otherwise provided by law, any person who knowingly removes, defaces, covers, alters or destroys a National Crime Information Center owner identification number from the personal property of another without permission is guilty of a misdemeanor punishable by a fine not to exceed four hundred dollars ($400), imprisonment in the county jail not to exceed one year, or both.

(b) This section shall not apply to any action taken by an authorized person to dispose of property pursuant to Article 1 of Chapter 4 of Title 6 of Part 4 of Division 3 of the Civil Code or pursuant to Chapter 12 of Title 10 of Part 2 of this code.

538d. Misrepresenting Oneself as a Peace Officer, Etc.

(a) Any person other than one who by law is given the authority of a peace officer, who willfully wears, exhibits, or uses the authorized uniform, insignia, emblem, device, label, certificate, card, or writing, of a peace officer, with the intent of fraudulently impersonating a peace officer, or of fraudulently inducing the belief that he or she is a peace officer, is guilty of a misdemeanor.

(b)(1) Any person, other than the one who by law is given the authority of a peace officer, who willfully wears, exhibits, or uses the badge of a peace officer with the intent of fraudulently impersonating a peace officer, or of fraudulently inducing the belief that he or she is a peace officer, is guilty of a misdemeanor punishable by imprisonment in a county jail not to exceed one year, by a fine not to exceed two thousand dollars ($2,000), or by both that imprisonment and fine.

(2) Any person who willfully wears or uses any badge that falsely purports to be authorized for the use of one who by law is given the authority of a peace officer, or which so resembles the authorized badge of a peace officer as would deceive any ordinary reasonable person into believing that it is authorized for the use of one who by law is given the authority of a peace officer, for the purpose of fraudulently impersonating a peace officer, or of fraudulently inducing the belief that he or she is a peace officer, is guilty of a misdemeanor punishable by imprisonment in a county jail not to exceed one year, by a fine not to exceed two thousand dollars ($2,000), or by both that imprisonment and fine.

(c) Any person who willfully wears, exhibits, or uses, or who willfully makes, sells, loans, gives, or transfers to another, any badge, insignia, emblem, device, or any label, certificate, card, or writing, which falsely purports to be authorized for the use of one who by law is given the authority of a peace officer, or which so resembles the authorized badge, insignia, emblem, device, label, certificate, card, or writing of a peace officer as would deceive an ordinary reasonable person into believing that it is authorized for the use of one who by law is given the authority of a peace officer, is guilty of a misdemeanor, except that any person who makes or sells any badge under the circumstances described in this subdivision is subject to a fine not to exceed fifteen thousand dollars ($15,000). *(AM '98, '00)*

538e. Fireman, Fraudulent Personation of

Any person, other than an officer or member of a fire department, who willfully wears, exhibits, or uses the authorized badge, insignia, emblem, device, label, certificate, card, or writing of an officer or member of a fire department or a deputy state fire marshal, with the intent of fraudulently personating an officer or member of a fire department or the Office of the State Fire Marshal, or of fraudulently inducing the belief that he is an officer or member of a fire department or the Office of the State Fire Marshal, is guilty of a misdemeanor.

Any person who willfully wears, exhibits, or uses any badge, insignia, emblem, device, or any label, certificate, card, or writing, which falsely purports to be for the use of an officer or member of a fire department or deputy state fire marshal, or which so resembles the authorized badge, insignia, emblem, device, label, certificate, card, or writing of an officer or member of a fire department as would deceive an ordinary reasonable person into believing that it is authorized for use by an officer or member of a fire department or a deputy state fire marshal, is guilty of a misdemeanor.

Any person who, for the purpose of selling, leasing or otherwise disposing of merchandise, supplies or equipment used in fire prevention or suppression, falsely represents, in any manner whatsoever, to any other person that he is a fire marshal, fire inspector or member of a fire department, or that he has the approval, endorsement or authorization of any fire marshal, fire inspector or fire department, or member thereof, is guilty of a misdemeanor.

538f. Public Utility Employee, False Representation as

Any person, other than an employee of a public utility or district as defined in Sections 216 and 11503 of the Public Utilities Code, respectively, who willfully presents himself or herself to a utility or district customer with the intent of fraudulently personating an employee of a public utility or district, or of fraudulently inducing the belief that he or she is an employee of a public utility or district, is guilty of a misdemeanor and shall be punished by imprisonment in a county jail not to exceed six months, or by a fine not to exceed one thousand dollars ($1,000), or by both that fine and imprisonment. Nothing in this section shall be construed to prohibit conduct that arguably constitutes protected activity under state labor law or the National Labor Relations Act (Title 29, United States Code, Section 151 and following).

548. Defrauding Insurer

(a) Every person who willfully injures, destroys, secretes, abandons, or disposes of any property which at the time is insured against loss or damage by theft, or embezzlement, or any casualty with intent to defraud or prejudice the insurer, whether the property is the property or in the possession of such person or any other person, is punishable by imprisonment in the state prison for two, three, or five years and by a fine not exceeding fifty thousand dollars ($50,000).

For purposes of this section, "casualty" does not include fire.

(b) Any person who violates subdivision (a) and who has a prior conviction of the offense set forth in that subdivision, in Section 550 of this code, or in former Section 556 or former Section 1871.1 of the Insurance Code, shall receive a two-year enhancement for each prior conviction in addition to the sentence provided under subdivision (a). The existence of any fact which would subject a person to a penalty enhancement shall be alleged in the information or indictment and either admitted by the defendant in open court, or found to be true by the jury trying the issue of guilt or by the court where guilt is established by plea of guilty or nolo contendere or by trial by the court sitting without a jury.

549. False Insurance Claim Pending; Solicit, Etc. Any Business

Any firm, corporation, partnership, or association, or any person acting in his or her individual capacity, or in his or her capacity as a public or private employee, who solicits, accepts, or refers any business to or from any individual or entity with the knowledge that, or with reckless disregard for whether, the individual or entity for or from whom the solicitation or referral is made, or the individual or entity who is solicited or referred, intends to violate Section 550 of this code or Section 1871.4 of the Insurance Code is guilty of a crime, punishable upon a first conviction by imprisonment in the county jail for not more than one year or by imprisonment in the state prison for 16 months, two years, or three years, or by a fine not exceeding fifty thousand dollars ($50,000), or by both that imprisonment and fine. A second or subsequent conviction is punishable by imprisonment in the state prison or by imprisonment in the state prison and a fine of fifty thousand dollars ($50,000). *(AM '00)*

550. False or Fraudulent Claims

(a) It is unlawful to do any of the following, or to aid, abet, solicit, or conspire with any person to do any of the following:

(1) Knowingly present or cause to be presented any false or fraudulent claim for the payment of a loss or injury, including payment of a loss or injury under a contract of insurance.

(2) Knowingly present multiple claims for the same loss or injury, including presentation of multiple claims to more than one insurer, with an intent to defraud.

(3) Knowingly cause or participate in a vehicular collision, or any other vehicular accident, for the purpose of presenting any false or fraudulent claim.

(4) Knowingly present a false or fraudulent claim for the payments of a loss for theft, destruction, damage, or conversion of a motor vehicle, a motor vehicle part, or contents of a motor vehicle.

(5) Knowingly prepare, make, or subscribe any writing, with the intent to present or use it, or to allow it to be presented, in support of any false or fraudulent claim.

(6) Knowingly make or cause to be made any false or fraudulent claim for payment of a health care benefit.

(7) Knowingly submit a claim for a health care benefit that was not used by, or on behalf of, the claimant.

(8) Knowingly present multiple claims for payment of the same health care benefit with an intent to defraud.

(9) Knowingly present for payment any undercharges for health care benefits on behalf of a specific claimant unless any known overcharges for health care benefits for that claimant are presented for reconciliation at that same time.

(10) For purposes of paragraphs (6) to (9), inclusive, a claim or a claim for payment of a health care benefit also means a claim or claim for payment submitted by or on the behalf of a provider of any workers' compensation health benefits under the Labor Code.

(b) It is unlawful to do, or to knowingly assist or conspire with any person to do, any of the following:

(1) Present or cause to be presented any written or oral statement as part of, or in support of or opposition to, a claim for payment or other benefit pursuant to an insurance policy, knowing that the statement contains any false or misleading information concerning any material fact.

(2) Prepare or make any written or oral statement that is intended to be presented to any insurer or any insurance claimant in connection with, or in support of or opposition to, any claim or payment or other benefit pursuant to an insurance policy, knowing that the statement contains any false or misleading information concerning any material fact.

(3) Conceal, or knowingly fail to disclose the occurrence of, an event that affects any person's initial or continued right or entitlement to any insurance benefit or payment, or the amount of any benefit or payment to which the person is entitled.

(4) Prepare or make any written or oral statement, intended to be presented to any insurer or producer for the purpose of obtaining a motor vehicle insurance policy, that the person to be the insured resides or is domiciled in this state when, in fact, that person resides or is domiciled in a state other than this state.

(c)(1) Every person who violates paragraph (1), (2), (3), (4), or (5) of subdivision (a) is guilty of a felony punishable by imprisonment in the state prison for two, three, or five years, and by a fine not exceeding fifty thousand dollars ($50,000), unless the value of the fraud exceeds fifty thousand dollars ($50,000), in which event the fine may not exceed double of the value of the fraud.

(2) Every person who violates paragraph (6), (7), (8), or (9) of subdivision (a) is guilty of a public offense.

(A) Where the claim or amount at issue exceeds four hundred dollars ($400), the offense is punishable by imprisonment in the state prison for two, three, or five years, or by a fine not exceeding fifty thousand dollars ($50,000), or by both that imprisonment and fine, unless the value of the fraud exceeds fifty thousand dollars ($50,000), in which event the fine may not exceed double the value of the fraud, or by imprisonment in a county jail not to exceed one year, by a fine of not more than one thousand dollars ($1,000), or by both that imprisonment and fine.

(B) Where the claim or amount at issue is four hundred dollars ($400) or less, the offense is punishable by imprisonment in a county jail not to exceed six months, or by a fine of not more than one thousand dollars ($1,000), or by both that imprisonment and fine, unless the aggregate amount of the claims or amount at issue exceeds four hundred dollars ($400) in any 12-consecutive-month period, in which case the claims or amounts may be charged as in subparagraph (A).

(3) Every person who violates paragraph (1), (2), (3), or (4) of subdivision (b) shall be punished by imprisonment in the state prison for two, three, or five years, or by a fine not exceeding fifty thousand dollars ($50,000), unless the value of the fraud exceeds fifty thousand dollars ($50,000), in which event the fine may not exceed double the value of the fraud, or by both that imprisonment and fine; or by imprisonment in a county jail not to exceed one year, or by a fine of not more than one thousand five hundred dollars ($1,500), or by both that imprisonment and fine.

(d) Notwithstanding any other provision of law, probation shall not be granted to, nor shall the execution or imposition of a sentence be suspended for, any adult person convicted of felony violations of this section who previously has been convicted of felony violations of this section or Section 548, or of Section 1871.4 of the Insurance Code, or former Section 556 of the Insurance Code, or former Section 1871.1 of the Insurance Code as an adult under charges separately brought and tried two or more times. The existence of any fact that would make a person ineligible for probation under this subdivision shall be alleged in the information or indictment, and either admitted by the defendant in an open court, or found to be true by the jury trying the issue of guilt or by the court where guilt is established by plea of guilty or nolo contendere or by trial by the court sitting without a jury.

Except when the existence of the fact was not admitted or found to be true or the court finds that a prior felony conviction was invalid, the court shall not strike or dismiss any prior felony convictions alleged in the information or indictment.

This subdivision does not prohibit the adjournment of criminal proceedings pursuant to Division 3 (commencing with Section 3000) or Division 6 (commencing with Section 6000) of the Welfare and Institutions Code.

(e) Except as otherwise provided in subdivision (f), any person who violates subdivision (a) or (b) and who has a prior felony conviction of an offense set forth in either subdivision (a) or (b), in Section 548, in Section 1871.4 of the Insurance Code, in former Section 556 of the Insurance Code, or in former Section 1871.1 of the Insurance Code shall receive a two-year enhancement for each prior felony conviction in addition to the sentence provided in subdivision (c). The existence of any fact that would subject a person to a penalty enhancement shall be alleged in the information or indictment and either admitted by the defendant in open court, or found to be true by the jury trying the issue of guilt or by the court where guilt is established by plea of guilty or nolo contendere or by trial by the court sitting without a jury. Any person who violates this section shall be subject to appropriate orders of restitution pursuant to Section 13967 of the Government Code.

(f) Any person who violates paragraph (3) of subdivision (a) and who has two prior felony convictions for a violation of paragraph (3) of subdivision (a) shall receive a five-year enhancement in addition to the sentence provided in subdivision (c). The existence of any fact that would subject a person to a penalty enhancement shall be alleged in the information or indictment and either admitted by the defendant in open court, or found to be true by the jury trying the issue of guilt or by the court where guilt is established by plea of guilty or nolo contendere or by trial by the court sitting without a jury.

(g) Except as otherwise provided in Section 12022.7, any person who violates paragraph (3) of subdivision (a) shall receive a two-year enhancement for each person other than an accomplice who suffers serious bodily injury resulting from the vehicular collision or accident in a violation of paragraph (3) of subdivision (a).

(h) This section shall not be construed to preclude the applicability of any other provision of criminal law or equitable remedy that applies or may apply to any act committed or alleged to have been committed by a person.

(i) Any fine imposed pursuant to this section shall be doubled if the offense was committed in connection with any claim pursuant to any automobile insurance policy in an auto insurance fraud crisis area designated by the Insurance Commissioner pursuant to Article 4.6 (commencing with Section 1874.90) of Chapter 12 of Part 2 of Division 1 of the Insurance Code. *(AM '99, '00)*

555. Entry Without Permission

It is unlawful to enter or remain upon any posted property without the written permission of the owner, tenant, or occupant in legal possession or control thereof. Every person who enters or remains upon posted property without such written permission is guilty of a separate offense for each day during any portion of which he enters or remains upon such posted property.

555.1. Destruction of Signs

It is unlawful, without authority, to tear down, deface or destroy any sign posted pursuant to this article.

555.2. Loitering - Picketing

It is unlawful to loiter in the immediate vicinity of any posted property. This section does not prohibit picketing in such immediate vicinity or any lawful activity by which the public is informed of the existence of an alleged labor dispute.

556. Place Advertising Sign on Public Property Without Permission

It is a misdemeanor for any person to place or maintain, or cause to be placed or maintained without lawful permission upon any property of the State, or of a city or of a county, any sign, picture, transparency, advertisement, or mechanical device which is used for the purpose of advertising or which advertises or brings to notice any person, article of merchandise, business or profession, or anything that is to be or has been sold, bartered, or given away.

556.1. Place Advertising Sign on Private Property Without Permission

It is a misdemeanor for any person to place or maintain or cause to be placed or maintained upon any property in which he has no estate or right of possession any sign, picture, transparency, advertisement, or mechanical device which is used for the purpose of advertising, or which advertises or brings to notice any person, article of merchandise, business or profession, or anything that is to be or has been sold, bartered, or even away, without the consent of the owner, lessee, or person in lawful possession of such property before such sign, picture, transparency, advertisement, or mechanical device is placed upon the property.

565. Brand Registrations; Unauthorized Use, Possession, Obliteration or Destruction

It is a misdemeanor, punishable by a fine not exceeding one thousand dollars ($1,000), or by imprisonment in the county jail not exceeding six months, or both, for an unauthorized person to possess or use, or to obliterate or destroy the brand registration upon, containers (including milk cases), cabinets, or other dairy equipment, which have a value of four hundred dollars ($400) or less, when the containers, cabinets, or other dairy equipment are marked with a brand that is registered pursuant to Chapter 10 (commencing with Section 34501) of Part 1 of Division 15 of the Food and Agricultural Code. "Unauthorized person" shall have the meaning of that term as defined in Section 34564 of the Food and Agricultural Code.

566. Brand Registrations; Unauthorized Use, Possession, Obliteration or Destruction

It is a felony, punishable by a fine not exceeding one thousand five hundred dollars ($1,500), or by imprisonment, or both, for an unauthorized person to possess or use, or to obliterate or destroy the brand registration upon, containers (including milk cases), cabinets, or other dairy equipment, which have a value in excess of four hundred dollars ($400), when the containers, cabinets, or other dairy equipment are marked with a brand that is registered pursuant to Chapter 10 (commencing with Section 34501) of Part 1 of Division 15 of the Food and Agricultural Code. "Unauthorized person" shall have the meaning of that term as defined in Section 34564 of the Food and Agricultural Code.

587. Injuring or Obstructing Railroad Tracks, Rights-of-Way or Structures

Every person who maliciously, either:

1. Removes, displaces, injures, or destroys any part of any railroad, whether for steam or horse cars, or any track of any railroad, or any branch or branchway, switch, turnout, bridge, viaduct, culvert, embankment, station house, or other structure or fixture, or any part thereof, attached to or connected with any railroad; or,

2. Places any obstruction upon the rails or track of any railroad, or of any switch, branch, branchway, or turnout connected with any railroad; is punishable by imprisonment in the state prison, or in the county jail not exceeding one year.

587a. Injuring Brakes or Appliances on Cars or Engines

Every person, who, without being thereunto duly authorized by the owner, lessee, or person or corporation engaged in the operation of any railroad, shall manipulate or in anyway tamper or interfere with any airbrake or other device, appliance or apparatus in or upon any car or locomotive upon such railroad, and used or provided for use in the operation of such car or locomotive, or of any train upon such railroad, or with any switch, signal or other appliance or apparatus used or provided for use in the operation of such railroad, shall be deemed guilty of a misdemeanor.

587b. Riding Engine or Train Without Authority

Every person, who shall, without being thereunto authorized by the owner, lessee, person or corporation operating any railroad, enter into, climb upon, hold to, or in any manner attach himself to any locomotive, locomotive engine, tender, freight or passenger car upon such railroad, or any portion of any train thereon, shall be deemed guilty of a misdemeanor, and, upon conviction thereof shall be punished by a fine not exceeding fifty dollars ($50), or by imprisonment not exceeding 30 days, or by both such fine and imprisonment.

587c. Evading Payment of Fare

Every person who fraudulently evades, or attempts to evade the payment of his fare, while traveling upon any railroad, shall be deemed guilty of a misdemeanor, and upon conviction thereof, shall be punished by a fine of not more than five hundred dollars, or imprisonment not exceeding six months or by both such fine and imprisonment.

587.1. Unauthorized Moving of Locomotives

(a) Every person who maliciously moves or causes to be moved, without authorization, any locomotive, is guilty of a misdemeanor punishable by imprisonment in the county jail not exceeding one year.

(b) Every person who maliciously moves or causes to be moved, without authorization, any locomotive, when the moving creates a substantial likelihood of causing personal injury or death to another, is guilty of a public offense punishable by imprisonment in the state prison, or in the county jail not exceeding one year.

588. Injuring Public Road or Bridge

Every person who negligently, willfully or maliciously digs up, removes, displaces, breaks down or otherwise injures or destroys any state or other public highway or bridge, or any private way, laid out by authority of law, or bridge upon any such highway or private way, or who negligently, willfully or maliciously sprinkles, drains, diverts or in any manner permits water from any sprinkler, ditch, canal, flume, or reservoir to flow upon or saturate by seepage any public highway, which act tends to damage such highway or tends to be a hazard to traffic thereon, shall be guilty of a misdemeanor. This section shall not apply to the natural flow of surface or flood waters that are not diverted, accelerated or concentrated by such person.

588a. Depositing Glass, Tacks, Etc., on Public Highway

Any person who throws or deposits any oil, glass bottle, glass, nails, tacks, hoops, wire, cans, or any other substance likely to injure any person, animal or vehicle upon any public highway in the State of California shall be guilty of a misdemeanor; provided, however, that any person who willfully deposits any such substance upon any public highway in the State of California with the intent to cause great bodily injury to other persons using the highway shall be guilty of a felony.

588b. Removing Barriers, Notices or Danger Signals on Closed Road

Any person who willfully breaks down, removes, injures, or destroys any barrier or obstruction erected or placed in or upon any road or highway by the authorities in charge thereof, or by any authorized contractor engaged in the construction or maintenance thereof, or who tears down, defaces, removes, or destroys any warnings, notices, or directional signs erected, placed or posted in, upon, or adjacent to any road or highway, or who extinguishes, removes, injures, or destroys any warning light or lantern, or reflectorized warning or directional sign, erected, placed or maintained by any such authority in, upon or adjacent to any such road or highway, shall be guilty of a misdemeanor.

590. Injuring Road Signs or Guide Posts

Every person who maliciously removes, destroys, injures, breaks or defaces any mile post, board or stone, or guide post erected on or near any highway, or any inscription thereon, is guilty of a misdemeanor.

591. Injuring or Tapping Telegraph, Telephone, or Cable Television Line

A person who unlawfully and maliciously takes own, removes, injures, or obstructs any line of telegraph, telephone, or cable television, or any other line used to conduct electricity, or any part thereof, or appurtenances or apparatus connected therewith, or severs any wire thereof, or makes any unauthorized connection with any line, other than a telegraph, telephone, or cable television line, used to conduct electricity, or any part thereof, or appurtenances or apparatus connected therewith, is punishable by imprisonment in the state prison, or by a fine not exceeding five hundred dollars ($500) or imprisonment in the county jail not exceeding one year.

592. Taking or Polluting Water by Injuring Ditch or Canal

(a) Every person who shall, without authority of the owner or managing agent, and with intent to defraud, take water from any canal, ditch, flume or reservoir used for the purpose of holding or conveying water for manufacturing, agricultural, mining, irrigation or generation of power, or domestic uses is guilty of a misdemeanor.

(b) If the total retail value of all the water taken is more than four hundred dollars ($400), or if the defendant has previously been convicted of an offense under this section or any former section that would be an offense under this section, or of an offense under the laws of another state or of the United States that would have been an offense under this section if committed in this state, then the violation is punishable by imprisonment in the county jail for not more than one year, or in state prison.

593. Injuring Electric Power Line

Every person who unlawfully and maliciously takes down, removes, injures, interferes with, or obstructs any line erected or maintained by proper authority for the purpose of transmitting electricity for light, heat, or power, or any part thereof, or any insulator or crossarm, appurtenance or apparatus connected therewith, or severs or in any way interferes with any wire, cable, or current thereof, is punishable by imprisonment in the state prison, or by fine not exceeding one thousand dollars ($1,000), or imprisonment in the county jail not exceeding one year.

593a. Driving Iron or Other Hard Substance Into Trees, Saw-Logs, or Other Wood

(a) Every person who maliciously drives or places, in any tree, saw-log, shingle-bolt, or other wood, any iron, steel, ceramic, or other substance sufficiently hard to injure saws, knowing that the tree is intended to be harvested or that the sawlog, shingle-bolt, or other wood is intended to be manufactured into any kind of lumber or other wood product, is guilty of a felony.

(b) Any person who violates subdivision (a) and causes bodily injury to another person other than an accomplice shall, in addition and consecutive to the punishment prescribed for that felony, be punished by an additional prison term of three years.

593b. Tower or Pole Climbing

Every person who shall, without the written permission of the owner, lessee, or person or corporation operating any electrical transmission line, distributing line or system, climb upon any pole, tower or other structure which is a part of such line or system and is supporting or is designed to support a wire or wires, cable or cables, for the transmission or distribution of electric energy, shall be deemed guilty of a misdemeanor; provided, that nothing herein shall apply to employees of either privately or publicly owned public utilities engaged in the performance of their duties.

593c. Interference or Obstruction of Flow of Gas or Other Hazardous Liquids

Every person who willfully and maliciously breaks, digs up, obstructs, interferes with, removes or injures any pipe or main or hazardous liquid pipeline erected, operated, or maintained for the purpose of transporting, conveying or distributing gas or other hazardous liquids for light, heat, power or any other purpose, or any part thereof, or any valve, meter, holder, compressor, machinery, appurtenance, equipment or apparatus connected with any such main or pipeline, or used in connection with or affecting the operation thereof or the conveying of gas or hazardous liquid therethrough, or shuts off, removes, obstructs, injures, or in any way interferes with any valve or fitting installed on, connected to, or operated in connection with any such main or pipeline, or controlling or affecting the flow of gas or hazardous liquid through any such main or pipeline, is guilty of a felony.

593d. Unauthorized Connection With Cable Television System

(a) Except as provided in subdivision (e), any person who, for the purpose of intercepting, receiving, or using any program or other service carried by a multichannel video or information services provider that the person is not authorized by that provider to receive or use, commits any of the following acts is guilty of a public offense:

(1) Knowingly and willfully makes or maintains an unauthorized connection or connections, whether physically, electrically, electronically, or inductively, to any cable, wire, or other component of a multichannel video or information services provider's system or to a cable, wire or other media, or receiver that is attached to a multichannel video or information services provider's system.

(2) Knowingly and willfully purchases, possesses, attaches, causes to be attached, assists others in attaching, or maintains the attachment of any unauthorized device or devices to any cable, wire, or other component of a multichannel video or information services provider's system or to a cable, wire or other media, or receiver that is attached to a multichannel video or information services provider's system.

(3) Knowingly and willfully makes or maintains any modification or alteration to any device installed with the authorization of a multichannel video or information services provider.

(4) Knowingly and willfully makes or maintains any modifications or alterations to an access device that authorizes services or knowingly and willfully obtains an unauthorized access device and uses the modified, altered, or unauthorized access device to obtain services from a multichannel video or information services provider.

For purposes of this section, each purchase, possession, connection, attachment, or modification shall constitute a separate violation of this section.

(b) Except as provided in subdivision (e), any person who knowingly and willfully manufactures, assembles, modifies, imports into this state, distributes, sells, offers to sell, advertises for sale, or possesses for any of these purposes, any device or kit for a device, designed, in whole or in part, to decrypt, decode, descramble, or otherwise make intelligible any encrypted, encoded, scrambled, or other nonstandard signal carried by a multichannel video or information services provider, unless the device has been granted an equipment authorization by the Federal Communications Commission (FCC), is guilty of a public offense.

For purposes of this subdivision, "encrypted, encoded, scrambled, or other nonstandard signal" means any type of signal or transmission that is not intended to produce an intelligible program or service without the use of a special device, signal, or information provided by the multichannel video or information services provider or its agents to authorized subscribers.

(c) Every person who knowingly and willfully makes or maintains an unauthorized connection or connections with, whether physically, electrically, electronically, or inductively, or who attaches, causes to be attached, assists others in attaching, or maintains any attachment to, any cable, wire, or other component of a multichannel video or information services provider's system, for the purpose of interfering with, altering, or degrading any multichannel video or information service being transmitted to others, or for the purpose of transmitting or broadcasting any program or other service not intended to be transmitted or broadcast by the multichannel video or information services provider, is guilty of a public offense.

For purposes of this section, each transmission or broadcast shall constitute a separate violation of this section.

(d)(1) Any person who violates subdivision (a) shall be punished by a fine not exceeding one thousand dollars ($1,000), by imprisonment in a county jail not exceeding 90 days, or by both that fine and imprisonment.

(2) Any person who violates subdivision (b) shall be punished as follows:

(A) If the violation involves the manufacture, assembly, modification, importation into this state, distribution, advertisement for sale, or possession for sale or for any of these purposes, of 10 or more of the items described in subdivision (b), or the sale or offering for sale of five or more items for financial gain, the person shall be punished by imprisonment in a county jail not exceeding one year, or in the state prison, by a fine not exceeding two hundred fifty thousand dollars ($250,000), or by both that imprisonment and fine.

(B) If the violation involves the manufacture, assembly, modification, importation into this state, distribution, advertisement for sale, or possession for sale or for any of these purposes, of nine or less of the items described in subdivision (b), or the sale or offering for sale of four or less items for financial gain, shall upon a conviction of a first offense, be punished by imprisonment in a county jail not exceeding one year, by a fine not exceeding twenty-five thousand dollars ($25,000), or by both that imprisonment and fine. A second or subsequent conviction shall be punished by imprisonment in a county jail not exceeding one year, or in the state prison, by a fine not exceeding one hundred thousand dollars ($100,000), or by both that imprisonment and fine.

(3) Any person who violates subdivision (c) shall be punished by a fine not exceeding ten thousand dollars ($10,000), by imprisonment in a county jail, or by both that fine and imprisonment.

(e) Any device or kit described in subdivision (a) or (b) seized under warrant or incident to a lawful arrest, upon the conviction of a person for a violation of subdivision (a) or (b), may be destroyed as contraband by the sheriff.

(f) Any person who violates this section shall be liable in a civil action to the multichannel video or information services provider for the greater of the following amounts:

(1) Five thousand dollars ($5,000).

(2) Three times the amount of actual damages, if any, sustained by the plaintiff plus reasonable attorney's fees.

A defendant who prevails in the action shall be awarded his or her reasonable attorney's fees.

(g) Any multichannel video or information services provider may, in accordance with the provisions of Chapter 3 (commencing with Section 525) of Title 7 of Part 2 of the Code of Civil Procedure, bring an action to enjoin and restrain any violation of this section, and may in the same action seek damages as provided in subdivision ***(f).

(h) It is not a necessary prerequisite to an action pursuant to this section that the plaintiff has suffered, or be threatened with, actual damages.

(i) For the purposes of this section, a "multichannel video or information services provider" means a franchised or otherwise duly licensed cable television system, video dialtone system, Multichannel Multipoint Distribution Service system, Direct Broadcast Satellite system, or other system providing video or information services that are distributed via cable, wire, radio frequency, or other media. A video dialtone system is a platform operated by a public utility telephone corporation for the transport of video programming as authorized by the Federal Communications Commission pursuant to FCC Docket No. 87-266, and any subsequent decisions related to that docket, subject to any rules promulgated by the FCC pursuant to those decisions. *(AM '01)*

593f. Unauthorized Devices, Plans, Etc. for Decoding Certain Transmissions

Every person who for profit knowingly and willfully manufactures, distributes, or sells any device or plan or kit for a device, or printed circuit containing circuitry for decoding or addressing with the purpose or intention of facilitating decoding or addressing of any over-the-air transmission by a Multi-point Distribution Service or Instructional Television Fixed Service made pursuant to authority granted by the Federal Communications Commission which is not authorized by the Multi-point Distribution Service or the Instructional Television Fixed Service is guilty of a misdemeanor punishable by a fine not exceeding two thousand five hundred dollars ($2,500) or by imprisonment in the county jail not exceeding 90 days, or both.

593g. Possession of Substance Hard Enough to Injure Saws or Wood Manufacturing Equipment

Every person who, with the intent to use it in a violation of Section 593a, possesses any iron, steel, ceramic, or other substance sufficiently hard to injure saws or wood manufacturing or processing equipment, shall be punished by imprisonment in the county jail not to exceed one year.

MALICIOUS MISCHIEF

594. Vandalism

(a) Every person who maliciously commits any of the following acts with respect to any real or personal property not his or her own, in cases other than those specified by state law, is guilty of vandalism:

(1) Defaces with graffiti or other inscribed material.

(2) Damages.

(3) Destroys.

Whenever a person violates this subdivision with respect to real property, vehicles, signs, fixtures, furnishings, or property belonging to any public entity, as defined by Section 811.2 of the Government Code, or the federal government, it shall be a permissive inference that the person neither owned the property nor had the permission of the owner to deface, damage, or destroy the property.

(b)(1) If the amount of defacement, damage, or destruction is four hundred dollars ($400) or more, vandalism is punishable by imprisonment in the state prison or in a county jail not exceeding one year, or by a fine of not more than ten thousand dollars ($10,000), or if the amount of defacement, damage, or destruction is ten thousand dollars ($10,000) or more, by a fine of not more than fifty thousand dollars ($50,000), or by both that fine and imprisonment.

(2)(A) If the amount of defacement, damage, or destruction is less than four hundred dollars ($400), vandalism is punishable by imprisonment in a county jail not exceeding one year, or by a fine of not more than one thousand dollars ($1,000), or by both that fine and imprisonment.

(B) If the amount of defacement, damage, or destruction is less than four hundred dollars ($400), and the defendant has been previously convicted of vandalism or affixing graffiti or other inscribed material under Section 594, 594.3, 594.4, 640.5, 640.6, or 640.7, vandalism is punishable by imprisonment in a county jail for not more than one year, or by a fine of not more than five thousand dollars ($5,000), or by both that fine and imprisonment.

(c)(1) Upon conviction of any person under this section for acts of vandalism consisting of defacing property with graffiti or other inscribed materials, the court may, in addition to any punishment imposed under subdivision (b), order the defendant to clean up, repair, or replace the damaged property himself or herself, or order the defendant, and his or her parents or guardians if the defendant is a minor, to keep the damaged property or another specified property in the community free of graffiti for up to one year. Participation of a parent or guardian is not required under this subdivision if the court deems this participation to be detrimental to the defendant, or if the parent or guardian is a single parent who must care for young children.

(2) Any city, county, or city and county may enact an ordinance that provides for all of the following:

(A) That upon conviction of any person pursuant to this section for acts of vandalism, the court may, in addition to any punishment imposed under subdivision (b), provided that the court determines that the defendant has the ability to pay any law enforcement costs not exceeding two hundred fifty dollars ($250), order the defendant to pay all or part of the costs not to exceed two hundred fifty dollars ($250) incurred by a law enforcement agency in identifying and apprehending the defendant. The law enforcement agency shall provide evidence of, and bear the burden of establishing, the reasonable costs that it incurred in identifying and apprehending the defendant.

(B) The law enforcement costs authorized to be paid pursuant to this subdivision are in addition to any other costs incurred or recovered by the law enforcement agency, and payment of these costs does not in any way limit, preclude, or restrict any other right, remedy, or action otherwise available to the law enforcement agency.

(d) If a minor is personally unable to pay a fine levied for acts prohibited by this section, the parent of that minor shall be liable for payment of the fine. A court may waive payment of the fine, or any part thereof, by the parent upon a finding of good cause.

(e) As used in this section, the term "graffiti or other inscribed material"includes any unauthorized inscription, word, figure, mark, or design, that is written, marked, etched, scratched, drawn, or painted on real or personal property.

(f) The court may order any person ordered to perform community service or graffiti removal pursuant to paragraph (1) of subdivision (c) to undergo counseling.

(g) No amount paid by a defendant in satisfaction of a criminal matter shall be applied in satisfaction of the law enforcement costs that may be imposed pursuant to this section until all outstanding base fines, state and local penalty assessments, restitution orders, and restitution fines have been paid.

(h) This section shall remain in effect until January 1, 2002, and as of that date is repealed, unless a later enacted statute that is enacted before January 1, 2002, deletes or extends that date. *(AM '99, '00)*

594. Vandalism

(a) Every person who maliciously commits any of the following acts with respect to any real or personal property not his or her own, in cases other than those specified by state law, is guilty of vandalism:

(1) Defaces with graffiti or other inscribed material.

(2) Damages.

(3) Destroys.

Whenever a person violates this subdivision with respect to real property, vehicles, signs, fixtures, furnishings, or property belonging to any public entity, as defined by Section 811.2 of the Government Code, or the federal government, it shall be a permissive inference that the person neither owned the property nor had the permission of the owner to deface, damage, or destroy the property.

(b)(1) If the amount of defacement, damage, or destruction is four hundred dollars ($400) or more, vandalism is punishable by imprisonment in the state prison or in a county jail not exceeding one year, or by a fine of not more than ten thousand dollars ($10,000), or if the amount of defacement, damage, or destruction is ten thousand dollars ($10,000) or more, by a fine of not more than fifty thousand dollars ($50,000), or by both that fine and imprisonment.

(2)(A) If the amount of defacement, damage, or destruction is less than four hundred dollars ($400), vandalism is punishable by imprisonment in a county jail not exceeding one year, or by a fine of not more than one thousand dollars ($1,000), or by both that fine and imprisonment.

(B) If the amount of defacement, damage, or destruction is less than four hundred dollars ($400), and the defendant has been previously convicted of vandalism or affixing graffiti or other inscribed material under Section 594, 594.3, 594.4, 640.5, 640.6, or 640.7, vandalism is punishable by imprisonment in a county jail for not more than one year, or by a fine of not more than five thousand dollars ($5,000), or by both that fine and imprisonment.

(c) Upon conviction of any person under this section for acts of vandalism consisting of defacing property with graffiti or other inscribed materials, the court may, in addition to any punishment imposed under subdivision (b), order the defendant to clean up, repair, or replace the damaged property himself or herself, or order the defendant, and his or her parents or guardians if the defendant is a minor, to keep the damaged property or another specified property in the community free of graffiti for up to one year. Participation of a parent or guardian is not required under this subdivision if the court deems this participation to be detrimental to the defendant, or if the parent or guardian is a single parent who must care for young children.

(d) If a minor is personally unable to pay a fine levied for acts prohibited by this section, the parent of that minor shall be liable for payment of the fine. A court may waive payment of the fine, or any part thereof, by the parent upon a finding of good cause.

(e) As used in this section, the term "graffiti or other inscribed material" includes any unauthorized inscription, word, figure, mark, or design, that is written, marked, etched, scratched, drawn, or painted on real or personal property.

(f) The court may order any person ordered to perform community service or graffiti removal pursuant to paragraph (1) of subdivision (c) to undergo counseling.

(g) This section shall become operative on January 1, 2002.

594.1. Giving, Selling Aerosol Containers of Paint to Minors

(a)(1) It shall be unlawful for any person, firm, or corporation, except a parent of legal guardian, to sell or give or in any way furnish to another person, who is in fact under the age of 18 years, any aerosol container of paint that is capable of defacing property without first obtaining bona fide evidence of majority and identity.

(2) For purposes of this subdivision, "bona fide evidence of majority and identity" is any document evidencing the age and identity of an individual which has been issued by a federal, state, or local governmental entity, and includes, but is not limited to, a motor vehicle operator's license, a registration certificate issued under the federal Selective Service Act, or an identification card issued to a member of the armed forces.

(3) This subdivision shall not apply to the furnishing of six ounces or less of an aerosol container of paint to a minor for the minor's use or possession under the supervision of the minor's parent, guardian, instructor, or employer.

(4) Aerosol containers of paint or related substances may be furnished for use in school-related activities that are part of the instructional program when used under controlled and supervised situations within the classroom or on the site of a supervised project. These containers may not leave the supervised site and shall be inventoried by the instructor. This use shall comply with Section 32060 of the Education Code regarding the safe use of toxic art supplies in schools.

(b) It shall be unlawful for any person under the age of 18 years to purchase an aerosol container of paint that is capable of defacing property.

(c) Every retailer selling or offering for sale in this state aerosol containers of paint capable of defacing property shall post in a conspicuous place a sign in letters at least three-eighths of an inch high stating: "Any person who maliciously defaces real or personal property with paint is guilty of vandalism which is punishable by a fine, imprisonment, or both."

(d) It is unlawful for any person to carry on his or her person and in plain view to the public an aerosol container of paint while in any posted public facility, park, playground, swimming pool, beach or recreational area, other than a highway, street, alley, or way, unless he or she has first received valid authorization from the governmental entity which has jurisdiction over the public area.

As used in this subdivision, "posted" means a sign placed in a reasonable location or locations stating it is a misdemeanor to possess a spray can of paint in that public facility, park, playground, swimming pool, beach or recreational area without valid authorization.

(e)(1) It is unlawful for any person under the age of 18 years to possess an aerosol container of paint for the purpose of defacing property while on any public highway, street, alley, or way, or other public place, regardless of whether that person is or is not in any automobile, vehicle, or other conveyance.

(2) As a condition of probation for any violation of this subdivision, the court may order a defendant convicted of a violation of this subdivision to perform community service as follows:

(A) For a first conviction under this subdivision, community service not to exceed 100 hours over a period not to exceed 90 days during a time other than his or her hours of school attendance or employment.

(B) If the person has a prior conviction under this subdivision, community service not to exceed 200 hours over a period of 180 days during a time other than his or her hours of school attendance or employment.

(C) If the person has two prior convictions under this subdivision, community service not to exceed 300 hours over a period not to exceed 240 days during a time other than his or her hours of school attendance or employment.

(f) Violation of any provision of this section is a misdemeanor. Upon conviction of any person under this section, the court may, in addition to any other punishment imposed, if the jurisdiction has adopted a graffiti abatement program as defined in subdivision (f) of Section 594, order the defendant, and his or her parents or guardians if the defendant is a minor, to keep the damaged property or another specified property in the community free of graffiti, as follows:

(1) For a first conviction under this section, for 90 days.

(2) If the defendant has a prior conviction under this section, for 180 days.

(3) If the defendant has two or more prior convictions under this section, for 240 days.

Participation of a parent or guardian is not required under this subdivision if the court deems this participation to be detrimental to the defendant, or if the parent or guardian is a single parent who must care for young children.

(g) The court may order any person ordered to perform community service or graffiti removal pursuant to subdivision (e) or (f) to undergo counseling.

594.2. Possession of Vandalism Tools

(a) Every person who possesses a masonry or glass drill bit, a carbide drill bit, a glass cutter, a grinding stone, an awl, a chisel, a carbide scribe, an aerosol paint container, a felt tip marker, or any other marking substance with the intent to commit vandalism or graffiti, is guilty of a misdemeanor.

(b) As a condition of probation for any violation of this section, the court may order the defendant to perform community service not to exceed 90 hours during a time other than his or her hours of school attendance or employment.

(c) For the purposes of this section:

(1) "Felt tip marker"means any broad-tipped marker pen with a tip exceeding three-eighths of one inch in width, or any similar implement containing an ink that is not water soluble.

(2) "Marking substance"means any substance or implement, other than aerosol paint containers and felt tip markers, that could be used to draw, spray, paint, etch, or mark.

594.3. Vandalism - Place of Worship or Cemetery

(a) Any person who knowingly commits any act of vandalism to a church, synagogue, building owned and occupied by a religious educational institution, or other place primarily used as a place of worship where religious services are regularly conducted or a cemetery is guilty of a crime punishable by imprisonment in the state prison or by imprisonment in the county jail for not exceeding one year.

(b) Any person who knowingly commits any act of vandalism to a church, synagogue, building owned and occupied by a religious educational institution, or other place primarily used as a place of worship where religious services are regularly conducted or a cemetery, which is shown to have been committed by reason of the race, color, religion, or national origin of another individual or group of individuals and to have been committed for the purpose of intimidating and deterring persons from freely exercising their religious beliefs, is guilty of a felony punishable by imprisonment in the state prison. *(AM '00)*

594.35. Vandalism to Cemetery or Mortuary Property, etc.; Penalties

Every person is guilty of a crime and punishable by imprisonment in the state prison or by imprisonment in a county jail for not exceeding one year, who maliciously does any of the following:

(a) Destroys, cuts, mutilates, effaces, or otherwise injures, tears down, or removes any tomb, monument, memorial, or marker in a cemetery, or any gate, door, fence, wall, post or railing, or any inclosure for the protection of a cemetery or mortuary or any property in a cemetery or mortuary.

(b) Obliterates any grave, vault, niche, or crypt.

(c) Destroys, cuts, breaks or injures any mortuary building or any building, statuary, or ornamentation within the limits of a cemetery.

(d) Disturbs, obstructs, detains or interferes with any person carrying or accompanying human remains to a cemetery or funeral establishment, or engaged in a funeral service, or an interment. *(AD '00)*

594.4. Use Butyric Acid, or Similar Chemical, To Injure Property

(a) Any person who willfully and maliciously injects into or throws upon, or otherwise defaces, damages, destroys, or contaminates, any structure with butyric acid, or any other similar noxious or caustic chemical or substance, is guilty of a public offense, punishable by imprisonment in the state prison or in a county jail, by a fine as specified in subdivision (b), or by both that imprisonment and fine.

(b)(1) If the amount of the defacement, damage, destruction, or contamination is fifty thousand dollars ($50,000) or more, by a fine of not more than fifty thousand dollars ($50,000).

(2) If the amount of the defacement, damage, destruction, or contamination is five thousand dollars ($5,000) or more, but less than fifty thousand dollars ($50,000), by a fine of not more than ten thousand dollars ($10,000).

(3) If the amount of defacement, damage, destruction, or contamination is four hundred dollars ($400) or more, but less than five thousand dollars ($5,000), by a fine of not more than five thousand dollars ($5,000).

(4) If the amount of the defacement, damage, destruction, or contamination is less than four hundred dollars ($400), by a fine of not more than one thousand dollars ($1,000).

(c) For purposes of this section, "structure"includes any house or other building being used at the time of the offense for a dwelling or for commercial purposes.

596. Poisoning Animals

Every person who, without the consent of the owner, willfully administers poison to any animal, the property of another, or exposes any poisonous substance, with the intent that the same shall be taken or swallowed by any such animal, is guilty of a misdemeanor.

However, the provisions of this section shall not apply in the case of a person who exposes poisonous substances upon premises or property owned or controlled by him for the purpose of controlling or destroying predatory animals or livestock-killing dogs and if, prior to or during the placing out of such poisonous substances, he shall have posted upon the property conspicuous signs located at intervals of distance not greater than one-third of a mile apart, and in any case not less than three such signs having words with letters at least one inch high reading "Warning- Poisoned bait placed out on these premises,"which signs shall be kept in place until the poisonous substances have been removed. Whenever such signs have been conspicuously located upon the property or premises owned or controlled by him as hereinabove provided, such person shall not be charged with any civil liability to another party in the event that any domestic animal belonging to such party becomes injured or killed by trespassing or partaking of the poisonous substance or substances so placed.

596.7. Inhumane Treatment of Rodeo Animals

(a) For purposes of this section, "rodeo"means a public performance featuring competition between persons, which includes four or more of the following events: bareback bronc riding, saddle bronc riding, bull riding, calf roping, steer wrestling, or team roping.

(b) The management of any professionally sanctioned or amateur rodeo that intends to perform in any city, county, or city and county shall ensure that there is a veterinarian licensed to practice in this state present at all times during the performances of the rodeo, or a veterinarian licensed to practice in the state who is on-call and able to arrive at the rodeo within one hour after a determination has been made that there is an injury which requires treatment to be provided by a veterinarian.

(c)(1) The attending or on-call veterinarian shall have complete access to the site of any event in the rodeo that uses animals.

(2) The attending or on-call veterinarian may, for good cause, declare any animal unfit for use in any rodeo event.

(d)(1) Any animal that is injured during the course of, or as a result of, any rodeo event shall receive immediate examination and appropriate treatment by the attending veterinarian or shall begin receiving examination and appropriate treatment by a veterinarian licensed to practice in this state within one hour of the determination of the injury requiring veterinary treatment.

(2) The attending or on-call veterinarian shall submit a brief written listing of any animal injury requiring veterinary treatment to the Veterinary Medical Board within 48 hours of the conclusion of the rodeo.

(3) The rodeo management shall ensure that there is a conveyance available at all times for the immediate and humane removal of any injured animal.

(e) The rodeo management shall ensure that no electric prod or similar device is used on any animal once the animal is in the holding chute, unless necessary to protect the participants and spectators of the rodeo.

(f) A violation of this section is an infraction and shall be punishable as follows:

(1) A fine of not less than five hundred dollars ($500) and not more than two thousand dollars ($2,000) for a first violation.

(2) A fine of not less than one thousand five hundred dollars ($1,500) and not more than five thousand dollars ($5,000) for a second or subsequent violation. *(AD '00)*

597. Killing, Maiming, or Abusing Animals

(a) Except as provided in subdivision (c) of this section or Section 599c, every person who maliciously and intentionally maims, mutilates, tortures, or wounds a living animal, or maliciously and intentionally kills an animal, is guilty of an offense punishable by imprisonment in the state prison, or by a fine of not more than twenty thousand dollars ($20,000), or by both the fine and imprisonment, or, alternatively, by imprisonment in a county jail for not more than one year, or by a fine of not more than twenty thousand dollars ($20,000), or by both the fine and imprisonment.

(b) Except as otherwise provided in subdivision (a) or (c), every person who overdrives, overloads, drives when overloaded, overworks, tortures, torments, deprives of necessary sustenance, drink, or shelter, cruelly beats, mutilates, or cruelly kills any animal, or causes or procures any animal to be so overdriven, overloaded, driven when overloaded, overworked, tortured, tormented, deprived of necessary sustenance, drink, shelter, or to be cruelly beaten, mutilated, or cruelly killed; and whoever, having the charge or custody of any animal, either as owner or otherwise, subjects any animal to needless suffering, or inflicts unnecessary cruelty upon the animal, or in any manner abuses any animal, or fails to provide the animal with proper food, drink, or shelter or protection from the weather, or who drives, rides, or otherwise uses the animal when unfit for labor, is, for every such offense, guilty of a crime punishable as a misdemeanor or as a felony or alternatively punishable as a misdemeanor or a felony and by a fine of not more than twenty thousand dollars ($20,000).

(c) Every person who maliciously and intentionally maims, mutilates, or tortures any mammal, bird, reptile, amphibian, or fish as described in subdivision (d), is guilty of an offense punishable by imprisonment in the state prison, or by a fine of not more than twenty thousand dollars ($20,000), or by both the fine and imprisonment, or, alternatively, by imprisonment in the county jail for not more than one year, by a fine of not more than twenty thousand dollars ($20,000), or by both the fine and imprisonment.

(d) Subdivision (c) applies to any mammal, bird, reptile, amphibian, or fish which is a creature described as follows:

(1) Endangered species or threatened species as described in Chapter 1.5 (commencing with Section 2050) of Division 3 of the Fish and Game Code.

(2) Fully protected birds described in Section 3511 of the Fish and Game Code.

(3) Fully protected mammals described in Chapter 8 (commencing with Section 4700) of Part 3 of Division 4 of the Fish and Game Code.

(4) Fully protected reptiles and amphibians described in Chapter 2 (commencing with Section 5050) of Division 5 of the Fish and Game Code.

(5) Fully protected fish as described in Section 5515 of the Fish and Game Code.

This subdivision does not supersede or affect any provisions of law relating to taking of the described species, including, but not limited to, Section 12008 of the Fish and Game Code.

(e) For the purposes of subdivision (c), each act of malicious and intentional maiming, mutilating, or torturing a separate specimen of a creature described in subdivision (d) is a separate offense. If any person is charged with a violation of subdivision (c), the proceedings shall be subject to Section 12157 of the Fish and Game Code.

(f)(1) Upon the conviction of a person charged with a violation of this section by causing or permitting an act of cruelty, as defined in Section 599b, all animals lawfully seized and impounded with respect to the violation by a peace officer, officer of a humane society, or officer of a pound or animal regulation department of a public agency shall be adjudged by the court to be forfeited and shall thereupon be awarded to the impounding officer for proper disposition. A person convicted of a violation of this section by causing or permitting an act of cruelty, as defined in Section 599b, shall be liable to the impounding officer for all costs of impoundment from the time of seizure to the time of proper disposition.

(2) Mandatory seizure or impoundment shall not apply to animals in properly conducted scientific experiments or investigations performed under the authority of the faculty of a regularly incorporated medical college or university of this state.

(g) Notwithstanding any other provision of law, if a defendant is granted probation for a conviction under this section, the court shall order the defendant to pay for, and successfully complete, counseling, as determined by the court, designed to evaluate and treat behavior or conduct disorders. If the court finds that the defendant is financially unable to pay for that counseling, the court may develop a sliding fee schedule based upon the defendant's ability to pay. An indigent defendant may negotiate a deferred payment schedule, but shall pay a nominal fee if the defendant has the ability to pay the nominal fee. County mental health departments or Medi-Cal shall be responsible for the costs of counseling required by this section only for those persons who meet the medical necessity criteria for mental health managed care pursuant to Section 1830.205 of Title 7 of the California Code of Regulations or the targeted population criteria specified in Section 5600.3 of the Welfare and Institutions Code. The counseling specified in this subdivision shall be in addition to any other terms and conditions of probation, including any term of imprisonment and any fine. This provision specifies a mandatory additional term of probation and is not to be utilized as an alternative in lieu of imprisonment in the state prison or county jail when such a sentence is otherwise appropriate. If the court does not order custody as a condition of probation for a conviction under this section, the court shall specify on the court record the reason or reasons for not ordering custody. This subdivision shall not apply to cases involving police dogs or horses as described in Section 600. *(AM '98)*

597a. Cruelty in Transporting Animals

Whoever carries or causes to be carried in or upon any vehicle or otherwise any domestic animal in a cruel and inhuman manner, or knowingly and willfully authorizes or permits it to be subjected to unnecessary torture, suffering, or cruelty of any kind, is guilty of a misdemeanor; and whenever any such person is taken into custody therefor by any officer, such officer must take charge of such vehicle and ifs contents, together with the horse or team attached to such vehicle, and deposit the same in some place of custody; and any necessary expenses incurred for taking care of and keeping the same, is a lien thereon, to be paid before the same can be lawfully recovered; and if such expense, or any part thereof, remains unpaid, it may be recovered, by the person incurring the same, of the owner of such domestic animal, in an action therefor.

597b. Fighting Animals or Birds - Worrying Animals

Any person who, for amusement or gain, causes any bull, bear, cock, or other animal, not including any dog, to fight with like kind of animal or creature, or causes any such animal, including any dog, to fight with a different kind of animal or creature, or with any human being; or who, for amusement or gain, worries or injures any such bull, bear, cock, dog or other animal, or causes any such bull, bear, cock, or other animal, not including any dog, to worry or injure each other; and any person who permits the same to be done on any premises under his charge or control; and any person who aids, abets, or is present at such fighting or worrying of such animal or creature, as a spectator, is guilty of a misdemeanor.

597c. Training Animals to Fight, Attending Training Quarters or Fight; Exceptions

Whoever owns, possesses, keeps, or trains any bird or animal, with the intent that such bird or animal shall be engaged in an exhibition of fighting, or is present at any place, building, or tenement, where preparations are being made for an exhibition of the fighting of birds or animals, with the intent to be present at such exhibition, or is present at such exhibition, is guilty of a misdemeanor. This section shall not apply to an exhibition of fighting of a dog with another dog.

597d. Arrest of Attendants or Promoters of Animal or Bird Fight Without Warrant

Any sheriff, police, or peace officer, or officer qualified as provided in Section 14502 of the Corporations Code, may enter any place, building, or tenement, where there is an exhibition of the fighting of birds or animals, or where preparations are being made for such an exhibition, and, without a warrant, arrest all persons present.

597e.　Impounding Animal With Insufficient Food and Water

Any person who impounds, or causes to be impounded in any pound, any domestic animal, shall supply it during such confinement with a sufficient quantity of good and wholesome food and water, and in default thereof, is guilty of a misdemeanor. In case any domestic animal is at any time so impounded and continues to be without necessary food and water for more than 12 consecutive hours, it is lawful for any person, from time to time, as may be deemed necessary, to enter into and upon any pound in which the animal is confined, and supply it with necessary food and water so long as it remains so confined. Such person is not liable for the entry and may collect the reasonable cost of the food and water from the owner of the animal, and the animal is subject to enforcement of a money judgment for the reasonable cost of such food and water.

597g.　Poling of Horses

(a) Poling a horse is a method of training horses to jump which consists of (1) forcing, persuading, or enticing a horse to jump in such manner that one or more of its legs will come in contact with an obstruction consisting of any kind of wire, or a pole, stick, rope or other object with brads, nails, tacks or other sharp points imbedded therein or attached thereto or (2) raising, throwing or moving a pole, stick, wire, rope or other object, against one or more of the legs of a horse while it is jumping an obstruction so that the horse, in either case, is induced to raise such leg or legs higher in order to clear the obstruction. Tripping a horse is an act that consists of the use of any wire, pole, stick, rope, or other object or apparatus whatsoever to cause a horse to fall or lose its balance. The poling or tripping of any horse is unlawful and any person violating the provisions of this section is guilty of a misdemeanor.

(b) It is a misdemeanor for any person to intentionally trip or fell an equine by the legs by any means whatsoever for the purposes of entertainment or sport.

(c) This section does not apply to the lawful laying down of a horse for medical or identification purposes, nor shall the section be construed as condemning or limiting any cultural or historical activities, except those prohibited herein.

597i.　Manufacture, Sale or Possession of Cock Fighting Implements

It shall be unlawful for anyone to manufacture, buy, sell, barter, exchange, or have in his possession any of the implements commonly known as gaffs or slashers, or any other sharp implement designed to be attached in place of the natural spur of a gamecock or other fighting bird. Anyone violating any of the provisions of this section shall be guilty of a misdemeanor and upon conviction thereof shall, in addition to any judgment or sentence imposed by the court, forfeit possession or ownership of such implements.

597j.　Owning, Possessing or Keeping Any Cock With Intention to Engage in Fighting

Any person who owns, possesses or keeps any cock with the intent that such cock shall be used or engaged by himself or by his vendee or by any other person in any exhibition of fighting is guilty of a misdemeanor.

597k.　Use of Bristle or Tack Bur on Animals

Anyone who, having care, custody or control of any horse or other animal, uses what is known as the bristle bur, tack bur, or other like device, by whatsoever name known or designated, on such horse or other animal for any purpose whatsoever, is guilty of a misdemeanor and is punishable by a fine of not less than fifty dollars ($50) nor more than five hundred dollars ($500), or by imprisonment in the county jail for not less than 10 days nor more than 175 days, or by both such fine and imprisonment.

597l.　Pet Shops - Definitions - Care of Animals and Premises

It shall be unlawful for any person who operates a pet shop to fail to do all of the following:

(1) Maintain the facilities used for the keeping of pet animals in a sanitary condition.

(2) Provide proper heating and ventilation for the facilities used for the keeping of pet animals.

(3) Provide adequate nutrition for, and humane care and treatment of, all pet animals under his care and control.

(4) Take reasonable care to release for sale, trade, or adoption only those pet animals which are free of disease or injuries.

(5) Provide adequate space appropriate to the size, weight and specie of pet animals.

(b) As used in this section:

(1) "Pet animals" means dogs, cats, monkeys, and other primates, rabbits, birds, guinea pigs, hamsters, mice, snakes, iguanas, turtles, and any other species of animal sold or retained for the purpose of being kept as a household pet.

(2) "Pet shop" means every place or premises where pet animals are kept for the purpose of either wholesale or retail sale. "Pet shop" does not include any place or premises where pet animals are occasionally sold.

(c) Any person who violates any provision of this section is guilty of a misdemeanor and is punishable by a fine of not to exceed one thousand dollars ($1,000), or by imprisonment in the county jail for not more than 90 days, or by both such fine and imprisonment.

597o. Transportation of Equine Requirements

(a) Any person who transports an equine in a vehicle to slaughter shall meet the following requirements:

(1) The vehicle shall have sufficient clearance to allow the equine to be transported in a standing position with its head in a normal upright position above its withers.

(2) Any ramps and floors in the vehicle shall be covered with a nonskid surface to prevent the equine from slipping.

(3) The sides and overhead of the vehicle shall be constructed to withstand the weight of any equine which may put pressure against the sides or overhead.

(5) Any compartments in the interior of the vehicle shall be constructed of smooth materials and shall contain no protrusions or sharp objects.

(6) The size of the vehicle shall be appropriate for the number of equine being transported and the welfare of the equine shall not be jeopardized by overloading.

(7) Stallions shall be segregated during transportation to slaughter

(8) Diseased, sick, blind, dying, or otherwise disabled equine shall not be transported out of state.

(9) Any equine being transported shall be able to bear weight on all four feet.

(10) Unweaned foals shall not be transported.

(11) Mares in their last trimester of pregnancy shall not be transported.

(12) The person shall notify a humane officer having jurisdiction 72 hours before loading the equine in order that the humane officer may perform a thorough inspection of the vehicle to determine if all requirements of this section have been satisfied.

(b)(1) Any person who violates this section is guilty of a misdemeanor and is subject to a fine of one hundred dollars ($100) per equine being transported.

(2) Any person who violates this section for a second or subsequent time is guilty of a misdemeanor and shall be fined five hundred dollars ($500) per equine being transported.

(c) Whenever a person is taken into custody by an officer for a violation of this section, the officer shall take charge of the vehicle and its contents and deposit the property in some place of custody.

(d)(1) Any necessary expense incurred for taking care of and keeping the property described in subdivision (c) is a lien thereon, to be paid before the property can be lawfully recovered.

(2) If the expense, or any part thereof, remains unpaid, it may be recovered by the person incurring the expense from the owner of the equine in an action thereon.

(e) For the purposes of this section, "equine" means any horse, pony, burro, or mule.

597s. Abandoning Animal

(a) Every person who willfully abandons any animal is guilty of a misdemeanor.

(b) This section shall not apply to the release or rehabilitation and release of native California wildlife pursuant to statute or regulations of the California Department of Fish and Game. *(AM '99)*

597t. Mistreatment of Confined Animals

Every person who keeps an animal confined in an enclosed area shall provide it with an adequate exercise area. If the animal is restricted by a leash, rope, or chain, the leash, rope, or chain shall be affixed in such a manner that it will prevent the animal from becoming entangled or injured and permit the animal's access to adequate shelter, food, and water. Violation of this section constitutes a misdemeanor.

This section shall not apply to an animal which is in transit, in a vehicle, or in the immediate control of a person.

597x. Transportation of Live Animals

(a) Notwithstanding Section 18734 of the Food and Agricultural Code or any other provision of law, it is unlawful for any person to sell, attempt to sell, load, cause to be loaded, transport, or attempt to transport any live horse, mule, burro, or pony that is disabled, if the animal is intended to be sold, loaded, or transported for commercial slaughter out of the state.

(b) For the purposes of this section, "disabled animal" includes, but is not limited to, any animal that has broken limbs, is unable to stand and balance itself without assistance, cannot walk, or is severely injured.

(c) A person who violates this section is guilty of a misdemeanor and subject to the same penalties imposed upon a person convicted of a misdemeanor under section 597a.

597.1. Failing to Care for Animals

(a) Every owner, driver, or keeper of any animal who permits the animal to be in any building, enclosure, lane, street, square, or lot of any city, county, city and county, or judicial district without proper care and attention is guilty of a misdemeanor. Any peace officer, humane society officer, or animal control officer shall take possession of the stray or abandoned animal and shall provide care and treatment for the animal until the animal is deemed to be in suitable condition to be returned to the owner. When the officer has reasonable grounds to believe that very prompt action is required to protect the health or safety of the animal or the health or safety of others, the officer shall immediately seize the animal and comply with subdivision (f). In all other cases, the officer shall comply with the provisions of subdivision (g). The cost of caring for and treating any animal properly seized under this subdivision shall constitute a lien on the animal and the animal shall not be returned to its owner until the charges are paid, if the seizure is upheld pursuant to this section.

(b) Every sick, disabled, infirm, or crippled animal, except a dog or cat, that is abandoned in any city, county, city and county, or judicial district may be killed by the officer if, after a reasonable search, no owner of the animal can be found. It shall be the duty of all peace officers, humane society officers, and animal control officers to cause the animal to be killed or rehabilitated and placed in a suitable home on information that the animal is stray or abandoned. The officer may likewise take charge of any animal, including a dog or cat, that by reason of lameness, sickness, feebleness, or neglect, is unfit for the labor it is performing, or that in any other manner is being cruelly treated, and provide care and treatment for the animal until it is deemed to be in a suitable condition to be returned to the owner. When the officer has reasonable grounds to believe that very prompt action is required to protect the health or safety of an animal or the health or safety of others, the officer shall immediately seize the animal and comply with subdivision (f). In all other cases, the officer shall comply with subdivision (g). The cost of caring for and treating any animal properly seized under this subdivision shall constitute a lien on the animal and the animal shall not be returned to its owner until the charges are paid.

(c) Any peace officer, humane society officer, or animal control officer shall convey all injured cats and dogs found without their owners in a public place directly to a veterinarian known by the officer to be a veterinarian who ordinarily treats dogs and cats for a determination of whether the animal shall be immediately and humanely destroyed or shall be hospitalized under proper care and given emergency treatment.

If the owner does not redeem the animal within the locally prescribed waiting period, the veterinarian may personally perform euthanasia on the animal. If the animal is treated and recovers from its injuries, the veterinarian may keep the animal for purposes of adoption, provided the responsible animal control agency has first been contacted and has refused to take possession of the animal.

Whenever any animal is transferred to a veterinarian in a clinic, such as an emergency clinic that is not in continuous operation, the veterinarian may, in turn, transfer the animal to an appropriate facility.

If the veterinarian determines that the animal shall be hospitalized under proper care and given emergency treatment, the costs of any services that are provided pending the owner's inquiry to the responsible agency, department, or society shall be paid from the dog license fees, fines, and fees for impounding dogs in the city, county, or city and county in which the animal was licensed or, if the animal is unlicensed, shall be paid by the jurisdiction in which the animal was found, subject to the provision that this cost be repaid by the animal's owner. The cost of caring for and treating any animal seized under this subdivision shall constitute a lien on the animal and the animal shall not be returned to the owner until the charges are paid. No veterinarian shall be criminally or civilly liable for any decision that he or she makes or for services that he or she provides pursuant to this subdivision.

(d) An animal control agency that takes possession of an animal pursuant to subdivision (c) shall keep records of the whereabouts of the animal from the time of possession to the end of the animal's impoundment, and those records shall be available for inspection by the public upon request for three years after the date the animal's impoundment ended.

(e) Notwithstanding any other provision of this section, any peace officer, humane society officer, or any animal control officer may, with the approval of his or her immediate superior, humanely destroy any stray or abandoned animal in the field in any case where the animal is too severely injured to move or where a veterinarian is not available and it would be more humane to dispose of the animal.

(f) Whenever an officer authorized under this section seizes or impounds an animal based on a reasonable belief that prompt action is required to protect the health or safety of the animal or the health or safety of others, the officer shall, prior to the commencement of any criminal proceedings authorized by this section, provide the owner or keeper of the animal, if known or ascertainable after reasonable investigation, with the opportunity for a postseizure hearing to determine the validity of the seizure or impoundment, or both.

(1) The agency shall cause a notice to be affixed to a conspicuous place where the animal was situated or personally deliver a notice of the seizure or impoundment, or both, to the owner or keeper within 48 hours, excluding weekends and holidays. The notice shall include all of the following:

(A) The name, business address, and telephone number of the officer providing the notice.

(B) A description of the animal seized, including any identification upon the animal.

(C) The authority and purpose for the seizure, or impoundment, including the time, place, and circumstances under which the animal was seized.

(D) A statement that, in order to receive a postseizure hearing, the owner or person authorized to keep the animal, or his or her agent, shall request the hearing by signing and returning an enclosed declaration of ownership or right to keep the animal to the agency providing the notice within 10 days, including weekends and holidays, of the date of the notice. The declaration may be returned by personal delivery or mail.

(E) A statement that the cost of caring for and treating any animal properly seized under this section is a lien on the animal and that the animal shall not be returned to the owner until the charges are paid, and that failure to request or to attend a scheduled hearing shall result in liability for this cost.

(2) The postseizure hearing shall be conducted within 48 hours of the request, excluding weekends and holidays. The seizing agency may authorize its own officer or employee to conduct the hearing if the hearing officer is not the same person who directed the seizure or impoundment of the animal and is not junior in rank to that person. The agency may utilize the services of a hearing officer from outside the agency for the purposes of complying with this section.

(3) Failure of the owner or keeper, or of his or her agent, to request or to attend a scheduled hearing shall result in a forfeiture of any right to a postseizure hearing or right to challenge his or her liability for costs incurred.

(4) The agency, department, or society employing the person who directed the seizure shall be responsible for the costs incurred for caring and treating the animal, if it is determined in the postseizure hearing that the seizing officer did not have reasonable grounds to believe very prompt action, including seizure of the animal, was required to protect the health or safety of the animal or the health or safety of others. If it is determined the seizure was justified, the owner or keeper shall be personally liable to the seizing agency for the cost of the seizure and care of the animal, the charges for the seizure and care of the animal shall be a lien on the animal, and the animal shall not be returned to its owner until the charges are paid and the seizing agency or hearing officer has determined that the animal is physically fit or the owner demonstrates to the seizing agency's or the hearing officer's satisfaction that the owner can and will provide the necessary care.

(g) Where the need for immediate seizure is not present and prior to the commencement of any criminal proceedings authorized by this section, the agency shall provide the owner or keeper of the animal, if known or ascertainable after reasonable investigation, with the opportunity for a hearing prior to any seizure or impoundment of the animal. The owner shall produce the animal at the time of the hearing unless, prior to the hearing, the owner has made arrangements with the agency to view the animal upon request of the agency, or unless the owner can provide verification that the animal was humanely destroyed. Any person who willfully fails to produce the animal or provide the verification is guilty of an infraction, punishable by a fine of not less than two hundred fifty dollars ($250) nor more than one thousand dollars ($1,000).

(1) The agency shall cause a notice to be affixed to a conspicuous place where the animal was situated or personally deliver a notice stating the grounds for believing the animal should be seized under subdivision (a) or (b). The notice shall include all of the following:

(A) The name, business address, and telephone number of the officer providing the notice.

(B) A description of the animal to be seized, including any identification upon the animal.

(C) The authority and purpose for the possible seizure or impoundment.

(D) A statement that, in order to receive a hearing prior to any seizure, the owner or person authorized to keep the animal, or his or her agent, shall request the hearing by signing and returning the enclosed declaration of ownership or right to keep the animal to the officer providing the notice within two days, excluding weekends and holidays, of the date of the notice.

(E) A statement that the cost of caring for and treating any animal properly seized under this section is a lien on the animal, that any animal seized shall not be returned to the owner until the charges are paid, and that failure to request or to attend a scheduled hearing shall result in a conclusive determination that the animal may properly be seized and that the owner shall be liable for the charges.

(2) The preseizure hearing shall be conducted within 48 hours, excluding weekends and holidays, after receipt of the request. The seizing agency may authorize its own officer or employee to conduct the hearing if the hearing officer is not the same person who requests the seizure or impoundment of the animal and is not junior in rank to that person. The agency may utilize the services of a hearing officer from outside the agency for the purposes of complying with this section.

(3) Failure of the owner or keeper, or his or her agent, to request or to attend a scheduled hearing shall result in a forfeiture of any right to a preseizure hearing or right to challenge his or her liability for costs incurred pursuant to this section.

(4) The hearing officer, after the hearing, may affirm or deny the owner's or keeper's right to custody of the animal and, if reasonable grounds are established, may order the seizure or impoundment of the animal for care and treatment.

(h) If any animal is properly seized under this section, the owner or keeper shall be personally liable to the seizing agency for the cost of the seizure and care of the animal. Furthermore, if the charges for the seizure or impoundment and any other charges permitted under this section are not paid within 14 days of the seizure, or, if the owner, within 14 days of notice of availability of the animal to be returned, fails to pay charges permitted under this section and take possession of the animal, the animal shall be deemed to have been abandoned and may be disposed of by the impounding officer.

(i) If the animal requires veterinary care and the humane society or public agency is not assured, within 14 days of the seizure of the animal, that the owner will provide the necessary care, the animal shall not be returned to its owner and shall be deemed to have been abandoned and may be disposed of by the impounding officer. A veterinarian may humanely destroy an impounded animal without regard to the prescribed holding period when it has been determined that the animal has incurred severe injuries or is incurably crippled. A veterinarian also may immediately humanely destroy an impounded animal afflicted with a serious contagious disease unless the owner or his or her agent immediately authorizes treatment of the animal by a veterinarian at the expense of the owner or agent.

(j) No animal properly seized under this section shall be returned to its owner until, in the determination of the seizing agency or hearing officer, the animal is physically fit or the owner can demonstrate to the seizing agency's or hearing officer's satisfaction that the owner can and will provide the necessary care.

(k) Upon the conviction of a person charged with a violation of this section, or Section 597 or 597a, all animals lawfully seized and impounded with respect to the violation shall be adjudged by the court to be forfeited and shall thereupon be transferred to the impounding officer or appropriate public entity for proper adoption or other disposition. A person convicted of a violation of this section shall be personally liable to the seizing agency for all costs of impoundment from the time of seizure to the time of proper disposition. Upon conviction, the court shall order the convicted person to make payment to the appropriate public entity for the costs incurred in the housing, care, feeding, and treatment of the seized or impounded animals. Each person convicted in connection with a particular animal may be held jointly and severally liable for restitution for that particular animal. The payment shall be in addition to any other fine or sentence ordered by the court.

The court may also order, as a condition of probation, that the convicted person be prohibited from owning, possessing, caring for, or having any contact with, animals of any kind and require the convicted person to immediately deliver all animals in his or her possession to a designated public entity for adoption or other lawful disposition or provide proof to the court that the person no longer has possession, care, or control of any animals. In the event of the acquittal or final discharge without conviction of the arrested person, the court shall, on demand, direct the release of seized or impounded animals upon a showing of proof of ownership. Any questions regarding ownership shall be determined in a separate hearing by the court where the criminal case was finally adjudicated and the court shall hear testimony from any persons who may assist the court in determining ownership of the animal. If the owner is determined to be unknown or the owner is prohibited or unable to retain possession of the animals for any reason, the court shall order the animals to be released to the appropriate public entity for adoption or other lawful disposition. This section is not intended to cause the release of any animal, bird, reptile, amphibian, or fish, seized or impounded pursuant to any other statute, ordinance, or municipal regulation. This section shall not prohibit the seizure or impoundment of animals as evidence as provided for under any other provision of law.

(l) It shall be the duty of all peace officers, humane society officers, and animal control officers to use all currently acceptable methods of identification, both electronic and otherwise, to determine the lawful owner or caretaker of any seized or impounded animal. It shall also be their duty to make reasonable efforts to notify the owner or caretaker of the whereabouts of the animal and any procedures available for the lawful recovery of the animal and, upon the owner's and caretaker's initiation of recovery procedures, retain custody of the animal for a reasonable period of time to allow for completion of the recovery process. Efforts to locate or contact the owner or caretaker and communications with persons claiming to be the owner or caretaker shall be recorded and maintained and be made available for public inspection. *(AM '98)*

597.3. Cruelty to Animals; Live Animal Market Requiements [Renumbered from 597.2]

(a) Every person who operates a live animal market shall do all of the following:

(1) Provide that no animal will be dismembered, flayed, cut open, or have its skin, scales, feathers, or shell removed while the animal is still alive.

(2) Provide that no live animals will be confined, held, or displayed in a manner that results, or is likely to result, in injury, starvation, dehydration, or suffocation.

(b) As used in this section:

(1) "Animal"means frogs, turtles, and birds sold for the purpose of human consumption, with the exception of poultry.

(2) "Live animal market"means a retail food market where, in the regular course of business, animals are stored alive and sold to consumers for the purpose of human consumption.

(c) Any person who fails to comply with any requirement of subdivision (a) shall for the first violation, be given a written warning in a written language that is understood by the person receiving the warning. A second or subsequent violation of subdivision (a) shall be an infraction, punishable by a fine of not less than two hundred fifty dollars ($250), nor more than one thousand dollars ($1,000). However, a fine paid for a second violation of subdivision (a) shall be deferred for six months if a course is available that is administered by a state or local agency on state law and local ordinances relating to live animal markets. If the defendant successfully completes that course within six months of entry of judgment, the fine shall be waived. The state or local agency may charge the participant a fee to take the course, not to exceed one hundred dollars ($100). *(RN '01)*

597.5.　Dog Fights - Training, Conducting, Attending

(a) Any person who does any of the following is guilty of a felony and is punishable by imprisonment in a state prison for 16 months, or two or three years, or by a fine not to exceed fifty thousand dollars ($50,000), or by both such fine and imprisonment:

(1) Owns, possesses, keeps, or trains any dog, with the intent that the dog shall be engaged in an exhibition of fighting with another dog.

(2) For amusement or gain, causes any dog to fight with another dog, or causes any dogs to injure each other.

(3) Permits any act in violation of paragraph (1) or (2) to be done on any premises under his or her charge or control, or aids or abets that act.

(b) Any person who is knowingly present, as a spectator, at any place, building, or tenement where preparations are being made for an exhibition of the fighting of dogs, with the intent to be present at those preparations, or is knowingly present at that exhibition or at any other fighting or injuring as described in paragraph (2) of subdivision (a), with the intent to be present at such exhibition, fighting, or injuring, is guilty of a misdemeanor.

(c) Nothing in this section shall prohibit any of the following:

(1) The use of dogs in the management of livestock, as defined by Section 14205 of the Food and Agricultural Code, by the owner of the livestock or his or her employees or agents or other persons in lawful custody thereof.

(2) The use of dogs in hunting as permitted by the Fish and Game Code, including, but not limited to, Sections 3286, 3509, 3510, 4002, and 4756, and by the rules and regulations of the Fish and Game Commission.

(3) The training of dogs or the use of equipment in the training of dogs for any purpose not prohibited by law.

598.　Killing Birds or Robbing Nests in Cemeteries

Every person who, within any public cemetery or burying-ground, kills, wounds, or traps any bird, or destroys any bird's nest other than swallows'nests, or removes any eggs or young birds from any nest, is guilty of a misdemeanor.

598b.　Possession, Buying, Selling, Etc. of Pet for Food

(a) Every person is guilty of a misdemeanor who possesses, imports into, or exports from, this state, sells, buys, gives away, or accepts any carcass or part of any carcass of any animal traditionally or commonly kept as a pet or companion with the intent of using or having another person use any part of that carcass for food.

(b) Every person is guilty of a misdemeanor who possesses, imports into, or exports from, this state, sells, buys, gives away, or accepts any animal traditionally or commonly kept as a pet or companion with the intent of killing or having another person kill that animal for the purpose of using or having another person use any part of the animal for food.

(c) This section shall not be construed to interfere with the production, marketing, or disposal of any livestock, poultry, fish, shellfish, or any other agricultural commodity produced in this state. Nor shall this section be construed to interfere with the lawful killing of wildlife, or the lawful killing of any other animal under the laws of this state pertaining to game animals.

600. Harming, Interfering With or Obstructing Peace Officer's Horse or Dog

(a) Any person who willfully and maliciously and with no legal justification strikes, beats, kicks, cuts, stabs, shoots with a firearm, administers any poison or other harmful or stupefying substance to, or throws, hurls, or projects at, or places any rock, object, or other substance which is used in such a manner as to be capable of producing injury and likely to produce injury, on or in the path of, any horse being used by, or any dog under the supervision of, any peace officer in the discharge or attempted discharge of his or her duties, is guilty of a public offense. If the injury inflicted is a serious injury, as defined in subdivision (c), the person shall be punished by imprisonment in the state prison for 16 months, two or three years, or in a county jail for not exceeding one year, or by a fine not exceeding two thousand dollars ($2,000), or by both a fine and imprisonment. If the injury inflicted is not a serious injury, the person shall be punished by imprisonment in the county jail for not exceeding one year, or by a fine not exceeding one thousand dollars ($1,000), or by both a fine and imprisonment.

(b) Any person who willfully and maliciously and with no legal justification interferes with or obstructs any horse or dog being used by any peace officer in the discharge or attempted discharge of his or her duties by frightening, teasing, agitating, harassing, or hindering the horse or dog shall be punished by imprisonment in a county jail for not exceeding one year, or by a fine not exceeding one thousand dollars ($1,000), or by both a fine and imprisonment.

(c) Any person who, in violation of this section, and with intent to inflict such injury or death, personally causes the death, destruction, or serious physical injury including bone fracture, loss or impairment of function of any bodily member, wounds requiring extensive suturing, or serious crippling, of any horse or dog, shall, upon conviction of a felony under this section, in addition and consecutive to the punishment prescribed for the felony, be punished by an additional term of imprisonment in the state prison for one year.

(d) Any person who, in violation of this section, and with the intent to inflict such injury, personally causes great bodily injury, as defined in Section 12022.7, to any person not an accomplice, shall, upon conviction of a felony under this section, in addition and consecutive to the punishment prescribed for the felony, be punished by an additional term of imprisonment in the state prison for two years unless the conduct described in this subdivision is an element of any other offense of which the person is convicted or receives an enhancement under Section 12022.7.

(e) In any case in which a defendant is convicted of a violation of this section, the defendant shall be ordered to make restitution to the agency owning the animal and employing the peace officer for any veterinary bills, replacement costs of the animal if it is disabled or killed, and the salary of the peace officer for the period of time his or her services are lost to the agency. *(AM '00)*

600.2 Allow Dog To Injure or Kill Guide, Signal, or Service Dog While In Discharge of Duties

(a) It is unlawful and constitutes an infraction for any person to permit any dog which is owned, harbored, or controlled by him or her to cause injury to or the death of any guide, signal, or service dog, as defined by Section 54.1 of the Civil Code, while the guide, signal, or service dog is in discharge of its duties.

(b) In any case in which a defendant is convicted of a violation of this section, the defendant shall be ordered to make restitution to the disabled person who has custody or ownership of the guide, signal, or service dog for any veterinary bills and replacement costs of the dog if it is disabled or killed.

600.5 Cause Injury or Death of Guide, Signal, or Service Dog

(a) Any person who intentionally causes injury to or the death of any guide, signal, or service dog, as defined by Section 54.1 of the Civil Code, while the dog is in discharge of its duties, is guilty of a misdemeanor, punishable by imprisonment in the county jail not exceeding one year, or by a fine not exceeding five thousand dollars ($5,000), or by both a fine and imprisonment.

(b) In any case in which a defendant is convicted of a violation of this section, the defendant shall be ordered to make restitution to the disabled person who has custody or ownership of the dog for any veterinary bills and replacement costs of the dog if it is disabled or killed.

601. Trespass With Threat to Cause Serious Bodily Injury

(a) Any person is guilty of trespass who makes a credible threat to cause serious bodily injury, as defined in subdivision (a) of Section 417.6, to another person with the intent to place that other person in reasonable fear for his or her safety, or the safety of his or her immediate family, as defined in subdivision (i) of Section 646.9, and who does any of the following:

(1) Within 30 days of the threat, unlawfully enters into the residence or real property contiguous to the residence of the person threatened without lawful purpose, and with the intent to execute the threat against the target of the threat.

(2) Within 30 days of the threat, knowing that the place is the threatened person's workplace, unlawfully enters into the workplace of the person threatened and carries out an act or acts to locate the threatened person within the workplace premises without lawful purpose, and with the intent to execute the threat against the target of the threat.

(b) Subdivision (a) shall not apply if the residence, real property, or workplace described in paragraph (1) or (2) that is entered is the residence, real property, or workplace of the person making the threat.

(c) This section shall not apply to any person who is engaged in labor union activities which are permitted to be carried out on the property by the California Agricultural Labor Relations Act, Part 3.5 (commencing with Section 1140) of Division 2 of the Labor Code, or by the National Labor Relations Act.

(d) A violation of this section shall be punishable by imprisonment in the state prison, or by imprisonment in a county jail not exceeding one year, or by a fine not exceeding two thousand dollars ($2,000), or by both a fine and imprisonment.

602. Trespassing

Except as provided in Section 602.8, every person who willfully commits a trespass by any of the following acts is guilty of a misdemeanor:

(a) Cutting down, destroying, or injuring any kind of wood or timber standing or growing upon the lands of another.

(b) Carrying away any kind of wood or timber lying on those lands.

(c) Maliciously injuring or severing from the freehold of another anything attached to it, or its produce.

(d) Digging, taking, or carrying away from any lot situated within the limits of any incorporated city, without the license of the owner or legal occupant, any earth, soil, or stone.

(e) Digging, taking, or carrying away from land in any city or town laid down on the map or plan of the city, or otherwise recognized or established as a street, alley, avenue, or park, without the license of the proper authorities, any earth, soil, or stone.

(f) Maliciously tearing down, damaging, mutilating, or destroying any sign, signboard, or notice placed upon, or affixed to, any property belonging to the state, or to any city, county, city and county, town or village, or upon any property of any person, by the state or by an automobile association, which sign, signboard or notice is intended to indicate or designate a road, or a highway, or is intended to direct travelers from one point to another, or relates to fires, fire control, or any other matter involving the protection of the property, or putting up, affixing, fastening, printing, or painting upon any property belonging to the state, or to any city, county, town, or village, or dedicated to the public, or upon any property of any person, without license from the owner, any notice, advertisement, or designation of, or any name for any commodity, whether for sale or otherwise, or any picture, sign, or device intended to call attention to it.

(g) Entering upon any lands owned by any other person whereon oysters or other shellfish are planted or growing; or injuring, gathering, or carrying away any oysters or other shellfish planted, growing, or on any such lands, whether covered by water or not, without the license of the owner or legal occupant; or destroying or removing, or causing to be removed or destroyed, any stakes, marks, fences, or signs intended to designate the boundaries and limits of any such lands.

(h) Willfully opening, tearing down, or otherwise destroying any fence on the enclosed land of another, or opening any gate, bar, or fence of another and willfully leaving it open without the written permission of the owner, or maliciously tearing down, mutilating, or destroying any sign, signboard, or other notice forbidding shooting on private property.

(i) Building fires upon any lands owned by another where signs forbidding trespass are displayed at intervals not greater than one mile along the exterior boundaries and at all roads and trails entering the lands, without first having obtained written permission from the owner of the lands or the owner's agent, or the person in lawful possession.

(j) Entering any lands, whether unenclosed or enclosed by fence, for the purpose of injuring any property or property rights or with the intention of interfering with, obstructing, or injuring any lawful business or occupation carried on by the owner of the land, the owner's agent or by the person in lawful possession.

(k) Entering any lands under cultivation or enclosed by fence, belonging to, or occupied by, another, or entering upon uncultivated or unenclosed lands where signs forbidding trespass are displayed at intervals not less than three to the mile along all exterior boundaries and at all roads and trails entering the lands without the written permission of the owner of the land, the owner's agent or of the person in lawful possession, and

(1) Refusing or failing to leave the lands immediately upon being requested by the owner of the land, the owner's agent or by the person in lawful possession to leave the lands, or

(2) Tearing down, mutilating, or destroying any sign, signboard, or notice forbidding trespass or hunting on the lands, or

(3) Removing, injuring, unlocking, or tampering with any lock on any gate on or leading into the lands, or

(4) Discharging any firearm.

(l) Entering and occupying real property or structures of any kind without the consent of the owner, the owner's agent, or the person in lawful possession.

(m) Driving any vehicle, as defined in Section 670 of the Vehicle Code, upon real property belonging to, or lawfully occupied by, another and known not to be open to the general public, without the consent of the owner, the owner's agent, or the person in lawful possession. This subdivision shall not apply to any person described in Section 22350 of the Business and Professions Code who is making a lawful service of process, provided that upon exiting the vehicle, the person proceeds immediately to attempt the service of process, and leaves immediately upon completing the service of process or upon the request of the owner, the owner's agent, or the person in lawful possession.

(n) Refusing or failing to leave land, real property, or structures belonging to or lawfully occupied by another and not open to the general public, upon being requested to leave by (1) a peace officer at the request of the owner, the owner's agent, or the person in lawful possession, and upon being informed by the peace officer that he or she is acting at the request of the owner, the owner's agent, or the person in lawful possession, or (2) the owner, the owner's agent, or the person in lawful possession. The owner, the owner's agent, or the person in lawful possession shall make a separate request to the peace officer on each occasion when the peace officer's assistance in dealing with a trespass is requested. However, a single request for a peace officer's assistance may be made to cover a limited period of time not to exceed 30 days and identified by specific dates, during which there is a fire hazard or the owner, owner's agent or person in lawful possession is absent from the premises or property. In addition, a single request for a peace officer's assistance may be made for a period not to exceed six months when the premises or property is closed to the public and posted as being closed. However, this subdivision shall not be applicable to persons engaged in lawful labor union activities which are permitted to be carried out on the property by the California Agricultural Labor Relations Act, Part 3.5 (commencing with Section 1140) of Division 2 of the Labor Code, or by the National Labor Relations Act. For purposes of this section, land, real property, or structures owned or operated by any housing authority for tenants as defined under Section 34213.5 of the Health and Safety Code constitutes property not open to the general public; however, this subdivision shall not apply to persons on the premises who are engaging in activities protected by the California or United States Constitution, or to persons who are on the premises at the request of a resident or management and who are not loitering or otherwise suspected of violating or actually violating any law or ordinance.

(o) Entering upon any lands declared closed to entry as provided in Section 4256 of the Public Resources Code, if the closed areas shall have been posted with notices declaring the closure, at intervals not greater than one mile along the exterior boundaries or along roads and trails passing through the lands.

(p) Refusing or failing to leave a public building of a public agency during those hours of the day or night when the building is regularly closed to the public upon being requested to do so by a regularly employed guard, watchman, or custodian of the public agency owning or maintaining the building or property, if the surrounding circumstances are such as to indicate to a reasonable person that the person has no apparent lawful business to pursue.

(q) Knowingly skiing in an area or on a ski trail which is closed to the public and which has signs posted indicating the closure.

(r) Refusing or failing to leave a hotel or motel, where he or she has obtained accommodations and has refused to pay for those accommodations, upon request of the proprietor or manager, and the occupancy is exempt, pursuant to subdivision (b) of Section 1940 of the Civil Code, from Chapter 2 (commencing with Section 1940) of Title 5 of Part 4 of Division 3 of the Civil Code. For purposes of this subdivision, occupancy at a hotel or motel for a continuous period of 30 days or less shall, in the absence of a written agreement to the contrary, or other written evidence of a periodic tenancy of indefinite duration, be exempt from Chapter 2 (commencing with Section 1940) of Title 5 of Part 4 of Division 3 of the Civil Code.

(s) Entering upon private property, including contiguous land, real property, or structures thereon belonging to the same owner, whether or not generally open to the public, after having been informed by a peace officer at the request of the owner, the owner's agent, or the person in lawful possession, and upon being informed by the peace officer that he or she is acting at the request of the owner, the owner's agent, or the person in lawful possession, that the property is not open to the particular person; or refusing or failing to leave the property upon being asked to leave the property in the manner provided in this subdivision.

This subdivision shall apply only to a person who has been convicted of a violent felony, as specified in subdivision (c) of Section 667.5, committed upon the particular private property. A single notification or request to the person as set forth above shall be valid and enforceable under this subdivision unless and until rescinded by the owner, the owner's agent, or the person in lawful possession of the property.

(t)(1) Knowingly entering, by an unauthorized person, upon any airport operations area if the area has been posted with notices restricting access to authorized personnel only and the postings occur not greater than every 150 feet along the exterior boundary.

(2) Any person convicted of a violation of paragraph (1) shall be punished as follows:

(A) By a fine not exceeding one hundred dollars ($100).

(B) By imprisonment in the county jail not exceeding six months, or by a fine not exceeding one thousand dollars ($1,000), or both, if the person refuses to leave the airport operations area after being requested to leave by a peace officer.

(C) By imprisonment in the county jail not exceeding six months, or by a fine not exceeding one thousand dollars ($1,000), or both, for a second or subsequent offense.

(3) As used in this subdivision the following definitions shall control:

(A) "Airport operations area" means that part of the airport used by aircraft for landing, taking off, surface maneuvering, loading and unloading, refueling, parking, or maintenance, where aircraft support vehicles and facilities exist, and which is not for public use or public vehicular traffic.

(B) "Authorized personnel"means any person who has a valid airport identification card issued by the airport operator or has a valid airline identification card recognized by the airport operator, or any person not in possession of an airport or airline identification card who is being escorted for legitimate purposes by a person with an airport or airline identification card.

(C) "Airport"means any facility whose function is to support commercial aviation.

(u) Refusing or failing to leave a battered women's shelter at any time after being requested to leave by a managing authority of the shelter.

(1) A person who is convicted of violating this subdivision shall be punished by imprisonment in a county jail for not more than one year.

(2) The court may order a defendant who is convicted of violating this subdivision to make restitution to a battered woman in an amount equal to the relocation expenses of the battered woman and her children if those expenses are incurred as a result of trespass by the defendant at a battered women's shelter. *(AM '00)*

602.1. Interfering with Business

(a) Any person who intentionally interferes with any lawful business or occupation carried on by the owner or agent of a business establishment open to the public, by obstructing or intimidating those attempting to carry on business, or their customers, and who refuses to leave the premises of the business establishment after being requested to leave by the owner or the owner's agent, or by a peace officer acting at the request of the owner or owner's agent, is guilty of a misdemeanor, punishable by imprisonment in a county jail for up to 90 days, or by a fine of up to four hundred dollars ($400), or by both that imprisonment and fine.

(b) Any person who intentionally interferes with any lawful business carried on by the employees of a public agency open to the public, by obstructing or intimidating those attempting to carry on business, or those persons there to transact business with the public agency, and who refuses to leave the premises of the public agency after being requested to leave by the office manager or a supervisor of the public agency, or by a peace officer acting at the request of the office manager or a supervisor of the public agency, is guilty of a misdemeanor, punishable by imprisonment in a county jail for up to 90 days, or by a fine of up to four hundred dollars ($400), or by both that imprisonment and fine.

(c) This section shall not apply to any of the following persons:

(1) Any person engaged in lawful labor union activities that are permitted to be carried out on the property by state or federal law.

(2) Any person on the premises who is engaging in activities protected by the California Constitution or the United States Constitution.

(d) Nothing in this section shall be deemed to supersede the application of any other law.

602.3. Lodging in Dwelling House

(a) A lodger who is subject to Section 1946.5 of the Civil Code and who remains on the premises of an owner-occupied dwelling unit after receipt of a notice terminating the hiring, and expiration of the notice period, provided in Section 1946.5 of the Civil Code is guilty of an infraction and may, pursuant to Section 837, be arrested for the offense by the owner, or in the event the owner is represented by a court-appointed conservator, executor, or administrator, by the owner's representative. Notwithstanding Section 853.5, the requirement of that section for release upon a written promise to appear shall not preclude an assisting peace officer from removing the person from the owner-occupied dwelling unit.

(b) The removal of a lodger from a dwelling unit by the owner pursuant to subdivision (a) is not a forcible entry under the provisions of Section 1159 of the code of Civil Procedure and shall not be the basis of civil liability under that section.

(c) Chapter 5 (commencing with Section 1980) of Title 5 of Part 4 of Division 3 of the Civil Code applies to any personal property of the lodger which remains on the premises following the lodger's removal from the premises pursuant to this section.

(d) Nothing in this section shall be construed to limit the owner's right to have a lodger removed under other provisions of law.

(e) Except as provided in subdivision (b), nothing in this section shall be construed to limit or affect in any way any cause of action an owner or lodger may have for damages for any breach of the contract of the parties respecting the lodging.

(f) This section applies only to owner-occupied dwellings where a single lodger resides. Nothing in this section shall be construed to determine or affect in any way the rights of persons residing as lodgers in an owner-occupied dwelling where more than one lodger resides.

602.4.   Unauthorized Entry or Sales of Goods at Airports

Every person who enters or remains on airport property owned by a city, county, or city and county but located in another county, and sells, peddles, or offers for sale any goods, merchandise, property, or services of any kind whatsoever, to members of the public, including transportation services, other than charter limousines licensed by the Public Utilities Commission, on or from the airport property, without the express written consent of the governing board of the airport property, or its duly authorized representative, is guilty of a misdemeanor.

Nothing in this section affects the power of a county, city, or city and county to regulate the sale, peddling or offering for sale of goods, merchandise, property, or services.

602.5.   Unauthorized Entry of Dwelling

(a) Every person other than a public officer or employee acting within the course and scope of his or her employment in performance of a duty imposed by law, who enters or remains in any noncommercial dwelling house, apartment, or other residential place without consent of the owner, his or her agent, or the person in lawful possession thereof, is guilty of a misdemeanor.

(b) Every person other than a public officer or an employee acting within the course and scope of his employment in performance of a duty imposed by law, who, without the consent of the owner, his or her agent, or the person in lawful possession thereof, enters or remains in any noncommercial dwelling house, apartment, or other residential place while a resident, or another person authorized to be in the dwelling, is present at any time during the course of the incident is guilty of aggravated trespass punishable by imprisonment in a county jail for not more than one year or by a fine of not more than one thousand dollars ($1,000), or by both that fine and imprisonment.

(c) If the court grants probation, it may order a person convicted of a misdemeanor under subdivision (b) to up to three years of supervised probation. It shall be a condition of probation that the person participate in counseling, as designated by the court.

(d) If a person is convicted of a misdemeanor under subdivision (b), the sentencing court shall also consider issuing an order restraining the defendant from any contact with the victim, that may be valid for up to three years, as determined by the court. In determining the length of the restraining order, the court shall consider, among other factors, the seriousness of the facts before the court, the probability of future violations, and the safety of the victim and his or her immediate family.

(e) Nothing in this section shall preclude prosecution under Section 459 or any other provision of law. *(AM '00)*

602.6   Unauthorized Entry or Refusal to Leave Fair Buildings or Grounds

Every person who enters or remains in, or upon, any state, county, district, or citrus fruit fair buildings or grounds, when the buildings or grounds are not open to the general public, after having been ordered or directed by a peace officer or a fair manager to leave the building or grounds and when the order or direction to leave is issued after determination that the person has no apparent lawful business or other legitimate reason for remaining on the property, and fails to identify himself or herself and account for his or her presence, is guilty of a misdemeanor.

602.7.   Unauthorized Peddling on Rapid Transit District Property or Vehicles

Every person who enters or remains on any property, facility, or vehicle owned by the San Francisco Bay Area Rapid Transit District or the Southern California Rapid Transit District, and sells or peddles any goods, merchandise, property, or services of any kind whatsoever on the property, facilities, or vehicles, without the express written consent of the governing board of the San Francisco Bay Area Rapid Transit

District or the governing board of the Southern California Rapid Transit District, or its duly authorized representatives, is guilty of an infraction.

Nothing in this section affects the power of a county, city, transit district, or city and county to regulate the sale or peddling of goods, merchandise, property, or services.

602.8. Trespass - Entering Cultivated, Fenced or Posted Land

(a) Any person who without the written permission of the landowner, the owner's agent or of the person in lawful possession of the land, willfully enters any lands under cultivation or enclosed by fence, belonging to, or occupied by, another, or who willfully enters upon uncultivated or unenclosed lands where signs forbidding trespass are displayed at intervals not less than three to the mile along all exterior boundaries and at all roads and trails entering the lands, is guilty of an infraction or a misdemeanor.

(b) Any person convicted of a violation of subdivision (a) shall be punished as follows:

(1) For a first offense, punished as an infraction by a fine of ten dollars ($10).

(2) For a second offense on any contiguous land of the same owner, punished as an infraction by a fine of not less than one hundred dollars ($100) nor more than two hundred fifty dollars ($250).

(3) For a third or subsequent offense on, any contiguous land of the same owner, by imprisonment in the county jail not exceeding six months, or by fine not exceeding one thousand dollars ($1,000), or both.

(c) Subdivision (a) shall not apply to any of the following:

(1) Any person engaged in lawful labor union activities which are permitted to be carried out on property by the California Agricultural Labor Relations Act, Part 3.5 of Division 2 of the Labor Code, or by the National Labor Relations Act.

(2) Any person on the premises who is engaging in activities protected by the California or United States Constitution.

(3) Any person described in Section 22350 of the Business and Professions Code who is making a lawful service of process.

(d) For any infraction charged pursuant to this section, the defendant shall have the option to forfeit bail in lieu of making a court appearance. Notwithstanding subdivision (e) of Section 853.6, if the offender elects to forfeit bail pursuant to this subdivision, no further proceedings shall be had in the case.

602.9. Claim Ownership or Possess Residential Dwelling Without Owner's Consent for Purpose of Renting or Selling to Another

(a) Except as provided in subdivision (c), any person who, without the owner's or owner's agent's consent, claims ownership or claims or takes possession of a residential dwelling for the purpose of renting that dwelling to another is guilty of a misdemeanor punishable by imprisonment in a county jail not exceeding six months, or by a fine not exceeding one thousand dollars ($1,000), or by both such imprisonment and fine. Each violation is a separate offense.

(b) Except as provided in subdivision (c), any person who, without the owner's or owner's agent's consent, causes another person to enter or remain in any residential dwelling for the purpose of renting that dwelling to another, is guilty of a misdemeanor punishable by imprisonment in a county jail not exceeding six months, or by a fine not exceeding one thousand dollars ($1,000), or by both such imprisonment and fine. Each violation is a separate offense.

(c) This section does not apply to any tenant, subtenant, lessee, sublessee, or assignee, nor to any other hirer having a lawful occupancy interest in the residential dwelling. *(AD '98)*

602.10. Physical Obstruction of Student or Teacher From Attending or Instructing at the University of California, California State University, or Community Colleges

Every person who, by physical force and with the intent to prevent attendance or instruction, willfully obstructs or attempts to obstruct any student or teacher seeking to attend or instruct classes at any of the campuses or facilities owned, controlled, or administered by the Regents of the University of California, the Trustees of the California State University, or the governing board of a community college district shall be punished by a fine not exceeding five hundred dollars ($500), by imprisonment in a county jail for a period of not exceeding one year, or by both such fine and imprisonment.

As used in this section, "physical force"includes, but is not limited to, use of one's person, individually or in concert with others, to impede access to, or movement within, or otherwise to obstruct the students and teachers of the classes to which the premises are devoted.

602.11. Obstruct Entry/Exit of Health Facility, Church, or School

(a) Any person, alone or in concert with others, who intentionally prevents an individual from entering or exiting a health care facility, place of worship, or school by physically detaining the individual or physically obstructing the individual's passage shall be guilty of a misdemeanor punishable by imprisonment in the county jail, or a fine of not more than two hundred fifty dollars ($250), or both, for the first offense; and imprisonment in the county jail for not less than five days and a fine of not more than five hundred dollars ($500) for the second offense; and imprisonment in the county jail for not less than 30 days and a fine of not more than two thousand dollars ($2,000) for a third or subsequent offense. However, the court may order the defendant to perform community service, in lieu of any fine or any imprisonment imposed under this section, if it determines that paying the fine would result in undue hardship to the defendant or his or her dependents.

(b) As used in subdivision (a), the following terms have the following meanings:

(1) "Physically"does not include speech.

(2) "Health care facility"means a facility licensed pursuant to Chapter 1 (Commencing with Section 1200) of Division 2 of the Health and Safety code, a health facility licensed pursuant to Chapter 2 (commencing with Section 1250) of Division 2 of the Health and Safety Code, or any facility where medical care is regularly provided to individuals by persons licensed under Division 2 (commencing with Section 500) of the Business and Professions Code, the Osteopathic Act, or the Chiropractic Initiative Act.

(3) "Person"does not include an officer, employee, or agent of the health care facility, or a law enforcement officer, acting in the course of his or her employment.

(c) This section shall not be interpreted to prohibit any lawful activities permitted under the laws of the State of California or by the National Labor Relations Act in connection with a labor dispute.

603. Forcible Entry or Injury to Dwelling House, Etc.

Every person other than a peace officer engaged in the performance of his duties as such who forcibly and without the consent of the owner, representative of the owner, lessee or representative of the lessee thereof, enters a dwelling house, cabin, or other building occupied or constructed for occupation by humans, and who damages, injures or destroys any property of value in, around or appertaining to such dwelling house, cabin or other building, is guilty of a misdemeanor.

607. Injuring Hydro-Power Equipment

Every person who willfully and maliciously cuts, breaks, injures or destroys, or who, without the authority of the owner or managing agent, operates any gate or control of, any bridge, dam, canal, flume, aqueduct, levee, embankment, reservoir, or other structure erected to create hydraulic power, or to drain or reclaim any swamp, overflow, tide or marsh land, or to store or conduct water for mining, manufacturing, reclamation, or agricultural purposes, or for the supply of the inhabitants of any city or town, or any embankment necessary to the same, or either of them, or willfully or maliciously makes, or causes to be made, any aperture or plows up the bottom or sides in such dam, canal, flume, aqueduct, reservoir, embankment, levee, or structure, with intent to injure or destroy the same; or draws up, cuts or injures any piles fixed in the ground for the purpose of securing any sea bank, sea wall, any dock, quay, jetty, or lock; or who, between the first day of October and the fifteenth day of April of each year, plows up or loosens the soil in the bed on the side of any natural water course, reclamation ditch, or drainage ditch, with an intent to destroy the same without removing such soil within 24 hours from such water course, reclamation ditch, or drainage ditch, or who, between the fifteenth day of April and the first day of October of each year, plows up or loosens the soil in the bed or on the sides of the natural water course, reclamation ditch, or drainage ditch, with an intent to destroy the same and does not remove therefrom the soil so plowed up or loosened before the first day of October next thereafter, is guilty of vandalism under Section 594. Nothing in this section shall be construed so as to in any manner prohibit any person from digging or removing soil from any water course, reclamation ditch, or drainage ditch for the purpose of mining.

610. Endangering Navigation by Masked or False Lights

Every person who unlawfully masks, alters, or removes any light or signal, or willfully exhibits any light or signal, with intent to bring any vessel into danger, is punishable by imprisonment in the state prison.

616. Tampering With Posted Legal Notice

Every person who intentionally defaces, obliterates, tears down, or destroys any copy or transcript, or extract from or of any law of the United States or of this State, or any proclamation, advertisement, or notification set up at any place in this State, by authority of any law of the United States or of this State, or by order of any Court, before the expiration of the time for which the same was to remain set up, is punishable by fine not less than twenty nor more than one hundred dollars, or by imprisonment in the County Jail not more than one month.

620. Altering Telegram or Phone Message

Every person who willfully alters the purport, effect, or meaning of a telegraphic or telephonic message to the injury of another, is punishable by imprisonment in the state prison, or in the county jail not exceeding one year, or by fine not exceeding ten thousand dollars ($10,000), or by both such fine and imprisonment.

622½. Willful Injury of Any Archeological or Historical Object

Every person, not the owner thereof, who willfully injures, disfigures, defaces, or destroys any object or thing of archeological or historical interest or value, whether situated on private lands or within any public park or place, is guilty of a misdemeanor.

624. Injuring Water Facilities or Pipes

Every person who willfully breaks, digs up, obstructs, or injures any pipe or main for conducting water, or any works erected for supplying buildings with water, or any appurtenances or appendages connected thereto, is guilty of a misdemeanor.

625b. Tampering With or Removing Parts From Aircraft

(a) Every person who willfully injures or tampers with any aircraft or the contents or parts thereof, or removes any part of or from an aircraft without the consent of the owner, and every person who, with intent to commit any malicious mischief, injury or other crime, climbs into or upon an aircraft or attempts to manipulate any of the controls, starting mechanism, brakes or other mechanism or device of an aircraft while it is at rest and unattended or who sets in motion any aircraft while it is at rest and unattended, is guilty of a misdemeanor and upon conviction shall be punished by imprisonment for not more than six months or by a fine of not more than one thousand dollars ($1,000), or by both such fine and imprisonment.

(b) Every person who willfully and maliciously damages, injures, or destroys any aircraft, or the contents or any part thereof, in such a manner as to render the aircraft unsafe for those flight operations for which it is designed and equipped is punishable by imprisonment in the state prison, or by imprisonment in a county jail not exceeding one year, or by a fine not exceeding ten thousand dollars ($10,000), or by both such fine and imprisonment.

625c. Tampering With Passenger Transit Vehicle or System

Any person who, with the intent to cause great bodily injury to another person, willfully removes, tampers with, injures or destroys any passenger transit vehicle or the contents or parts thereof, or who willfully removes, tampers with or destroys, or places an obstruction upon any part of the transit system, including its right-of-way, structures, fixtures, tracks, switches or controls, or who willfully sets a vehicle in motion while it is at rest and unattended is guilty of a felony.

MISCELLANEOUS CRIMES

626. Definitions - Miscellaneous Crimes - Schools

(a) As used in this chapter:

(1) "University"means the University of California, and includes any affiliated institution thereof and any campus or facility owned, operated, or controlled by the Regents of the University of California.

(2) "State university"means any California state university, and includes any campus or facility owned, operated, or controlled by the Trustees of the California State University.

(3) "Community college"means any public community college established pursuant to the Education Code.

(4) "School"means any elementary school, junior high school, four year high school, senior high school, adult school or any branch thereof, opportunity school, continuation high school, regional occupational center, evening high school, or technical school or any public right-of-way situated immediately adjacent to school property or any other place if a teacher and one or more students are required to be at that place in connection with assigned school activities.

(5) "Chief administrative officer"means:

(i) The president of the university or a state university, the Chancellor of the California State University, or the officer designated by the Regents of the University of California or pursuant to authority granted by the Regents of the University of California to administer and be the officer in charge of a campus or other facility owned, operated, or controlled by the Regents of the University of California, or the superintendent of a community college district.

(ii) For a school: the principal of the school; or a person who possesses a standard supervision credential or a standard administrative credential and who is designated by the principal; or a person who carries out the same functions as a person who possesses a credential and who is designated by the principal.

(b) For the purpose of determining the penalty to be imposed pursuant to this chapter, the court may consider a written report from the Department of Justice containing information from its records showing prior convictions; and the communication is prima facie evidence of the convictions, if the defendant admits them, regardless of whether or not the complaint commencing the proceedings has alleged prior convictions.

626.2. Unauthorized Student or Employee Willfully Entering Campus

Every student or employee who, after a hearing, has been suspended or dismissed from a community college, a state university, the university, or a school for disrupting the orderly operation of the campus or facility of such institution, and as a condition of such suspension or dismissal has been denied access to the campus or facility, or both, of the institution for the period of the suspension or in the case of dismissal for a period not to exceed one year; who has been served by registered or certified mail, at the last address given by such person, with a written notice of such suspension or dismissal and condition; and who willfully and knowingly enters upon the campus or facility of the institution to which he or she has been denied access, without the express written permission of the chief administrative officer of the campus or facility, is guilty of a misdemeanor and shall be punished as follows;

(1) Upon a first conviction, by a fine of not exceeding five hundred dollars ($500), by imprisonment in the county jail for a period of not more than six months, or by both such fine and imprisonment.

(2) If the defendant has been previously convicted once of a violation of any offense defined in this chapter or Section 415.5, by imprisonment in the county jail for a period of not less than 10 days or more than six months, or by both such imprisonment and a fine of not exceeding five hundred dollars ($500), and shall not be released on probation, parole, or any other basis until he or she has served not less than 10 days.

(3) If the defendant has been previously convicted two or more times of a violation of any offense defined in this chapter or Section 415.5, by imprisonment in the county jail for a period of not less than 90 days or more than six months, or by both such imprisonment and a fine of not exceeding five hundred dollars ($500), and shall not be released on probation, parole, or any other basis until he or she has served not less than 90 days.

Knowledge shall be presumed if notice has been given as prescribed in this section. The presumption established by this section is a presumption affecting the burden of proof.

626.4. Authority of Chief Administrative Officer to Revoke Authority of Person to Remain on Campus - Reinstatement

(a) The chief administrative officer of a campus or other facility of a community college, a state university, the university, or a school, or an officer or employee designated by the chief administrative officer to maintain order on such campus or facility, may notify a person that consent to remain on the campus or other facility under the control of the chief administrative officer has been withdrawn whenever there is reasonable cause to believe that such person has willfully disrupted the orderly operation of such campus or facility.

(b) Whenever consent is withdrawn by any authorized officer or employee, other than the chief administrative officer, such officer or employee shall as soon as is reasonably possible submit a written report to the chief administrative officer. The report shall contain all of the following:

(1) The description of the person from whom consent was withdrawn, including, if available, the person's name, address, and phone number.

(2) A statement of the facts giving rise to the withdrawal of consent.

If the chief administrative officer or, in the chief administrative officer's absence, a person designated by him or her for this purpose, upon reviewing the report, finds that there was reasonable cause to believe that such person has willfully disrupted the orderly operation of the campus or facility, he or she may enter written confirmation upon the report of the action taken by the officer or employee. If the chief administrative officer or, in the chief administrative officer's absence, the person designated by him or her, does not confirm the action of the officer or employee within 24 hours after the time that consent was withdrawn, the action of the officer or employee shall be deemed void and of no force or effect, except that any arrest made during such period shall not for this reason be deemed not to have been made for probable cause.

(c) Consent shall be reinstated by the chief administrative officer whenever he or she has reason to believe that the presence of the person from whom consent was withdrawn will not constitute a substantial and material threat to the orderly operation of the campus or facility. In no case shall consent be withdrawn for longer than 14 days from the date upon which consent was initially withdrawn. The person from whom consent has been withdrawn may submit a written request for a hearing on the withdrawal within the two-week period. The written request shall state the address to which notice of hearing is to be sent. The chief administrative officer shall grant such a hearing not later than seven days from the date of receipt of the request and shall immediately mail a written notice of the time, place, and date of such hearing to such person.

(d) Any person who has been notified by the chief administrative officer of a campus or other facility of a community college, a state university, the university, or a school, or by an officer or employee designated by the chief administrative officer to maintain order on such campus or facility, that consent to remain on the campus or facility has been withdrawn pursuant to subdivision (a); who has not had such consent reinstated; and who willfully and knowingly enters or remains upon such campus or facility during the period for which consent has been withdrawn is guilty of a misdemeanor. This subdivision does not apply to any person who enters or remains on such campus or facility for the sole purpose of applying to the chief administrative officer for the reinstatement of consent or for the sole purpose of attending a hearing on the withdrawal.

(e) This section shall not affect the power of the duly constituted authorities of a community college, a state university, the university, or a school, to suspend, dismiss, or expel any student or employee at the college, state university, university, or school.

(f) Any person convicted under this section shall be punished as follows:

(1) Upon a first conviction, by a fine of not exceeding five hundred dollars ($500), by imprisonment in the county jail for a period of not more than six months, or by both such fine and imprisonment.

(2) If the defendant has been previously convicted once of a violation of any offense defined in this chapter or Section 415.5, by imprisonment in the county jail for a period of not less than 10 days or more than

six months, or by both such imprisonment and a fine of not exceeding five hundred dollars ($500), and shall not be released on probation, parole, or any other basis until he or she has served not less than 10 days.

(3) If the defendant has been previously convicted two or more times of a violation of any offense defined in this chapter or Section 415.5, by imprisonment in the county jail for a period of not less than 90 days or more than six months, or by both such imprisonment and a fine of not exceeding five hundred dollars ($500), and shall not be released on probation, parole, or any other basis until he or she has served not less than 90 days.

(g) This section shall not affect the rights of representatives of employee organizations to enter, or remain upon, school grounds while actually engaged in activities related to representation, as provided for in Chapter 10.7 of Division 4 of Title 1 of the Government Code.

626.6. Interfering With Peaceful Conduct of Campus - Failure to Leave or Reentering Campus by Person Not a Student, Officer or Employee

(a) If a person who is not a student, officer or employee of a college or university and who is not required by his or her employment to be on the campus or any other facility owned, operated, or controlled by the governing board of that college or university, enters a campus or facility, and it reasonably appears to the chief administrative officer of the campus or facility, or to an officer or employee designated by the chief administrative officer to maintain order on the campus or facility, that the person is committing any act likely to interfere with the peaceful conduct of the activities of the campus or facility, or has entered the campus or facility for the purpose of committing any such act, the chief administrative officer or his or her designee may direct the person to leave the campus or facility. If that person fails to do so or if the person willfully and knowingly reenters upon the campus or facility within seven days after being directed to leave, he or she is guilty of a misdemeanor and shall be punished as follows:

(1) Upon a first conviction, by a fine of not more than five hundred dollars ($500), by imprisonment in the county jail for a period of not more than six months, or by both that fine and imprisonment.

(2) If the defendant has been previously convicted once of a violation of any offense defined in this chapter or Section 415.5, by imprisonment in the county jail for a period of not less than 10 days or more than six months, or by both that imprisonment and a fine of not more than five hundred dollars ($500), and shall not be released on probation, parole, or any other basis until he or she has served not less than 10 days.

(3) If the defendant has been previously convicted two or more times of a violation of any offense defined in this chapter or Section 415.5, by imprisonment in the county jail for a period of not less than 90 days or more than six months, or by both that imprisonment and a fine of not more than five hundred dollars ($500), and shall not be released on probation, parole, or any other basis until he or she has served not less than 90 days.

(b) The provisions of this section shall not be utilized to impinge upon the lawful exercise of constitutionally protected rights of freedom of speech or assembly.

(c) When a person is directed to leave pursuant to subdivision (a), the person directing him or her to leave shall inform the person that if he or she reenters the campus or facility within seven days he or she will be guilty of a crime.

626.7. Entering School Campus or Facility - Interfere with Peaceful Conduct - Removal and Reentry

(a) If a person who is not a student, officer, or employee of a public school, and who is not required by his or her employment to be on the campus or any other facility owned, operated, or controlled by the governing board of that school, enters a campus or facility, and it reasonably appears to the chief administrative officer of the campus or facility, or to an officer or employee designated by the chief administrative officer to maintain order on the campus or facility, that the person is committing any act likely to interfere with the peaceful conduct of the activities of the campus or facility, or has entered the campus or facility for the purpose of committing any such act, the chief administrative officer or his or her designee may direct the person to leave the campus or facility. If that person fails to do so or if the person willfully and knowingly reenters upon the campus or facility within 30 days after being directed to leave, or within seven days if the person is a parent or guardian of a student attending that school, he or she is guilty of a misdemeanor and shall be punished as follows:

(1) Upon a first conviction, by a fine of not more than five hundred dollars ($500), by imprisonment in a county jail for a period of not more than six months, or by both that fine and imprisonment.

(2) If the defendant has been previously convicted once of a violation of any offense defined in this chapter or Section 415.5, by imprisonment in a county jail for a period of not less than 10 days or more than six months, or by both that imprisonment and a fine of not more than five hundred dollars ($500), and the defendant shall not be released on probation, parole, or any other basis until he or she has served not less than 10 days.

(3) If the defendant has been previously convicted two or more times of a violation of any offense defined in this chapter or Section 415.5, by imprisonment in a county jail for a period of not less than 90 days or more than six months, or by both that imprisonment and a fine of not more than five hundred dollars ($500), and the defendant shall not be released on probation, parole, or any other basis until he or she has served not less than 90 days.

For purposes of this section, a representative of a school employee organization engaged in activities related to representation, as provided for in Chapter 10.7 (commencing with Section 3540) of Division 4 of Title 1 of the Government Code, shall be deemed a person required by his or her employment to be in a school building or on the grounds of a school.

(b) The provisions of this section shall not be utilized to impinge upon the lawful exercise of constitutionally protected rights of freedom of speech or assembly.

(c) When a person is directed to leave pursuant to subdivision (a), the person directing him or her to leave shall inform the person that if he or she reenters the campus or facility within the number of days prescribed by subdivision (a) he or she will be guilty of a crime.

(d) Notwithstanding any other subdivision of this section, the chief administrative officer, or his or her designee, shall allow a person previously directed to leave the campus or facility pursuant to this section to reenter the campus if the person is a parent or guardian of a pupil enrolled at the campus or facility who has to retrieve the pupil for disciplinary reasons, for medical attention, or for a family emergency.

626.8. Person Upon or Near School Ground Without Lawful Business - Interfering With Peaceful Conduct

(a) Any person who comes into any school building or upon any school ground, or street, sidewalk, or public way adjacent thereto, without lawful business thereon, and whose presence or acts interfere with the peaceful conduct of the activities of the school or disrupt the school or its pupils or school activities, or any specified sex offender who comes into any school building or upon any school ground, or street, sidewalk, or public way adjacent thereto, unless the person is a parent or guardian of a child attending that school, or is a student at the school or has prior written permission for the entry from the chief administrative officer of that school, is guilty of a misdemeanor if he or she does any of the following:

(1) Remains there after being asked to leave by the chief administrative official of that school or his or her designated representative, or by a person employed as a member of a security or police department of a school district pursuant to Section 39670 of the Education Code, or a city police officer, or sheriff or deputy sheriff, or a Department of the California Highway Patrol peace officer.

(2) Reenters or comes upon that place within seven days of being asked to leave by a person specified in paragraph (1).

(3) Has otherwise established a continued pattern of unauthorized entry.

This section shall not be utilized to impinge upon the lawful exercise of constitutionally protected rights of freedom of speech or assembly.

(b) Punishment for violation of this section shall be as follows:

(1) Upon a first conviction by a fine of not exceeding five hundred dollars ($500), by imprisonment in the county jail for a period of not more than six months, or by both the fine and imprisonment.

(2) If the defendant has been previously convicted once of a violation of any offense defined in this chapter or Section 415.5, by imprisonment in the county jail for a period of not less than 10 days or more than

six months, or by both imprisonment and a fine of not exceeding five hundred dollars ($500), and shall not be released on probation, parole, or any other basis until he or she has served not less than 10 days.

(3) If the defendant has been previously convicted two or more times of a violation of any offense defined in this chapter or Section 415.5, by imprisonment in the county jail for a period of not less than 90 days or more than six months, or by both imprisonment and a fine of not exceeding five hundred dollars ($500), and shall not be released on probation, parole, or any other basis until he or she has served not less than 90 days.

(c) As used in this section, the following definitions govern the meaning of the following words and phrases:

(1) "Specified sex offender"means any person required to register pursuant to Section 290, who has been convicted of a violation of Section 220, 261, 266, 267, 272, 288, or 289, or of subdivision (c), (d), or (f) of Section 286, or of subdivision (c), (d), or (f) of Section 288a, or of an attempt to commit any of these offenses.

(2) "Lawful business"means a reason for being present upon school property which is not otherwise prohibited by statute, by ordinance, or by any regulation adopted pursuant to statute or ordinance.

(3) "Continued pattern of unauthorized entry"means that on at least two prior occasions in the same school year the defendant came into any school building or upon any school ground, or street, sidewalk, or public way adjacent thereto, without lawful business thereon, and his or her presence or acts interfered with the peaceful conduct of the activities of the school or disrupted the school or its pupils or school activities, and the defendant was asked to leave by a person specified in paragraph (1) of subdivision (a).

(4) In the case of a specified sex offender, "continued pattern of unauthorized entry"means that on at least two prior occasions in the same school year the defendant came into any school building or upon any school ground, or street, sidewalk, or public way adjacent thereto, and the defendant was asked to leave by a person specified in paragraph (1) of subdivision (a).

(5) "School"means any preschool or school having any of grades kindergarten through 12.

(d) When a person is directed to leave pursuant to paragraph (1) of subdivision (a), the person directing him or her to leave shall inform the person that if he or she reenters the place within seven days he or she will be guilty of a crime.

626.85. Drug Offender On School Grounds

(a) Any specified drug offender who, at any time, comes into any school building or upon any school ground, or adjacent street, sidewalk, or public way, unless the person is a parent or guardian of a child attending that school and his or her presence is during any school activity, or is a student at the school and his or her presence is during any school activity, or has prior written permission for the entry from the chief administrative officer of that school, is guilty of a misdemeanor if he or she does any of the following:

(1) Remains there after being asked to leave by the chief administrative officer of that school or his or her designated representative, or by a person employed as a member of a security or police department of a school district pursuant to Section 39670 of the Education Code, or a city police officer, sheriff, or a Department of the California Highway Patrol peace officer.

(2) Reenters or comes upon that place within seven days of being asked to leave by a person specified in paragraph (1) of subdivision (a).

(3) Has otherwise established a continued pattern of unauthorized entry.

This section shall not be utilized to impinge upon the lawful exercise of constitutionally protected rights of freedom of speech or assembly, or to prohibit any lawful act, including picketing, strikes, or collective bargaining.

(b) Punishment for violation of this section shall be as follows:

(1) Upon a first conviction, by a fine not exceeding one thousand dollars ($1,000), by imprisonment in the county jail for a period of not more than six months, or by both that fine and imprisonment.

(2) If the defendant has been previously convicted once of a violation of any offense defined in this chapter or Section 415.5, by imprisonment in the county jail for a period of not less than 10 days or more than six months, or by both imprisonment and a fine not exceeding one thousand dollars ($1,000), and the de-

fendant shall not be released on probation, parole, or any other basis until he or she has served not less than 10 days.

(3) If the defendant has been previously convicted two or more times of a violation of any offense defined in this chapter or Section 415.5, by imprisonment in the county jail for a period of not less than 90 days or more than six months, or by both imprisonment and a fine not exceeding one thousand dollars ($1,000), and the defendant shall not be released on probation, parole, or any other basis until he or she has served not less than 90 days.

(c) As used in this section:

(1) "Specified drug offender"means any person who, within the immediately preceding three years, has a felony or misdemeanor conviction of either:

(A) Unlawful sale, or possession for sale, of any controlled substance, as defined in Section 11007 of the Health and Safety Code.

(B) Unlawful use, possession, or being under the influence of any controlled substance, as defined in Section 11007 of the Health and Safety Code, where that conviction was based on conduct which occurred, wholly or partly, in any school building or upon any school ground, or adjacent street, sidewalk, or public way.

(2) "Continued pattern of unauthorized entry"means that on at least two prior occasions in the same calendar year the defendant came into any school building or upon any school ground, or adjacent street, sidewalk, or public way, and the defendant was asked to leave by a person specified in paragraph (1) of subdivision (a).

(3) "School"means any preschool or school having any of grades kindergarten to 12, inclusive.

(4) "School activity"means and includes any school session, any extracurricular activity or event sponsored by or participated in by the school, and the 30-minute periods immediately preceding and following any session, activity, or event.

(d) When a person is directed to leave pursuant to paragraph (1) of subdivision (a), the person directing him or her to leave shall inform the person that if he or she reenters the place he or she will be guilty of a crime.

626.9. Bringing or Possessing Firearm on Grounds of Public School, College, or University

(a) This section shall be known, and may be cited, as the Gun-Free School Zone Act of 1995.

(b) Any person who possesses a firearm in a place that the person knows, or reasonably should know, is a school zone, as defined in paragraph (1) of subdivision (e), unless it is with the written permission of the school district superintendent, his or her designee, or equivalent school authority, shall be punished as specified in subdivision (f).

(c) Subdivision (b) does not apply to the possession of a firearm under any of the following circumstances:

(1) Within a place of residence or place of business or on private property, if the place of residence, place of business, or private property is not part of the school grounds and the possession of the firearm is otherwise lawful.

(2) When the firearm is an unloaded pistol, revolver, or other firearm capable of being concealed on the person and is in a locked container or within the locked trunk of a motor vehicle.

This section does not prohibit or limit the otherwise lawful transportation of any other firearm, other than a pistol, revolver, or other firearm capable of being concealed on the person, in accordance with state law.

(3) When the person possessing the firearm reasonably believes that he or she is in grave danger because of circumstances forming the basis of a current restraining order issued by a court against another person or persons who has or have been found to pose a threat to his or her life or safety. This subdivision may not apply when the circumstances involve a mutual restraining order issued pursuant to Division 10 (commencing with Section 6200) of the Family Code absent a factual finding of a specific threat to the person's life or

safety. Upon a trial for violating subdivision (b), the trier of a fact shall determine whether the defendant was acting out of a reasonable belief that he or she was in grave danger.

(4) When the person is exempt from the prohibition against carrying a concealed firearm pursuant to subdivision (b), (d), (e), or (h) of Section 12027.

(d) Except as provided in subdivision (b), it shall be unlawful for any person, with reckless disregard for the safety of another, to discharge, or attempt to discharge, a firearm in a school zone, as defined in paragraph (1) of subdivision (e).

The prohibition contained in this subdivision does not apply to the discharge of a firearm to the extent that the conditions of paragraph (1) of subdivision (c) are satisfied.

(e) As used in this section, the following definitions shall apply:

(1) "School zone"means an area in, or on the grounds of, a public or private school providing instruction in kindergarten or grades 1 to 12, inclusive, or within a distance of 1,000 feet from the grounds of the public or private school.

(2) "Firearm"has the same meaning as that term is given in Section 12001.

(3) "Locked container"has the same meaning as that term is given in subdivision (c) of Section 12026.1.

(4) "Concealed firearm"has the same meaning as that term is given in Sections 12025 and 12026.1.

(f)(1) Any person who violates subdivision (b) by possessing a firearm in, or on the grounds of, a public or private school providing instruction in kindergarten or grades 1 to 12, inclusive, shall be punished by imprisonment in the state prison for two, three, or five years.

(2) Any person who violates subdivision (b) by possessing a firearm within a distance of 1,000 feet from the grounds of a public or private school providing instruction in kindergarten or grades 1 to 12, inclusive, shall be punished as follows:

(A) By imprisonment in the state prison for two, three, or five years, if any of the following circumstances apply:

(i) If the person previously has been convicted of any felony, or of any crime made punishable by Chapter 1 (commencing with Section 12000) of Title 2 of Part 4.

(ii) If the person is within a class of persons prohibited from possessing or acquiring a firearm pursuant to Section 12021 or 12021.1 of this code or Section 8100 or 8103 of the Welfare and Institutions Code.

(iii) If the firearm is any pistol, revolver, or other firearm capable of being concealed upon the person and the offense is punished as a felony pursuant to Section 12025.

(B) By imprisonment in a county jail for not more than one year or by imprisonment in the state prison for two, three, or five years, in all cases other than those specified in subparagraph (A).

(3) Any person who violates subdivision (d) shall be punished by imprisonment in the state prison for three, five, or seven years.

(g)(1) Every person convicted under this section for a misdemeanor violation of subdivision (b) who has been convicted previously of a misdemeanor offense enumerated in Section 12001.6 shall be punished by imprisonment in a county jail for not less than three months, or if probation is granted or if the execution or imposition of sentence is suspended, it shall be a condition thereof that he or she be imprisoned in a county jail for not less than three months.

(2) Every person convicted under this section of a felony violation of subdivision (b) or (d) who has been convicted previously of a misdemeanor offense enumerated in Section 12001.6, if probation is granted or if the execution of sentence is suspended, it shall be a condition thereof that he or she be imprisoned in a county jail for not less than three months.

(3) Every person convicted under this section for a felony violation of subdivision (b) or (d) who has been convicted previously of any felony, or of any crime made punishable by Chapter 1 (commencing with Section 12000) of Title 2 of Part 4, if probation is granted or if the execution or imposition of sentence is suspended, it shall be a condition thereof that he or she be imprisoned in a county jail for not less than three months.

(4) The court shall apply the three-month minimum sentence specified in this subdivision, except in unusual cases where the interests of justice would best be served by granting probation or suspending the exe-

cution or imposition of sentence without the minimum imprisonment required in this subdivision or by granting probation or suspending the execution or imposition of sentence with conditions other than those set forth in this subdivision, in which case the court shall specify on the record and shall enter on the minutes the circumstances indicating that the interests of justice would best be served by this disposition.

(h) Notwithstanding Section 12026, any person who brings or possesses a loaded firearm upon the grounds of a campus of, or buildings owned or operated for student housing, teaching, research, or administration by, a public or private university or college, that are contiguous or are clearly marked university property, unless it is with the written permission of the university or college president, his or her designee, or equivalent university or college authority, shall be punished by imprisonment in the state prison for two, three, or four years. Notwithstanding subdivision (k), a university or college shall post a prominent notice at primary entrances on noncontiguous property stating that firearms are prohibited on that property pursuant to this subdivision.

(i) Notwithstanding Section 12026, any person who brings or possesses a firearm upon the grounds of a campus of, or buildings owned or operated for student housing, teaching, research, or administration by, a public or private university or college, that are contiguous or are clearly marked university property, unless it is with the written permission of the university or college president, his or her designee, or equivalent university or college authority, shall be punished by imprisonment in the state prison for one, two, or three years. Notwithstanding subdivision (k), a university or college shall post a prominent notice at primary entrances on noncontiguous property stating that firearms are prohibited on that property pursuant to this subdivision.

(j) For purposes of this section, a firearm shall be deemed to be loaded when there is an unexpended cartridge or shell, consisting of a case that holds a charge of powder and a bullet or shot, in, or attached in any manner to, the firearm, including, but not limited to, in the firing chamber, magazine, or clip thereof attached to the firearm. A muzzle-loader firearm shall be deemed to be loaded when it is capped or primed and has a powder charge and ball or shot in the barrel or cylinder.

(k) This section does not require that notice be posted regarding the proscribed conduct.

(l) This section does not apply to a duly appointed peace officer as defined in Chapter 4.5 (commencing with Section 830) of Title 3 of Part 2, a full-time paid peace officer of another state or the federal government who is carrying out official duties while in California, any person summoned by any of these officers to assist in making arrests or preserving the peace while he or she is actually engaged in assisting the officer, a member of the military forces of this state or of the United States who is engaged in the performance of his or her duties, a person holding a valid license to carry the firearm pursuant to Article 3 (commencing with Section 12050) of Chapter 1 of Title 2 of Part 4, or an armored vehicle guard, engaged in the performance of his or her duties, as defined in subdivision (e) of Section 7521 of the Business and Professions Code.

(m) This section does not apply to a security guard authorized to carry a loaded firearm pursuant to Section 12031.

(n) This section does not apply to an existing shooting range at a public or private school or university or college campus.

(o) This section does not apply to an honorably retired peace officer authorized to carry a concealed or loaded firearm pursuant to subdivision (a) or (i) of Section 12027 or paragraph (1) or (8) of subdivision (b) of Section 12031. *(AM '99)*

626.95. Possess/Brandish Firearm Where Children Gather

(a) Any person who is in violation of paragraph (2) of subdivision (a), or subdivision (b), of Section 417, or Section 12025 or 12031, upon the grounds of or within a playground, or a public or private youth center during hours in which the facility is open for business, classes, or school-related programs, or at any time when minors are using the facility, knowing that he or she is on or within those grounds, shall be punished by imprisonment in the state prison or one, two, or three years, or in a county jail not exceeding one year.

(b) State and local authorities are encouraged to cause signs to be posted around playgrounds and youth centers giving warning or prohibition of the possession of firearms upon the grounds of or within playgrounds or youth centers.

(c) For purposes of this section, the following definitions shall apply:

(1) "Playground" means any park or recreational area specifically designed to be used by children that has play equipment installed, including public grounds designed for athletic activities such as baseball, football, soccer, or basketball, or any similar facility located on public or private school grounds, or on city or county parks.

(2) "Youth center" means any public or private facility that is used to host recreational or social activities for minors while minors are present.

(d) It is the Legislature's intent that only an actual conviction of a felony of one of the offenses specified in this section would subject a person to firearms disabilities under the federal Gun Control Act of 1968 (P.L. 90-618; 18 U.S.C. Section 921).

626.10. Knives, Razors, Tasers, Stun Guns, Etc. on School Grounds - Exceptions

(a) Any person, except a duly appointed peace officer as defined in Chapter 4.5 (commencing with Section 830) of Title 3 of Part 2, a full-time paid peace officer of another state or the federal government who is carrying out official duties while in this state, a person summoned by any officer to assist in making arrests or preserving the peace while the person is actually engaged in assisting any officer, or a member of the military forces of this state or the United States who is engaged in the performance of his or her duties, who brings or possesses any dirk, dagger, ice pick, knife having a blade longer than 2 1/2 inches, folding knife with a blade that locks into place, a razor with an unguarded blade, a taser, or a stun gun, as defined in subdivision (a) of Section 244.5, any instrument that expels a metallic projectile such as a BB or a pellet, through the force of air pressure, CO2 pressure, or spring action, or any spot marker gun, upon the grounds of, or within, any public or private school providing instruction in kindergarten or any of grades 1 to 12, inclusive, is guilty of a public offense, punishable by imprisonment in a county jail not exceeding one year, or by imprisonment in the state prison.

(b) Any person, except a duly appointed peace officer as defined in Chapter 4.5 (commencing with Section 830) of Title 3 of Part 2, a full-time paid peace officer of another state or the federal government who is carrying out official duties while in this state, a person summoned by any officer to assist in making arrests or preserving the peace while the person is actually engaged in assisting any officer, or a member of the military forces of this state or the United States who is engaged in the performance of his or her duties, who brings or possesses any dirk, dagger, ice pick, or knife having a fixed blade longer than 2 1/2 inches upon the grounds of, or within, any private university, the University of California, the California State University, or the California Community Colleges is guilty of a public offense, punishable by imprisonment in a county jail not exceeding one year, or by imprisonment in the state prison.

(c) Subdivisions (a) and (b) do not apply to any person who brings or possesses a knife having a blade longer than 2 1/2 inches or a razor with an unguarded blade upon the grounds of, or within, a public or private school providing instruction in kindergarten or any of grades 1 to 12, inclusive, or any private university, state university, or community college at the direction of a faculty member of the private university, state university, or community college, or a certificated or classified employee of the school for use in a private university, state university, community college, or school-sponsored activity or class.

(d) Subdivisions (a) and (b) do not apply to any person who brings or possesses an ice pick, a knife having a blade longer than 2 1/2 inches, or a razor with an unguarded blade upon the grounds of, or within, a public or private school providing instruction in kindergarten or any of grades 1 to 12, inclusive, or any private university, state university, or community college for a lawful purpose within the scope of the person's employment.

(e) Subdivision (b) does not apply to any person who brings or possesses an ice pick or a knife having a fixed blade longer than 2 1/2 inches upon the grounds of, or within, any private university, state university, or community college for lawful use in or around a residence or residential facility located upon those grounds or for lawful use in food preparation or consumption.

(f) Subdivision (a) does not apply to any person who brings an instrument that expels a metallic projectile such as a BB or a pellet, through the force of air pressure, CO_2 pressure, or spring action, or any spot marker gun upon the grounds of, or within, a public or private school providing instruction in kindergarten or any of grades 1 to 12, inclusive, if the person has the written permission of the school principal or his or her designee.

(g) Any certificated or classified employee or school peace officer of a public or private school providing instruction in kindergarten or any of grades 1 to 12, inclusive, may seize any of the weapons described in subdivision (a), and any certificated or classified employee or school peace officer of any private university, state university, or community college may seize any of the weapons described in subdivision (b), from the possession of any person upon the grounds of, or within, the school if he or she knows, or has reasonable cause to know, the person is prohibited from bringing or possessing the weapon upon the grounds of, or within, the school.

(h) As used in this section, "dirk" or "dagger" means a knife or other instrument with or without a handguard that is capable of ready use as a stabbing weapon that may inflict great bodily injury or death.

627.1. Definitions - Access to School Grounds

As used in this chapter, with regard to a public school:

(a) An "outsider" is any person other than:

(1) A student of the school; except that a student who is currently suspended from the school shall be deemed an outsider for purposes of this chapter.

(2) A parent or guardian of a student of the school.

(3) An officer or employee of the school district that maintains the school.

(4) A public employee whose employment requires him or her to be on school grounds, or any person who is on school grounds at the request of the school.

(5) A representative of a school employee organization who is engaged in activities related to the representation of school employees.

(6) An elected public official.

(7) A person who comes within the provisions of Section 1070 of the Evidence Code by virtue of his or her current employment or occupation.

(b) "School grounds" are the buildings and grounds of the public school.

(c) "School hours" extend from one hour before classes begin until one hour after classes end.

(d) "Principal" is the chief administrative officer of the public school.

(e) "Designee" is a person whom the principal has authorized to register outsiders pursuant to this chapter.

(f) "Superintendent" is the superintendent of the school district that maintains the school or a person (other than the principal or someone employed under the principal's supervision) who the superintendent has authorized to conduct hearings pursuant to Section 627.5.

627.2. Registration of Outsiders Required

No outsider shall enter or remain on school grounds during school hours without having registered with the principal or designee, except to proceed expeditiously to the office of the principal or designee for the purpose of registering. If signs posted in accordance with Section 627.6 restrict the entrance or route that outsiders may use to reach the office of the principal or designee, an outsider shall comply with such signs.

627.6. Signs - Notice of Registration Requirement

At each entrance to the school grounds of every public school at which this chapter is in force, signs shall be posted specifying the hours during which registration is required pursuant to Section 627.2, stating where the office of the principal or designee is located and what route to take to that office, and setting forth the applicable requirements of Section 627.2 and the penalties for violation of this chapter.

627.7. Failure or Refusal to Leave School Grounds Promptly

(a) It is a misdemeanor punishable by imprisonment in the county jail not to exceed six months, or by a fine not to exceed five hundred dollars ($500), or by both, for an outsider to fail or refuse to leave the school grounds promptly after the principal, designee, or school security officer has requested the outsider to leave or to fail to remain off the school grounds for 7 days after being requested to leave, if the outsider does any of the following:

(1) Enters or remains on school grounds without having registered as required by Section 627.2.

(2) Enters or remains on school grounds after having been denied registration pursuant to subdivision (a) of Section 627.4.

(3) Enters or remains on school grounds after having registration revoked pursuant to subdivision (b) of Section 627.4.

(b) The provisions of this section shall not be utilized to impinge upon the lawful exercise of constitutionally protected rights of freedom of speech or assembly.

(c) When a person is directed to leave pursuant to subdivision (a), the person directing him or her to leave shall inform the person that if he or she reenters the place within 7 days he or she will be guilty of a crime.

631. Wiretapping

(a) Any person who, by means of any machine, instrument, or contrivance, or in any other manner, intentionally taps, or makes any unauthorized connection, whether physically, electrically, acoustically, inductively, or otherwise, with any telegraph or telephone wire, line, cable, or instrument, including the wire, line, cable, or instrument of any internal telephonic communication system, or who willfully and without the consent of all parties to the communication, or in any unauthorized manner, reads, or attempts to read, or to learn the contents or meaning of any message, report, or communication while the same is in transit or passing over any such wire, line, or cable, or is being sent from, or received at any place within this state; or who uses, or attempts to use, in any manner, or for any purpose, or to communicate in any way, any information so obtained, or who aids, agrees with, employs, or conspires with any person or persons to unlawfully do, or permit, or cause to be done any of the acts or things mentioned above in this section, is punishable by a fine not exceeding two thousand five hundred dollars ($2,500), or by imprisonment in the county jail not exceeding one year, or by imprisonment in the state prison, or by both a fine and imprisonment in the county jail or in the state prison. If the person has previously been convicted of a violation of this section or Section 632, 632.5, 632.6, 632.7, or 636, he or she is punishable by a fine not exceeding ten thousand dollars ($10,000), or by imprisonment in the county jail not exceeding one year, or by imprisonment in the state prison, or by both a fine and imprisonment in the county jail or in the state prison.

(b) This section shall not apply (1) to any public utility engaged in the business of providing communications services and facilities, or to the officers, employees or agents thereof, where the acts otherwise prohibited herein are for the purpose of construction, maintenance, conduct or operation of the services and facilities of the public utility, or (2) to the use of any instrument, equipment, facility, or service furnished and used pursuant to the tariffs of a public utility, or (3) to any telephonic communication system used for communication exclusively within a state, county, city and county, or city correctional facility.

(c) Except as proof in an action or prosecution for violation of this section, no evidence obtained in violation of this section shall be admissible in any judicial, administrative, legislative or other proceeding.

632. Eavesdropping on or Recording Confidential Communications

(a) Every person who, intentionally and without the consent of all parties to a confidential communication, by means of any electronic amplifying or recording device, eavesdrops upon or records the confidential communication, whether the communication is carried on among the parties in the presence of one another or by means of a telegraph, telephone, or other device, except a radio, shall be punished by a fine not exceeding two thousand five hundred dollars ($2,500), or imprisonment in the county jail not exceeding one year, or in the state prison, or by both that fine and imprisonment. If the person has previously been convicted of a violation of this section or Section 631, 632.5, 632.6, 632.7, or 636, the person shall be punished by a fine not exceeding ten thousand dollars ($10,000), by imprisonment in the county jail not exceeding one year, or in the state prison, or by both that fine and imprisonment.

(b) The term "person"includes an individual, business association, partnership, corporation, limited liability company, or other legal entity, and an individual acting or purporting to act for or on behalf of any government or subdivision thereof, whether federal, state, or local, but excludes an individual known by all parties to a confidential communication to be overhearing or recording the communication.

(c) The term "confidential communication"includes any communication carried on in circumstances as may reasonably indicate that any party to the communication desires it to be confined to the parties thereto, but excludes a communication made in a public gathering or in any legislative, judicial, executive or administrative proceeding open to the public, or in any other circumstance in which the parties to the communication may reasonably expect that the communication may be overheard or recorded.

(d) Except as proof in an action or prosecution for violation of this section, no evidence obtained as a result of eavesdropping upon or recording a confidential communication in violation of this section shall be admissible in any judicial, administrative, legislative, or other proceeding.

(e) This section does not apply (1) to any public utility engaged in the business of providing communications services and facilities, or to the officers, employees or agents thereof, where the acts otherwise prohibited by this section are for the purpose of construction, maintenance, conduct or operation of the services and facilities of the public utility, or (2) to the use of any instrument, equipment, facility, or service furnished and used pursuant to the tariffs of a public utility, or (3) to any telephonic communication system used for communication exclusively within a state, county, city and county, or city correctional facility.

(f) This section does not apply to the use of hearing aids and similar devices, by persons afflicted with impaired hearing, for the purpose of overcoming the impairment to permit the hearing of sounds ordinarily audible to the human ear.

632.5.   Intercepting or Receiving Cellular Radio Telephone Communication

(a) Every person who, maliciously and without the consent of all parties to the communication, intercepts, receives, or assists in intercepting or receiving a communication transmitted between cellular radio telephones or between any cellular radio telephone and a landline telephone shall be punished by a fine not exceeding two thousand five hundred dollars ($2,500), by imprisonment in the county jail not exceeding one year or in the state prison, or by both that fine and imprisonment. If the person has been previously convicted of a violation of this section or Section 631, 632, 632.7, or 636, the person shall be punished by a fine not exceeding ten thousand dollars ($10,000), by imprisonment in the county jail not exceeding one year or in the state prison, or by both that fine and imprisonment.

(b) In the following instances, this section shall not apply:

(1) To any public utility engaged in the business of providing communications services and facilities, or to the officers, employees, or agents thereof, where the acts otherwise prohibited are for the purpose of construction, maintenance, conduct, or operation of the services and facilities of the public utility.

(2) To the use of any instrument, equipment, facility, or service furnished and used pursuant to the tariffs of the public utility.

(3) To any telephonic communication system used for communication exclusively within a state, county, city and county, or city correctional facility.

(c) As used in this section and Section 635, "cellular radio telephone"means a wireless telephone authorized by the Federal Communications Commission to operate in the frequency bandwidth reserved for cellular radio telephones.

632.6.   Eavesdropping on Cordless Telephone Communications

(a) Every person who, maliciously and without the consent of all parties to the communication, intercepts, receives, or assists in intercepting or receiving a communication transmitted between cordless telephones as defined in subdivision (c), between any cordless telephone and a landline telephone, or between a cordless telephone and a cellular telephone shall be punished by a fine not exceeding two thousand five hundred dollars ($2,500), by imprisonment in the county jail not exceeding one year, or in the state prison, or by both that fine and imprisonment. If the person has been convicted previously of a violation of Section

631, 632, 632.5, 632.7, or 636, the person shall be punished by a fine not exceeding ten thousand dollars ($10,000), or by imprisonment in the county jail not exceeding one year, or in the state prison, or by both that fine and imprisonment.

(b) This section shall not apply in any of the following instances:

(1) To any public utility engaged in the business of providing communications services and facilities, or to the officers, employees, or agents thereof, where the acts otherwise prohibited are for the purpose of construction, maintenance, conduct, or operation of the services and facilities of the public utility.

(2) To the use of any instrument, equipment, facility, or service furnished and used pursuant to the tariffs of the public utility.

(3) To any telephonic communications system used for communication exclusively within a state, county, city and county, or city correctional facility.

(c) As used in this section and Section 635, "cordless telephone"means a two-way low power communication system consisting of two parts "base"unit which connects to the public switched telephone network and a handset or "remote"unit which are connected by a radio link and authorized by the Federal Communications Commission to operate in the frequency bandwidths reserved for cordless telephones.

632.7. Recording of Unlawfully Intercepted Communications

(a) Every person who, without the consent of all parties to a communication, intercepts or receives and intentionally records, or assists in the interception or reception and intentional recordation of, a communication transmitted between two cellular radio telephones, a cellular radio telephone and a landline telephone, two cordless telephones, a cordless telephone and a landline telephone, or a cordless telephone and cellular radio telephone, shall be punished by a fine not exceeding two thousand five hundred dollars ($2,500), or by imprisonment in a county jail not exceeding one year, or in the state prison, or by both that fine and imprisonment. If the person has been convicted previously of a violation of this section or Section 631, 632, 632.5, 632.6, or 636, the person shall be punished by a fine not exceeding ten thousand dollars ($10,000), by imprisonment in a county jail not exceeding one year, or in the state prison, or by both that fine and imprisonment.

(b) This section shall not apply to any of the following:

(1) To any public utility engaged in the business of providing communications services and facilities, or to the officers, employees, or agents thereof, where the acts otherwise prohibited are for the purpose of construction, maintenance, conduct, or operation of the services and facilities of the public utility.

(2) The use of any instrument, equipment, facility, or service furnished and used pursuant to the tariffs of the public utility.

(3) Any telephonic communications system used for communication exclusively within a state, county, city and county, or city correctional facility.

(c) As used in this section, each of the following terms have the following meaning:

(1) "Cellular radio telephone"means a wireless telephone authorized by the Federal Communications Commission to operate in the frequency bandwidth reserved for cellular radio telephones.

(2) "Cordless telephone"means a two-way, low power communication system consisting of two parts, a "base"unit which connects to the public switched telephone network and a handset or "remote"unit, that are connected by a radio link and authorized by the Federal Communications Commission to operate in the frequency bandwidths reserved for cordless telephones.

(3) "Communication"includes, but is not limited to, communications transmitted by voice, data, or image, including facsimile.

633. Law Enforcement Officers - Limited Exemption From Prohibition Against Overhearing or Recording Communications

Nothing in Section 631, 632, 632.5, 632.6, or 632.7 prohibits the Attorney General, any district attorney, or any assistant, deputy, or investigator of the Attorney General or any district attorney, any officer of the CHP, any chief of police, assistant chief of police, or police officer of a city or city and county, any sheriff, under-sheriff, or deputy sheriff regularly employed and paid as such of a county, or any person acting pursuant to the direction of one of these law enforcement officers acting within the scope of his or her authority, from overhearing or recording any communication which they could lawfully overhear or record prior to the effective date of this chapter.

Nothing in Section 631, 632, 632.5, 632.6, or 632.7 renders inadmissible any evidence obtained by the above-named persons by means of overhearing or recording any communication which they could lawfully overhear or record prior to the effective date of this chapter.

633.1. Airport Law Enforcement Officers - Exemption From Prohibition Against Recording Telephone Communications

(a) Nothing in Section 631, 632, 632.5, 632.6, or 632.7 prohibits any person regularly employed as an airport law enforcement officer, as described in subdivision (d) of Section 830.33, acting within the scope of his or her authority, from recording any communication which is received on an incoming telephone line, for which the person initiating the call utilized a telephone number known to the public to be a means of contacting airport law enforcement officers. In order for a telephone call to be recorded under this subdivision, a series of electronic tones shall be used, placing the caller on notice that his or her telephone call is being recorded.

(b) Nothing in Section 631, 632, 632.5, 632.6, or 632.7 renders inadmissible any evidence obtained by an officer described in subdivision (a) if the evidence was received by means of recording any communication which is received on an incoming public telephone line, for which the person initiating the call utilized a telephone number known to the public to be a means of contacting airport law enforcement officers.

(c) This section shall only apply to airport law enforcement officers who are employed at an airport which maintains regularly scheduled international airport service and which maintains permanent facilities of the United States Customs Service.

633.5. Confidential Communications Recorded by One Party as Evidence of Felony - Admissibility

Nothing in Section 631, 632, 632.5, 632.6, or 632.7 prohibits one party to a confidential communication from recording the communication for the purpose of obtaining evidence reasonably believed to relate to the commission by another party to the communication of the crime of extortion, kidnapping, bribery, any felony involving violence against the person, or a violation of Section 653m. Nothing in Section 631, 632, 632.5, 632.6, or 632.7 renders any evidence so obtained inadmissible in a prosecution for extortion, kidnapping, bribery, any felony involving violence against the person, a violation of Section 653m, or any crime in connection therewith.

634. Trespassing for Purpose of Committing Invasion of Privacy

Any person who trespasses on property for the purpose of committing any act, or attempting to commit any act, in violation of Section 631, 632, 632.5, 632.6, 632.7, or 636 shall be punished by a fine not exceeding two thousand five hundred dollars ($2,500), by imprisonment in the county jail not exceeding one year or in the state prison, or by both that fine and imprisonment. If the person has previously been convicted of a violation of this section or Section 631, 632, 632.5, 632.6, 632.7, or 636, the person shall be punished by a fine not exceeding ten thousand dollars ($10,000), by imprisonment in the county jail not exceeding one year or in the state prison, or by both that fine and imprisonment.

635. Manufacturing or Selling Devices Intended for Eavesdropping or Interception of Radio Telephone Communications

(a) Every person who manufactures, assembles, sells, offers for sale, advertises for sale, possesses, transports, imports, or furnishes to another any device which is primarily or exclusively designed or intended for eavesdropping upon the communication of another, or any device which is primarily or exclusively designed or intended for the unauthorized interception or reception of communications between cellular radio telephones or between a cellular radio telephone and a landline telephone in violation of Section 632.5, or communications between cordless telephones or between a cordless telephone and a landline telephone in violation of Section 632.6, shall be punished by a fine not exceeding two thousand five hundred dollars ($2,500), by imprisonment in the county jail not exceeding one year, or in the state prison, or by both that fine and imprisonment. If the person has previously been convicted of a violation of this section, the person shall be punished by a fine not exceeding ten thousand dollars ($10,000), by imprisonment in the county jail not exceeding one year, or in the state prison, or by both that fine and imprisonment.

(b) This section does not apply to either of the following:

(1) An act otherwise prohibited by this section when performed by any of the following:

(A) A communication utility or an officer, employee or agent thereof for the purpose of construction, maintenance, conduct, or operation of, or otherwise incident to the use of, the services or facilities of the utility.

(B) A state, county, or municipal law enforcement agency or an agency of the federal government.

(C) A person engaged in selling devices specified in subdivision (a) for use by, or resale to, agencies of a foreign government under terms approved by the federal government, communication utilities, state, county, or municipal law enforcement agencies, or agencies of the federal government.

(2) Possession by a subscriber to communication utility service of a device specified in subdivision (a) furnished by the utility pursuant to its tariffs.

636. Eavesdropping on or Recording Conversation Between Person in Custody and His Attorney, Religious Advisor or Physician

(a) Every person who, without permission from all parties to the conversation, eavesdrops on or records, by means of an electronic device, a conversation, or any portion thereof, between a person who is in the physical custody of a law enforcement officer or other public officer, or who is on the property of a law enforcement agency or other public agency, and that person's attorney, religious adviser, or licensed physician, is guilty of a felony.

(b) Every person who, intentionally and without permission from all parties to the conversation, nonelectronically eavesdrops upon a conversation, or any portion thereof, that occurs between a person who is in the physical custody of a law enforcement officer or other public officer and that person's attorney, religious adviser, or licensed physician, is guilty of a public offense. This subdivision applies to conversations that occur in a place, and under circumstances, where there exists a reasonable expectation of privacy, including a custody holding area, holding area, or anteroom.

This subdivision does not apply to conversations that are inadvertently overheard or that take place in a courtroom or other room used for adjudicatory proceedings. A person who is convicted of violating this subdivision shall be punished by imprisonment in the state prison, or in the county jail for a term not to exceed one year, or by a fine not to exceed two thousand five hundred dollars ($2,500), or by both that fine and imprisonment.

(c) This section shall not apply to any employee of a public utility engaged in the business of providing service and facilities for telephone or telegraph communications while engaged in the construction, maintenance, conduct, or operation of the service or facilities of that public utility who listens in to conversations for the limited purpose of testing or servicing equipment.

636.5. Interception and Divulgence of Police Radio Communication

Any person not authorized by the sender, who intercepts any public safety radio service communication, by use of a scanner or any other means, for the purpose of using that communication to assist in the commission of a criminal offense or to avoid or escape arrest, trial, conviction, or punishment or who divulges to any person he or she knows to be a suspect in the commission of any criminal offense, the existence, contents, substance, purport, effect or meaning of that communication concerning the offense with the intent that the suspect may avoid or escape from arrest, trial, conviction, or punishment is guilty of a misdemeanor.

Nothing in this section shall preclude prosecution of any person under Section 31 or 32.

As used in this section, "public safety radio service communication"means a communication authorized by the Federal Communications Commission to be transmitted by a station in the public safety radio service. *(AM '99)*

637. Wrongful Disclosure of Telegraphic or Telephonic Communication

Every person not a party to a telegraphic or telephonic communication who willfully discloses the contents of a telegraphic or telephonic message, or any part thereof, addressed to another person, without the permission of such person, unless directed so to do by the lawful order of a court, is punishable by imprisonment in the state prison, or in the county jail not exceeding one year, or by fine not exceeding five thousand dollars ($5,000), or by both fine and imprisonment.

637.1. Wrongful Obtaining of Telegraphic or Telephonic Communication

Every person not connected with any telegraph or telephone office who, without the authority or consent of the person to whom the same may be directed, willfully opens any sealed envelope enclosing a telegraphic or telephonic message, addressed to another person, with the purpose of learning the contents of such message, or who fraudulently represents another person and thereby procures to be delivered to himself any telegraphic or telephonic message addressed to such other person, with the intent to use, destroy, or detain the same from the person entitled to receive such message, is punishable as provided in Section 637.

637.3. Use of Voice Prints or Voice Stress Analyzers Prohibited

(a) No person or entity in this state shall use any system which examines or records in any manner voice prints or other voice stress patterns of another person to determine the truth or falsity of statements made by such other person without his or her express written consent given in advance of the examination or recordation.

(b) This section shall not apply to any peace officer, as defined in Section 830, while he is carrying out his official duties.

(c) Any person who has been injured by a violator of this section may bring an action against the violator for his actual damages or one thousand dollars ($1,000), whichever is greater.

637.6. Release of Personal Information - Carpooling Program

(a) No person who, in the course of business, acquires or has access to personal information concerning an individual, including, but not limited to, the individual's residence address, employment address, or hours of employment, for the purpose of assisting private entities in the establishment or implementation of carpooling or ridesharing programs, shall disclose that information to any other person or use that information for any other purpose without the prior written consent of the individual.

(b) As used in this section, "carpooling or ridesharing programs" include, but shall not be limited to, the formation of carpools, vanpools, buspools, the provision of transit routes, rideshare research, and the development of other demand management strategies such as variable working hours and telecommuting.

(c) Any person who violates this section is guilty of a misdemeanor, punishable by imprisonment in the county jail for not exceeding one year, or by a fine of not exceeding one thousand dollars ($1,000), or by both that imprisonment and fine.

637.7. Use of Electronic Tracking Device to Locate or Track a Person Prohibited

(a) No person or entity in this state shall use an electronic tracking device to determine the location or movement of a person.

(b) This section shall not apply when the registered owner, lessor, or lessee of a vehicle has consented to the use of the electronic tracking device with respect to that vehicle.

(c) This section shall not apply to the lawful use of an electronic tracking device by a law enforcement agency.

(d) As used in this section, "electronic tracking device" means any device attached to a vehicle or other movable thing that reveals its location or movement by the transmission of electronic signals.

(e) A violation of this section is a misdemeanor.

(f) A violation of this section by a person, business, firm, company, association, partnership, or corporation licensed under Division 3 (commencing with Section 5000) of the Business and Professions Code shall constitute grounds for revocation of the license issued to that person, business, firm, company, association, partnership, or corporation, pursuant to the provisions that provide for the revocation of the license as set forth in Division 3 (commencing with Section 5000) of the Business and Professions Code. *(AD '98)*

637.9. Misuse of Mailing Lists

(a) Any person who, in the course of business, provides mailing lists, computerized or telephone-based reference services, or similar products or services utilizing lists, as defined, knowingly does any of the following is guilty of a misdemeanor:

(1) Fails, prior to selling or distributing a list to a first-time buyer, to obtain the buyer's name, address, telephone number, tax identification number if the buyer is a for profit entity, a sample of the type of material to be distributed using the list, or to make a good-faith effort to verify the nature and legitimacy of the business or organization to which the list is being sold or distributed.

(2) Knowingly provides access to personal information about children to any person who he or she knows is registered or required to register as a sex offender.

(b) Any person who uses personal information about a child that was obtained for commercial purposes to directly contact the child or the child's parent to offer a commercial product or service to the child and who knowingly fails to comply with the parent's request to take steps to limit access to personal information about a child only to authorized persons is guilty of a misdemeanor.

(c) Any person who knowingly distributes or receives any personal information about a child with knowledge that the information will be used to abuse or physically harm the child is guilty of a misdemeanor.

(d)(1) List brokers shall, upon a written request from a parent that specifically identifies the child, provide the parent with procedures that the parent must follow in order to withdraw consent to use personal information relating to his or her child. Any list broker who fails to discontinue disclosing personal information about a child within 20 days after being so requested in writing by the child's parent, is guilty of a misdemeanor.

(2) Any person who, through the mail, markets or sells products or services directed to children, shall maintain a list of all individuals, and their addresses, who have requested in writing that the person discontinue sending any marketing or sales materials to the individual or the individual's child or children. No person who is obligated to maintain that list shall cause any marketing or sales materials, other than those that are already in the process of dissemination, to be sent to any individual's child or children, after that individual has made that written request. Any person who is subject to the provisions of this paragraph, who fails to comply with the requirements of this paragraph or who violates the provisions of this paragraph is guilty of a misdemeanor.

(e) The following shall be exempt from subdivisions (a) and (b):

(1) Any federal, state, or local government agency or law enforcement agency.

(2) The National Center for Missing and Exploited Children.

(3) Any educational institution, consortia, organization, or professional association, which shall include, but not be limited to, the California community colleges; the California State University, and each campus, branch, and function thereof; each campus, branch, and function of the University of California; the California Maritime Academy; or any independent institution of higher education accredited by an agency recognized by the federal Department of Education. For the purposes of this paragraph, "independent institution of higher education" means any nonpublic higher education institution that grants undergraduate degrees, graduate degrees, or both undergraduate and graduate degrees, is formed as a nonprofit corporation in this state, and is accredited by an agency recognized by the federal Department of Education; or any private postsecondary vocational institution registered, approved, or exempted by the Bureau of Private Postsecondary Vocational Education.

(4) Any nonprofit organization that is exempt from taxation under Section 23701d of the Revenue and Taxation Code.

(f) As used in this section:

(1) "Child" means a person who is under 16 years of age.

(2) "Parent" shall include a legal guardian.

(3) "Personal information"means any information that identifies a child and that would suffice to locate and contact the child, including, but not limited to, the name, postal or electronic mail address, telephone number, social security number, date of birth, physical description of the child, or family income.

(4) "List"may include, but is not limited to, a collection of name and address records of individuals sharing a common interest, purchase history, demographic profile, membership, or affiliation. *(AD '98)*

639. Bribing Financial Institution Employee to Obtain Credit

Every person who gives, offers, or agrees to give to any director, officer, or employee of a financial institution any emolument, gratuity, or reward, or any money, property, or thing of value for his own personal benefit or of personal advantage, for procuring or endeavoring to procure for any person a loan or extension of credit from such financial institution is guilty of a felony.

As used in this section and Section 639a, "financial institution"means any person or persons engaged in the business of making loans or extending credit or procuring the making of loans or extension of credit, including, but not limited to, state and federal banks, savings and loan associations, trust companies, industrial loan companies, personal property brokers, consumer finance lenders, commercial finance lenders, credit unions, escrow companies, title insurance companies, insurance companies, small business investment companies, pawnbrokers, and retirement funds.

As used in this section and Section 639a the word "person"includes any person, firm, partnership, association, corporation, limited liability company, company, syndicate, estate, trust, business trust, or organization of any kind.

639a. Financial Institution Employee Accepting Bribe

Any officer, director or employee of a financial institution who asks, receives, consents, or agrees to receive any commission, emolument, gratuity, or reward or any money, property, or thing of value for his own personal benefit or of personal advantage for procuring or endeavoring to procure for any person a loan from such financial institution is guilty of a felony.

640. Infractions Committed on or in Facilities or Vehicles of a Public Transportation System

(a) Any of the acts described in subdivision (b) is an infraction punishable by a fine not to exceed two hundred fifty dollars ($250) and by community service for a total time not to exceed 48 hours over a period not to exceed 30 days, during a time other than during his or her hours of school attendance or employment, when committed on or in any of the following:

(1) Any facility or vehicle of a public transportation system as defined by Section 99211 of the Public Utilities Code.

(2) Any facility of, or vehicle operated by any entity subsidized by, the Department of Transportation.

(3) Any leased or rented facility or vehicle for which any of the entities described in paragraph (1) or (2) incur costs of cleanup, repair, or replacement as a result of any of those acts.

(b)(1) Evasion of the payment of any fare of the system.

(2) Misuse of any transfer, pass, ticket, or token with the intent to evade the payment of any fare.

(3) Playing sound equipment on or in any system facility or vehicle.

(4) Smoking, eating, or drinking in or on any system facility or vehicle in those areas where those activities are prohibited by that system.

(5) Expectorating upon any system facility or vehicle.

(6) Willfully disturbing others on or in any system facility or vehicle by engaging in boisterous or unruly behavior.

(7) Carrying any explosive or acid, flammable liquid, or toxic or hazardous material in any public transit facility or vehicle.

(8) Urinating or defecating in any system facility or vehicle, except in a lavatory. However, this paragraph shall not apply to any person who cannot comply with this paragraph as a result of a disability, age, or a medical condition.

(9)(A) Willfully blocking the free movement of another person in any system facility or vehicle.

(B) This paragraph (9) shall not be interpreted to affect any lawful activities permitted or first amendment rights protected under the laws of this state or applicable federal law, including, but not limited to, laws related to collective bargaining, labor relations, or labor disputes.

(10) Skateboarding, roller skating, bicycle riding, or roller blading in any system facility, vehicle, or parking structure. This paragraph does not apply to any activity that is necessary for utilization of the transit facility by a bicyclist, including, but not limited to, any activity that is necessary for parking a bicycle or transporting a bicycle aboard a transit vehicle, if that activity is conducted with the permission of the transit agency in a manner that does not interfere with the safety of the bicyclist or other patrons of the transit facility.

(11)(A) Unauthorized use of a discount ticket or failure to present, upon request from a transit system representative, acceptable proof of eligibility to use a discount ticket, in accordance with Section 99155 of the Public Utilities Code and posted system identification policies when entering or exiting a transit station or vehicle. Acceptable proof of eligibility must be clearly defined in the posting.

(B) In the event that an eligible discount ticket user is not in possession of acceptable proof at the time of request, any citation issued shall be held for a period of 72 hours to allow the user to produce acceptable proof. If the proof is provided, the citation shall be voided. If the proof is not produced within that time period, the citation shall be processed. *(AM '00)*

640a. Beating Vending or Slot Machine

1. Any person who shall knowingly and willfully operate, or cause to be operated, or who shall attempt to operate, or attempt to cause to be operated, any automatic vending machine, slot machine or other receptacle designed to receive lawful coin of the United States of America in connection with the sale, use or enjoyment of property or service, by means of a slug or any false, counterfeited, mutilated, sweated or foreign coin, or by any means, method, trick or device whatsoever not lawfully authorized by the owner, lessee or licensee of such machine or receptacle, or who shall take, obtain or receive from or in connection with any automatic vending machine, slot machine or other receptacle designed to receive lawful coin of the United States of America in connection with the sale, use or enjoyment of property or service, any goods, wares, merchandise, gas, electric current, article of value, or the use or enjoyment of any musical instrument, phonograph or other property, without depositing in and surrendering to such machine or receptacle lawful coin of the United States of America to the amount required therefor by the owner, lessee or licensee of such machine or receptacle, shall be guilty of a misdemeanor.

2. Any person who, with intent to cheat or defraud the owner, lessee, licensee or other person entitled to the contents of any automatic vending machine, slot machine or other receptacle, depository or contrivance designed to receive lawful coin of the United States of America in connection with the sale, use or enjoyment of property or service, or who, knowing or having cause to believe that the same is intended for unlawful use, shall manufacture for sale, or sell or give away any slug, device or substance whatsoever intended or calculated to be placed or deposited in any such automatic vending machine, slot machine or other receptacle, depository or contrivance, shall be guilty of a misdemeanor.

640b. Beating Pay Phone

1. Any person who knowingly, willfully and with intent to defraud the owner, lessee or licensee of any coin-box telephone, shall operate or cause to be operated, attempt to operate, or attempt to cause to be operated, any coin-box telephone by means of any slug or any false, counterfeited, mutilated, sweated or foreign coin, or by any means, method, trick or device whatsoever not lawfully authorized by such owner, lessee or licensee, or any person who, knowingly, willfully and with intent to defraud the owner, lessee or licensee of any coin-box telephone, shall take, obtain or receive from or in connection with any such coin-box telephone, the use or enjoyment of any telephone or telegraph facilities or service, without depositing in or surrendering to such coin-box telephone lawful coin of the United States of America to the amount required therefor by such owner, lessee or licensee, shall be guilty of a misdemeanor.

2. Any person who, with the intent to cheat or defraud the owner, lessee or licensee or other person entitled to the contents of any coin-box telephone, or who, knowing or having cause to believe that the same is intended for unlawful use, shall manufacture for sale, or sell or give away any slug, device or substance

whatsoever intended or calculated to be placed or deposited in any such coin-box telephone, shall be guilty of a misdemeanor.

640.5. Graffiti on Public Vehicles or Facilities

(a)(1) Any person who defaces with graffiti or other inscribed material the interior or exterior of the facilities or vehicles of a governmental entity, as defined by Section 811.2 of the Government Code, or the interior or exterior of the facilities or vehicles of a public transportation system as defined by Section 99211 of the Public Utilities Code, or the interior or exterior of the facilities of or vehicles operated by entities subsidized by the Department of Transportation or the interior or exterior of any leased or rented facilities or vehicles for which any of the above entities incur costs of less than two hundred fifty dollars ($250) for cleanup, repair, or replacement is guilty of an infraction, punishable by a fine not to exceed one thousand dollars($1,000) and by a minimum of 48 hours of community service for a total time not to exceed 200 hours over a period not to exceed 180 days, during a time other than his or her hours of school attendance or employment. This subdivision does not preclude application of Section 594.

(2) In lieu of the community service required pursuant to paragraph (1), the court may, if a jurisdiction has adopted a graffiti abatement program as defined in subdivision (f) of Section 594, order the defendant, and his or her parents or guardians if the defendant is a minor, to keep a specified property in the community free of graffiti for 90 days. Participation of a parent or guardian is not required under this paragraph if the court deems this participation to be detrimental to the defendant, or if the parent or guardian is a single parent who must care for young children.

(b)(1) If the person has been convicted previously of an infraction under subdivision (a) or has a prior conviction of Section 594, 594.3, 594.4, 640.6, or 640.7, the offense is a misdemeanor, punishable by imprisonment in a county jail not to exceed six months, by a fine not to exceed two thousand dollars($2,000), or by both that imprisonment and fine. As a condition of probation, the court shall order the defendant to perform a minimum of 96 hours of community service not to exceed 400 hours over a period not to exceed 350 days during a time other than   his or her hours of school attendance or employment.

(2) In lieu of the community service required pursuant to paragraph (1), the court may, if a jurisdiction has adopted a graffiti abatement program as defined in subdivision (f) of Section 594, order the defendant, and his or her parents or guardians if the defendant is a minor, as a condition of probation, to keep a specified property in the community free of graffiti for 180 days. Participation of a parent or guardian is not required under this paragraph if the court deems this participation to be detrimental to the defendant, or if the parent or guardian is a single parent who must care for young children.

(c)(1) Every person who, having been convicted previously under this section or Section 594, 594.3, 594.4, 640.6, or 640.7, or any combination of these offenses, on two separate occasions, and having been incarcerated pursuant to a sentence, a conditional sentence, or a grant of probation for at least one of the convictions, is subsequently convicted under this section, shall be punished by imprisonment in a county jail not to exceed one year, by a fine not to exceed three thousand dollars ($3,000), or by both that imprisonment and fine. As a condition of probation, the court may order the defendant to perform community service not to exceed 600 hours over a period not to exceed 480 days during a time other than his or her hours of school attendance or employment.

(2) In lieu of the community service that may be ordered pursuant to paragraph (1), the court may, if a jurisdiction has adopted a graffiti abatement program as defined in subdivision (f) of Section 594, order the defendant, and his or her parents or guardians if the defendant is a minor, as a condition of probation, to keep a specified property in the community free of graffiti for 240 days. Participation of a parent or guardian is not required under this paragraph if the court deems this participation to be detrimental to the defendant, or if the parent or guardian is a single parent who must care for young children.

(d)(1) Upon conviction of any person under subdivision (a), the court, in addition to any punishment imposed pursuant to subdivision (a), (b), or (c), at the victim's option, may order the defendant to perform the necessary labor to clean up, repair, or replace the property damaged by that person.

(2) If a minor is personally unable to pay any fine levied for violating subdivision (a), (b), or (c), the parent or legal guardian of the minor shall be liable for payment of the fine. A court may waive payment of the fine or any part thereof by the parent or legal guardian upon a finding of good cause.

(e) Any fine levied for a violation of subdivision (a), (b), or (c) shall be credited by the county treasurer pursuant to Section 1463.29 to the governmental entity having jurisdiction over, or responsibility for, the facility or vehicle involved, to be used for removal of the graffiti or other inscribed material or replacement or repair of the property defaced by the graffiti or other inscribed material. Before crediting these fines to the appropriate governmental entity, the county may determine the administrative costs it has incurred pursuant to this section, and retain an amount equal to those costs.

Any community service which is required pursuant to subdivision (a), (b), or (c) of a person under the age of 18 years may be performed in the presence, and under the direct supervision, of the person's parent or legal guardian.

(f) As used in this section, the term "graffiti or other inscribed material" includes any unauthorized inscription, word, figure, mark, or design that is written, marked, etched, scratched, drawn, or painted on real or personal property.

(g) The court may order any person ordered to perform community service or graffiti removal pursuant to subdivision (a), (b), (c), or (d) to undergo counseling.

640.6. Graffiti on Real or Personal Property

(a)(1) Except as provided in Section 640.5, any person who defaces with graffiti or other inscribed material any real or personal property not his or her own, when the amount of the defacement, damage, or destruction is less than two hundred fifty dollars ($250), is guilty of an infraction, punishable by a fine not to exceed one thousand dollars($1,000). This subdivision does not preclude application of Section 594.

In addition to the penalty set forth in this section, the court shall order the defendant to perform a minimum of 48 hours of community service not to exceed 200 hours over a period not to exceed 180 days during a time other than his or her hours of school attendance or employment.

(2) In lieu of the community service required pursuant to paragraph (1), the court may, if a jurisdiction has adopted a graffiti abatement program as defined in subdivision (f) of Section 594, order the defendant, and his or her parents or guardians if the defendant is a minor, to keep a specified property in the community free of graffiti for 90 days. Participation of a parent or guardian is not required under this paragraph if the court deems this participation to be detrimental to the defendant, or if the parent or guardian is a single parent who must care for young children.

(b)(1) If the person has been convicted previously of an infraction under subdivision (a) or has a prior conviction of Section 594, 594.3, 594.4, 640.5, or 640.7, the offense is a misdemeanor, punishable by not to exceed six months in a county jail, by a fine not to exceed two thousand dollars($2,000), or by both that imprisonment and fine. As a condition of probation, the court shall order the defendant to perform a minimum of 96 hours of community service not to exceed 400 hours over a period not to exceed 350 days during a time other than his or her hours of school attendance or employment.

(2) In lieu of the community service required pursuant to paragraph (1), the court may, if a jurisdiction has adopted a graffiti abatement program as defined in subdivision (f) of Section 594, order the defendant, and his or her parents or guardians if the defendant is a minor, as a condition of probation, to keep a specified property in the community free of graffiti for 180 days. Participation of a parent or guardian is not required under this paragraph if the court deems this participation to be detrimental to the defendant, or if the parent or guardian is a single parent who must care for young children.

(c)(1) Every person who, having been convicted previously under this section or Section 594, 594.3, 594.4, 640.5, or 640.7, or any combination of these offenses, on two separate occasions, and having been incarcerated pursuant to a sentence, a conditional sentence, or a grant of probation for at least one of the convictions, is subsequently convicted under this section, shall be punished by imprisonment in a county jail not to exceed one year, by a fine not to exceed three thousand dollars ($3,000), or by both that imprisonment and fine. As a condition of probation, the court may order the defendant to perform community service not to exceed 600 hours over a period not to exceed 480 days during a time other than his or her hours of school attendance or employment.

(2) In lieu of the community service that may be ordered pursuant to paragraph (1), the court may, if a jurisdiction has adopted a graffiti abatement program as defined in subdivision (f) of Section 594, order the defendant, and his or her parents or guardians if the defendant is a minor, as a condition of probation, to keep a specified property in the community free of graffiti for 240 days. Participation of a parent or guardian is not required under this paragraph if the court deems this participation to be detrimental to the defendant, or if the parent or guardian is a single parent who must care for young children.

(d) Upon conviction of any person under subdivision (a), the court, in addition to any punishment imposed pursuant to subdivision (a), (b), or (c), at the victim's option, may order the defendant to perform the necessary labor to clean up, repair, or replace the property damaged by that person.

(e) If a minor is personally unable to pay any fine levied for violating subdivision (a), (b), or (c), the parent or legal guardian of the minor shall be liable for payment of the fine. A court may waive payment of the fine or any part thereof by the parent or legal guardian upon a finding of good cause.

Any community service which is required pursuant to subdivision (a), (b), or (c) of a person under the age of 18 years may be performed in the presence, and under the direct supervision, of the person's parent or legal guardian.

(f) As used in this section, the term "graffiti or other inscribed material" includes any unauthorized inscription, word, figure, mark, or design that is written, marked, etched, scratched, drawn, or painted on real or personal property.

(g) The court may order any person ordered to perform community service or graffiti removal pursuant to subdivision (a), (b), (c), or (d) to undergo counseling.

640.7 Vandalism on or Near Highway

Any person who violates Section 594, 640.5, or 640.6 on or within 100 feet of a highway, or its appurtenances, including, but not limited to, guardrails, signs, traffic signals, snow poles, and similar facilities, excluding signs naming streets, is guilty of a misdemeanor, punishable by imprisonment in a county jail not exceeding six months, or by a fine not exceeding one thousand dollars ($1,000), or by both that imprisonment and fine. A second conviction is punishable by imprisonment in a county jail not exceeding one year, or by a fine not exceeding one thousand dollars ($1,000), or by both that imprisonment and fine. *(AM '98)*

641.3. Commercial Bribery

(a) Any employee who solicits, accepts, or agrees to accept money or any thing of value from a person other than his or her employer, other than in trust for the employer, corruptly and without the knowledge and consent of the employer, in return for using or agreeing to use his or her position for the benefit of that other person, and any person who offers or gives an employee money or any thing of value under those circumstances, is guilty of commercial bribery.

(b) This section does not apply where the amount of money or monetary worth of the thing of value is one hundred dollars ($100) or less.

(c) Commercial bribery is punishable by imprisonment in the county jail for not more than one year if the amount of the bribe is one thousand dollars ($1,000) or less, or by imprisonment in the county jail, or in the state prison for 16 months, or two or three years if the amount of the bribe exceeds one thousand dollars ($1,000).

(d) For purposes of this section:

(1) "Employee" means an officer, director, agent, trustee, partner, or employee.

(2) "Employer" means a corporation, association, organization, trust, partnership, or sole proprietorship.

(3) "Corruptly" means that the person specifically intends to injure or defraud (A) his or her employer, (B) the employer of the person to whom he or she offers, gives, or agrees to give the money or a thing of value, (C) the employer of the person from whom he or she requests, receives, or agrees to receive the money or a thing of value, or (D) a competitor of any such employer.

Legislative Note: This act does not apply to acts or practices involving financial institutions defined in Sections 102 and 3360 of the Financial Code to the extent that these acts or practices are prohibited by Chapter 18 of Division 1 of the Financial Code.

641.4. Commercial Bribery: Payment as Inducement for Placement or Referral of Title Business

(a) An employee of a title insurer, underwritten title company, or controlled escrow company who corruptly violates Section 12404 of the Insurance Code by paying, directly or indirectly, a commission, compensation, or other consideration to a licensee, as defined in Section 10011 of the Business and Professions Code, or a licensee who corruptly violates Section 10177.4 of the Business and Professions Code by receiving from an employee of a title insurer, underwritten title company, or controlled escrow company a commission, compensation, or other consideration, as an inducement for the placement or referral of title business, is guilty of commercial bribery.

(b) For purposes of this section, commercial bribery is punishable by imprisonment in a county jail for not more than one year, or by a fine of ten thousand dollars ($10,000) for each unlawful transaction, or by both a fine and imprisonment.

(c) For purposes of this section, "title business" has the same meaning as that used in Section 12404 of the Insurance Code.

(d) This section shall not preclude prosecution under any other law.

(e) This section shall not be construed to supersede or affect Section 641.3. A person may be charged with a violation of this section and Section 641.3. However, a defendant may not be punished under this section and Section 641.3 for the same act that constitutes a violation of both this section and Section 641.3.

642. Removing and Keeping Articles From Corpse

Every person who willfully and maliciously removes and keeps possession of and appropriates for his own use articles of value from a dead human body, the theft of which articles would be petty theft is guilty of a misdemeanor, or if the theft of the articles would be grand theft, a felony. This section shall not apply to articles removed at the request or direction of one of the persons enumerated in section 7111 of the Health and Safety Code.

643. Disposal of Fetal Remains

No person knowingly shall dispose of fetal remains in a public or private dump, refuse, or disposal site or place open to public view. For the purposes of this section, "fetal remains" means the lifeless product of conception regardless of the duration of the pregnancy. Any violation of this section is a misdemeanor.

646.9. Stalking and Threatening Bodily Injury

(a) Any person who willfully, maliciously, and repeatedly follows or harasses another person and who makes a credible threat with the intent to place that person in reasonable fear for his or her safety, or the safety of his or her immediate family, is guilty of the crime of stalking, punishable by imprisonment in a county jail for not more than one year or by a fine of not more than one thousand dollars ($1,000), or by both that fine and imprisonment, or by imprisonment in the state prison.

(b) Any person who violates subdivision (a) when there is a temporary restraining order, injunction, or any other court order in effect prohibiting the behavior described in subdivision (a) against the same party, shall be punished by imprisonment in the state prison for two, three, or four years.

(c)(1) Every person who, after having been convicted of a felony under Section 273.5, 273.6, or 422, commits a violation of subdivision (a) shall be punished by imprisonment in a county jail for not more than one year, or by a fine of not more than one thousand dollars ($1,000), or by both that fine and imprisonment, or by imprisonment in the state prison for two, three, or five years.

(2) Every person who, after having been convicted of a felony under subdivision (a), commits a violation of this section shall be punished by imprisonment in the state prison for two, three, or five years.

(d) In addition to the penalties provided in this section, the sentencing court may order a person convicted of a felony under this section to register as a sex offender pursuant to subparagraph (E) of paragraph (2) of subdivision (a) of Section 290.

(e) For the purposes of this section, "harasses"means a knowing and willful course of conduct directed at a specific person that seriously alarms, annoys, torments, or terrorizes the person, and that serves no legitimate purpose. This course of conduct must be such as would cause a reasonable person to suffer substantial emotional distress, and must actually cause substantial emotional distress to the person.

(f) For purposes of this section, "course of conduct"means a pattern of conduct composed of a series of acts over a period of time, however short, evidencing a continuity of purpose. Constitutionally protected activity is not included within the meaning of "course of conduct."

(g) For the purposes of this section, "credible threat"means a verbal or written threat, including that performed through the use of an electronic communication device, or a threat implied by a pattern of conduct or a combination of verbal, written, or electronically communicated statements and conduct made with the intent to place the person that is the target of the threat in reasonable fear for his or her safety or the safety of his or her family and made with the apparent ability to carry out the threat so as to cause the person who is the target of the threat to reasonably fear for his or her safety or the safety of his or her family. It is not necessary to prove that the defendant had the intent to actually carry out the threat. The present incarceration of a person making the threat shall not be a bar to prosecution under this section.

(h) For purposes of this section, the term "electronic communication device"includes, but is not limited to, telephones, cellular phones, computers, video recorders, fax machines, or pagers. "Electronic communication"has the same meaning as the term defined in Subsection 12 of Section 2510 of Title 18 of the United States Code.

(i) This section shall not apply to conduct that occurs during labor picketing.

(j) If probation is granted, or the execution or imposition of a sentence is suspended, for any person convicted under this section, it shall be a condition of probation that the person participate in counseling, as designated by the court. However, the court, upon a showing of good cause, may find that the counseling requirement shall not be imposed.

(k) The sentencing court also shall consider issuing an order restraining the defendant from any contact with the victim, that may be valid for up to 10 years, as determined by the court. It is the intent of the Legislature that the length of any restraining order be based upon the seriousness of the facts before the court, the probability of future violations, and the safety of the victim and his or her immediate family.

(l) For purposes of this section, "immediate family"means any spouse, parent, child, any person related by consanguinity or affinity within the second degree, or any other person who regularly resides in the household, or who, within the prior six months, regularly resided in the household.

(m) The court shall consider whether the defendant would benefit from treatment pursuant to Section 2684. If it is determined to be appropriate, the court shall recommend that the Department of Corrections make a certification as provided in Section 2684. Upon the certification, the defendant shall be evaluated and transferred to the appropriate hospital for treatment pursuant to Section 2684. *(AM '98, '00)*

646.91. Emergency Protective Order - Stalking

(a) Notwithstanding any other law, a judicial officer may issue an ex parte emergency protective order where a peace officer, as defined in Section 830.1, 830.2, or 830.32, asserts reasonable grounds to believe that a person is in immediate and present danger of stalking based upon the person's allegation that he or she has been willfully, maliciously, and repeatedly followed or harassed by another person who has made a credible threat with the intent of placing the person who is the target of the threat in reasonable fear for his or her safety, or the safety of his or her immediate family, within the meaning of Section 646.9.

(b) A peace officer who requests an emergency protective order shall reduce the order to writing and sign it.

(c) An emergency protective order shall include all of the following:

(1) A statement of the grounds asserted for the order.

(2) The date and time the order expires.

(3) The address of the superior court for the district or county in which the protected party resides.

(4) The following statements, which shall be printed in English and Spanish:

(A) "To the protected person: This order will last until the date and time noted above. If you wish to seek continuing protection, you will have to apply for an order from the court at the address noted above. You may seek the advice of an attorney as to any matter connected with your application for any future court orders. The attorney should be consulted promptly so that the attorney may assist you in making your application."

(B) "To the restrained person: This order will last until the date and time noted above. The protected party may, however, obtain a more permanent restraining order from the court. You may seek the advice of an attorney as to any matter connected with the application. The attorney should be consulted promptly so that the attorney may assist you in responding to the application."

(d) An emergency protective order may be issued under this section only if the judicial officer finds both of the following:

(1) That reasonable grounds have been asserted to believe that an immediate and present danger of stalking, as defined in Section 646.9, exists.

(2) That an emergency protective order is necessary to prevent the occurrence or reoccurrence of the stalking activity.

(e) An emergency protective order may include either of the following specific orders as appropriate:

(1) A harassment protective order as described in Section 527.6 of the Code of Civil Procedure.

(2) A workplace violence protective order as described in Section 527.8 of the Code of Civil Procedure.

(f) An emergency protective order shall be issued without prejudice to any person.

(g) An emergency protective order expires at the earlier of the following times:

(1) The close of judicial business on the fifth court day following the day of its issuance.

(2) The seventh calendar day following the day of its issuance.

(h) A peace officer who requests an emergency protective order shall do all of the following:

(1) Serve the order on the restrained person, if the restrained person can reasonably be located.

(2) Give a copy of the order to the protected person, or, if the protected person is a minor child, to a parent or guardian of the protected child if the parent or guardian can reasonably be located, or to a person having temporary custody of the child.

(3) File a copy of the order with the court as soon as practicable after issuance.

(i) A peace officer shall use every reasonable means to enforce an emergency protective order.

(j) A peace officer who acts in good faith to enforce an emergency protective order is not civilly or criminally liable.

(k) A peace officer who requests an emergency protective order under this section shall carry copies of the order while on duty.

(l) A peace officer described in subdivision (a) or (b) of Section 830.32 who requests an emergency protective order pursuant to this section shall also notify the sheriff or police chief of the city in whose jurisdiction the peace officer's college or school is located after issuance of the order.

(m) "Judicial officer, "as used in this section, means a judge, commissioner, or referee.

(n) Nothing in this section shall be construed to permit a court to issue an emergency protective order prohibiting speech or other activities that are constitutionally protected or protected by the laws of this state or by the United States or activities occurring during a labor dispute, as defined by Section 527.3 of the Code of Civil Procedure, including but not limited to, picketing and hand billing.

(o) The Judicial Council shall develop forms, instructions, and rules for the scheduling of hearings and other procedures established pursuant to this section.

(p) Any intentional disobedience of any emergency protective order granted under this section is punishable pursuant to Section 166. Nothing in this subdivision shall be construed to prevent punishment under Section 646.9, in lieu of punishment under this section, if a violation of Section 646.9 is also pled and proven. *(AM '99)*

647. Disorderly Conduct Defined

Every person who commits any of the following acts is guilty of disorderly conduct, a misdemeanor:

(a) Who solicits anyone to engage in or who engages in lewd or dissolute conduct in any public place or in any place open to the public or exposed to public view.

(b) Who solicits or who agrees to engage in or who engages in any act of prostitution. A person agrees to engage in an act of prostitution when, with specific intent to so engage, he or she manifests an acceptance of an offer or solicitation to so engage, regardless of whether the offer or solicitation was made by a person who also possessed the specific intent to engage in prostitution. No agreement to engage in an act of prostitution shall constitute a violation of this subdivision unless some act, in addition to the agreement, is done within this state in furtherance of the commission of an act of prostitution by the person agreeing to engage in that act. As used in this subdivision, "prostitution" includes any lewd act between persons for money or other consideration.

(c) Who accosts other persons in any public place or in any place open to the public for the purpose of begging or soliciting alms.

(d) Who loiters in or about any toilet open to the public for the purpose of engaging in or soliciting any lewd or lascivious or any unlawful act.

(e) Who loiters or wanders upon the streets or from place to place without apparent reason or business and who refuses to identify himself or herself and to account for his or her presence when requested by any peace officer so to do, if the surrounding circumstances would indicate to a reasonable person that the public safety demands this identification.

(f) Who is found in any public place under the influence of intoxicating liquor, any drug, controlled substance, toluene, or any combination of any intoxicating liquor, drug, controlled substance, or toluene, in such a condition that he or she is unable to exercise care for his or her own safety or the safety of others, or by reason of his or her being under the influence of intoxicating liquor, any drug, controlled substance, toluene, or any combination of any intoxicating liquor, drug, or toluene, interferes with or obstructs or prevents the free use of any street, sidewalk, or other public way.

(g) When a person has violated subdivision (f) of this section, a peace officer, if he or she is reasonably able to do so, shall place the person, or cause him or her to be placed, in civil protective custody. The person shall be taken to a facility, designated pursuant to Section 5170 of the Welfare and Institutions Code, for the 72-hour treatment and evaluation of inebriates. A peace officer may place a person in civil protective custody with that kind and degree of force which would be lawful were he or she effecting an arrest for a misdemeanor without a warrant. No person who has been placed in civil protective custody shall thereafter be subject to any criminal prosecution or juvenile court proceeding based on the facts giving rise to this placement. This subdivision shall not apply to the following persons:

(1) Any person who is under the influence of any drug, or under the combined influence of intoxicating liquor and any drug.

(2) Any person who a peace officer has probable cause to believe has committed any felony, or who has committed any misdemeanor in addition to subdivision (f) of this section.

(3) Any person who a peace officer in good faith believes will attempt escape or will be unreasonably difficult for medical personnel to control.

(h) Who loiters, prowls, or wanders upon the private property of another, at any time, without visible or lawful business with the owner or occupant. As used in this subdivision, "loiter" means to delay or linger without a lawful purpose for being on the property and for the purpose of committing a crime as opportunity may be discovered.

(i) Who, while loitering, prowling, or wandering upon the private property of another, at any time, peeks in the door or window of any inhabited building or structure, without visible or lawful business with the owner or occupant.

(j) Who lodges in any building, structure, vehicle, or place, whether public or private, without the permission of the owner or person entitled to the possession or in control of it.

(k)(1) Any person who looks through a hole or opening, into, or otherwise views, by means of any instrumentality, including, but not limited to, a periscope, telescope, binoculars, camera, motion picture camera, or camcorder, the interior of a bathroom, changing room, fitting room, dressing room, or tanning booth, or the interior of any other area in which the occupant has a reasonable expectation of privacy, with the intent to invade the privacy of a person or persons inside. This subdivision shall not apply to those areas of a private business used to count currency or other negotiable instruments.

(2) Any person who uses a concealed camcorder, motion picture camera, or photographic camera of any type, to secretly videotape, film, photograph, or record by electronic means, another, identifiable person under or through the clothing being worn by that other person, for the purpose of viewing the body of, or the undergarments worn by, that other person, without the consent or knowledge of that other person, with the intent to arouse, appeal to, or gratify the lust, passions, or sexual desires of that person and invade the privacy of that other person, under circumstances in which the other person has a reasonable expectation of privacy.

In any accusatory pleading charging a violation of subdivision (b), if the defendant has been once previously convicted of a violation of that subdivision, the previous conviction shall be charged in the accusatory pleading. If the previous conviction is found to be true by the jury, upon a jury trial, or by the court, upon a court trial, or is admitted by the defendant, the defendant shall be imprisoned in a county jail for a period of not less than 45 days and shall not be eligible for release upon completion of sentence, on probation, on parole, on work furlough or work release, or on any other basis until he or she has served a period of not less than 45 days in a county jail. In all cases in which probation is granted, the court shall require as a condition thereof that the person be confined in a county jail for at least 45 days. In no event does the court have the power to absolve a person who violates this subdivision from the obligation of spending at least 45 days in confinement in a county jail.

In any accusatory pleading charging a violation of subdivision (b), if the defendant has been previously convicted two or more times of a violation of that subdivision, each such previous conviction shall be charged in the accusatory pleading. If two or more of these previous convictions are found to be true by the jury, upon a jury trial, or by the court, upon a court trial, or are admitted by the defendant, the defendant shall be imprisoned in a county jail for a period of not less than 90 days and shall not be eligible for release upon completion of sentence, on probation, on parole, on work furlough or work release, or on any other basis until he or she has served a period of not less than 90 days in a county jail. In all cases in which probation is granted, the court shall require as a condition thereof that the person be confined in a county jail for at least 90 days. In no event does the court have the power to absolve a person who violates this subdivision from the obligation of spending at least 90 days in confinement in a county jail.

In addition to any punishment prescribed by this section, a court may suspend, for not more than 30 days, the privilege of the person to operate a motor vehicle pursuant to Section 13201.5 of the Vehicle Code for any violation of subdivision (b) that was committed within 1,000 feet of a private residence and with the use of a vehicle. In lieu of the suspension, the court may order a person's privilege to operate a motor vehicle restricted, for not more than six months, to necessary travel to and from the person's place of employment or education. If driving a motor vehicle is necessary to perform the duties of the person's employment, the court may also allow the person to drive in that person's scope of employment. *(AM '99)*

647b. Loitering Around Adult Schools

Every person who loiters about any school in which adults are in attendance at courses established pursuant to Chapter 10 of Part 28 of the Education Code, and who annoys or molests any person in attendance therein shall be punished by a fine of not exceeding one thousand dollars ($1,000) or by imprisonment in the county jail for not exceeding six months, or by both such fine and imprisonment.

647c. Obstructing Movement on Street or Public Place

Every person who willfully and maliciously obstructs the free movement of any person on any street, sidewalk, or other public place or on or in any place open to the public is guilty of a misdemeanor.

Nothing in this section affects the power of a county or a city to regulate conduct upon a street, sidewalk, or other public place or on or in a place open to the public.

647e.   Counties May Prohibit Open Containers in Certain Locations

(a) A city, county, or city and county may by local ordinance provide that no person who has in his or her possession any bottle, can or other receptacle containing any alcoholic beverage which has been opened, or a seal broken, or the contents of which have been partially removed, shall enter, be, or remain on the posted premises of, including the posted parking lot immediately adjacent to, any retail package off-sale alcoholic beverage licensee licensed pursuant to Division 9 of the Business and Professions Code, or on any public sidewalk immediately adjacent to the licensed and posted premises. Any person violating any provision of such an ordinance shall be guilty of an infraction.

(b) As used in subdivision (a), "posted premises"means those premises which are subject to licensure under any retail package off-sale alcoholic beverage license, the parking lot immediately adjacent to the licensed premises and any public sidewalk immediately adjacent to the licensed premises on which clearly visible notices indicate to the patrons of the licensee and parking lot and to persons on the public sidewalk, that the provisions of subdivision (a) are applicable. Any local ordinance adopted pursuant to this section shall require posting of the premises.

(c) The provisions of this section shall not apply to a private residential parking lot which is immediately adjacent to the posted premises.

Nothing in this section shall affect the power of a county or a city, or city and county, to regulate the possession of an opened alcoholic beverage in any public place or in a place open to the public.

647.6.   Child Molesters

(a) Every person who annoys or molests any child under the age of 18 shall be punished by a fine not exceeding one thousand dollars ($1,000), by imprisonment in a county jail not exceeding one year, or by both the fine and imprisonment.

(b) Every person who violates this section after having entered, without consent, an inhabited dwelling house, or trailer coach as defined in Section 635 of the Vehicle Code, or the inhabited portion of any other building, shall be punished by imprisonment in the state prison, or in a county jail not exceeding one year.

(c)(1) Every person who violates this section shall be punished upon the second and each subsequent conviction by imprisonment in the state prison.

(2) Every person who violates this section after a previous felony conviction under Section 261, 264.1, 269, 285, 286, 288a, 288.5, or 289, any of which involved a minor under the age of 16 years, or a previous felony conviction under this section, a conviction under Section 288, or a felony conviction under Section 311.4 involving a minor under the age of 14 years shall be punished by imprisonment in the state prison for two, four, or six years.

(d)(1) In any case in which a person is convicted of violating this section and probation is granted, the court shall require counseling as a condition of probation, unless the court makes a written statement in the court record, that counseling would be inappropriate or ineffective.

(2) In any case in which a person is convicted of violating this section, and as a condition of probation, the court prohibits the defendant from having contact with the victim, the court order prohibiting contact shall not be modified except upon the request of the victim and a finding by the court that the modification is in the best interest of the victim. As used in this paragraph, "contact with the victim"includes all physical contact, being in the presence of the victim, communication by any means, any communication by a third party acting on behalf of the defendant, and any gifts. *(AM '00)*

647.7.   Disorderly Conduct; Subsequent Offense

(a) In any case in which a person is convicted of violating subdivision (i) or (k) of Section 647, the court may require counseling as a condition of probation.   Any defendant so ordered to be placed in a counseling program shall be responsible for paying the expense of his or her participation in the counseling program as determined by the court.   The court shall take into consideration the ability of the defendant to pay, and no defendant shall be denied probation because of his or her inability to pay.

(b) Every person who, having been convicted of violating subdivision (i) or (k) of Section 647, commits a second or subsequent violation of subdivision (i) or (k) of Section 647, shall be punished by imprisonment in a county jail not exceeding one year, by a fine not exceeding one thousand dollars ($1,000), or by both that fine and imprisonment.

648. Uttering and Passing Counterfeit Paper

Every person who makes, issues, or puts in circulation any bill, check, ticket, certificate, promissory note, or the paper of any bank, to circulate as money, except as authorized by the laws of the United States, for the first offense, is guilty of a misdemeanor, and for each and every subsequent offense, is guilty of felony.

648a. Tokens or Slugs Imitating Coins

(a) Every person who has in his or her possession for any illegal purpose or who makes, sells, issues, or puts in circulation any slug or token that does not conform to the limitations on size, shape, weight, construction, and use specified in subdivision (b) is guilty of a misdemeanor. The term "slug"and the term "token,"as used in this section, mean any piece of metal or other material not a coin of the United States or a foreign country. However, tokens sold by and accepted as fares by electric railways and lettered checks having a returnable trade value shall not be subject to the provisions of this section.

(b)(1) The slug or token shall either be clearly identified with the name and location of the establishment from which it originates on at least one side or shall contain an identifying mark or logo that clearly indicates the identity of the manufacturer.

(2) The slug or token shall not be within any of the following diameter ranges in inches:

(A) 0.680-0.775.

(B) 0.810-0.860.

(C) 0.910-0.980.

(D) 1.018-1.068.

(E) 1.180-1.230.

(F) 1.475-1.525.

(3) The slug or token shall not be manufactured from a three-layered material consisting of a copper-nickel alloy clad on both sides of a pure core, nor from a copper-based material except if the total of zinc, nickel, aluminum, magnesium, and other alloying materials is at least 20 percent of the token's weight.

(4) The slug or token shall not possess sufficient magnetic properties so as to be accepted by a coin mechanism.

(5) The design on the slug or token shall not resemble any current or past foreign or United States coinage.

(6) Establishments using these slugs or tokens shall prominently and conspicuously post signs on their premises notifying patrons that federal law prohibits the use of the slugs or tokens outside the premises for any monetary purpose.

(7) The issuing establishment shall not accept slugs or tokens as payment for any goods or services offered by the establishment with the exception of the specific use for which the slugs or tokens were designed.

649. Unlawful to Misdirect Prospective Hotel Guest

Any person engaged in the transportation of persons by taxicab or other means of conveyance who knowingly misdirects a prospective guest of any hotel, inn, boardinghouse or lodginghouse or knowingly takes such a prospective guest to a hotel, inn, boardinghouse or lodginghouse different from that of his instructions from such prospective guest is guilty of a misdemeanor.

649a. Fraud in Procuring Hotel Guests

Any person engaged in the operation of any hotel, inn, boardinghouse or lodginghouse who pays another any compensation for inducing or attempting to induce, by false statement or misrepresentation, prospective guests of a given hotel, inn, boardinghouse or lodginghouse to enter, lodge at or become a guest of any other hotel, inn, boardinghouse or lodginghouse is guilty of a misdemeanor.

651.　Selling Food Stamps

It is a misdemeanor for any person to buy, receive, sell, give away, dispose of, exchange or barter any Federal order stamps except for the foods or cotton goods for which they are issued.

This section does not apply to any person buying, receiving, selling, giving away, disposing of, exchanging or bartering any Federal order stamps subsequent to the redemption of such stamps in the manner provided by State or Federal law for the foods or cotton goods for which they are issued.

As used in this section, Federal order stamps refers to stamps issued by the United States Department of Agriculture or its duly authorized agent for food and surplus food or cotton and surplus cotton.

652.　Body Piercing - Person Under the Age of 18 Years

(a) It shall be an infraction for any person to perform or offer to perform body piercing upon a person under the age of 18 years, unless the body piercing is performed in the presence of, or as directed by a notarized writing by, the person's parent or guardian.

(b) This section does not apply to the body piercing of an emancipated minor.

(c) As used in this section, "body piercing"means the creation of an opening in the body of a human being for the purpose of inserting jewelry or other decoration. This includes, but is not limited to, piercing of a lip, tongue, nose, or eyebrow. "Body piercing"does not include the piercing of an ear.

(d) Neither the minor upon whom the body piercing was performed, nor the parent or guardian of that minor, nor any other minor is liable for punishment under this section.

(e) This section shall remain in effect only until January 1, 2005, and as of that date is repealed, unless a later enacted statute, that is enacted before January 1, 2005, deletes or extends that date.

653.　Tattooing Minor

Every person who tattoos or offers to tattoo a person under the age of 18 years is guilty of a misdemeanor.

As used in this section, to "tattoo"means to insert pigment under the surface of the skin of a human being, by pricking with a needle or otherwise, so as to produce an indelible mark or figure visible through the skin.

This section is not intended to apply to any act of a licensed practitioner of the healing arts performed in the course of his practice.

653d.　Sale of Mining Machinery; Bill of Sale and Record of Sale Required

Every person who sells machinery used or to be used for mining purposes who fails to give to the buyer, at the time of sale, a bill of sale for the machinery, or who fails to keep a written record of the sale, giving the date thereof, describing the machinery, and showing the name and address of the buyer, and every buyer of such machinery, if in this State, who fails to keep a record of his purchase of such machinery, giving the name and address of the seller, describing the machinery, and showing the date of the purchase, is guilty of a misdemeanor.

653f.　Solicitation to Commit Felony

(a) Every person who, with the intent that the crime be committed, solicits another to offer or accept or join in the offer or acceptance of a bribe, or to commit or join in the commission of carjacking, robbery, burglary, grand theft, receiving stolen property, extortion, perjury, subornation of perjury, forgery, kidnapping, arson or assault with a deadly weapon or instrument or by means of force likely to produce great bodily injury, or, by the use of force or a threat of force, to prevent or dissuade any person who is or may become a witness from attending upon, or testifying at, any trial, proceeding, or inquiry authorized by law, is punishable by imprisonment in the county jail not more than one year or in the state prison, or by fine of not more than ten thousand dollars ($10,000), or the amount which could have been assessed for commission of the offense itself, whichever is greater, or by both the fine and imprisonment.

(b) Every person who, with the intent that the crime be committed, solicits another to commit or join in the commission of murder is punishable by imprisonment in the state prison for three, six, or nine years.

(c) Every person who, with the intent that the crime be committed, solicits another to commit rape by force or violence, sodomy by force or violence, oral copulation by force or violence, or any violation of Section 264.1, 288, or 289, is punishable by imprisonment in a state prison for two, three or four years.

(d) Every person who, with the intent that the crime be committed, solicits another to commit an offense specified in Section 11352, 11379, 11379.5, 11379.6, or 11391 of the Health and Safety Code shall be punished by imprisonment in the county jail not exceeding six months. Every person, who, having been convicted of soliciting another to commit an offense specified in this subdivision, is subsequently convicted of the proscribed solicitation, then the person convicted of the subsequent offense is punishable by imprisonment in a county jail not exceeding one year, or in the state prison.

This subdivision does not apply where the term of imprisonment imposed under other provisions of law would result in a longer term of imprisonment.

(e) Every person who, with the intent that the crime be committed, solicits another to commit an offense specified in Section 14014 of the Welfare & Institutions Code shall be punished by imprisonment in a county jail for not exceeding six months. Every person who, having been convicted of soliciting another to commit an offense specified in this subdivision, is subsequently convicted of the proscribed solicitation, shall be punished by imprisonment in a county jail not exceeding one year, or in the state prison.

(f) An offense charged in violation of subdivision (a), (b), or (c) shall be proven by the testimony of two witnesses, or of one witness and corroborating circumstances. An offense charged in violation of subdivision (d) shall be proven by the testimony of one witness and corroborating circumstances.

653g. Loitering About Place Where Children Congregate Punishable as Vagrancy

Every person who loiters about any school or public place at or near which children attend or normally congregate and who remains at any school or public place at or near which children attend or normally congregate, or who reenters or comes upon a school or place within 72 hours, after being asked to leave by the chief administrative official of that school or, in the absence of the chief administrative official, the person acting as the chief administrative official, or by a member of the security patrol of the school district who has been given authorization, in writing, by the chief administrative official of that school to act as his or her agent in performing this duty, or a city police officer, or sheriff or deputy sheriff, or Department of the California Highway Patrol peace officer is a vagrant, and is punishable by a fine of not exceeding one thousand dollars ($1,000) or by imprisonment in the county jail for not exceeding six months, or by both the fine and the imprisonment.

As used in this section, "loiter" means to delay, to linger, or to idle about a school or public place without lawful business for being present.

653h. Sound Recordings

(a) Every person is guilty of a public offense punishable as provided in subdivisions (b) and (c), who:

(1) Knowingly and willfully transfers or causes to be transferred any sounds that have been recorded on a phonograph record, disc, wire, tape, film or other article on which sounds are recorded, with intent to sell or cause to be sold, or to use or cause to be used for commercial advantage or private financial gain through public performance, the article on which the sounds are so transferred, without the consent of the owner.

(2) Transports for monetary or like consideration within this state or causes to be transported within this state any such article with the knowledge that the sounds thereon have been so transferred without the consent of the owner.

(b) Any person who has been convicted of a violation of subdivision (a), shall be punished by imprisonment in the county jail not to exceed one year, by imprisonment in the state prison for two, three, or five years, or by a fine not to exceed two hundred fifty thousand dollars ($250,000), or by both, if the offense involves the transfer or transportation, or conduct causing that transfer or transportation, of not less than 1,000 of the articles described in subdivision (a).

(c) Any person who has been convicted of any other violation of subdivision (a) not described in subdivision (b), shall be punished by imprisonment in the county jail not to exceed one year, or by a fine of not more than twenty-five thousand dollars ($25,000), or by both. A second or subsequent conviction under subdivision (a) not described in subdivision (b) shall be punished by imprisonment in the state prison or by a fine not to exceed one hundred thousand dollars ($100,000), or by both.

(d) Every person who offers for sale or resale, or sells or resells, or causes the sale or resale, or rents, or possesses for these purposes, any article described in subdivision (a) with knowledge that the sounds thereon have been so transferred without the consent of the owner is guilty of a public offense.

(1) A violation of subdivision (d) involving not less than 100 of those articles shall be punishable by imprisonment in a county jail not to exceed one year or by a fine not to exceed ten thousand dollars ($10,000), or by both. A second or subsequent conviction for the conduct described in this paragraph shall be punishable by imprisonment in the county jail not to exceed one year or in the state prison, or by a fine not to exceed twenty-five thousand dollars ($25,000), or by both.

(2) A person who has been convicted of any violation of this subdivision not described in paragraph (1) shall be punished by imprisonment in the county jail not to exceed six months or by a fine not to exceed five thousand dollars ($5,000), or by both. A second conviction for the conduct described in this paragraph shall be punishable by imprisonment in the county jail not to exceed one year or by a fine not to exceed ten thousand dollars ($10,000), or by both. A third or subsequent conviction for the conduct described in this paragraph shall be punishable by imprisonment in the county jail not to exceed one year or in the state prison, or by a fine not to exceed twenty-five thousand dollars ($25,000), or by both.

(e) As used in this section, "person" means any individual, partnership, partnership's member or employee, corporation, limited liability company, association or corporation or association employee, officer or director; "owner" means the person who owns the original master recording embodied in the master phonograph record, master disc, master tape, master film or other article used for reproducing recorded sounds on phonograph records, discs, tapes, films or other articles on which sound is or can be recorded, and from which the transferred recorded sounds are directly or indirectly derived; and "master recording" means the original fixation of sounds upon a recording from which copies can be made.

(f) This section shall neither enlarge nor diminish the right of parties in private litigation.

(g) This section does not apply to any person engaged in radio or television broadcasting who transfers, or causes to be transferred, any such sounds (other than from the sound track of a motion picture) intended for, or in connection with broadcast transmission or related uses, or for archival purposes.

(h) This section does not apply to any not-for-profit educational institution or any federal or state governmental entity, if the institution or entity has as a primary purpose the advancement of the public's knowledge and the dissemination of information regarding America's musical cultural heritage, provided that this purpose is clearly set forth in the institution's or entity's charter, bylaws, certificate of incorporation, or similar document, and the institution or entity has, prior to the transfer, made a good faith effort to identify and locate the owner or owners of the sound recordings to be transferred and, provided that the owner or owners could not be and have not been located. Nothing in this section shall be construed to relieve an institution or entity of its contractual or other obligation to compensate the owners of sound recordings to be transferred. In order to continue the exemption permitted by this subdivision, the institution or entity shall make continuing efforts to locate such owners and shall make an annual public notice of the fact of the transfers in newspapers of general circulation serving the jurisdictions where the owners were incorporated or doing business at the time of initial affixations. The institution or entity shall keep on file a record of the efforts made to locate such owners for inspection by appropriate governmental agencies.

(i) This section applies only to such articles that were initially mastered prior to February 15, 1972.

653i. Leave Scene of Skiing Accident

Any person who is involved in a skiing accident and who leaves the scene of the accident knowing or having reason to believe that any other person involved in the accident is in need of medical and other assistance, except to notify the proper authorities or to obtain assistance, shall be guilty of an infraction punishable by fine not exceeding one thousand dollars ($1,000).

653j. Solicitation of Minor to Commit Felony

(a) Every person 18 years of age or older who, in any voluntary manner, solicits, induces, encourages, or intimidates any minor with the intent that the minor shall commit a felony in violation of paragraph (1) of subdivision (c) of Section 136.1 or Section 187, 211, 215, 245, 246, 451, 459, or 520 of the Penal Code, or Section 10851 of the Vehicle Code, shall be punished by imprisonment in the state prison for a period of three, five, or seven years. If the minor is 16 years of age or older at the time of the offense, this section shall only apply when the adult is at least five years older than the minor at the time the offense is committed.

(b) In no case shall the court impose a sentence pursuant to subdivision (a) which exceeds the maximum penalty prescribed for the felony offense for which the minor was solicited, induced, encouraged, or intimidated to commit.

(c) Whenever a sentence is imposed under subdivision (a), the court shall consider the severity of the underlying crime as one of the circumstances in aggravation.

653k. Switchblade Knives

Every person who possesses in the passenger's or driver's area of any motor vehicle in any public place or place open to the public, carries upon his or her person, and every person who sells, offers for sale, exposes for sale, loans, transfers, or gives to any other person a switchblade knife having a blade two or more inches in length is guilty of a misdemeanor.

For the purposes of this section, "switchblade knife" means a knife having the appearance of a pocketknife and includes a spring-blade knife, snap-blade knife, gravity knife or any other similar type knife, the blade or blades of which are two or more inches *** in length and which can be released automatically by a flick of a button, pressure on the handle, flip of the wrist or other mechanical device, or is released by the weight of the blade or by any type of mechanism whatsoever. "Switchblade knife" does not include a knife that *** opens with one hand utilizing thumb pressure applied solely to the blade of the knife or a thumb stud attached to the blade, provided that the knife has a detent or other mechanism that provides resistance that must be overcome in opening the blade, or that biases the blade back toward its closed position.

For purposes of this section, "passenger's or driver's area" means that part of a motor vehicle which is designed to carry the driver and passengers, including any interior compartment or space therein. *(AM '01)*

653l. 911 Line; Annoying Calls [Renumbered 653x]

653m. Obscene or Threatening Phone Calls

(a) Every person who, with intent to annoy, telephones or makes contact by means of an electronic communication device with another and addresses to or about the other person any obscene language or addresses to the other person any threat to inflict injury to the person or property of the person addressed or any member of his or her family, is guilty of a misdemeanor. Nothing in this subdivision shall apply to telephone calls or electronic contacts made in good faith.

(b) Every person who makes repeated telephone calls or makes repeated contact by means of an electronic communication device with intent to annoy another person at his or her residence, is, whether or not conversation ensues from making the telephone call or electronic contact, guilty of a misdemeanor. Nothing in this subdivision shall apply to telephone calls or electronic contacts made in good faith.

(c) Every person who makes repeated telephone calls or makes repeated contact by means of an electronic communication device with the intent to annoy another person at his or her place of work is guilty of a misdemeanor punishable by a fine of not more than one thousand dollars ($1,000), or by imprisonment in a county jail for not more than one year, or by both that fine and imprisonment. Nothing in this subdivision shall apply to telephone calls or electronic contacts made in good faith. This subdivision applies only if one or both of the following circumstances exist:

(1) There is a temporary restraining order, an injunction, or any other court order, or any combination of these court orders, in effect prohibiting the behavior described in this section.

(2) The person makes repeated telephone calls or makes repeated contact by means of an electronic communication device with the intent to annoy another person at his or her place of work, totaling more than

10 times in a 24-hour period, whether or not conversation ensues from making the telephone call or electronic contact, and the repeated telephone calls or electronic contacts are made to the workplace of an adult or fully emancipated minor who is a spouse, former spouse, cohabitant, former cohabitant, or person with whom the person has a child or has had a dating or engagement relationship or is having a dating or engagement relationship.

(d) Any offense committed by use of a telephone may be deemed to have been committed where the telephone call or calls were made or received. Any offense committed by use of an electronic communication device or medium, including the Internet, may be deemed to have been committed when the electronic communication or communications were originally sent or first viewed by the recipient.

(e) Subdivision (a), (b), or (c) is violated when the person acting with intent to annoy makes a telephone call requesting a return call and performs the acts prohibited under subdivision (a), (b), or (c) upon receiving the return call.

(f) If probation is granted, or the execution or imposition of sentence is suspended, for any person convicted under this section, the court may order as a condition of probation that the person participate in counseling.

(g) For purposes of this section, the term "electronic communication device" includes, but is not limited to, telephones, cellular phones, computers, video recorders, fax machines, or pagers. "Electronic communication" has the same meaning as the term defined in Subsection 12 of Section 2510 of Title 18 of the United States Code. *(AM '99)*

653n. Installation or Maintenance of a Two-Way Mirror Permitting Observation of Certain Areas

Any person who installs or who maintains after April 1, 1970, any two-way mirror permitting observation of any restroom, toilet, bathroom, washroom, shower, locker room, fitting room, motel room, or hotel room, is guilty of a misdemeanor.

This section does not apply to such areas (a) in state or local public penal, correctional, custodial, or medical institutions which are used by, or for the treatment of, persons who are committed or voluntarily confined to such institutions or voluntarily receive treatment therein; (b) in private custodial or medical institutions, which are used by, or for the treatment of, persons who are committed or voluntarily confined to such institutions or voluntarily receive treatment therein; (c) in public or private treatment facilities which are used by, or for the treatment of, persons who are committed or voluntarily confined to such facilities or voluntarily receive treatment therein; (d) in buildings operated by state or local law enforcement agencies; or (e) in public or private educational institutions.

"Two-way mirror" as used in this section means a mirror or other surface which permits any person on one side thereof to see through it under certain conditions of lighting, while any person on the other side thereof or other surface at that time can see only the usual mirror or other surface reflection.

653x. Misuse 911 Emergency Line to Annoy or Harass

(a) Any person who telephones the 911 emergency line with the intent to annoy or harass another person is guilty of a misdemeanor punishable by a fine of not more than one thousand dollars ($1,000), by imprisonment in a county jail for not more than six months, or by both the fine and imprisonment. Nothing in this section shall apply to telephone calls made in good faith.

(b) An intent to annoy or harass is established by proof of repeated calls over a period of time, however short, that are unreasonable under the circumstances.

(c) Upon conviction of a violation of this section, a person also shall be liable for all reasonable costs incurred by any unnecessary emergency response.

653.1. Electrically Conductive Balloons

(a) No person shall sell or distribute any balloon which is constructed of electrically conductive material, and filled with a gas lighter than air without:

(1) Affixing an object of sufficient weight to the balloon or its appurtenance to counter the lift capability of the balloon.

(2) Affixing a statement on the balloon, or ensuring that a statement is so affixed, that warns the consumer about the risk if the balloon comes in contact with electrical power lines.

(3) A printed identification of the manufacturer of the balloon.

(b) No person shall sell or distribute any balloon filled with a gas lighter than air, which is attached to an electrically conductive string, tether, streamer, or other electrically conductive appurtenance.

(c) No person shall sell or distribute any balloon which is constructed of electrically conductive material and filled with a gas lighter than air, which, is attached to another balloon constructed of electrically conductive material and filled with a gas lighter than air.

(d) No person or group shall release, outdoors, balloons made of electrically conductive material and filled with a gas lighter than air, as part of a public or civic event, promotional activity, or product advertisement.

(e) Any person who violates subdivision (a), (b), (c), or (d) shall be guilty of an infraction punishable by a fine not exceeding one hundred dollars ($100). Any person who violates subdivision (a), (b), (c), or (d) who has been previously convicted twice of violating subdivision (a), (b), (c), or (d) shall be guilty of a misdemeanor.

(f) This section shall not apply to manned hot air balloons, or to balloons used in governmental or scientific research projects.

653.20. Loiter for Prostitution - Definitions

For purposes of this chapter, the following definitions apply:

(a) "Commit prostitution"means to engage in sexual conduct for money or other consideration, but does not include sexual conduct engaged in as a part of any stage performance, play, or other entertainment open to the public.

(b) "Public place"means an area open to the public, or an alley, plaza, park, driveway, or parking lot, or an automobile, whether moving or not, or a building open to the general public, including one which serves food or drink, or provides entertainment, or the doorways and entrances to a building or dwelling, or the grounds enclosing a building or dwelling.

(c) "Loiter"means to delay or linger without a lawful purpose for being on the property and for the purpose of committing a crime as opportunity may be discovered.

653.22. Loitering for the Purpose of Engaging in a Prostitution Offense

(a) It is unlawful for any person to loiter in any public place with the intent to commit prostitution. This intent is evidenced by acting in a manner and under circumstances which openly demonstrate the purpose of inducing, enticing, or soliciting prostitution, or procuring another to commit prostitution.

(b) Among the circumstances that may be considered in determining whether a person loiters with the intent to commit prostitution are that the person:

(1) Repeatedly beckons to, stops, engages in conversations with, or attempts to stop or engage in conversations with passersby, indicative of soliciting for prostitution.

(2) Repeatedly stops or attempts to stop motor vehicles by hailing the drivers, waving arms, or making any other bodily gestures, or engages or attempts to engage the drivers or passengers of the motor vehicles in conversation, indicative of soliciting for prostitution.

(3) Has been convicted of violating this section, subdivision (a) or (b) of Section 647, or any other offense relating to or involving prostitution, within five years of the arrest under this section.

(4) Circles an area in a motor vehicle and repeatedly beckons to, contacts, or attempts to contact or stop pedestrians or other motorists, indicative of soliciting for prostitution.

(5) Has engaged, within six months prior to the arrest under this section, in any behavior described in this subdivision, with the exception of paragraph (3), or in any other behavior indicative of prostitution activity.

(c) The list of circumstances set forth in subdivision (b) is not exclusive. The circumstances set forth in subdivision (b) should be considered particularly salient if they occur in an area that is known for prostitution activity. Any other relevant circumstances may be considered in determining whether a person has the requisite intent. Moreover, no one circumstance or combination of circumstances is in itself determinative of intent. Intent must be determined based on an evaluation of the particular circumstances of each case.

653.23. Prostitution - Direct, Supervise, Recruit, or Otherwise Aid Another or Collect or Receive Proceeds Earned from Prostitution Committed by Another

(a) It is unlawful for any person to do either of the following:

(1) Direct, supervise, recruit, or otherwise aid another person in the commission of a violation of subdivision (b) of Section 647 or subdivision (a) of Section 653.22.

(2) Collect or receive all or part of the proceeds earned from an act or acts of prostitution committed by another person in violation of subdivision (b) of Section 647.

(b) Among the circumstances that may be considered in determining whether a person is in violation of subdivision (a) are that the person does the following:

(1) Repeatedly speaks or communicates with another person who is acting in violation of subdivision (a) of Section 653.22.

(2) Repeatedly or continuously monitors or watches another person who is acting in violation of subdivision (a) of Section 653.22.

(3) Repeatedly engages or attempts to engage in conversation with pedestrians or motorists to solicit, arrange, or facilitate an act of prostitution between the pedestrians or motorists and another person who is acting in violation of subdivision (a) of Section 653.22.

(4) Repeatedly stops or attempts to stop pedestrians or motorists to solicit, arrange, or facilitate an act of prostitution between pedestrians or motorists and another person who is acting in violation of subdivision (a) of Section 653.22.

(5) Circles an area in a motor vehicle and repeatedly beckons to, contacts, or attempts to contact or stop pedestrians or other motorists to solicit, arrange, or facilitate an act of prostitution between the pedestrians or motorists and another person who is acting in violation of subdivision (a) of Section 653.22.

(6) Receives or appears to receive money from another person who is acting in violation of subdivision (a) of Section 653.22.

(7) Engages in any of the behavior described in paragraphs (1) to (6), inclusive, in regard to or on behalf of two or more persons who are in violation of subdivision (a) of Section 653.22.

(8) Has been convicted of violating this section, subdivision (a) or (b) of Section 647, subdivision (a) of Section 653.22, Section 266h, or 266i, or any other offense relating to or involving prostitution within five years of the arrest under this section.

(9) Has engaged, within six months prior to the arrest under subdivision (a), in any behavior described in this subdivision, with the exception of paragraph (8), or in any other behavior indicative of prostitution activity.

(c) The list of circumstances set forth in subdivision (b) is not exclusive. The circumstances set forth in subdivision (b) should be considered particularly salient if they occur in an area that is known for prostitution activity. Any other relevant circumstances may be considered. Moreover, no one circumstance or combination of circumstances is in itself determinative. A violation of subdivision (a) shall be determined based on an evaluation of the particular circumstances of each case.

(d) Nothing in this section shall preclude the prosecution of a suspect for a violation of Section 266h or 266i or for any other offense, or for a violation of this section in conjunction with a violation of Section 266h or 266i or any other offense. *(AD '98)*

TITLE 16 - GENERAL PROVISIONS

659. Aiding in Misdemeanor

Whenever an act is declared a misdemeanor, and no punishment for counseling or aiding in the commission of such act is expressly prescribed by law, every person who counsels or aids another in the commission of such act is guilty of a misdemeanor.

664. Attempts - Defined

Every person who attempts to commit any crime, but fails, or is prevented or intercepted in its perpetration, shall be punished where no provision is made by law for the punishment of those attempts, as follows:

(a) If the crime attempted is punishable by imprisonment in the state prison, the person guilty of the attempt shall be punished by imprisonment in the state prison for one-half the term of imprisonment prescribed upon a conviction of the offense attempted. However, if the crime attempted is willful, deliberate, and premeditated murder, as defined in Section 189, the person guilty of that attempt shall be punished by imprisonment in the state prison for life with the possibility of parole. If the crime attempted is any other one in which the maximum sentence is life imprisonment or death, the person guilty of the attempt shall be punished by imprisonment in the state prison for five, seven, or nine years. The additional term provided in this section for attempted willful, deliberate, and premeditated murder shall not be imposed unless the fact that the attempted murder was willful, deliberate, and premeditated is charged in the accusatory pleading and admitted or found to be true by the trier of fact.

(b) If the crime attempted is punishable by imprisonment in a county jail, the person guilty of the attempt shall be punished by imprisonment in a county jail for a term not exceeding one-half the term of imprisonment prescribed upon a conviction of the offense attempted.

(c) If the offense so attempted is punishable by a fine, the offender convicted of that attempt shall be punished by a fine not exceeding one-half the largest fine which may be imposed upon a conviction of the offense attempted.

(d) If a crime is divided into degrees, an attempt to commit the crime may be of any of those degrees, and the punishment for the attempt shall be determined as provided by this section.

(e) Notwithstanding subdivision (a), if attempted murder is committed upon a peace officer or firefighter, as those terms are defined in paragraphs (7) and (9) of subdivision (a) of Section 190.2, and the person who commits the offense knows or reasonably should know that the victim is such a peace officer or firefighter engaged in the performance of his or her duties, the person guilty of the attempt shall be punished by imprisonment in the state prison for life with the possibility of parole.

This subdivision shall apply if it is proven that a direct but ineffectual act was committed by one person toward killing another human being and the person committing the act harbored express malice aforethought, namely, a specific intent to unlawfully kill another human being. The Legislature finds and declares that this paragraph is declaratory of existing law.

(f) Notwithstanding subdivision (a), if the elements of subdivision (e) are proven in an attempted murder and it is also proven that the attempted murder was willful, deliberate, premeditated, and admitted or found to be true by the trier of fact, the person guilty of the attempt shall be punished by imprisonment in the state prison for 15 years to life. Article 2.5 (commencing with Section 2930) of Chapter 7 of Title 1 of Part 3 shall not apply to reduce this minimum term of 15 years in state prison, and the person shall not be released prior to serving 15 years' confinement.

666. Petit Theft with Prior Theft Conviction

Every person who, having been convicted of petty theft, grand theft, auto theft under Section 10851 of the Vehicle Code, burglary, carjacking, robbery, or a felony violation of Section 496 and having served a term therefor in any penal institution or having been imprisoned therein as a condition of probation for that offense, is subsequently convicted of petty theft, then the person convicted of that subsequent offense is punishable by imprisonment in the county jail not exceeding one year, or in the state prison. *(AM '00)*

CRIMINAL PROCEDURE

827.1. Citation and Release in Lieu of Physical Arrest

A person who is specified or designated in a warrant of arrest for a misdemeanor offense may be released upon the issuance of a citation, in lieu of physical arrest, unless one of the following conditions exists:

(a) The misdemeanor cited in the warrant involves violence.

(b) The misdemeanor cited in the warrant involves a firearm.

(c) The misdemeanor cited in the warrant involves resisting arrest.

(d) The misdemeanor cited in the warrant involves giving false information to a peace officer.

(e) The person arrested is a danger to himself or herself or others due to intoxication or being under the influence of drugs or narcotics.

(f) The person requires medical examination or medical care or was otherwise unable to care for his or her own safety.

(g) The person has other ineligible charges pending against him or her.

(h) There is reasonable likelihood that the offense or offenses would continue or resume, or that the safety of persons or property would be immediately endangered by the release of the person.

(i) The person refuses to sign the notice to appear.

(j) The person cannot provide satisfactory evidence of personal identification.

(k) The warrant of arrest indicates that the person is not eligible to be released on a citation.

The issuance of a citation under this section shall be undertaken in the manner set forth in Sections 853.6 to 853.8, inclusive.

830. Peace Officer Defined

Any person who comes within the provisions of this chapter and who otherwise meets all standards imposed by law on a peace officer is a peace officer, and notwithstanding any other provision of law, no person other than those designated in this chapter is a peace officer. The restriction of peace officer functions of any public officer or employee shall not affect his or her status for purposes of retirement.

830.1. Designation of Peace Officer - Scope of Authority

(a) Any sheriff, undersheriff, or deputy sheriff, employed in that capacity, of a county, any chief of police of a city or chief, director, or chief executive officer of a consolidated municipal public safety agency which performs police functions, any police officer, employed in that capacity and appointed by the chief of police or chief, director, or chief executive of a public safety agency, of a city, any chief of police, or police officer of a district (including police officers of the San Diego Unified Port District ***Harbor Police) authorized by statute to maintain a police department, any marshal or deputy marshal of a municipal court, any port warden or special officer of the Harbor Department of the City of Los Angeles, or any inspector or investigator employed in that capacity in the office of a district attorney, is a peace officer. The authority of these peace officers extends to any place in the state, as follows:

(1) As to any public offense committed or which there is probable cause to believe has been committed within the political subdivision which employs the peace officer.

(2) Where the peace officer has the prior consent of the chief of police or chief, director, or chief executive officer of a consolidated municipal public safety agency, or person authorized by him or her to give consent, if the place is within a city or of the sheriff, or person authorized by him or her to give consent, if the place is within a county.

(3) As to any public offense committed or which there is probable cause to believe has been committed in the peace officer's presence, and with respect to which there is immediate danger to person or property, or of the escape of the perpetrator of the offense.

(b) Special agents and Attorney General investigators of the Department of Justice are peace officers, and those assistant chiefs, deputy chiefs, chiefs, deputy directors, and division directors designated as peace officers by the Attorney General are peace officers. The authority of these peace officers extends to any place in the state where a public offense has been committed or where there is probable cause to believe one has been committed.

(c) Any deputy sheriff of a county of the first class, and any deputy sheriff of the ***Counties of Riverside and San Diego, who is employed to perform duties exclusively or initially relating to custodial assignments with responsibilities for maintaining the operations of county custodial facilities, including the custody, care, supervision, security, movement, and transportation of inmates, is a peace officer whose authority extends to any place in the state only while engaged in the performance of the duties of his or her respective employment and for the purpose of carrying out the primary function of employment relating to his or her custodial assignments, or when performing other law enforcement duties directed by his or her employing agency during a local state of emergency. *(AM '01)*

830.2. Persons Who Are Peace Officers With Authority Any Place in the State

The following persons are peace officers whose authority extends to any place in the state:

(a) Any member of the Department of the California Highway Patrol including those members designated under subdivision (a) of Section 2250.1 of the Vehicle Code, provided that the primary duty of the peace officer is the enforcement of any law relating to the use or operation of vehicles upon the highways, or laws pertaining to the provision of police services for the protection of state officers, state properties, and the occupants of state properties, or both, as set forth in the Vehicle Code and Government Code.

(b) A member of the University of California Police Department appointed pursuant to Section 92600 of the Education Code, provided that the primary duty of the peace officer shall be the enforcement of the law within the area specified in Section 92600 of the Education Code.

(c) A member of the California State University Police Departments appointed pursuant to Section 89560 of the Education Code, provided that the primary duty of the peace officer shall be the enforcement of the law within the area specified in Section 89560 of the Education Code.

(d)(1) Any member of the Law Enforcement and Investigations Unit of the Department of Corrections, provided that the primary duties of the peace officer shall be the investigation or apprehension of parolees, parole violators, or escapees from state institutions, the transportation of those persons, and the coordination of those activities with other criminal justice agencies.

(2) Any member of the Office of Internal Affairs of the Department of Corrections, provided that the primary duties shall be criminal investigations of Department of Corrections personnel and the coordination of those activities with other criminal justice agencies. For purposes of this subdivision the member of the Office of Internal Affairs shall possess certification from the Commission on Peace Officer Standards and Training for investigators, or have completed training pursuant to Section 6126.1 of the Penal Code.

(e) Employees of the Department of Fish and Game designated by the director, provided that the primary duty of those peace officers shall be the enforcement of the law as set forth in Section 856 of the Fish and Game Code.

(f) Employees of the Department of Parks and Recreation designated by the director pursuant to Section 5008 of the Public Resources Code, provided that the primary duty of the peace officer shall be the enforcement of the law as set forth in Section 5008 of the Public Resources Code.

(g) The Director of Forestry and Fire Protection and employees or classes of employees of the Department of Forestry and Fire Protection designated by the director pursuant to Section 4156 of the Public Resources Code, provided that the primary duty of the peace officer shall be the enforcement of the law as that duty is set forth in Section 4156 of the Public Resources Code.

(h) Persons employed by the Department of Alcoholic Beverage Control for the enforcement of Division 9 (commencing with Section 23000) of the Business and Professions Code and designated by the Director of Alcoholic Beverage Control, provided that the primary duty of any of these peace officers shall be the enforcement of the laws relating to alcoholic beverages, as that duty is set forth in Section 25755 of the Business and Professions Code.

(i) Marshals and police appointed by the Board of Directors of the California Exposition and State Fair pursuant to Section 3332 of the Food and Agricultural Code, provided that the primary duty of the peace officers shall be the enforcement of the law as prescribed in that section.

(j) The Inspector General, pursuant to Section 6125, and the Chief Deputy Inspector General In Charge, the Senior Deputy Inspector General, the Deputy Inspector General, and those employees of the Inspector General as designated by the Inspector General, are peace officers, provided that the primary duty of these peace officers shall be conducting audits of investigatory practices and other audits, as well as conducting investigations, of the Department of Corrections, the Department of the Youth Authority, the Board of Prison Terms, the Youthful Offender Parole Board, or the Board of Corrections. *(AM '99)*

830.3. Peace Officers and Their Respective Duties

The following persons are peace officers whose authority extends to any place in the state for the purpose of performing their primary duty or when making an arrest pursuant to Section 836 of the Penal Code as to any public offense with respect to which there is immediate danger to person or property, or of the escape of the perpetrator of that offense, or pursuant to Section 8597 or 8598 of the Government Code. These peace officers may carry firearms only if authorized and under those terms and conditions as specified by their employing agencies:

(a) Persons employed by the Division of Investigation of the Department of Consumer Affairs and investigators of the Medical Board of California and the Board of Dental Examiners, who are designated by the Director of Consumer Affairs, provided that the primary duty of these peace officers shall be the enforcement of the law as that duty is set forth in Section 160 of the Business and Professions Code. The Director of Consumer Affairs shall designate as peace officers seven persons who shall at the time of their designation be assigned to the investigations unit of the Board of Dental Examiners.

(b) Voluntary fire wardens designated by the Director of Forestry and Fire Protection pursuant to Section 4156 of the Public Resources Code, provided that the primary duty of these peace officers shall be the enforcement of the law as that duty is set forth in Section 4156 of that code.

(c) Employees of the Department of Motor Vehicles designated in Section 1655 of the Vehicle Code, provided that the primary duty of these peace officers shall be the enforcement of the law as that duty is set forth in Section 1655 of that code.

(d) Investigators of the California Horse Racing Board designated by the board, provided that the primary duty of these peace officers shall be the enforcement of Chapter 4 (commencing with Section 19400) of Division 8 of the Business and Professions Code and Chapter 10 (commencing with Section 330) of Title 9 of Part 1 of this code.

(e) The State Fire Marshal and assistant or deputy state fire marshals appointed pursuant to Section 13103 of the Health and Safety Code, provided that the primary duty of these peace officers shall be the enforcement of the law as that duty is set forth in Section 13104 of that code.

(f) Inspectors of the food and drug section designated by the chief pursuant to subdivision (a) of Section 106500 of the Health and Safety Code, provided that the primary duty of these peace officers shall be the enforcement of the law as that duty is set forth in Section 106500 of that code.

(g) All investigators of the Division of Labor Standards Enforcement designated by the Labor Commissioner, provided that the primary duty of these peace officers shall be the enforcement of the law as prescribed in Section 95 of the Labor Code.

(h) All investigators of the State Departments of Health Services, Social Services, Mental Health, Developmental Services, and Alcohol and Drug Programs, the Department of Toxic Substances Control, the Office of Statewide Health Planning and Development, and the Public Employees'Retirement System, provided that the primary duty of these peace officers shall be the enforcement of the law relating to the duties of his or her department, or office. Notwithstanding any other provision of law, investigators of the Public Employees'Retirement System shall not carry firearms.

(i) The Chief of the Bureau of Fraudulent Claims of the Department of Insurance and those investigators designated by the chief, provided that the primary duty of those investigators shall be the enforcement of Section 550.

(j) Employees of the Department of Housing and Community Development designated under Section 18023 of the Health and Safety Code, provided that the primary duty of these peace officers shall be the enforcement of the law as that duty is set forth in Section 18023 of that code.

(k) Investigators of the office of the Controller, provided that the primary duty of these investigators shall be the enforcement of the law relating to the duties of that office. Notwithstanding any other law, except as authorized by the Controller, the peace officers designated pursuant to this subdivision shall not carry firearms.

(l) Investigators of the Department of Corporations designated by the Commissioner of Corporations, provided that the primary duty of these investigators shall be the enforcement of the provisions of law administered by the Department of Corporations. Notwithstanding any other provision of law, the peace officers designated pursuant to this subdivision shall not carry firearms.

(m) Persons employed by the Contractors'State License Board designated by the Director of Consumer Affairs pursuant to Section 7011.5 of the Business and Professions Code, provided that the primary duty of these persons shall be the enforcement of the law as that duty is set forth in Section 7011.5, and in Chapter 9 (commencing with Section 7000) of Division 3, of that code. The Director of Consumer Affairs may designate as peace officers not more than three persons who shall at the time of their designation be assigned to the special investigations unit of the board. Notwithstanding any other provision of law, the persons designated pursuant to this subdivision shall not carry firearms.

(n) The chief and coordinators of the Law Enforcement Division of the Office of Emergency Services.

(o) Investigators of the office of the Secretary of State designated by the Secretary of State, provided that the primary duty of these peace officers shall be the enforcement of the law as prescribed in Chapter 3 (commencing with Section 8200) of Division 1 of Title 2 of, and Section 12172.5 of, the Government Code. Notwithstanding any other provision of law, the peace officers designated pursuant to this subdivision shall not carry firearms.

(p) The Deputy Director for Security designated by Section 8880.38 of the Government Code, and all lottery security personnel assigned to the California State Lottery and designated by the director, provided that the primary duty of any of those peace officers shall be the enforcement of the laws related to assuring the integrity, honesty, and fairness of the operation and administration of the California State Lottery.

(q) Investigators employed by the Investigation Division of the Employment Development Department designated by the director of the department, provided that the primary duty of those peace officers shall be the enforcement of the law as that duty is set forth in Section 317 of the Unemployment Insurance Code. Notwithstanding any other provision of law, the peace officers designated pursuant to this subdivision shall not carry firearms.

(r) The chief and assistant chief of museum security and safety of the California Science Center, as designated by the executive director pursuant to Section 4108 of the Food and Agricultural Code, provided that the primary duty of those peace officers shall be the enforcement of the law as that duty is set forth in Section 4108 of the Food and Agricultural Code.

(s) Employees of the Franchise Tax Board designated by the board, provided that the primary duty of these peace officers shall be the enforcement of the law as set forth in Chapter 9 (commencing with Section 19701) of Part 10.2 of Division 2 of the Revenue and Taxation Code.

(t) Notwithstanding any other provision of this section, a peace officer authorized by this section shall not be authorized to carry firearms by his or her employing agency until that agency has adopted a policy on the use of deadly force by those peace officers, and until those peace officers have been instructed in the employing agency's policy on the use of deadly force.

Every peace officer authorized pursuant to this section to carry firearms by his or her employing agency shall qualify in the use of the firearms at least every six months.

(u) Investigators of the Department of Managed Health Care designated by the Director of the Department of Managed Health Care, provided that the primary duty of these investigators shall be the enforcement of the provisions of laws administered by the Director of the Department of Managed Health Care. Notwithstanding any other provision of law, the peace officers designated pursuant to this subdivision shall not carry firearms. *(AM '99, '00)*

830.31. Los Angeles County Safety Officers; Park Rangers; Los Angeles Department of General Services Security Officers; Housing Authority Patrol Officers

The following persons are peace officers whose authority extends to any place in the state for the purpose of performing their primary duty or when making an arrest pursuant to Section 836 as to any public offense with respect to which there is immediate danger to person or property, or of the escape of the perpetrator of that offense, or pursuant to Section 8597 or 8598 of the Government Code. These peace officers may carry firearms only if authorized, and under the terms and conditions specified, by their employing agency.

(a) A safety police officer of the County of Los Angeles, if the primary duty of the officer is the enforcement of the law in or about properties owned, operated, or administered by his or her employing agency or when performing necessary duties with respect to patrons, employees, and properties of his or her employing agency.

(b) A person designated by a local agency as a park ranger and regularly employed and paid in that capacity, if the primary duty of the officer is the protection of park and other property of the agency and the preservation of the peace therein.

(c)(1) A peace officer of the Department of General Services of the City of Los Angeles designated by the general manager of the department, if the primary duty of the officer is the enforcement of the law in or about properties owned, operated, or administered by his or her employing agency or when performing necessary duties with respect to patrons, employees, and properties of his or her employing agency.

(2) A peace officer designated pursuant to this subdivision, and authorized to carry firearms by his or her employing agency, shall satisfactorily complete the introductory course of firearm training required by Section 832 and shall requalify in the use of firearms every six months.

(3) Notwithstanding any other provision of law, a peace officer designated pursuant to this subdivision who is authorized to carry a firearm by his or her employing agency while on duty, shall not be authorized to carry a firearm when he or she is not on duty.

(d) A housing authority patrol officer employed by the housing authority of a city, district, county, or city and county or employed by the police department of a city and county, if the primary duty of the officer is the enforcement of the law in or about properties owned, operated, or administered by his or her employing agency or when performing necessary duties with respect to patrons, employees, and properties of his or her employing agency.

830.32. Community College and School District Police

The following persons are peace officers whose authority extends to any place in the state for the purpose of performing their primary duty or when making an arrest pursuant to Section 836 as to any public offense with respect to which there is immediate danger to person or property, or of the escape of the perpetrator of that offense, or pursuant to Section 8597 or 8598 of the Government Code. Those peace officers may carry firearms only if authorized and under terms and conditions specified by their employing agency.

(a) Members of a California Community College police department appointed pursuant to Section 72330 of the Education Code, if the primary duty of the police officer is the enforcement of the law as prescribed in Section 72330 of the Education Code.

(b) Persons employed as members of a police department of a school district pursuant to Section 38000 of the Education Code, if the primary duty of the police officer is the enforcement of the law as prescribed in Section 38000 of the Education Code.

(c) Any peace officer employed by a K-12 public school district or California Community College district who has completed training as prescribed by subdivision (f) of Section 832.3 shall be designated a school police officer. *(AM '98, '00)*

830.33. BART, Harbor, Port, Transit, Airport, and Railroad Police

The following persons are peace officers whose authority extends to any place in the state for the purpose of performing their primary duty or when making an arrest pursuant to Section 836 as to any public offense with respect to which there is immediate danger to person or property, or of the escape of the perpetrator of that offense, or pursuant to Section 8597 or 8598 of the Government Code. Those peace officers may carry firearms only if authorized and under terms and conditions specified by their employing agency.

(a) A member of the San Francisco Bay Area Rapid Transit District Police Department appointed pursuant to Section 28767.5 of the Public Utilities Code, if the primary duty of the peace officer is the enforcement of the law in or about properties owned, operated, or administered by the district or when performing necessary duties with respect to patrons, employees, and properties of the district.

(b) Harbor or port police regularly employed and paid in that capacity by a county, city, or district other than peace officers authorized under Section 830.1, if the primary duty of the peace officer is the enforcement of the law in or about the properties owned, operated, or administered by the harbor or port or when performing necessary duties with respect to patrons, employees, and properties of the harbor or port.

(c) Transit police officers or peace officers of a county, city, transit development board, or district, if the primary duty of the peace officer is the enforcement of the law in or about properties owned, operated, or administered by the employing agency or when performing necessary duties with respect to patrons, employees, and properties of the employing agency.

(d) Any person regularly employed as an airport law enforcement officer by a city, county, or district operating the airport or by a joint powers agency, created pursuant to Article 1 (commencing with Section 6500) of Chapter 5 of Division 7 of Title 1 of the Government Code, operating the airport, if the primary duty of the peace officer is the enforcement of the law in or about properties owned, operated, and administered by the employing agency or when performing necessary duties with respect to patrons, employees, and properties of the employing agency.

(e) Any railroad police officer commissioned by the Governor pursuant to Section 8226 of the Public Utilities Code, if the primary duty of the peace officer is the enforcement of the law in or about properties owned, operated, or administered by the employing agency or when performing necessary duties with respect to patrons, employees, and properties of the employing agency.

830.34. Municipal Utility District or County Water District Security Officers - Security Director of City and County Public Utilities Commission

The following persons are peace officers whose authority extends to any place in the state for the purpose of performing their primary duty or when making an arrest pursuant to Section 836 as to any public offense with respect to which there is immediate danger to person or property, or of the escape of the perpetrator of that offense, or pursuant to Section 8597 or 8598 of the Government Code. Those peace officers may carry firearms only if authorized and under terms and conditions specified by their employing agency.

(a) Persons designated as a security officer by a municipal utility district pursuant to Section 12820 of the Public Utilities Code, if the primary duty of the officer is the protection of the properties of the utility district and the protection of the persons thereon.

(b) Persons designated as a security officer by a county water district pursuant to Section 30547 of the Water Code, if the primary duty of the officer is the protection of the properties of the county water district and the protection of the persons thereon.

(c) The security director of the public utilities commission of a city and county, if the primary duty of the security director is the protection of the properties of the commission and the protection of the persons thereon.

830.35. Welfare Fraud or Child Support Investigators - Coroners and Deputy Coroners

The following persons are peace officers whose authority extends to any place in the state for the purpose of performing their primary duty or when making an arrest pursuant to Section 836 as to any public offense with respect to which there is immediate danger to person or property, or of the escape of the perpetrator of that offense, or pursuant to Section 8597 or 8598 of the Government Code. Those peace officers may carry firearms only if authorized and under terms and conditions specified by their employing agency.

(a) A welfare fraud investigator or inspector, regularly employed and paid in that capacity by a county, if the primary duty of the peace officer is the enforcement of the provisions of the Welfare and Institutions Code.

(b) A child support investigator or inspector, regularly employed and paid in that capacity by a district attorney's office, if the primary duty of the peace officer is the enforcement of the provisions of the Family Code and Section 270.

(c) The coroner and deputy coroners, regularly employed and paid in that capacity, of a county, if the primary duty of the peace officer are those duties set forth in Sections 27469 and 27491 to 27491.4, inclusive, of the Government Code. *(AM '00)*

830.36.　Sergeant-at-Arms of House of Legislature - Bailiffs of Supreme Court and Courts of Appeal - Court Service Officer in County of Third Class

The following persons are peace officers whose authority extends to any place in the state for the purpose of performing their primary duty or when making an arrest pursuant to Section 836 as to any public offense with respect to which there is immediate danger to person or property, or of the escape of the perpetrator of that offense, or pursuant to Section 8597 or 8598 of the Government Code. Those peace officers may carry firearms only if authorized and under terms and conditions specified by their employing agency.

(a)　The Sergeant-at-Arms of each house of the Legislature, if the primary duty of the peace officer is the enforcement of the law in or about properties owned, operated, or administered by the employing agency or when performing necessary duties with respect to patrons, employees, and properties of the employing agency.

(b)　Marshals of the Supreme Court and bailiffs of the courts of appeal, and coordinators of security for the judicial branch, if the primary duty of the peace officer is the enforcement of the law in or about properties owned, operated, or administered by the employing agency or when performing necessary duties with respect to patrons, employees, and properties of the employing agency.

(c)　Court service officer in a county of the second class and third class, if the primary duty of the peace officer is the enforcement of the law in or about properties owned, operated, or administered by the employing agency or when performing necessary duties with respect to patrons, employees, and properties of the employing agency. *(AM '99)*

830.37.　Fire Department Arson Investigators - Other Fire Department Personnel

The following persons are peace officers whose authority extends to any place in the state for the purpose of performing their primary duty or when making an arrest pursuant to Section 836 as to any public offense with respect to which there is immediate danger to person or property, or of the escape of the perpetrator of that offense, or pursuant to Section 8597 or 8598 of the Government Code. These peace officers may carry firearms only if authorized and under terms and conditions specified by their employing agency.

(a)　Members of an arson-investigating unit, regularly paid and employed in that capacity, of a fire department or fire protection agency of a county, city, city and county, district, or the state, if the primary duty of these peace officers is the detection and apprehension of persons who have violated any fire law or committed insurance fraud.

(b)　Members other than members of an arson-investigating unit, regularly paid and employed in that capacity, of a fire department or fire protection agency of a county, city, city and county, district, or the state, if the primary duty of these peace officers, when acting in that capacity, is the enforcement of laws relating to fire prevention or fire suppression.

(c)　Voluntary fire wardens as are designated by the Director of Forestry and Fire Protection pursuant to Section 4156 of the Public Resources Code, provided that the primary duty of these peace officers shall be the enforcement of the law as that duty is set forth in Section 4156 of that code.

(d)　Firefighter/security guards by the Military Department, if the primary duty of the peace officer is the enforcement of the law in or about properties owned, operated, or administered by the employing agency or when performing necessary duties with respect to patrons, employees, and properties of the employing agency.

830.38.　State Mental Hospital Officers

The officers of a state hospital under the jurisdiction of the State Department of Mental Health or the State Department of Developmental Services appointed pursuant to Section 4313 or 4493 of the Welfare and Institutions Code, are peace officers whose authority extends to any place in the state for the purpose of performing their primary duty or when making an arrest pursuant to Section 826 as to any public offense with respect to which there is immediate danger to person or property, or of the escape of the perpetrator of that offense, or pursuant to Section 8597 or 8598 of the Government Code provided that the primary duty of the peace officers shall be the enforcement of the law as set forth in Sections 4311, 4313, 4491, and

4493 of the Welfare and Institutions Code. Those peace officers may carry firearms only if authorized and under terms and conditions specified by their employing agency.

830.39. Conditional Powers of Out-of-State Police Officers in California

(a) Any regularly employed law enforcement officer of the Oregon State Police, the Nevada Department of Motor Vehicles and Public Safety, or the Arizona Department of Public Safety is a peace officer in this state if all of the following conditions are met:

(1) The officer is providing, or attempting to provide, law enforcement services within this state on the state or county highways and areas immediately adjacent thereto, within a distance of up to 50 statute miles of the contiguous border of this state and the state employing the officer.

(2) The officer is providing, or attempting to provide, law enforcement services pursuant to either of the following:

(A) In response to a request for services initiated by a member of the CHP.

(B) In response to a reasonable belief that emergency law enforcement services are necessary for the preservation of life, and a request for services by a member of the CHP is impractical to obtain under the circumstances. In those situations, the officer shall obtain authorization as soon as practical.

(3) The officer is providing, or attempting to provide, law enforcement services for the purpose of assisting a member of the CHP to provide emergency service in response to misdemeanor or felony criminal activity, pursuant to the authority of a peace officer as provided in subdivision (a) of Section 830.2, or, in the event of highway-related traffic accidents, emergency incidents or other similar public safety problems, whether or not a member of the CHP is present at the scene of the event. Nothing in this section shall be construed to confer upon the officer the authority to enforce traffic or motor vehicle infractions.

(4) An agreement pursuant to Section 2403.5 of the Vehicle Code is in effect between the CHP and the agency of the adjoining state employing the officer, the officer acts in accordance with that agreement, and the agreement specifies that the officer and employing agency of the adjoining state shall be subject to the same civil immunities and liabilities as a peace officer and his or her employing agency in this state.

(5) The officer receives no separate compensation from this state for providing law enforcement services within this state.

(6) The adjoining state employing the officer confers similar rights and authority upon a member of the CHP who renders assistance within that state.

(b) Whenever, pursuant to Nevada law, Nevada correctional officer is working or supervising Nevada inmates who are performing conservation-related projects or fire suppression duties within California, the correctional officer may maintain custody of the inmates in California, and retake any inmate who should escape in California, to the same extent as if the correctional officer were a peace officer in this state and the inmate had been committed to his or her custody in proceedings under California law.

(c) Notwithstanding any other provision of law, any person who is acting as a peace officer in this state in the manner described in this section shall be deemed to have met the requirements of Section 1031 of the Government Code and the selection and training standards of the Commission of Peace Officers Standards and Training if the officer has completed the basic training required for peace officers in his or her state.

(d) In no case shall a peace officer of an adjoining state be authorized to provide services within California jurisdiction during any period in which the regular law enforcement agency of the jurisdiction is involved in a labor dispute.

830.4. Authority of National Guard, Guards and Messengers of Treasurer's Office, and Security Officers of Department of Justice, and Hastings College of Law to Carry Firearms

The following persons are peace officers whose authority extends to any place in the state for the purpose of performing their duties under the conditions as specified by statute. Those peace officers may carry firearms only if authorized and under terms and conditions specified by their employing agency.

(a) Members of the California National Guard have the powers of peace officers when they are involved in any or all the following:

(1) Called or ordered into active state service by the Governor pursuant to the provisions of Section 143 or 146 of the Military and Veterans Code.

(2) Serving within the area wherein military assistance is required.

(3) Directly assisting civil authorities in any of the situations specified in Section 143 or 146.

The authority of the peace officer under this subdivision extends to the area wherein military assistance is required as to a public offense committed or which there is reasonable cause to believe has been committed within that area. The requirements of Section 1031 of the Government Code are not applicable under those circumstances.

(b) Guards and messengers of the Treasurer's office when performing assigned duties as a guard or messenger.

(c) Security officers of the Department of Justice when performing assigned duties as security officers.

(d) Security officers of Hastings College of the Law. These officers shall have authority of peace officers only within the City and County of San Francisco. Notwithstanding any other provisions of law, the peace officers designated by this subdivision shall not be authorized by this subdivision to carry firearms either on or off duty. Notwithstanding any other provision of law, the act which designated the persons described in this subdivision as peace officers shall serve only to define those persons as peace officers, the extent of their jurisdiction, and the nature and scope of their authority, powers, and duties, and there shall be no change in the status of those persons for purposes of retirement, workers'compensation or similar injury or death benefits, or other employee benefits.

830.5. Parole and Correctional Officers; When Carrying Firearm Permitted

The following persons are peace officers whose authority extends to any place in the state while engaged in the performance of the duties of their respective employment and for the purpose of carrying out the primary function of their employment or as required under Sections 8597, 8598, and 8617 of the Government Code. Except as specified in this section, these peace officers may carry firearms only if authorized and under those terms and conditions specified by their employing agency:

(a) A parole officer of the Department of Corrections or the Department of the Youth Authority, probation officer, deputy probation officer, or a board coordinating parole agent employed by the Youthful Offender Parole Board. Except as otherwise provided in this subdivision, the authority of these parole or probation officers shall extend only as follows:

(1) To conditions of parole or of probation by any person in this state on parole or probation.

(2) To the escape of any inmate or ward from a state or local institution.

(3) To the transportation of persons on parole or probation.

(4) To violations of any penal provisions of law which are discovered while performing the usual or authorized duties of his or her employment.

(5) To the rendering of mutual aid to any other law enforcement agency.

For the purposes of this subdivision, "parole agent"shall have the same meaning as parole officer of the Department of Corrections or of the Department of the Youth Authority.

Any parole officer of the Department of Corrections, the Department of the Youth Authority, or the Youthful Offender Parole Board is authorized to carry firearms, but only as determined by the director on a case-by-case or unit-by-unit basis and only under those terms and conditions specified by the director or chairperson. The Department of the Youth Authority shall develop a policy for arming peace officers of the Department of the Youth Authority who comprise "high-risk transportation details"or "high-risk escape details"no later than June 30, 1995. This policy shall be implemented no later than December 31, 1995.

The Department of the Youth Authority shall train and arm those peace officers who comprise tactical teams at each facility for use during "high-risk escape details."

(b) A correctional officer employed by the Department of Corrections or any employee of the Department of the Youth Authority having custody of wards or the Inspector General of the Youth and Adult Correctional Agency or any internal affairs investigator under the authority of the Inspector General or any employee of the Department of Corrections designated by the Director of Corrections or any correctional counselor series employee of the Department of Corrections or any medical technical assistant series employee designated by the Director of Corrections or designated by the Director of Corrections and employed by the State Department of Mental Health to work in the California Medical Facility or employee of the Board of Prison Terms designated by the Secretary of the Youth and Adult Correctional Agency or employee of the Department of the Youth Authority designated by the Director of the Youth Authority or any superintendent, supervisor, or employee having custodial responsibilities in an institution operated by a probation department, or any transportation officer of a probation department.

(c) The following persons may carry a firearm while not on duty: a parole officer of the Department of Corrections or the Department of the Youth Authority, a correctional officer or correctional counselor employed by the Department of Corrections or any employee of the Department of the Youth Authority having custody of wards or any employee of the Department of Corrections designated by the Director of Corrections. A parole officer of the Youthful Offender Parole Board may carry a firearm while not on duty only when so authorized by the chairperson of the board and only under the terms and conditions specified by the chairperson. Nothing in this section shall be interpreted to require licensure pursuant to Section 12025. The director or chairperson may deny, suspend, or revoke for good cause a person's right to carry a firearm under this subdivision. That person shall, upon request, receive a hearing, as provided for in the negotiated grievance procedure between the exclusive employee representative and the Department of Corrections, the Department of the Youth Authority, or the Youthful Offender Parole Board, to review the director's or the chairperson's decision.

(d) Persons permitted to carry firearms pursuant to this section, either on or off duty, shall meet the training requirements of Section 832 and shall qualify with the firearm at least quarterly. It is the responsibility of the individual officer or designee to maintain his or her eligibility to carry concealable firearms off duty. Failure to maintain quarterly qualifications by an officer or designee with any concealable firearms carried off duty shall constitute good cause to suspend or revoke that person's right to carry firearms off duty.

(e) The Department of Corrections shall allow reasonable access to its ranges for officers and designees of either department to qualify to carry concealable firearms off duty. The time spent on the range for purposes of meeting the qualification requirements shall be the person's own time during the person's off-duty hours.

(f) The Director of Corrections shall promulgate regulations consistent with this section.

(g) "High-risk transportation details" and "high-risk escape details" as used in this section shall be determined by the Director of the Youth Authority, or his or her designee. The director, or his or her designee, shall consider at least the following in determining "high-risk transportation details" and "high-risk escape details": protection of the public, protection of officers, flight risk, and violence potential of the wards.

(h) "Transportation detail" as used in this section shall include transportation of wards outside the facility, including, but not limited to, court appearances, medical trips, and interfacility transfers. *(AM '01)*

830.6. Peace Officer Powers: Reserve or Auxiliary Peace Officers; Person Summoned to Aid Uniformed Peace Officer

(a)(1) Whenever any qualified person is deputized or appointed by the proper authority as a reserve or auxiliary sheriff or city police officer, a reserve deputy sheriff, a reserve deputy marshal, a reserve police officer of a regional park district or of a transit district, a reserve park ranger, a reserve harbor or port police officer of a county, city, or district as specified in Section 663.5 of the Harbors and Navigation Code, a reserve deputy of the Department of Fish and Game, a reserve special agent of the Department of Justice, a reserve officer of a community service district which is authorized under subdivision (h) of Section 61600 of the Government Code to maintain a police department or other police protection, a reserve officer of a school district police department under Section 35021.5 of the Education Code, or a reserve officer of a police protection district formed under Part 1 (commencing with Section 20000) of Division 14 of the Health and Safety Code, and is assigned specific police functions by that authority, the person is a peace officer, if the person qualifies as set forth in Section 832.6. The authority of a person designated as a peace officer pursuant to this paragraph extends only for the duration of the person's specific assignment. A reserve park ranger or a transit, harbor, or port district reserve officer may carry firearms only if authorized by, and under those terms and conditions as are specified by, his or her employing agency.

(2) Whenever any qualified person is deputized or appointed by the proper authority as a reserve or auxiliary sheriff or city police officer, a reserve deputy sheriff, a reserve deputy marshal, a reserve park ranger, a reserve police officer of a regional park district, transit district, or a school district, a reserve harbor or port police officer of a county, city, or district as specified in Section 663.5 of the Harbors and Navigation Code, a reserve officer of a community service district that is authorized under subdivision (h) of Section 61600 of the Government Code to maintain a police department or other police protection, or a reserve officer of a police protection district formed under Part 1 (commencing with Section 20000) of Division 14 of the Health and Safety Code, and is so designated by local ordinance or, if the local agency is not authorized to act by ordinance, by resolution, either individually or by class, and is assigned to the prevention and detection of crime and the general enforcement of the laws of this state by that authority, the person is a peace officer, if the person qualifies as set forth in paragraph (1) of subdivision (a) of Section 832.6. The authority of a person designated as a peace officer pursuant to this paragraph includes the full powers and duties of a peace officer as provided by Section 830.1. A transit, harbor, or port district reserve police officer, or a city or county reserve peace officer who is not provided with the powers and duties authorized by Section 830.1, has the powers and duties authorized in Section 830.33, or in the case of a reserve park ranger, the powers and duties that are authorized in Section 830.31, and a school district reserve police officer has the powers and duties authorized in Section 830.32.

(b) Whenever any person designated by a Native American tribe recognized by the United States Secretary of the Interior is deputized or appointed by the county sheriff as a reserve or auxiliary sheriff or a reserve deputy sheriff, and is assigned to the prevention and detection of crime and the general enforcement of the laws of this state by the county sheriff, the person is a peace officer, if the person qualifies as set forth in paragraph (1) of subdivision (a) of Section 832.6. The authority of a peace officer pursuant to this subdivision includes the full powers and duties of a peace officer as provided by Section 830.1.

(c) Whenever any person is summoned to the aid of any uniformed peace officer, the summoned person is vested with the powers of a peace officer that are expressly delegated to him or her by the summoning officer or that are otherwise reasonably necessary to properly assist the officer.

830.7. Persons Who May Exercise the Power of Arrest

The following persons are not peace officers but may exercise the powers of arrest of a peace officer as specified in Section 836 during the course and within the scope of their employment, if they successfully complete a course in the exercise of those powers pursuant to Section 832:

(a) Persons designated by a cemetery authority pursuant to Section 8325 of the Health and Safety Code.

(b) Persons regularly employed as security officers for independent institutions of higher education, recognized under subdivision (b) of Section 66010 of the Education Code, if the institution has concluded a memorandum of understanding, permitting the exercise of that authority, with the sheriff or the chief of police within whose jurisdiction the institution lies.

(c) Persons regularly employed as security officers for health facilities, as defined in Section 1250 of the Health and Safety Code, that are owned and operated by cities, counties, and cities and counties, if the facility has concluded a memorandum of understanding, permitting the exercise of that authority, with the sheriff or the chief of police within whose jurisdiction the facility lies.

(d) Employees or classes of employees of the California Department of Forestry and Fire Protection designated by the Director of Forestry and Fire Protection, provided that the primary duty of the employee shall be the enforcement of the law as that duty is set forth in Section 4156 of the Public Resources Code.

(e) Persons regularly employed as inspectors, supervisors, or security officers for transit districts, as defined in Section 99213 of the Public Utilities Code, if the district has concluded a memorandum of understanding permitting the exercise of that authority, with, as applicable, the sheriff, the chief of police, or the Department of the California Highway Patrol within whose jurisdiction the district lies. For the purposes of this subdivision, the exercise of peace officer authority may include the authority to remove a vehicle from a railroad right-of-way as set forth in Section 22656 of the Vehicle Code.

(f) Nonpeace officers regularly employed as county parole officers pursuant to Section 3089.

(g) Persons appointed by the Executive Director of the California Science Center pursuant to Section 4108 of the Food and Agricultural Code.

(h) Persons regularly employed as investigators by the Department of Transportation for the City of Los Angeles and designated by local ordinance as public officers, to the extent necessary to enforce laws related to public transportation, and authorized by a memorandum of understanding with the chief of police, permitting the exercise of that authority. For the purposes of this subdivision, "investigator"means an employee defined in Section 53075.61 of the Government Code authorized by local ordinance to enforce laws related to public transportation. Transportation investigators authorized by this section shall not be deemed "peace officers"for purposes of Sections 241 and 243. *(AM '99)*

830.8. Federal Officers Powers in California

(a) Federal criminal investigators and law enforcement officers are not California peace officers, but may exercise the powers of arrest of a peace officer in any of the following circumstances:

(1) Any circumstances specified in Section 836 or Section 5150 of the Welfare and Institutions Code for violations of state or local laws.

(2) When these investigators and law enforcement officers are engaged in the enforcement of federal criminal laws and exercise the arrest powers only incidental to the performance of these duties.

(3) When requested by a California law enforcement agency to be involved in a joint task force or criminal investigation.

(4) When probable cause exists to believe there is any public offense that involves immediate danger to persons or property.

In all of these instances, the provisions of Section 847 shall apply. These investigators and law enforcement officers, prior to the exercise of these arrest powers, shall have been certified by their agency heads as having satisfied the training requirements of Section 832, or the equivalent thereof.

This subdivision does not apply to federal officers of the Bureau of Land Management or the Forest Service of the Department of Agriculture. These officers have no authority to enforce California statutes without the written consent of the sheriff or the chief of police in whose jurisdiction they are assigned.

(b) Duly authorized federal employees who comply with the training requirements set forth in Section 832 are peace officers when they are engaged in enforcing applicable state or local laws on property owned or possessed by the United States government, or on any street, sidewalk, or property adjacent thereto, and with the written consent of the sheriff or the chief of police, respectively, in whose jurisdiction the property is situated.

(c) National park rangers are not California peace officers but may exercise the powers of arrest of a peace officer as specified in Section 836 and the powers of a peace officer specified in Section 5150 of the Welfare and Institutions Code for violations of state or local laws provided these rangers are exercising the arrest powers incidental to the performance of their federal duties or providing or attempting to provide law enforcement services in response to a request initiated by California state park rangers to assist in preserving the peace and protecting state parks and other property for which California state park rangers are responsible. National park rangers, prior to the exercise of these arrest powers, shall have been certified by their agency heads as having satisfactorily completed the training requirements of Section 832.3, or the equivalent thereof.

(d) Notwithstanding any other provision of law, during a state of war emergency or a state of emergency, as defined in Section 8558 of the Government Code, federal criminal investigators and law enforcement officers who are assisting California law enforcement officers in carrying out emergency operations are not deemed California peace officers, but may exercise the powers of arrest of a peace officer as specified in Section 836 and the powers of a peace officer specified in Section 5150 of the Welfare and Institutions

Code for violations of state or local laws. In these instances, the provisions of Section 847 and of Section 8655 of the Government Code shall apply.

(e)(1) Any qualified person who is appointed as a Washoe tribal law enforcement officer is not a California peace officer, but may exercise the powers of a Washoe tribal peace officer when engaged in the enforcement of Washoe tribal criminal laws against any person who is an Indian, as defined in subsection (a) of Section 450b of Title 25 of the United States Code, on Washoe tribal land. The respective prosecuting authorities, in consultation with law enforcement agencies, may agree on who shall have initial responsibility for prosecution of specified infractions. This subdivision is not meant to confer cross-deputized status as California peace officers, nor to confer California peace officer status upon Washoe tribal law enforcement officers when enforcing state or local laws in the State of California. Nothing in this section shall be construed to impose liability upon or to require indemnification by the County of Alpine or the State of California for any act performed by an officer of the Washoe Tribe. Washoe tribal law enforcement officers shall have the right to travel to and from Washoe tribal lands within California in order to carry out tribal duties.

(2) Washoe tribal law enforcement officers are exempted from the provisions of subdivision (a) of Section 12025 and subdivision (a) of Section 12031 while performing their official duties on their tribal lands or while proceeding by a direct route to or from the tribal lands. Tribal law enforcement vehicles are deemed to be emergency vehicles within the meaning of Section 30 of the Vehicle Code while performing official police services.

(3) As used in this subdivision, the term "Washoe tribal lands" includes the following:

(A) All lands located in the County of Alpine within the limits of the reservation created for the Washoe Tribe of Nevada and California, notwithstanding the issuance of any patent and including rights-of-way running through the reservation and all tribal trust lands.

(B) All Indian allotments, the Indian titles to which have not been extinguished, including rights-of-way running through the same.

(4) As used in this subdivision, the term "Washoe tribal law" refers to the laws codified in the Law and Order Code of the Washoe Tribe of Nevada and California, as adopted by the Tribal Council of the Washoe Tribe of Nevada and California.

830.9. Animal Control Officers - Powers and Training Requirements

Animal control officers are not peace officers but may exercise the powers of arrest of a peace officer as specified in Section 836 and the power to serve warrants as specified in Sections 1523 and 1530 during the course and within the scope of their employment, if those officers receive a course in the exercise of those powers pursuant to Section 832. That part of the training course specified in Section 832 pertaining to the carrying and use of firearms shall not be required for any animal control officer whose employing agency prohibits the use of firearms.

For the purposes of this section, "firearms" includes capture guns, blowguns, carbon dioxide operated rifles and pistols, air guns, handguns, rifles, and shotguns.

830.10. Uniformed Peace Officer - Identification

Any uniformed peace officer shall wear a badge, nameplate, or other device which bears clearly on its face the identification number or name of the officer.

830.11. State Banking and Real Estate Investigators

(a) The following persons are not peace officers but may exercise the powers of arrest of a peace officer as specified in Section 836 and the power to serve warrants as specified in Sections 1523 and 1530 during the course and within the scope of their employment, if they receive a course in the exercise of those powers pursuant to Section 832. The authority and powers of the persons designated under this section shall extend to any place in the state:

(1) Persons employed by the Department of Financial Institutions designated by the Commissioner of Financial Institutions, provided that the primary duty of these persons shall be the enforcement of, and investigations relating to, the provisions of law administered by the Commissioner of Financial Institutions.

(2) Persons employed by the Department of Real Estate designated by the Real Estate Commissioner, provided that the primary duty of these persons shall be the enforcement of the laws set forth in Part 1 (commencing with Section 10000) and Part 2 (commencing with Section 11000) of Division 4 of the Business and Professions Code. The Real Estate Commissioner may designate persons under this section, who at the time of their designation, are assigned to the Special Investigations Unit, internally known as the Crisis Response Team.

(3) Persons employed by the State Lands Commission designated by the executive officer, provided that the primary duty of these persons shall be the enforcement of the law relating to the duties of the State Lands Commission.

(4) Persons employed as investigators of the Investigations Bureau of the Department of Insurance, who are designated by the Chief of the Investigations Bureau, provided that the primary duty of these persons shall be the enforcement of the Insurance Code and other laws relating to persons and businesses, licensed and unlicensed by the Department of Insurance, who are engaged in the business of insurance.

(5) Persons employed as investigators and investigator supervisors of the Consumer Services Division or the Rail Safety and Carrier Division of the Public Utilities Commission who are designated by the commission's executive director and approved by the commission, provided that the primary duty of these persons shall be the enforcement of the law as that duty is set forth in Section 308.5 of the Public Utilities Code.

(b) Notwithstanding any other provision of law, persons designated pursuant to this section shall not carry firearms.

(c) Persons designated pursuant to this section shall be included as "peace officers of the state" under paragraph (2) of subdivision (c) of Section 11105 for the purpose of receiving state summary criminal history information and shall be furnished that information on the same basis as peace officers of the state designated in paragraph (2) of subdivision (c) of Section 11105. *(AM '99)*

830.12. Litter Control Officers, Vehicle Abatement Officers, Registered Sanitarians, and Solid Waste Specialists - Powers

Notwithstanding any other provision of law, persons designated by a local agency as litter control officers, vehicle abatement officers, registered sanitarians, and solid waste specialists, are not peace officers, may not exercise the powers of arrest of a peace officer, as specified in Section 836, and shall not be authorized to carry or use firearms within the scope and course of their employment. These persons may, however, be authorized by the governing board of the particular local agency to issue citations involving violations of laws relating to abandoned vehicles and littering.

831. Custodial Officers as City or County Public Officers

(a) A custodial officer is a public officer, not a peace officer, employed by a law enforcement agency of a city or county who has the authority and responsibility for maintaining custody of prisoners and performs tasks related to the operation of a local detention facility used for the detention of persons usually pending arraignment or upon court order either for their own safekeeping or for the specific purpose of serving a sentence therein.

(b) A custodial officer shall have no right to carry or possess firearms in the performance of his prescribed duties.

(c) Each person described in this section as a custodial officer shall, within 90 days following the date of the initial assignment to such position, satisfactorily complete the training course specified in Section 832. In addition, each person designated as a custodial officer shall, within 180 days following the date of the initial assignment as a custodial officer, satisfactorily complete the jail operations course prescribed by the Board of Corrections pursuant to Section 6030. Persons designated as custodial officers, before the expiration of the 90- and 180-day periods described in this subdivision, who have not yet completed the required training, may perform the duties of a custodial officer only while under the direct supervision of a peace officer as described in Section 830.1, who has completed the training prescribed by the Commission on Peace Officer Standards and Training, or a custodial officer who has completed the training required in this section.

(d) At any time 20 or more custodial officers are on duty, there shall be at least one peace officer, as described in Section 830.1, on duty at the same time to supervise the performance of the custodial officers.

(e) This section shall not be construed to confer any authority upon any custodial officer except while on duty.

(f) A custodial officer may use reasonable force in establishing and maintaining custody of persons delivered to him by a law enforcement officer; may make arrests for misdemeanors and felonies within the local detention facility pursuant to a duly issued warrant; may release without further criminal process persons arrested for intoxication; and may release misdemeanants on citation to appear in lieu of or after booking.

831.5. Custodial Officers as County Public Officers

(a) As used in this section, a custodial officer is a public officer, not a peace officer, employed by a law enforcement agency of San Diego County, Fresno County, Kern County, Stanislaus County, Riverside County, Santa Clara County, or a county having a population of 425,000 or less who has the authority and responsibility for maintaining custody of prisoners and performs tasks related to the operation of a local detention facility used for the detention of persons usually pending arraignment or upon court order either for their own safekeeping or for the specific purpose of serving a sentence therein. Custodial officers of a county shall be employees of, and under the authority of, the sheriff, except in counties in which the sheriff, as of July 1, 1993, is not in charge of and the sole and exclusive authority to keep the county jail and the prisoners in it. A custodial officer includes a person designated as a correctional officer, jailer, or other similar title. The duties of a custodial officer may include the serving of warrants, court orders, writs, and subpoenas in the detention facility or under circumstances arising directly out of maintaining custody of prisoners and related tasks. In counties having a population of 100,000 or less, a custodial officer may be assigned by the sheriff as a court bailiff on an interim basis, and, when under the direction of the sheriff, a custodial officer assigned as a court bailiff may carry or possess firearms.

(b) Notwithstanding any other provision of law, during a state of emergency as defined in Section 8558 of the Government Code, a custodial officer may be assigned limited law enforcement responsibilities under the supervision of a peace officer. While on this assignment, the custodial officer may exercise the powers of arrest pursuant to Section 836.5.

(c) A custodial officer has no right to carry or possess firearms in the performance of his or her prescribed duties, except, under the direction of the sheriff or chief of police, while assigned as a court bailiff or engaged in transporting prisoners, guarding hospitalized prisoners, or suppressing jail riots, lynchings, escapes, or rescues in or about a detention facility falling under the care and custody of the sheriff or chief of police.

(d) Each person described in this section as a custodial officer shall, within 90 days following the date of the initial assignment to that position, satisfactorily complete the training course specified in Section 832. In addition, each person designated as a custodial officer shall, within one year following the date of the initial assignment as a custodial officer, have satisfactorily met the minimum selection and training standards prescribed by the Board of Corrections pursuant to Section 6035. Persons designated as custodial officers, before the expiration of the 90-day and one-year periods described in this subdivision, who have not yet completed the required training, shall not carry or possess firearms in the performance of their prescribed duties, but may perform the duties of a custodial officer only while under the direct supervision of a peace officer, as described in Section 830.1, who has completed the training prescribed by the Commission on Peace Officer Standards and Training, or a custodial officer who has completed the training required in this section.

(e) At any time 20 or more custodial officers are on duty, there shall be at least one peace officer, as described in Section 830.1, on duty at the same time to supervise the performance of the custodial officers.

(f) This section shall not be construed to confer any authority upon any custodial officer except while on duty.

(g) A custodial officer may use reasonable force in establishing and maintaining custody of persons delivered to him or her by a law enforcement officer, may make arrests for misdemeanors and felonies within the local detention facility pursuant to a duly issued warrant, may make warrantless arrests pursuant to

Section 836.5 only during the duration of his or her job, may release without further criminal process persons arrested for intoxication, and may release misdemeanants on citation to appear in lieu of or after booking.

(h) Custodial officers employed by the Santa Clara County Department of Corrections are authorized to perform the following additional duties in the facility:

(1) Arrest a person without a warrant whenever the custodial officer has reasonable cause to believe that the person to be arrested has committed a misdemeanor or felony in the presence of the officer that is a violation of a statute or ordinance that the officer has the duty to enforce.

(2) Search property, cells, prisoners, or visitors.

(3) Conduct strip or body cavity searches of prisoners pursuant to Section 4030.

(4) Conduct searches and seizures pursuant to a duly issued warrant.

(5) Segregate prisoners.

(6) Classify prisoners for the purpose of housing or participation in supervised activities.

These duties may be performed at the Santa Clara Valley Medical Center as needed and only as they directly relate to guarding inpatient, in-custody inmates. This subdivision shall not be construed to authorize the performance of any law enforcement activity involving any person other than the inmate or his or her visitors.

(i) Nothing in this section shall authorize a custodial officer to carry or possess a firearm when the officer is not on duty.

(j) It is the intent of the Legislature that this section, as it relates to Santa Clara County, enumerate specific duties of custodial officers (known as "correctional officers"in Santa Clara County) and to clarify the relationships of the correctional officers and deputy sheriffs in Santa Clara County. These duties are the same duties of the custodial officers prior to the date of enactment of Senate Bill 1019 of the 1999-2000 Regular Session of the Legislature pursuant to local rules and judicial decisions. It is further the intent of the Legislature that all issues regarding compensation for custodial officers remain subject to the collective bargaining process between the County of Santa Clara and the authorized bargaining representative for the custodial officers. However, nothing in this section shall be construed to assert that the duties of custodial officers are equivalent to the duties of deputy sheriffs nor to affect the ability of the county to negotiate pay that reflects the different duties of custodial officers and deputy sheriffs.

(k) This section shall remain in effect only until January 1, 2003, and as of that date is repealed, unless a later enacted statute, that is enacted before January 1, 2003, deletes or extends that date. *(AM '99)*

831.6. Transportation Officers as Public Officers

(a) A transportation officer is a public officer, not a peace officer, appointed on a contract basis by a peace officer to transport a prisoner or prisoners.

(b) A transportation officer shall have the authority of a public officer, and shall have the right to carry or possess firearms, only while engaged in the transportation of a prisoner or prisoners for the duration of the contract.

(c) Each person described in this section as a transportation officer shall, prior to the transportation of any prisoner, have satisfactorily completed the training course specified in Section 832.

(d) A transportation officer may use reasonable force in establishing and maintaining custody of persons delivered to him or her by a peace officer.

832.5. Citizens' Complaints Against Peace Officers

(a) Each department or agency in this state that employs peace officers shall establish a procedure to investigate complaints by members of the public against the personnel of these departments or agencies, and shall make a written description of the procedure available to the public.

(b) Complaints and any reports or findings relating to these complaints shall be retained for a period of at least five years. All complaints retained pursuant to this subdivision may be maintained either in the officer's general personnel file or in a separate file designated by the department or agency as provided by department or agency policy, in accordance with all applicable requirements of law. However, prior to any official determination regarding promotion, transfer, or disciplinary action by an officer's employing department or agency, the complaints described by subdivision (c) shall be removed from the officer's general personnel file and placed in separate file designated by the department or agency, in accordance with all applicable requirements of law.

(c) Complaints by members of the public that are determined by the peace officer's employing agency to be frivolous, as defined in Section 128.5 of the Code of Civil Procedure, or unfounded or exonerated, or any portion of a complaint that is determined to be frivolous, unfounded, or exonerated, shall not be maintained in that officer's general personnel file. However, these complaints shall be retained in other, separate files that shall be deemed personnel records for purposes of the California Public Records Act (Chapter 3.5 (commencing with Section 6250) of Division 7 of Title 1 of the Government Code) and Section 1043 of the Evidence Code.

(1) Management of the peace officer's employing agency shall have access to the files described in this subdivision.

(2) Management of the peace officer's employing agency shall not use the complaints contained in these separate files for punitive or promotional purposes except as permitted by subdivision (f) of Section 3304 of the Government Code.

(3) Management of the peace officer's employing agency may identify any officer who is subject to the complaints maintained in these files which require counseling or additional training. However, if a complaint is removed from the officer's personnel file, any reference in the personnel file to the complaint or to a separate file shall be deleted.

(d) As used in this section, the following definitions apply:

(1) "General personnel file"means the file maintained by the agency containing the primary records specific to each officer's employment, including evaluations, assignments, status changes, and imposed discipline.

(2) "Unfounded"means that the investigation clearly established that the allegation is not true.

(3) "Exonerated"means that the investigation clearly established that the actions of the peace officer that formed the basis for the complaint are not violations of law or department policy. *(AM '98)*

832.6. Limitations on Powers of Persons Deputized or Appointed Under Section 830.6; Commission's Functions

(a) Every person deputized or appointed, as described in subdivision (a) of Section 830.6, shall have the powers of a peace officer only when the person is any of the following:

(1) A level I reserve officer deputized or appointed pursuant to paragraph (1) or (2) of subdivision (a) or subdivision (b) of Section 830.6 and assigned to the prevention and detection of crime and the general enforcement of the laws of this state, whether or not working alone, and the person has completed the basic training course for deputy sheriffs and police officers prescribed by the Commission on Peace Officer Standards and Training. For level I reserve officers appointed prior to January 1, 1997, the basic training requirement shall be the course that was prescribed at the time of their appointment. Reserve officers appointed pursuant to this paragraph shall satisfy the continuing professional training requirement prescribed by the commission.

(2) A level II reserve officer assigned to the prevention and detection of crime and the general enforcement of the laws of this state while under the immediate supervision of a peace officer who has completed the basic training course for deputy sheriffs and police officers prescribed by the Commission on Peace Officer Standards and Training, and the level II reserve officer has completed the course required by Section 832 and any other training prescribed by the commission.

Level II reserve officers appointed pursuant to this paragraph may be assigned, without immediate supervision, to those limited duties that are authorized for level III reserve officers pursuant to paragraph (3). Reserve officers appointed pursuant to this paragraph shall satisfy the continuing professional training requirement prescribed by the commission.

(3) Level III reserve officers may be deployed and are authorized only to carry out limited support duties not requiring general law enforcement powers in their routine performance. Those limited duties shall include traffic control, security at parades and sporting events, report taking, evidence transportation, park-

ing enforcement, and other duties that are not likely to result in physical arrests. Level III reserve officers while assigned these duties shall be supervised in the accessible vicinity by a level I reserve officer or a full-time, regular peace officer employed by a law enforcement agency authorized to have reserve officers. Level III reserve officers may transport prisoners without immediate supervision. Those persons shall have completed the training required under Section 832 and any other training prescribed by the commission for those persons.

(4) A person assigned to the prevention and detection of a particular crime or crimes or to the detection or apprehension of a particular individual or individuals while working under the supervision of a California peace officer in a county adjacent to the state border who possesses a basic certificate issued by the Commission on Peace Officer Standards and Training, and the person is a law enforcement officer who is regularly employed by a local or state law enforcement agency in an adjoining state and has completed the basic training required for peace officers in his or her state.

(5) For purposes of this section, a reserve officer who has previously satisfied the training requirements pursuant to this section, and has served as a level I or II reserve officer within the three-year period prior to the date of a new appointment shall be deemed to remain qualified as to the Commission on Peace Officer Standards and Training requirements if that reserve officer accepts a new appointment at the same or lower level with another law enforcement agency. If the reserve officer has more than a three-year break in service, he or she shall satisfy current training requirements.

This training shall fully satisfy any other training requirements required by law, including those specified in Section 832.

In no case shall a peace officer of an adjoining state provide services within a California jurisdiction during any period in which the regular law enforcement agency of the jurisdiction is involved in a labor dispute.

(b) Notwithstanding subdivision (a), a person who is issued a level I reserve officer certificate before January 1, 1981, shall have the full powers and duties of a peace officer as provided by Section 830.1 if so designated by local ordinance or, if the local agency is not authorized to act by ordinance, by resolution, either individually or by class, if the appointing authority determines the person is qualified to perform general law enforcement duties by reason of the person's training and experience. Persons who were qualified to be issued the level I reserve officer certificate before January 1, 1981, and who state in writing under penalty of perjury that they applied for but were not issued the certificate before January 1, 1981, may be issued the certificate before July 1, 1984. For purposes of this section, certificates so issued shall be deemed to have the full force and effect of any level I reserve officer certificate issued prior to January 1, 1981.

(c) In carrying out this section, the commission:

(1) May use proficiency testing to satisfy reserve training standards.

(2) Shall provide for convenient training to remote areas in the state.

(3) Shall establish a professional certificate for reserve officers as defined in paragraph (1) of subdivision (a) and may establish a professional certificate for reserve officers as defined in paragraphs (2) and (3) of subdivision (a).

(4) Shall facilitate the voluntary transition of reserve officers to regular officers with no unnecessary redundancy between the training required for level I and level II reserve officers.
***

(d) In carrying out paragraphs (1) and (3) of subdivision (c), the commission may establish and levy appropriate fees, provided the fees do not exceed the cost for administering the respective services. These fees shall be deposited in the Peace Officers'Training Fund established by Section 13520.

(e) The commission shall include an amount in its annual budget request to carry out this section. *(AM '01)*

833.   Search for Dangerous Weapons

A peace officer may search for dangerous weapons any person whom he has legal cause to arrest, whenever he has reasonable cause to believe that the person possesses a dangerous weapon. If the officer finds a dangerous weapon, he may take and keep it until the completion of the questioning, when he shall either return it or arrest the person. The arrest may be for the illegal possession of the weapon.

833.5. Possession of Dangerous Weapons - Search, Seizure and Arrest

(a) In addition to any other detention permitted by law, if a peace officer has reasonable cause to believe that a person has a firearm or other deadly weapon with him or her in violation of any provision of law relating to firearms or deadly weapons the peace officer may detain that person to determine whether a crime relating to firearms or deadly weapons has been committed.

For purposes of this section "reasonable cause to detain" requires that the circumstances known or apparent to the officer must include specific and articulable facts causing him or her to suspect that some offense relating to firearms or deadly weapons has taken place or is about to occur and that the person he or she intends to detain is involved in that offense. The circumstances must be such as would cause any reasonable peace officer in like position, drawing when appropriate on his or her training and experience, to suspect the same offense and the same involvement by the person in question.

(b) Incident to any detention permitted pursuant to subdivision (a), a peace officer may conduct a limited search of the person for firearms or weapons if the peace officer reasonably concludes that the person detained may be armed and presently dangerous to the peace officer or others. Any firearm or weapon seized pursuant to a valid detention or search pursuant to this section shall be admissible in evidence in any proceeding for any purpose permitted by law.

(c) This section shall not be construed to otherwise limit the authority of a peace officer to detain any person or to make an arrest based on reasonable cause.

(d) This section shall not be construed to permit a peace officer to conduct a detention or search of any person at the person's residence or place of business absent a search warrant or other reasonable cause to detain or search.

(e) If a firearm or weapon is seized pursuant to this section and the person from whom it was seized owned the firearm or weapon and is convicted of a violation of any offense relating to the possession of such firearm or weapon, the court shall order the firearm or weapon to be deemed a nuisance and disposed of in the manner provided by Section 12028.

834. Arrest Defined

An arrest is taking a person into custody, in a case and in the manner authorized by law. An arrest may be made by a peace-officer or by a private person.

834a. Duty to Refrain From Resisting Arrest

If a person has knowledge, or by the exercise of reasonable care, should have knowledge, that he is being arrested by a peace officer, it is the duty of such person to refrain from using force or any weapon to resist such arrest.

834b. Cooperation with U.S. Immigration and Naturalization Service Required

(a) Every law enforcement agency in California shall fully cooperate with the United States Immigration and Naturalization Service regarding any person who is arrested if he or she is suspected of being present in the United States in violation of federal immigration laws.

(b) With respect to any such person who is arrested, and suspected of being present in the United States in violation of federal immigration laws, every law enforcement agency shall do the following:

(1) Attempt to verify the legal status of such person as a citizen of the United States, an alien lawfully admitted as a permanent resident, an alien lawfully admitted for a temporary period of time or as an alien who is present in the United States in violation of immigration laws. The verification process may include, but shall not be limited to, questioning the person regarding his or her date and place of birth, and entry into the United States, and demanding documentation to indicate his or her legal status.

(2) Notify the person of his or her apparent status as an alien who is present in the United States in violation of federal immigration laws and inform him or her that, apart from any criminal justice proceedings, he or she must either obtain legal status or leave the United States.

(3) Notify the Attorney General of California and the United States Immigration and Naturalization Service of the apparent illegal status and provide any additional information that may be requested by any other public entity.

(c) Any legislative, administrative, or other action by a city, county, or other legally authorized local governmental entity with jurisdictional boundaries, or by a law enforcement agency, to prevent or limit the cooperation required by subdivision (a) is expressly prohibited. *(AD '94)*

834c. Arrest of Foreign National; Advisement and Notification Requirements

(a)(1) In accordance with federal law and the provisions of this section, every peace officer, upon arrest and booking or detention for more than two hours of a known or suspected foreign national, shall advise the foreign national that he or she has a right to communicate with an official from the consulate of his or her country, except as provided in subdivision (d). If the foreign national chooses to exercise that right, the peace officer shall notify the pertinent official in his or her agency or department of the arrest or detention and that the foreign national wants his or her consulate notified.

(2) The law enforcement official who receives the notification request pursuant to paragraph (1) shall be guided by his or her agency's procedures in conjunction with the Department of State Guidelines Regarding Foreign Nationals Arrested or Detained in the United States, and make the appropriate notifications to the consular officers at the consulate of the arrestee.

(3) The law enforcement official in charge of the custodial facility where an arrestee subject to this subdivision is located shall ensure that the arrestee is allowed to communicate with, correspond with, and be visited by, a consular officer of his or her country.

(b) The 1963 Vienna Convention on Consular Relations Treaty was signed by 140 nations, including the United States, which ratified the agreement in 1969. This treaty guarantees that individuals arrested or detained in a foreign country must be told by police "without delay" that they have a right to speak to an official from their country's consulate and if an individual chooses to exercise that right a law enforcement official is required to notify the consulate.

(c) California law enforcement agencies shall ensure that policy or procedure and training manuals incorporate language based upon provisions of the treaty that set forth requirements for handling the arrest and booking or detention for more than two hours of a foreign national pursuant to this section prior to December 31, 2000.

(d) Countries requiring mandatory notification under Article 36 of the Vienna Convention shall be notified as set forth in this section without regard to an arrested or detained foreign national's request to the contrary. Those countries, as identified by the United States Department of State on July 1, 1999, are as follows:

(1) Antigua and Barbuda.
(2) Armenia.
(3) Azerbaijan.
(4) The Bahamas.
(5) Barbados.
(6) Belarus.
(7) Belize.
(8) Brunei.
(9) Bulgaria.
(10) China.
(11) Costa Rica.
(12) Cyprus.
(13) Czech Republic.
(14) Dominica.
(15) Fiji.
(16) The Gambia.
(17) Georgia.

(18) Ghana.
(19) Grenada.
(20) Guyana.
(21) Hong Kong.
(22) Hungary.
(23) Jamaica.
(24) Kazakhstan.
(25) Kiribati.
(26) Kuwait.
(27) Kyrgyzstan.
(28) Malaysia.
(29) Malta.
(30) Mauritius.
(31) Moldova.
(32) Mongolia.
(33) Nigeria.
(34) Philippines.
(35) Poland (nonpermanent residents only).
(36) Romania.
(37) Russia.
(38) Saint Kitts and Nevis.
(39) Saint Lucia.
(40) Saint Vincent and the Grenadines.
(41) Seychelles.
(42) Sierra Leone.
(43) Singapore.
(44) Slovakia.
(45) Tajikistan.
(46) Tanzania.
(47) Tonga.
(48) Trinidad and Tobago.
(49) Turkmenistan.
(50) Tuvalu.
(51) Ukraine.
(52) United Kingdom.
(53) U.S.S.R.
(54) Uzbekistan.
(55) Zambia.
(56) Zimbabwe.

However, any countries requiring notification that the above list does not identify because the notification requirement became effective after July 1, 1999, shall also be required to be notified. *(AD '99)*

835. How Arrest is Made - Restraint Limited to Necessity

An arrest is made by an actual restraint of the person, or by submission to the custody of an officer. The person arrested may be subjected to such restraint as is reasonable for his arrest and detention.

835a. Use of Reasonable Force to Effect Arrest

Any peace officer who has reasonable cause to believe that the person to be arrested has committed a public offense may use reasonable force to effect the arrest, to prevent escape or to overcome resistance.

A peace officer who makes or attempts to make an arrest need not retreat or desist from his efforts by reason of the resistance or threatened resistance of the person being arrested; nor shall such officer be deemed an aggressor or lose his right to self-defense by the use of reasonable force to effect the arrest or to prevent escape or to overcome resistance.

836. Arrest by Peace Officer

(a) A peace officer may arrest a person in obedience to a warrant, or, pursuant to the authority granted to him or her by Chapter 4.5 (commencing with Section 830) of Title 3 of Part 2, without a warrant, may arrest a person whenever any of the following circumstances occur:

(1) The officer has probable cause to believe that the person to be arrested has committed a public offense in the officer's presence.

(2) The person arrested has committed a felony, although not in the officer's presence.

(3) The officer has probable cause to believe that the person to be arrested has committed a felony, whether or not a felony, in fact, has been committed.

(b) Any time a peace officer is called out on a domestic violence call, it shall be mandatory that the officer make a good faith effort to inform the victim of his or her right to make a citizen's arrest. This information shall include advising the victim how to safely execute the arrest.

(c)(1) When a peace officer is responding to a call alleging a violation of a domestic violence protective or restraining order issued under the Family Code, Section 527.6 of the Code of Civil Procedure, Section 213.5 of the Welfare and Institutions Code, Section 136.2 of this code, or paragraph (2) of subdivision (a) of Section 1203.097 of this code, or of a domestic violence protective or restraining order issued by the court of another state, tribe, or territory and the peace officer has probable cause to believe that the person against whom the order is issued has notice of the order and has committed an act in violation of the order, the officer shall, consistent with subdivision (b) of Section 13701, make a lawful arrest of the person without a warrant and take that person into custody whether or not the violation occurred in the presence of the arresting officer. The officer shall, as soon as possible after the arrest, confirm with the appropriate authorities or the Domestic Violence Protection Order Registry maintained pursuant to Section 6380 of the Family Code that a true copy of the protective order has been registered, unless the victim provides the officer with a copy of the protective order.

(2) The person against whom a protective order has been issued shall be deemed to have notice of the order if the victim presents to the officer proof of service of the order, the officer confirms with the appropriate authorities that a true copy of the proof of service is on file, or the person against whom the protective order was issued was present at the protective order hearing or was informed by a peace officer of the contents of the protective order.

(3) In situations where mutual protective orders have been issued under Division 10 (commencing with Section 6200) of the Family Code, liability for arrest under this subdivision applies only to those persons who are reasonably believed to have been the primary aggressor. In those situations, prior to making an arrest under this subdivision, the peace officer shall make reasonable efforts to identify, and may arrest, the primary aggressor involved in the incident. The primary aggressor is the person determined to be the most significant, rather than the first, aggressor. In identifying the primary aggressor, an officer shall consider (A) the intent of the law to protect victims of domestic violence from continuing abuse, (B) the threats creating fear of physical injury, (C) the history of domestic violence between the persons involved, and (D) whether either person involved acted in self-defense.

(d) Notwithstanding paragraph (1) of subdivision (a), if a suspect commits an assault or battery upon a current or former spouse, fiance, fiancee, a current or former cohabitant as defined in Section 6209 of the Family Code, a person with whom the suspect currently is having or has previously had an engagement or dating relationship, as defined in paragraph (10) of subdivision (f) of Section 243, a person with whom the suspect has parented a child, or is presumed to have parented a child pursuant to the Uniform Parentage Act (Part 3 (commencing with Section 7600) of Division 12 of the Family Code), a child of the suspect, a child whose parentage by the suspect is the subject of an action under the Uniform Parentage Act, a child of a person in one of the above categories, or any other person related to the suspect by consanguinity or affinity within the second degree, a peace officer may arrest the suspect without a warrant where both of the following circumstances apply:

(1) The peace officer has probable cause to believe that the person to be arrested has committed the assault or battery, whether or not it has in fact been committed.

(2) The peace officer makes the arrest as soon as probable cause arises to believe that the person to be arrested has committed the assault or battery, whether or not it has in fact been committed.

(e) In addition to the authority to make an arrest without a warrant pursuant to paragraphs (1) and (3) of subdivision (a), a peace officer may, without a warrant, arrest a person for a violation of Section 12025 when all of the following apply:

(1) The officer has reasonable cause to believe that the person to be arrested has committed the violation of Section 12025.

(2) The violation of Section 12025 occurred within an airport, as defined in Section 21013 of the Public Utilities Code, in an area to which access is controlled by the inspection of persons and property.

(3) The peace officer makes the arrest as soon as reasonable cause arises to believe that the person to be arrested has committed the violation of Section 12025. *(AM '99, '00)*

836.1. Arrest Without Warrant - Battery on Firefighter, EMT or Paramedic

When a person commits an assault or battery against the person of a firefighter, emergency medical technician, or mobile intensive care paramedic while that person is on duty engaged in the performance of his or her duties in violation of subdivision (b) of Section 241 or subdivision (b) of Section 243, a peace officer may, without a warrant, arrest the person who commits the assault or battery:

(a) Whenever the peace officer has reasonable cause to believe that the person to be arrested has committed the assault or battery, although the assault or battery was not committed in the peace officer's presence.

(b) Whenever the peace officer has reasonable cause to believe that the person to be arrested has committed the assault or battery, whether or not the assault or battery has in fact been committed.

836.3. Arrest of Escaped Prisoner

A peace officer may make an arrest in obedience to a warrant delivered to him, or may, without a warrant, arrest a person who, while charged with or convicted of a misdemeanor, has escaped from any county or city jail, prison, industrial farm or industrial road camp or from the custody of the officer or person in charge of him while engaged on any county road or other county work or going to or returning from such county road or other county work or from the custody of any officer or person in whose lawful custody he is when such escape is not by force or violence.

836.5. Arrest by Public Officer or Employee

(a) A public officer or employee, when authorized by ordinance, may arrest a person without a warrant whenever the officer or employee has reasonable cause to believe that the person to be arrested has committed a misdemeanor in the presence of the officer or employee that is a violation of a statute or ordinance that the officer or employee has the duty to enforce.

(b) There shall be no civil liability on the part of, and no cause of action shall arise against, any public officer or employee acting pursuant to subdivision (a) and within the scope of his or her authority for false arrest or false imprisonment arising out of any arrest that is lawful or that the public officer or employee, at the time of the arrest, had reasonable cause to believe was lawful. No officer or employee shall be deemed an aggressor or lose his or her right to self-defense by the use of reasonable force to effect the arrest, prevent escape, or overcome resistance.

(c) In any case in which a person is arrested pursuant to subdivision (a) and the person arrested does not demand to be taken before a magistrate, the public officer or employee making the arrest shall prepare a written notice to appear and release the person on his or her promise to appear, as prescribed by Chapter 5C (commencing with Section 853.5). The provisions of that chapter shall thereafter apply with reference to any proceeding based upon the issuance of a written notice to appear pursuant to this authority.

(d) The governing body of a local agency, by ordinance, may authorize its officers and employees who have the duty to enforce a statute or ordinance to arrest persons for violations of the statute or ordinance as provided in subdivision (a).

(e) For purposes of this section, "ordinance"includes an order, rule, or regulation of any air pollution control district.

(f) For purposes of this section, a "public officer or employee"includes an officer or employee of a non-profit transit corporation wholly owned by a local agency and formed to carry out the purposes of the local agency.

836.6. Escape or Attempt After Remand or Arrest

(a) It is unlawful for any person who is remanded by a magistrate or judge of any court in this state to the custody of a sheriff, marshal, or other police agency, to thereafter escape or attempt to escape from that custody.

(b) It is unlawful for any person who has been lawfully arrested by any peace officer and who knows, or by the exercise of reasonable care should have known, that he or she has been so arrested, to thereafter escape or attempt to escape from that peace officer.

(c) Any person who violates subdivision (a) or (b) is guilty of a misdemeanor, punishable by imprisonment in a county jail not to exceed one year. However, if the escape or attempted escape is by force or violence, and the person proximately causes a peace officer serious bodily injury, the person shall be punished by imprisonment in a county jail not to exceed one year.

837. Arrest by Private Person

A private person may arrest another:
1. For a public offense committed or attempted in his presence.
2. When the person arrested has committed a felony, although not in his presence.
3. When a felony has been in fact committed, and he has reasonable cause for believing the person arrested to have committed it.

838. Arrest for Acts in Presence of Magistrate

A magistrate may orally order a peace officer or private person to arrest any one committing or attempting to commit a public offense in the presence of such magistrate.

839. Summoning Assistance to Make Arrest

Any person making an arrest may orally summon as many persons as he deems necessary to aid him therein.

840. Time of Day Arrest May Be Made

An arrest for the commission of a felony may be made on any day and at any time of the day or night. An arrest for the commission of a misdemeanor or an infraction cannot be made between the hours of 10 o'clock p.m. of any day and 6 o'clock a.m. of the succeeding day, unless:

(1) The arrest is made without a warrant pursuant to Section 836 or 837.

(2) The arrest is made in a public place.

(3) The arrest is made when the person is in custody pursuant to another lawful arrest.

(4) The arrest is made pursuant to a warrant which, for good cause shown, directs that it may be served at any time of the day or night.

841. Notice of Authority and Intent to Arrest

The person making the arrest must inform the person to be arrested of the intention to arrest him, of the cause of the arrest, and the authority to make it, except when the person making the arrest has reasonable cause to believe that the person to be arrested is actually engaged in the commission of or an attempt to commit an offense, or the person to be arrested is pursued immediately after its commission, or after an escape.

The person making the arrest must, on request of the person he is arresting, inform the latter of the offense for which he is being arrested.

842. Showing Warrant on Demand

An arrest by a peace officer acting under a warrant is lawful even though the officer does not have the warrant in his possession at the time of the arrest, but if the person arrested so requests it, the warrant shall be shown to him as soon as practicable.

843. Overcoming Resistance or Preventing Escape

When the arrest is being made by an officer under the authority of a warrant, after information of the intention to make the arrest, if the person to be arrested either flees or forcibly resists, the officer may use all necessary means to effect the arrest.

844. Breaking Doors or Windows to Make Arrest

To make an arrest, a private person, if the offense is a felony, and in all cases a peace officer, may break open the door or window of the house in which the person to be arrested is, or in which they have reasonable grounds for believing the person to be, after having demanded admittance and explained the purpose for which admittance is desired.

845. Breaking Door or Window When Leaving Place of Arrest

Any person who has lawfully entered a house for the purpose of making an arrest, may break open the door or window thereof if detained therein, when necessary for the purpose of liberating himself, and an officer may do the same, when necessary for the purpose of liberating a person who, acting in his aid, lawfully entered for the purpose of making an arrest, and is detained therein.

846. Taking Weapon From Accused

Any person making an arrest may take from the person arrested all offensive weapons which he may have about his person, and must deliver them to the magistrate before whom he is taken.

847. Duty of Private Person to Deliver Arrested Person to Magistrate or Peace Officer; Limitations on Liability of Peace Officer for False Arrest or Imprisonment

A private person who has arrested another for the commission of a public offense must, without unnecessary delay, take the person arrested before a magistrate, or deliver him or her to a peace officer. There shall be no civil liability on the part of, and no cause of action shall arise against, any peace officer or federal criminal investigator or law enforcement officer described in subdivision (a) or (d) of Section 830.8, acting within the scope of his or her authority, for false arrest or false imprisonment arising out of any arrest when any one of the following circumstances exist:

(a) The arrest was lawful or when the peace officer, at the time of the arrest had reasonable cause to believe the arrest was lawful.

(b) When the arrest was made pursuant to a charge made, upon reasonable cause, of the commission of a felony by the person to be arrested.

(c) When the arrest was made pursuant to the requirements of Section 142, 838, or 839.

847.5. Proceedings for Arrest of Fugitive Admitted to Bail in Another State

If a person has been admitted to bail in another state, escapes bail, and is present in this State, the bail bondsman or other person who is bail for such fugitive, may file with a magistrate in the county where the fugitive is present an affidavit stating the name and whereabouts of the fugitive, the offense with which the alleged fugitive was charged or of which he was convicted, the time and place of same, and the particulars in which the fugitive has violated the terms of his bail, and may request the issuance of a warrant for arrest of the fugitive, and the issuance, after hearing, of an order authorizing the affiant to return the fugitive to the jurisdiction from which he escaped bail. The magistrate may require such additional evidence under oath as he deems necessary to decide the issue. If he concludes that there is probable cause for believing that the person alleged to be a fugitive is such, he may issue a warrant for his arrest. The magistrate shall notify the district attorney of such action and shall direct him to investigate the case and determine the facts of the matter. When the fugitive is brought before him pursuant to the warrant, the magistrate shall set a time and place for hearing, and shall advise the fugitive of his right to counsel and to produce evidence at the hearing. He may admit the fugitive to bail pending the hearing. The district attorney shall appear at the hearing. If, after hearing, the magistrate is satisfied from the evidence that the person is a fugitive he may issue an order authorizing affiant to return the fugitive to the jurisdiction from which he escaped bail.

A bondsman or other person who is bail for a fugitive admitted to bail in another state who takes the fugitive into custody, except pursuant to an order issued under this section, is guilty of a misdemeanor.

848. Officer to Proceed as Warrant Directs

An officer making an arrest, in obedience to a warrant, must proceed with the person arrested as commanded by the warrant, or as provided by law.

849. Duty of Officer to Take Accused Before Magistrate - Release From Custody

(a) When an arrest is made without a warrant by a peace officer or private person, the person arrested, if not otherwise released, shall, without unnecessary delay, be taken before the nearest or most accessible magistrate in the county in which the offense is triable, and a complaint stating the charge against the arrested person shall be laid before such magistrate.

(b) Any peace officer may release from custody, instead of taking such person before a magistrate, any person arrested without a warrant whenever:

(1) He or she is satisfied that there are insufficient grounds for making a criminal complaint against the person arrested.

(2) The person arrested was arrested for intoxication only, and no further proceedings are desirable.

(3) The person was arrested only for being under the influence of a controlled substance or drug and such person is delivered to a facility or hospital for treatment and no further proceedings are desirable.

(c) Any record of arrest of a person released pursuant to paragraphs (1) and (3) of subdivision (b) shall include a record of release. Thereafter, such arrest shall not be deemed an arrest, but a detention only.

851.5. Arrested Person May Make Telephone Call

(a) Immediately upon being booked, and, except where physically impossible, no later than three hours after arrest, an arrested person has the right to make at least three completed telephone calls, as described in subdivision. (b).

The arrested person shall be entitled to make at least three such calls at no expense if the calls are completed to telephone numbers within the local calling area.

(b) At any police facility or place where an arrestee is detained, a sign containing the following information in bold block type shall be posted in a conspicuous place:

That the arrestee has the right to free telephone calls within the local dialing area, or at his own expense if outside the local area, to three of the following:

(1) An attorney of his choice or, if he has no funds, the public defender or other attorney assigned by the court to assist indigents, whose telephone number shall be posted. This phone call shall not be monitored, eavesdropped upon, or recorded.

(2) A bail bondsman.

(3) A relative or other person.

(c) These telephone calls shall be given immediately upon request, or as soon as practicable.

(d) This provision shall not abrogate a law enforcement officer's duty to advise a suspect of his right to counsel or of any other right.

(e) Any public officer or employee who willfully deprives an arrested person of any right granted by this section is guilty of a misdemeanor.

853.5. Arrest for Infraction - Release Provisions

Except as otherwise provided by law, in any case in which a person is arrested for an offense declared to be an infraction, the person may be released according to the procedures set forth by this chapter for the release of persons arrested for an offense declared to be a misdemeanor. In all cases, except as specified in Sections 40302, 40303, 40305, and 40305.5 of the Vehicle Code, in which a person is arrested for an infraction, a peace officer shall only require the arrestee to present his driver's license or other satisfactory evidence of his identity for examination and to sign a written promise to appear. If the arrestee does not have a driver's license or other satisfactory evidence of identity in his or her possession, the officer may require the arrestee to place a right thumbprint, or a left thumbprint or fingerprint if the person has a missing or disfigured right thumb, on the promise to appear. This thumbprint or fingerprint shall not be used to create a data base. Only if the arrestee refuses to present such identification or, refuses to sign such a written promise sign a written promise, has no satisfactory identification, or refuses to provide a thumbprint or fingerprint may the arrestee be taken into custody.

853.6. Citation for Misdemeanors; Release or Nonrelease; Penalty for Alteration or Concealment of Citation

(a) In any case in which a person is arrested for an offense declared to be a misdemeanor, including a violation of any city or county ordinance, and does not demand to be taken before a magistrate, that person shall, instead of being taken before a magistrate, be released according to the procedures set forth by this chapter. If the person is released, the officer or superior shall prepare in duplicate a written notice to appear in court, containing the name and address of the person, the offense charged, and the time when, and place where, the person shall appear in court. If, pursuant to subdivision (i), the person is not released prior to being booked and the officer in charge of the booking or his or her superior determines that the person should be released, the officer or superior shall prepare a written notice to appear in a court.

In any case in which a person is arrested for a misdemeanor violation of a protective court order involving domestic violence, as defined in subdivision (b) of Section 13700, the person shall be taken before a magistrate instead of being released according to the procedures set forth in this chapter, unless the arresting officer determines that there is not a reasonable likelihood that the offense will continue or resume or that the safety of persons or property would be imminently endangered by release of the person arrested. Prior to adopting these provisions, each city, county, or city and county shall develop a protocol to assist officers to determine when arrest and release is appropriate, rather than taking the arrested person before a magistrate. The county shall establish a committee to develop the protocol, consisting of, at a minimum, the police chief or county sheriff within the jurisdiction, the district attorney, county counsel, city attorney, representatives from domestic violence shelters, domestic violence councils, and other relevant community agencies.

Nothing in this subdivision shall be construed to affect a defendant's ability to be released on bail or on his or her own recognizance.

(b) Unless waived by the person, the time specified in the notice to appear shall be at least 10 days after arrest if the duplicate notice is to be filed by the officer with the magistrate.

(c) The place specified in the notice shall be the court of the magistrate before whom the person would be taken if the requirement of taking an arrested person before a magistrate were complied with, or shall be an officer authorized by that court to receive a deposit of bail.

(d) The officer shall deliver one copy of the notice to appear to the arrested person, and the arrested person, in order to secure release, shall give his or her written promise to appear in court as specified in the notice by signing the duplicate notice which shall be retained by the officer, and the officer may require the arrested person, if he or she has no satisfactory identification, to place a right thumbprint, or a left thumbprint or fingerprint if the person has a missing or disfigured right thumb, on the promise to appear. This thumbprint or fingerprint shall not be used to create a data base. Upon the signing of the duplicate notice, the arresting officer shall immediately release the person arrested from custody.

(e) The officer shall, as soon as practicable, file the duplicate notice, as follows:

(1) It shall be filed with the magistrate if the offense charged is an infraction.

(2) It shall be filed with the magistrate if the prosecuting attorney has previously directed the officer to do so.

(3) The duplicate notice and underlying police reports in support of the charge or charges shall be filed with the prosecuting attorney in cases other than those specified in paragraphs (1) and (2).

If the duplicate notice is filed with the prosecuting attorney, he or she, within his or her discretion, may initiate prosecution by filing the notice or a formal complaint with the magistrate specified in the duplicate notice within 25 days from the time of arrest. If the prosecution is not to be initiated, the prosecutor shall send notice to the person arrested at the address on the notice to appear. The failure by the prosecutor to file the notice or formal complaint within 25 days of the time of the arrest shall not bar further prosecution of the misdemeanor charged in the notice to appear. However, any further prosecution shall be preceded by a new and separate citation or an arrest warrant.

Upon the filing of the notice with the magistrate by the officer, or the filing of the notice or formal complaint by the prosecutor, the magistrate may fix the amount of bail which in his or her judgment, in accordance with Section 1275, is reasonable and sufficient for the appearance of the defendant and shall indorse upon the notice a statement signed by him or her in the form set forth in Section 815a. The defendant may, prior to the date upon which he or she promised to appear in court, deposit with the magistrate the amount of bail set by the magistrate. At the time the case is called for arraignment before the magistrate, if the defendant does not appear, either in person or by counsel, the magistrate may declare the bail forfeited, and may, in his or her discretion, order that no further proceedings shall be had in the case, unless the defendant has been charged with violation of Section 374.3 or 374.7 of this code or of Section 11357, 11360, or 13002 of the Health and Safety Code, or a violation punishable under Section 5008.7 of the Public Resources Code, and he or she has previously been convicted of a violation of that section or a violation which is punishable under that section, except in cases where the magistrate finds that undue hardship will be imposed upon the defendant by requiring him or her to appear, the magistrate may declare the bail forfeited and order that no further proceedings be had in the case.

Upon the making of the order that no further proceedings be had, all sums deposited as bail shall immediately be paid into the county treasury for distribution pursuant to Section 1463.

(f) No warrant shall be issued for the arrest of a person who has given a written promise to appear in court, unless and until he or she has violated that promise or has failed to deposit bail, to appear for arraignment, trial, or judgment or to comply with the terms and provisions of the judgment, as required by law.

(g) The officer may book the arrested person prior to release or indicate on the citation that the arrested person shall appear at the arresting agency to be booked or indicate on the citation that the arrested person shall appear at the arresting agency to be fingerprinted prior to the date the arrested person appears in court. If it is indicated on the citation that the arrested person shall be booked or fingerprinted prior to the date of the person's court appearance, the arresting agency at the time of booking or fingerprinting shall provide the arrested person with verification of the booking or fingerprinting by either making an entry on the citation or providing the arrested person a verification form established by the arresting agency. If it is indicated on the citation that the arrested person is to be booked or fingerprinted, the magistrate, judge, or court shall, before the proceedings begin, order the defendant to provide verification that he or she was booked or fingerprinted by the arresting agency. If the defendant cannot produce the verification, the magistrate, judge, or court shall require that the defendant be booked or fingerprinted by the arresting agency before the next court appearance, and that the defendant provide the verification at the next court appearance unless both parties stipulate that booking or fingerprinting is not necessary.

(h) A peace officer shall use the written notice to appear procedure set forth in this section for any misdemeanor offense in which the officer has arrested a person without a warrant pursuant to Section 836 or in which he or she has taken custody of a person pursuant to Section 847.

(i) Whenever any person is arrested by a peace officer for a misdemeanor, that person shall be released according to the procedures set forth by this chapter unless one of the following is a reason for nonrelease, in which case the arresting officer may release the person, or the arresting officer shall indicate, on a form to be established by his or her employing law enforcement agency, which of the following was a reason for the non-release:

(1) The person arrested was so intoxicated that he or she could have been a danger to himself or herself or to others.

(2) The person arrested required medical examination or medical care or was otherwise unable to care for his or her own safety.

(3) The person was arrested under one or more of the circumstances listed in Sections 40302 and 40303 of the Vehicle Code.

(4) There were one or more outstanding arrest warrants for the person.

(5) The person could not provide satisfactory evidence of personal identification.

(6) The prosecution of the offense or offenses for which the person was arrested, or the prosecution of any other offense or offenses, would be jeopardized by immediate release of the person arrested.

(7) There was a reasonable likelihood that the offense or offenses would continue or resume, or that the safety of persons or property would be imminently endangered by release of the person arrested.

(8) The person arrested demanded to be taken before a magistrate or refused to sign the notice to appear.

(9) There is reason to believe that the person would not appear at the time and place specified in the notice. The basis for this determination shall be specifically stated.

The form shall be filed with the arresting agency as soon as practicable and shall be made available to any party having custody of the arrested person, subsequent to the arresting officer, and to any person authorized by law to release him or her from custody before trial.

(j) Once the arresting officer has prepared the written notice to appear and has delivered a copy to the person arrested, the officer shall deliver the remaining original and all copies as provided by subdivision (e).

Any person, including the arresting officer and any member of the officer's department or agency, or any peace officer, who alters, conceals, modifies, nullifies, or destroys, or causes to be altered, concealed, modified, nullified, or destroyed, the face side of the remaining original or any copy of a citation that was retained by the officer, for any reason, before it is filed with the magistrate or with a person authorized by the magistrate to receive deposit of bail, is guilty of a misdemeanor.

If, after an arrested person has signed and received a copy of a notice to appear, the arresting officer determines that, in the interest of justice, the citation or notice should be dismissed, the arresting agency may recommend, in writing, to the magistrate that the charges be dismissed. The recommendation shall cite the reasons for the recommendation and shall be filed with the court.

If the magistrate makes a finding that there are grounds for dismissal, the finding shall be entered in the record and the charges dismissed.

Under no circumstances shall a personal relationship with any officer, public official, or law enforcement agency be grounds for dismissal.

(k) For purposes of this section, the term "arresting agency" includes any other agency designated by the arresting agency to provide booking or fingerprinting services.

1026.4. Escape From Mental Health Facility

(a) Every person committed to a state hospital or other public or private mental health facility pursuant to the provisions of Section 1026, who escapes from or who escapes while being conveyed to or from the state hospital or facility, is punishable by imprisonment in the county jail not to exceed one year or in a state prison for a determinate term of one year and one day. The term of imprisonment imposed pursuant to this section shall be served consecutively to any other sentence or commitment.

(b) The medical director or person in charge of a state hospital or other public or private mental health facility to which a person has been committed pursuant to the provisions of Section 1026 shall promptly notify the chief of police of the city in which the hospital or facility is located, or the sheriff of the county if the hospital or facility is located in an unincorporated area, of the escape of the person, and shall request the assistance of the chief of police or sheriff in apprehending the person, and shall within 48 hours of the escape of the person orally notify the court that made the commitment, the prosecutor in the case, and the Department of Justice of the escape.

1203.2a. Defendant Released on Probation Imprisoned in This or Any Other State; Procedures

If any defendant who has been released on probation is committed to a prison in this state or another state for another offense, the court which released him or her on probation shall have jurisdiction to impose sentence, if no sentence has previously been imposed for the offense for which he or she was granted probation, in the absence of the defendant, on the request of the defendant made through his or her counsel, or by himself or herself in writing, if such writing is signed in the presence of the warden of the prison in which he or she is confined or the duly authorized representative of the warden, and the warden or his or her representative attests both that the defendant has made and signed such request and that he or she states that he or she wishes the court to impose sentence in the case in which he or she was released on probation, in his or her absence and without him or her being represented by counsel.

The probation officer may, upon learning of the defendant's imprisonment, and must within 30 days after being notified in writing by the defendant or his or her counsel, or the warden or duly authorized representative of the prison in which the defendant is confined, report such commitment to the court which released him or her on probation.

Upon being informed by the probation officer of the defendant's confinement, or upon receipt from the warden or duly authorized representative of any prison in this state or another state of a certificate showing that the defendant is confined in prison, the court shall issue its commitment if sentence has previously been imposed. If sentence has not been previously imposed and if the defendant has requested the court through counsel or in writing in the manner herein provided to impose sentence in the case in which he or she was released on probation in his or her absence and without the presence of counsel to represent him or her, the court shall impose sentence and issue its commitment, or shall make other final order terminating its jurisdiction over the defendant in the case in which the order of probation was made. If the case is one in which sentence has previously been imposed, the court shall be deprived of jurisdiction over defendant if it does not issue its commitment or make other final order terminating its jurisdiction over defendant in the case within 60 days after being notified of the confinement. If the case is one in which sentence has not previously been imposed, the court is deprived of jurisdiction over defendant if it does not impose sentence and issue its commitment or make other final order terminating its jurisdiction over defendant in the case within 30 days after defendant has, in the manner prescribed by this section, requested imposition of sentence.

Upon imposition of sentence hereunder the commitment shall be dated as of the date upon which probation was granted. If the defendant is then in a state prison for an offense committed subsequent to the one upon which he or she has been on probation, the term of imprisonment of such defendant under a commitment issued hereunder shall commence upon the date upon which defendant was delivered to prison under commitment for his or her subsequent offense. Any terms ordered to be served consecutively shall be served as otherwise provided by law.

In the event the probation officer fails to report such commitment to the court or the court fails to impose sentence as herein provided, the court shall be deprived thereafter of all jurisdiction it may have retained in the granting of probation in said case.

Bail Fugitive Recovery Persons Act

1299. Article Title

This article shall be known as the Bail Fugitive Recovery Persons Act. *(AD '99)*

1299.01. Definitions

For purposes of this article, the following terms shall have the following meanings:

(a) "Bail fugitive" means a defendant in a pending criminal case who has been released from custody under a financially secured appearance, cash, or other bond and has had that bond declared forfeited, or a defendant in a pending criminal case who has violated a bond condition whereby apprehension and reincarceration are permitted.

(b) "Bail" means a person licensed by the Department of Insurance pursuant to Section 1800 of the Insurance Code.

(c) "Depositor of bail" means a person or entity who has deposited money or bonds to secure the release of a person charged with a crime or offense.

(d) "Bail fugitive recovery person" means a person who is provided written authorization pursuant to Sections 1300 and 1301 by the bail or depositor of bail, and is contracted to investigate, surveil, locate, and arrest a bail fugitive for surrender to the appropriate court, jail, or police department, and any person who is employed to assist a bail or depositor of bail to investigate, surveil, locate, and arrest a bail fugitive for surrender to the appropriate court, jail, or police department. *(AD '99)*

1299.02. Arrest of Bail Fugitive by Non-Peace Officer; Conditions

(a) No person, other than a certified law enforcement officer, shall be authorized to apprehend, detain, or arrest a bail fugitive unless that person meets one of the following conditions:

(1) Is a bail as defined in subdivision (b) of Section 1299.01 or a depositor of bail as defined in subdivision (c) of Section 1299.01.

(2) Is a bail fugitive recovery person as defined in subdivision (d) of Section 1299.01.

(3) Holds a bail license issued by a state other than California or is authorized by another state to transact and post bail and is in compliance with the provisions of Section 847.5 with respect to the arrest of a bail fugitive.

(4) Is licensed as a private investigator as provided in Chapter 11.3 (commencing with Section 7512) of Division 3 of the Business and Professions Code.

(5) Holds a private investigator license issued by another state, is authorized by the bail or depositor of bail to apprehend a bail fugitive, and is in compliance with the provisions of Section 847.5 with respect to the arrest of a bail fugitive.

(b) This article shall not prohibit an arrest pursuant to Sections 837, 838, and 839. *(AD '99)*

1299.04. License Requirements - Bail Agent, Permittee or Solicitor

(a) A bail fugitive recovery person, a bail agent, bail permittee, or bail solicitor who contracts his or her services to another bail agent or surety as a bail fugitive recovery person for the purposes specified in subdivision (d) of Section 1299.01, and any bail agent, bail permittee, or bail solicitor who obtains licensing after January 1, 2000, and who engages in the arrest of a defendant pursuant to Section 1301 shall comply with the following requirements:

(1) The person shall be at least 18 years of age.

(2) The person shall have completed a 40-hour power of arrest course certified by the Commission on Peace Officer Standards and Training pursuant to Section 832. Completion of the course shall be for educational purposes only and not intended to confer the power of arrest of a peace officer or public officer, or agent of any federal, state, or local government, unless the person is so employed by a governmental agency.

(3) The person shall have completed a minimum of 12 hours of classroom education certified pursuant to Section 1810.7 of the Insurance Code.

(4) The person shall have completed a course of training in the exercise of the power to arrest offered pursuant to Section 7583.7 of the Business and Professions Code.

(5) The person shall not have been convicted of a felony.

(b) Upon completion of any course or training program required by this section, an individual authorized by Section 1299.02 to apprehend a bail fugitive shall carry certificates of completion with him or her at all times in the course of performing his or her duties under this article. *(AD '99)*

1299.05. All Applicable Laws to be Obeyed

In performing a bail fugitive apprehension, an individual authorized by Section 1299.02 to apprehend a bail fugitive shall comply with all laws applicable to that apprehension. *(AD '99)*

1299.06. Documentation Required Prior to Apprehension of Bail Fugitive

Before apprehending a bail fugitive, an individual authorized by Section 1299.02 to apprehend a bail fugitive shall have in his or her possession proper documentation of authority to apprehend issued by the bail or depositor of bail as prescribed in Sections 1300 and 1301. The authority to apprehend document shall include all of the following information: the name of the individual authorized by Section 1299.02 to apprehend a bail fugitive and any fictitious name, if applicable; the address of the principal office of the individual authorized by Section 1299.02 to apprehend a bail fugitive; and the name and principal business address of the bail agency, surety company, or other party contracting with the individual authorized by Section 1299.02 to apprehend a bail fugitive. *(AD '99)*

1299.07. Representation as Sworn Law Enforcement Officer Prohibited

(a) An individual authorized by Section 1299.02 to apprehend a bail fugitive shall not represent himself or herself in any manner as being a sworn law enforcement officer.

(b) An individual authorized by Section 1299.02 to apprehend a bail fugitive shall not wear any uniform that represents himself or herself as belonging to any part or department of a federal, state, or local government. Any uniform shall not display the words United States, Bureau, Task Force, Federal, or other substantially similar words that a reasonable person may mistake for a government agency.

(c) An individual authorized by Section 1299.02 to apprehend a bail fugitive shall not wear or otherwise use a badge that represents himself or herself as belonging to any part or department of the federal, state, or local government.

(d) An individual authorized by Section 1299.02 to apprehend a bail fugitive shall not use a fictitious name that represents himself or herself as belonging to any federal, state, or local government. *(AD '99)*

1299.08. Notification of Local Law Enforcement Agency Required; Six Hour Limit

(a) Except under exigent circumstances, an individual authorized by Section 1299.02 to apprehend a bail fugitive shall, prior to and no more than six hours before attempting to apprehend the bail fugitive, notify the local police department or sheriff's department of the intent to apprehend a bail fugitive in that jurisdiction by:

(1) Indicating the name of an individual authorized by Section 1299.02 to apprehend a bail fugitive entering the jurisdiction.

(2) Stating the approximate time an individual authorized by Section 1299.02 to apprehend a bail fugitive will be entering the jurisdiction and the approximate length of the stay.

(3) Stating the name and approximate location of the bail fugitive.

(b) If an exigent circumstance does arise and prior notification is not given as provided in subdivision (a), an individual authorized by Section 1299.02 to apprehend a bail fugitive shall notify the local police department or sheriff's department immediately after the apprehension, and upon request of the local jurisdiction, shall submit a detailed explanation of those exigent circumstances within three working days after the apprehension is made.

(c) This section shall not preclude an individual authorized by Section 1299.02 to apprehend a bail fugitive from making or attempting to make a lawful arrest of a bail fugitive on bond pursuant to Section 1300 or 1301. The fact that a bench warrant is not located or entered into a warrant depository or system shall not affect a lawful arrest of the bail fugitive.

(d) For the purposes of this section, notice may be provided to a local law enforcement agency by telephone prior to the arrest or, after the arrest has taken place, if exigent circumstances exist. In that case the name or operator number of the employee receiving the notice information shall be obtained and retained by the bail, depositor of bail, or bail fugitive recovery person. *(AD '99)*

1299.09. Forced Entry to Premises Prohibited; Section 844 Exception

(a) An individual authorized by Section 1299.02 to apprehend a bail fugitive shall not forcibly enter a premises except as provided for in Section 844.

(b) Nothing in subdivision (a) shall be deemed to authorize an individual authorized by Section 12099.02 to apprehend a bail fugitive to apprehend, detain, or arrest any person except as otherwise authorized pursuant to Chapter 5 (commencing with Section 833) of Title 3 of Part 2, or any other provision of law. *(AD '99)*

1299.10. Firearms - Carrying Prohibited Unless Licensed

An individual authorized by Section 1299.02 to apprehend a bail fugitive shall not carry a firearm or other weapon unless in compliance with the laws of the state. *(AD '99)*

1299.11. Violation of Article a Misdemeanor

Any person who violates this act, or who conspires with another person to violate this act, or who hires an individual to apprehend a bail fugitive, knowing that the individual is not authorized by Section 1299.02

to apprehend a bail fugitive, is guilty of a misdemeanor punishable by a fine of five thousand dollars ($5,000) or by imprisonment in the county jail not to exceed one year, or by both that imprisonment and fine. *(AD '99)*

1299.12. Article Repeals 1-1-2005

This article shall remain in effect only until January 1, 2005, and as of that date is repealed, unless a later enacted statute, that is enacted before January 1, 2005, deletes or extends that date. *(AD '99)*

1299.13. Private Investigators not Exempted from Licensure

Nothing in this article is intended to exempt from licensure persons otherwise required to be licensed as private investigators pursuant to Chapter 11.3 (commencing with Section 7512) of Division 3 of the Business and Professions Code. *(AD '99)*

COUNTY JAILS, FARMS & CAMPS

4011.7. Removal of Guard From Hospitalized Prisoner; Escape

Notwithstanding the provisions of Sections 4011 and 4011.5, when it appears that the prisoner in need of medical or surgical treatment necessitating hospitalization or in need of medical or hospital care was arrested for, charged with, or convicted of an offense constituting a misdemeanor, the court in proceedings under Section 4011 or the sheriff or jailer in action taken under Section 4011.5 may direct that the guard be removed from the prisoner while he is in the hospital. If such direction is given, any such prisoner who knowingly escapes or attempts to escape from such hospital shall upon conviction thereof be guilty of a misdemeanor and punishable by imprisonment for not to exceed one year in the county jail if such escape or attempt to escape was not by force or violence. However, if such escape is by force or violence such prisoner shall be guilty of a felony and punishable by imprisonment in the state prison, or in the county jail for not exceeding one year; provided, that when such second term of imprisonment is to be served in the county jail it shall commence from the time such prisoner would otherwise be discharged from such jail.

4024.3. Required Participation in Work Release Program

(a) Notwithstanding any other law, the board of supervisors of any county in which the average daily inmate population is 90 percent of the county's correctional system's mandated capacity may authorize the sheriff or other official in charge of county correctional facilities to operate a program under which any person committed to the facility is required to participate in a work release program pursuant to criteria described in subdivision (b) of Section 4024.2. Participants in this work release program shall receive any sentence reduction credits that they would have received had they served their sentences in a county correctional facility. Priority for participation in the work release program shall be given to inmates who volunteer to participate in the program.

(b) For purposes of this section, all of the following definitions apply:

(1) "County correctional system's mandated capacity" means the total capacity of all jails and other correctional facilities for the permanent housing of adult inmates within the county.

(2) "Mandated capacity" of any facility is the capacity for that facility as established by court order or the facility's rated capacity as established by the Board of Corrections, whichever is less.

(3) "Average daily jail population" is the average total number of inmates incarcerated within the county jail system computed on an annual basis.

(c)(1) The board of supervisors may prescribe reasonable rules and regulations under which a work release program authorized under this section is operated and may provide that participants wear clothing of a distinctive character while performing the work. A person shall be advised by written notice to appear before the sheriff or at the educational, vocational, or substance abuse program at a time and place specified in the notice and shall sign an acknowledgement that the sheriff may immediately retake the person into custody to serve the balance of his or her sentence if the person fails to appear for the program at the time and place designated in the notice, does not perform the work or activity assigned, or for any other reason is no longer a fit subject for release under this section. A copy of the notice and acknowledgement shall be delivered to the person and a copy shall be retained by the sheriff.

(2) Any person who willfully fails to appear at the time and place specified in the notice is guilty of a misdemeanor.

(3) Whenever a peace officer has reasonable cause to believe the person has failed to appear at the time and place specified in the notice or fails to appear or work at the time and place agreed to or has failed to perform the work assigned, the peace officer may, without a warrant, retake the person into custody, or the court may issue an arrest warrant for the retaking of the person into custody, to complete the remainder of the original sentence. A peace officer may not retake a person into custody under this subdivision, without a warrant for arrest, unless the officer has a written order to do so, signed by the sheriff or other person in charge of the work release program, that describes with particularity the person to be retaken.

(d) Nothing in this section shall be construed to require the sheriff or other official in charge to assign a person to a work release program pursuant to this section if it appears from the record that the person has refused to perform satisfactorily as assigned or has not satisfactorily complied with the reasonable rules and regulations governing the assignment or any other order of the court.

(e) A person shall be eligible for work release under this section only if the sheriff or other official in charge concludes that the person is a fit subject therefor.

(f) The board of supervisors may prescribe a program administrative fee, not to exceed the pro rata cost of administration, to be paid by each person according to his or her ability to pay.

4030. Regulation of Body and Strip Searches

(a) The Legislature finds and declares that law enforcement policies and practices for conducting strip or body cavity searches of detained persons vary widely throughout California. Consequently, some people have been arbitrarily subjected to unnecessary strip and body cavity searches after arrests for minor misdemeanor and infraction offenses. Some present search practices violate state and federal constitutional rights to privacy and freedom from unreasonable searches and seizures.

It is the intent of the Legislature in enacting this section to protect the state and federal constitutional rights of the people of California by establishing a statewide policy strictly limiting strip and body cavity searches.

(b) The provisions of this section shall apply only to pre-arraignment detainees arrested for infraction or misdemeanor offenses and to any minor detained prior to a detention hearing on the grounds that he or she is a person described in Section 300, 601, or 602 of the Welfare and Institutions Code alleged to have committed a misdemeanor or infraction offense. The provisions of this section shall not apply to any person in the custody of the Director of the Dept. of Corrections or the Director of the Youth Authority.

(c) As used in this section, "strip search"means a search which requires a person to remove or arrange some or all of his or her clothing so as to permit a visual inspection of the underclothing, breasts, buttocks, or genitalia of such person.

(d) As used in this section:

(1) "Body cavity"only means the stomach or rectal cavity of a person, and vagina of a female person.

(2) "Visual body cavity search"means visual inspection of a body cavity.

(3) "Physical body cavity search"means physical intrusion into a body cavity for the purpose of discovering any object concealed in the body cavity.

(e) Notwithstanding any other provision of law, including Section 40304.5 of the Vehicle Code, when a person is arrested and taken into custody, that person may be subjected to patdown searches, metal detector searches, and thorough clothing searches in order to discover and retrieve concealed weapons and contraband substances prior to being placed in a booking cell.

(f) No person arrested and held in custody on a misdemeanor or infraction offense, except those involving weapons, controlled substances or violence nor any minor detained prior to a detention hearing on the grounds that he or she is a person described in Section 300, 601 or 602 of the Welfare and Institutions Code, except for those minors alleged to have committed felonies or offenses involving weapons, controlled substances or violence, shall be subjected to a strip search or visual body cavity search prior to placement in the general jail population, unless a peace officer has determined there is reasonable suspicion based on specific and articulable facts to believe such person is concealing a weapon or contraband, and a strip search will result in the discovery of the weapon or contraband. No strip search or visual body cavity search or both may be conducted without the prior written authorization of the supervising officer on duty. The authorization shall include the specific and articulable facts and circumstances upon which the reasonable suspicion determination was made by the supervisor.

(g)(1) Except pursuant to the provisions of paragraph (2), no person arrested and held in custody on a misdemeanor or infraction offense not involving weapons, controlled substances or violence, shall be confined in the general jail population unless all of the following are true:

(i) The person is not cited and released.

(ii) The person is not released on his/her own recognizance pursuant to Article 9 of Chapter 1 of Title 10 of Part 2.

(iii) The person is not able to post bail within a reasonable time not less than three hours.

(2) No person may be housed in the general jail population prior to release pursuant to the provisions of paragraph (1) unless a documented emergency exists and there is no reasonable alternative to such placement. Such person shall be placed in the general population only upon prior written authorization documenting the specific facts and circumstances of the emergency. The written authorization shall be signed by the uniformed supervisor of the facility or by a uniformed watch commander. Any person confined in the general jail population pursuant to paragraph (1) shall retain all rights to release on citation, his or her own recognizance, or bail which were preempted as a consequence of the emergency.

(h) No person arrested on a misdemeanor or infraction offense, nor any minor described in subdivision (b), shall be subjected to a physical body cavity search except under the authority of a search warrant issued by a magistrate specifically authorizing the physical body cavity search.

(i) A copy of the prior written authorization required by subdivisions (f) and (g) and the search warrant required by subdivision (h) shall be placed in the agency's records and made available, on request, to the person searched or his or her authorized representative. With regard to any strip, visual or body search, the time, date and place of the search, the name and sex of the person conducting the search and a statement of the results of the search, including a list of any items removed from the person searched, shall be recorded in the agency's records and made available, upon request, to the person searched or his or her authorized representative.

(j) Persons conducting a strip search or a visual body cavity search shall not touch the breasts, buttocks, or genitalia of the person being searched.

(k) A physical body cavity search shall be conducted under sanitary conditions, and only by a physician, nurse practitioner, registered nurse, licensed vocational nurse or emergency medical technician Level II licensed to practice in this state. Any physician engaged in providing health care to detainees and inmates of the facility may conduct physical body cavity searches.

(l) All persons conducting or otherwise present during a strip search or visual or physical body cavity search shall be of the same sex as the person being searched, except for physicians or licensed medical personnel.

(m) All strip, visual and physical body cavity searches shall be conducted in an area of privacy so that the search cannot be observed by persons not participating in the search. Persons are considered to be participating in the search if their official duties relative to search procedure require them to be present at the time the search is conducted.

(n) A person who knowingly and willfully authorizes or conducts a strip, visual or physical body cavity search in violation of this section is guilty of a misdemeanor.

(o) Nothing in this section shall be construed as limiting any common law or statutory rights of any person regarding any action for damages or injunctive relief, or as precluding the prosecution under another provision of law of any peace officer or other person who has violated this section.

(p) Any person who suffers damage or harm as a result of a violation of this section may bring a civil action to recover actual damages, or one thousand dollars ($1,000), whichever is greater. In addition, the court may, in its discretion, award punitive damages, equitable relief as it deems necessary and proper, and costs, including reasonable attorney's fees.

4131.5.　Battery Upon Noninmate

Every person confined in, sentenced to, or serving a sentence in, a city or county jail, industrial farm, or industrial road camp in this state, who commits a battery upon the person of any individual who is not himself a person confined or sentenced therein, is guilty of a public offense and is punishable by imprisonment in a state prison, or in a county jail for not more than one year.

4133.　Boundary - Escapes

The boundary of every industrial farm established under the provisions of this article shall be marked by a fence, hedge or by some other visible line. Every person confined on any industrial farm who escapes therefrom or attempts to escape therefrom shall upon conviction thereof be imprisoned in a state prison, or in the county jail or industrial farm for not to exceed one year. Any such imprisonment shall begin at the expiration of the imprisonment in effect at the time of the escape.

OFFENSES RELATING TO PRISONS AND PRISONERS

4501.1.　Battery by Gassing by Prison Inmate - Required Reports

(a) Every person confined in the state prison who commits a battery by gassing upon the person of any peace officer, as defined in Chapter 4.5 (commencing with Section 830) of Title 3 of Part 2, or employee of the state prison is guilty of aggravated battery and shall be punished by imprisonment in a county jail or by imprisonment in the state prison for two, three, or four years. Every state prison inmate convicted of a felony under this section shall serve his or her term of imprisonment as prescribed in Section 4501.5.

(b) For purposes of this section, "gassing" means intentionally placing or throwing, or causing to be placed or thrown, upon the person of another, any human excrement or other bodily fluids or bodily substances or any mixture containing human excrement or other bodily fluids or bodily substances that results in actual contact with the person's skin or membranes.

(c) The warden or other person in charge of the state prison shall use every available means to immediately investigate all reported or suspected violations of subdivision (a), including, but not limited to, the use of forensically acceptable means of preserving and testing the suspected gassing substance to confirm the presence of human excrement or other bodily fluids or bodily substances. If there is probable cause to believe that the inmate has violated subdivision (a), the chief medical officer of the state prison or his or her designee, may, when he or she deems it medically necessary to protect the health of an officer or employee who may have been subject to a violation of this section, order the inmate to receive an examination or test for hepatitis or tuberculosis or both hepatitis and tuberculosis on either a voluntary or involuntary basis immediately after the event, and periodically thereafter as determined to be necessary by the medical officer in order to ensure that further hepatitis or tuberculosis transmission does not occur. These decisions shall be consistent with an occupational exposure as defined by the Center for Disease Control and Prevention. The results of any examination or test shall be provided to the officer or employee who has been subject to a reported or suspected violation of this section. Nothing in this subdivision shall be construed to otherwise supersede the operation of Title 8 (commencing with Section 7500). Any person performing tests, transmitting test results, or disclosing information pursuant to this section shall be immune from civil liability for any action taken in accordance with this section.

(d) The warden or other person in charge of the state prison shall refer all reports for which there is probable cause to believe that the inmate has violated subdivision (a) to the local district attorney for prosecution.

(e) The Department of Corrections shall report to the Legislature, by January 1, 2000, its findings and recommendations on gassing incidents at the state prison and the medical testing authorized by this section. The report shall include, but not be limited to, all of the following:

(1) The total number of gassing incidents at each state prison facility up to the date of the report.

(2) The disposition of each gassing incident, including the administrative penalties imposed, the number of incidents that are prosecuted, and the results of those prosecutions, including any penalties imposed.

(3) A profile of the inmates who commit the aggravated batteries, including the number of inmates who have one or more prior serious or violent felony convictions.

(4) Efforts that the department has taken to limit these incidents, including staff training and the use of protective clothing and goggles.

(5) The results and costs of the medical testing authorized by this section.

(f) Nothing in this section shall preclude prosecution under both this section and any other provision of law. *(AM '98, '00)*

4502. Possession of Deadly Weapons by Person Confined, Conveyed, or in Custody

(a) Every person who, while at or confined in any penal institution, while being conveyed to or from any penal institution, or while under the custody of officials, officers, or employees of any penal institution, possesses or carries upon his or her person or has under his or her custody or control any instrument or weapon of the kind commonly known as a blackjack, slungshot, billy, sandclub, sandbag, or metal knuckles, any explosive substance, or fixed ammunition, any dirk or dagger or sharp instrument, any pistol, revolver, or other firearm, or any tear gas or tear gas weapon, is guilty of a felony and shall be punished by imprisonment in the state prison for two, three, or four years, to be served consecutively.

(b) Every person who, while at or confined in any penal institution, while being conveyed to or from any penal institution, or while under the custody of officials, officers, or employees of any penal institution, manufactures or attempts to manufacture any instrument or weapon of the kind commonly known as a blackjack, slungshot, billy, sandclub, sandbag, or metal knuckles, any explosive substance, or fixed ammunition, any dirk or dagger or sharp instrument, any pistol, revolver, or other firearm, or any tear gas or tear gas weapon, is guilty of a felony and shall be punished by imprisonment in the state prison for 16 months, or two or three years, to be served consecutively.

(c) For purposes of this section, "penal institution" means the state prison, a prison road camp, prison forestry camp, or other prison camp or farm, or a county jail or county road camp.

4530. Escape or Attempt to Escape From Prison

(a) Every prisoner confined in a state prison who, by force or violence, escapes or attempts to escape therefrom and every prisoner committed to a state prison who, by force or violence, escapes or attempts to escape while being conveyed to or from such prison or any other state prison, or any prison road camp, prison forestry camp, or other prison camp or prison farm or any other place while under the custody of prison officials, officers or employees; or who, by force or violence, escapes or attempts to escape from any prison road camp, prison forestry camp, or other prison camp or prison farm or other place while under the custody of prison officials, officers or employees; or who, by force or violence, escapes or attempts to escape while at work outside or away from prison under custody of prison officials, officers, or employees, is punishable by imprisonment in a state prison for a term of two, four, or six years. The second term of imprisonment of a person convicted under this subdivision shall commence from the time he would otherwise have been discharged from prison. No additional probation report shall be required with respect to such offense.

(b) Every prisoner who commits an escape or attempts an escape as described in subdivision (a), without force or violence, is punishable by imprisonment in the state prison for 16 months, or two or three years to be served consecutively. No additional probation report shall be required with respect to such offense.

(c) The willful failure of a prisoner who is employed or continuing his education, or who is authorized to secure employment or education, or who is temporarily released pursuant to Section 2690, 2910, or 6254, or Section 3306 of the Welfare and Institutions Code, to return to the place of confinement not later than the expiration of a period during which he or she is authorized to be away from the place of confinement, is an escape from the place of confinement punishable as provided in this section. A conviction of a violation of this subdivision, not involving force or violence, shall not be charged as a prior felony conviction in any subsequent prosecution for a public offense.

4532. Escape or Attempt to Escape From County or City Jail, Industrial Farm or Road Camp

(a)(1) Every prisoner arrested and booked for, charged with, or convicted of a misdemeanor, and every person committed under the terms of Section 5654, 5656, or 5677 of the Welfare and Institutions Code as an inebriate, who is confined in any county or city jail, prison, industrial farm, or industrial road camp, is engaged on any county road or other county work, is in the lawful custody of any officer or person, is employed or continuing in his or her regular educational program or authorized to secure employment or education away from the place of confinement, pursuant to the Cobey Work Furlough Law (Section 1208), is authorized for temporary release for family emergencies or for purposes preparatory to his or her return to the community pursuant to Section 4018.6, or is a participant in a home detention program pursuant to Section 1203.016, and who thereafter escapes or attempts to escape from the county or city jail, prison, industrial farm, or industrial road camp or from the custody of the officer or person in charge of him or her while engaged in or going to or returning from the county work or from the custody of any officer or person in whose lawful custody he or she is, or from the place of confinement in a home detention program pursuant to Section 1203.016, is guilty of a felony and, if the escape or attempt to escape was not by force or violence, is punishable by imprisonment in the state prison for a determinate term of one year and one day, or in a county jail not exceeding one year.

(2) If the escape or attempt to escape described in paragraph (1) is committed by force or violence, the person is guilty of a felony, punishable by imprisonment in the state prison for two, four, or six years to be served consecutively, or in a county jail not exceeding one year. When the second term of imprisonment is to be served in a county jail, it shall commence from the time the prisoner otherwise would have been discharged from jail.

(3) A conviction of a violation of this subdivision, or a violation of subdivision (b) involving a participant of a home detention program pursuant to Section 1203.016, that is not committed by force or violence, shall not be charged as a prior felony conviction in any subsequent prosecution for a public offense.

(b)(1) Every prisoner arrested and booked for, charged with, or convicted of a felony, and every person committed by order of the juvenile court, who is confined in any county or city jail, prison, industrial farm, or industrial road camp, is engaged on any county road or other county work, is in the lawful custody of any officer or person, or is confined pursuant to Section 4011.9, is a participant in a home detention program pursuant to Section 1203.016, who escapes or attempts to escape from a county or city jail, prison, industrial farm, or industrial road camp or from the custody of the officer or person in charge of him or her while engaged in or going to or returning from the county work or from the custody of any officer or person in whose lawful custody he or she is, or from confinement pursuant to Section 4011.9, or from the place of confinement in a home detention program pursuant to Section 1203.016, is guilty of a felony and, if the escape or attempt to escape was not by force or violence, is punishable by imprisonment in the state prison for 16 months, two years, or three years, to be served consecutively, or in a county jail not exceeding one year.

(2) If the escape or attempt to escape described in paragraph (1) is committed by force or violence, the person is guilty of a felony, punishable by imprisonment in the state prison for a full term of two, four, or six years to be served consecutively to any other term of imprisonment, commencing from the time the person otherwise would have been released from imprisonment and the term shall not be subject to reduction pursuant to subdivision (a) of Section 1170.1, or in a county jail for a consecutive term not to exceed one year, that term to commence from the time the prisoner otherwise would have been discharged from jail.

(c)(1) Except in unusual cases where the interests of justice would best be served if the person is granted probation, probation shall not be granted to any person who is convicted of a felony offense under this section in that he or she escaped or attempted to escape from a secure main jail facility, from a court building, or while being transported between the court building and the jail facility.

(2) In any case in which a person is convicted of a violation of this section designated as a misdemeanor, he or she shall be confined in a county jail for not less than 90 days nor more than one year except in unusual cases where the interests of justice would best be served by the granting of probation.

(3) For the purposes of this subdivision, "main jail facility"means the facility used for the detention of persons pending arraignment, after arraignment, during trial, and upon sentence or commitment. The facility shall not include an industrial farm, industrial road camp, work furlough facility, or any other nonsecure facility used primarily for sentenced prisoners. As used in this subdivision, "secure"means that the facility contains an outer perimeter characterized by the use of physically restricting construction, hardware, and procedures designed to eliminate ingress and egress from the facility except through a closely supervised gate or doorway.

(4) If the court grants probation under this subdivision, it shall specify the reason or reasons for that order on the court record.

(5) Any sentence imposed under this subdivision shall be served consecutive to any other sentence in effect or pending.

(d) The willful failure of a prisoner, whether convicted of a felony or a misdemeanor, to return to his or her place of confinement no later than the expiration of the period that he or she was authorized to be away from that place of confinement, is an escape from that place of confinement. This subdivision applies to a prisoner who is employed or continuing in his or her regular educational program, authorized to secure employment or education pursuant to the Cobey Work Furlough Law (Section 1208), authorized for temporary release for family emergencies or for purposes preparatory to his or her return to the community pursuant to Section 4018.6, or permitted to participate in a home detention program pursuant to Section 1203.016. A prisoner convicted of a misdemeanor who willfully fails to return to his or her place of confinement under this subdivision shall be punished as provided in paragraph (1) of subdivision (a). A prisoner convicted of a felony who willfully fails to return to his or her place of confinement shall be punished as provided in paragraph (1) of subdivision (b). *(AM '98)*

4536. Escape from Mental Health Facility

(a) Every person committed to a state hospital or other public or private mental health facility as a mentally disordered sex offender, who escapes from or who escapes while being conveyed to or from such state hospital or other public or private mental health facility, is punishable by imprisonment in the state prison or in the county jail not to exceed one year. The term imposed pursuant to this section shall be served consecutively to any other sentence or commitment.

(b) The medical director or person in charge of a state hospital or other public or private mental health facility to which a person has been committed as a mentally disordered sex offender shall promptly notify the chief of police of the city in which the hospital or facility is located, or the sheriff of the county if the hospital or facility is located in an unincorporated area, of the escape of the person, and shall request the assistance of the chief of police or sheriff in apprehending the person, and shall, within 48 hours of the escape of the person, orally notify the court that made the commitment, the prosecutor in the case, and the Department of Justice of the escape.

4536.5. Sexually Violent Predator; Notification of Escape from Hospital or Mental Health Facility

The medical director or person in charge of a state hospital or other public or private mental health facility to which a person has been committed under the provisions of Article 4 (commencing with Section 6600) of Chapter 2 of Part 2 of the Welfare and Institutions Code, shall promptly notify the Department of Corrections'Sexually Violent Predator Parole Coordinator, the chief of police of the city in which the hospital or facility is located, or the sheriff of the county if the hospital or facility is located in an unincorporated area, of the escape of the person, and shall request the assistance of the chief of police or sheriff in apprehending the person, and shall, within 48 hours of the escape of the person, orally notify the court that made the commitment, the prosecutor in the case, and the Department of Justice of the escape. *(AM '99)*

4550. Penalties for Rescue or Attempt to Rescue

Every person who rescues or attempts to rescue, or aids another person in rescuing or attempting to rescue any prisoner from any prison, or prison road camp or any jail or county road camp, or from any officer or person having him in lawful custody, is punishable as follows:

1. If such prisoner was in custody upon a conviction of a felony punishable with death: by imprisonment in the state prison for two, three or four years;

2. If such prisoner was in custody otherwise than as specified in subsection 1 hereof: by imprisonment in the state prison, or by imprisonment in the county jail not to exceed one year.

4570. Unauthorized Communication With Prisoners, or Taking From or Bringing in Letters, Etc.

Every person who, without the permission of the warden or other officer in charge of any State prison, or prison road camp, or prison forestry camp, or other prison camp or prison farm or any other place where prisoners of the State prison are located under the custody of prison officials, officers or employees, or any jail, or any county road camp in the State, communicates with any prisoner or person detained therein, or brings therein or takes therefrom any letter, writing, literature, or reading matter to or from any prisoner or person confined therein, is guilty of a misdemeanor.

4570.1. Unauthorized Transportation of Prisoner

Every person who, without permission of the peace officer or corrections officer in charge of any vehicle, bus, van or automobile used for the transportation of prisoners, delivers a written communication to any prisoner or person detained therein, or being escorted to or from that vehicle, or takes from or gives to the prisoner any item, is guilty of a misdemeanor.

4570.5. False Identification to Secure Admission to Prison, Camp, Farm, or Jail

Every person who falsely identifies himself either verbally or by presenting any fraudulent written instrument to prison officials, officers, or employees of any state prison, prison road camp, or prison forestry camp, or other prison camp or prison farm, or any jail, or any county industrial farm, or any county road camp, for the purpose of securing admission to the premises or grounds of any such prison, camp, farm, or jail, and such person would not otherwise qualify for admission, is guilty of a misdemeanor.

4571. Unauthorized Entry on Prison or Jail Grounds by an Ex-Convict

Every person who, having been previously convicted of a felony and confined in any State prison in this State, without the consent of the warden or other officer in charge of any State prison or prison road camp, or prison forestry camp, or other prison camp or prison farm or any other place where prisoners of the State prison are located under the custody of prison officials, officers or employees, or any jail or any county road camp in this State, comes upon the grounds of any such institution, or lands belonging or adjacent thereto, is guilty of a felony.

4573. Smuggling Controlled Substances or Liquor Into Prison or Jail

Except when otherwise authorized by law, or when authorized by the person in charge of the prison or other institution referred to in this section or by an officer of the institution empowered by the person in charge of the institution to give the authorization, any person, who knowingly brings or sends into, or knowingly assists in bringing into, or sending into, any state prison, prison road camp, prison forestry camp, or other prison camp or prison farm or any other place where prisoners of the state are located under the custody of prison officials, officers or employees, into any county, city and county, or city jail, road camp, farm or other place where prisoners or inmates are located under custody of any sheriff, chief of police, peace officer, probation officer or employees, or within the grounds belonging to the institution, any controlled substance, the possession of which is prohibited by Division 10 of the Health and Safety Code, any device, contrivance, instrument, or paraphernalia intended to be used for unlawfully injecting or consuming a controlled substance, is guilty of a felony punishable by imprisonment in the state prison for two, three, or four years. The prohibitions and sanctions addressed in this section shall be clearly and prominently posted outside of, and at the entrance to, the grounds of all detention facilities under the jurisdiction of, or operated by, the state or any city, county, or city and county.

4573.5. Bring Drugs or Alcoholic Beverages Into Penal Institutions

Any person who knowingly brings into any state prison or other institution under the jurisdiction of the Dept. of Corrections, or into any prison camp, prison farm, or any other place where prisoners or inmates of these institutions are located under the custody of prison or institution officials, officers, or employees, or into any county, city and county, or city jail, road camp, farm or any other institution or place where prisoners or inmates are being held under the custody of any sheriff, chief of police, peace officer, probation officer, or employees, or within the grounds belonging to any institution or place, any alcoholic beverage, any drugs, other than controlled substances, in any manner, shape, form, dispenser, or container, or any device, contrivance, instrument, or paraphernalia intended to be used for unlawfully injecting or consuming any drug other than controlled substances, without having authority so to do by the rules of the Dept. of Corrections, the rules of the prison, institution, camp, farm, place, or jail, or by the specific authorization of the warden, superintendent, jailer, or other person in charge of the prison, jail, institution, camp, farm, or place, is guilty of a felony. The prohibitions and sanctions addressed in this section shall be clearly and prominently posted outside of, and at the entrance to, the grounds of all detention facilities under the jurisdiction of, or operated by, the state or any city, county, or city and county.

4573.6. Possess Controlled Substances, Drugs, etc. Where Prisoners Are Kept

Any person who knowingly has in his or her possession in any state prison, prison road camp, prison forestry camp, or other prison camp or prison farm or any place where prisoners of the state are located under the custody of prison officials, officers, or employees, or in any county, city and county, or city jail, road camp, farm, or any place or institution, where prisoners or inmates are being held under the custody of any sheriff, chief of police, peace officer, probation officer, or employees, or within the grounds belonging to any jail, road camp, farm, place or institution, any controlled substances, the possession of which is prohibited by Division 10 of the Health and Safety Code, any device, contrivance, instrument, or paraphernalia intended to be used for unlawfully injecting or consuming controlled substances, without being authorized to so possess the same by the rules of the Dept. of Corrections, rules of the prison or jail, institution, camp, farm or place, or by the specific authorization of the warden, superintendent, jailer, or other person in charge of the prison, jail, institution, camp, farm or place, is guilty of a felony punishable by imprisonment in the state prison for two, three, or four years. The prohibitions and sanctions addressed in this section shall be clearly and prominently posted outside of, and at the entrance to, the grounds of all detention facilities under the jurisdiction of, or operated by, the state or any city, county, or city and county.

4573.8. Possession of Alcoholic Beverages, Drugs, etc. in Prison, Camp or Jail

Any person who knowingly has in his or her possession in any state prison, prison road camp, prison forestry camp, or other prison camp or prison farm or any place where prisoners of the state are located under the custody of prison officials, officers, or employees, or in any county, city and county, or city jail, road camp, farm, or any place or institution, where prisoners or inmates are being held under the custody of any sheriff, chief of police, peace officer, probation officer, or employees, or within the grounds belonging to any jail, road camp, farm, place, or institution, drugs in any manner, shape, form, dispenser, or container, any device, contrivance, instrument, or paraphernalia intended to be used for unlawfully injecting or consuming drugs, or alcoholic beverages, without being authorized to possess the same by rules of the Dept. of Corrections, rules of the prison or jail, institution, camp, farm, or place, or by the specific authorization of the warden, superintendent, jailer, or other person in charge of the prison, jail, institution, camp, farm, or place, is guilty of a felony. The prohibitions and sanctions addressed in this section shall be clearly and prominently posted outside of, and at the entrance to, the grounds of all detention facilities under the jurisdiction of, or operated by, the state or any city, county, or city and county.

4573.9. Controlled Substances - Sell, Furnish, etc. in Prison, Camp or Jail

Notwithstanding any other provision of law, any person, other than a person held in custody, who sells, furnishes, administers, or gives away, or offers to sell, furnish, administer, or give away to any person held in custody in any state prison or other institution under the jurisdiction of the Dept. of Corrections, or in any prison camp, prison farm, or any other place where prisoners or inmates of these institutions are located under the custody of prison institution officials, officers, or employees, or in any county, city and county, or city jail, road camp, farm, or any other institution or place where prisoners or inmates are being held under the custody of any sheriff, chief of police, peace officer, probation officer, or employees, or within the grounds belonging to any institution or place, any controlled substance, the possession of which is prohibited by Division 10 of the Health and Safety Code, if the recipient is not authorized to possess the same by the rules of the Dept. of Corrections, rules of the prison or jail, institution, camp, farm, or place, or by the specific authorization of the warden, superintendent, jailer, or other person in charge of the prison, jail, institution, camp, farm, or place, is guilty of a felony punishable by imprisonment in the state prison for two, four, or six years. The prohibitions and sanctions addressed in this section shall be clearly and prominently posted outside of, and at the entrance to, the grounds of all detention facilities under the jurisdiction of, or operated by, the state or any city, county, or city and county.

4574. Smuggling Firearms, Deadly Weapon, or Tear Gas Weapon Into Prison or Jail

(a) Except when otherwise authorized by law, or when authorized by the person in charge of the prison or other institution referred to in this section or by an officer of the institution empowered by the person in charge of the institution to give such authorization, any person, who knowingly brings or sends into, or knowingly assists in bringing into, or sending into, any state prison or prison road camp or prison forestry camp, or other prison camp or prison farm or any other place where prisoners of the state prison are located under the custody of prison officials, officers or employees, or any jail or any county road camp in this state, or within the grounds belonging or adjacent to any such institution, any firearms, deadly weapons, or explosives, and any person who, while lawfully confined in a jail or county road camp possesses therein any firearm, deadly weapon, explosive, tear gas or tear gas weapon, is guilty of a felony and punishable by imprisonment in the state prison for two, three, or four years.

(b) Except as provided in subdivision (a), any person who knowingly brings or sends into such places any tear gas or tear gas weapons which results in the release of such tear gas or use of such weapon is guilty of a felony and punishable by imprisonment in the state prison for two, three, or four years.

(c) Except as provided in subdivision (a), any person who knowingly brings or sends into such places any tear gas or tear gas weapons is guilty of a misdemeanor and punishable by imprisonment in the county jail not exceeding six months, or by fine not exceeding one thousand dollars ($1,000), or by both such fine and imprisonment.

4600. Destroying or Injuring Prison or Jail

(a) Every person who willfully and intentionally breaks down, pulls down, or otherwise destroys or injures any jail, prison, or any public property in any jail or prison, is punishable by a fine not exceeding ten thousand dollars ($10,000), and by imprisonment in the state prison, except that where the damage or injury to any city, city and county, or county jail property or prison property is determined to be four hundred dollars ($400) or less, that person is guilty of a misdemeanor.

(b) In any case in which a person is convicted of violating this section, the court may order the defendant to make restitution to the public entity that owns the property damaged by the defendant. The court shall specify in the order that the public entity that owns the property damaged by the defendant shall not enforce the order until the defendant satisfies all outstanding fines, penalties, assessments, restitution fines, and restitution orders.

INVESTIGATION & CONTROL OF CRIMES & CRIMINALS

11165. Child Defined

As used in this article "child" means a person under the age of 18 years.

11165.1. Sexual Abuse, Sexual Assault, Sexual Exploitation Defined

As used in this article, "sexual abuse"means sexual assault or sexual exploitation as defined by the following:

(a) "Sexual assault"means conduct in violation of one or more of the following sections: Section 261 (rape), subdivision (d) of Section 261.5 (statutory rape), 264.1 (rape in concert), 285 (incest), 286 (sodomy), subdivision (a) or (b), or paragraph (1) of subdivision (c) of Section 288 (lewd or lascivious acts upon a child), 288a (oral copulation), 289 (sexual penetration), or 647.6 (child molestation).

(b) Conduct described as "sexual assault"includes, but is not limited to, all of the following:

(1) Any penetration, however slight, of the vagina or anal opening of one person by the penis of another person, whether or not there is the emission of semen.

(2) Any sexual contact between the genitals or anal opening of one person and the mouth or tongue of another person.

(3) Any intrusion by one person into the genitals or anal opening of another person, including the use of any object for this purpose, except that, it does not include acts performed for a valid medical purpose.

(4) The intentional touching of the genitals or intimate parts (including the breasts, genital area, groin, inner thighs, and buttocks) or the clothing covering them, of a child, or of the perpetrator by a child, for purposes of sexual arousal or gratification, except that, it does not include acts which may reasonably be construed to be normal caretaker responsibilities; interactions with, or demonstrations of affection for, the child; or acts performed for a valid medical purpose.

(5) The intentional masturbation of the perpetrator's genitals in the presence of a child.

(c) "Sexual exploitation"refers to any of the following:

(1) Conduct involving matter depicting a minor engaged in obscene acts in violation of Section 311.2 (preparing, selling, or distributing obscene matter) or subdivision (a) of Section 311.4 (employment of minor to perform obscene acts).

(2) Any person who knowingly promotes, aids, or assists, employs, uses, persuades, induces, or coerces a child, or any person responsible for a child's welfare, who knowingly permits or encourages a child to engage in, or assist others to engage in, prostitution or a live performance involving obscene sexual conduct, or to either pose or model alone or with others for purposes of preparing a film, photograph, negative, slide, drawing, painting, or other pictorial depiction, involving obscene sexual conduct. For the purpose of this section, "person responsible for a child's welfare"means a parent, guardian, foster parent, or a licensed administrator or employee of a public or private residential home, residential school, or other residential institution.

(3) Any person who depicts a child in, or who knowingly develops, duplicates, prints, or exchanges, any film, photograph, video tape, negative, or slide in which a child is engaged in an act of obscene sexual conduct, except for those activities by law enforcement and prosecution agencies and other persons described in subdivisions (c) and (e) of Section 311.3. *(AM '00)*

11165.2. Neglect, Severe Neglect, General Neglect Defined

As used in this article, "neglect"means the negligent treatment or the maltreatment of a child by a person responsible for the child's welfare under circumstances indicating harm or threatened harm to the child's health or welfare. The term includes both acts and omissions on the part of the responsible person.

(a) "Severe neglect"means the negligent failure of a person having the care or custody of a child to protect the child from severe malnutrition or medically diagnosed nonorganic failure to thrive. "Severe neglect"also means those situations of neglect where any person having the care or custody of a child willfully causes or permits the person or health of the child to be placed in a situation such that his or her person or health is endangered, as proscribed by Section 11165.3, including the intentional failure to provide adequate food, clothing, shelter, or medical care.

(b) "General neglect"means the negligent failure of a person having the care or custody of a child to provide adequate food, clothing, shelter, medical care, or supervision where no physical injury to the child has occurred.

For the purposes of this chapter, a child receiving treatment by spiritual means as provided in Section 16509.1 of the Welfare and Institutions Code or not receiving specified medical treatment for religious reasons, shall not for that reason alone be considered a neglected child. An informed and appropriate medical decision made by parent or guardian after consultation with a physician or physicians who have examined the minor does not constitute neglect.

11165.3. Willful Cruelty or Unjustifiable Punishment of Child Defined

As used in this article, "willful cruelty or unjustifiable punishment of a child" means a situation where any person willfully causes or permits any child to suffer, or inflicts thereon, unjustifiable physical pain or mental suffering, or having the care or custody of any child, willfully causes or permits the person or health of the child to be placed in a situation such that his or her person or health is endangered.

11165.4. Unlawful Corporal Punishment or Injury Defined

As used in this article, "unlawful corporal punishment or injury" means a situation where any person willfully inflicts upon any child any cruel or inhuman corporal punishment or injury resulting in a traumatic condition. It does not include an amount of force that is reasonable and necessary for a person employed by or engaged in a public school to quell a disturbance threatening physical injury to person or damage to property, for purposes of self-defense, or to obtain possession of weapons or other dangerous objects within the control of the pupil, as authorized by Section 49001 of the Education Code. It also does not include the exercise of the degree of physical control authorized by Section 44807 of the Education Code. It also does not include an injury caused by reasonable and necessary force used by a peace officer acting within the course and scope of his or her employment as a peace officer.

11165.5. Abuse in Out-of-Home Care Defined

As used in this article, the term "abuse or neglect in out-of-home care" includes <u>physical injury inflicted upon a child by another person by other than accidental means</u>, sexual abuse as defined in Section 11165.1, neglect as defined in Section 11165.2, unlawful corporal punishment or injury as defined in Section 11165.4, or the willful cruelty or unjustifiable punishment of a child, as defined in Section 11165.3, where the person responsible for the child's welfare is a licensee, administrator, or employee of any facility licensed to care for children, or an administrator or employee of a public or private school or other institution or agency. "Abuse or neglect in out-of-home care" does not include an injury caused by reasonable and necessary force used by a peace officer acting within the course and scope of his or her employment as a peace officer. *(AM '01)*

11165.6. Child Abuse Defined

As used in this article, <u>the term</u> "child abuse *** <u>or neglect" includes</u> physical injury *** inflicted by other than accidental means *** <u>upon</u> a child by another person***, sexual abuse as defined in Section 11165.1, neglect as defined in Section 11165.2, willful cruelty or unjustifiable punishment as defined in Section 11165.3, <u>and</u> unlawful corporal punishment or injury as defined in Section 11165.4***. "Child abuse or neglect" does not include a mutual affray between minors. "Child abuse or neglect" does not include an injury caused by reasonable and necessary force used by a peace officer acting within the course and scope of his or her employment as a peace officer. *(AM '01)*

11165.7. Mandated Reporter Defined

(a) As used in this article, "mandated reporter" is defined as any of the following:

(1) A teacher.

(2) An instructional aide.

(3) A teacher's aide or teacher's assistant employed by any public or private school.

(4) A classified employee of any public school.

(5) An administrative officer or supervisor of child welfare and attendance, or a certificated pupil personnel employee of any public or private school.

(6) An administrator of a public or private day camp.

(7) An administrator or employee of a public or private youth center, youth recreation program, or youth organization.

(8) An administrator or employee of a public or private organization whose duties require direct contact and supervision of children.

(9) Any employee of a county office of education or the California Department of Education, whose duties bring the employee into contact with children on a regular basis.

(10) A licensee, an administrator, or an employee of a licensed community care or child day care facility.

(11) A headstart teacher.

(12) A licensing worker or licensing evaluator employed by a licensing agency as defined in Section 11165.11.

(13) A public assistance worker.

(14) An employee of a child care institution, including, but not limited to, foster parents, group home personnel, and personnel of residential care facilities.

(15) A social worker, probation officer, or parole officer.

(16) An employee of a school district police or security department.

(17) Any person who is an administrator or presenter of, or a counselor in, a child abuse prevention program in any public or private school.

(18) A district attorney investigator, inspector, or family support officer unless the investigator, inspector, or officer is working with an attorney appointed pursuant to Section 317 of the Welfare and Institutions Code to represent a minor.

(19) A peace officer, as defined in Chapter 4.5 (commencing with Section 830) of Title 3 of Part 2, who is not otherwise described in this section.

(20) A firefighter, except for *** volunteer firefighters.

(21) A physician, surgeon, psychiatrist, psychologist, dentist, resident, intern, podiatrist, chiropractor, licensed nurse, dental hygienist, optometrist, marriage, family and child counselor, clinical social worker, or any other person who is currently licensed under Division 2 (commencing with Section 500) of the Business and Professions Code.

(22) Any emergency medical technician I or II, paramedic, or other person certified pursuant to Division 2.5 (commencing with Section 1797) of the Health and Safety Code.

(23) A psychological assistant registered pursuant to Section 2913 of the Business and Professions Code.

(24) A marriage, family and child therapist trainee, as defined in subdivision (c) of Section 4980.03 of the Business and Professions Code.

(25) An unlicensed marriage, family, and child therapist intern registered under Section 4980.44 of the Business and Professions Code.

(26) A state or county public health employee who treats a minor for venereal disease or any other condition.

(27) A coroner.

(28) A medical examiner, or any other person who performs autopsies.

(29) A commercial film and photographic print processor, as specified in subdivision (e) of Section 11166. As used in this article, "commercial film and photographic print processor" means any person who develops exposed photographic film into negatives, slides, or prints, or who makes prints from negatives or slides, for compensation. The term includes any employee of such a person; it does not include a person who develops film or makes prints for a public agency.

(30) A child visitation monitor. As used in this article, "child visitation monitor" means any person who, for financial compensation, acts as monitor of a visit between a child and any other person when the monitoring of that visit has been ordered by a court of law.

(31) An animal control officer or humane society officer. For the purposes of this article, the following terms have the following meanings:

(A) "Animal control officer" means any person employed by a city, county, or city and county for the purpose of enforcing animal control laws or regulations.

(B) "Humane society officer" means any person appointed or employed by a public or private entity as a humane officer who is qualified pursuant to Section 14502 or 14503 of the Corporations Code.

(32) A clergy member, as specified in subdivision (c) of Section 11166. As used in this article, "clergy member" means a priest, minister, rabbi, religious practitioner, or similar functionary of a church, temple, or recognized denomination or organization.

(33) Any employee of any police department, county sheriff's department, county probation department, or county welfare department.

(34) An employee or volunteer of a Court Appointed Special Advocate program, as defined in Rule 1424 of the Rules of Court.

(b) Volunteers of public or private organizations whose duties require direct contact and supervision of children are encouraged to obtain training in the identification and reporting of child abuse.

(c) Training in the duties imposed by this article shall include training in child abuse identification and training in child abuse reporting. As part of that training, school districts shall provide to all employees being trained a written copy of the reporting requirements and a written disclosure of the employees' confidentiality rights.

(d) School districts that do not train *** their employees specified in subdivision (a) in the duties of *** mandated reporters under the child abuse reporting laws shall report to the State Department of Education the reasons why this training is not provided.

(e) The absence of training shall not excuse a mandated reporter from the duties imposed by this article. *(AM '01)*

11165.8. Health Practitioner Defined [Repealed Stats. 2000]

11165.9. Where Reports Are to be Made; Processing by Receiving Agency

Reports of suspected child abuse or neglect shall be made by mandated reporters to any police department*** or sheriff's department, not including a school district police or security department, county probation department, if designated by the county to receive mandated reports, or the county welfare department.*** Any of those agencies shall accept a report of suspected child abuse or neglect whether offered by a mandated reporter or another person, or *** referred by another agency, even if the agency to whom the report is being made lacks subject matter or geographical jurisdiction to investigate the reported case, unless the agency can immediately electronically transfer the call to an agency with proper jurisdiction. When an agency takes a report about a case of suspected child abuse or neglect in which that agency lacks jurisdiction, the agency shall immediately refer the case by telephone, fax, or electronic transmission to an agency with proper jurisdiction. *(AM '01)*

11165.10. Commercial Film and Photographic Print Processor Defined c

11165.11. Licensing Agency Defined

As used in this article, "licensing agency" means the State Department of Social Services office responsible for the licensing and enforcement of the California Community Care Facilities Act (Chapter 3 of Division 2 of the Health and Safety Code), the California Child Day Care Act (Chapter 3.4 of Division 2 of the Health and Safety Code), and Chapter 3.5 of Division 2 of the Health and Safety Code), or the county licensing agency which has contracted with the state for performance of those duties.

11165.12. Unfounded Report" Defined

As used in this article, the following definitions shall control:

(a) "Unfounded report" means a report which is determined by the investigator who conducted the investigation to be false, to be inherently improbable, to involve an accidental injury, or not to constitute child abuse or neglect, as defined in Section 11165.6.

(b) "Substantiated report" means a report which is determined by the investigator who conducted the investigation, based upon some credible evidence, to constitute child abuse or neglect, as defined in Section 11165.6.

(c) "Inconclusive report"means a report which is determined by the investigator who conducted the investigation not to be unfounded, but in which the findings are inconclusive and there is insufficient evidence to determine whether child abuse or neglect, as defined in Section 11165.6, has occurred. *(AM '00)*

11165.15. Child Visitation Monitor" Defined [Repealed Stats. 2000]

11165.16 Animal Control, Humane Society Officer Defined [Repealed Stats. 2000]

11166. Persons Authorized or Required to Report Child Abuse; Method of Reporting

(a) Except as provided in subdivision (c), a mandated reporter shall make a report to an agency specified in Section 11165.9 whenever the mandated reporter, in his or her professional capacity or within the scope of his or her employment, has knowledge of or observes a child whom the mandated reporter knows or reasonably suspects has been the victim of child abuse or neglect. The mandated reporter shall make a report to the agency immediately or as soon as is practicably possible by telephone, and the mandated reporter shall prepare and send a written report thereof within 36 hours of receiving the information concerning the incident.

(1) For the purposes of this article, "reasonable suspicion"means that it is objectively reasonable for a person to entertain a suspicion, based upon facts that could cause a reasonable person in a like position, drawing, when appropriate, on his or her training and experience, to suspect child abuse or neglect. For the purpose of this article, the pregnancy of a minor does not, in and of itself, constitute a basis for a reasonable suspicion of sexual abuse.

(2) The agency shall be notified and a report shall be prepared and sent even if the child has expired, regardless of whether or not the possible abuse was a factor contributing to the death, and even if suspected child abuse was discovered during an autopsy.

(3) A report made by a mandated reporter pursuant to this section shall be known as a mandated report.

(b) Any mandated reporter who fails to report an incident of known or reasonably suspected child abuse or neglect as required by this section is guilty of a misdemeanor punishable by up to six months confinement in a county jail or by a fine of one thousand dollars ($1,000) or by both that fine and punishment.

(c)(1) A clergy member who acquires knowledge or a reasonable suspicion of child abuse or neglect during a penitential communication is not subject to subdivision (a). For the purposes of this subdivision, "penitential communication"means a communication, intended to be in confidence, including, but not limited to, a sacramental confession, made to a clergy member who, in the course of the discipline or practice of his or her church, denomination, or organization, is authorized or accustomed to hear those communications, and under the discipline, tenets, customs, or practices of his or her church, denomination, or organization, has a duty to keep those communications secret.

(2) Nothing in this subdivision shall be construed to modify or limit a clergy member's duty to report known or suspected child abuse or neglect when the clergy member is acting in some other capacity that would otherwise make the clergy member a mandated reporter.

(d) Any commercial film and photographic print processor who has knowledge of or observes, within the scope of his or her professional capacity or employment, any film, photograph, videotape, negative, or slide depicting a child under the age of 16 years engaged in an act of sexual conduct, shall report the instance of suspected child abuse to the law enforcement agency having jurisdiction over the case immediately, or as soon as practically possible, by telephone, and shall prepare and send a written report of it with a copy of the film, photograph, videotape, negative, or slide attached within 36 hours of receiving the information concerning the incident. As used in this subdivision, "sexual conduct"means any of the following:

(1) Sexual intercourse, including genital-genital, oral-genital, anal-genital, or oral-anal, whether between persons of the same or opposite sex or between humans and animals.

(2) Penetration of the vagina or rectum by any object.

(3) Masturbation for the purpose of sexual stimulation of the viewer.

(4) Sadomasochistic abuse for the purpose of sexual stimulation of the viewer.

(5) Exhibition of the genitals, pubic, or rectal areas of any person for the purpose of sexual stimulation of the viewer.

(e) Any other person who has knowledge of or observes a child whom he or she knows or reasonably suspects has been a victim of child abuse or neglect may report the known or suspected instance of child abuse or neglect to an agency specified in Section 11165.9.

(f) When two or more persons, who are required to report, jointly have knowledge of a known or suspected instance of child abuse or neglect, and when there is agreement among them, the telephone report may be made by a member of the team selected by mutual agreement and a single report may be made and signed by the selected member of the reporting team. Any member who has knowledge that the member designated to report has failed to do so shall thereafter make the report.

(g)(1) The reporting duties under this section are individual, and no supervisor or administrator may impede or inhibit the reporting duties, and no person making a report shall be subject to any sanction for making the report. However, internal procedures to facilitate reporting and apprise supervisors and administrators of reports may be established provided that they are not inconsistent with this article.

(2) The internal procedures shall not require any employee required to make reports pursuant to this article to disclose his or her identity to the employer.

(3) Reporting the information regarding a case of possible child abuse or neglect to an employer, supervisor, school principal, school counselor, *** coworker, or other person shall not be a substitute for making a mandated report to an agency specified in Section 11165.9.

(h) A county probation or welfare department shall immediately, or as soon as practically possible, report by telephone, fax, or *** electronic transmission to the law enforcement agency having jurisdiction over the case, to the agency given the responsibility for investigation of cases under Section 300 of the Welfare and Institutions Code, and to the district attorney's office every known or suspected instance of child abuse or neglect, as defined in Section 11165.6, except acts or omissions coming within subdivision (b) of Section 11165.2, or reports made pursuant to Section 11165.13 based on risk to a child which relates solely to the inability of the parent to provide the child with regular care due to the parent's substance abuse, which shall be reported only to the county welfare or probation department. A county probation or welfare department also shall send, fax, or electronically transmit a written report thereof within 36 hours of receiving the information concerning the incident to any agency to which it *** makes a telephone report under this subdivision. ***

(i) A law enforcement agency shall immediately, or as soon as practically possible, report by telephone to the agency given responsibility for investigation of cases under Section 300 of the Welfare and Institutions Code and to the district attorney's office every known or suspected instance of child abuse or neglect reported to it, except acts or omissions coming within subdivision (b) of Section 11165.2, which shall be reported only to the county welfare or probation department. A law enforcement agency shall report to the county welfare or probation department every known or suspected instance of child abuse or neglect reported to it which is alleged to have occurred as a result of the action of a person responsible for the child's welfare, or as the result of the failure of a person responsible for the child's welfare to adequately protect the minor from abuse when the person responsible for the child's welfare knew or reasonably should have known that the minor was in danger of abuse. A law enforcement agency also shall send, fax, or electronically transmit a written report thereof within 36 hours of receiving the information concerning the incident to any agency to which it *** makes a telephone report under this subdivision. *(AM '01)*

11166.1. Report of Child Abuse - Notification of Licensing Office Within 24 Hours

(a) When an agency receives a report pursuant to Section 11166 that contains either of the following, it shall, within 24 hours, notify the licensing office with jurisdiction over the facility:

(1) A report of abuse alleged to have occurred in facilities licensed to care for children by the State Department of Social Services.

(2) A report of the death of a child who was, at the time of death, living at, enrolled in, or regularly attending a facility licensed to care for children by the State Department of Social Services, unless the circumstances of the child's death are clearly unrelated to the child's care at the facility.

The agency shall send the licensing agency a copy of its investigation and any other pertinent materials.

(b) Any employee of an agency specified in Section 11165.9 who has knowledge of, or observes in his or her professional capacity or within the scope of his or her employment, a child in protective custody whom he or she knows or reasonably suspects has been the victim of child abuse or neglect shall, within 36 hours, send or have sent to the attorney who represents the child in dependency court, a copy of the report prepared in accordance with Section 11166. The agency shall maintain a copy of the written report. All information requested by the attorney for the child or the child's guardian ad litem shall be provided by the agency within 30 days of the request. *(AM '98, '00)*

11166.2. Immediate Telephone Report by Child Protective Agency

In addition to the reports required under Section 11166, any agency specified in Section 11165.9 shall immediately or as soon as practically possible report by telephone, fax, or electronic transmission to the appropriate licensing agency every known or suspected instance of child abuse or neglect when the instance of abuse or neglect occurs while the child is being cared for in a child day care facility, involves a child day care licensed staff person, or occurs while the child is under the supervision of a community care facility or involves a community care facility licensee or staff person. The agency shall also send, fax, or electronically transmit a written report thereof within 36 hours of receiving the information concerning the incident to any agency to which it *** makes a telephone report under this subdivision. The agency shall send the licensing agency a copy of its investigation report and any other pertinent materials. *(AM '01)*

11167. Information Contained in Child Abuse Reports; Identity of Informant Confidential

(a) Reports of suspected child abuse or neglect pursuant to Section 11166 shall include, if known, the name, business address, and telephone number of the mandated reporter, and the capacity that makes the person a mandated reporter; the child's name and address, present location, and, where applicable, school, grade, and class; the names, addresses, and telephone numbers of the child's parents or guardians; the information that gave rise to the reasonable suspicion of child abuse or neglect and the source or sources of that information; and the name, address, telephone number, and other relevant personal information about the person or persons who might have abused or neglected the child. The mandated reporter shall make a report even if some of this information is not known or is uncertain to him or her.

(b) Information relevant to the incident of child abuse or neglect may *** be given to an investigator from an agency that is investigating the known or suspected case of child abuse or neglect.

(c) Information relevant to the incident of child abuse or neglect, including the investigation report and other pertinent materials, may be given to the licensing agency when it is investigating a known or suspected case of child abuse or neglect.

(d)(1) The identity of all persons who report under this article shall be confidential and disclosed only among agencies receiving or investigating mandated reports, to the district attorney in a criminal prosecution or in an action initiated under Section 602 of the Welfare and Institutions Code arising from alleged child abuse, or to counsel appointed pursuant to subdivision (c) of Section 317 of the Welfare and Institutions Code, or to the county counsel or district attorney in a proceeding under Part 4 (commencing with Section 7800) of Division 12 of the Family Code or Section 300 of the Welfare and Institutions Code, or to a licensing agency when abuse or neglect in out-of-home care is reasonably suspected, or when those persons waive confidentiality, or by court order.

(2) No agency or person listed in this subdivision shall disclose the identity of any person who reports under this article to that person's employer, except with the employee's consent or by court order.

(e) Persons who may report pursuant to subdivision ***(e) of Section 11166 are not required to include their names. *(AM '01)*

11167.5. Confidential Reports Required by 11166 and 11166.2 - Disclosure

(a) The reports required by Sections 11166 and 11166.2 shall be confidential and may be disclosed only as provided in subdivision (b). Any violation of the confidentiality provided by this article is a misdemeanor punishable by imprisonment in a county jail not to exceed six months, by a fine of five hundred dollars ($500), or by both that imprisonment and fine.

(b) Reports of suspected child abuse or neglect and information contained therein may be disclosed only to the following:

(1) Persons or agencies to whom disclosure of the identity of the reporting party is permitted under Section 11167.

(2) Persons or agencies to whom disclosure of information is permitted under subdivision (b) of Section 11170.

(3) Persons or agencies with whom investigations of child abuse or neglect are coordinated under the regulations promulgated under Section 11174.

(4) Multidisciplinary personnel teams as defined in subdivision (d) of Section 18951 of the Welfare and Institutions Code.

(5) Persons or agencies responsible for the licensing of facilities which care for children, as specified in Section 11165.7.

(6) The State Department of Social Services or any county licensing agency which has contracted with the state, as specified in paragraph (3) of subdivision (b) of Section 11170, when an individual has applied for a community care license or child day care license, or for employment in an out-of-home care facility, or when a complaint alleges child abuse or neglect by an operator or employee of an out-of-home care facility.

(7) Hospital scan teams. As used in this paragraph, "hospital scan team" means a team of three or more persons established by a hospital, or two or more hospitals in the same county, consisting of health care professionals and representatives of law enforcement and child protective services, the members of which are engaged in the identification of child abuse or neglect. The disclosure authorized by this section includes disclosure among all hospital scan teams.

(8) Coroners and medical examiners when conducting a postmortem examination of a child.

(9) The Board of Prison Terms, who may subpoena an employee of a county welfare department who can provide relevant evidence and reports that both (A) are not unfounded, pursuant to Section 11165.12, and (B) concern only the current incidents upon which parole revocation proceedings are pending against a parolee charged with child abuse or neglect. The reports and information shall be confidential pursuant to subdivision (d) of Section 11167.

(10) Personnel from an agency responsible for making a placement of a child pursuant to Section 361.3 of, and Article 7 (commencing with Section 305) of Chapter 2 of Part 1 of Division 2 of, the Welfare and Institutions Code.

(11) Persons who have been identified by the Department of Justice as listed in the Child Abuse Central Index pursuant to subdivision (c) of Section 11170. Nothing in this paragraph shall preclude a submitting agency prior to disclosure from redacting the name, address, and telephone number of a witness, person who reports under this article, or victim in order to maintain confidentiality as required by law.

(12) Out-of-state law enforcement agencies conducting an investigation of child abuse or neglect only when an agency makes the request for reports of suspected child abuse or neglect in writing and on official letterhead, identifying the suspected abuser or victim by name. The request shall be signed by the department supervisor of the requesting law enforcement agency. The written request shall cite the out-of-state statute or interstate compact provision that requires that the information contained within these reports is to be disclosed only to law enforcement, prosecutorial entities, or multidisciplinary investigative teams, and shall cite the criminal penalties for unlawful disclosure provided by the requesting state or the applicable interstate compact provision. In the absence of both (1) a specific out-of-state statute or interstate compact provision that requires that the information contained within these reports be disclosed only to law enforcement, prosecutorial entities, or multidisciplinary investigative teams, and (2) criminal penalties equivalent to the penalties in California for unlawful disclosure, access shall be denied.

(13) Persons who have verified with the Department of Justice that they are listed in the Child Abuse Central Index as provided by subdivision (e) of Section 11170. Disclosure under this section shall be subject to the California Public Records Act (Chapter 3.5 (commencing with Section 6250) of Division 7 of Title 1 of the Government Code). Nothing in this section prohibits a submitting agency prior to disclosure from redacting the name, address, and telephone number of a witness, person who reports under this article, or victim to maintain confidentiality as required by law.

(14) Each chairperson of a county child death review team, or his or her designee, to whom disclosure of information is permitted under this article, relating to the death of one or more children and any prior child abuse or neglect investigation reports maintained involving the same victim, siblings, or suspects. Local child death review teams may share any relevant information regarding case reviews involving child death with other child death review teams.

(c) Authorized persons within county health departments shall be permitted to receive copies of any reports made by health practitioners, as defined in Section 11165.8, pursuant to Section 11165.13, and copies of assessments completed pursuant to Sections 123600 and 123605 of the Health and Safety Code, to the extent permitted by federal law. Any information received pursuant to this subdivision is protected by subdivision (e).

(d) Nothing in this section requires the Department of Justice to disclose information contained in records maintained under Section 11169 or under the regulations promulgated pursuant to Section 11174, except as otherwise provided in this article.

(e) This section shall not be interpreted to allow disclosure of any reports or records relevant to the reports of child abuse or neglect if the disclosure would be prohibited by any other provisions of state or federal law applicable to the reports or records relevant to the reports of child abuse or neglect. *(AM '98, '00)*

11172. No Liability for Reporting Known or Suspected Child Abuse; Failure to Report Child Abuse

(a) No mandated reporter *** shall be civilly or criminally liable for any report required or authorized by this article. Any other person reporting a known or suspected instance of child abuse or neglect shall not incur civil or criminal liability as a result of any report authorized by this article unless it can be proven that a false report was made and the person knew that the report was false or was made with reckless disregard of the truth or falsity of the report, and any person who makes a report of child abuse or neglect known to be false or with reckless disregard of the truth or falsity of the report is liable for any damages caused. No person required to make a report pursuant to this article, nor any person taking photographs at his or her direction, shall incur any civil or criminal liability for taking photographs of a suspected victim of child abuse or neglect, or causing photographs to be taken of a suspected victim of child abuse or neglect, without parental consent, or for disseminating the photographs with the reports required by this article. However, this section shall not be construed to grant immunity from this liability with respect to any other use of the photographs.

(b) Any person, who, pursuant to a request from a government agency investigating a report of suspected child abuse or neglect, provides the requesting agency with access to the victim of a known or suspected instance of child abuse or neglect shall not incur civil or criminal liability as a result of providing that access.

(c) The Legislature finds that even though it has provided immunity from liability to persons required *** or authorized to make reports pursuant to this article, that immunity does not eliminate the possibility that actions may be brought against those persons based upon required or authorized reports ***. In order to further limit the financial hardship that those persons may incur as a result of fulfilling their legal responsibilities, it is necessary that they not be unfairly burdened by legal fees incurred in defending those actions. Therefore, a mandated reporter may present a claim to the State Board of Control for reasonable attorney's fees and costs incurred in any action against that person on the basis of making a report required or authorized by this article if the court has dismissed the action upon a demurrer or motion for summary judgment made by that person, or if he or she prevails in the action. The State Board of Control shall allow that claim if the requirements of this subdivision are met, and the claim shall be paid from an appropriation to be made for that purpose. Attorney's fees awarded pursuant to this section shall not exceed an hourly rate greater than the rate charged by the Attorney General of the State of California at the time the award is made and shall not exceed an aggregate amount of fifty thousand dollars ($50,000).

This subdivision shall not apply if a public entity has provided for the defense of the action pursuant to Section 995 of the Government Code.

(d) A court may award attorney's fees and costs to a commercial film and photographic print processor when a suit is brought against the processor because of a disclosure mandated by this article and the court finds this suit to be frivolous.

***

(AM '01)

11174.3. Interview of Suspected Child Abuse Victim on School Premises

(a) Whenever a representative of a government agency investigating suspected child abuse or neglect or the State Department of Social Services deems it necessary, a suspected victim of child abuse or neglect may be interviewed during school hours, on school premises, concerning a report of suspected child abuse or neglect that occurred within the child's home or out-of-home care facility. The child shall be afforded the option of being interviewed in private or selecting any adult who is a member of the staff of the school, including any certificated or classified employee or volunteer aide, to be present at the interview. A representative of the agency investigating suspected child abuse or neglect or the State Department of Social Services shall inform the child of that right prior to the interview.

The purpose of the staff person's presence at the interview is to lend support to the child and enable him or her to be as comfortable as possible. However, the member of the staff so elected shall not participate in the interview. The member of the staff so present shall not discuss the facts or circumstances of the case with the child. The member of the staff so present, including, but not limited to, a volunteer aide, is subject to the confidentiality requirements of this article, a violation of which is punishable as specified in Section 11167.5. A representative of the school shall inform a member of the staff so selected by a child of the requirements of this section prior to the interview. A staff member selected by a child may decline the request to be present at the interview. If the staff person selected agrees to be present, the interview shall be held at a time during school hours when it does not involve an expense to the school. Failure to comply with the requirements of this section does not affect the admissibility of evidence in a criminal or civil proceeding.

(b) The Superintendent of Public Instruction shall notify each school district and each agency specified in Section 11165.9 to receive mandated reports, and the State Department of Social Services shall notify each of its employees who participate in the investigation of reports of child abuse or neglect, of the requirements of this section. *(AM '98, '00)*

11411. Terrorizing

(a) Any person who places or displays a sign, mark, symbol, emblem, or other physical impression, including, but not limited to, a Nazi swastika on the private property of another, without authorization, for the purpose of terrorizing the owner or occupant of that private property or in reckless disregard of the risk of terrorizing the owner or occupant of that private property shall be punished by imprisonment in the county jail not to exceed one year, by a fine not to exceed five thousand dollars ($5,000), or by both the fine and imprisonment for the first conviction and by imprisonment in the county jail not to exceed one year, by a fine not to exceed fifteen thousand dollars ($15,000), or by both the fine and imprisonment for any subsequent conviction.

(b) Any person who engages in a pattern of conduct for the purpose of terrorizing the owner or occupant of private property or in reckless disregard of terrorizing the owner or occupant of that private property, by placing or displaying a sign, mark, symbol, emblem, or other physical impression, including, but not limited to, a Nazi swastika, on the private property of another on two or more occasions, shall be punished by imprisonment in the state prison for 16 months or 2 or 3 years, by a fine not to exceed ten thousand dollars ($10,000), or by both the fine and imprisonment, or by imprisonment in a county jail not to exceed one year, by a fine not to exceed five thousand dollars ($5,000), or by both the fine and imprisonment. A violation of this subdivision shall not constitute felonious conduct for purposes of Section 186.22.

(c) Any person who burns or desecrates a cross or other religious symbol, knowing it to be a religious symbol, on the private property of another without authorization for the purpose of terrorizing the owner or occupant of that private property or in reckless disregard of the risk of terrorizing the owner or occupant of that private property, or who burns, desecrates, or destroys a cross or other religious symbol, knowing it to be a religious symbol, on the property of a primary school, junior high school, or high school for the purpose of terrorizing any person who attends or works at the school or who is otherwise associated with the school, shall be punished by imprisonment in the state prison for 16 months or 2 or 3 years, by a fine of not more than ten thousand dollars ($10,000), or by both the fine and imprisonment, or by imprisonment in a county jail not to exceed one year, by a fine not to exceed five thousand dollars ($5,000), or by both the fine and imprisonment for the first conviction and by imprisonment in the state prison for 16 months or 2 or 3 years, by a fine of not more than ten thousand dollars ($10,000), or by both the fine and imprisonment, or by imprisonment in a county jail not to exceed one year, by a fine not to exceed fifteen thousand dollars ($15,000), or by both the fine and imprisonment for any subsequent conviction.

(d) As used in this section, "terrorize"means to cause a person of ordinary emotions and sensibilities to fear for personal safety.

(e) The provisions of this section are severable. If any provision of this section or its application is held invalid, that invalidity shall not affect other provisions or applications that can be given effect without the invalid provision or application. *(AM '98)*

11412. Religious Terrorism

Any person who, with intent to cause, attempts to cause or causes another to refrain from exercising his or her religion or from engaging in a religious service by means of a threat, directly communicated to such person, to inflict an unlawful injury upon any person or property, and it reasonably appears to the recipient of the threat that such threat could be carried out is guilty of a felony.

11413. Use of Explosives in Acts of Terrorism in Specified Places

(a) Any person who explodes, ignites, or attempts to explode or ignite any destructive device or any explosive, or who commits arson, in or about any of the places listed in subdivision (b), for the purpose of terrorizing another or in reckless disregard of terrorizing another is guilty of a felony, and shall be punished by imprisonment in the state prison for three, five, or seven years, and a fine not exceeding ten thousand dollars ($10,000).

(b) Subdivision (a) applies to the following places:

(1) Any health facility licensed under Chapter 2 (commencing with Section 1250) of Division 2 of the Health and Safety Code, or any place where medical care is provided by a licensed health care professional.

(2) Any church, temple, synagogue, or other place of worship.

(3) The buildings, offices, and meeting sites of organizations that counsel for or against abortion or among whose major activities are lobbying, publicizing, or organizing with respect to public or private issues relating to abortion.

(4) Any place at which a lecture, film-showing, or other private meeting or presentation that educates or propagates with respect to abortion practices or policies, whether on private property or at a meeting site authorized for specific use by a private group on public property, is taking place.

(5) Any bookstore or public or private library.

(6) Any building or facility designated as a courthouse.

(7) The home or office of a judicial officer.

(8) Any building or facility regularly occupied by county probation department personnel in which the employees perform official duties of the probation department.

(9) Any private property, if the property was targeted because of the race, color, religion, ancestry, national origin, disability, gender, or sexual orientation of the owner or occupant of the property.

(10) Any public or private school providing instruction in kindergarten or grades 1 to 12, inclusive.

(c) As used in this section, "judicial officer"means a magistrate, judge, justice, commissioner, referee, or any person appointed by a court to serve in one of these capacities, of any state or federal court located in this state.

(d) As used in this section, "terrorizing"means to cause a person of ordinary emotions and sensibilities to fear for personal safety.

(e) Nothing in this section shall be construed to prohibit the prosecution of any person pursuant to Section 12303.3 or any other provision of law in lieu of prosecution pursuant to this section.

11414. Harass Child Due To Parent's Employment

(a) Any person who intentionally harasses the child or ward of any other person because of that person's employment, is guilty of a misdemeanor.

(b) For purposes of this section, the following definitions shall apply:

(1) "Child"and "ward"mean a person under the age of 16 years.

(2) "Harasses"means knowing and willful conduct directed at a specific child that seriously alarms, annoys, torments, or terrorizes the child, and that serves no legitimate purpose. The conduct must be such as would cause a reasonable child to suffer substantial emotional distress, and actually cause the victim to suffer substantial emotional distress.

(c) A second conviction under this section shall be punished by imprisonment in a county jail for not less than five days. A third or subsequent conviction under this section shall be punished by imprisonment in a county jail for not less than 30 days.

The Hertzberg-Alarcon California Prevention of Terrorism Act

11415. Article Title

This article shall be known and may be cited as the Hertzberg-Alarcon California Prevention of Terrorism Act. *(AD '99)*

11416. Legislative Finding and Declaration

The Legislature hereby finds and declares that the threat of terrorism involving weapons of mass destruction, including, but not limited to, chemical, biological, nuclear, or radiological agents, is a significant public safety concern. The Legislature also recognizes that terrorism involving weapons of mass destruction could result in an intentional disaster placing residents of California in great peril. The Legislature also finds it necessary to sanction the possession, manufacture, use, or threatened use of chemical, biological, nuclear, or radiological weapons, as well as the intentional use or threatened use of industrial or commercial chemicals as weapons against persons or animals. *(AD '99)*

11417. Definitions

(a) For the purposes of this article, the following terms have the following meanings:

(1) "Weapon of mass destruction"includes chemical warfare agents, weaponized biological or biologic warfare agents, nuclear agents, radiological agents, or the intentional release of industrial agents as a weapon.

(2) "Chemical Warfare Agents"includes, but is not limited to, the following weaponized agents, or any analog of these agents:

(A) Nerve agents, including Tabun (GA), Sarin (GB), Soman (GD), GF, and VX.

(B) Choking agents, including Phosgene (CG) and Diphosgene (DP).

(C) Blood agents, including Hydrogen Cyanide (AC), Cyanogen Chloride (CK), and Arsine (SA).

(D) Blister agents, including mustards (H, HD (sulfur mustard), HN-1, HN-2, HN-3 (nitrogen mustard)), arsenicals, such as Lewisite (L), urticants, such as CX; and incapacitating agents, such as BZ.

(3) "Weaponized biological or biologic warfare agents"include weaponized pathogens, such as bacteria, viruses, rickettsia, yeasts, fungi, or genetically engineered pathogens, toxins, vectors, and endogenous biological regulators (EBRs).

(4) "Nuclear or radiological agents"includes any improvised nuclear device (IND) which is any explosive device designed to cause a nuclear yield; any radiological dispersal device (RDD) which is any explosive device utilized to spread radioactive material; or a simple radiological dispersal device (SRDD) which is any act or container designed to release radiological material as a weapon without an explosion.

(5) "Vector"means a living organism or a molecule, including a recombinant molecule, or a biological product that may be engineered as a result of biotechnology, that is capable of carrying a biological agent or toxin to a host.

(6) "Weaponization"is the deliberate processing, preparation, packaging, or synthesis of any substance for use as a weapon or munition. "Weaponized agents"are those agents or substances prepared for dissemination through any explosive, thermal, pneumatic, or mechanical means.

(b) The intentional release of a dangerous chemical or hazardous material generally utilized in an industrial or commercial process shall be considered use of a weapon of mass destruction when a person knowingly utilizes those agents with the intent to cause harm and the use places persons or animals at risk of serious injury, illness, or death, or endangers the environment.

(c) The lawful use of chemicals for legitimate mineral extraction, industrial, agricultural, or commercial purposes is not proscribed by this article.

(d) No university, research institution, private company, individual, or hospital engaged in scientific or public health research and, as required, registered with the Centers for Disease Control and Prevention (CDC) pursuant to Part 113 (commencing with Section 113.1) of Subchapter E of Chapter 1 of Title 9 or pursuant to Part 72 (commencing with Section 72.1) of Subchapter E of Chapter 1 of Title 42 of the Code of Federal Regulations, or any successor provisions, shall be subject to this article. *(AD '99)*

11418. Weapon of Mass Destruction; Possession, Development, Production, etc.; Punishment

(a)(1) Any person, without lawful authority, who possesses, develops, manufactures, produces, transfers, acquires, or retains any weapon of mass destruction, shall be *** punished by imprisonment in the state prison for 3, 6, or 9 years***.

(2) Any person who commits a violation of paragraph (1) and who has been previously convicted of Section 11411, 11412, 11413, 11460, 12303.1, 12303.2, or 12303.3 shall be punished by imprisonment in the state prison for *** 4, 8, or 12 years.

(b)(1) Any person who uses or directly employs against another person a weapon of mass destruction in a form that may cause widespread, disabling illness, or injury in human beings shall be punished by ***imprisonment in the state prison for life.

(2) Any person who uses a weapon of mass destruction in a form that may cause widespread damage to and disruption of the water or food supply shall be punished by imprisonment in the state prison for *** 4, 8, or 12 years, and by a fine of not more than one hundred thousand dollars ($100,000).

(3) Any person who maliciously uses against animals or crops a weapon of mass destruction in a form that may cause widespread damage to and substantial diminution in the value of stock animals or crops shall be punished by a fine of not more than one hundred thousand dollars ($100,000), or by imprisonment in the state prison for 4, 8, or 12 years, or *** by both that fine and imprisonment.

(c) Any person who uses a weapon of mass destruction in a form that may cause widespread and significant damage to public natural resources, including coastal waterways and beaches, public parkland, surface waters, ground water, and wildlife, shall be punished by imprisonment in the state prison for 3, 4, or 6 years.

(d) Any person who uses recombinant technology or any other biological advance to create new pathogens or more virulent forms of existing pathogens for the purposes specified in this section, shall be punished by imprisonment in a county jail for up to one year or in the state prison for 3, 6, or 9 years, or by a fine of not more than two hundred fifty thousand dollars ($250,000), or by both that fine and imprisonment.

(e) Nothing in this section shall be construed to prevent punishment instead pursuant to any other provision of law that imposes a greater or more severe punishment. *(AM '01)*

11418.5. Weapon of Mass Destruction; Threaten to Use; Sustained Fear Defined

(a) Any person who knowingly threatens to use a weapon of mass destruction, with the specific intent that the statement, made verbally, in writing, or by means of an electronic communication device, is to be taken as a threat, even if there is no intent of actually carrying it out, which, on its face and under the circumstances in which it is made, is so unequivocal, immediate, and specific as to convey to the person threatened, a gravity of purpose and an immediate prospect of execution of the threat, and thereby causes that person reasonably to be in sustained fear for his or her own safety, or for his or her immediate family's safety, which results in an isolation, quarantine, or decontamination effort, shall be punished by imprisonment in a county jail for up to one year or in the state prison for 3, 4, or 6 years, or by a fine of not more than two hundred fifty thousand dollars ($250,000), or by both that fine and imprisonment.

(b) For the purposes of this section, "sustained fear" can be established by, but is not limited to, conduct such as evacuation of any building by any occupant, evacuation of any school by any employee or student, evacuation of any home by any resident or occupant, or any other action taken in direct response to the threat to use a weapon of mass destruction.

(c) The fact that the person who allegedly violated this section did not actually possess a biological agent, toxin, or chemical weapon does not constitute a defense to the crime specified in this section.

(d) Nothing in this section shall be construed to prevent punishment instead pursuant to any other provision of law that imposes a greater or more severe punishment. *(AD '99)*

11419. Possession of Restricted Biological Agents; Penalty

(a) Any person or entity possessing any of the restricted biological agents enumerated in subdivision (b) shall be punished by a fine of not more than two hundred fifty thousand dollars ($250,000), imprisonment in the state prison for 4, 8, or 12 years, or by both that fine and imprisonment.

(b) For the purposes of this section, "restricted biological agents" means the following:

(1) Viruses: Crimean-Congo hemorrhagic fever virus, eastern equine encephalitis virus, ebola viruses, equine morbilli virus, lassa fever virus, marburg virus, Rift Valley fever virus, South African hemorrhagic fever viruses (Junin, Machupo, Sabia, Flexal, Guanarito), tick-borne encephalitis complex viruses, variola major virus (smallpox virus), Venezuelan equine encephalitis virus, viruses causing hantavirus pulmonary syndrome, yellow fever virus.

(2) Bacteria: bacillus anthracis (commonly known as anthrax), brucella abortus, brucella melitensis, brucella suis, burkholderia (pseudomonas) mallei, burkholderia (pseudomonas) pseudomallei, clostridium botulinum, francisella tularensis, yersinia pestis (commonly known as plague).

(3) Rickettsiae: coxiella burnetii, rickettsia prowazekii, rickettsia rickettsii.

(4) Fungi: coccidioides immitis.

(5) Toxins: abrin, aflatoxins, botulinum toxins, clostridium perfringens epsilon toxin, conotoxins, diacetoxyscirpenol, ricin, saxitoxin, shigatoxin, staphylococcal enterotoxins, tetrodotoxin, T-2 toxin.

(c)(1) This section shall not apply to any physician, veterinarian, pharmacist, or licensed medical practitioner authorized to dispense a prescription under Section 11026 of the Health and Safety Code, or universities, research institutions, or pharmaceutical corporations, or any person possessing the agents pursuant to a lawful prescription issued by a person defined in Section 11026 of the Health and Safety Code, if the person possesses vaccine strains of the viral agents Junin virus strain #1, Rift Valley fever virus strain MP-12, Venezuelan equine encephalitis virus strain TC-83 and yellow fever virus strain 17-D; any vaccine strain described in Section 78.1 of Subpart A of Part 78 of Subchapter C of Chapter 1 of Title 9 of the Code of Federal Regulations, or any successor provisions, and any toxin for medical use, inactivated for use as vaccines, or toxin preparation for biomedical research use at a median lethal dose for vertebrates of more than 100 ng/kg, as well as any national standard toxin required for biologic potency testing as described in Part 113 (commencing with Section 113.1) of Subchapter E of Chapter 1 of Title 9 of the Code of Federal Regulations, or any successor provisions.

(2) For the purposes of this section, no person shall be deemed to be in possession of an agent if the person is naturally exposed to, or innocently infected or contaminated with, the agent.

(d) Any peace officer who encounters any of the restricted agents mentioned above shall immediately notify and consult with a local public health officer to ensure proper consideration of any public health risk.

(e) Nothing in this section shall be construed to prevent punishment instead pursuant to any other provision of law that imposes a greater or more severe punishment. *(AD '99)*

11460. Participating in Paramilitary Organization

(a) Any two or more persons who assemble as a paramilitary organization for the purpose of practicing with weapons shall be punished by imprisonment in the county jail for not more than one year or by a fine of not more than one thousand dollars ($1,000), or by both.

As used in this subdivision, "paramilitary organization"means an organization which is not an agency of the United States government or of the State of California, or which is not a private school meeting the requirements set forth in Section 12154 of the Education Code, but which engages in instruction or training in guerrilla warfare or sabotage, or which, as an organization, engages in rioting or the violent disruption of, or the violent interference with, school activities.

(b)(1) Any person who teaches or demonstrates to any other person the use, application, or making of any firearm, explosive, or destructive device, or technique capable of causing injury or death to persons, knowing or having reason to know or intending that such objects or techniques will be unlawfully employed for use in, or in the furtherance of a civil disorder, or any person who assembles with one or more other persons for the purpose of training with, practicing with, or being instructed in the use of any firearm, explosive, or destructive device, or technique capable of causing injury or death to persons, with the intent to cause or further a civil disorder, shall be punished by imprisonment in the county jail for not more than one year or by a fine of not more than one thousand dollars ($1,000), or by both.

Nothing in this subdivision shall make unlawful any act of any peace officer or a member of the military forces of this state or of the United States, performed in the lawful course of his official duties.

(2) As used in this section:

(A) "Civil disorder"means any disturbance involving acts of violence which cause an immediate danger of or results in damage or injury to the property or person of any other individual.

(B) "Destructive device"has the same meaning as in Section 12301.

(C) "Explosive"has the same meaning as in Section 12000 of the Health and Safety Code.

(D) "Firearm"means any device designed to be used as a weapon, or which may readily be converted to a weapon, from which is expelled a projectile by the force of any explosion or other form of combustion, or the frame or receiver of any such weapon.

(E) "Peace officer"means any peace officer or other officer having the powers of arrest of a peace officer, specified in Chapter 4.5 of Title 3 of Part 2.

CONTROL OF DEADLY WEAPONS

12001. Firearms Defined

(a)(1) As used in this title, the terms "pistol,""revolver,"and "firearm capable of being concealed upon the person"shall apply to and include any device designed to be used as a weapon, from which is expelled a projectile by the force of any explosion, or other form of combustion, and *** that has a barrel less than 16 inches in length. These terms also include any device that has a barrel 16 inches or more in length which is designed to be interchanged with a barrel less than 16 inches in length.

(2) As used in this title, the term "handgun"means any "pistol,""revolver,"or "firearm capable of being concealed upon the person."

(b) As used in this title, "firearm"means any device, designed to be used as a weapon, from which is expelled through a barrel a projectile by the force of any explosion or other form of combustion.

(c) As used in Sections 12021, 12021.1, 12070, 12071, 12072, 12073, 12078, *** 12101, and 12801 of this code, and Sections 8100, 8101, and 8103 of the Welfare and Institutions Code, the term "firearm"includes the frame or receiver of the weapon.

(d) For the purposes of Sections 12025 and 12031, the term "firearm"also shall include any rocket, rocket propelled projectile launcher, or similar device containing any explosive or incendiary material whether or not the device is designed for emergency or distress signaling purposes.

(e) For purposes of Sections 12070, 12071, and paragraph ***(8) of subdivision (a), and subdivisions (b), (c), (d), and (f) of Section 12072, the term "firearm"does not include an unloaded firearm that is defined as an "antique firearm"in Section 921(a)(16) of Title 18 of the United States Code.

(f) Nothing shall prevent a device defined as a "handgun," "pistol,""revolver,"or "firearm capable of being concealed upon the person"from also being found to be a short-barreled shotgun or a short-barreled rifle, as defined in Section 12020.

(g) For purposes of Sections 12551 and 12552, the term "BB device"means any instrument that expels a metallic projectile, such as a BB or a pellet, through the force of air pressure, CO_2 pressure, or spring action, or any spot marker gun.

(h) As used in this title, "wholesaler"means any person who is licensed as a dealer pursuant to Chapter 44 (commencing with Section 921) of Title 18 of the United States Code and the regulations issued pursuant thereto who sells, transfers, or assigns firearms, or parts of firearms, to persons who are licensed as manufacturers, importers, or gunsmiths pursuant to Chapter 44 (commencing with Section 921) of Title 18 of the United States Code, or persons licensed pursuant to Section 12071, and includes persons who receive finished parts of firearms and assemble them into completed or partially completed firearms in furtherance of that purpose.

"Wholesaler"shall not include a manufacturer, importer, or gunsmith who is licensed to engage in those activities pursuant to Chapter 44 (commencing with Section 921) of Title 18 of the United States Code or a person licensed pursuant to Section 12071 and the regulations issued pursuant thereto. A wholesaler also does not include those persons dealing exclusively in grips, stocks, and other parts of firearms that are not frames or receivers thereof.

(i) As used in Section 12071, 12072, or 12084, "application to purchase"means any of the following:

(1) The initial completion of the register by the purchaser, transferee, or person being loaned the firearm as required by subdivision (b) of Section 12076.

(2) The initial completion of the LEFT by the purchaser, transferee, or person being loaned the firearm as required by subdivision (d) of Section 12084.

(3) The initial completion and transmission to the department of the record of electronic or telephonic transfer by the dealer on the purchaser, transferee, or person being loaned the firearm as required by subdivision (c) of Section 12076.

(j) For purposes of Section 12023, a firearm shall be deemed to be "loaded"whenever both the firearm and the unexpended ammunition capable of being discharged from the firearm are in the immediate possession of the same person.

(k) For purposes of Sections 12021, 12021.1, 12025, 12070, *** 12072, 12073, 12078, *** 12101, and 12801 of this code, and Sections 8100, 8101, and 8103 of the Welfare and Institutions Code, notwithstanding the fact that the term "any firearm"may be used in those sections, each firearm or the frame or receiver of the same shall constitute a distinct and separate offense under those sections.

(l) For purposes of Section 12020, a violation of that section as to each firearm, weapon, or device enumerated therein shall constitute a distinct and separate offense.

(m) Each application that requires any firearms eligibility determination involving the issuance of any license, permit, or certificate pursuant to this title shall include two copies of the applicant's fingerprints on forms prescribed by the Department of Justice. One copy of the fingerprints may be submitted to the United States Federal Bureau of Investigation.

(n) As used in this chapter, a "personal handgun importer"means an individual who meets all of the following criteria:

(1) He or she is not a person licensed pursuant to Section 12071.

(2) He or she is not a licensed manufacturer of firearms pursuant to Chapter 44 (commencing with Section 921) of Title 18 of the United States Code.

(3) He or she is not a licensed importer of firearms pursuant to Chapter 44 (commencing with Section 921) of Title 18 of the United States Code and the regulations issued pursuant thereto.

(4) He or she is the owner of a pistol, revolver, or other firearm capable of being concealed upon the person.

(5) He or she acquired that pistol, revolver, or other firearm capable of being concealed upon the person outside of California.

(6) He or she moves into this state on or after January 1, 1998, as a resident of this state.

(7) He or she intends to possess that pistol, revolver, or other firearm capable of being concealed upon the person within this state on or after January 1, 1998.

(8) The pistol, revolver, or other firearm capable of being concealed upon the person was not delivered to him or her by a person licensed pursuant to Section 12071 who delivered that firearm following the procedures set forth in Section 12071 and subdivision (c) of Section 12072.

(9) He or she, while a resident of this state, had not previously reported his or her ownership of that pistol, revolver, or other firearm capable of being concealed upon the person to the Department of Justice in a manner prescribed by the department that included information concerning him or her and a description of the firearm.

(10) The pistol, revolver, or other firearm capable of being concealed upon the person is not a firearm that is prohibited by subdivision (a) of Section 12020.

(11) The pistol, revolver, or other firearm capable of being concealed upon the person is not an assault weapon, as defined in Section 12276 or 12276.1.

(12) The pistol, revolver, or other firearm capable of being concealed upon the person is not a machinegun, as defined in Section 12200.

(13) The person is 18 years of age or older.

(o) For purposes of paragraph (6) of subdivision (n):

(1) Except as provided in paragraph (2), residency shall be determined in the same manner as is the case for establishing residency pursuant to Section 12505 of the Vehicle Code.

(2) In the case of members of the *** Armed Forces of the United States, residency shall be deemed to be established when he or she was discharged from active service in this state.

(p) As used in this code, "basic firearms safety certificate"means a certificate issued by the Department of Justice pursuant to Article 8 (commencing with Section 12800) of Chapter 6 of Title 2 of Part 4, prior to January 1, 2003.

(q) As used in this code, "handgun safety certificate"means a certificate issued by the Department of Justice pursuant to Article 8 (commencing with Section 12800) of Chapter 6 of Title 2 of Part 4, as that article is operative on or after January 1, 2003. *(AM '01)*

12001.1.   Manufacture, Sale, etc. of Undetectable Knife

(a) Any person in this state who commercially manufactures or causes to be commercially manufactured, or who knowingly imports into the state for commercial sale, keeps for commercial sale, or offers or exposes for commercial sale, any undetectable knife is guilty of a misdemeanor. As used in this section, an "undetectable knife"means any knife or other instrument with or without a handguard that is capable of ready use as a stabbing weapon that may inflict great bodily injury or death that is commercially manufactured to be used as a weapon and is not detectable by a metal detector set at standard calibration.

(b) Notwithstanding any other provision of law, commencing January 1, 2000, all knives or other instrument with or without a handguard that is capable of ready use as a stabbing weapon that may inflict great bodily injury or death that are commercially manufactured in this state that utilize materials that are not detectable by a metal detector shall be manufactured to include materials that will ensure they are detectable by a metal detector set at standard calibration.

(c) This section shall not apply to the manufacture or importation of undetectable knives for sale to a law enforcement or military entity nor shall this section apply to the subsequent sale of these knives to a law enforcement or military entity.

(d) This section shall not apply to the manufacture or importation of undetectable knives for sale to federal, state, and local historical societies, museums, and institutional collections which are open to the public, provided that the undetectable knives are properly housed and secured from unauthorized handling, nor shall this section apply to the subsequent sale of the knives to these societies, museums, and collections. *(AD '99)*

12001.5. Short-Barreled Shotguns and Short-Barreled Rifles

Except as expressly provided in Section 12020, and solely in accordance with Section 12020, no person may manufacture, import into this state, keep for sale, offer for sale, give, lend, or possess any short-barreled shotgun or short-barreled rifle, as defined in Section 12020, and nothing else in this chapter shall be construed as authorizing the manufacture, importation into the state, keeping for sale, offering for sale, or giving, lending, or possession of any short-barreled shotgun or short-barreled rifle, as defined in Section 12020.

12002. Law Enforcement Equipment Exempt

(a) Nothing in this chapter prohibits police officers, special police officers, peace officers, or law enforcement officers from carrying any wooden club, baton, or any equipment authorized for the enforcement of law or ordinance in any city or county.

(b) Nothing in this chapter prohibits a uniformed security guard, regularly employed and compensated *** by a person engaged in any lawful business, while actually employed and engaged in protecting and preserving property or life within the scope of his or her employment, from carrying any wooden club or baton if the uniformed security guard has satisfactorily completed a course of instruction certified by the Department of Consumer Affairs in the carrying and use of the club or baton. The training institution certified by the Department of Consumer Affairs to present this course, whether public or private, is authorized to charge a fee covering the cost of the training.

(c) The Department of Consumer Affairs, in cooperation with the Commission on Peace Officer Standards and Training, shall develop standards for a course in the carrying and use of the club or baton.

(d) Any uniformed security guard who successfully completes a course of instruction under this section is entitled to receive a permit to carry and use a club or baton within the scope of his or her employment, issued by the Department of Consumer Affairs. The department may authorize certified training institutions to issue permits to carry and use a club or baton. A fee in the amount provided by law shall be charged by the Department of Consumer Affairs to offset the costs incurred by the department in course certification, quality control activities associated with the course, and issuance of the permit.

(e) Any person who has received a permit or certificate which indicates satisfactory completion of a club or baton training course approved by the Commission on Peace Officer Standards and Training prior to January 1, 1983, shall not be required to obtain a baton or club permit or complete a course certified by the Department of Consumer Affairs.

(f) Any person employed as a county sheriff's or police security officer, as defined in Section 831.4, shall not be required to obtain a club or baton permit or to complete a course certified by the Department of Consumer Affairs in the carrying and use of a club or baton, provided that the person completes a course approved by the Commission on Peace Officer Standards and Training in the carrying and use of the club or baton, within 90 days of employment.

(g) Nothing in this chapter prohibits an animal control officer, as described in Section 830.9, from carrying any wooden club or baton if the animal control officer has satisfactorily completed a course of instruction certified by the Department of Consumer Affairs in the carrying and use of the club or baton. The training institution certified by the Department of Consumer Affairs to present this course, whether public or private, is authorized to charge a fee covering the cost of the training. *(AM '01)*

12020. Manufacture, Importation, Sale, or Possession of Disguised Firearms or Other Deadly Weapons Prohibited; Carrying Concealed Weapons Prohibited; Exceptions

(a) Any person in this state who does any of the following is punishable by imprisonment in a county jail not exceeding one year or in the state prison:

(1) Manufactures or causes to be manufactured, imports into the state, keeps for sale, or offers or exposes for sale, or who gives, lends, or possesses any cane gun or wallet gun, any undetectable firearm, any firearm which is not immediately recognizable as a firearm, any camouflaging firearm container, any ammunition which contains or consists of any flechette dart, any bullet containing or carrying an explosive agent, any ballistic knife, any multiburst trigger activator, any nunchaku, any short-barreled shotgun, any short-bar-

reled rifle, any metal knuckles, any belt buckle knife, any leaded cane, any zip gun, any shuriken, any unconventional pistol, any lipstick case knife, any cane sword, any shobi-zue, any air gauge knife, any writing pen knife, any metal military practice handgrenade or metal replica handgrenade, or any instrument or weapon of the kind commonly known as a blackjack, slungshot, billy, sandclub, sap, or sandbag.

(2) Commencing January 1, 2000, manufactures or causes to be manufactured, imports into the state, keeps for sale, or offers or exposes for sale, or who gives, or lends, any large-capacity magazine.

(3) Carries concealed upon his or her person any explosive substance, other than fixed ammunition.

(4) Carries concealed upon his or her person any dirk or dagger.

However, a first offense involving any metal military practice handgrenade or metal replica handgrenade shall be punishable only as an infraction unless the offender is an active participant in a criminal street gang as defined in the Street Terrorism and Enforcement and Prevention Act (Chapter 11 (commencing with Section 186.20) of Title 7 of Part 1). A bullet containing or carrying an explosive agent is not a destructive device as that term is used in Section 12301.

(b) Subdivision (a) does not apply to any of the following:

(1) The sale to, purchase by, or possession of short-barreled shotguns or short-barreled rifles by police departments, sheriffs'offices, marshals'offices, the California Highway Patrol, the Department of Justice, or the military or naval forces of this state or of the United States for use in the discharge of their official duties or the possession of short-barreled shotguns and short-barreled rifles by peace officer members of a police department, sheriff's office, marshal's office, the California Highway Patrol, or the Department of Justice when on duty and the use is authorized by the agency and is within the course and scope of their duties and the peace officer has completed a training course in the use of these weapons certified by the Commission on Peace Officer Standards and Training.

(2) The manufacture, possession, transportation or sale of short-barreled shotguns or short-barreled rifles when authorized by the Department of Justice pursuant to Article 6 (commencing with Section 12095) of this chapter and not in violation of federal law.

(3) The possession of a nunchaku on the premises of a school which holds a regulatory or business license and teaches the arts of self-defense.

(4) The manufacture of a nunchaku for sale to, or the sale of a nunchaku to, a school which holds a regulatory or business license and teaches the arts of self-defense.

(5) Any antique firearm. For purposes of this section, "antique firearm"means any firearm not designed or redesigned for using rimfire or conventional center fire ignition with fixed ammunition and manufactured in or before 1898 (including any matchlock, flintlock, percussion cap, or similar type of ignition system or replica thereof, whether actually manufactured before or after the year 1898) and also any firearm using fixed ammunition manufactured in or before 1898, for which ammunition is no longer manufactured in the United States and is not readily available in the ordinary channels of commercial trade.

(6) Tracer ammunition manufactured for use in shotguns.

(7) Any firearm or ammunition which is a curio or relic as defined in Section 178.11 of Title 27 of the Code of Federal Regulations and which is in the possession of a person permitted to possess the items pursuant to Chapter 44 (commencing with Section 921) of Title 18 of the United States Code and the regulations issued pursuant thereto. Any person prohibited by Section 12021, 12021.1, or 12101 of this code or Section 8100 or 8103 of the Welfare and Institutions Code from possessing firearms or ammunition who obtains title to these items by bequest or intestate succession may retain title for not more than one year, but actual possession of these items at any time is punishable pursuant to Section 12021, 12021.1, or 12101 of this code or Section 8100 or 8103 of the Welfare and Institutions Code. Within the year, the person shall transfer title to the firearms or ammunition by sale, gift, or other disposition. Any person who violates this paragraph is in violation of subdivision (a).

(8) Any other weapon as defined in subsection (e) of Section 5845 of Title 26 of the United States Code and which is in the possession of a person permitted to possess the weapons pursuant to the federal Gun Control Act of 1968 (Public Law 90-618), as amended, and the regulations issued pursuant thereto. Any person prohibited by Section 12021, 12021.1, or 12101 of this code or Section 8100 or 8103 of the Wel-

fare and Institutions Code from possessing these weapons who obtains title to these weapons by bequest or intestate succession may retain title for not more than one year, but actual possession of these weapons at any time is punishable pursuant to Section 12021, 12021.1, or 12101 of this code or Section 8100 or 8103 of the Welfare and Institutions Code. Within the year, the person shall transfer title to the weapons by sale, gift, or other disposition. Any person who violates this paragraph is in violation of subdivision (a). The exemption provided in this subdivision does not apply to pen guns.

(9) Instruments or devices that are possessed by federal, state, and local historical societies, museums, and institutional collections which are open to the public, provided that these instruments or devices are properly housed, secured from unauthorized handling, and, if the instrument or device is a firearm, unloaded.

(10) Instruments or devices, other than short-barreled shotguns or short-barreled rifles, that are possessed or utilized during the course of a motion picture, television, or video production or entertainment event by an authorized participant therein in the course of making that production or event or by an authorized employee or agent of the entity producing that production or event.

(11) Instruments or devices, other than short-barreled shotguns or short-barreled rifles, that are sold by, manufactured by, exposed or kept for sale by, possessed by, imported by, or lent by persons who are in the business of selling instruments or devices listed in subdivision (a) solely to the entities referred to in paragraphs (9) and (10) when engaging in transactions with those entities.

(12) The sale to, possession of, or purchase of any weapon, device, or ammunition, other than a short-barreled rifle or short-barreled shotgun, by any federal, state, county, city and county, or city agency that is charged with the enforcement of any law for use in the discharge of their official duties, or the possession of any weapon, device, or ammunition, other than a short-barreled rifle or short-barreled shotgun, by peace officers thereof when on duty and the use is authorized by the agency and is within the course and scope of their duties.

(13) Weapons, devices, and ammunition, other than a short-barreled rifle or short-barreled shotgun, that are sold by, manufactured by, exposed*** or kept for sale by, possessed by, imported by, or lent by, persons who are in the business of selling weapons, devices, and ammunition listed in subdivision (a) solely to the entities referred to in paragraph (12) when engaging in transactions with those entities.

(14) The manufacture for, sale to, exposing or keeping for sale to, importation of, or lending of wooden clubs or batons to special police officers or uniformed security guards authorized to carry any wooden club or baton pursuant to Section 12002 by entities that are in the business of selling wooden batons or clubs to special police officers and uniformed security guards when engaging in transactions with those persons.

(15) Any plastic toy handgrenade, or any metal military practice handgrenade or metal replica handgrenade that is a relic, curio, memorabilia, or display item, that is filled with a permanent inert substance or that is otherwise permanently altered in a manner that prevents ready modification for use as a grenade.

(16) Any instrument, ammunition, weapon, or device listed in subdivision (a) that is not a firearm that is found and possessed by a person who meets all of the following:

(A) The person is not prohibited from possessing firearms or ammunition pursuant to Section 12021 or 12021.1 or paragraph (1) of subdivision (b) of Section 12316 of this code or Section 8100 or 8103 of the Welfare and Institutions Code.

(B) The person possessed the instrument, ammunition, weapon, or device no longer than was necessary to deliver or transport the same to a law enforcement agency for that agency's disposition according to law.

(C) If the person is transporting the listed item, he or she is transporting the listed item to a law enforcement agency for disposition according to law.

(17) Any firearm, other than a short-barreled rifle or short-barreled shotgun, that is found and possessed by a person who meets all of the following:

(A) The person is not prohibited from possessing firearms or ammunition pursuant to Section 12021 or 12021.1 or paragraph (1) of subdivision (b) of Section 12316 of this code or Section 8100 or 8103 of the Welfare and Institutions Code.

(B) The person possessed the firearm no longer than was necessary to deliver or transport the same to a law enforcement agency for that agency's disposition according to law.

(C) If the person is transporting the firearm, he or she is transporting the firearm to a law enforcement agency for disposition according to law.

(D) Prior to transporting the firearm to a law enforcement agency, he or she has given prior notice to that law enforcement agency that he or she is transporting the firearm to that law enforcement agency for disposition according to law.

(E) The firearm is transported in a locked container as defined in subdivision (d) of Section 12026.2.

(18) The possession of any weapon, device, or ammunition, by a forensic laboratory or any authorized agent or employee thereof in the course and scope of his or her authorized activities.

(19) The sale of, giving of, lending of, importation into this state of, or purchase of, any large-capacity magazine to or by any federal, state, county, city and county, or city agency that is charged with the enforcement of any law, for use by agency employees in the discharge of their official duties whether on or off duty, and where the use is authorized by the agency and is within the course and scope of their duties.

(20) The sale to, lending to, transfer to, purchase by, receipt of, or importation into this state of, a large capacity magazine by a sworn peace officer as defined in Chapter 4.5 (commencing with Section 830) of Title 3 of Part 2 who is authorized to carry a firearm in the course and scope of his or her duties.

(21) The sale or purchase of any large-capacity magazine to or by a person licensed pursuant to Section 12071.

(22) The loan of a lawfully possessed large-capacity magazine between two individuals if all of the following conditions are met:

(A) The person being loaned the large-capacity magazine is not prohibited by Section 12021, 12021.1, or 12101 of this code or Section 8100 or 8103 of the Welfare and Institutions Code from possessing firearms or ammunition.

(B) The loan of the large-capacity magazine occurs at a place or location where the possession of the large-capacity magazine is not otherwise prohibited and the person who lends the large-capacity magazine remains in the accessible vicinity of the person to whom the large-capacity magazine is loaned.

(23) The importation of a large-capacity magazine by a person who lawfully possessed the large-capacity magazine in the state prior to January 1, 2000, lawfully took it out of the state, and is returning to the state with the large-capacity magazine previously lawfully possessed in the state.

(24) The lending or giving of any large-capacity magazine to a person licensed pursuant to Section 12071, or to a gunsmith, for the purposes of maintenance, repair, or modification of that large-capacity magazine.

(25) The return to its owner of any large-capacity magazine by a person specified in paragraph (24).

(26) The importation into this state of, or sale of, any large-capacity magazine by a person who has been issued a permit to engage in those activities pursuant to Section 12079, when those activities are in accordance with the terms and conditions of that permit.

(27) The sale of, giving of, lending of, importation into this state of, or purchase of, any large-capacity magazine, to or by entities that operate armored vehicle businesses pursuant to the laws of this state.

(28) The lending of large-capacity magazines by the entities specified in paragraph (27) to their authorized employees, while in the course and scope of their employment for purposes that pertain to the entity's armored vehicle business.

(29) The return of those large-capacity magazines to those entities specified in paragraph (27) by those employees specified in paragraph (28).

(30)(A) The manufacture of a large-capacity magazine for any federal, state, county, city and county, or city agency that is charged with the enforcement of any law, for use by agency employees in the discharge of their official duties whether on or off duty, and where the use is authorized by the agency and is within the course and scope of their duties.

(B) The manufacture of a large-capacity magazine for use by a sworn peace officer as defined in Chapter 4.5 (commencing with Section 830) of Title 3 of Part 2 who is authorized to carry a firearm in the course and scope of his or her duties.

(C) The manufacture of a large-capacity magazine for export or for sale to government agencies or the military pursuant to applicable federal regulations.

(31) The loan of a large-capacity magazine for use solely as a prop for a motion picture, television, or video production.

(32) The purchase of a large-capacity magazine by the holder of a special weapons permit issued pursuant to Section 12095, 12230, 12250, 12286, or 12305, for any of the following purposes:

(A) For use solely as a prop for a motion picture, television, or video production.

(B) For export pursuant to federal regulations.

(C) For resale to law enforcement agencies, government agencies, or the military, pursuant to applicable federal regulations.

(c)(1) As used in this section, a "short-barreled shotgun" means any of the following:

(A) A firearm which is designed or redesigned to fire a fixed shotgun shell and having a barrel or barrels of less than 18 inches in length.

(B) A firearm which has an overall length of less than 26 inches and which is designed or redesigned to fire a fixed shotgun shell.

(C) Any weapon made from a shotgun (whether by alteration, modification, or otherwise) if that weapon, as modified, has an overall length of less than 26 inches or a barrel or barrels of less than 18 inches in length.

(D) Any device which may be readily restored to fire a fixed shotgun shell which, when so restored, is a device defined in subparagraphs (A) to (C), inclusive.

(E) Any part, or combination of parts, designed and intended to convert a device into a device defined in subparagraphs (A) to (C), inclusive, or any combination of parts from which a device defined in subparagraphs (A) to (C), inclusive, can be readily assembled if those parts are in the possession or under the control of the same person.

(2) As used in this section, a "short-barreled rifle" means any of the following:

(A) A rifle having a barrel or barrels of less than 16 inches in length.

(B) A rifle with an overall length of less than 26 inches.

(C) Any weapon made from a rifle (whether by alteration, modification, or otherwise) if that weapon, as modified, has an overall length of less than 26 inches or a barrel or barrels of less than 16 inches in length.

(D) Any device which may be readily restored to fire a fixed cartridge which, when so restored, is a device defined in subparagraphs (A) to (C), inclusive.

(E) Any part, or combination of parts, designed and intended to convert a device into a device defined in subparagraphs (A) to (C), inclusive, or any combination of parts from which a device defined in subparagraphs (A) to (C), inclusive, may be readily assembled if those parts are in the possession or under the control of the same person.

(3) As used in this section, a "nunchaku" means an instrument consisting of two or more sticks, clubs, bars or rods to be used as handles, connected by a rope, cord, wire, or chain, in the design of a weapon used in connection with the practice of a system of self-defense such as karate.

(4) As used in this section, a "wallet gun" means any firearm mounted or enclosed in a case, resembling a wallet, designed to be or capable of being carried in a pocket or purse, if the firearm may be fired while mounted or enclosed in the case.

(5) As used in this section, a "cane gun" means any firearm mounted or enclosed in a stick, staff, rod, crutch, or similar device, designed to be, or capable of being used as, an aid in walking, if the firearm may be fired while mounted or enclosed therein.

(6) As used in this section, a "flechette dart" means a dart, capable of being fired from a firearm, *** that measures approximately one inch in length, with tail fins *** that take up approximately five-sixteenths of an inch of the body.

(7) As used in this section, "metal knuckles"means any device or instrument made wholly or partially of metal which is worn for purposes of offense or defense in or on the hand and which either protects the wearer's hand while striking a blow or increases the force of impact from the blow or injury to the individual receiving the blow. The metal contained in the device may help support the hand or fist, provide a shield to protect it, or consist of projections or studs which would contact the individual receiving a blow.

(8) As used in this section, a "ballistic knife"means a device that propels a knifelike blade as a projectile by means of a coil spring, elastic material, or compressed gas. Ballistic knife does not include any device which propels an arrow or a bolt by means of any common bow, compound bow, crossbow, or underwater spear gun.

(9) As used in this section, a "camouflaging firearm container"means a container which meets all of the following criteria:

(A) It is designed and intended to enclose a firearm.

(B) It is designed and intended to allow the firing of the enclosed firearm by external controls while the firearm is in the container.

(C) It is not readily recognizable as containing a firearm.

"Camouflaging firearm container"does not include any camouflaging covering used while engaged in lawful hunting or while going to or returning from a lawful hunting expedition.

(10) As used in this section, a "zip gun"means any weapon or device which meets all of the following criteria:

(A) It was not imported as a firearm by an importer licensed pursuant to Chapter 44 (commencing with Section 921) of Title 18 of the United States Code and the regulations issued pursuant thereto.

(B) It was not originally designed to be a firearm by a manufacturer licensed pursuant to Chapter 44 (commencing with Section 921) of Title 18 of the United States Code and the regulations issued pursuant thereto.

(C) No tax was paid on the weapon or device nor was an exemption from paying tax on that weapon or device granted under Section 4181 and *** Subchapters F (commencing with Section 4216) and G (commencing with Section 4221) of Chapter 32 of Title 26 of the United States Code, as amended, and the regulations issued pursuant thereto.

(D) It is made or altered to expel a projectile by the force of an explosion or other form of combustion.

(11) As used in this section, a "shuriken"means any instrument, without handles, consisting of a metal plate having three or more radiating points with one or more sharp edges and designed in the shape of a polygon, trefoil, cross, star, diamond, or other geometric shape for use as a weapon for throwing.

(12) As used in this section, an "unconventional pistol"means a firearm that does not have a rifled bore and has a barrel or barrels of less than 18 inches in length or has an overall length of less than 26 inches.

(13) As used in this section, a "belt buckle knife"is a knife which is made an integral part of a belt buckle and consists of a blade with a length of at least 21/2 inches.

(14) As used in this section, a "lipstick case knife"means a knife enclosed within and made an integral part of a lipstick case.

(15) As used in this section, a "cane sword"means a cane, swagger stick, stick, staff, rod, pole, umbrella, or similar device, having concealed within it a blade that may be used as a sword or stiletto.

(16) As used in this section, a "shobi-zue"means a staff, crutch, stick, rod, or pole concealing a knife or blade within it which may be exposed by a flip of the wrist or by a mechanical action.

(17) As used in this section, a "leaded cane"means a staff, crutch, stick, rod, pole, or similar device, unnaturally weighted with lead.

(18) As used in this section, an "air gauge knife"means a device that appears to be an air gauge but has concealed within it a pointed, metallic shaft that is designed to be a stabbing instrument which is exposed by mechanical action or gravity which locks into place when extended.

(19) As used in this section, a "writing pen knife"means a device that appears to be a writing pen but has concealed within it a pointed, metallic shaft that is designed to be a stabbing instrument which is exposed by

mechanical action or gravity which locks into place when extended or the pointed, metallic shaft is exposed by the removal of the cap or cover on the device.

(20) As used in this section, a "rifle"means a weapon designed or redesigned, made or remade, and intended to be fired from the shoulder and designed or redesigned and made or remade to use the energy of the explosive in a fixed cartridge to fire only a single projectile through a rifled bore for each single pull of the trigger.

(21) As used in this section, a "shotgun"means a weapon designed or redesigned, made or remade, and intended to be fired from the shoulder and designed or redesigned and made or remade to use the energy of the explosive in a fixed shotgun shell to fire through a smooth bore either a number of projectiles (ball shot) or a single projectile for each pull of the trigger.

(22) As used in this section, an "undetectable firearm"means any weapon which meets one of the following requirements:

(A) When, after removal of grips, stocks, and magazines, it is not as detectable as the Security Exemplar, by walk-through metal detectors calibrated and operated to detect the Security Exemplar.

(B) When any major component of which, when subjected to inspection by the types of X-ray machines commonly used at airports, does not generate an image that accurately depicts the shape of the component. Barium sulfate or other compounds may be used in the fabrication of the component.

(C) For purposes of this paragraph, the terms "firearm,""major component,"and "Security Exemplar" have the same meanings as those terms are defined in Section 922 of Title 18 of the United States Code.

All firearm detection equipment newly installed in nonfederal public buildings in this state shall be of a type identified by either the United States Attorney General, the Secretary of Transportation, or the Secretary of the Treasury, as appropriate, as available state-of-the-art equipment capable of detecting an undetectable firearm, as defined, while distinguishing innocuous metal objects likely to be carried on one's person sufficient for reasonable passage of the public.

(23) As used in this section, a "multiburst trigger activator"means one of the following devices:

(A) A device designed or redesigned to be attached to a semiautomatic firearm which allows the firearm to discharge two or more shots in a burst by activating the device.

(B) A manual or power-driven trigger activating device constructed and designed so that when attached to a semiautomatic firearm it increases the rate of fire of that firearm.

(24) As used in this section, a "dirk"or "dagger"means a knife or other instrument with or without a handguard that is capable of ready use as a stabbing weapon that may inflict great bodily injury or death. A nonlocking folding knife, a folding knife that is not prohibited by Section 653k, or a pocketknife is capable of ready use as a stabbing weapon that may inflict great bodily injury or death only if the blade of the knife is exposed and locked into position.

(25) As used in this section, "large-capacity magazine"means any ammunition feeding device with the capacity to accept more than 10 rounds, but shall not be construed to include *** any of the following:

(A) A feeding device that has been permanently altered so that it cannot accommodate more than 10 rounds ***.

(B) A .22 caliber tube ammunition feeding device.

(C) A tubular magazine that is contained in a lever-action firearm.

(d) Knives carried in sheaths which are worn openly suspended from the waist of the wearer are not concealed within the meaning of this section. *(AM '01)*

12020.3.   Sale, etc. of Bright Orange or Bright Green Firearms

Any person who, for commercial purposes, purchases, sells, manufacturers, ships, transports, distributes, or receives a firearm, where the coloration of the entire exterior surface of the firearm is bright orange or bright green, either singly, in combination, or as the predominant color in combination with other colors in any pattern, is liable for a civil fine in an action brought by the city attorney of the city or the district attorney for the county of not more than ten thousand dollars ($10,000). *(AD '00)*

12020.5. Advertising Sale of Weapons

It shall be unlawful for any person, as defined in Section 12277, to advertise the sale of any weapon or device whose possession is prohibited by Section 12020, 12220, 12280, 12303, 12320, 12321, 12355, or 12520 in any newspaper, magazine, circular, form letter, or open publication that is published, distributed, or circulated in this state, or on any billboard, card, label, or other advertising medium, or by means of any other advertising device.

12021. Convicts, Persons Convicted of Offenses Involving Violent Use of Firearms, and Addicts Prohibited From Possessing Firearms

(a)(1) Any person who has been convicted of a felony under the laws of the United States, of the State of California, or any other state, government, or country, or of an offense enumerated in subdivision (a), (b), or (d) of Section 12001.6, or who is addicted to the use of any narcotic drug, who owns or has in his or her possession or under his or her custody or control any firearm is guilty of a felony.

(2) Any person who has two or more convictions for violating paragraph (2) of subdivision (a) of Section 417 and who owns or has in his or her possession or under his or her custody or control any firearm is guilty of a felony.

(b) Notwithstanding subdivision (a), any person who has been convicted of a felony or of an offense enumerated in Section 12001.6, when that conviction results from certification by the juvenile court for prosecution as an adult in an adult court under Section 707 of the Welfare and Institutions Code, who owns or has in his or her possession or under his or her custody or control any firearm is guilty of a felony.

(c)(1) Except as provided in subdivision (a) or paragraph (2) of this subdivision, any person who has been convicted of a misdemeanor violation of Section 71, 76, 136.1, 136.5, or 140, subdivision (d) of Section 148, Section 171b, 171c, 171d, 186.28, 240, 241, 242, 243, 244.5, 245, 245.5, 246, 246.3, 247, 273.5, 273.6, 417, 417.1, 417.2, 417.6, 422, 626.9, 646.9, 12023, or 12024, subdivision (b) or (d) of Section 12034, Section 12040, subdivision (b) of Section 12072, subdivision (a) of former Section 12100, Section 12220, 12320, or 12590, or Section 8100, 8101, or 8103 of the Welfare and Institutions Code, any firearm-related offense pursuant to Sections 871.5 and 1001.5 of the Welfare and Institutions Code, or of the conduct punished in paragraph (3) of subdivision (g) of Section 12072, and who, within 10 years of the conviction, owns, or has in his or her possession or under his or her custody or control, any firearm is guilty of a public offense, which shall be punishable by imprisonment in a county jail not exceeding one year or in the state prison, by a fine not exceeding one thousand dollars ($1,000), or by both that imprisonment and fine. The court, on forms prescribed by the Department of Justice, shall notify the department of persons subject to this subdivision. However, the prohibition in this paragraph may be reduced, eliminated, or conditioned as provided in paragraph (2) or (3).

(2) Any person employed as a peace officer described in Section 830.1, 830.2, 830.31, 830.32, 830.33, or 830.5 whose employment or livelihood is dependent on the ability to legally possess a firearm, who is subject to the prohibition imposed by this subdivision because of a conviction under Section 273.5, 273.6, or 646.9, may petition the court only once for relief from this prohibition. The petition shall be filed with the court in which the petitioner was sentenced. If possible, the matter shall be heard before the same judge that sentenced the petitioner. Upon filing the petition, the clerk of the court shall set the hearing date and shall notify the petitioner and the prosecuting attorney of the date of the hearing. Upon making each of the following findings, the court may reduce or eliminate the prohibition, impose conditions on reduction or elimination of the prohibition, or otherwise grant relief from the prohibition as the court deems appropriate:

(A) Finds by a preponderance of the evidence that the petitioner is likely to use a firearm in a safe and lawful manner.

(B) Finds that the petitioner is not within a prohibited class as specified in subdivision (a), (b), (d), (e), or (g) or Section 12021.1, and the court is not presented with any credible evidence that the petitioner is a person described in Section 8100 or 8103 of the Welfare and Institutions Code.

(C) Finds that the petitioner does not have a previous conviction under this subdivision no matter when the prior conviction occurred.

In making its decision, the court shall consider the petitioner's continued employment, the interest of justice, any relevant evidence, and the totality of the circumstances. The court shall require, as a condition of granting relief from the prohibition under this section, that the petitioner agree to participate in counseling as deemed appropriate by the court. Relief from the prohibition shall not relieve any other person or entity from any liability that might otherwise be imposed. It is the intent of the Legislature that courts exercise broad discretion in fashioning appropriate relief under this paragraph in cases in which relief is warranted. However, nothing in this paragraph shall be construed to require courts to grant relief to any particular petitioner. It is the intent of the Legislature to permit persons who were convicted of an offense specified in Section 273.5, 273.6, or 646.9 to seek relief from the prohibition imposed by this subdivision.

(3) Any person who is subject to the prohibition imposed by this subdivision because of a conviction of an offense prior to that offense being added to paragraph (1)*** may petition the court only once for relief from this prohibition. The petition shall be filed with the court in which the petitioner was sentenced. If possible, the matter shall be heard before the same judge that sentenced the petitioner. Upon filing the petition, the clerk of the court shall set the hearing date and notify the petitioner and the prosecuting attorney of the date of the hearing. Upon making each of the following findings, the court may reduce or eliminate the prohibition, impose conditions on reduction or elimination of the prohibition, or otherwise grant relief from the prohibition as the court deems appropriate:

(A) Finds by a preponderance of the evidence that the petitioner is likely to use a firearm in a safe and lawful manner.

(B) Finds that the petitioner is not within a prohibited class as specified in subdivision (a), (b), (d), (e), or (g) or Section 12021.1, and the court is not presented with any credible evidence that the petitioner is a person described in Section 8100 or 8103 of the Welfare and Institutions Code.

(C) Finds that the petitioner does not have a previous conviction under this subdivision, no matter when the prior conviction occurred.

In making its decision, the court may consider the interest of justice, any relevant evidence, and the totality of the circumstances. It is the intent of the Legislature that courts exercise broad discretion in fashioning appropriate relief under this paragraph in cases in which relief is warranted. However, nothing in this paragraph shall be construed to require courts to grant relief to any particular petitioner.

(4) Law enforcement officials who enforce the prohibition specified in this subdivision against a person who has been granted relief pursuant to paragraph (2) or (3)*** shall be immune from any liability for false arrest arising from the enforcement of this subdivision unless the person has in his or her possession a certified copy of the court order that granted the person relief from the prohibition. This immunity from liability shall not relieve any person or entity from any other liability that might otherwise be imposed.

(d)(1) Any person who, as an express condition of probation, is prohibited or restricted from owning, possessing, controlling, receiving, or purchasing a firearm and who owns, or has in his or her possession or under his or her custody or control, any firearm but who is not subject to subdivision (a) or (c) is guilty of a public offense, which shall be punishable by imprisonment in a county jail not exceeding one year or in the state prison, by a fine not exceeding one thousand dollars ($1,000), or by both that imprisonment and fine. The court, on forms provided by the Department of Justice, shall notify the department of persons subject to this subdivision. The notice shall include a copy of the order of probation and a copy of any minute order or abstract reflecting the order and conditions of probation.

(2) For any person who is subject to subdivision (a), (b), or (c), the court shall, at the time judgment is imposed, provide on a form supplied by the Department of Justice, a notice to the defendant prohibited by this section from owning, possessing or having under his or her custody or control, any firearm. The notice shall inform the defendant of the prohibition regarding firearms and include a form to facilitate the transfer of firearms. Failure to provide the notice shall not be a defense to a violation of this section.

(e) Any person who (1) is alleged to have committed an offense listed in subdivision (b) of Section 707 of the Welfare and Institutions Code, an offense described in subdivision (b) of Section 1203.073, or any offense enumerated in paragraph (1) of subdivision (c), and (2) is subsequently adjudged a ward of the juvenile court within the meaning of Section 602 of the Welfare and Institutions Code because the person committed an offense listed in subdivision (b) of Section 707 of the Welfare and Institutions Code, an offense described in subdivision (b) of Section 1203.073, or any offense enumerated in paragraph (1) of subdivision (c) shall not own, or have in his or her possession or under his or her custody or control, any firearm until the age of 30 years. A violation of this subdivision shall be punishable by imprisonment in a county jail not exceeding one year or in the state prison, by a fine not exceeding one thousand dollars ($1,000), or by both that imprisonment and fine. The juvenile court, on forms prescribed by the Department of Justice, shall notify the department of persons subject to this subdivision. Notwithstanding any other law, the forms required to be submitted to the department pursuant to this subdivision may be used to determine eligibility to acquire a firearm.

(f) Subdivision (a) shall not apply to a person who has been convicted of a felony under the laws of the United States unless either of the following criteria is satisfied:

(1) Conviction of a like offense under California law can only result in imposition of felony punishment.

(2) The defendant was sentenced to a federal correctional facility for more than 30 days, or received a fine of more than one thousand dollars ($1,000), or received both punishments.

(g)(1) Every person who purchases or receives, or attempts to purchase or receive, a firearm knowing that he or she is subject to a protective order as defined in Section 6218 of the Family Code, Section 136.2, or a temporary restraining order or injunction issued pursuant to Section 527.6 or 527.8 of the Code of Civil Procedure, is guilty of a public offense, which shall be punishable by imprisonment in a county jail not exceeding one year or in the state prison, by a fine not exceeding one thousand dollars ($1,000), or by both that imprisonment and fine. This subdivision does not apply unless the copy of the restraining order personally served on the person against whom the restraining order is issued contains a notice in bold print stating (1) that the person is prohibited from purchasing or receiving or attempting to purchase or receive a firearm and (2) specifying the penalties for violating this subdivision, or a court has provided actual verbal notice of the firearm prohibition and penalty as provided in Section 6304 of the Family Code.

(2) Every person who owns or possesses a firearm knowing that he or she is prohibited from owning or possessing a firearm by the provisions of a protective order as defined in Section 6218 of the Family Code, Section 136.2 of the Penal Code, or a temporary restraining order or injunction issued pursuant to Section 527.6 or 527.8 of the Code of Civil Procedure, is guilty of a public offense, which shall be punishable by imprisonment in a county jail not exceeding one year, by a fine not exceeding one thousand dollars ($1,000), or by both that imprisonment and fine. This subdivision does not apply unless a copy of the restraining order personally served on the person against whom the restraining order is issued contains a notice in bold print stating (1) that the person is prohibited from owning or possessing or attempting to own or possess a firearm and (2) specifying the penalties for violating this subdivision, or a court has provided actual verbal notice of the firearm prohibition and penalty as provided in Section 6304 of the Family Code.(3) Judicial Council shall provide notice on all protective orders that the respondent is prohibited from owning, possessing, purchasing, or receiving a firearm while the protective order is in effect and that the firearm shall be relinquished to the local law enforcement agency for that jurisdiction or sold to a licensed gun dealer, and that proof of surrender or sale shall be filed within a specified time of receipt of the order. The order shall also state on its face the expiration date for relinquishment.

(4) If probation is granted upon conviction of a violation of this subdivision, the court shall impose probation consistent with the provisions of Section 1203.097.

(h)(1) A violation of subdivision (a), (b), (c), (d), or (e) is justifiable where all of the following conditions are met:

(A) The person found the firearm or took the firearm from a person who was committing a crime against him or her.

(B) The person possessed the firearm no longer than was necessary to deliver or transport the firearm to a law enforcement agency for that agency's disposition according to law.

(C) If the firearm was transported to a law enforcement agency, it was transported in accordance with paragraph (18) of subdivision (a) of Section 12026.2.

(D) If the firearm is being transported to a law enforcement agency, the person transporting the firearm has given prior notice to the law enforcement agency that he or she is transporting the firearm to the law enforcement agency for disposition according to law.

(2) Upon the trial for violating subdivision (a), (b), (c), (d), or (e), the trier of fact shall determine whether the defendant was acting within the provisions of the exemption created by this subdivision.

(3) The defendant has the burden of proving by a preponderance of the evidence that he or she comes within the provisions of the exemption created by this subdivision. *(AM '01)*

12021.1. Person Previously Convicted of Violent Offense Prohibited From Possessing Firearms

(a) Notwithstanding subdivision (a) of Section 12021, any person who has been previously convicted of any of the offenses listed in subdivision (b) and who owns or has in his or her possession or under his or her custody or control any firearm is guilty of a felony. A dismissal of an accusatory pleading pursuant to Section 1203.4a involving an offense set forth in subdivision (b) does not affect the finding of a previous conviction. If probation is granted, or if the imposition or execution of sentence is suspended, it shall be a condition of the probation or suspension that the defendant serve at least six months in a county jail.

(b) As used in this section, a violent offense includes any of the following:

(1) Murder or voluntary manslaughter.

(2) Mayhem.

(3) Rape.

(4) Sodomy by force, violence, duress, menace, or threat of great bodily harm.

(5) Oral copulation by force, violence, duress, menace, or threat of great bodily harm.

(6) Lewd acts on a child under the age of 14 years.

(7) Any felony punishable by death or imprisonment in the state prison for life.

(8) Any other felony in which the defendant inflicts great bodily injury on any person, other than an accomplice, that has been charged and proven, or any felony in which the defendant uses a firearm which use has been charged and proven.

(9) Attempted murder.

(10) Assault with intent to commit rape or robbery.

(11) Assault with a deadly weapon or instrument on a peace officer.

(12) Assault by a life prisoner on a noninmate.

(13) Assault with a deadly weapon by an inmate.

(14) Arson.

(15) Exploding a destructive device or any explosive with intent to injure.

(16) Exploding a destructive device or any explosive causing great bodily injury.

(17) Exploding a destructive device or any explosive with intent to murder.

(18) Robbery.

(19) Kidnapping.

(20) Taking of a hostage by an inmate of a state prison.

(21) Attempt to commit a felony punishable by death or imprisonment in the state prison for life.

(22) Any felony in which the defendant personally used a dangerous or deadly weapon.

(23) Escape from a state prison by use of force or violence.

(24) Assault with a deadly weapon or force likely to produce great bodily injury.

(25) Any felony violation of Section 186.22.

(26) Any attempt to commit a crime listed in this subdivision other than an assault.

(27) Any offense enumerated in subdivision (a), (b), or (d) of Section 12001.6.

(28) Carjacking.

(29) Any offense enumerated in subdivision (c) of Section 12001.6 if the person has two or more convictions for violating paragraph (2) of subdivision (a) of Section 417.

(c) Any person previously convicted of any of the offenses listed in subdivision (b) which conviction results from certification by the juvenile court for prosecution as an adult in adult court under the provisions of Section 707 of the Welfare and Institutions Code, who owns or has in his or her possession or under his or her custody or control any firearm is guilty of a felony. If probation is granted, or if the imposition or execution of sentence is suspended, it shall be a condition of the probation or suspension that the defendant serve at least six months in a county jail.

(d) The court shall apply the minimum sentence as specified in subdivisions (a) and (c) except in unusual cases where the interests of justice would best be served by granting probation or suspending the imposition or execution of sentence without the imprisonment required by subdivisions (a) and (c), or by granting probation or suspending the imposition or execution of sentence with conditions other than those set forth in subdivisions (a) and (c), in which case the court shall specify on the record and shall enter on the minutes the circumstances indicating that the interests of justice would best be served by the disposition.

12022.2. Commit or Attempt Felony While in Possession of Firearm and Metal Penetrating Ammunition; Wearing Bullet Resistant Vest

(a) Any person who, while armed with a firearm in the commission or attempted commission of any felony, has in his or her immediate possession ammunition for the firearm designed primarily to penetrate metal or armor, shall upon conviction of that felony or attempted felony, in addition and consecutive to the punishment prescribed for the felony or attempted felony, be punished by an additional term of 3, 4, or 10 years. The court shall order the middle term unless there are circumstances in aggravation or mitigation. The court shall state the reasons for its enhancement choice on the record at the time of the sentence.

(b) Any person who wears a body vest in the commission or attempted commission of a violent offense, as defined in subdivision (b) of Section 12021.1, shall, upon conviction of that felony or attempted felony, in addition and consecutive to the punishment prescribed for the felony or attempted felony of which he or she has been convicted, be punished by an additional term of one, two, or five years. The court shall order the middle term unless there are circumstances in aggravation or mitigation. The court shall state the reasons for its enhancement choice on the record at the time of the sentence.

(c) As used in this section, "body vest" means any bullet-resistant material intended to provide ballistic and trauma protection for the wearer.

12023. Possession of Deadly Weapon Prima Facie Evidence of Intent to Commit Felony

(a) Every person who carries a loaded firearm with the intent to commit a felony is guilty of armed criminal action.

(b) Armed criminal action is punishable by imprisonment in a county jail not exceeding one year, or in the state prison.

12024. Possession of Deadly Weapon with Intent to Commit Assault

Every person having upon him or her any deadly weapon, with intent to assault another, is guilty of a misdemeanor.

12025. Carry Concealed Firearm Without License

(a) A person is guilty of carrying a concealed firearm when he or she does any of the following:

(1) Carries concealed within any vehicle which is under his or her control or direction any pistol, revolver, or other firearm capable of being concealed upon the person.

(2) Carries concealed upon his or her person any pistol, revolver, or other firearm capable of being concealed upon the person.

(3) Causes to be carried concealed within any vehicle in which he or she is an occupant any pistol, revolver, or other firearm capable of being concealed upon the person.

(b) Carrying a concealed firearm in violation of this section is punishable, as follows:

(1) Where the person previously has been convicted of any felony, or of any crime made punishable by this chapter, as a felony.

(2) Where the firearm is stolen and the person knew or had reasonable cause to believe that it was stolen, as a felony.

(3) Where the person is an active participant in a criminal street gang, as defined in subdivision (a) of Section 186.22, under the Street Terrorism Enforcement and Prevention Act (Chapter 11 (commencing with Section 186.20) of Title 7 of Part 1), as a felony.

(4) Where the person is not in lawful possession of the firearm, as defined in this section, or the person is within a class of persons prohibited from possessing or acquiring a firearm pursuant to Section 12021 or 12021.1 of this code or Section 8100 or 8103 of the Welfare and Institutions Code, as a felony.

(5) Where the person has been convicted of a crime against a person or property, or of a narcotics or dangerous drug violation, by imprisonment in the state prison, or by imprisonment in a county jail not to exceed one year, by a fine not to exceed one thousand dollars ($1,000), or by both that imprisonment and fine.

(6) By imprisonment in the state prison, or by imprisonment in a county jail not to exceed one year, by a fine not to exceed one thousand dollars ($1,000), or by both that fine and imprisonment if both of the following conditions are met:

(A) Both the pistol, revolver, or other firearm capable of being concealed upon the person and the unexpended ammunition capable of being discharged from that firearm are either in the immediate possession of the person or readily accessible to that person, or the pistol, revolver, or other firearm capable of being concealed upon the person is loaded as defined in subdivision (g) of Section 12031.

(B) The person is not listed with the Department of Justice pursuant to paragraph (1) of subdivision (c) of Section 11106, as the registered owner of that pistol, revolver, or other firearm capable of being concealed upon the person.

(7) In all cases other than those specified in paragraphs (1) to (6), inclusive, by imprisonment in a county jail not to exceed one year, by a fine not to exceed one thousand dollars ($1,000), or by both that imprisonment and fine.

(c) A peace officer may arrest a person for a violation of paragraph (6) of subdivision (b) if the peace officer has probable cause to believe that the person is not listed with the Department of Justice pursuant to paragraph (1) of subdivision (c) of Section 11106 as the registered owner of the pistol, revolver, or other firearm capable of being concealed upon the person, and one or more of the conditions in subparagraph (A) of paragraph (6) of subdivision (b) is met.

(d)(1) Every person convicted under this section who previously has been convicted of a misdemeanor offense enumerated in Section 12001.6 shall be punished by imprisonment in a county jail for at least three months and not exceeding six months, or, if granted probation, or if the execution or imposition of sentence is suspended, it shall be a condition thereof that he or she be imprisoned in a county jail for at least three months.

(2) Every person convicted under this section who has previously been convicted of any felony, or of any crime made punishable by this chapter, if probation is granted, or if the execution or imposition of sentence is suspended, it shall be a condition thereof that he or she be imprisoned in a county jail for not less than three months.

(e) The court shall apply the three-month minimum sentence as specified in subdivision (d), except in unusual cases where the interests of justice would best be served by granting probation or suspending the imposition or execution of sentence without the minimum imprisonment required in subdivision (d) or by granting probation or suspending the imposition or execution of sentence with conditions other than those set forth in subdivision (d), in which case, the court shall specify on the record and shall enter on the minutes the circumstances indicating that the interests of justice would best be served by that disposition.

(f) Firearms carried openly in belt holsters are not concealed within the meaning of this section.

(g) For purposes of this section, "lawful possession of the firearm"means that the person who has possession or custody of the firearm either lawfully owns the firearm or has the permission of the lawful owner or a person who otherwise has apparent authority to possess or have custody of the firearm. A person who takes a firearm without the permission of the lawful owner or without the permission of a person who has lawful custody of the firearm does not have lawful possession of the firearm.

(h)(1) The district attorney of each county shall submit annually a report on or before June 30, to the Attorney General consisting of profiles by race, age, gender, and ethnicity of any person charged with a felony or a misdemeanor under this section and any other offense charged in the same complaint, indictment, or information.

(2) The Attorney General shall submit annually, a report on or before December 31, to the Legislature compiling all of the reports submitted pursuant to paragraph (1).

(3) This subdivision shall remain operative until January 1, 2005, and as of that date shall be repealed. *(AM '99)*

12025.5. Justifiable Possession of a Firearm

(a) A violation of Section 12025 is justifiable when a person who possesses a firearm reasonably believes that he or she is in grave danger because of circumstances forming the basis of a current restraining order issued by a court against another person or persons who has or have been found to pose a threat to his or her life or safety. This section may not apply when the circumstances involve a mutual restraining order issued pursuant to Division 10 (commencing with Section 6200) of the Family Code absent a factual finding of a specific threat to the person's life or safety. It is not the intent of the Legislature to limit, restrict, or narrow the application of current statutory or judicial authority to apply this or other justifications to defendants charged with violating Section 12025 or of committing other similar offenses.

(b) Upon trial for violating Section 12025, the trier of fact shall determine whether the defendant was acting out of a reasonable belief that he or she was in grave danger.

12026. Possession at Residence, Place of Business, or Private Property

(a) Section 12025 shall not apply to or affect any citizen of the United States or legal resident over the age of 18 years who resides or is temporarily within this state, and who is not within the excepted classes prescribed by Section 12021 or 12021.1 of this code or Section 8100 or 8103 of the Welfare and Institutions Code, who carries, either openly or concealed, anywhere within the citizen's or legal resident's place of residence, place of business, or on private property owned or lawfully possessed by the citizen or legal resident any pistol, revolver, or other firearm capable of being concealed upon the person.

(b) No permit or license to purchase, own, possess, keep, or carry, either openly or concealed, shall be required of any citizen of the United States or legal resident over the age of 18 years who resides or is temporarily within this state, and who is not within the excepted classes prescribed by Section 12021 or 12021.1 of this code or Section 8100 or 8103 of the Welfare and Institutions Code, to purchase, own, possess, keep, or carry, either openly or concealed, a pistol, revolver, or other firearm capable of being concealed upon the person within the citizen's or legal resident's place of residence, place of business, or on private property owned or lawfully possessed by the citizen or legal resident.

(c) Nothing in this section shall be construed as affecting the application of Section 12031.

12026.1. Transportation in Trunk or Locked Container

(a) Section 12025 shall not be construed to prohibit any citizen of the United States over the age of 18 years who resides or is temporarily within this state, and who is not within the excepted classes prescribed by Section 12021 or 12021.1 of this code or Section 8100 or 8103 of the Welfare and Institutions Code, from transporting or carrying any pistol, revolver, or other firearm capable of being concealed upon the person, provided that the following applies to the firearm:

(1) The firearm is within a motor vehicle and it is locked in the vehicle's trunk or in a locked container in the vehicle other than the utility or glove compartment.

(2) The firearm is carried by the person directly to or from any motor vehicle for any lawful purpose and, while carrying the firearm, the firearm is contained within a locked container.

(b) The provisions of this section do not prohibit or limit the otherwise lawful carrying or transportation of any pistol, revolver, or other firearm capable of being concealed upon the person in accordance with this chapter.

(c) As used in this section, "locked container" means a secure container which is fully enclosed and locked by a padlock, key lock, combination lock, or similar locking device.

12026.2. Miscellaneous Exceptions to Prohibitions Against Concealed Firearms

(a) Section 12025 does not apply to, or affect, any of the following:

(1) The possession of a firearm by an authorized participant in a motion picture, television, or video production or entertainment event when the participant lawfully uses the firearm as part of that production or event or while going directly to, or coming directly from, that production or event.

(2) The possession of a firearm in a locked container by a member of any club or organization, organized for the purpose of lawfully collecting and lawfully displaying pistols, revolvers, or other firearms, while the member is at meetings of the clubs or organizations or while going directly to, and coming directly from, those meetings.

(3) The transportation of a firearm by a participant when going directly to, or coming directly from, a recognized safety or hunter safety class, or a recognized sporting event involving that firearm.

(4) The transportation of a firearm by a person listed in Section 12026 directly between any of the places mentioned in Section 12026.

(5) The transportation of a firearm by a person when going directly to, or coming directly from, a fixed place of business or private residential property for the purpose of the lawful repair or the lawful transfer, sale, or loan of that firearm.

(6) The transportation of a firearm by a person listed in Section 12026 when going directly from the place where that person lawfully received that firearm to that person's place of residence or place of business or to private property owned or lawfully possessed by that person.

(7) The transportation of a firearm by a person when going directly to, or coming directly from, a gun show, swap meet, or similar event to which the public is invited, for the purpose of displaying that firearm in a lawful manner.

(8) The transportation of a firearm by an authorized employee or agent of a supplier of firearms when going directly to, or coming directly from, a motion picture, television, or video production or entertainment event for the purpose of providing that firearm to an authorized participant to lawfully use as a part of that production or event.

(9) The transportation of a firearm by a person when going directly to, or coming directly from, a target range, which holds a regulatory or business license, for the purposes of practicing shooting at targets with that firearm at that target range.

(10) The transportation of a firearm by a person when going directly to, or coming directly from, a place designated by a person authorized to issue licenses pursuant to Section 12050 when done at the request of the issuing agency so that the issuing agency can determine whether or not a license should be issued to that person to carry that firearm.

(11) The transportation of a firearm by a person when going directly to, or coming directly from, a law enforcement agency for the purpose of a lawful transfer, sale, or loan of that firearm pursuant to Section 12084.

(12) The transportation of a firearm by a person when going directly to, or coming directly from, a lawful camping activity for the purpose of having that firearm available for lawful personal protection while at the lawful campsite. This paragraph shall not be construed to override the statutory authority granted to the Department of Parks and Recreation or any other state or local governmental agencies to promulgate rules and regulations governing the administration of parks and campgrounds.

(13) The transportation of a firearm by a person in order to comply with subdivision (c) or (i) of Section 12078 as it pertains to that firearm.

(14) The transportation of a firearm by a person in order to utilize subdivision (l) of Section 12078 as it pertains to that firearm.

(15) The transportation of a firearm by a person when going directly to, or coming directly from, a gun show or event, as defined in Section 178.100 of Title 27 of the Code of Federal Regulations, for the purpose of lawfully transferring, selling, or loaning that firearm in accordance with subdivision (d) of Section 12072.

(16) The transportation of a firearm by a person in order to utilize paragraph (3) of subdivision (a) of Section 12078 as it pertains to that firearm.

(17) The transportation of a firearm by a person who finds the firearm in order to comply with Article 1 (commencing with Section 2080) of Chapter 4 of Division 3 of the Civil Code as it pertains to that firearm and if that firearm is being transported to a law enforcement agency, the person gives prior notice to the law enforcement agency that he or she is transporting the firearm to the law enforcement agency.

(18) The transportation of a firearm by a person who finds the firearm and is transporting it to a law enforcement agency for disposition according to law, if he or she gives prior notice to the law enforcement agency that he or she is transporting the firearm to the law enforcement agency for disposition according to law.

(19) The transportation of a firearm by a person in order to comply with paragraph (2) of subdivision (f) of Section 12072 as it pertains to that firearm.

(20) The transportation of a firearm by a person in order to comply with paragraph (3) of subdivision (f) of Section 12072 as it pertains to that firearm.

(21) The transportation of a firearm by a person for the purpose of obtaining an identification number or mark assigned for that firearm from the Department of Justice pursuant to Section 12092.

(b) In order for a firearm to be exempted under subdivision (a), while being transported to or from a place, the firearm shall be unloaded, kept in a locked container, as defined in subdivision (d), and the course of travel shall include only those deviations between authorized locations as are reasonably necessary under the circumstances.

(c) This section does not prohibit or limit the otherwise lawful carrying or transportation of any pistol, revolver, or other firearm capable of being concealed upon the person in accordance with this chapter.

(d) As used in this section, "locked container" means a secure container which is fully enclosed and locked by a padlock, key lock, combination lock, or similar locking device. The term "locked container" does not include the utility or glove compartment of a motor vehicle. *(AM '98)*

12027. Exceptions to Carrying Concealed Firearms

Section 12025 does not apply to, or affect, any of the following:

(a)(1)(A) Any peace officer, listed in Section 830.1 or 830.2, or subdivision (a) of Section 830.33, whether active or honorably retired, other duly appointed peace officers, honorably retired peace officers listed in subdivision (c) of Section 830.5, other honorably retired peace officers who during the course and scope of their employment as peace officers were authorized to, and did, carry firearms, full-time paid peace officers of other states and the federal government who are carrying out official duties while in California, or any person summoned by any of these officers to assist in making arrests or preserving the peace while he or she is actually engaged in assisting that officer. Any peace officer described in this paragraph who has been honorably retired shall be issued an identification certificate by the law enforcement agency from which the officer has retired. The issuing agency may charge a fee necessary to cover any reasonable expenses incurred by the agency in issuing certificates pursuant to this subdivision. As used in this section and Section 12031, the term "honorably retired" includes all peace officers who have qualified for, and have accepted, a service or disability retirement. For purposes of this section and Section 12031, the term "honorably retired" does not include an officer who has agreed to a service retirement in lieu of termination.

(B) Any officer, except an officer listed in Section 830.1 or 830.2, subdivision (a) of Section 830.33, or subdivision (c) of Section 830.5 who retired prior to January 1, 1981, shall have an endorsement on the identification certificate stating that the issuing agency approves the officer's carrying of a concealed firearm.

(C) No endorsement or renewal endorsement issued pursuant to paragraph (2) shall be effective unless it is in the format set forth in subparagraph (D), except that any peace officer listed in subdivision (f) of Section 830.2 or in subdivision (c) of Section 830.5, who is retired between January 2, 1981, and on or before December 31, 1988, and who is authorized to carry a concealed firearm pursuant to this section, shall not be required to have an endorsement in the format set forth in subparagraph (D) until the time of the issuance, on or after January 1, 1989, of a renewal endorsement pursuant to paragraph (2).

(D) A certificate issued pursuant to this paragraph for persons who are not listed in Section 830.1 or 830.2, subdivision (a) of Section 830.33, or subdivision (c) of Section 830.5 or for persons retiring after January 1, 1981, shall be in the following format: it shall be on a 2X3 inch card, bear the photograph of the retiree, the retiree's name, address, date of birth, the date that the retiree retired, name and address of the agency from which the retiree retired, have stamped on it the endorsement "CCW Approved"and the date the endorsement is to be renewed.

(E) For purposes of this section and Section 12031, "CCW"means "carry concealed weapons."

(2) A retired peace officer, except an officer listed in Section 830.1 or 830.2, subdivision (a) of Section 830.33, or subdivision (c) of Section 830.5 who retired prior to January 1, 1981, shall petition the issuing agency for the renewal of his or her privilege to carry a concealed firearm every five years. An honorably retired peace officer listed in Section 830.1 or 830.2, subdivision (a) of Section 830.33, or subdivision (c) of Section 830.5 who retired prior to January 1, 1981, shall not be required to obtain an endorsement from the issuing agency to carry a concealed firearm. The agency from which a peace officer is honorably retired may, upon initial retirement of that peace officer, or at any time subsequent thereto, deny or revoke for good cause the retired officer's privilege to carry a concealed firearm. A peace officer who is listed in Section 830.1 or 830.2, subdivision (a) of Section 830.33, or subdivision (c) of Section 830.5 who retired prior to January 1, 1981, shall have his or her privilege to carry a concealed firearm denied or revoked by having the agency from which the officer retired stamp on the officer's identification certificate "No CCW privilege."

(3) An honorably retired peace officer who is listed in subdivision (c) of Section 830.5 and authorized to carry concealed firearms by this subdivision shall meet the training requirements of Section 832 and shall qualify with the firearm at least annually. The individual retired peace officer shall be responsible for maintaining his or her eligibility to carry a concealed firearm. The Department of Justice shall provide subsequent arrest notification pursuant to Section 11105.2 regarding honorably retired peace officers listed in subdivision (c) of Section 830.5 to the agency from which the officer has retired.

(b) The possession or transportation of unloaded pistols, revolvers, or other firearms capable of being concealed upon the person as merchandise by a person who is engaged in the business of manufacturing, importing, wholesaling, repairing, or dealing in firearms and who is licensed to engage in that business or the authorized representative or authorized agent of that person while engaged in the lawful course of the business.

(c) Members of the Army, Navy, Air Force, Coast Guard, or Marine Corps of the United States, or the National Guard, when on duty, or organizations which are by law authorized to purchase or receive those weapons from the United States or this state.

(d) The carrying of unloaded pistols, revolvers, or other firearms capable of being concealed upon the person by duly authorized military or civil organizations while parading, or the members thereof when going to and from the places of meeting of their respective organizations.

(e) Guards or messengers of common carriers, banks, and other financial institutions while actually employed in and about the shipment, transportation, or delivery of any money, treasure, bullion, bonds, or other thing of value within this state.

(f) Members of any club or organization organized for the purpose of practicing shooting at targets upon established target ranges, whether public or private, while the members are using pistols, revolvers, or other firearms capable of being concealed upon the person upon the target ranges, or transporting these firearms unloaded when going to and from the ranges.

(g) Licensed hunters or fishermen carrying pistols, revolvers, or other firearms capable of being concealed upon the person while engaged in hunting or fishing, or transporting those firearms unloaded when going to or returning from the hunting or fishing expedition.

(h) Transportation of unloaded firearms by a person operating a licensed common carrier or an authorized agent or employee thereof when transported in conformance with applicable federal law.

(i) Upon approval of the sheriff of the county in which they reside, honorably retired federal officers or agents of federal law enforcement agencies, including, but not limited to, the Federal Bureau of Investigation, the Secret Service, the United States Customs Service, the Federal Bureau of Alcohol, Tobacco, and

Firearms, the Federal Bureau of Narcotics, the Drug Enforcement Administration, the United States Border Patrol, and officers or agents of the Internal Revenue Service who were authorized to carry weapons while on duty, who were assigned to duty within the state for a period of not less than one year, or who retired from active service in the state.

Retired federal officers or agents shall provide the sheriff with certification from the agency from which they retired certifying their service in the state, the nature of their retirement, and indicating the agency's concurrence that the retired federal officer or agent should be accorded the privilege of carrying a concealed firearm.

Upon that approval, the sheriff shall issue a permit to the retired federal officer or agent indicating that he or she may carry a concealed firearm in accordance with this subdivision. The permit shall be valid for a period not exceeding five years, shall be carried by the retiree while carrying a concealed firearm, and may be revoked for good cause.

The sheriff of the county in which the retired federal officer or agent resides may require recertification prior to a permit renewal, and may suspend the privilege for cause. The sheriff may charge a fee necessary to cover any reasonable expenses incurred by the county.

(j) The carrying of a pistol, revolver, or other firearm capable of being concealed upon the person by a person who is authorized to carry that weapon in a concealed manner pursuant to Article 3 (commencing with Section 12050). *(AM '98)*

12027.1. Retired Peace Officer; Removal of Concealed Firearm Permit

(a)(1)(A)(i) Any peace officer employed by an agency and listed in Section 830.1 or 830.2 or subdivision (c) of Section 830.5 who retired after January 1, 1981, shall have an endorsement on the identification certificate stating that the issuing agency approves the officer's carrying of a concealed and loaded firearm.

(ii) Any peace officer listed in Section 830.1 or 830.2 or subdivision (c) of Section 830.5 who retired prior to January 1, 1981, is authorized to carry a concealed and loaded firearm if the agency issued the officer an identification certificate and the certificate has not been stamped as specified in paragraph (2) of subdivision (a) of Section 12027.

(iii) Peace officers not listed in clause (i) or (ii) who were authorized to, and did, carry firearms during the course and scope of their employment as peace officers, shall have an endorsement on the identification certificate stating that the issuing agency approves the officer's carrying of a concealed and loaded firearm.

(B) An identification certificate authorizing the officer to carry a concealed and loaded firearm or an endorsement on the certificate may be revoked or denied by the issuing agency only upon a showing of good cause. Good cause shall be determined at a hearing, as specified in subdivision (d).

(2) A retired peace officer may have his or her privileges to carry a concealed firearm revoked or denied by violating any departmental rule, or state or federal law that, if violated by an officer on active duty, would result in that officer's arrest, suspension, or removal from the agency.

(b)(1) An identification certificate authorizing the officer to carry a concealed and loaded firearm or an endorsement may be revoked or denied by the issuing agency only upon a showing of good cause. Good cause shall be determined at a hearing, as specified in subdivision (d).

(2) An identification certificate authorizing the officer to carry a concealed and loaded firearm or an endorsement may be revoked only after a hearing, as specified in subdivision (d). Any retired peace officer whose identification certificate authorizing the officer to carry a concealed and loaded firearm or an endorsement is to be revoked shall have 15 days to respond to the notice of the hearing. Notice of the hearing shall be served either personally on the retiree or sent by first-class mail, postage prepaid, return receipt requested to the retiree's last known place of residence. Upon the date the agency receives the signed registered receipt or upon the date the agency receives personally on the retiree, the retiree shall have 15 days to respond to the notification. A retired peace officer who fails to respond to the notice of the hearing shall forfeit his or her right to respond.

(3) An identification certificate authorizing the officer to carry a concealed and loaded firearm or an endorsement may be denied prior to a hearing. If a hearing is not conducted prior to the denial of an endorsement, a retired peace officer, within 15 days of the denial, shall have the right to request a hearing. A retired

peace officer who fails to request a hearing pursuant to this paragraph shall forfeit his or her right to the hearing.

(c) A retired peace officer, when notified of the revocation of his or her privilege to carry a concealed and loaded firearm, after the hearing, or upon forfeiting his or her right to a hearing, shall immediately surrender to the issuing agency his or her identification certificate. The issuing agency shall reissue a new identification certificate without an endorsement. However, if the peace officer retired prior to January 1, 1981, and was at the time of his or her retirement a peace officer listed in Section 830.1 or 830.2 or subdivision (c) of Section 830.5, the issuing agency shall stamp on the identification certificate "No CCW privilege."

(d) Any hearing conducted under this section shall be held before a three-member hearing board. One member of the board shall be selected by the agency and one member shall be selected by the retired peace officer or his or her employee organization. The third member shall be selected jointly by the agency and the retired peace officer or his or her employee organization.

Any decision by the board shall be binding on the agency and the retired peace officer.

(e) No peace officer who is retired after January 1, 1989, because of a psychological disability shall be issued an endorsement to carry a concealed firearm pursuant to this section.

12028.5. Taking Temporary Custody of Firearm at Scene of Domestic Violence Incident

(a) As used in this section, the following definitions shall apply:

(1) "Abuse" means any of the following:

(A) Intentionally or recklessly to cause or attempt to cause bodily injury.

(B) Sexual assault.

(C) To place a person in reasonable apprehension of imminent serious bodily injury to that person or to another.

(D) To molest, attack, strike, stalk, destroy personal property, or violate the terms of a domestic violence protective order issued pursuant to Part 4 (commencing with Section 6300) of Division 10 of the Family Code.

(2) "Domestic violence" means abuse perpetrated against any of the following persons:

(A) A spouse or former spouse.

(B) A cohabitant or former cohabitant, as defined in Section 6209 of the Family Code.

(C) A person with whom the respondent is having or has had a dating or engagement relationship.

(D) A person with whom the respondent has had a child, where the presumption applies that the male parent is the father of the child of the female parent under the Uniform Parentage Act (Part 3 (commencing with Section 7600) of Division 12 of the Family Code).

(E) A child of a party or a child who is the subject of an action under the Uniform Parentage Act, where the presumption applies that the male parent is the father of the child to be protected.

(F) Any other person related by consanguinity or affinity within the second degree.

(3) "Deadly weapon" means any weapon, the possession or concealed carrying of which is prohibited by Section 12020.

(b) A sheriff, undersheriff, deputy sheriff, marshal, deputy marshal, or police officer of a city, as defined in subdivision (a) of Section 830.1, a peace officer of the Department of the California Highway Patrol, as defined in subdivision (a) of Section 830.2, a member of the University of California Police Department, as defined in subdivision (b) of Section 830.2, an officer listed in Section 830.6 while acting in the course and scope of his or her employment as a peace officer, a member of a California State University Police Department, as defined in subdivision (c) of Section 830.2, a peace officer of the Department of Parks and Recreation, as defined in subdivision (f) of Section 830.2, a peace officer, as defined in subdivision (d) of Section 830.31, a peace officer as defined in subdivisions (a) and (b) of Section 830.32, and a peace officer, as defined in Section 830.5, who is at the scene of a domestic violence incident involving a threat to human life or a physical assault, shall take temporary custody of any firearm or other deadly weapon in plain sight or discovered pursuant to a consensual search as necessary for the protection of the peace officer or other persons present. Upon taking custody of a firearm or other deadly weapon, the officer shall give the owner or person who possessed the firearm a receipt. The receipt shall describe the firearm or other deadly weapon and list any identification or serial number on the firearm. The receipt shall indicate where the firearm or other deadly weapon can be recovered and the date after which the owner or possessor can recover the firearm or other deadly weapon. No firearm or other deadly weapon shall be held less than 48 hours. Except as provided in subdivision (e), if a firearm or other deadly weapon is not retained for use as evidence related to criminal charges brought as a result of the domestic violence incident or is not retained because it was illegally possessed, the firearm or other deadly weapon shall be made available to the owner or person who was in lawful possession 48 hours after the seizure or as soon thereafter as possible, but no later than 72 hours after the seizure. In any civil action or proceeding for the return of firearms or ammunition or other deadly weapon seized by any state or local law enforcement agency and not returned within 72 hours following the initial seizure, except as provided in subdivision (c), the court shall allow reasonable attorney's fees to the prevailing party.

(c) Any peace officer, as defined in subdivisions (a) and (b) of Section 830.32, who takes custody of a firearm or deadly weapon pursuant to this section shall deliver the firearm within 24 hours to the city police department or county sheriff's office in the jurisdiction where the college or school is located.

(d) Any firearm or other deadly weapon which has been taken into custody that has been stolen shall be restored to the lawful owner, as soon as its use for evidence has been served, upon his or her identification of the firearm or other deadly weapon and proof of ownership.

(e) Any firearm or other deadly weapon taken into custody and held by a police, university police, or sheriff's department or by a marshal's office, by a peace officer of the Department of the California Highway Patrol, as defined in subdivision (a) of Section 830.2, by a peace officer of the Department of Parks and Recreation, as defined in subdivision (f) of Section 830.2, by a peace officer, as defined in subdivision (d) of Section 830.31, or by a peace officer, as defined in Section 830.5, for longer than 12 months and not recovered by the owner or person who has lawful possession at the time it was taken into custody, shall be considered a nuisance and sold or destroyed as provided in subdivision (c) of Section 12028. Firearms or other deadly weapons not recovered within 12 months due to an extended hearing process as provided in subdivision (j), are not subject to destruction until the court issues a decision, and then only if the court does not order the return of the firearm or other deadly weapon to the owner.

(f) In those cases where a law enforcement agency has reasonable cause to believe that the return of a firearm or other deadly weapon would be likely to result in endangering the victim or the person reporting the assault or threat, the agency shall advise the owner of the firearm or other deadly weapon, and within 30 days of the seizure, initiate a petition in superior court to determine if the firearm or other deadly weapon should be returned. The law enforcement agency may make an ex parte application stating good cause for an order extending the time to file a petition. Including any extension of time granted in response to an ex parte request, a petition must be filed within 60 days of the date of seizure of the firearm.

(g) The law enforcement agency shall inform the owner or person who had lawful possession of the firearm or other deadly weapon, at that person's last known address by registered mail, return receipt requested, that he or she has 30 days from the date of receipt of the notice to respond to the court clerk to confirm his or her desire for a hearing, and that the failure to respond shall result in a default order forfeiting the confiscated firearm or other deadly weapon. For the purposes of this subdivision, the person's last known address shall be presumed to be the address provided to the law enforcement officer by that person at the time of the family violence incident. In the event the person whose firearm or other deadly weapon was seized does not reside at the last address provided to the agency, the agency shall make a diligent, good faith effort to learn the whereabouts of the person and to comply with these notification requirements.

(h) If the person requests a hearing, the court clerk shall set a hearing no later than 30 days from receipt of that request. The court clerk shall notify the person, the law enforcement agency involved, and the district attorney of the date, time, and place of the hearing. Unless it is shown by clear and convincing evidence that the return of the firearm or other deadly weapon would result in endangering the victim or the person reporting the assault or threat, the court shall order the return of the firearm or other deadly weapon and shall award reasonable attorney's fees to the prevailing party.

(i) If the person does not request a hearing or does not otherwise respond within 30 days of the receipt of the notice, the law enforcement agency may file a petition for an order of default and may dispose of the firearm or other deadly weapon as provided in Section 12028.

(j) If, at the hearing, the court does not order the return of the firearm or other deadly weapon to the owner or person who had lawful possession, that person may petition the court for a second hearing within 12 months from the date of the initial hearing. If the owner or person who had lawful possession does not petition the court within this 12-month period for a second hearing or is unsuccessful at the second hearing in gaining return of the firearm or other deadly weapon, the firearm or other deadly weapon may be disposed of as provided in Section 12028.

(k) The law enforcement agency, or the individual law enforcement officer, shall not be liable for any act in the good faith exercise of this section. *(AM '99, '00)*

12031. Loaded Firearm: Carrying in Public Place or in Vehicle

(a)(1) A person is guilty of carrying a loaded firearm when he or she carries a loaded firearm on his or her person or in a vehicle while in any public place or on any public street in an incorporated city or in any public place or on any public street in a prohibited area of unincorporated territory.

(2) Carrying a loaded firearm in violation of this section is punishable, as follows:

(A) Where the person previously has been convicted of any felony, or of any crime made punishable by this chapter, as a felony.

(B) Where the firearm is stolen and the person knew or had reasonable cause to believe that it was stolen, as a felony.

(C) Where the person is an active participant in a criminal street gang, as defined in subdivision (a) of Section 186.22, under the Street Terrorism Enforcement and Prevention Act (Chapter 11 (commencing with Section 186.20) of Title 7 of Part 1), as a felony.

(D) Where the person is not in lawful possession of the firearm, as defined in this section, or is within a class of persons prohibited from possessing or acquiring a firearm pursuant to Section 12021 or 12021.1 of this code or Section 8100 or 8103 of the Welfare and Institutions Code, as a felony.

(E) Where the person has been convicted of a crime against a person or property, or of a narcotics or dangerous drug violation, by imprisonment in the state prison, or by imprisonment in a county jail not to exceed one year, by a fine not to exceed one thousand dollars ($1,000), or by both that imprisonment and fine.

(F) Where the person is not listed with the Department of Justice pursuant to Section 11106, as the registered owner of the pistol, revolver, or other firearm capable of being concealed upon the person, by imprisonment in the state prison, or by imprisonment in a county jail not to exceed one year, or by a fine not to exceed one thousand dollars ($1,000), or both that fine and imprisonment.

(G) In all cases other than those specified in subparagraphs (A) to (F), inclusive, as a misdemeanor, punishable by imprisonment in a county jail not to exceed one year, by a fine not to exceed one thousand dollars ($1,000), or by both that imprisonment and fine.

(3) For purposes of this section, "lawful possession of the firearm" means that the person who has possession or custody of the firearm either lawfully acquired and lawfully owns the firearm or has the permission of the lawful owner or person who otherwise has apparent authority to possess or have custody of the firearm. A person who takes a firearm without the permission of the lawful owner or without the permission of a person who has lawful custody of the firearm does not have lawful possession of the firearm.

(4) Nothing in this section shall preclude prosecution under Sections 12021 and 12021.1 of this code, Section 8100 or 8103 of the Welfare and Institutions Code, or any other law with a greater penalty than this section.

(5)(A) Notwithstanding paragraphs (2) and (3) of subdivision (a) of Section 836, a peace officer may make an arrest without a warrant:

(i) When the person arrested has violated this section, although not in the officer's presence.

(ii) Whenever the officer has reasonable cause to believe that the person to be arrested has violated this section, whether or not this section has, in fact, been violated.

(B) A peace officer may arrest a person for a violation of subparagraph (F) of paragraph (2), if the peace officer has probable cause to believe that the person is carrying a loaded pistol, revolver, or other firearm capable of being concealed upon the person in violation of this section and that person is not listed with the Department of Justice pursuant to paragraph (1) of subdivision (c) of Section 11106 as the registered owner of that pistol, revolver, or other firearm capable of being concealed upon the person.

(6)(A) Every person convicted under this section who has previously been convicted of an offense enumerated in Section 12001.6, or of any crime made punishable under this chapter, shall serve a term of at least three months in a county jail, or, if granted probation or if the execution or imposition of sentence is suspended, it shall be a condition thereof that he or she be imprisoned for a period of at least three months.

(B) The court shall apply the three-month minimum sentence except in unusual cases where the interests of justice would best be served by granting probation or suspending the imposition or execution of sentence without the minimum imprisonment required in this subdivision or by granting probation or suspending the imposition or execution of sentence with conditions other than those set forth in this subdivision, in which case, the court shall specify on the record and shall enter on the minutes the circumstances indicating that the interests of justice would best be served by that disposition.

(7) A violation of this section which is punished by imprisonment in a county jail not exceeding one year shall not constitute a conviction of a crime punishable by imprisonment for a term exceeding one year for the purposes of determining federal firearms eligibility under Section 922(g)(1) of Title 18 of the United States Code.

(b) Subdivision (a) shall not apply to any of the following:

(1) Peace officers listed in Section 830.1 or 830.2, or subdivision (a) of Section 830.33, whether active or honorably retired, other duly appointed peace officers, honorably retired peace officers listed in subdivision (c) of Section 830.5, other honorably retired peace officers who during the course and scope of their employment as peace officers were authorized to, and did, carry firearms, full-time paid peace officers of other states and the federal government who are carrying out official duties while in California, or any person summoned by any of those officers to assist in making arrests or preserving the peace while the person is actually engaged in assisting that officer. Any peace officer described in this paragraph who has been honorably retired shall be issued an identification certificate by the law enforcement agency from which the officer has retired. The issuing agency may charge a fee necessary to cover any reasonable expenses incurred by the agency in issuing certificates pursuant to this paragraph and paragraph (3).

Any officer, except an officer listed in Section 830.1 or 830.2, subdivision (a) of Section 830.33, or subdivision (c) of Section 830.5 who retired prior to January 1, 1981, shall have an endorsement on the identification certificate stating that the issuing agency approves the officer's carrying of a loaded firearm.

No endorsement or renewal endorsement issued pursuant to paragraph (2) shall be effective unless it is in the format set forth in subparagraph (D) of paragraph (1) of subdivision (a) of Section 12027, except that any peace officer listed in subdivision (f) of Section 830.2 or in subdivision (c) of Section 830.5, who is retired between January 2, 1981, and on or before December 31, 1988, and who is authorized to carry a loaded firearm pursuant to this section, shall not be required to have an endorsement in the format set forth in subparagraph (D) of paragraph (1) of subdivision (a) of Section 12027 until the time of the issuance, on or after January 1, 1989, of a renewal endorsement pursuant to paragraph (2).

(2) A retired peace officer, except an officer listed in Section 830.1 or 830.2, subdivision (a) of Section 830.33, or subdivision (c) of Section 830.5 who retired prior to January 1, 1981, shall petition the issuing agency for renewal of his or her privilege to carry a loaded firearm every five years. An honorably retired peace officer listed in Section 830.1 or 830.2, subdivision (a) of Section 830.33, or subdivision (c) of Section 830.5 who retired prior to January 1, 1981, shall not be required to obtain an endorsement from the issuing agency to carry a loaded firearm. The agency from which a peace officer is honorably retired may, upon initial retirement of the peace officer, or at any time subsequent thereto, deny or revoke for good cause the retired officer's privilege to carry a loaded firearm. A peace officer who is listed in Section 830.1 or

830.2, subdivision (a) of Section 830.33, or subdivision (c) of Section 830.5 who is retired prior to January 1, 1981, shall have his or her privilege to carry a loaded firearm denied or revoked by having the agency from which the officer retired stamp on the officer's identification certificate "No CCW privilege."

(3) An honorably retired peace officer who is listed in subdivision (c) of Section 830.5 and authorized to carry loaded firearms by this subdivision shall meet the training requirements of Section 832 and shall qualify with the firearm at least annually. The individual retired peace officer shall be responsible for maintaining his or her eligibility to carry a loaded firearm. The Department of Justice shall provide subsequent arrest notification pursuant to Section 11105.2 regarding honorably retired peace officers listed in subdivision (c) of Section 830.5 to the agency from which the officer has retired.

(4) Members of the military forces of this state or of the United States engaged in the performance of their duties.

(5) Persons who are using target ranges for the purpose of practice shooting with a firearm or who are members of shooting clubs while hunting on the premises of those clubs.

(6) The carrying of pistols, revolvers, or other firearms capable of being concealed upon the person by persons who are authorized to carry those weapons pursuant to Article 3 (commencing with Section 12050) of Chapter 1 of Title 2 of Part 4.

(7) Armored vehicle guards, as defined in Section 7521 of the Business and Professions Code, (A) if hired prior to January 1, 1977, or (B) if hired on or after that date, if they have received a firearms qualification card from the Department of Consumer Affairs, in each case while acting within the course and scope of their employment.

(8) Upon approval of the sheriff of the county in which they reside, honorably retired federal officers or agents of federal law enforcement agencies, including, but not limited to, the Federal Bureau of Investigation, the Secret Service, the United States Customs Service, the Federal Bureau of Alcohol, Tobacco, and Firearms, the Federal Bureau of Narcotics, the Drug Enforcement Administration, the United States Border Patrol, and officers or agents of the Internal Revenue Service who were authorized to carry weapons while on duty, who were assigned to duty within the state for a period of not less than one year, or who retired from active service in the state.

Retired federal officers or agents shall provide the sheriff with certification from the agency from which they retired certifying their service in the state, the nature of their retirement, and indicating the agency's concurrence that the retired federal officer or agent should be accorded the privilege of carrying a loaded firearm.

Upon approval, the sheriff shall issue a permit to the retired federal officer or agent indicating that he or she may carry a loaded firearm in accordance with this paragraph. The permit shall be valid for a period not exceeding five years, shall be carried by the retiree while carrying a loaded firearm, and may be revoked for good cause.

The sheriff of the county in which the retired federal officer or agent resides may require recertification prior to a permit renewal, and may suspend the privilege for cause. The sheriff may charge a fee necessary to cover any reasonable expenses incurred by the county.

(c) Subdivision (a) shall not apply to any of the following who have completed a regular course in firearms training approved by the Commission on Peace Officer Standards and Training:

(1) Patrol special police officers appointed by the police commission of any city, county, or city and county under the express terms of its charter who also, under the express terms of the charter, (A) are subject to suspension or dismissal after a hearing on charges duly filed with the commission after a fair and impartial trial, (B) are not less than 18 years of age or more than 40 years of age, (C) possess physical qualifications prescribed by the commission, and (D) are designated by the police commission as the owners of a certain beat or territory as may be fixed from time to time by the police commission.

(2) The carrying of weapons by animal control officers or zookeepers, regularly compensated as such by a governmental agency when acting in the course and scope of their employment and when designated by a local ordinance or, if the governmental agency is not authorized to act by ordinance, by a resolution, either individually or by class, to carry the weapons, or by persons who are authorized to carry the weapons pur-

suant to Section 14502 of the Corporations Code, while actually engaged in the performance of their duties pursuant to that section.

(3) Harbor police officers designated pursuant to Section 663.5 of the Harbors and Navigation Code.

(d) Subdivision (a) shall not apply to any of the following who have been issued a certificate pursuant to Section 12033. The certificate shall not be required of any person who is a peace officer, who has completed all training required by law for the exercise of his or her power as a peace officer, and who is employed while not on duty as a peace officer.

(1) Guards or messengers of common carriers, banks, and other financial institutions while actually employed in and about the shipment, transportation, or delivery of any money, treasure, bullion, bonds, or other thing of value within this state.

(2) Guards of contract carriers operating armored vehicles pursuant to California Highway Patrol and Public Utilities Commission authority (A) if hired prior to January 1, 1977, or (B) if hired on or after January 1, 1977, if they have completed a course in the carrying and use of firearms which meets the standards prescribed by the Department of Consumer Affairs.

(3) Private investigators and private patrol operators who are licensed pursuant to Chapter 11.5 (commencing with Section 7512) of, and alarm company operators who are licensed pursuant to Chapter 11.6 (commencing with Section 7590) of, Division 3 of the Business and Professions Code, while acting within the course and scope of their employment.

(4) Uniformed security guards or night watch persons employed by any public agency, while acting within the scope and course of their employment.

(5) Uniformed security guards, regularly employed and compensated in that capacity by persons engaged in any lawful business, and uniformed alarm agents employed by an alarm company operator, while actually engaged in protecting and preserving the property of their employers or on duty or en route to or from their residences or their places of employment, and security guards and alarm agents en route to or from their residences or employer-required range training. Nothing in this paragraph shall be construed to prohibit cities and counties from enacting ordinances requiring alarm agents to register their names.

(6) Uniformed employees of private patrol operators and private investigators licensed pursuant to Chapter 11.5 (commencing with Section 7512) of Division 3 of the Business and Professions Code, while acting within the course and scope of their employment.

(e) In order to determine whether or not a firearm is loaded for the purpose of enforcing this section, peace officers are authorized to examine any firearm carried by anyone on his or her person or in a vehicle while in any public place or on any public street in an incorporated city or prohibited area of an unincorporated territory. Refusal to allow a peace officer to inspect a firearm pursuant to this section constitutes probable cause for arrest for violation of this section.

(f) As used in this section, "prohibited area"means any place where it is unlawful to discharge a weapon.

(g) A firearm shall be deemed to be loaded for the purposes of this section when there is an unexpended cartridge or shell, consisting of a case that holds a charge of powder and a bullet or shot, in, or attached in any manner to, the firearm, including, but not limited to, in the firing chamber, magazine, or clip thereof attached to the firearm; except that a muzzle-loader firearm shall be deemed to be loaded when it is capped or primed and has a powder charge and ball or shot in the barrel or cylinder.

(h) Nothing in this section shall prevent any person engaged in any lawful business, including a nonprofit organization, or any officer, employee, or agent authorized by that person for lawful purposes connected with that business, from having a loaded firearm within the person's place of business, or any person in lawful possession of private property from having a loaded firearm on that property.

(i) Nothing in this section shall prevent any person from carrying a loaded firearm in an area within an incorporated city while engaged in hunting, provided that the hunting at that place and time is not prohibited by the city council.

(j)(1) Nothing in this section is intended to preclude the carrying of any loaded firearm, under circumstances where it would otherwise be lawful, by a person who reasonably believes that the person or property of himself or herself or of another is in immediate, grave danger and that the carrying of the weapon is necessary for the preservation of that person or property. As used in this subdivision, "immediate"means the brief interval before and after the local law enforcement agency, when reasonably possible, has been notified of the danger and before the arrival of its assistance.

(2) A violation of this section is justifiable when a person who possesses a firearm reasonably believes that he or she is in grave danger because of circumstances forming the basis of a current restraining order issued by a court against another person or persons who has or have been found to pose a threat to his or her life or safety. This paragraph may not apply when the circumstances involve a mutual restraining order issued pursuant to Division 10 (commencing with Section 6200) of the Family Code absent a factual finding of a specific threat to the person's life or safety. It is not the intent of the Legislature to limit, restrict, or narrow the application of current statutory or judicial authority to apply this or other justifications to defendants charged with violating Section 12025 or of committing other similar offenses.

Upon trial for violating this section, the trier of fact shall determine whether the defendant was acting out of a reasonable belief that he or she was in grave danger.

(k) Nothing in this section is intended to preclude the carrying of a loaded firearm by any person while engaged in the act of making or attempting to make a lawful arrest.

(l) Nothing in this section shall prevent any person from having a loaded weapon, if it is otherwise lawful, at his or her place of residence, including any temporary residence or campsite.

(m)(1) The district attorney of each county shall submit annually a report on or before June 30, to the Attorney General consisting of profiles by race, age, gender, and ethnicity of any person charged with a felony or a misdemeanor under this section and any other offense charged in the same complaint, indictment, or information.

(2) The Attorney General shall submit annually, a report on or before December 31, to the Legislature compiling all of the reports submitted pursuant to paragraph (1).

(3) This subdivision shall remain operative only until January 1, 2005. *(AM '99)*

12034. Prohibition of Firearms in Vehicles; Discharging Firearm From Vehicle

(a) It is a misdemeanor for a driver of any motor vehicle or the owner of any motor vehicle, whether or not the owner of the vehicle is occupying the vehicle, knowingly to permit any other person to carry into or bring into the vehicle a firearm in violation of Section 12031 of this code or Section 2006 of the Fish and Game Code.

(b) Any driver or owner of any vehicle, whether or not the owner of the vehicle is occupying the vehicle, who knowingly permits any other person to discharge any firearm from the vehicle is punishable by imprisonment in the county jail for not more than one year or in state prison for 16 months or two or three years.

(c) Any person who willfully and maliciously discharges a firearm from a motor vehicle at another person other than an occupant of a motor vehicle is guilty of a felony punishable by imprisonment in state prison for three, five, or seven years.

(d) Except as provided in Section 3002 of the Fish and Game Code, any person who willfully and maliciously discharges a firearm from a motor vehicle is guilty of a public offense punishable by imprisonment in the county jail for not more than one year or in the state prison.

12035. Definitions

(a) As used in this section, the following definitions shall apply:

(1) "Locking device"means a device that is designed to prevent the firearm from functioning and when applied to the firearm, renders the firearm inoperable.

(2) "Loaded firearm"has the same meaning as set forth in subdivision (g) of Section 12031.

(3) "Child"means a person under *** 18 years of age.

(4) "Great bodily injury"has the same meaning as set forth in Section 12022.7.

(5) "Locked container"has the same meaning as set forth in subdivision (d) of Section 12026.2.

(b)(1) Except as provided in subdivision (c), a person commits the crime of "criminal storage of a firearm of the first degree"if he or she keeps any loaded firearm within any *** premises that are under his or her custody or control and he or she knows or reasonably should know that a child is likely to gain access to the firearm without the permission of the child's parent or legal guardian and the child obtains access to the firearm and thereby causes death or great bodily injury to himself, herself, or any other person.

(2) Except as provided in subdivision (c), a person commits the crime of "criminal storage of a firearm of the second degree"if he or she keeps any loaded firearm within any *** premises that are under his or her custody or control and he or she knows or reasonably should know that a child is likely to gain access to the firearm without the permission of the child's parent or legal guardian and the child obtains access to the firearm and thereby causes injury, other than great bodily injury, to himself, herself, or any other person, or carries the firearm either to a public place or in violation of Section 417.

(c) Subdivision (b) shall not apply whenever any of the following occurs:

(1) The child obtains the firearm as a result of an illegal entry to any premises by any person.

(2) The firearm is kept in a locked container or in a location that a reasonable person would believe to be secure.

(3) The firearm is carried on the person or within such a close proximity thereto so that the individual can readily retrieve and use the firearm as if carried on the person.

(4) The firearm is locked with a locking device that has rendered the firearm inoperable.

(5) The person is a peace officer or a member of the *** Armed Forces or National Guard and the child obtains the firearm during, or incidental to, the performance of the person's duties.

(6) The child obtains, or obtains and discharges, the firearm in a lawful act of self-defense or defense of another person, or persons.

(7) The person who keeps a loaded firearm on any premise *** that is under his or her custody or control has no reasonable expectation, based on objective facts and circumstances, that a child is likely to be present on the *** premises.

(d) Criminal storage of a firearm is punishable as follows:

(1) Criminal storage of a firearm in the first degree, by imprisonment in the state prison for 16 months, or *** two or *** three years, by a fine not exceeding ten thousand dollars ($10,000), or by both that imprisonment and fine; or by imprisonment in a county jail not exceeding one year, by a fine not exceeding one thousand dollars ($1,000), or by both that fine and imprisonment ***.

(2) Criminal storage of a firearm in the second degree, by imprisonment in a county jail not exceeding one year, by a fine not exceeding one thousand dollars ($1,000), or by both that imprisonment and fine.

(e) If the person who allegedly violated this section is the parent or guardian of a child who is injured or who dies as the result of an accidental shooting, the district attorney shall consider, among other factors, the impact of the injury or death on the person alleged to have violated this section when deciding whether to prosecute an alleged violation. It is the Legislature's intent that a parent or guardian of a child who is injured or who dies as the result of an accidental shooting shall be prosecuted only in those instances in which the parent or guardian behaved in a grossly negligent manner or where similarly egregious circumstances exist. This subdivision shall not otherwise restrict, in any manner, the factors that a district attorney may consider when deciding whether to prosecute alleged violations of this section.

(f) If the person who allegedly violated this section is the parent or guardian of a child who is injured or who dies as the result of an accidental shooting, no arrest of the person for the alleged violation of this section shall occur until at least seven days after the date upon which the accidental shooting occurred.

In addition to the limitation contained in this subdivision, a law enforcement officer shall consider the health status of a child who suffers great bodily injury as the result of an accidental shooting prior to arresting a person for a violation of this section, if the person to be arrested is the parent or guardian of the injured child. The intent of this subdivision is to encourage law enforcement officials to delay the arrest of a parent or guardian of a seriously injured child while the child remains on life-support equipment or is in a similarly critical medical condition.

(g)(1) The fact that the person who allegedly violated this section attended a firearm safety training course prior to the purchase of the firearm that is obtained by a child in violation of this section shall be considered a mitigating factor by a district attorney when he or she is deciding whether to prosecute the alleged violation.

(2) In any action or trial commenced under this section, the fact that the person who allegedly violated this section attended a firearm safety training course prior to the purchase of the firearm that is obtained by a child in violation of this section, shall be admissible.

(h) Every person licensed under Section 12071 shall post within the licensed premises the notice required by paragraph (7) of subdivision (b) of that section, disclosing the duty imposed by this section upon any person who keeps a loaded firearm. *(AM '01)*

12036. Keeping Pistol, Revolver, Etc. Within Premise; Access by Person Under Age of 18 Years

(a) As used in this section, the following definitions shall apply:

(1) "Locking device"means a device that is designed to prevent the firearm from functioning and when applied to the firearm, renders the firearm inoperable.

(2) "Child"means a person under the age of *** 18 years.

(3) "Off-premises"means premises other than the premises where the firearm was stored.

(4) "Locked container"has the same meaning as set forth in subdivision (d) of Section 12026.2.

(b) A person who keeps a pistol, revolver, or other firearm capable of being concealed upon the person, loaded or unloaded, within any *** premises that *** are under his or her custody or control and he or she knows or reasonably should know that a child is likely to gain access to that firearm without the permission of the child's parent or legal guardian and the child obtains access to that firearm and thereafter carries that firearm off-premises, shall be punished by imprisonment in a county jail not exceeding one year, by a fine not exceeding one thousand dollars ($1,000), or by both that imprisonment and fine.

(c) A person who keeps any firearm within any premises that is under his or her custody or control and he or she knows or reasonably should know that a child is likely to gain access to the firearm without the permission of the child's parent or legal guardian and the child obtains access to the firearm and thereafter carries that firearm off-premises to any public or private preschool, elementary school, middle school, high school, or to any school-sponsored event, activity, or performance whether occurring on school grounds or elsewhere, shall be punished by imprisonment in a county jail not exceeding one year, by a fine not exceeding five thousand dollars ($5,000), or by both that imprisonment and fine.

(d) A pistol, revolver, or other firearm capable of being concealed upon the person that a child gains access to and carries off-premises in violation of this section shall be deemed "used in the commission of any misdemeanor as provided in this code or any felony"for the purpose of subdivision (b) of Section 12028 regarding the authority to confiscate firearms and other deadly weapons as a nuisance.

***(e) This section shall not apply if any one of the following circumstances exists:

(1) The child obtains the pistol, revolver, or other firearm capable of being concealed upon the person as a result of an illegal entry into any premises by any person.

(2) The pistol, revolver, or other firearm capable of being concealed upon the person is kept in a locked container or in a location that a reasonable person would believe to be secure.

(3) The pistol, revolver, or other firearm capable of being concealed upon the person is locked with a locking device that has rendered the firearm inoperable.

(4) The pistol, revolver, or other firearm capable of being concealed upon a person is carried on the person within such a close range that the individual can readily retrieve and use the firearm as if carried on the person.

(5) The person is a peace officer or a member of the *** Armed Forces or National Guard and the child obtains the pistol, revolver, or other firearm capable of being concealed upon the person during, or incidental to, the performance of the person's duties.

(6) The child obtains, or obtains and discharges, the pistol, revolver, or other firearm capable of being concealed upon the person in a lawful act of self-defense or defense of another person or persons.

(7) The person who keeps a pistol, revolver, or other firearm capable of being concealed upon the person has no reasonable expectation, based on objective facts and circumstances, that a child is likely to be present on the premises.

***(f) If the person who allegedly violated this section is the parent or guardian of a child who is injured or who dies as the result of an accidental shooting, the district attorney shall consider, among other factors, the impact of the injury or death on the person alleged to have violated this section when deciding whether to prosecute the alleged violation. It is the Legislature's intent that a parent or guardian of a child who is injured or who dies as the result of an accidental shooting shall be prosecuted only in those instances in which the parent or guardian behaved in a grossly negligent manner or where similarly egregious circumstances exist. This subdivision shall not otherwise restrict, in any manner, the factors that a district attorney may consider when deciding whether to prosecute alleged violations of this section.

***(g) If the person who allegedly violated this section is the parent or guardian of a child who is injured or who dies as the result of an accidental shooting, no arrest of the person for the alleged violation of this section shall occur until at least seven days after the date upon which the accidental shooting occurred.

In addition to the limitation contained in this subdivision, a law enforcement officer shall consider the health status of a child who suffers great bodily injury as the result of an accidental shooting prior to arresting a person for a violation of this section, if the person to be arrested is the parent or guardian of the injured child. The intent of this subdivision is to encourage law enforcement officials to delay the arrest of a parent or guardian of a seriously injured child while the child remains on life-support equipment or is in a similarly critical medical condition.

***(h)(1) The fact that the person who allegedly violated this section attended a firearm safety training course prior to the purchase of the firearm that is obtained by a child in violation of this section shall be considered a mitigating factor by a district attorney when he or she is deciding whether to prosecute the alleged violation.

(2) In any action or trial commenced under this section, the fact that the person who allegedly violated this section attended a firearm safety training course prior to the purchase of the firearm that is obtained by a child in violation of this section, shall be admissible.

***(i) Every person licensed under Section 12071 shall post within the licensed premises the notice required by paragraph (7) of subdivision (b) of that section, disclosing the duty imposed by this section upon any person who keeps *** any firearm. *(AM '01)*

12070. Selling, Leasing, Transferring, Advertising, or Offering Firearm Without License

(a) No person shall sell, lease, or transfer firearms unless he or she has been issued a license pursuant to Section 12071. Any person violating this section is guilty of a misdemeanor.

(b) Subdivision (a) does not include any of the following:

(1) The sale, lease, or transfer of any firearm by a person acting pursuant to operation of law, a court order, or pursuant to the Enforcement of Judgments Law (Title 9 (commencing with Section 680.010) of Part 2 of the Code of Civil Procedure), or by a person who liquidates a personal firearm collection to satisfy a court judgment.

(2) A person acting pursuant to subdivision (e) of Section 186.22a or subdivision (c) of Section 12028.

(3) The sale, lease, or transfer of a firearm by a person who obtains title to the firearm by intestate succession or by bequest or as a surviving spouse pursuant to Chapter 1 (commencing with Section 13500) of Part 2 of Division 8 of the Probate Code, provided the person disposes of the firearm within 60 days of receipt of the firearm.

(4) The infrequent sale, lease, or transfer of firearms.

(5) The sale, lease, or transfer of used firearms other than pistols, revolvers, or other firearms capable of being concealed upon the person, at gun shows or events, as specified in subparagraph (B) of paragraph (1) of subdivision (b) of Section 12071, by a person other than a licensee or dealer, provided the person has a valid federal firearms license and a current certificate of eligibility issued by the Department of Justice, as specified in Section 12071, and provided all the sales, leases, or transfers fully comply with subdivision (d) of Section 12072. However, the person shall not engage in the sale, lease, or transfer of used firearms other than pistols, revolvers, or other firearms capable of being concealed upon the person at more than 12 gun shows or events in any calendar year and shall not sell, lease, or transfer more than 15 used firearms other

than pistols, revolvers, or other firearms capable of being concealed upon the person at any single gun show or event. In no event shall the person sell more than 75 used firearms other than pistols, revolvers, or other firearms capable of being concealed upon the person in any calendar year.

A person described in this paragraph shall be known as a "Gun Show Trader."

The Department of Justice shall adopt regulations to administer this program and shall recover the full costs of administration from fees assessed applicants.

As used in this paragraph, the term "used firearm" means a firearm that has been sold previously at retail and is more than three years old.

(6) The activities of a law enforcement agency pursuant to Section 12084.

(7) Deliveries, sales, or transfers of firearms between or to importers and manufacturers of firearms licensed to engage in business pursuant to Chapter 44 (commencing with Section 921) of Title 18 of the United States Code and the regulations issued pursuant thereto.

(8) The sale, delivery, or transfer of firearms by manufacturers or importers licensed pursuant to Chapter 44 (commencing with Section 921) of Title 18 of the United States Code and the regulations issued pursuant thereto to dealers or wholesalers.

(9) Deliveries and transfers of firearms made pursuant to Section 12028, 12028.5, or 12030.

(10) The loan of a firearm for the purposes of shooting at targets, if the loan occurs on the premises of a target facility which holds a business or regulatory license or on the premises of any club or organization organized for the purposes of practicing shooting at targets upon established ranges, whether public or private, if the firearm is at all times kept within the premises of the target range or on the premises of the club or organization.

(11) Sales, deliveries, or transfers of firearms by manufacturers, importers, or wholesalers licensed pursuant to Chapter 44 (commencing with Section 921) of Title 18 of the United States Code and the regulations issued pursuant thereto to persons who reside outside this state who are licensed pursuant to Chapter 44 (commencing with Section 921) of Title 18 of the United States Code and the regulations issued pursuant thereto, if the sale, delivery, or transfer is in accordance with Chapter 44 (commencing with Section 921) of Title 18 of the United States Code and the regulations issued pursuant thereto.

(12) Sales, deliveries, or transfers of firearms by persons who reside outside this state and are licensed outside this state pursuant to Chapter 44 (commencing with Section 921) of Title 18 of the United States Code and the regulations issued pursuant thereto to wholesalers, manufacturers, or importers, if the sale, delivery, or transfer is in accordance with Chapter 44 (commencing with Section 921) of Title 18 of the United States Code and the regulations issued pursuant thereto.

(13) Sales, deliveries, or transfers of firearms by wholesalers to dealers.

(14) Sales, deliveries, or transfers of firearms by persons who reside outside this state to persons licensed pursuant to Section 12071, if the sale, delivery, or transfer is in accordance with Chapter 44 (commencing with Section 921) of Title 18 of the United States Code, and the regulations issued pursuant thereto.

(15) Sales, deliveries, or transfers of firearms by persons who reside outside this state and are licensed pursuant to Chapter 44 (commencing with Section 921) of Title 18 of the United States Code and the regulations issued pursuant thereto to dealers, if the sale, delivery, or transfer is in accordance with Chapter 44 (commencing with Section 921) of Title 18 of the United States Code and the regulations issued pursuant thereto.

(16) The delivery, sale, or transfer of an unloaded firearm by one wholesaler to another wholesaler if that firearm is intended as merchandise in the receiving wholesaler's business.

(17) The loan of an unloaded firearm or the loan of a firearm loaded with blank cartridges for use solely as a prop for a motion picture, television, or video production or entertainment or theatrical event.

(18) The delivery of an unloaded firearm that is a curio or relic, as defined in Section 178.11 of Title 27 of the Code of Federal Regulations, by a person licensed as a collector pursuant to Chapter 44 (commencing with Section 921) of Title 18 of the United States Code and the regulations issued pursuant thereto with a current certificate of eligibility issued pursuant to Section 12071 to a dealer.

(c)(1) As used in this section, "infrequent" means:

(A) For pistols, revolvers, and other firearms capable of being concealed upon the person, less than six transactions per calendar year. For this purpose, "transaction" means a single sale, lease, or transfer of any number of pistols, revolvers, or other firearms capable of being concealed upon the person.

(B) For firearms other than pistols, revolvers, or other firearms capable of being concealed upon the person, occasional and without regularity.

(2) As used in this section, "operation of law" includes, but is not limited to, any of the following:

(A) The executor or administrator of an estate, if the estate includes firearms.

(B) A secured creditor or an agent or employee thereof when the firearms are possessed as collateral for, or as a result of, a default under a security agreement under the Commercial Code.

(C) A levying officer, as defined in Section 481.140, 511.060, or 680.260 of the Code of Civil Procedure.

(D) A receiver performing his or her functions as a receiver, if the receivership estate includes firearms.

(E) A trustee in bankruptcy performing his or her duties, if the bankruptcy estate includes firearms.

(F) An assignee for the benefit of creditors performing his or her functions as an assignee, if the assignment includes firearms.

(G) A transmutation of property between spouses pursuant to Section 850 of the Family Code.

(H) Firearms received by the family of a police officer or deputy sheriff from a local agency pursuant to Section 50081 of the Government Code.

(I) The transfer of a firearm by a law enforcement agency to the person who found the firearm where the delivery is to the person as the finder of the firearm pursuant to Article 1 (commencing with Section 2080) of Chapter 4 of Division 3 of the Civil Code. *(AM '98)*

12072. Transfer of Concealable Deadly Weapon

(a)(1) No person, corporation, or firm shall knowingly supply, deliver, sell, or give possession or control of a firearm to any person within any of the classes prohibited by Section 12021 or 12021.1.

(2) No person, corporation, or dealer shall sell, supply, deliver, or give possession or control of a firearm to any person whom he or she has cause to believe to be within any of the classes prohibited by Section 12021 or 12021.1 of this code or Section 8100 or 8103 of the Welfare and Institutions Code.

(3)(A) No person, corporation, or firm shall sell, loan, or transfer a firearm to a minor, nor sell a handgun to an individual under 21 years of age.

(B) Subparagraph (A) shall not apply to or affect those circumstances set forth in subdivision (p) of Section 12078.

(4) No person, corporation, or dealer shall sell, loan, or transfer a firearm to any person whom he or she knows or has cause to believe is not the actual purchaser or transferee of the firearm, or to any person who is not the person actually being loaned the firearm, if the person, corporation, or dealer has either of the following:

(A) Knowledge that the firearm is to be subsequently loaned, sold, or transferred to avoid the provisions of subdivision (c) or (d).

(B) Knowledge that the firearm is to be subsequently loaned, sold, or transferred to avoid the requirements of any exemption to the provisions of subdivision (c) or (d).

(5) No person, corporation, or dealer shall acquire a firearm for the purpose of selling, transferring, or loaning the firearm, if the person, corporation, or dealer has either of the following:

(A) In the case of a dealer, intent to violate subdivision (b) or (c).

(B) In any other case, intent to avoid either of the following:

(i) The provisions of subdivision (d).

(ii) The requirements of any exemption to the provisions of subdivision (d).

(6) The dealer shall comply with the provisions of paragraph (18) of subdivision (b) of Section 12071.

(7) The dealer shall comply with the provisions of paragraph (19) of subdivision (b) of Section 12071.

(8) No person shall sell or otherwise transfer his or her ownership in a pistol, revolver, or other firearm capable of being concealed upon the person unless the firearm bears either:

(A) The name of the manufacturer, the manufacturer's make or model, and a manufacturer's serial number assigned to that firearm.

(B) The identification number or mark assigned to the firearm by the Department of Justice pursuant to Section 12092.

(9)(A) No person shall make an application to purchase more than one pistol, revolver, or other firearm capable of being concealed upon the person within any 30-day period.

(B) Subparagraph (A) shall not apply to any of the following:

(i) Any law enforcement agency.

(ii) Any agency duly authorized to perform law enforcement duties.

(iii) Any state or local correctional facility.

(iv) Any private security company licensed to do business in California.

(v) Any person who is properly identified as a full-time paid peace officer, as defined in Chapter 4.5 (commencing with Section 830) of Title 3 of Part 2, and who is authorized to, and does carry a firearm during the course and scope of his or her employment as a peace officer.

(vi) Any motion picture, television, or video production company or entertainment or theatrical company whose production by its nature involves the use of a firearm.

(vii) Any person who may, pursuant to Section 12078, claim an exemption from the waiting period set forth in subdivision (c) of this section.

(viii) Any transaction conducted through a licensed firearms dealer pursuant to Section 12082.

(ix) Any transaction conducted through a law enforcement agency pursuant to Section 12084.

(x) Any person who is licensed as a collector pursuant to Chapter 44 (commencing with Section 921) of Title 18 of the United States Code and the regulations issued pursuant thereto and who has a current certificate of eligibility issued to him or her by the Department of Justice pursuant to Section 12071.

(xi) The exchange of a pistol, revolver, or other firearm capable of being concealed upon the person where the dealer purchased that firearm from the person seeking the exchange within the 30-day period immediately preceding the date of exchange or replacement.

(xii) The replacement of a pistol, revolver, or other firearm capable of being concealed upon the person when the person's pistol, revolver, or other firearm capable of being concealed upon the person was lost or stolen, and the person reported that firearm lost or stolen prior to the completion of the application to purchase to any local law enforcement agency of the city, county, or city and county in which he or she resides.

(xiii) The return of any pistol, revolver, or other firearm capable of being concealed upon the person to its owner.

(b) No person licensed under Section 12071 shall supply, sell, deliver, or give possession or control of a pistol, revolver, or firearm capable of being concealed upon the person to any person under the age of 21 years or any other firearm to a person under the age of 18 years.

(c) No dealer, whether or not acting pursuant to Section 12082, shall deliver a firearm to a person, as follows:

(1) Within 10 days of the application to purchase, or, after notice by the department pursuant to subdivision (d) of Section 12076, within 10 days of the submission to the department of any correction to the application, or within 10 days of the submission to the department of any fee required pursuant to subdivision (e) of Section 12076, whichever is later.

(2) Unless unloaded and securely wrapped or unloaded and in a locked container.

(3) Unless the purchaser, transferee, or person being loaned the firearm presents clear evidence of his or her identity and age, as defined in Section 12071, to the dealer.

(4) Whenever the dealer is notified by the Department of Justice that the person is in a prohibited class described in Section 12021 or 12021.1 of this code or Section 8100 or 8103 of the Welfare and Institutions Code.

(5)<~(A) Commencing April 1, 1994, and until January 1, 2003, no pistol, revolver, or other firearm capable of being concealed upon the person shall be delivered unless the purchaser, transferee, or person being loaned the firearm presents to the dealer a basic firearms safety certificate.

(B) Commencing January 1, 2003, no handgun shall be delivered unless the purchaser, transferee, or person being loaned the handgun presents a handgun safety certificate to the dealer.

(6) No pistol, revolver, or other firearm capable of being concealed upon the person shall be delivered whenever the dealer is notified by the Department of Justice that within the preceding 30-day period the purchaser has made another application to purchase a pistol, revolver, or other firearm capable of being concealed upon the person and that the previous application to purchase involved none of the entities specified in subparagraph (B) of paragraph (9) of subdivision (a).

(d) Where neither party to the transaction holds a dealer's license issued pursuant to Section 12071, the parties to the transaction shall complete the sale, loan, or transfer of that firearm through either of the following:

(1) A licensed firearms dealer pursuant to Section 12082.

(2) A law enforcement agency pursuant to Section 12084.

(e) No person may commit an act of collusion relating to Article 8 (commencing with Section 12800) of Chapter 6. For purposes of this section and Section 12071, collusion may be proven by any one of the following factors:

(1) Answering a test applicant's questions during an objective test relating to *** firearms safety.

(2) Knowingly grading the examination falsely.

(3) Providing an advance copy of the test to an applicant.

(4) Taking or allowing another person to take the basic firearms safety course for one who is the applicant for *** a basic firearms safety certificate or a handgun safety certificate.

(5) Allowing another to take the objective test for the applicant, purchaser, or transferee.

(6) Using or allowing another to use one's identification, proof of residency, or thumbprint.

(7) Allowing others to give unauthorized assistance during the examination.

*** (8) Reference to unauthorized materials during the examination and cheating by the applicant.

***(9) Providing originals or photocopies of the objective test, or any version thereof, to any person other than as *** authorized by the department.

(f)(1) No person who is licensed pursuant to Chapter 44 (commencing with Section 921) of Title 18 of the United States Code shall deliver, sell, or transfer a firearm to a person who is licensed pursuant to Chapter 44 (commencing with Section 921) of Title 18 of the United States Code and whose licensed premises are located in this state unless one of the following conditions is met:

(A) The person presents proof of licensure pursuant to Section 12071 to that person.

(B) The person presents proof that he or she is exempt from licensure under Section 12071 to that person, in which case the person also shall present proof that the transaction is also exempt from the provisions of subdivision (d).

(2)(A) On or after January 1, 1998, within 60 days of bringing a pistol, revolver, or other firearm capable of being concealed upon the person into this state, a personal handgun importer shall do one of the following:

(i) Forward by prepaid mail or deliver in person to the Department of Justice, a report prescribed by the department including information concerning that individual and a description of the firearm in question.

(ii) Sell or transfer the firearm in accordance with the provisions of subdivision (d) or in accordance with the provisions of an exemption from subdivision (d).

(iii) Sell or transfer the firearm to a dealer licensed pursuant to Section 12071.

(iv) Sell or transfer the firearm to a sheriff or police department.

(B) If the personal handgun importer sells or transfers the pistol, revolver, or other firearm capable of being concealed upon the person pursuant to subdivision (d) of Section 12072 and the sale or transfer cannot be completed by the dealer to the purchaser or transferee, and the firearm can be returned to the personal handgun importer, the personal handgun importer shall have complied with the provisions of this paragraph.

(C) The provisions of this paragraph are cumulative and shall not be construed as restricting the application of any other law. However, an act or omission punishable in different ways by this section and different provisions of the Penal Code shall not be punished under more than one provision.

(D)(i) On and after January 1, 1998, the department shall conduct a public education and notification program regarding this paragraph to ensure a high degree of publicity of the provisions of this paragraph.

(ii) As part of the public education and notification program described in this subparagraph, the department shall do all of the following:

(I) Work in conjunction with the Department of Motor Vehicles to ensure that any person who is subject to this paragraph is advised of the provisions of this paragraph, and provided with blank copies of the report described in clause (i) of subparagraph (A) at the time that person applies for a California driver's license or registers his or her motor vehicle in accordance with the Vehicle Code.

(II) Make the reports referred to in clause (i) of subparagraph (A) available to dealers licensed pursuant to Section 12071.

(III) Make the reports referred to in clause (i) of subparagraph (A) available to law enforcement agencies.

(IV) Make persons subject to the provisions of this paragraph aware of the fact that reports referred to in clause (i) of subparagraph (A) may be completed at either the licensed premises of dealers licensed pursuant to Section 12071 or at law enforcement agencies, that it is advisable to do so for the sake of accuracy and completeness of the reports, that prior to transporting a pistol, revolver, or other firearm capable of being concealed upon the person to a law enforcement agency in order to comply with subparagraph (A), the person should give prior notice to the law enforcement agency that he or she is doing so, and that in any event, the pistol, revolver, or other firearm capable of being concealed upon the person should be transported unloaded and in a locked container.

(iii) Any costs incurred by the department to implement this paragraph shall be absorbed by the department within its existing budget and the fees in the Dealers'Record of Sale Special Account allocated for implementation of this subparagraph pursuant to Section 12076.

(3) Where a person who is licensed as a collector pursuant to Chapter 44 (commencing with Section 921) of Title 18 of the United States Code and the regulations issued pursuant thereto, whose licensed premises are within this state, acquires a pistol, revolver, or other firearm capable of being concealed upon the person that is a curio or relic, as defined in Section 178.11 of Title 27 of the Code of Federal Regulations, outside of this state, takes actual possession of that firearm outside of this state pursuant to the provisions of subsection (j) of Section 923 of Title 18 of the United States Code, as amended by Public Law 104-208, and transports that firearm into this state, within five days of that licensed collector transporting that firearm into this state, he or she shall report to the department in a format prescribed by the department his or her acquisition of that firearm.

(4)(A) It is the intent of the Legislature that a violation of paragraph (2) or (3) shall not constitute a "continuing offense"and the statute of limitations for commencing a prosecution for a violation of paragraph (2) or (3) commences on the date that the applicable grace period specified in paragraph (2) or (3) expires.

(B) Paragraphs (2) and (3) shall not apply to a person who reports his or her ownership of a pistol, revolver, or other firearm capable of being concealed upon the person after the applicable grace period specified in paragraph (2) or (3) expires if evidence of that violation arises only as the result of the person submitting the report described in paragraph (2) or (3).

(g)(1) Except as provided in paragraph (2) ***, (3), or (5), a violation of this section is a misdemeanor.

(2) If any of the following circumstances apply, a violation of this section is punishable by imprisonment in the state prison for two, three, or four years.

(A) If the violation is of paragraph (1) of subdivision (a).

(B) If the defendant has a prior conviction of violating the provisions, other than paragraph (9) of subdivision (a), of this section or former Section 12100 of this code or Section 8101 of the Welfare and Institutions Code.

(C) If the defendant has a prior conviction of violating any offense specified in subdivision (b) of Section 12021.1 or of a violation of Section 12020, 12220, or 12520, or of former Section 12560.

(D) If the defendant is in a prohibited class described in Section 12021 or 12021.1 of this code or Section 8100 or 8103 of the Welfare and Institutions Code.

(E) A violation of this section by a person who actively participates in a "criminal street gang" as defined in Section 186.22.

(F) A violation of subdivision (b) involving the delivery of any firearm to a person who the dealer knows, or should know, is a minor.

(3) If any of the following circumstances apply, a violation of this section shall be punished by imprisonment in a county jail not exceeding one year or in the state prison, or by a fine not to exceed one thousand dollars ($1,000), or by both *** that fine and imprisonment.

(A) A violation of paragraph (2), (4), or (5)*** of subdivision (a).

(B) A violation of paragraph (3) of subdivision (a) involving the sale, loan, or transfer of a pistol, revolver, or other firearm capable of being concealed upon the person to a minor.

(C) A violation of subdivision (b) involving the delivery of a pistol, revolver, or other firearm capable of being concealed upon the person.

(D) A violation of paragraph (1), (3), (4), ***(5), or (6) of subdivision (c) involving a pistol, revolver, or other firearm capable of being concealed upon the person.

(E) A violation of subdivision (d) involving a pistol, revolver, or other firearm capable of being concealed upon the person.

(F) A violation of subdivision (e).

(4) If both of the following circumstances apply, an additional term of imprisonment in the state prison for one, two, or three years shall be imposed in addition and consecutive to the sentence prescribed***.

(A) A violation of paragraph (2) of subdivision (a) or subdivision (b).

(B) The firearm transferred in violation of paragraph (2) of subdivision (a) or subdivision (b) is used in the subsequent commission of a felony for which a conviction is obtained and the prescribed sentence is imposed.

(5)(A) A first violation of paragraph (9) of subdivision (a) is an infraction punishable by a fine of fifty dollars ($50).

(B) A second violation of paragraph (9) of subdivision (a) is an infraction punishable by a fine of one hundred dollars ($100).

(C) A third or subsequent violation of paragraph (9) of subdivision (a) is a misdemeanor.

(D) For purposes of this paragraph each application to purchase a pistol, revolver, or other firearm capable of being concealed upon the person in violation of paragraph (9) of subdivision (a) shall be deemed a separate offense. *(AM '01)*

Firearms Safety Devices

12087. Article Title

This article shall be known and may be cited as the "Aroner-Scott-Hayden Firearms Safety Act of 1999." *(AD '99)*

12087.5. Legislative Findings

The Legislature makes the following findings:

(a) In the years 1987 to 1996, nearly 2,200 children in the United States under the age of 15 years died in unintentional shootings. In 1996 alone, 138 children were shot and killed unintentionally. Thus, more than 11 children every month, or one child every three days, were shot or killed unintentionally in firearms-related incidents.

(b) The United States leads the industrialized world in the rates of children and youth lost to unintentional, firearms-related deaths. A 1997 study from the federal Centers for Disease Control and Prevention reveals that for unintentional firearm-related deaths for children under the age of 15, the rate in the United States was nine times higher than in 25 other industrialized countries combined.

(c) While the number of unintentional deaths from firearms is an unacceptable toll on America's children, nearly eight times that number are treated in U.S. hospital emergency rooms each year for nonfatal unintentional gunshot wounds.

(d) A study of unintentional firearm deaths among children in California found that unintentional gunshot wounds most often involve handguns.

(e) A study in the December 1995 issue of the Archives of Pediatric and Adolescent Medicine found that children as young as three years old are strong enough to fire most commercially available handguns. The study revealed that 25 percent of three to four year olds and 70 percent of five to six year olds had sufficient finger strength to fire 59 (92 percent) of the 64 commonly available handguns referenced in the study.

(f) The Government Accounting Office (GAO), in its March 1991 study, "Accidental Shootings: Many Deaths and Injuries Caused by Firearms Could be Prevented,"estimates that 31 percent of accidental deaths caused by firearms might be prevented by the addition of two safety devices: a child-resistant safety device that automatically engages and a device that indicates whether the gun is loaded. According to the study results, of the 107 unintentional firearms-related fatalities the GAO examined for the calendar years 1988 and 1989, eight percent could have been prevented had the firearm been equipped with a child-resistant safety device. This eight percent represents instances in which children under the age of six unintentionally shot and killed themselves or other persons.

(g) Currently, firearms are the only products manufactured in the United Stated that are not subject to minimum safety standards.

(h) A 1997 public opinion poll conducted by the National Opinion Research Center at the University of Chicago in conjunction with the Johns Hopkins Center for Gun Policy and Research found that 74 percent of Americans support safety regulation of the firearms industry.

(i) Some currently available trigger locks and other similar devices are inadequate to prevent the accidental discharge of the firearms to which they are attached, or to prevent children from gaining access to the firearm. *(AD '99)*

12088. Certification of Laboratories; DOJ to Publish Roster of Approved Devices

Effective January 1, 2001:

(a) The Department of Justice shall certify laboratories to verify compliance with standards for firearms safety devices set forth in Section 12088.2.

(b) The Department of Justice may charge any laboratory that is seeking certification to test firearms safety devices a fee not exceeding the costs of certification, including costs associated with the development and approval of regulations and standards pursuant to Section 12088.2.

(c) The certified laboratory shall, at the manufacturer's or dealer's expense, test the firearms safety device and submit a copy of the final test report directly to the Department of Justice along with the firearms safety device. The department shall notify the manufacturer or dealer of its receipt of the final test report and the department's determination as to whether the firearms safety device tested may be sold in this state.

(d) On and after July 1, 2001, the Department of Justice shall compile, publish, and thereafter maintain a roster listing all of the safety devices that have been tested by a certified testing laboratory, have been determined to meet the department's standards for firearms safety devices and may be sold in this state.

(e) The roster shall list, for each firearms safety device, the manufacturer, model number, and model name. *(AD '99)*

12088.1. Approved Firearm Safety Device Required

Effective January 1, 2002:

(a) All firearms sold or transferred in this state by a licensed firearms dealer, including private transfers through a dealer, and all firearms manufactured in this state, shall include or be accompanied by a firearms safety device that is listed on the Department of Justice's roster of approved firearms safety devices.

(b) All firearms sold or transferred in this state by a licensed firearms dealer, including private transfers through a dealer, and all firearms manufactured in this state shall be accompanied with warning language or labels as described in Section 12088.3.

(c) The sale or transfer of a firearm shall be exempt from subdivision (a) if both of the following apply:

(1) The purchaser or transferee owns a gun safe that meets the standards set forth in Section 12088.2. Gun safes shall not be required to be tested, and therefore may meet the standards without appearing on the Department of Justice roster.

(2) The purchaser or transferee presents an original receipt for purchase of the gun safe, or other proof of purchase or ownership of the gun safe as authorized by the Attorney General, to the firearms dealer. The dealer shall maintain a copy of this receipt or proof of purchase with the dealers' record of sales of firearms.

(d) The sale or transfer of a firearm shall be exempt from subdivision (a) if all of the following apply:

(1) The purchaser or transferee purchases an approved safety device no more than 30 days prior to the day the purchaser or transferee takes possession of the firearm.

(2) The purchaser or transferee presents the approved safety device to the firearms dealer when picking up the firearm.

(3) The purchaser or transferee presents an original receipt to the firearms dealer which shows the date of purchase, the name, and the model number of the safety device.

(4) The firearms dealer verifies that the requirements in (1) to (3), inclusive, have been satisfied.

(5) The firearms dealer maintains a copy of the receipt along with the dealers' record of sales of firearms. *(AD '99)*

12088.2. Firearm Safety Devices; Regulations to Implement Minimum Standards

(a) No later than January 1, 2000, the Attorney General shall commence development of regulations to implement a minimum safety standard for firearms safety devices and gun safes to significantly reduce the risk of firearms-related injuries to children 17 years of age and younger. The final standard shall do all of the following:

(1) Address the risk of injury from unintentional gunshot wounds.

(2) Address the risk of injury from self-inflicted gunshot wounds by unauthorized users.

(3) Include provisions to ensure that all firearms safety devices and gun safes are reusable and of adequate quality and construction to prevent children and unauthorized users from firing the firearm and to ensure that these devices cannot be readily removed from the firearm or that the firearm cannot be readily removed from the gun safe except by an authorized user utilizing the key, combination, or other method of access intended by the manufacturer of the device.

(4) Include additional provisions as appropriate.

(b) The Attorney General may consult, for the purposes of guidance in development of the standards, test protocols such as those described in Title 16 (commencing with Part 1700) of the Code of Federal Regulations, relating to poison prevention packaging standards. These protocols may be consulted to provide suggestions for potential methods to utilize in developing standards and shall serve as guidance only. The Attorney General shall also give appropriate consideration to the use of devices that are not detachable, but are permanently installed and incorporated into the design of a firearm. The Attorney General shall adopt and issue regulations implementing a final standard not later than January 1, 2001. The Attorney General shall report to the Legislature on these standards by January 1, 2001. The final standard shall be effective January 1, 2002. *(AD '99)*

12088.3.   Firearms Packaging and Descriptive Materials; Required Warning Label

(a) The packaging of any firearm and any descriptive materials that accompany any firearm sold or transferred in this state, or delivered for sale in this state, by any licensed manufacturer, or licensed dealer, shall bear a label containing the following warning statement:

WARNING Children are attracted to and can operate firearms that can cause severe injuries or death. Prevent child access by always keeping guns locked away and unloaded when not in use. If you keep a loaded firearm where a child obtains and improperly uses it, you may be fined or sent to prison.

A yellow triangle containing an exclamation mark shall appear immediately before the word "Warning" on the label.

(b) If the firearm is sold or transferred without accompanying packaging, the warning label or notice shall be affixed to the firearm itself by a method to be prescribed by regulation of the Attorney General.

(c) The warning statement required under subdivisions (a) and (b) shall be:

(1) Displayed in its entirety on the principal display panel of the firearm's package, and on any descriptive materials that accompany the firearm.

(2) Displayed in both English and Spanish in conspicuous and legible type in contrast by typography, layout, or color with other printed matter on that package or descriptive materials in a manner consistent with Part 1500.121 of Title 16, of the Code of Federal Regulations, or successor regulations thereto. *(AD '99)*

12088.4.   Recall by Attorney General of Safety Device Not in Conformance with Standards

If at any time the Attorney General determines that a gun safe or firearms safety device subject to the provisions of this article and sold after January 1, 2002, does not conform with the standards required by subdivision (a) of Section 12088.1 or Section 12088.2, the Attorney General may order the recall and replacement of the gun safe or firearms safety device, or order that the gun safe or firearm safety device be brought into conformity with those requirements. If the firearms safety device cannot be separated from the firearm without damaging the firearm, the Attorney General may order the recall and replacement of the firearm. If the firearms safety device can be separated and reattached to the firearm without damaging the firearm, the licensed manufacturer or licensed firearms dealer shall immediately provide a conforming replacement as instructed by the Attorney General. *(AD '99)*

12088.5.   Required Report by Investigating Law Enforcement Agency

Each lead law enforcement agency investigating an incident shall report to the State Department of Health Services any information obtained that reasonably supports the conclusion that:

(a) A child 18 years of age or younger suffered an unintentional or self-inflicted gunshot wound inflicted by a firearm that was sold or transferred in this state, or manufactured in this state.

(b) Whether as a result of that incident the child died, suffered serious injury, or was treated for an injury by a medical professional. *(AD '99)*

12088.6.   Penalties

Any violation of Section 12088.1 or Section 12088.3 is punishable by a fine of one thousand dollars ($1,000). On the second violation of any of those sections, the licensed firearm manufacturer shall be ineligible to manufacture, or the licensed firearm dealer shall be ineligible to sell, firearms in this state for 30 days, and shall be punished by a fine of one thousand dollars ($1,000). On the third violation of any of those sections, a firearm manufacturer shall be permanently ineligible to manufacture firearms in this state. On the third violation of any of those sections, a licensed firearm dealer shall be permanently ineligible to sell firearms in this state. *(AD '99)*

12088.7.   Compliance with Standards not Relief from Liability

Compliance with the requirements set forth in this article shall not relieve any person from liability to any other person as may be imposed pursuant to common law, statutory law, or local ordinance. *(AD '99)*

12088.8. Antique Firearm; Exclusion

(a) This article does not apply to the commerce of any firearm defined as an "antique firearm"in paragraph (16) of subsection (a) of Section 921 of Title 18 of the United States Code.

(b) This article shall not apply to the commerce of any firearm intended to be used by a salaried, full-time peace officer as defined in Chapter 4.5 (commencing with Section 830) of Title 3 of Part 2 for purposes of law enforcement. Nothing in this article shall preclude local governments, local agencies, or state law enforcement agencies from requiring their peace officers to store their firearms in gun safes or attach firearms safety devices to those firearms. *(AD '99)*

12088.9. Additional Transfer Fee; Firearm Safety Account

(a) The Department of Justice may require each dealer to charge each firearm purchaser or transferee a fee not to exceed one dollar ($1) for each firearm transaction. The fee shall be for the purpose of supporting department program costs related to this act, including the establishment, maintenance, and upgrading of related data base systems and public rosters.

(b) There is hereby created within the General Fund the Firearm Safety Account. Revenue from the fee imposed by subdivision (a) shall be deposited into the Firearm Safety Account and shall be available for expenditure by the Department of Justice upon appropriation by the Legislature. Expenditures from the Firearm Safety Account shall be limited to program expenditures as defined by subdivision (a). *(AD '99)*

12090. Altering or Effacing Identifying Marks on Firearms

Any person who changes, alters, removes or obliterates the name of the maker, model, manufacturer's number, or other mark of identification, including any distinguishing number or mark assigned by the Department of Justice on any pistol, revolver, or any other firearm, without first having secured written permission from the department to make such change, alteration or removal shall be punished by imprisonment in the state prison.

12091. Possession of Firearms With Altered Identifying Marks

Possession of any pistol or revolver upon which the name of the maker, model, manufacturer's number or other mark of identification has been changed, altered, removed, or obliterated, shall be presumptive evidence that the possessor has changed, altered, removed, or obliterated the same.

12092. Assignment of Identifying Mark

The Department of Justice upon request may assign a distinguishing number or mark of identification to any firearm whenever it is without a manufacturer's number, or other mark of identification or whenever the manufacturer's number or other mark of identification or the distinguishing number or mark assigned by the department has been destroyed or obliterated.

12093. Restoration of Identifying Mark

Any person may place or stamp on any pistol, revolver, or other firearm any number or identifying indicium, provided the number or identifying indicium does not change, alter, remove, or obliterate the manufacturer's name, number, model, or other mark of identification. This section does not prohibit restoration by the owner of the name of the maker, model, or of the original manufacturer's number or other mark of identification when such restoration is authorized by the department, nor prevent any manufacturer from placing in the ordinary course of business the name of the maker, model, manufacturer's number, or other mark of identification upon a new firearm.

12094. Purchase or Sale of Firearm Without Identifying Mark

(a) Any person with knowledge of any change, alteration, removal, or obliteration described herein, who buys, receives, disposes of, sells, offers for sale, or has in his or her possession any pistol, revolver, or other firearm which has had the name of the maker, model, or the manufacturer's number or other mark of identification including any distinguishing number or mark assigned by the Department of Justice changed, altered, removed, or obliterated is guilty of a misdemeanor.

(b) Subdivision (a) does not apply to any of the following:

(1) The acquisition or possession of a firearm described in subdivision (a) by any member of the military forces of *** this state or of the United States, while on duty and acting within the scope and course of his or her employment.

(2) The acquisition or possession of a firearm described in subdivision (a) by any peace officer described in Chapter 4.5 (commencing with Section 830) of Title 3 of Part 2, while on duty and acting within the scope and course of his or her employment.

(3) The acquisition or possession of a firearm described in subdivision (a) by any employee of a forensic laboratory, while on duty and acting within the scope and course of his or her employment.

(4) The possession and disposition of a firearm described in subdivision (a) by a person who meets*** all of the following:

(A) He or she is not prohibited from possessing firearms or ammunition pursuant to Section 12021 or 12021.1 or paragraph (1) of subdivision (b) of Section 12316 of this code, or Section 8100 or 8103 of the Welfare and Institutions Code.

(B) The person possessed the firearm no longer than was necessary to deliver the same to a law enforcement agency for that agency's disposition according to law.

(C) If the person is transporting the firearm, he or she is transporting the firearm to a law enforcement agency in order to deliver the firearm to the law enforcement agency for the agency's disposition according to law.

(D) If the person is transporting the firearm to a law enforcement agency, he or she has given prior notice to the law enforcement agency that he or she is transporting the firearm to that law enforcement agency for that agency's disposition according to law.

(E) The firearm is transported in a locked container as defined in subdivision (d) of Section 12026.2. *(AM '01)*

12101. Possession of Pistol, Revolver, or Live Ammunition by Minor

(a)(1) A minor shall not possess a pistol, revolver, or other firearm capable of being concealed upon the person.

(2) Paragraph (1) shall not apply if one of the following circumstances exists:

(A) The minor is accompanied by his or her parent or legal guardian, and the minor is actively engaged in, or is in direct transit to or from, a lawful, recreational sport, including, but not limited to, competitive shooting, or agricultural, ranching, or hunting activity, or a motion picture, television, or video production, or entertainment or theatrical event, the nature of which involves this use of a firearm.

(B) The minor is accompanied by a responsible adult, the minor has the prior written consent of his or her parent or legal guardian, and the minor is actively engaged in, or is in direct transit to or from, a lawful, recreational sport, including, but not limited to, competitive shooting, or agricultural, ranching, or hunting activity, or a motion picture, television, or video production, or entertainment or theatrical event, the nature of which involves the use of a firearm.

(C) The minor is at least 16 years of age, the minor has the prior written consent of his or her parent or legal guardian and the minor is actively engaged in, or is in direct transit to or from, a lawful recreational sport, including, but not limited to, competitive shooting, or agricultural, ranching, or hunting activity, or a motion picture, television, or video production, or entertainment or theatrical event, the nature of which involves the use of a firearm.

(D) The minor has the prior written consent of his or her parent or legal guardian, the minor is on lands owned or lawfully possessed by his or her parent or legal guardian, and the minor is actively engaged in, or is in direct transit to or from, a lawful, recreational sport, including, but not limited to, competitive shooting, or agricultural, ranching, or hunting activity, or a motion picture, television, or video production, or entertainment or theatrical event, the nature of which involves the use of a firearm.

(b)(1) A minor shall not possess live ammunition.

(2) Paragraph (1) shall not apply if one of the following circumstances exists:

(A) The minor has the written consent of his or her parent or legal guardian to possess live ammunition.

(B) The minor is accompanied by his or her parent or legal guardian.

(C) The minor is actively engaged in, or is going to or from, a lawful, recreational sport, including, but not limited to, competitive shooting, or agricultural, ranching, or hunting activity, the nature of which involves the use of a firearm.

(c) Every minor who violates this section shall be punished as follows:

(1) By imprisonment in the state prison or in a county jail if one of the following applies:

(A) The minor has been found guilty previously of violating this section.

(B) The minor has been found guilty previously of an offense specified in subdivision (b) of Section 12021.1 or in Section 12020, 12220, 12520, or 12560.

(C) The minor has been found guilty of a violation of paragraph (1) of subdivision (a).

(2) Violations of this section other than those violations specified in paragraph (1) shall be punishable as a misdemeanor.

(d) In a proceeding to enforce this section brought pursuant to Article 14 (commencing with Section 601) of Chapter 2 of Part 1 of the Welfare and Institutions Code, the court may require the custodial parent or legal guardian of a minor who violates this section to participate in classes on parenting education that meet the requirements established in Section 16507.7 of the Welfare and Institutions Code.

(e) As used in this section, "responsible adult"means a person at least 21 years of age who is not within a class of persons prohibited from owning or possessing firearms by virtue of Section 12021 or 12021.1 of this code, or Section 8100 or 8103 of the Welfare and Institutions Code.

(f) It is not the intent of the Legislature in enacting the amendments to this section or to Section 12078 to expand or narrow the application of current statutory or judicial authority as to the rights of minors to be loaned or to possess live ammunition or a firearm for the purpose of self-defense or the defense of others.

12125. Manufacture, Sale, etc. of Unsafe Handgun

(a) Commencing January 1, 2001, any person in this state who manufactures or causes to be manufactured, imports into the state for sale, keeps for sale, offers or exposes for sale, gives, or lends any unsafe handgun shall be punished by imprisonment in a county jail not exceeding one year.

(b) This section shall not apply to any of the following:

(1) The manufacture in this state, or importation into this state, of any prototype pistol, revolver, or other firearm capable of being concealed upon the person when the manufacture or importation is for the sole purpose of allowing an independent laboratory certified by the Department of Justice pursuant to Section 12130 to conduct an independent test to determine whether that pistol, revolver, or other firearm capable of being concealed upon the person is prohibited by this chapter, and, if not, for the department to add the firearm to the roster of pistols, revolvers, and other firearms capable of being concealed upon the person that may be sold in this state pursuant to Section 12131.

(2) The importation or lending of a pistol, revolver, or other firearm capable of being concealed upon the person by employees or authorized agents determining whether the weapon is prohibited by this section.

(3) Firearms listed as curios or relics, as defined in Section 178.11 of Title 27 of the Code of Federal Regulations.

(4) The sale to, purchase by, or possession of any pistol, revolver or other firearm capable of being concealed upon the person by the Department of Justice, any police department, any sheriff's official, any marshal's office, the Youth and Adult Correctional Agency, the California Highway Patrol, any district attorney's office, and the military or naval forces of this state or of the United States for use in the discharge of their official duties. Nor shall anything in this section prohibit the possession of any pistol, revolver, or other firearm capable of being concealed upon the person by sworn members of these agencies, whether the sworn member is on or off duty, or an individual who is retired from service with a law enforcement agency and who is not otherwise prohibited from possessing a concealable firearm upon his or her retirement.

(c) Violations of subdivision (a) are cumulative with respect to each handgun and shall not be construed as restricting the application of any other law. However, an act or omission punishable in different ways by this section and other provisions of law shall not be punished under more than one provision, but the penalty to be imposed shall be determined as set forth in Section 654. *(AD '99)*

12200. Machinegun Defined

The term "machinegun"as used in this chapter means any weapon which shoots, is designed to shoot, or can readily be restored to shoot, automatically more than one shot, without manual reloading, by a single function of the trigger. The term shall also include the frame or receiver of any such weapon, any part designed and intended solely and exclusively, or combination of parts designed and intended, for use in converting a weapon into a machinegun, and any combination of parts from which a machinegun can be assembled if such parts are in the possession or under the control of a person. The term also includes any weapon deemed by the federal Bureau of Alcohol, Tobacco, and Firearms as readily convertible to a machinegun under Chapter 53 (commencing with Section 5801) of Title 26 of the United States Code. *(AM '00)*

12220. Sale, Possession or Transportation Illegal

(a) Any person, firm, or corporation, who within this state possesses or knowingly transports a machine gun, except as authorized by this chapter, is guilty of a public offense and upon conviction thereof shall be punished by imprisonment in the state prison, or by a fine not to exceed ten thousand dollars ($10,000), or by both such fine and imprisonment.

(b) Any person, firm, or corporation who within this state intentionally converts a firearm into a machine gun, or who sells, or offers for sale, or knowingly manufactures a machine gun, except as authorized by this chapter, is punishable by imprisonment in the state prison for four, six, or eight years.

12276. "Assault Weapons" Defined

As used in this chapter, "assault weapon"shall mean the following designated semiautomatic firearms:

(a) All of the following specified rifles:

(1) All AK series including, but not limited to, the models identified as follows:

(A) Made in China AK, AKM, AKS, AK47, AK47S, 56, 56S, 84S, and 86S.

(B) Norinco 56, 56S, 84S, and 86S.

(C) Poly Technologies AKS and AK47.

(D) MAADI AK47 and ARM.

(2) UZI and Galil.

(3) Beretta AR-70.

(4) CETME Sporter

(5) Colt AR-15 series.

(6) Daewoo K-l, K-2, Max 1, Max 2, AR 100, and AR 110C.

(7) Fabrique Nationale FAL, LAR, FNC, 308 Match, and Sporter.

(8) MAS 223.

(9) HK-91, HK-93, HK-94, HK-PSG-l.

(10) The following MAC types:

(A) RPB Industries Inc. sM10 and sM11.

(B) SWD Incorporated M11.

(11) SKS with detachable magazine.

(12) SIG AMT, PE-57, SG 550, and SG 551.

(13) Springfield Armory BM59 and SAR-48.

(14) Sterling MK-6.

(15) Steyer AUG.

(16) Valmet M62S, M71S, and M78S.

(17) Armalite AR-180.

(18) Bushmaster Assault Rifle.

(19) Calico M-900.

(20) J&R ENG M-68.

(21) Weaver Arms Nighthawk.

(b) All of the following specified pistols:

(1) UZI.

(2) Encom MP-9 and MP-45.

(3) The following MAC types:

(A) RPB Industries Inc. sM10 and sM11.

(B) SWD Incorporated M-11.

(C) Advance Armament Inc. M-11.

(D) Military Armament Corp. Ingram M-11.

(4) Intratec TEC-9.

(5) Sites Spectre.

(6) Sterling MK-7.

(7) Calico M-950.

(8) Bushmaster Pistol.

(c) All of the following specified shotguns:

(1) Franchi SPAS 12 and LAW 12.

(2) Striker 12.

(3) The Streetsweeper type S/S Inc. SS/12

(d) Any firearm declared by a court pursuant to Section 12276.5 to be an assault weapon that is specified as an assault weapon in a list promulgated pursuant to Section 12276.5.

(e) The term "series" includes all other models that are only variations, with minor differences, of those models listed in subdivision (a), regardless of the manufacturer.

(f) This section is declaratory of existing law, as amended, and a clarification of the law and the Legislature's intent which bans the weapons enumerated in this section, the weapons included in the list promulgated by the Attorney General pursuant to Section 12276.5, and any other models which are only variations of those weapons with minor differences, regardless of the manufacturer. The Legislature has defined assault weapons as the types, series, and models listed in this section because it was the most effective way to identify and restrict a specific class of semiautomatic weapons.

12276.1. Assault Weapon; Additional Definitions

(a) Notwithstanding Section 12276, "assault weapon" shall also mean any of the following:

(1) A semiautomatic, centerfire rifle that has the capacity to accept a detachable magazine and any one of the following:

(A) A pistol grip that protrudes conspicuously beneath the action of the weapon.

(B) A thumbhole stock.

(C) A folding or telescoping stock.

(D) A grenade launcher or flare launcher.

(E) A flash suppressor.

(F) A forward pistol grip.

(2) A semiautomatic, centerfire rifle that has a fixed magazine with the capacity to accept more than 10 rounds.

(3) A semiautomatic, centerfire rifle that has an overall length of less than 30 inches.

(4) A semiautomatic pistol that has the capacity to accept a detachable magazine and any one of the following:

(A) A threaded barrel, capable of accepting a flash suppressor, forward handgrip, or silencer.

(B) A second handgrip.

(C) A shroud that is attached to, or partially or completely encircles, the barrel that allows the bearer to fire the weapon without burning his or her hand, except a slide that encloses the barrel.

(D) The capacity to accept a detachable magazine at some location outside of the pistol grip.

(5) A semiautomatic pistol with a fixed magazine that has the capacity to accept more than 10 rounds.

(6) A semiautomatic shotgun that has both of the following:

(A) A folding or telescoping stock.

(B) A pistol grip that protrudes conspicuously beneath the action of the weapon, thumbhole stock, or vertical handgrip.

(7) A semiautomatic shotgun that has the ability to accept a detachable magazine.

(8) Any shotgun with a revolving cylinder.

(b) The Legislature finds a significant public purpose in exempting pistols that are designed expressly for use in Olympic target shooting events. Therefore, those pistols that are sanctioned by the International Olympic Committee and by USA Shooting, the national governing body for international shooting competition in the United States, and that are used for Olympic target shooting purposes at the time the act adding this subdivision is enacted, and that would otherwise fall within the definition of "assault weapon" pursuant to this section are exempt, as provided in subdivision (c).

(c) "Assault weapon" does not include either of the following:

(1) Any antique firearm.

(2) Any of the following pistols, because they are consistent with the significant public purpose expressed in subdivision (b):

MANUFACTURER	MODEL	CALIBER
BENELLI	MP90	.22LR
BENELLI	MP90	.32 S&W LONG
BENELLI	MP95	.22LR
BENELLI	MP95	.32 S&W LONG
HAMMERLI	280	.22LR
HAMMERLI	280	.32 S&W LONG
HAMMERLI	SP20	.22LR
HAMMERLI	SP20	.32 S&W LONG
PARDINI	GPO	.22 SHORT
PARDINI	GP-SCHUMANN	.22 SHORT
PARDINI	HP	.32 S&W LONG
PARDINI	MP	.32 S&W LONG
PARDINI	SP	.22LR
PARDINI	SPE	.22LR
WALTHER	GSP	.22LR
WALTHER	GSP	.32 S&W LONG
WALTHER	OSP	.22 SHORT
WALTHER	OSP-2000	.22 SHORT

(d) The following definitions shall apply under this section:

(1) "Magazine" shall mean any ammunition feeding device.

(2) "Capacity to accept more than 10 rounds" shall mean capable of accommodating more than 10 rounds, but shall not be construed to include a feeding device that has been permanently altered so that it cannot accommodate more than 10 rounds.

(3) "Antique firearm" means any firearm manufactured prior to January 1, 1899.

(e) This section shall become operative January 1, 2000. *(AD '99; AM '00)*

12280. Manufacture, Transportation, Sale, or Possession of Assault Weapon

(a)(1) Any person who, within this state, manufactures or causes to be manufactured, distributes, transports, or imports into the state, keeps for sale, or offers or exposes for sale, or who gives or lends any assault weapon, except as provided by this chapter, is guilty of a felony, and upon conviction shall be punished by imprisonment in the state prison for four, six, or eight years.

(2) In addition and consecutive to the punishment imposed under paragraph (1), any person who transfers, lends, sells, or gives any assault weapon to a minor in violation of paragraph (1) shall receive an enhancement of one year.

(b) Except as provided in Section 12288, and in subdivisions (c) and (d), any person who, within this state, possesses any assault weapon, except as provided in this chapter, is guilty of a public offense and upon conviction shall be punished by imprisonment in the state prison, or in a county jail, not exceeding one year. However, if the person presents proof that he or she lawfully possessed the assault weapon prior to June 1, 1989, or prior to the date it was specified as an assault weapon, and has since either registered the firearm and any other lawfully obtained firearm specified by Section 12276 or 12276.5 pursuant to Section 12285 or relinquished them pursuant to Section 12288, a first-time violation of this subdivision shall be an infraction punishable by a fine of up to five hundred dollars ($500), but not less than three hundred fifty dollars ($350), if the person has otherwise possessed the firearm in compliance with subdivision (c) of Section 12285. In these cases, the firearm shall be returned unless the court finds in the interest of public safety, after notice and hearing, that the assault weapon should be destroyed pursuant to Section 12028.

(c) A first-time violation of subdivision (b) shall be an infraction punishable by a fine of up to five hundred dollars ($500), if the person was found in possession of no more than two firearms in compliance with subdivision (c) of Section 12285 and the person meets all of the following conditions:

(1) The person proves that he or she lawfully possessed the assault weapon prior to the date it was defined as an assault weapon pursuant to Section 12276.1.

(2) The person is not found in possession of a firearm specified as an assault weapon pursuant to Section 12276 or Section 12276.5.

(3) The person has not previously been convicted of violating this section.

(4) The person was found to be in possession of the assault weapons within one year following the end of the one-year registration period established pursuant to subdivision (a) of Section 12285.

(5) The person has since registered the firearms and any other lawfully obtained firearms defined by Section 12276.1, pursuant to Section 12285, except as provided for by this section, or relinquished them pursuant to Section 12288.

(d) Firearms seized pursuant to subdivision (c) shall be returned unless the court finds in the interest of public safety, after notice and hearing, that the assault weapon should be destroyed pursuant to Section 12028.

(e) Notwithstanding Section 654 or any other provision of law, any person who commits another crime while violating this section may receive an additional, consecutive punishment of one year for violating this section in addition and consecutive to the punishment, including enhancements, which is prescribed for the other crime.

(f) Subdivisions (a) and (b) shall not apply to the sale to, purchase by, or possession of assault weapons by the Department of Justice, police departments, sheriffs'offices, marshals'offices, the Youth and Adult Corrections Agency, the Department of the California Highway Patrol, district attorneys'offices, Department of Fish and Game, Department of Parks and Recreation, or the military or naval forces of this state or of the United States, or any federal law enforcement agency for use in the discharge of their official duties.

(g)(1) Subdivision (b) shall not prohibit the possession or use of assault weapons by sworn peace officer members of those agencies specified in subdivision (f) for law enforcement purposes, whether on or off duty.

(2) Subdivisions (a) and (b) shall not prohibit the delivery, transfer, or sale of an assault weapon to, or the possession of an assault weapon by, a sworn peace officer member of an agency specified in subdivision (f), provided that the peace officer is authorized by his or her employer to posses or receive the assault weapon. Required authorization is defined as verifiable written certification from the head of the agency, identifying the recipient or possessor of the assault weapon as a peace officer and authorizing him or her to receive or possess the specific assault weapon. For this exemption to apply, in the case of a peace officer who possesses or receives the assault weapon prior to January 1, 2002, the officer shall register the assault weapon pursuant to Section 12285 on or before April 1, 2002; in the case of a peace officer who possesses or receives the assault weapon on or after January 1, 2002, the officer shall register the assault weapon pursuant to Section 12285 not later than 90 days after possession or receipt. The peace officer must include with the registration, a copy of the authorization required pursuant to this paragraph.

(3) Nothing in this section shall be construed to limit or prohibit the delivery, transfer, or sale of an assault weapon to, or the possession of an assault weapon by, a member of a federal law enforcement agency provided that person is authorized by the employing agency to possess the assault weapon.

(h) Subdivisions (a) and (b) shall not prohibit the sale or transfer of assault weapons by an entity specified in subdivision (f) to a person, upon retirement, who retired as a sworn officer from that entity.

(i) Subdivision (b) shall not apply to the possession of an assault weapon by a retired peace officer who received that assault weapon pursuant to subdivision (h).

(j) Subdivision (b) shall not apply to the possession of an assault weapon, as defined in Section 12276, by any person during the 1990 calendar year, during the 90-day period immediately after the date it was specified as an assault weapon pursuant to Section 12276.5, or during the one-year period after the date it was defined as an assault weapon pursuant to Section 12276.1, if all of the following are applicable:

(1) The person is eligible under this chapter to register the particular assault weapon.

(2) The person lawfully possessed the particular assault weapon described in paragraph (1) prior to June 1, 1989, if the weapon is specified as an assault weapon pursuant to Section 12276, or prior to the date it was specified as an assault weapon pursuant to Section 12276.5, or prior to the date it was defined as an assault weapon pursuant to Section 12276.1.

(3) The person is otherwise in compliance with this chapter.

(k) Subdivisions (a) and (b) shall not apply to the manufacture by persons who are issued permits pursuant to Section 12287 of assault weapons for sale to the following:

(1) Exempt entities listed in subdivision (f).

(2) Entities and persons who have been issued permits pursuant to Section 12286.

(3) Entities outside the state who have, in effect, a federal firearms dealer's license solely for the purpose of distribution to an entity listed in paragraphs (4) to (6), inclusive.

(4) Federal military and law enforcement agencies.

(5) Law enforcement and military agencies of other states.

(6) Foreign governments and agencies approved by the United States State Department.

(l) Subdivision (a) shall not apply to a person who is the executor or administrator of an estate that includes an assault weapon registered under Section 12285 or that was possessed pursuant to subdivision (g) or (i) which is disposed of as authorized by the probate court, if the disposition is otherwise permitted by this chapter.

(m) Subdivision (b) shall not apply to a person who is the executor or administrator of an estate that includes an assault weapon registered under Section 12285 or that was possessed pursuant to subdivision (g) or (i), if the assault weapon is possessed at a place set forth in paragraph (1) of subdivision (c) of Section 12285 or as authorized by the probate court.

(n) Subdivision (a) shall not apply to:

(1) A person who lawfully possesses and has registered an assault weapon pursuant to this chapter, or who lawfully possesses an assault weapon pursuant to subdivision (i), who lends that assault weapon to another if all the following apply:

(A) The person to whom the assault weapon is lent is 18 years of age or over and is not in a class of persons prohibited from possessing firearms by virtue of Section 12021 or 12021.1 of this code or Section 8100 or 8103 of the Welfare and Institutions Code.

(B) The person to whom the assault weapon is lent remains in the presence of the registered possessor of the assault weapon, or the person who lawfully possesses an assault weapon pursuant to subdivision (i).

(C) The assault weapon is possessed at any of the following locations:

(i) While on a target range that holds a regulatory or business license for the purpose of practicing shooting at that target range.

(ii) While on the premises of a target range of a public or private club or organization organized for the purpose of practicing shooting at targets.

(iii) While attending any exhibition, display, or educational project that is about firearms and that is sponsored by, conducted under the auspices of, or approved by a law enforcement agency or a nationally or state recognized entity that fosters proficiency in, or promotes education about, firearms.

(2) The return of an assault weapon to the registered possessor, or the lawful possessor, which is lent by the same pursuant to paragraph (1).

(o) Subdivision (b) shall not apply to the possession of an assault weapon by a person to whom an assault weapon is lent pursuant to subdivision (n).

(p) Subdivisions (a) and (b) shall not apply to the possession and importation of an assault weapon into this state by a nonresident if all of the following conditions are met:

(1) The person is attending or going directly to or coming directly from an organized competitive match or league competition that involves the use of an assault weapon.

(2) The competition or match is conducted on the premises of one of the following:

(i) A target range that holds a regulatory or business license for the purpose of practicing shooting at that target range.

(ii) A target range of a public or private club or organization that is organized for the purpose of practicing shooting at targets.

(3) The match or competition is sponsored by, conducted under the auspices of, or approved by, a law enforcement agency or a nationally or state recognized entity that fosters proficiency in, or promotes education about, firearms.

(4) The assault weapon is transported in accordance with Section 12026.1 or 12026.2.

(5) The person is 18 years of age or over and is not in a class of persons prohibited from possessing firearms by virtue of Section 12021 or 12021.1 of this code or Section 8100 or 8103 of the Welfare and Institutions Code.

(q) Subdivision (b) shall not apply to any of the following persons:

(1) A person acting in accordance with Section 12286.

(2) A person who has a permit to possess an assault weapon issued pursuant to Section 12286 when he or she is acting in accordance with Section 12285 or 12286.

(r) Subdivisions (a) and (b) shall not apply to any of the following persons:

(1) A person acting in accordance with Section 12285.

(2) A person acting in accordance with Section 12286 or 12290.

(s) Subdivision (b) shall not apply to the registered owner of an assault weapon possessing that firearm in accordance with subdivision (c) of Section 12285.

(t) Subdivision (a) shall not apply to the importation into this state of an assault weapon by the registered owner of that assault weapon, if it is in accordance with the provisions of subdivision (c) of Section 12285.

(u) As used in this chapter, the date a firearm is an assault weapon is the earliest of the following:

(1) The effective date of an amendment to Section 12276 that adds the designation of the specified firearm.

(2) The effective date of the list promulgated pursuant to Section 12276.5 that adds or changes the designation of the specified firearm.

(3) The operative date of Section 12276.1, as specified in subdivision ***(d) of that section. *(AM'01)*

12285. Registration of Assault Weapons; Restrictions on Transfer, Possession, and Use

(a) Any person who lawfully possesses an assault weapon, as defined in Section 12276, prior to June 1, 1989, shall register the firearm by January 1, 1991, and any person who lawfully possessed an assault weapon prior to the date it was specified as an assault weapon pursuant to Section 12276.5 shall register the firearm within 90 days with the Department of Justice pursuant to those procedures that the department may establish. Except as provided in subdivision (a) of Section 12280, any person who lawfully possessed an assault weapon prior to the date it was defined as an assault weapon pursuant to Section 12276.1, and which was not specified as an assault weapon under Section 12276 or 12276.5, shall register the firearm within one year of the effective date of Section 12276.1, with the department pursuant to those procedures that the department may establish. The registration shall contain a description of the firearm that identifies it uniquely, including all identification marks, the full name, address, date of birth, and thumbprint of the owner, and any other information that the department may deem appropriate. The department may charge a fee for registration of up to twenty dollars ($20) per person but not to exceed the actual processing costs of the department. After the department establishes fees sufficient to reimburse the department for processing costs, fees charged shall increase at a rate not to exceed the legislatively approved annual cost-of-living adjustment for the department's budget or as otherwise increased through the Budget Act.

(b)(1) Except as provided in paragraph (2), no assault weapon possessed pursuant to this section may be sold or transferred on or after January 1, 1990, to anyone within this state other than to a licensed gun dealer, as defined in subdivision (c) of Section 12290, or as provided in Section 12288. Any person who (A) obtains title to an assault weapon registered under this section or that was possessed pursuant to subdivision (g) or (i) of Section 12280 by bequest or intestate succession, or (B) lawfully possessed a firearm subsequently declared to be an assault weapon pursuant to Section 12276.5, or subsequently defined as an assault weapon pursuant to Section 12276.1, shall, within 90 days, render the weapon permanently inoperable, sell the weapon to a licensed gun dealer, obtain a permit from the Department of Justice in the same manner as specified in Article 3 (commencing with Section 12230) of Chapter 2, or remove the weapon from this state. A person who lawfully possessed a firearm that was subsequently declared to be an assault weapon pursuant to Section 12276.5 may alternatively register the firearm within 90 days of the declaration issued pursuant to subdivision (f) of Section 12276.5.

(2) A person moving into this state, otherwise in lawful possession of an assault weapon, shall do one of the following:

(A) Prior to bringing the assault weapon into this state, that person shall first obtain a permit from the Department of Justice in the same manner as specified in Article 3 (commencing with Section 12230) of Chapter 2.

(B) The person shall cause the assault weapon to be delivered to a licensed gun dealer, as defined in subdivision (c) of Section 12290, in this state in accordance with Chapter 44 (commencing with Section 921) of Title 18 of the United States Code and the regulations issued pursuant thereto. If the person obtains a permit from the Department of Justice in the same manner as specified in Article 3 (commencing with Section 12230) of Chapter 2, the dealer shall redeliver that assault weapon to the person. If the licensed gun dealer, as defined in subdivision (c) of Section 12290, is prohibited from delivering the assault weapon to a person pursuant to this paragraph, the dealer shall possess or dispose of the assault weapon as allowed by this chapter.

(c) A person who has registered an assault weapon under this section may possess it only under any of the following conditions unless a permit allowing additional uses is first obtained under Section 12286:

(1) At that person's residence, place of business, or other property owned by that person, or on property owned by another with the owner's express permission.

(2) While on the premises of a target range of a public or private club or organization organized for the purpose of practicing shooting at targets.

(3) While on a target range that holds a regulatory or business license for the purpose of practicing shooting at that target range.

(4) While on the premises of a shooting club which is licensed pursuant to the Fish and Game Code.

(5) While attending any exhibition, display, or educational project which is about firearms and which is sponsored by, conducted under the auspices of, or approved by a law enforcement agency or a nationally or state recognized entity that fosters proficiency in, or promotes education about, firearms.

(6) While on publicly owned land if the possession and use of a firearm described in Section 12276 or 12276.1 is specifically permitted by the managing agency of the land.

(7) While transporting the assault weapon between any of the places mentioned in this subdivision, or to any licensed gun dealer, as defined in subdivision (c) of Section 12290, for servicing or repair pursuant to subdivision (b) of Section 12290, if the assault weapon is transported as required by Section 12026.1.

(d) No person who is under the age of 18 years, no person who is prohibited from possessing a firearm by Section 12021 or 12021.1, and no person described in Section 8100 or 8103 of the Welfare and Institutions Code may register or possess an assault weapon.

(e) The department's registration procedures shall provide the option of joint registration for assault weapons owned by family members residing in the same household.

(f) For 90 days following January 1, 1992, a forgiveness period shall exist to allow persons specified in subdivision (b) of Section 12280 to register with the Department of Justice assault weapons that they lawfully possessed prior to June 1, 1989.

(g) Any person who registered a firearm as an assault weapon pursuant to the provisions of law in effect prior to January 1, 2000, where the assault weapon is thereafter defined as an assault weapon pursuant to Section 12276.1, shall be deemed to have registered the weapon for purposes of this chapter and shall not be required to reregister the weapon pursuant to this section.

(h) Any person who registers his or her assault weapon during the 90-day forgiveness period described in subdivision (f), and any person whose registration form was received by the Department of Justice after January 1, 1991, and who was issued a temporary registration prior to the end of the forgiveness period, shall not be charged with a violation of subdivision (b) of Section 12280, if law enforcement becomes aware of that violation only as a result of the registration of the assault weapon. This subdivision shall have no effect upon persons charged with a violation of subdivision (b) of Section 12280 of the Penal Code prior to January 1, 1992, provided that law enforcement was aware of the violation before the weapon was registered. *(AM '99)*

12301. Destructive Device Defined

(a) The term "destructive device,"as used in this chapter, shall include any of the following weapons:

(1) Any projectile containing any explosive or incendiary material or any other chemical substance, including, but not limited to, that which is commonly known as tracer or incendiary ammunition, except tracer ammunition manufactured for use in shotguns.

(2) Any bomb, grenade, explosive missile, or similar device or any launching device therefor.

(3) Any weapon of a caliber greater than 0.60 caliber which fires fixed ammunition, or any ammunition therefor, other than a shotgun (smooth or rifled bore) conforming to the definition of a "destructive device"found in subsection (b) of Section 179.11 of Title 27 of the Code of Federal Regulations, shotgun ammunition (single projectile or shot), antique rifle, or an antique cannon. For purposes of this section, the term "antique cannon"means any cannon manufactured before January 1, 1899, which has been rendered incapable of firing or for which ammunition is no longer manufactured in the United States and is not readily available in the ordinary channels of commercial trade. The term "antique rifle"means a firearm conforming to the definition of an "antique firearm"in Section 179.11 of Title 27 of the Code of Federal Regulations.

(4) Any rocket, rocket-propelled projectile, or similar device of a diameter greater than 0.60 inch, or any launching device therefor, and any rocket, rocket-propelled projectile, or similar device containing any explosive or incendiary material or any other chemical substance, other than the propellant for such device, except such devices as are designed primarily for emergency or distress signaling purposes.

(5) Any breakable container which contains a flammable liquid with a flashpoint of 150 degrees Fahrenheit or less and has a wick or similar device capable of being ignited, other than a device which is commercially manufactured primarily for the purpose of illumination.

(6) Any sealed device containing dry ice (CO_2) or other chemically reactive substances assembled for the purpose of causing an explosion by a chemical reaction.

(b) The term "explosive,"as used in this chapter, shall mean any explosive defined in Section 12000 of the Health and Safety Code.

12303. Possession of Destructive Device Prohibited

Any person, firm, or corporation who, within this state, possesses any destructive device, other than fixed ammunition of a caliber greater than .60 caliber, except as provided by this chapter, is guilty of a public offense and upon conviction thereof shall be punished by imprisonment in the county jail for a term not to exceed one year, or in state prison, or by a fine not to exceed ten thousand dollars ($10,000) or by both such fine and imprisonment.

12303.1. Carrying or Placing Explosives on Transportation Vehicles

Every person who willfully does any of the following is guilty of a felony and is punishable by imprisonment in the state prison for two, four, or six years:

(a) Carries any explosive or destructive device on any vessel, aircraft, car, or other vehicle that transports passengers for hire.

(b) Places or carries any explosive or destructive device, while on board any such vessel, aircraft, car or other vehicle, in any hand baggage, roll, or other container.

(c) Places any explosive or destructive device in any baggage which is later checked with any common carrier.

12303.2. Possession of Destructive Device in Public Places

Every person who recklessly or maliciously has in his possession any destructive device or any explosive on a public street or highway, in or near any theater, hall, school, college, church, hotel, other public building, or private habitation, in, on, or near any aircraft, railway passenger train, car, cable road or cable car, vessel engaged in carrying passengers for hire, or other public place ordinarily passed by human beings is guilty of a felony, and shall be punishable by imprisonment in the state prison for a period of two, four, or six years.

12303.3. Explosion of Destructive Device

Every person who possesses, explodes, ignites, or attempts to explode or ignite any destructive device or any explosive with intent to injure, intimidate, or terrify any person, or with intent to wrongfully injure or destroy any property, is guilty of a felony, and shall be punished by imprisonment in the state prison for a period of three, five, or seven years.

12303.6. Sale or Transportation of Destructive Device Prohibited

Any person, firm, or corporation who, within this state, sells, offers for sale, or knowingly transports any destructive device, other than fixed ammunition of a caliber greater than .60 caliber, except as provided by this chapter, is guilty of a felony and is punishable by imprisonment in the state prison for two, three or four years.

12304. Punishment

Any person, firm or corporation who, within this state, sells, offers for sale, possesses or knowingly transports any fixed ammunition of a caliber greater than .60 caliber, except as provided in this chapter, is guilty of a public offense and upon conviction thereof shall be punished by imprisonment in the county jail for a term not to exceed six months or by a fine not to exceed one thousand dollars ($1,000), or by both such fine and imprisonment.

A second or subsequent conviction shall be punished by imprisonment in the county jail for a term not to exceed one year, or by imprisonment in the state prison, or by a fine not to exceed three thousand dollars ($3,000), or by both such fine and imprisonment.

12308. Explosion of Destructive Device With Intent to Commit Murder

Every person who explodes, ignites, or attempts to explode or ignite any destructive device or any explosive with intent to commit murder is guilty of a felony, and shall be punished by imprisonment in the state prison for life with the possibility of parole.

12309. Explosion of Destructive Device Which Causes Bodily Injury

Every person who willfully and maliciously explodes or ignites any destructive device or any explosive which causes bodily injury to any person is guilty of a felony, and shall be punished by imprisonment in the state prison for a period of five, seven, or nine years.

12310. Explosion of Destructive Device Which Causes Death, Mayhem or Great Bodily Injury

(a) Every person who willfully and maliciously explodes or ignites any destructive device or any explosive which causes the death of any person is guilty of a felony, and shall be punished by imprisonment in the state prison for life without the possibility of parole.

(b) Every person who willfully and maliciously explodes or ignites any destructive device or any explosive which causes mayhem or great bodily injury to any person is guilty of a felony, and shall be punished by imprisonment in the state prison for life.

12312. Intention to Make Destructive Device Without Valid Permit

Every person who possesses any substance, material, or any combination of substances or materials, with the intent to make any destructive device or any explosive without first obtaining a valid permit to make such destructive device or explosive, is guilty of a felony, and is punishable by imprisonment in the state prison for two, three, or four years.

12316. Sell Ammunition To Minor

(a)(1) Any person, corporation, or dealer who does either of the following shall be punished by imprisonment in a county jail for a term not to exceed six months, or by a fine not to exceed one thousand dollars ($1,000), or by both the imprisonment and fine.

(A) Sells any ammunition or reloaded ammunition to a person knowing that person to be under 18 years of age.

(B) Sells any ammunition or reloaded ammunition designed and intended for use in a pistol, revolver, or other firearm capable of being concealed upon the person to a person knowing that person to be under 21 years of age. As used in this subparagraph, "ammunition" means handgun ammunition as defined in subdivision (a) of Section 12323. Where ammunition or reloaded ammunition may be used in both a rifle and a handgun, federal law shall be considered for purposes of enforcing this subparagraph.

(2) Proof that a person, corporation, or dealer, or his or her agent or employee, demanded, was shown, and acted in reliance upon, bona fide evidence of majority and identity shall be a defense to any criminal prosecution under this subdivision. As used in this subdivision, "bona fide evidence of majority and identity" means a document issued by a federal, state, county, or municipal government, or subdivision or agency thereof, including, but not limited to, a motor vehicle operator's license, California state identification card, identification card issued to a member of the armed forces, or other form of identification that bears the name, date of birth, description, and picture of the person.

(b)(1) No person prohibited from owning or possessing a firearm under Section 12021 or 12021.1 of this code or Section 8100 or 8103 of the Welfare and Institutions Code shall own, possess, or have under his or her custody or control, any ammunition or reloaded ammunition.

(2) For purposes of this subdivision, "ammunition" shall include, but not be limited to, any bullet, cartridge, magazine, clip, speed loader, autoloader, or projectile capable of being fired from a firearm with a deadly consequence.

(3) A violation of this subdivision is punishable by imprisonment in a county jail not to exceed one year or in the state prison, by a fine not to exceed one thousand dollars ($1,000), or by both the fine and imprisonment.

(c) Unless it is with the written permission of the school district superintendent, his or her designee, or equivalent school authority, no person shall carry ammunition or reloaded ammunition onto school grounds, except sworn law enforcement officers acting within the scope of their duties or persons exempted under subparagraph (A) of paragraph (1) of subdivision (a) of Section 12027. This subdivision shall not apply to a duly appointed peace officer as defined in Chapter 4.5 (commencing with Section 830) of Title 3 of Part 2, a full-time paid peace officer of another state or the federal government who is carrying out official duties while in California, any person summoned by any of these officers to assist in making an arrest or preserving the peace while he or she is actually engaged in assisting the officer, a member of the military forces of this state or of the United States who is engaged in the performance of his or her duties, a person holding a valid license to carry the firearm pursuant to Article 3 (commencing with Section 12050) of Chapter 1 of Title 2 of Part 4, or an armored vehicle guard, who is engaged in the performance of his or her duties, as defined in subdivision (e) of Section 7521 of the Business and Professions Code. A violation of this subdivision is punishable by imprisonment in a county jail for a term not to exceed six months, a fine not to exceed one thousand dollars ($1,000), or both the imprisonment and fine.

(d)(1) A violation of paragraph (1) of subdivision (b) is justifiable where all of the following conditions are met:

(A) The person found the ammunition or reloaded ammunition or took the ammunition or reloaded ammunition from a person who was committing a crime against him or her.

(B) The person possessed the ammunition or reloaded ammunition no longer than was necessary to deliver or transport the ammunition or reloaded ammunition to a law enforcement agency for that agency's disposition according to law.

(C) The person is prohibited from possessing any ammunition or reloaded ammunition solely because that person is prohibited from owning or possessing a firearm only by virtue of Section 12021.

(2) Upon the trial for violating paragraph (1) of subdivision (b), the trier of fact shall determine whether the defendant is subject to the exemption created by this subdivision.

(3) The defendant has the burden of proving by a preponderance of the evidence that he or she is subject to the exemption provided by this subdivision.

12320. Possession of Metal Penetrating Ammunition

Any person, firm, or corporation who, within this state knowingly possesses any handgun ammunition designed primarily to penetrate metal or armor is guilty of a public offense and upon conviction thereof shall be punished by imprisonment in the state prison, or in the county jail for a term not to exceed one year, or by a fine not to exceed five thousand dollars ($5,000), or by both such fine and imprisonment.

12321. Metal Penetrating Ammunition; Manufacture, Importation, Sale or Transportation

Any person, firm, or corporation who, within this state, manufactures, imports, sells, offers to sell, or knowingly transports any handgun ammunition designed primarily to penetrate metal or armor is guilty of a felony and upon conviction thereof shall be punished by imprisonment in state prison, or by a fine not to exceed five thousand dollars ($5,000), or by both such fine and imprisonment.

12355. Boobytraps

(a) Except as provided in Chapter 2.5 any person who assembles, maintains, places, or causes to be placed a boobytrap device as described in subdivision (c) is guilty of a felony punishable by imprisonment in the state prison for two, three, or five years.

(b) Possession of any device with the intent to use the device as a boobytrap is punishable by imprisonment in state prison, or in a county jail not exceeding one year, or by a fine not exceeding five thousand dollars ($5,000), or by both that fine and imprisonment.

(c) For purposes of this section, "boobytrap" means any concealed or camouflaged device designed to cause great bodily injury when triggered by an action of any unsuspecting person coming across the device. Boobytraps may include, but are not limited to, guns, ammunition, or explosive devices attached to trip wires or other triggering mechanisms, sharpened stakes, and lines or wire with hooks attached.

12401. Tear Gas Defined

"Tear gas" as used in this chapter shall apply to and include all liquid, gaseous, or solid substances intended to produce temporary physical discomfort or permanent injury through being vaporized or otherwise dispersed in the air, but does not apply to, and shall not include, any substance registered as an economic poison as provided in Chapter 2 of Division 7 of the Agricultural Code provided that such substance is not intended to be used to produce discomfort or injury to human beings.

12402. Tear Gas Weapon Defined

The term "tear gas weapon" as used in this chapter shall apply to and include:

(a) Any shell, cartridge, or bomb capable of being discharged or exploded, when the discharge or explosion will cause or permit the release or emission of tear gases.

(b) Any revolvers, pistols, fountain pen guns, billies, or other form of device, portable or fixed, intended for the projection or release of tear gas except those regularly manufactured and sold for use with firearm ammunition.

12403. Possession by Peace Officers Exempt

Nothing in this chapter shall prohibit any person who is a peace officer, as defined in Chapter 4.5 (commencing with Section 830) of Title 3 of Part 2, from purchasing, possessing, transporting, or using any tear gas or tear gas weapon if the person has satisfactorily completed a course of instruction approved by the Commission on Peace Officer Standards and Training in the use of tear gas.

12403.1. Possession by Military and Naval Forces Exempt

Nothing in this chapter shall prohibit any member of the military and naval forces of this state or of the United States or any federal law enforcement officer from purchasing, possessing, or transporting any tear gas or tear gas weapon for official use in the discharge of his duties.

12403.5. Possession by Private Investigator or Private Patrol - Qualifications

Notwithstanding any other provision of law, a person holding a license as a private investigator or private patrol operator issued pursuant to Chapter 11 (commencing with Section 7500), Division 3 of the Business and Professions Code, or uniformed patrolmen employees of a private patrol operator, may purchase, possess, or transport any tear gas weapon, if it is used solely for defensive purposes in the course of the activity for which the license was issued and if the person has satisfactorily completed a course of instruction approved by the Department of Consumer Affairs in the use of tear gas. *(AM '99)*

12403.7. Possession by Others - Qualifications

Notwithstanding any other law, any person may purchase, possess, or use tear gas and tear gas weapons for the projection or release of tear gas if the tear gas and tear gas weapons are used solely for self-defense purposes, subject to the following requirements:

(a) No person convicted of a felony or any crime involving an assault under the laws of the United States, the State of California, or any other state, government, or country or convicted of misuse of tear gas under subdivision (g) shall purchase, possess, or use tear gas or tear gas weapons.

(b) No person who is addicted to any narcotic drug shall purchase, possess, or use tear gas or tear gas weapons.

(c) No person shall sell or furnish any tear gas or tear gas weapon to a minor.

(d) No person who is a minor shall purchase, possess, or use tear gas or tear gas weapons.

(e)(1) No person shall purchase, possess, or use any tear gas weapon that expels a projectile, or that expels the tear gas by any method other than an aerosol spray, or that contains more than 2.5 ounces net weight of aerosol spray.

(2) Every tear gas container and tear gas weapon that may be lawfully purchased, possessed, and used pursuant to this section shall have a label that states: "WARNING: The use of this substance or device for any purpose other than self-defense is a crime under the law. The contents are dangerous—use with care."

(3) After January 1, 1984, every tear gas container and tear gas weapon that may be lawfully purchased, possessed, and used pursuant to this section shall have a label that discloses the date on which the useful life of the tear gas weapon expires.

(4) Every tear gas container and tear gas weapon that may be lawfully purchased pursuant to this section shall be accompanied at the time of purchase by printed instructions for use.

(f) Effective March 1, 1994, every tear gas container and tear gas weapon that may be lawfully purchased, possessed, and used pursuant to this section shall be accompanied by an insert including directions for use, first aid information, safety and storage information, and explanation of the legal ramifications of improper use of the tear gas container or tear gas product.

(g) Any person who uses tear gas or tear gas weapons except in self-defense is guilty of a public offense and is punishable by imprisonment in a state prison for 16 months, or two or three years or in a county jail not to exceed one year or by a fine not to exceed one thousand dollars ($1,000), or by both the fine and imprisonment, except that, if the use is against a peace officer, as defined in Chapter 4.5 (commencing with Section 830) of Title 3 of Part 2, engaged in the performance of his or her official duties and the person committing the offense knows or reasonably should know that the victim is a peace officer, the offense is punishable by imprisonment in a state prison for 16 months or two or three years or by a fine of one thousand dollars ($1,000), or by both the fine and imprisonment.

12403.8. Possession by Minor - Qualifications

(a) Notwithstanding paragraph (4) of subdivision (a) of Section 12403.7, a minor who has attained the age of 16 years may purchase and possess tear gas or tear gas weapons pursuant to this chapter if he or she is accompanied by a parent or guardian, or has the written consent of his or her parent or guardian.

(b) Notwithstanding paragraph (3) of subdivision (a) of Section 12403.7, a person may sell or furnish tear gas or a tear gas weapon to a minor who has attained the age of 16 years and who is accompanied by a parent or guardian, or who presents a statement of consent signed by the minor's parent or guardian .

(c) Any civil liability of a minor arising out of his or her use of tear gas or a tear gas weapon other than for self-defense is imposed upon the person, parent, or guardian who signed the statement of consent specified in subdivision (b) who shall be jointly and severally liable with the minor for any damages proximately resulting from the negligent or wrongful act or omission of the minor in the use of the tear gas or a tear gas weapon.

12403.9. Custodial Officers - Carry While on Duty

Custodial officers of any county may carry tear gas weapons pursuant to Section 12403 only while on duty. These custodial officers may carry tear gas weapons while off duty only in accordance with all other laws.

12420. Sale, Possession or Transportation Prohibited

Any person, firm, or corporation who within this state knowingly sells or offers for sale, possesses, or transports any tear gas or tear gas weapon, except as permitted under the provisions of this chapter, is guilty of a public offense and upon conviction thereof shall be punishable by imprisonment in the county jail for not exceeding one year or by a fine not to exceed two thousand dollars ($2,000), or by both.

12421. Maker's Name and Serial Number

Each tear gas weapon sold, transported or possessed under the authority of this chapter shall bear the name of the manufacturer and a serial number applied by him.

12422. Alteration of Identification

Any person who changes, alters, removes or obliterates the name of the manufacturer, the serial number or any other mark of identification on any tear gas weapon is guilty of a public offense and, upon conviction, shall be punished by imprisonment in the state prison or by a fine of not more than two thousand dollars ($2,000) or by both.

Possession of any such weapon upon which the same shall have been changed, altered, removed, or obliterated, shall be presumptive evidence that such possessor has changed, altered, removed, or obliterated the same.

12500. Silencer Defined

The term "silencer" as used in this chapter means any device or attachment of any kind designed, used, or intended for use in silencing, diminishing, or muffling the report of a firearm. The term "silencer" also includes any combination of parts, designed or redesigned, and intended for use in assembling a silencer or fabricating a silencer and any part intended only for use in such assembly or fabrication.

12520. Possession Prohibited

Any person, firm or corporation who within this state possesses a silencer for firearms is guilty of a felony and upon conviction thereof shall be punished by imprisonment in the state prison or by a fine not to exceed ten thousand dollars ($10,000) or by both.

12551. Sale of BB Device to Minor

Every person who sells to a minor any BB device is guilty of a misdemeanor.

12580. Definition of Blowgun

"Blowgun,"as used in this article, means a hollow tube designed and intended to be used as a tube through which a dart is propelled by the force of the breath of the user.

12581. Ammunition

"Blowgun ammunition,"as used in this article, means a dart designed and intended for use in a blowgun.

12582. Manufacture, Sale, Possession, or Use

Any person who knowingly manufactures, sells, offers for sale, possesses, or uses a blowgun or blowgun ammunition in this state is guilty of a misdemeanor.

12583. Exemptions

Nothing in this article shall prohibit the sale to, purchase by, possession of, or use of blowguns or blowgun ammunition by zookeepers, animal control officers, Department of Fish and Game personnel, humane officers whose names are maintained in the county record of humane officers pursuant to Section 14502 of the Corporations Code, or veterinarians in the course and scope of their business in order to administer medicine to animals.

12590. Carrying Firearm or Deadly Weapon - Wearing Uniform of Peace Officer

(a) Any person who does any of the following acts while engaged in picketing, or other informational activities in a public place relating to a concerted refusal to work, is guilty of a misdemeanor:

(1) Carries concealed upon his person or within any vehicle which is under his or her control or direction any pistol, revolver, or other firearm capable of being concealed upon the person.

(2) Carries a loaded firearm upon his or her person or within any vehicle which is under his or her control or direction.

(3) Carries a deadly weapon.

(4) Wears the uniform of a peace officer, whether or not the person is a peace officer.

(b) This section shall not be construed to authorize or ratify any picketing or other informational activities not otherwise authorized by law.

(c) Section 12027 shall not be construed to authorize any conduct described in paragraph (1) of subdivision (a), nor shall subdivision (b) of Section 12031 be construed to authorize any conduct described in paragraph (2) of subdivision (a).

12650. "Stun Gun" Defined

"Stun gun"as used in this chapter shall include any time, except a taser, used or intended to be used as either an offensive or defensive weapon capable of temporarily immobilizing a person by the infliction of an electrical charge.

12651. Purchase, Possession, or Use of Stun Gun

Notwithstanding any other provision of law, any person may purchase, possess, or use a stun gun, subject to the following requirements:

(a) No person convicted of a felony or any crime involving an assault under the laws of the United States, of the State of California, or any other state, government, or country or convicted of misuse of a stun gun under Section 244.5, shall purchase, possess, or use stun guns.

(b) No person who is addicted to any narcotic drug shall purchase, possess, or use a stun gun.

(c) No person shall sell or furnish any stun gun to a minor unless the minor is at least 16 years of age and has the written consent of his or her parent or legal guardian.

Violation of this subdivision shall be a public offense punishable by a fifty dollar ($50) fine for the first offense. Any subsequent violation of this subdivision is a misdemeanor.

(d) No minor shall possess any stun gun unless the minor is at least 16 years of age and has the written consent of his or her parent or legal guardian.

13700. Definitions

As used in this title:

(a) "Abuse"means intentionally or recklessly causing or attempting to cause bodily injury, or placing another person in reasonable apprehension of imminent serious bodily injury to himself or herself, or another.

(b) "Domestic violence"means abuse committed against an adult or a fully emancipated minor who is a spouse, former spouse, cohabitant, former cohabitant, or person with whom the suspect has had a child or is having or has had a dating or engagement relationship. For purposes of this subdivision, "cohabitant" means two unrelated adult persons living together for a substantial period of time, resulting in some permanency of relationship. Factors that may determine whether persons are cohabiting include, but are not limited to, (1) sexual relations between the parties while sharing the same living quarters, (2) sharing of income or expenses, (3) joint use or ownership of property, (4) whether the parties hold themselves out as husband and wife, (5) the continuity of the relationship, and (6) the length of the relationship.

(c) "Officer"means any officer or employee of a local police department or sheriff's office, and any peace officer of the Department of the California Highway Patrol, the Department of Parks and Recreation, the University of California Police Department, or the California State University and College Police Departments, as defined in Section 830.2, a housing authority patrol officer, as defined in subdivision (d) of Section 830.31, or a peace officer as defined in subdivisions (a) and (b) of Section 830.32.

(d) "Victim"means a person who is a victim of domestic violence. *(AM '99)*

TITLE 12.5. DNA

14250. Department of Justice to Develop Missing Person DNA Database; Requirements

(a)(1) The Department of Justice shall develop a DNA data base for all cases involving the report of an unidentified deceased person or a high-risk missing person.

(2) The data base required in paragraph (1) shall be comprised of DNA data from genetic markers that are appropriate for human identification, but have no capability to predict biological function other than gender. These markers shall be selected by the department and may change as the technology for DNA typing progresses. The results of DNA typing shall be compatible with and uploaded into the CODIS DNA data base established by the Federal Bureau of Investigation. The sole purpose of this data base shall be to identify missing persons and shall be kept separate from the data base established under Chapter 6 (commencing with Section 295) of Title 9 of Part 1.

(3) The Department of Justice shall compare DNA samples taken from the remains of unidentified deceased persons with DNA samples taken from personal articles belonging to the missing person, or from the parents or appropriate relatives of high-risk missing persons.

(4) For the purpose of this data base, "high-risk missing person"means a person missing as a result of a stranger abduction, a person missing under suspicious circumstances, a person missing under unknown circumstances, or where there is reason to assume that the person is in danger, or deceased, and that person has been missing more than 30 days, or less than 30 days in the discretion of the investigating agency.

(b) The department shall develop standards and guidelines for the preservation and storage of DNA samples. Any agency that is required to collect samples from unidentified remains for DNA testing shall follow these standards and guidelines. These guidelines shall address all scientific methods used for the identification of remains, including DNA, anthropology, odontology, and fingerprints.

(c)(1) A coroner shall collect samples for DNA testing from the remains of all unidentified persons and shall send those samples to the Department of Justice for DNA testing and inclusion in the DNA data bank. After the department has taken a sample from the remains for DNA analysis and analyzed it, the remaining evidence shall be returned to the appropriate local coroner.

(2) After a report has been made of a person missing under high-risk circumstances, the responsible investigating law enforcement agency shall inform the parents or other appropriate relatives that they may give a voluntary sample for DNA testing or may collect a DNA sample from a personal article belonging to the missing person if available. The samples shall be taken by the appropriate law enforcement agency in a manner prescribed by the Department of Justice. The responsible investigating law enforcement agency shall wait no longer than 30 days after a report has been made to inform the parents or other relatives of their right to give a sample.

(3) The Department of Justice shall develop a standard release form that authorizes a mother, father, or other relative to voluntarily provide the sample. The release shall explain that DNA is to be used only for the purpose of identifying the missing person and that the DNA sample and profile will be destroyed upon request. No incentive or coercion shall be used to compel a parent or relative to provide a sample.

(4) The Department of Justice shall develop a model kit that law enforcement shall use when taking samples from parents and relatives.

(5) Before submitting the sample to the department for analysis, law enforcement shall reverify the status of the missing person. After 30 days has elapsed from the date the report was filed, law enforcement shall send the sample to the department for DNA testing and inclusion in the DNA data base, with a copy of the crime report, and any supplemental information.

(6) All retained samples and DNA extracted from a living person, and profiles developed therefrom, shall be used solely for the purpose of identification of the deceased's remains. All samples and DNA extracted from a living person, and profiles developed therefrom, shall be destroyed after a positive identification with the deceased's remains is made and a report is issued, unless any of the following has occurred:

(A) The coroner has made a report to a law enforcement agency pursuant to Section 27491.1 of the Government Code, that he or she has a reasonable ground to suspect that the identified person's death has been occasioned by another by criminal means.

(B) A law enforcement agency makes a determination that the identified person's death has been occasioned by another by criminal means.

(C) The evidence is needed in an active criminal investigation to determine whether the identified person's death has been occasioned by another by criminal means.

(D) A governmental entity is required to retain the material pursuant to Section 1417.9.

(7) Notwithstanding any other provisions of this section, upon the request of any living person who submits his or her DNA sample and profile pursuant to this section, including the parent or guardian of a child who submits a DNA sample of the child, the DNA sample shall be removed from the DNA data base.

(d) All DNA samples and profiles developed therefrom shall be confidential and shall only be disclosed to personnel of the Department of Justice, law enforcement officers, coroners, medical examiners, ***district attorneys, and persons who need access to a DNA sample for purposes of the prosecution or defense of a criminal case, except that a law enforcement officer *** or agency may publicly disclose the fact of a DNA profile match after taking reasonable measures to first notify the family of an unidentified deceased person or the family of a high-risk missing person that there has been an identification.

*** ***(e) All DNA, forensic identification profiles, and other identification information retained by the Department of Justice pursuant to this section are exempt from any law requiring disclosure of information to the public.

(f)(1) Any person who knowingly discloses DNA or other forensic identification information developed pursuant to this section to an unauthorized individual or agency, or for any purpose other than for identification or for use in a criminal investigation, prosecution, or defense, is guilty of a misdemeanor ***.

(2) A person who collects, processes, or stores DNA ***or DNA samples from a living person that are used for DNA testing *** pursuant to this section who does either of the following is liable in civil damages

to the donor of the DNA in the amount of five thousand dollars ($5,000) for each violation, plus attorney's fees and costs:

(A) Fails to destroy samples or DNA extracted from a living person pursuant to paragraph (6) of subdivision (c).

(B) Discloses DNA samples in violation of subdivision (d).

(g)(1) If a disclosure or failure to destroy samples described in paragraph (2) of subdivision (f) is made by an employee of the Department of Justice, the department shall be liable for those actions of its employee.

(2) Notwithstanding any other law, the remedy in this section shall be the sole and exclusive remedy against the department and its employees available to the donor of the DNA against the department and its employees.

(3) The department employee disclosing DNA or other forensic identification information or otherwise violating this section shall be absolutely immune from civil liability under this or any other law.

(h) It is not an unauthorized disclosure or violation of this section to release DNA and other forensic identification information as part of a judicial or administrative proceeding, to a jury or grand jury, or in a document filed with a court or administrative agency, or for this information to become part of the public transcript or record of proceedings.

(i) In order to maintain computer system security, the computer software and data base structures used by the DNA laboratory of the Department of Justice to implement this chapter are confidential. *(AM '01)*

14251. Funding of Missing Persons DNA Database

(a) The "Missing Persons DNA Data Base"shall be funded by a two dollar ($2) fee increase on death certificates issued by a local government agency or by the State of California. The issuing agencies may retain up to 5 percent of the funds from the fee increase for administrative costs. This fee increase shall remain in effect only until January 1, 2006, or when federal funding for operation of the data base becomes available if it becomes available before that date.

(b) Funds shall be directed on a quarterly basis to the "Missing Persons DNA Data Base Fund,"hereby established, to be administered by the department for establishing and maintaining laboratory infrastructure, DNA sample storage, DNA analysis, and labor costs for cases of missing persons and unidentified remains. Funds may also be distributed by the department to various counties for the purposes of pathology and exhumation as the department deems necessary. The department may also use those funds to publicize the data base for the purpose of contacting parents and relatives so that they may provide a DNA sample for training law enforcement officials about the data base and DNA sampling and for outreach.

(c) The department shall create an advisory committee, comprised of coroners and appropriate law enforcement officials, and interested stakeholders to prioritize the identification of the backlog of unidentified remains. The identification of the backlog may be outsourced to other laboratories at the department's discretion.

(d)(1) The death certificate fee increase shall begin and funds shall be directed to the Missing Persons DNA Data Base Fund beginning January 1, 2001. Funding for year one shall be used to develop the data base and laboratory infrastructure, and to establish Department of Justice protocols and personnel.

(2) The Department of Justice shall begin case analysis in 2002. The Department of Justice shall retain the authority to prioritize case analysis, giving priority to those cases involving children.

(3) If federal funding is made available, it shall be used to assist in the identification of the backlog of high-risk missing person cases and long-term unidentified remains.

(4) This section shall remain in effect only until January 1, 2006, and as of that date is repealed, unless a later enacted statute, that is enacted before January 1, 2006, deletes or extends that date. *(AD '00)*

This page intentionally left blank.

SELECTED PROVISIONS
FROM OTHER
CALIFORNIA
CODES

BUSINESS AND PROFESSIONS CODE

EDUCATION CODE

FAMILY CODE

HEALTH AND SAFETY CODE

PUBLIC RESOURCES CODE

WELFARE AND INSTITUTIONS CODE

BUSINESS & PROFESSIONS CODE

[For a more complete listing of DRUG violations, refer to LawTech's "DRUG LAW" book which lists
all California Codes that comprise the California Uniform
Controlled Substances Act.]

4060. Possession of Controlled Substance Without Prescription

No person shall possess any controlled substance, except that furnished to a person upon the prescription of a physician, dentist, podiatrist, or veterinarian, or furnished pursuant to a drug order issued by a *** certified nurse-midwife pursuant to Section *** 2746.51, a nurse practitioner pursuant to Section 2836.1, or a physician assistant pursuant to Section 3502.1. This section shall not apply to the possession of any controlled substance by a manufacturer, wholesaler, pharmacy, physician, podiatrist, dentist, veterinarian, *** certified nurse-midwife, nurse practitioner, or physician assistant, when in stock in containers correctly labeled with the name and address of the supplier or producer.

Nothing in this section authorizes a certified nurse-midwife, a nurse practitioner, or a physician assistant to order his or her own stock of dangerous drugs and devices. *(AM '01)*

4140. Unlawful Possession or Control

No person shall possess or have under his or her control any hypodermic needle or syringe except when acquired in accordance with this article.

4141. Permit Required for Sale

No person shall furnish hypodermic needles or syringes, by sale or otherwise, without a license issued by the board, except as otherwise provided by this article.

4142. Retail Sale Prohibited without Prescription

Except as otherwise provided by this article, no hypodermic needle or syringe shall be sold at retail except upon the prescription of a physician, dentist, veterinarian, or podiatrist.

4324. Prescription Forgery

(a) Every person who signs the name of another, or of a fictitious person, or falsely makes, alters, forges, utters, publishes, passes, or attempts to pass, as genuine, any prescription for any drugs is guilty of forgery and upon conviction thereof shall be punished by imprisonment in the state prison, or by imprisonment in the county jail for not more than one year.

(b) Every person who has in his or her possession any drugs secured by a forged prescription shall be punished by imprisonment in the state prison, or by imprisonment in the county jail for not more than one year.

4325. Unlawful Production or Possession of Prescription Blank

(a) No person other than a physician, dentist, podiatrist, veterinarian, pharmacist, or other person authorized by law to dispense, administer, or prescribe controlled substances, or the person's agent acting under authorization by the person to print prescription blanks, and acting in the regular practice of the person's profession, shall knowingly and willfully manufacture, copy, reproduce, or possess, or cause to be manufactured, copied, reproduced, or possessed, any prescription blank that purports to bear the name, address, and federal registry or other identifying information of a physician, dentist, podiatrist, veterinarian, or other person authorized by law to dispense, administer, or prescribe controlled substances.

(b) Every person who violates this section shall be guilty of a misdemeanor.

4326. Possession of Hypodermic Needle or Syringe by False Representation or Forgery; Allow Improper Use

(a) Any person who obtains a hypodermic needle or hypodermic syringe by a false or fraudulent representation or design or by a forged or fictitious name, or contrary to, or in violation of, any of the provisions of this chapter, is guilty of a misdemeanor.

(b) Any person who has obtained a hypodermic needle or hypodermic syringe from any person to whom a permit has been issued as provided in Article 9 (commencing with Section 4140) and who uses, or permits or causes, directly or indirectly, the hypodermic needle or hypodermic syringe to be used for any purpose other than that for which it was obtained is guilty of a misdemeanor and upon conviction thereof shall be punished by a fine not exceeding one thousand dollars ($1,000), or by imprisonment in a county jail not exceeding one year, or both a fine and imprisonment.

7582.26. Private Investigator or Patrol Operator - Prohibited Acts

(a) Any licensee or officer, director, partner, or manager of a licensee may divulge to any law enforcement officer or district attorney, or his or her representative, any information he or she may acquire as to any criminal offense, but he or she shall not divulge to any other person, except as he or she may be required by law so to do, any information acquired by him or her except at the direction of the employer or client for whom the information was obtained.

(b) No licensee or officer, director, partner, manager, or employee of a licensee shall knowingly make any false report to his or her employer or client for whom information was being obtained.

(c) No written report shall be submitted to a client except by the licensee, qualifying manager, or a person authorized by one or either of them, and the person submitting the report shall exercise diligence in ascertaining whether or not the facts and information in the report are true and correct.

(d) No licensee, or officer, director, partner, manager, or employee of a licensee, shall use a title, or wear a uniform, or use an insignia, or use an identification card, or make any statement with the intent to give an impression that he or she is connected in any way with the federal government, a state government, or any political subdivision of a state government.

(e) No licensee, or officer, director, partner, manager, or employee of a licensee, shall enter any private building or portion thereof, except premises commonly accessible to the public, without the consent of the owner or of the person in legal possession thereof.

(f) No private patrol licensee*** or officer, director, partner, manager, or employee of a private patrol licensee shall use or wear a badge, except while engaged in guard or patrol work and while wearing a *** distinctive uniform. A private patrol licensee or officer, director, partner, manager, or employee of a private patrol licensee wearing a distinctive uniform shall wear a patch on each *** shoulder of his or her uniform that reads "private security" and that includes the name of the private patrol company by which the person is employed or for which the person is a representative*** and a badge or cloth patch on the upper left breast of the uniform. All patches and badges worn on a distinctive uniform shall be of a standard design approved by the director and shall be clearly visible.

The director may assess a fine of two hundred fifty dollars ($250) per violation of this subdivision.

(g) No licensee shall permit an employee or agent in his or her own name to advertise, engage clients, furnish reports or present bills to clients, or in any manner whatever conduct business for which a license is required under this chapter. All business of the licensee shall be conducted in the name of and under the control of the licensee.

(h) No licensee shall use a fictitious name in connection with the official activities of the licensee's business.

(i) No private patrol operator licensee or officer, director, partner, or manager of a private patrol operator licensee, or person required to be registered as a security guard pursuant to this chapter shall use or wear a baton or exposed firearm as authorized by this chapter unless he or she is wearing a uniform which complies with the requirements of Section 7582.27. *(AM '01)*

22435.1. Requirements for Application of Section 22435.2

The provisions of Section 22435.2 shall apply when a shopping cart or a laundry cart has a sign permanently affixed to it that identifies the owner of the cart or the retailer, or both; notifies the public of the procedure to be utilized for authorized removal of the cart from the premises; notifies the public that the unauthorized removal of the cart from the premises or parking area of the retail establishment, or the unauthorized possession of the cart, is a violation of state law; and lists a valid telephone number or address for returning the cart removed from the premises or parking area to the owner or retailer.

22435.2.   **Shopping or Laundry Cart Theft**

It is unlawful to do any of the following acts, if a shopping cart or laundry cart has a permanently affixed sign as provided in Section 22435.1:

(a) To remove a shopping cart or laundry cart from the premises or parking area of a retail establishment with the intent to temporarily or permanently deprive the owner or retailer of possession of the cart.

(b) To be in possession of any shopping cart or laundry cart that has been removed from the premises or the parking area of a retail establishment, with the intent to temporarily or permanently deprive the owner or retailer of possession of the cart.

(c) To be in possession of any shopping cart or laundry cart with serial numbers removed, obliterated, or altered, with the intent to temporarily or permanently deprive the owner or retailer of possession of the cart.

(d) To leave or abandon a shopping cart or laundry cart at a location other than the premises or parking area of the retail establishment with the intent to temporarily or permanently deprive the owner or retailer of possession of the cart.

(e) To alter, convert, or tamper with a shopping cart or laundry cart, or to remove any part or portion thereof or to remove, obliterate or alter serial numbers on a cart, with the intent to temporarily or permanently deprive the owner or retailer of possession of the cart.

(f) To be in possession of any shipping cart or laundry cart while that cart is not located on the premises or parking lot of a retail establishment, with the intent to temporarily or permanently deprive the owner or retailer of possession of the cart.

22952.   **Department of Health Services Responsibilities - Tobacco Products**

On or before July 1, 1995, the State Department of Health Services shall do all of the following:

(a) Establish and develop a program to reduce the availability of tobacco products to persons under 18 years of age through the enforcement activities authorized by this division.

(b) Establish requirements that retailers of tobacco products post conspicuously, at each point of purchase, a notice stating that selling tobacco products to anyone under 18 years of age is illegal and subject to penalties. The notice shall also state that the law requires that all persons selling tobacco products check the identification of any purchaser of tobacco products who reasonably appears to be under 18 years of age. The warning signs shall include a toll-free telephone number to the state department for persons to report unlawful sales of tobacco products to minors.

(c) Provide that primary responsibility for enforcement of this division shall be with the state department. In carrying out its enforcement responsibilities, the state department shall conduct random, onsite sting inspections at retail sites and shall enlist the assistance of persons that are 15 and 16 years of age in conducting these enforcement activities. The state department may conduct onsite sting inspections in response to public complaints or at retail sites where violations have previously occurred, and investigate illegal sales of tobacco products to minors by telephone, mail, or the Internet. Participation in these enforcement activities by a person under 18 years of age shall not constitute a violation of subdivision (b) of Section 308 of the Penal Code for the person under 18 years of age, and the person under 18 years of age is immune from prosecution thereunder, or under any other provision of law prohibiting the purchase of these products by a person under 18 years of age.

(d) In accordance with Chapter 3.5 (commencing with Section 11340) of Part 1 of Division 3 of Title 2 of the Government Code, the state department shall adopt and publish guidelines for the use of persons under 18 years of age in inspections conducted pursuant to subdivision (c)*** that shall include, but not be limited to, all of the following:

(1) The state department and any local law enforcement agency under an enforcement delegation contract with the department may use persons under 18 years of age who are 15 or 16 years of age in random inspections to determine if sales of cigarettes or other tobacco products are being made to persons under 18 years of age.

(2) A photograph or video recording of the person under 18 years of age shall be taken prior to each inspection or shift of inspections and retained by the department or the local law enforcement agency under an enforcement delegation contract with the department for purposes of verifying appearances.

(3) The state department or a local law enforcement agency under an enforcement delegation contract with the department may use video recording equipment when conducting the inspections to record and document illegal sales or attempted sales.

(4) The person under 18 years of age, if questioned about his or her age, *** need not state his or her actual age *** but shall present a true and correct identification if verbally asked to present it. Any failure on the part of the person under 18 years of age to provide true and correct identification, if verbally asked for it, shall be a defense to any action pursuant to this section.

(5) The person under 18 years of age shall be under the supervision of a regularly employed peace officer during the inspection.

(6) All persons under 18 years of age used in this manner by the department or a local law enforcement agency under an enforcement delegation contract with the department shall display the appearance of a person under 18 years of age. It shall be a defense to any action under this division that the *** person's appearance was not that which could be generally expected of a person under 18 years of age, under the actual circumstances presented to the seller of the cigarettes or other tobacco products at the time of the alleged offense.

(7) Following the completion of the sale, *** the peace officer accompanying the person under 18 years of age shall reenter the retail establishment and inform the seller of the random inspection and *** following an attempted sale, the department shall notify the retail establishment of the inspection.

(8) Failure to comply with the procedures set forth in this subdivision shall be a defense to any action brought pursuant to this section.

(e) Be responsible for ensuring and reporting the *** state's compliance with Section 1926 of Title XIX of the federal Public Health Service Act (42 U.S.C. 300x-26) and any implementing regulations adopted in relation thereto by the United States Department of Health and Human Services. A copy of this report shall be made available to the Governor and the Legislature.

(f) Provide that any civil penalties imposed pursuant to Section 22958 shall be enforced against the owner or owners of the retail business and not the employees of the business. *(AM '01)*

23004. Alcoholic Beverage Defined

"Alcoholic beverage"includes alcohol, spirits, liquor, wine, beer, and every liquid or solid containing alcohol, spirits, wine, or beer, and which contains one-half of 1 percent or more of alcohol by volume and which is fit for beverage purposes either alone or when diluted, mixed, or combined with other substances.

23300. License Required

No person shall exercise the privilege or perform any act which a licensee may exercise or perform under the authority of a license unless the person is authorized to do so by a license issued pursuant to this division.

24046. License Must be Posted in Conspicuous Place

Upon receipt of any license, the licensee shall post it in a conspicuous place upon the licensed premises. Licenses issued for trains, boats or airplanes may, in lieu of being posted upon the train, boat, or airplane for which issued, be posted in such other place in this State as the department shall designate.

25601. Maintain a Disorderly houses

Every licensee, or agent or employee of a licensee, who keeps, permits to be used, or suffers to be used, in conjunction with a licensed premises, any disorderly house or place in which people abide or to which people resort, to the disturbance of the neighborhood, or in which people abide or to which people resort for purposes which are injurious to the public morals, health, convenience, or safety, is guilty of a misdemeanor.

25602. Sales to Intoxicated Person

(a) Every person who sells, furnishes, gives, or causes to be sold, furnished, or given away, any alcoholic beverage to any habitual or common drunkard or to any obviously intoxicated person is guilty of a misdemeanor.

(b) No person who sells, furnishes, gives, or causes to be sold, furnished, or given away, any alcoholic beverage pursuant to subdivision (a) of this section shall be civilly liable to any injured person or the estate of such person for injuries inflicted on that person as a result of intoxication by the consumer of such alcoholic beverage.

(c) The Legislature hereby declares that this section shall be interpreted so that the holdings in cases such as Vesely v. Sager (5 Cal.3d 153), Bernhard v. Harrah's Club (16 Cal.3d 313) and Coulter v. Superior Court (21 Cal.3d 144) be abrogated in favor of prior judicial interpretation finding the consumption of alcoholic beverages rather than the serving of alcoholic beverages as the proximate cause of injuries inflicted upon another by an intoxicated person.

25607. Possession of Unauthorized Beverages on Licensed Premises

(a) Except as provided in subdivision (b), it is unlawful for any person or licensee to have upon any premises for which a license has been issued any alcoholic beverages other than the alcoholic beverage which the licensee is authorized to sell at the premises under his or her license. It shall be presumed that all alcoholic beverages found or located upon premises for which licenses have been issued belong to the person or persons to whom the licenses were issued. Every person violating the provisions of this section is guilty of a misdemeanor. The department may seize any alcoholic beverages found in violation of this section.

(b) A bona fide public eating place for which an on-sale beer and wine license has been issued may have upon the premises brandy, rum, or liqueurs for use solely for cooking purposes.

25608. Possession of Alcoholic Beverage on School Property

Every person who possesses, consumes, sells, gives, or delivers to any other person, any alcoholic beverage in or on any public schoolhouse or any of the grounds thereof, is guilty of a misdemeanor. This section does not, however, make it unlawful for any person to acquire, possess, or use any alcoholic beverage in or on any public schoolhouse, or on any grounds thereof, if any of the following applies:

(a) The alcoholic beverage is acquired, possessed, or used in connection with a course of instruction given at the school and the person has been authorized to acquire, possess, or use it by the governing body or other administrative head of the school.

(b) The public schoolhouse is surplus school property and the grounds thereof are leased to a lessee which is a general law city with a population of less than 50,000, or the public schoolhouse is surplus school property and the grounds thereof are located in an unincorporated area and are leased to a lessee which is a civic organization, and the property is to be used for community center purposes and no public school education is to be conducted thereon by either the lessor or the lessee and the property is not being used by persons under the age of 21 years for recreational purposes at any time during which alcoholic beverages are being sold or consumed on the premises.

(c) The alcoholic beverages are acquired, possessed, or used during events at a college-owned or college-operated veterans stadium with a capacity of over 12,000 people, located in a county with a population of over six million people. As used in this subdivision, "events" mean football games sponsored by a college, other than a public community college, or other events sponsored by noncollege groups.

(d) The alcoholic beverages are acquired, possessed, or used during an event not sponsored by any college at a performing arts facility built on property owned by a community college district and leased to a nonprofit organization which is a public benefit corporation formed under Part 2 (commencing with Section 5110) of Division 2 of Title 1 of the Corporations Code. As used in this subdivision, "performing arts facility" means an auditorium with more than 300 permanent seats.

(e) The alcoholic beverage is wine for sacramental or other religious purposes and is used only during authorized religious services held on or before January 1, 1995.

(f) The alcoholic beverages are acquired, possessed, or used during an event at a community center owned by a community services district and the event is not held at a time when students are attending a public school sponsored activity at the center.

(g) The alcoholic beverage is wine which is acquired, possessed, or used during an event sponsored by a community college district or an organization operated for the benefit of the community college district where the college district maintains both an instructional program in viticulture on no less than five acres of land owned by the district and an instructional program in enology, which includes sales and marketing.

(h) The alcoholic beverage is acquired, possessed, or used at a professional minor league baseball game conducted at the stadium of a community college located in a county with a population of less than 250,000 inhabitants, and the baseball game is conducted pursuant to a contract between the community college district and a professional sports organization.

(i) The alcoholic beverages are acquired, possessed, or used during events at a college-owned or college-operated stadium with a capacity of over 18,900 people, located in a county of the 14th class. As used in this subdivision, "events"means fundraisers held to benefit a nonprofit corporation which has obtained a license pursuant to this division for the event. "Events"does not include football games or other athletic contests sponsored by any college or public community college.

Any person convicted of a violation of this section shall, in addition to the penalty imposed for the misdemeanor, be barred from having or receiving any privilege of the use of public school property which is accorded by Article 2 (commencing with Section 82537) of Chapter 8 of Part 49 of the Education Code.

25631. On- or Off-Sale Licensed Premises; Required Closing Hours

Any on- or off-sale licensee, or agent or employee of such licensee, who sells, gives, or delivers to any persons any alcoholic beverage or any person who knowingly purchases any alcoholic beverage between the hours of 2 o'clock a.m. and 6 o'clock a.m. of the same day, is guilty of a misdemeanor.

For the purposes of this section, on the day that a time change occurs from Pacific Standard Time to Pacific Daylight Time, or back again to Pacific Standard Time, "2 o'clock a.m."means two hours after 12 o'clock p.m. of the day preceding the day such change occurs.

25632. Licensee Permitting Consumption After Hours

Any retail licensee, or agent or employee of such licensee, who permits any alcoholic beverage to be consumed by any person on the licensee's licensed premises during any hours in which it is unlawful to sell, give, or deliver any alcoholic beverage for consumption on the premises is guilty of a misdemeanor.

25658. Alcoholic Beverages: Sales, etc. to Minors

(a) Except as otherwise provided in subdivision (c), every person who sells, furnishes, gives, or causes to be sold, furnished, or given away, any alcoholic beverage to any person under the age of 21 years is guilty of a misdemeanor.

(b) Any person under the age of 21 years who purchases any alcoholic beverage, or any person under the age of 21 years who consumes any alcoholic beverage in any on-sale premises, is guilty of a misdemeanor.

(c) Any person who violates subdivision (a) by purchasing an alcoholic beverage for a person under the age of 21 years and the person under the age of 21 years thereafter consumes the alcohol and thereby proximately causes great bodily injury or death to himself, herself, or any other person, is guilty of a misdemeanor.

(d) Any on-sale licensee who knowingly permits a person under the age of 21 years to consume any alcoholic beverage in the on-sale premises, whether or not the licensee has knowledge that the person is under the age of 21 years, is guilty of a misdemeanor.

(e)(1) Except as otherwise provided in paragraph (2) or (3), any person who violates this section shall be punished by a fine of two hundred fifty dollars ($250), no part of which shall be suspended, or the person shall be required to perform not less than 24 hours or more than 32 hours of community service during hours when the person is not employed and is not attending school, or a combination of fine and community service as determined by the court. A second or subsequent violation of subdivision (b) shall be punished by a fine of not more than five hundred dollars ($500), or the person shall be required to perform not less than 36 hours or more than 48 hours of community service during hours when the person is not employed and is not attending school, or a combination of fine and community service as determined by the court. It is the intent of the Legislature that the community service requirements prescribed in this section require service at an alcohol or drug treatment program or facility or at a county coroner's office, if available, in the area where the violation occurred or where the person resides.

(2) Any person who violates subdivision (a) by furnishing an alcoholic beverage, or causing an alcoholic beverage to be furnished, to a minor shall be punished by a fine of one thousand dollars ($1,000), no part of which shall be suspended, and the person shall be required to perform not less than 24 hours of community service during hours when the person is not employed and is not attending school.

(3) Any person who violates subdivision (c) shall be punished by imprisonment in a county jail for a minimum term of six months not to exceed one year, by a fine not exceeding one thousand dollars ($1,000), or by both imprisonment and fine.

(f) Persons under the age of 21 years may be used by peace officers in the enforcement of this section to apprehend licensees, or employees or agents of licensees, who sell alcoholic beverages to minors. Notwithstanding subdivision (b), any person under the age of 21 years who purchases or attempts to purchase any alcoholic beverage while under the direction of a peace officer is immune from prosecution for that purchase or attempt to purchase an alcoholic beverage. Guidelines with respect to the use of persons under the age of 21 years as decoys shall be adopted and published by the department in accordance with the rulemaking portion of the Administrative Procedure Act (Chapter 3.5 (commencing with Section 11340) of Part 1 of Division 3 of Title 2 of the Government Code). Law enforcement-initiated minor decoy programs in operation prior to the effective date of regulatory guidelines adopted by the department shall be authorized as long as the minor decoy displays to the seller of alcoholic beverages the appearance of a person under the age of 21 years. This subdivision shall not be construed to prevent the department from taking disciplinary action against a licensee who sells alcoholic beverages to a minor decoy prior to the department's final adoption of regulatory guidelines. After the completion of every minor decoy program performed under this subdivision, the law enforcement agency using the decoy shall notify licensees within 72 hours of the results of the program. When the use of a minor decoy results in the issuance of a citation, the notification required shall be given within 72 hours of the issuance of the citation. A law enforcement agency may comply with this requirement by leaving a written notice at the licensed premises addressed to the licensee, or by mailing a notice addressed to the licensee. *(AM '99)*

25658.5. Alcohol: Purchase by Person Under Age 21

Any person under the age of 21 years who attempts to purchase any alcoholic beverage from a licensee, or the licensee's agent or employee, is guilty of an infraction and shall be punished by a fine of not more than $100. A second or subsequent violation of this section shall be punished by a fine of not more than $250, or the person shall be required to perform up to 36 hours of community service during hours when the person is not employed or is not attending school, or a combination of fine and community service, as the court deems just.

25659.5. Sale of Keg Beer; Labeling Requirements

(a) Retail licensees selling keg beer for consumption off licensed premises shall place an identification tag on all kegs of beer at the time of sale and shall require the signing of a receipt for the keg of beer by the purchaser in order to allow kegs to be traced if the contents are used in violation of this article. The keg identification shall be in the form of a numbered label prescribed and supplied by the department that identifies the seller.

The receipt shall be on a form prescribed and supplied by the department and shall include the name and address of the purchaser and the purchaser's driver's license number or equivalent form of identification number. A retailer shall not return any deposit upon the return of any keg that does not have the identification label required pursuant to subdivision (a).

(b) Any licensee selling keg beer for off premise consumption who fails to require the signing of a receipt at the time of sale and fails to place a numbered identification label on the keg shall be subject to disciplinary action pursuant to this division. The licensee shall retain a copy of the receipt, which shall be retained on the licensed premise for a period of six months. The receipt records shall be available for inspection and copying by the department or other authorized law enforcement agency.

(c) Possession of a keg containing beer with knowledge that the keg is not identified as required by subdivision (a) is a misdemeanor.

(d) Any purchaser of keg beer who knowingly provides false information as required by subdivision (a) is guilty of a misdemeanor.

(e) The identification label required pursuant to subdivision (a) shall be constructed of material and made attachable in such a manner as to make the label easily removable for the purpose of cleaning and reusing the keg by a beer manufacturer.

(f) The department is authorized to charge a fee not to exceed the actual cost of supplying receipt forms and identification labels required pursuant to subdivision (a). Fees collected pursuant to this subdivision shall be deposited in the Alcohol Beverage Control Fund.

(g) As used in this section, "keg" means any brewery-sealed, individual container of beer having a liquid capacity of six gallons or more.

25660.　Bona fide Evidence of Majority and Identity; Demand as Defense to Prosecution

Bona fide evidence of majority and identity of the person is a document issued by a federal, state, county, or municipal government, or subdivision or agency thereof, including, but not limited to, a motor vehicle operator's license or an identification card issued to a member of the Armed Forces, which contains the name, date of birth, description, and picture of the person. Proof that the defendant-licensee, or his employee or agent, demanded, was shown and acted in reliance upon such bona fide evidence in any transaction, employment, use or permission forbidden by Sections 25658, 25663 or 25665 shall be a defense to any criminal prosecution therefor or to any proceedings for the suspension or revocation of any license based thereon.

25660.5.　Furnishing False Identification to Minors

Any person who sells, gives, or furnishes to any person under the age of 21 years any false or fraudulent written, printed, or photostatic evidence of the majority and identity of such person under the age of 21 years evidence of majority and identification of any other person is guilty of a misdemeanor.

25661.　Possession or Presentation of False Identification

Any person under 21 years who presents or offers to any licensee, his or her agent or employee, any written, printed, or photostatic evidence of age and identity which is false, fraudulent or not actually his or her own for the purpose of ordering, purchasing, attempting to purchase or otherwise procuring or attempting to procure, the serving of any alcoholic beverage, or who has in his or her possession any false or fraudulent written, printed, or photostatic evidence of age and identity, is guilty of a misdemeanor and shall be punished by a fine of at least two hundred fifty dollars ($250), no part of which shall be suspended; or the person shall be required to perform not less than 24 hours nor more than 32 hours of community service during hours when the person is not employed and is not attending school, or a combination of fine and community service as determined by the court.

25662.　Alcohol Seizure From Person Under Age 21

(a) Any person under the age of 21 years who has any alcoholic beverage in his or her possession on any street or highway or in any public place or in any place open to the public is guilty of a misdemeanor. This section does not apply to possession by a person under the age of 21 years making a delivery of an alcoholic beverage in pursuance of the order of his or her parent, responsible adult relative, or any other adult designated by the parent or legal guardian, or in pursuance of his or her employment. That person shall have a complete defense if he or she was following, in a timely manner, the reasonable instructions of his or her parent, legal guardian, responsible adult relative, or adult designee relating to disposition of the alcoholic beverage.

(b) Unless otherwise provided by law, where a peace officer has lawfully entered the premises, the peace officer may seize any alcoholic beverage in plain view that is in the possession of, or provided to, a person under the age of 21 years at social gatherings, when those gatherings are open to the public, 10 or more persons under the age of 21 years are participating, persons under the age of 21 years are consuming alcoholic beverages, and there is no supervision of the social gathering by a parent or guardian of one or more of the participants.

Where a peace officer has seized alcoholic beverages pursuant to this subdivision, the officer may destroy any alcoholic beverage contained in an opened container and in the possession of, or provided to, a person under the age of 21 years, and, with respect to alcoholic beverages in unopened containers, the officer shall impound those beverages for a period not to exceed seven working days pending a request for the release of those beverages by a person 21 years of age or older who is the lawful owner or resident of the property upon which the alcoholic beverages were seized. If no one requests release of the seized alcoholic beverages within that period, those beverages may be destroyed.

25663. Unlawful Employment of Minors

(a) Every person who employs or uses the services of any person under the age of 21 years in or on that portion of any premises, during business hours, which are primarily designed and used for the sale and service of alcoholic beverages for consumption on the premises is guilty of a misdemeanor.

(b) Any off-sale licensee who employs or uses the services of any person under the age of 18 years for sale of alcoholic beverages shall be subject to suspension or revocation of his or her license, except that a person under the age of 18 years may be employed or used for those purposes if that person is under the continuous supervision of a person 21 years of age or older.

25665. Presence of Minors in On-Sale Establishments

Any licensee under an on-sale license issued for public premises, as defined in Sec. 23039, who permits a person under the age of 21 years to enter and remain in the licensed premises without lawful business therein is guilty of a misdemeanor. Any person under the Age of 21 years who enters and remains in the licensed public premises without lawful business therein is guilty of a misdemeanor and shall be punished by a fine or not less than two hundred dollars ($200), no part of which shall be suspended.

25755. Inspection of Premises by Peace Officers; Requirements

(a) The director and the persons employed by the department for the administration and enforcement of this division are peace officers in the enforcement of the penal provisions of this division, the rules of the department adopted under the provisions of this division, and any other penal provisions of law of this state prohibiting or regulating the sale, exposing for sale, use, possession, giving away, adulteration, dilution, misbranding, or mislabeling of alcoholic beverages or intoxicating liquors, and these persons are authorized, while acting as peace officers, to enforce any penal provisions of law while in the course of their employment.

(b) The director, the persons employed by the department for the administration and enforcement of this division, peace officers listed in Section 830.1 of the Penal Code, and those officers listed in Section 830.6 of the Penal Code while acting in the course and scope of their employment as peace officers may, in enforcing the provisions of this division, visit and inspect the premises of any licensee at any time during which the licensee is exercising the privileges authorized by his or her license on the premises.

(c) Peace officers of the Department of the California Highway Patrol, members of the University of California and California State University police departments, and peace officers of the Department of Parks and Recreation, as defined in subdivisions (a), (b), (c), and (f) of Section 830.2 of the Penal Code, may, in enforcing this division, visit and inspect the premises of any licensee located on state property at any time during which the licensee is exercising the privileges authorized by his or her license on the premises.

(d) Any agents assigned to the Drug Enforcement Narcotics Team by the director shall have successfully completed a four-week course on narcotics enforcement approved by the Commission on Peace Officer Standards and Training. In addition, all other agents of the department shall successfully complete the four-week course on narcotics enforcement approved by the Commission on Peace Officer Standards and Training by June 1, 1995.

EDUCATION CODE

32210. Disturbing Schools

Any person who willfully disturbs any public school or any public school meeting is guilty of a misdemeanor, and shall be punished by a fine of not more than $500.

32211. Remain Upon School Grounds After Requested to Leave

(a) Any person who is not a student of the public school, a parent or guardian of a student of the public school, or an officer or employee of the school district maintaining the public school, or who is not required by his employment to be in a public school, or on the grounds of the public school, and who has entered any public school building or the grounds of any public school, during school hours, and who is requested either by the principal of the public school or by the designee of the principal to leave a public school building or public school grounds, shall promptly depart therefrom and shall not return thereto for at least 48 hours. A request that a person depart from a public school building or public school grounds shall be made by the principal or his designee exclusively on the basis that it appears reasonable to the principal or his designee to conclude that the continued presence of the person requested to depart would be disruptive of, or would interfere with, classes or other activities of the public school program.

(b) Any person who fails to leave a public school building or public school grounds promptly upon request of the principal of the public school or the designee of the principal made pursuant to subdivision (a) or who, after leaving a public school building or public school grounds pursuant to a request of the principal of the public school or the designee of the principal made pursuant to subdivision (a), returns thereto, except pursuant to subdivision (d), within 48 hours, is guilty of a misdemeanor and shall be punished pursuant to Penal Code Section 626.8.

(c) Any person who is requested pursuant to subdivision (a) to leave a public school building or school grounds may appeal to the superintendent of the school district in which the public school is located. Such an appeal shall be made not later than the second succeeding schoolday after the person has departed from the public school building or public school grounds. The superintendent shall, after reviewing the matter with the principal or his designee and the person seeking ingress to the public school during school hours, render his decision within 24 hours after the appeal is made, and such decision shall be binding upon both parties. A decision of the superintendent may be appealed by the person seeking ingress to the public school during public school hours to the governing board of the school district in which the public school is located. Such an appeal shall be made not later than the second succeeding schoolday after the superintendent has rendered his decision. The governing board of the school district shall consider and decide the appeal at its next scheduled regular or adjourned regular public meeting, and the decision of the governing board shall be final.

(d) Where the office of the superintendent of the school district or the office of the governing board of the school district is situated in the public school building or on the grounds of the public school from which a person has been requested, pursuant to subdivision (a), to depart, the person may enter the public school building or the grounds of the public school solely for the purpose of, and only to the extent necessary for, personally making at the office of the superintendent or the office of the governing board an appeal pursuant to subdivision (c).

(e) The governing board of every school district shall cause to have posted at every entrance to each school and grounds of the district a notice which shall set forth "school hours", which are hereby defined for the purposes of this section as the period commencing one hour before classes begin and one hour after classes end at any school, or as otherwise defined by the governing board of the school district.

(f) For the purposes of subdivision (a), a representative of a school employee organization engaged in activities related to representation, as defined by Section 7104, shall be deemed to be a person required by his employment to be in a school building or on the grounds of a school.

(g) Nothing in this section shall be construed as preempting any ordinance of any city, county, or city and county.

44810. Schools: Interference - Property Damage / Bodily Injury

Every minor over 16 years of age or adult who is not a pupil of the school, including but not limited to any such minor or adult who is the parent or guardian of a pupil of the school, who comes upon any school ground or into any schoolhouse and there willfully interferes with the discipline, good order, lawful conduct, or administration of any school class or activity of the school, with the intent to disrupt, obstruct or to inflict damage to property or bodily injury upon any person, is guilty of a misdemeanor, and is punishable by a fine of not less than $100, or by imprisonment in the county jail for not more than 6 months, or both.

44811. Disruption of Classwork or Extracurricular Activities

Any parent, guardian, or other person whose conduct in a place where a school employee is required to be in the course of his or her duties materially disrupts classwork or extracurricular activities or involves substantial disorder is guilty of a misdemeanor which is punishable by a fine not exceeding $100, by imprisonment in the county jail for a period of not more than 10 days, or both. This section does not apply to any otherwise lawful employee concerted activity, including, but not limited to, picketing and the distribution of handbills.

48264. Truants: Who May Arrest

The attendance supervisor or his or her designee, a peace officer, a school administrator or his or her designee, or a probation officer may arrest or assume temporary custody, during school hours, of any minor subject to compulsory full-time education or to compulsory continuation education found away from his or her home and who is absent from school without valid excuse within the county, city, or city and county, or school district.

48264.5. Truant; Peace Officer May Issue Written Warning: 4th Offense May Result in Ward Of Court Judgment

Any minor who is <u>required to be reported as</u> a truant pursuant to Section 48260 <u>or 48261 may be required to attend makeup classes conducted on one day of a weekend pursuant to subdivision (c) of Section 37223 and</u> is subject to the following:

(a) *** <u>The</u> first <u>time a</u> truancy <u>report is required</u>, the pupil may be personally given a written warning by any peace officer specified in Section 830.1 of the Penal Code. A record of the written warning may be kept at the school for a period of not less than two years, or until the pupil graduates, or transfers, from that school. If the pupil transfers, the record may be forwarded to any school receiving the pupil's school records. A record of the written warning may be maintained by the law enforcement agency in accordance with that law enforcement agency's policies and procedures.

(b) *** <u>The</u> second <u>time a</u> truancy <u>report is required</u> within the same school year, the pupil may be assigned by the school to an afterschool or weekend study program located within the same county as the pupil's school. If the pupil fails to successfully complete the assigned study program, the pupil shall be subject to subdivision (c).

(c) *** <u>The</u> third <u>time a</u> truancy <u>report is required</u> within the same school year, the pupil <u>shall be classified a habitual truant, as defined in Section 48262, and</u> may be referred to, and required to attend, an attendance review board or a truancy mediation program pursuant to Section 48263 or pursuant to Section 601.3 of the Welfare and Institutions Code. If the district does not have a truancy mediation program, the pupil may be required to attend a comparable program deemed acceptable by the school district's attendance supervisor. If the pupil does not successfully complete the truancy mediation program or other similar program, the pupil shall be subject to subdivision (d).

(d) *** <u>The</u> fourth <u>time a</u> truancy <u>is required to be reported</u> within the same school year, the pupil shall be *** within the jurisdiction of the juvenile court which may adjudge *** <u>the</u> pupil to be a ward of the court pursuant to Section 601 of the Welfare and Institutions Code. If the pupil is adjudged a ward of the court, the pupil shall be required to do one or more of the following:

(1) Performance at court-approved community services sponsored by either a public or private nonprofit agency for not less than 20 hours but not more than 40 hours over a period not to exceed 90 days, dur-

ing a time other than the pupil's hours of school attendance or employment. The probation officer shall report to the court the failure of the pupil to comply with this paragraph.

(2) Payment of a fine by the pupil of not more than one hundred dollars ($100) for which a parent or guardian of the pupil may be jointly liable.

(3) Attendance of a court-approved truancy prevention program.

(4) Suspension or revocation of driving privileges pursuant to Section 13202.7 of the Vehicle Code. This subdivision shall apply only to a pupil who has attended a school attendance review board program, a program operated by a probation department acting as a school attendance review board, or a truancy mediation program pursuant to subdivision (c). *(AM '01)*

FAMILY CODE

See Penal Code Sections 166(a)(4) or 273.6 for Protective Order Violations

6389. Protective Orders; Possession of Firearm by Subject Prohibited by Order

(a) A person subject to a protective order, as defined in Section 6218, shall not own, possess, purchase, or receive a firearm while that protective order is in effect.

(b) The Judicial Council shall provide a notice on all forms requesting a protective order that, at the hearing for a protective order, the respondent shall be ordered to relinquish possession or control of any firearms and not to purchase or receive or attempt to purchase or receive any firearms for a period not to exceed the duration of the restraining order.

(c) If the respondent is present in court at a duly noticed hearing, the court shall order the respondent to relinquish any firearm in that person's immediate possession or control, or subject to that person's immediate possession or control, within 24 hours of the order, by either surrendering the firearm to the control of local law enforcement officials, or by selling the firearm to a licensed gun dealer, as specified in Section 12071 of the Penal Code. If the respondent is not present at the hearing, the respondent shall relinquish the firearm within 48 hours after being served with the order. A person ordered to relinquish any firearm pursuant to this subdivision shall file with the court a receipt showing the firearm was surrendered to the local law enforcement agency or sold to a licensed gun dealer within 72 hours after receiving the order. In the event that it is necessary to continue the date of any hearing due to a request for a relinquishment order pursuant to this section, the court shall ensure that all applicable protective orders described in Section 6218 remain in effect or bifurcate the issues and grant the permanent restraining order pending the date of the hearing.

(d) If the respondent declines to relinquish possession of any firearm based upon the assertion of the right against self-incrimination, as provided by the Fifth Amendment to the United States Constitution and Section 15 of Article I of the California Constitution, the court may grant use immunity for the act of relinquishing the firearm required under this section.

(e) A local law enforcement agency may charge the respondent a fee for the storage of any firearm pursuant to this section. This fee shall not exceed the actual cost incurred by the local law enforcement agency for the storage of the firearm. For purposes of this subdivision, "actual cost" means expenses directly related to taking possession of a firearm, storing the firearm, and surrendering possession of the firearm to a licensed dealer as defined in Section 12071 of the Penal Code or to the respondent.

(f) The restraining order requiring a person to relinquish a firearm pursuant to subdivision (c) shall state on its face that the respondent is prohibited from owning, possessing, purchasing, or receiving a firearm while the protective order is in effect and that the firearm shall be relinquished to the local law enforcement agency for that jurisdiction or sold to a licensed gun dealer, and that proof of surrender or sale shall be filed with the court within a specified period of receipt of the order. The order shall also state on its face the expiration date for relinquishment. Nothing in this section shall limit a respondent's right under existing law to petition the court at a later date for modification of the order.

(g) The restraining order requiring a person to relinquish a firearm pursuant to subdivision (c) shall prohibit the person from possessing or controlling any firearm for the duration of the order. At the expiration of the order, the local law enforcement agency shall return possession of any surrendered firearm to the respondent, within five days after the expiration of the relinquishment order, unless the local law enforcement agency determines that (1) the firearm has been stolen, (2) the respondent is prohibited from possessing a firearm because the respondent is in any prohibited class for the possession of firearms, as defined in Sections 12021 and 12021.1 of the Penal Code and Sections 8100 and 8103 of the Welfare and Institutions Code, or (3) another successive restraining order is used against the respondent under this section. If the local law enforcement agency determines that the respondent is the legal owner of any firearm deposited with the local law enforcement agency and is prohibited from possessing any firearm, the respondent shall be entitled to sell or transfer the firearm to a licensed dealer as defined in Section 12071 of the Penal Code. If the firearm has been stolen, the firearm shall be restored to the lawful owner upon his or her identification of the firearm and proof of ownership.

(h) The court may, as part of the relinquishment order, grant an exemption from the relinquishment requirements of this section for a particular firearm if the respondent can show that a particular firearm is necessary as a condition of continued employment and that the current employer is unable to reassign the respondent to another position where a firearm is unnecessary. If an exemption is granted pursuant to this subdivision, the order shall provide that the firearm shall be in the physical possession of the respondent only during scheduled work hours and during travel to and from his or her place of employment. In any case involving a peace officer who as a condition of employment and whose personal safety depends on the ability to carry a firearm, a court may allow the peace officer to continue to carry a firearm, either on duty or off duty, if the court finds by a preponderance of the evidence that the officer does not pose a threat of harm. Prior to making this finding, the court shall require a mandatory psychological evaluation of the peace officer and may require the peace officer to enter into counseling or other remedial treatment program to deal with any propensity for domestic violence.

(i) During the period of the relinquishment order, a respondent is entitled to make one sale of all firearms that are in the possession of a local law enforcement agency pursuant to this section. A licensed gun dealer, who presents a local law enforcement agency with a bill of sale indicating that all firearms owned by the respondent that are in the possession of the local law enforcement agency have been sold by the respondent to the licensed gun dealer, shall be given possession of those firearms, at the location where a respondent's firearms are stored, within five days of presenting the local law enforcement agency with a bill of sale.

(j) The disposition of any unclaimed property under this section shall be made pursuant to Section 1413 of the Penal Code.

(k) The return of a firearm to any person pursuant to subdivision (g) shall not be subject to the requirements of subdivision (d) of Section 12072 of the Penal Code.

(l) If the respondent notifies the court that he or she owns a firearm that is not in his or her immediate possession, the court may limit the order to exclude that firearm if the judge is satisfied the respondent is unable to gain access to that firearm while the protective order is in effect.

(m) Any respondent to a protective order who violates any order issued pursuant to this section shall be punished under the provisions of subdivision (g) of Section 12021 of the Penal Code. *(AM '99)*

HEALTH & SAFETY CODE

[For a more complete listing of DRUG violations, refer to LawTech's "DRUG LAW" book, which lists all California Codes that comprise the California Uniform Controlled Substances Act.]

11014.5. Drug Paraphernalia

(a) "Drug paraphernalia"means all equipment, products and materials of any kind which are designed for use or marketed for use, in planting, propagating, cultivating, growing, harvesting, manufacturing, compounding, converting, producing, processing, preparing, testing, analyzing, packaging, repackaging, storing, containing, concealing, injecting, ingesting, inhaling, or otherwise introducing into the human body a controlled substance in violation of this division. It includes, but is not limited to:

(1) Kits designed for use or marketed for use in planting, propagating, cultivating, growing, or harvesting of any species of plant which is a controlled substance or from which a controlled substance can be derived.

(2) Kits designed for use or marketed for use in manufacturing, compounding, converting, producing, processing, or preparing controlled substances.

(3) Isomerization devices designed for use or marketed for use in increasing the potency of any species of plant which is a controlled substance.

(4) Testing equipment designed for use or marketed for use in identifying, or in analyzing the strength, effectiveness, or purity of controlled substances.

(5) Scales and balances designed for use or marketed for use in weighing or measuring controlled substances.

(6) Containers and other objects designed for use or marketed for use in storing or concealing controlled substances.

(7) Hypodermic syringes, needles, and other objects designed for use or marketed for use in parenterally injecting controlled substances into the human body.

(8) Objects designed for use or marketed for use in ingesting, inhaling, or otherwise introducing marijuana, cocaine, hashish, or hashish oil into the human body, such as:

(A) Carburetion tubes and devices.

(B) Smoking and carburetion masks.

(C) Roach clips, meaning objects used to hold burning material, such as a marijuana cigarette, that has become too small or too short to be held in the hand.

(D) Miniature cocaine spoons, and cocaine vials.

(E) Chamber pipes.

(F) Carburetor pipes.

(G) Electric pipes.

(H) Air-driven pipes.

(I) Chillums.

(J) Bongs.

(K) Ice pipes or chillers.

(b) For the purposes of this section, the phrase "marketed for use" means advertising, distributing, offering for sale, displaying for sale, or selling in a manner which promotes the use of equipment, products, or materials with controlled substances.

(c) In determining whether an object is drug paraphernalia, a court or other authority may consider, in addition to all other logically relevant factors, the following:

(1) Statements by an owner or by anyone in control of the object concerning its use.

(2) Instructions, oral or written, provided with the object concerning its use for ingesting, inhaling, or otherwise introducing a controlled substance into the human body.

(3) Descriptive materials accompanying the object which explain or depict its use.

(4) National and local advertising concerning its use.

(5) The manner in which the object is displayed for sale.

(6) Whether the owner, or anyone in control of the object, is a legitimate supplier of like or related items to the community, such as a licensed distributor or dealer of tobacco products.

(7) Expert testimony concerning its use.

(d) If any provision of this section or the application thereof to any person or circumstance is held invalid, it is the intent of the Legislature that the invalidity shall not affect other provisions or applications of the section which can be given effect without the invalid provision or application and to this end the provisions of this section are severable.

11153.5. Furnishing Controlled Substances for Other than Legitimate Medical Purpose

(a) No wholesaler or manufacturer, or agent or employee of a wholesaler or manufacturer, shall furnish controlled substances for other than legitimate medical purposes.

(b) Anyone who violates this section knowing, or having a conscious disregard for the fact, that the controlled substances are for other than a legitimate medical purpose shall be punishable by imprisonment in the state prison, or in the county jail not exceeding one year, or by a fine not exceeding twenty thousand dollars ($20,000), or by both a fine and imprisonment.

(c) Factors to be considered in determining whether a wholesaler or manufacturer, or agent or employee of a wholesaler or manufacturer, furnished controlled substances knowing or having a conscious disregard for the fact that the controlled substances are for other than legitimate medical purposes shall include, but not be limited to, whether the use of controlled substances was for purposes of increasing athletic ability or performance, the amount of controlled substances furnished, the previous ordering pattern of the customer (including size and frequency of orders), the type and size of the customer, and where and to whom the customer distributes the product.

11156. Dispensation or Prescription for Benefit of Addict

No person shall prescribe for or administer, or dispense a controlled substance to an addict or habitual user, or to any person representing himself as such, except as permitted by this division.

11157. False or Fictitious Prescriptions

No person shall issue a prescription that is false or fictitious in any respect.

11162.5. Counterfeit Blank Preseription

(a) Every person who counterfeits a prescription blank purporting to be an official prescription blank prepared and issued pursuant to Section 11161, or knowingly possesses more than three such counterfeited prescription blanks, shall be punished by imprisonment in the state prison or by imprisonment in the county jail for not more than one year.

(b) Every person who knowingly possesses three or fewer counterfeited prescription blanks purporting to be official prescription blanks prepared and issued pursuant to Section 11161, shall be guilty of a misdemeanor punishable by imprisonment in the county jail not exceeding six months, or by a fine not exceeding one thousand dollars ($1,000), or by both.

11166. Suspected Child Abuse Reporting Requirements

(a) Except as provided in subdivision (b), any child care custodian, health practitioner, employee of a child protective agency, child visitation monitor, firefighter, animal control officer, or humane society officer who has knowledge of or observes a child, in his or her professional capacity or within the scope of his or her employment, whom he or she knows or reasonably suspects has been the victim of child abuse, shall report the known or suspected instance of child abuse to a child protective agency immediately or as soon as practically possible by telephone and shall prepare and send a written report thereof within 36 hours of receiving the information concerning the incident. A child protective agency shall be notified and a report shall be prepared and sent even if the child has expired, regardless of whether or not the possible abuse was a factor contributing to the death, and even if suspected child abuse was discovered during an autopsy. For the purposes of this article, "reasonable suspicion" means that it is objectively reasonable for a person to entertain a suspicion, based upon facts that could cause a reasonable person in a like position, drawing, when appropriate, on his or her training and experience, to suspect child abuse. For the purpose of this article, the pregnancy of a minor does not, in and of itself, constitute a basis of reasonable suspicion of sexual abuse.

(b) Any child care custodian, health practitioner, employee of a child protective agency, child visitation monitor, firefighter, animal control officer, or humane society officer who has knowledge of or who reasonably suspects that mental suffering has been inflicted upon a child or that his or her emotional well-being is endangered in any other way, may report the known or suspected instance of child abuse to a child protective agency.

(c)(1) Except as provided in paragraph (2) and subdivision (d), any clergy member who has knowledge of or observes a child, in his or her professional capacity or within the scope of his or her duties, whom he or she knows or reasonably suspects has been the victim of child abuse, shall report the known or suspected instance of child abuse to a child protective agency immediately or as soon as practically possible by telephone and shall prepare and send a written report thereof within 36 hours of receiving the information concerning the incident. A child protective agency shall be notified and a report shall be prepared and sent even if the child has expired, regardless of whether or not the possible abuse was a factor contributing to the death.

(2) A clergy member who acquires knowledge or reasonable suspicion of child abuse during a penitential communication is not subject to paragraph (1). For the purposes of this subdivision, "penitential communication" means a communication, intended to be in confidence, including, but not limited to, a sacramental confession, made to a clergy member who, in the course of the discipline or practice of his or her church, denomination, or organization, is authorized or accustomed to hear those communications, and under the discipline, tenets, customs, or practices of his or her church, denomination, or organization, has a duty to keep those communications secret.

(3) Nothing in this subdivision shall be construed to modify or limit a clergy member's duty to report known or suspected child abuse when he or she is acting in the capacity of a child care custodian, health practitioner, employee of a child protective agency, child visitation monitor, firefighter, animal control officer, humane society officer, or commercial film print processor.

(d) Any member of the clergy who has knowledge of or who reasonably suspects that mental suffering has been inflicted upon a child or that his or her emotional well-being is endangered in any other way may report the known or suspected instance of child abuse to a child protective agency.

(e) Any commercial film and photographic print processor who has knowledge of or observes, within the scope of his or her professional capacity or employment, any film, photograph, videotape, negative, or slide depicting a child under the age of 16 years engaged in an act of sexual conduct, shall report the instance of suspected child abuse to the law enforcement agency having jurisdiction over the case immediately, or as soon as practically possible, by telephone, and shall prepare and send a written report of it with a copy of the film, photograph, videotape, negative, or slide attached within 36 hours of receiving the information concerning the incident. As used in this subdivision, "sexual conduct" means any of the following:

(1) Sexual intercourse, including genital-genital, oral-genital, anal-genital, or oral-anal, whether between persons of the same or opposite sex or between humans and animals.

(2) Penetration of the vagina or rectum by any object.

(3) Masturbation for the purpose of sexual stimulation of the viewer.

(4) Sadomasochistic abuse for the purpose of sexual stimulation of the viewer.

(5) Exhibition of the genitals, pubic, or rectal areas of any person for the purpose of sexual stimulation of the viewer.

(f) Any other person who has knowledge of or observes a child whom he or she knows or reasonably suspects has been a victim of child abuse may report the known or suspected instance of child abuse to a child protective agency.

(g) When two or more persons who are required to report are present and jointly have knowledge of a known or suspected instance of child abuse, and when there is agreement among them, the telephone report may be made by a member of the team selected by mutual agreement and a single report may be made and signed by the selected member of the reporting team. Any member who has knowledge that the member designated to report has failed to do so shall thereafter make the report.

(h) The reporting duties under this section are individual, and no supervisor or administrator may impede or inhibit the reporting duties, and no person making a report shall be subject to any sanction for making the report. However, internal procedures to facilitate reporting and apprise supervisors and administrators of reports may be established provided that they are not inconsistent with this article.

The internal procedures shall not require any employee required to make reports pursuant to this article to disclose his or her identity to the employer.

(i) A county probation or welfare department shall immediately, or as soon as practically possible, report by telephone to the law enforcement agency having jurisdiction over the case, to the agency given the responsibility for investigation of cases under Section 300 of the Welfare and Institutions Code, and to the district attorney's office every known or suspected instance of child abuse, as defined in Section 11165.6, except acts or omissions coming within subdivision (b) of Section 11165.2, or reports made pursuant to Section 11165.13 based on risk to a child which relates solely to the inability of the parent to provide the child with regular care due to the parent's substance abuse, which shall be reported only to the county welfare department. A county probation or welfare department also shall send a written report thereof within 36 hours of receiving the information concerning the incident to any agency to which it is required to make a telephone report under this subdivision.

A law enforcement agency shall immediately, or as soon as practically possible, report by telephone to the agency given responsibility for investigation of cases under Section 300 of the Welfare and Institutions Code and to the district attorney's office every known or suspected instance of child abuse reported to it, except acts or omissions coming within subdivision (b) of Section 11165.2, which shall be reported only to the county welfare department. A law enforcement agency shall report to the county welfare department every known or suspected instance of child abuse reported to it which is alleged to have occurred as a result of the action of a person responsible for the child's welfare, or as the result of the failure of a person responsible for the child's welfare to adequately protect the minor from abuse when the person responsible for the child's welfare knew or reasonably should have known that the minor was in danger of abuse. A law enforcement agency also shall send a written report thereof within 36 hours of receiving the information concerning the incident to any agency to which it is required to make a telephone report under this subdivision.

11173. Obtain Controlled Substance by Fraud, Deceit, Misrepresentation, Mislabeling

(a) No person shall obtain or attempt to obtain controlled substances, or procure or attempt to procure the administration of or prescription for controlled substances, (1) by fraud, deceit, misrepresentation, or subterfuge; or (2) by the concealment of a material fact.

(b) No person shall make a false statement in any prescription, order, report, or record, required by this division.

(c) No person, shall for the purpose of obtaining controlled substances, falsely assume the title of, or represent himself to be, a manufacturer, wholesaler, pharmacist, physician, dentist, veterinarian, registered nurse, physician's assistant, or other authorized person.

(d) No person shall affix any false or forged label to a package or receptacle containing controlled substances.

11350. Possession of Specified Controlled Substance

(a) Except as otherwise provided in this division, every person who possesses (1) any controlled substance specified in subdivision (b) or (c), or paragraph (1) of subdivision (f) of Section 11054, specified in paragraph (14), (15), or (20) of subdivision (d) of Section 11054, or specified in subdivision (b) or (c) of Section 11055, or specified in subdivision (h) of Section 11056, or (2) any controlled substance classified in Schedule III, IV, or V which is a narcotic drug, unless upon the written prescription of a physician, dentist, podiatrist, or veterinarian licensed to practice in this state, shall be punished by imprisonment in the state prison.

(b) Except as otherwise provided in this division, every person who possesses any controlled substance specified in subdivision (e) of Section 11054 shall be punished by imprisonment in the county jail for not more than one year or in the state prison.

(c) Except as otherwise provided in this division, whenever a person who possesses any of the controlled substances specified in subdivision (a) or (b), the judge may, in addition to any punishment provided for pursuant to subdivision (a) or (b), assess against that person a fine not to exceed seventy dollars ($70) with proceeds of this fine to be used in accordance with Section 1463.23 of the Penal Code. The court shall, however, take into consideration the defendant's ability to pay, and no defendant shall be denied probation because of his or her inability to pay the fine permitted under this subdivision.

(d) Except in unusual cases in which it would not serve the interest of justice to do so, whenever a court grants probation pursuant to a felony conviction under this section, in addition to any other conditions of probation which may be imposed, the following conditions of probation shall be ordered:

(1) For a first offense under this section, a fine of at least one thousand dollars ($1,000) or community service.

(2) For a second or subsequent offense under this section, a fine of at least two thousand dollars ($2,000) or community service.

(3) If a defendant does not have the ability to pay the minimum fines specified in paragraphs (1) and (2), community service shall be ordered in lieu of the fine. *(AM '00)*

11351. Possession or Purchase for Sale of Specified Controlled Substance

Except as otherwise provided in this division, every person who possesses for sale or purchases for purposes of sale (1) any controlled substance specified in subdivision (b), (c), or (e) of Section 11054, specified in paragraph (14), (15), or (20) of subdivision (d) of Section 11054, or specified in subdivision (b) or (c) of Section 11055, or specified in subdivision (h) of Section 11056, or (2) any controlled substance classified in Schedule III, IV, or V which is a narcotic drug, shall be punished by imprisonment in the state prison for two, three, or four years. *(AM '00)*

11351.5. Possession or Purchase of Cocaine (Other Than Cocaine Hydrochloride) for Sale

Except as otherwise provided in this division, every person who possesses for sale or purchases for purposes of sale cocaine base which is specified in paragraph (1) of subdivision (f) of Section 11054, shall be punished by imprisonment in the state prison for a period of three, four, or five years.

11352. Importing, Selling, Furnishing Controlled Substance

(a) Except as otherwise provided in this division, every person who transports, imports into this state, sells, furnishes, administers, or gives away, or offers to transport, import into this state, sell, furnish, administer, or give away, or attempts to import into this state or transport (1) any controlled substance specified in subdivision (b), (c), or (e), or paragraph (1) of subdivision (f) of Section 11054, specified in paragraph (14), (15), or (20) of subdivision (d) of Section 11054, or specified in subdivision (b) or (c) of Section 11055, or specified in subdivision (h) of Section 11056, or (2) any controlled substance classified in Schedule III, IV, or V which is a narcotic drug, unless upon the written prescription of a physician, dentist, podiatrist, or veterinarian licensed to practice in this state, shall be punished by imprisonment in the state prison for three, four, or five years.

(b) Notwithstanding the penalty provisions of subdivision (a), any person who transports for sale any controlled substances specified in subdivision (a) within this state from one county to another noncontiguous county shall be punished by imprisonment in the state prison for three, six, or nine years. *(AM '00)*

11353. Adult Inducing Minor to Violate Provisions

Every person 18 years of age or over, (a) who in any voluntary manner solicits, induces, encourages, or intimidates any minor with the intent that the minor shall violate any provision of this chapter or Section 11550 with respect to either (1) a controlled substance which is specified in subdivision (b), (c), or (e), or paragraph (1) of subdivision (f) of Section 11054, specified in paragraph (14), (15), or (20) of subdivision (d) of Section 11054, or specified in subdivision (b) or (c) of Section 11055, or specified in subdivision (h) of Section 11056, or (2) any controlled substance classified in Schedule III, IV, or V which is a narcotic drug, (b) who hires, employs, or uses a minor to unlawfully transport, carry, sell, give away, prepare for sale, or peddle any such controlled substance, or (c) who unlawfully sells, furnishes, administers, gives, or offers to sell, furnish, administer, or give, any such controlled substance to a minor, shall be punished by imprisonment in the state prison for a period of three, six, or nine years. *(AM '00)*

11353.5. Selling or Giving Controlled Substance to Minor

Except as authorized by law, any person 18 years of age or older who unlawfully prepares for sale upon school grounds or a public playground, a child day care facility, a church, or a synagogue, or sells or gives away a controlled substance, other than a controlled substance described in Section 11353 or 11380, to a minor upon the grounds of, or within, any school, child day care facility, public playground, church, or synagogue providing instruction in preschool, kindergarten, or any of grades 1 to 12, inclusive, or providing child care services, during hours in which those facilities are open for classes, school-related programs, or child care, or at any time when minors are using the facility where the offense occurs, or upon the grounds of a public playground during the hours in which school-related programs for minors are being conducted, or at any time when minors are using the facility where the offense occurs, shall be punished by imprisonment in the state prison for five, seven, or nine years. Application of this section shall be limited to persons at least five years older than the minor to whom he or she prepares for sale, sells, or gives away a controlled substance.

11353.7. Preparation for Sale or Sale of Substance to Minor in Public Place

Except as authorized by law, and except as provided otherwise in Sections 11353.1, 11353.6, and 11380.1 with respect to playgrounds situated in a public park, any person 18 years of age or older who unlawfully prepares for sale in a public park, including units of the state park system and state vehicular recreation areas, or sells or gives away a controlled substance to a minor under the age of 14 years in a public park, including units of the state park system and state vehicular recreation areas, during hours in which the public park, including units of the state park system and state vehicular recreation areas, is open for use, with knowledge that the person is a minor under the age of 14 years, shall be punished by imprisonment in the state prison for three, six, or nine years.

11354. Minor's Employment of Fellow Minor for Unlawful Transactions

(a) Every person under the age of 18 years who in any voluntary manner solicits, induces, encourages, or intimidates any minor with the intent that the minor shall violate any provision of this chapter or Section 11550, who hires, employs, or uses a minor to unlawfully transport, carry, sell, give away, prepare for sale, or peddle (1) any controlled substance specified in subdivision (b), (c), or (e), or paragraph (1) of subdivision (f) of Section 11054, specified in paragraph (14), (15), or (20) of subdivision (d) of Section 11054, or specified in subdivision (b) or (c) of Section 11055, or specified in subdivision (h) of Section 11056, or (2) any controlled substance classified in Schedule III, IV, or V which is a narcotic drug, or who unlawfully sells, furnishes, administers, gives, or offers to sell, furnish, administer, or give, any such controlled substance to a minor shall be punished by imprisonment in the state prison.

(b) This section is not intended to affect the jurisdiction of the juvenile court. *(AM '00)*

11355. Substance Provided in Lieu of Controlled Substance

Every person who agrees, consents, or in any manner offers to unlawfully sell, furnish, transport, administer, or give (1) any controlled substance specified in subdivision (b), (c), or (e), or paragraph (1) of subdivision (f) of Section 11054, specified in paragraph (13), (14), (15), or (20) of subdivision (d) of Section 11054, or specified in subdivision (b), or (c), or (g) of Section 11055, or specified in subdivision (h) of Section 11056, or (2) any controlled substance classified in Schedule III, IV, or V which is a narcotic drug to any person, or who offers, arranges, or negotiates to have any such controlled substance unlawfully sold, delivered, transported, furnished, administered, or given to any person and who then sells, delivers, furnishes, transports, administers, or gives, or offers, arranges, or negotiates to have sold, delivered, transported, furnished, administered, or given to any person any other liquid, substance, or material in lieu of any such controlled substance shall be punished by imprisonment in the county jail for not more than one year, or in the state prison. *(AM '00)*

11357. Unauthorized Possession of Marijuana

(a) Except as authorized by law, every person who possesses any concentrated cannabis shall be punished by imprisonment in the county jail for a period of not more than one year or by a fine of not more than five hundred dollars ($500), or by both such fine and imprisonment, or shall be punished by imprisonment in the state prison.

(b) Except as authorized by law, every person who possesses not more than 28.5 grams of marijuana, other than concentrated cannabis, is guilty of a misdemeanor and shall be punished by a fine of not more than one hundred dollars ($100). Notwithstanding other provisions of law, if such person has been previously convicted three or more times of an offense described in this subdivision during the two-year period immediately preceding the date of commission of the violation to be charged, the previous convictions shall also be charged in the accusatory pleading and, if found to be true by the jury upon a jury trial or by the court upon a court trial or if admitted by the person, the provisions of Sections 1000.1 and 1000.2 of the Penal Code shall be applicable to him, and the court shall divert and refer him for education, treatment, or rehabilitation, without a court hearing or determination or the concurrence of the district attorney, to an appropriate community program which will accept him. If the person is so diverted and referred he shall not be subject to the fine specified in this subdivision. If no community program will accept him, the person shall be subject to the fine specified in this subdivision. In any case in which a person is arrested for a violation of this subdivision and does not demand to be taken before a magistrate, such person shall be released by the arresting officer upon presentation of satisfactory evidence of identity and giving his written promise to appear in court, as provided in Section 853.6 of the Penal Code, and shall not be subjected to booking.

(c) Except as authorized by law, every person who possesses more than 28.5 grams of marijuana, other than concentrated cannabis, shall be punished by imprisonment in the county jail for a period of not more than six months or by a fine of not more than five hundred dollars ($500), or by both such fine and imprisonment.

(d) Except as authorized by law, every person 18 years of age or over who possesses not more than 28.5 grams of marijuana, other than concentrated cannabis, upon the grounds of, or within, any school providing instruction in kindergarten or any of grades 1 through 12 during hours the school is open for classes or school-related programs is guilty of a misdemeanor and shall be punished by a fine of not more than five hundred dollars ($500), or by imprisonment in the county jail for a period of not more than 10 days, or both.

(e) Except as authorized by law, every person under the age of 18 who possesses not more than 28.5 grams of marijuana, other than concentrated cannabis, upon the grounds of, or within, any school providing instruction in kindergarten or any of grades 1 through 12 during hours the school is open for classes or school-related programs is guilty of a misdemeanor and shall be subject to the following dispositions:

(1) A fine of not more than two hundred fifty dollars ($250), upon a finding that a first offense has been committed.

(2) A fine of not more than five hundred dollars ($500), or commitment to a juvenile hall, ranch, camp, forestry camp, or secure juvenile home for a period of not more than 10 days, or both, upon a finding that a second or subsequent offense has been committed.

11358. Unauthorized Planting, Cultivating or Processing

Every person who plants, cultivates, harvests, dries, or processes any marijuana or any part thereof, except as otherwise provided by law, shall be punished by imprisonment in the state prison.

11359. Possession for Sale

Every person who possesses for sale any marijuana, except as otherwise provided by law, shall be punished by imprisonment in the state prison.

11360. Transporting, Importing, Selling, Furnishing

(a) Except as otherwise provided by this section or as authorized by law, every person who transports, imports into this state, sells, furnishes, administers, or gives away, or offers to transport, import into this state, sell, furnish, administer, or give away, or attempts to import into this state or transport any marijuana shall be punished by imprisonment in the state prison for a period of two, three or four years.

(b) Except as authorized by law, every person who gives away, offers to give away, transports, offers to transport, or attempts to transport not more than 28.5 grams of marijuana, other than concentrated cannabis, is guilty of a misdemeanor and shall be punished by a fine of not more than one hundred dollars ($100). In any case in which a person is arrested for a violation of this subdivision and does not demand to be taken before a magistrate, such person shall be released by the arresting officer upon presentation of satisfactory evidence of identity and giving his written promise to appear in court, as provided in Section 853.6 of the Penal Code, and shall not be subjected to booking.

11361. Employment of Minors for Unlawful Transactions

(a) Every person 18 years of age or over who hires, employs, or uses a minor in unlawfully transporting, carrying, selling, giving away, preparing for sale, or peddling any marijuana, who unlawfully sells, or offers to sell, any marijuana to a minor, or who furnishes, administers, or gives, or offers to furnish, administer, or give any marijuana to a minor under 14 years of age, or who induces a minor to use marijuana in violation of law shall be punished by imprisonment in the state prison for a period of three, five, or seven years.

(b) Every person 18 years of age or over who furnishes, administers, or gives, or offers to furnish, administer, or give, any marijuana to a minor 14 years of age or older shall be punished by imprisonment in the state prison for a period of three, four, or five years.

11364. Possession of Opium Pipe, etc.

It is unlawful to possess an opium pipe or any device, contrivance, instrument, or paraphernalia used for unlawfully injecting or smoking (1) a controlled substance specified in subdivision (b), (c), or (e), or paragraph (1) or subdivision (f) of Section 11054, specified in paragraph (14), (15), or (20) of subdivision (d) of Section 11054, specified in subdivision (b) or (c) of Section 11055, or specified in paragraph (2) of subdivision (d) of Section 11055, or (2) a controlled substance which is a narcotic drug classified in Schedule III, IV, or V.

11364.7. Furnishing Drug Paraphernalia; Furnishing to Minors; Forfeiture of Business License

(a) Except as authorized by law, any person who delivers, furnishes, or transfers, possesses with intent to deliver, furnish, or transfer, or manufactures with the intent to deliver, furnish, or transfer, drug paraphernalia, knowing, or under circumstances where one reasonably should know, that it will be used to plant, propagate, cultivate, grow, harvest, compound, convert, produce, process, prepare, test, analyze, pack, repack, store, contain, conceal, inject, ingest, inhale, or otherwise introduce into the human body a controlled substance, except as provided in subdivision (b), in violation of this division, is guilty of a misdemeanor.

No public entity, its agents, or employees shall be subject to criminal prosecution for distribution of hypodermic needles or syringes to participants in clean needle and syringe exchange projects authorized by the public entity pursuant to a declaration of a local emergency due to the existence of a critical local public health crisis.

(b) Except as authorized by law, any person who manufactures with intent to deliver, furnish, or transfer drug paraphernalia knowing, or under circumstances where one reasonably should know, that it will be used to plant, propagate, cultivate, grow, harvest, manufacture, compound, convert, produce, process, prepare, test, analyze, pack, repack, store, contain, conceal, inject, ingest, inhale, or otherwise introduce into the human body cocaine, cocaine base, heroin, phencyclidine, or methamphetamine in violation of this division shall be punished by imprisonment in a county jail for not more than one year, or in the state prison.

(c) Except as authorized by law, any person, 18 years of age or over, who violates subdivision (a) by delivering, furnishing, or transferring drug paraphernalia to a person under 18 years of age who is at least three years his or her junior, or who, upon the grounds of a public or private elementary, vocational, junior high, or high school, possesses a hypodermic needle, as defined in paragraph (7) of subdivision (a) of Section 11014.5, with the intent to deliver, furnish, or transfer the hypodermic needle, knowing, or under circumstances where one reasonably should know, that it will be used by a person under 18 years of age to inject into the human body a controlled substance, is guilty of a misdemeanor and shall be punished by imprisonment in a county jail for not more than one year, by a fine of not more than one thousand dollars ($1,000), or by both that imprisonment and fine.

(d) The violation, or the causing or the permitting of a violation, of subdivision (a), (b), or (c) by a holder of a business or liquor license issued by a city, county, or city and county, or by the State of California, and in the course of the licensee's business shall be grounds for the revocation of that license.

(e) All drug paraphernalia defined in Section 11014.5 is subject to forfeiture and may be seized by any peace officer pursuant to Section 11471.

(f) If any provision of this section or the application thereof to any person or circumstance is held invalid, it is the intent of the Legislature that the invalidity shall not affect other provisions or applications of this section which can be given effect without the invalid provision or application and to this end the provisions of this section are severable. *(AM '99)*

11365. Visiting Place where Narcotics are being Used

(a) It is unlawful to visit or to be in any room or place where any controlled substances which are specified in subdivision (b), (c), or (e), or paragraph (1) of subdivision (f) of Sec. 11054, specified in paragraph (14), 15), or (20) of subdivision (d) of Sec. 11054, or specified in subdivision (b) or (c) or paragraph (2) of subdivision (d) of Sec. 11055, or which are narcotic drugs classified in Schedule III, IV, or V, are being unlawfully smoked or used with knowledge that such activity is occurring.

(b) This section shall apply only where the defendant aids, assists, or abets the perpetration of the unlawful smoking or use of a controlled substance specified in subdivision (a). This subdivision is declaratory of existing law as expressed in People v. Cressey (1970) 2 Cal. 3d 836.

11366. Maintenance of Location for Unlawful Activities

Every person who opens or maintains any place for the purpose of unlawfully selling, giving away, or using any controlled substance which is (1) specified in subdivision (b). (c), or (e), or paragraph (1) of subdivision (f) of Section 11054, specified in paragraph (13), (14), (15), or (20) of subdivision (d) of Section 11054, or specified in subdivision (b) or (c) of subdivision (d), or paragraph (3) of subdivision (e) of Section 11055, or (2) which is a narcotic drug classified in Schedule III, IV, or V, shall be punished by imprisonment in the county jail for a period of not more than one year or the state prison.

11366.5. Management of Location Used for Unlawful Manufacture or Storage of Controlled Substance

(a) Any person who has under his or her management or control any building, room, space, or enclosure, either as an owner, lessee, agent, employee, or mortgagee, who knowingly rents, leases, or makes available for use, with or without compensation, the building, room, space, or enclosure for the purpose of unlawfully manufacturing, storing, or distributing any controlled substance for sale or distribution shall be punished by imprisonment in the county jail for not more than one year, or in the state prison.

(b) Any person who has under his or her management or control any building, room, space, or enclosure, either as an owner, lessee, agent, employee. or mortgagee, who knowingly allows the building, room, space, or enclosure to be fortified to suppress law enforcement entry in order to further the sale of any amount of cocaine base as specified in paragraph (1) of subdivision (f) of Section 11054, cocaine as specified in paragraph (6) of subdivision (b) of Section 11055, heroin, phencyclidine, amphetamine, methamphetamine. or lysergic acid diethylamide and who obtains excessive profits from the use of the building, room, space or enclosure shall be punished by imprisonment in the state prison for two, three, or four years.

(c) Any person who violates subdivision (a) after previously being convicted of a violation of subdivision (a) shall be punished by imprisonment in the state prison for two, three, or four years.

(d) For the purposes of this section, "excessive profits" means the receipt of consideration of a value substantially higher than fair market value.

11366.6. Use of Location to Suppress Law Enforcement Entry in Order to Sell Controlled Substances

Any person who utilizes a building, room, space, or enclosure specifically designed to suppress law enforcement entry in order to sell, manufacture, or possess for sale any amount of cocaine base as specified in paragraph (1) of subdivision (f) of Section 11054, cocaine as specified in paragraph (6) of subdivision (b) of Section 11055, heroin, phencyclidine, amphetamine, methamphetamine, or lysergic acid diethylamide shall be punished by imprisonment in the state prison for three, four, or five years.

11366.7. Sale of Chemical or Laboratory Apparatus for Unlawful Use

(a) This section shall apply to the following:

(1) Any chemical or drug.

(2) Any laboratory apparatus or device.

(b) Any retailer or wholesaler who sells any item in paragraph (1) or (2) of subdivision (a) with knowledge or the intent that it will be used to unlawfully manufacture, compound, convert, process, or prepare a controlled substance for unlawful sale or distribution, shall be punished by imprisonment in a county jail for not more than one year, or in the state prison, or by a fine not exceeding twenty-five thousand dollars ($25,000), or by both that imprisonment and fine. Any fine collected pursuant to this section shall be distributed as specified in Section 1463.10 of the Penal Code.

11366.8. False Compartment in Vehicle for Smuggling Drugs

(a) Every person who possesses, uses, or controls a false compartment with the intent to store, conceal, smuggle, or transport a controlled substance within the false compartment shall be punished by imprisonment in a county jail for a term of imprisonment not to exceed one year or in the state prison.

(b) Every person who designs, constructs, builds, alters, or fabricates a false compartment for, or installs or attaches a false compartment to, a vehicle with the intent to store, conceal, smuggle, or transport a controlled substance shall be punished by imprisonment in the state prison for 16 months or two or three years.

(c) The term "vehicle" means any of the following vehicles without regard to whether the vehicles are private or commercial, including, but not limited to, cars, trucks, buses, aircraft, boats, ships, yachts, and vessels.

(d) The term "false compartment" means any box, container, space, or enclosure that is intended for use or designed for use to conceal, hide, or otherwise prevent discovery of any controlled substance within or attached to a vehicle, including, but not limited to, any of the following:

(1) False, altered, or modified fuel tanks.

(2) Original factory equipment of a vehicle that is modified, altered, or changed.

(3) Compartment, space, or box that is added to, or fabricated, made, or created from, existing compartments, spaces, or boxes within a vehicle.

11368. Forged or Altered Prescriptions

Every person who forges or alters a prescription or who issues or utters an altered prescription, or who issues or utters a prescription bearing a forged or fictitious signature for any narcotic drug, or who obtains any narcotic drug by any forged, fictitious, or altered prescription, or who has in possession any narcotic drug secured by a forged, fictitious, or altered prescription, shall be punished by imprisonment in the county jail for not less than six months nor more than one year, or in the state prison.

11369. Authority to Report Arrestee to INS

When there is reason to believe that any person arrested for a violation of Sec. 11350, 11351, 11351.5, 11352, 11353, 11355, 11357, 11359, 11360, 11361, 11363, 11368, Or 11550, may not be a citizen of the U.S., The arresting shall notify the appropriate agency of the United States having charge of deportation matters.

11370.1. Possession of Certain Controlled Substances

(a) Notwithstanding Section 11350 or 11377 or any other provision of law, every person who unlawfully possesses any amount of a substance containing cocaine base, a substance containing cocaine, a substance containing heroin, a substance containing methamphetamine, a crystalline substance containing phencyclidine, a liquid substance containing phencyclidine, plant material containing phencyclidine, or a hand-rolled cigarette treated with phencyclidine while armed with a loaded, operable firearm is guilty of a felony punishable by imprisonment in the state prison for two, three, or four years.

As used in this subdivision, "armed with"means having available for immediate offensive or defensive use.

(b) Except as provided in Section 1000 of the Penal Code, any person who is convicted under this section shall be ineligible for diversion under Chapter 2.5 (commencing with Section 1000) of Title 6 of Part 2 of the Penal Code.

11375. Possession for Sale of Certain Controlled Substances [A second Version Follows]

(a) As to the substances specified in subdivision (c), this section, and not Sections 11377, 11378, 11379, and 11380, shall apply.

(b)(1) Every person who possesses for sale, or who sells, any substance specified in subdivision (c) shall be punished by imprisonment in the county jail for a period of not more than one year or state prison.

(2) Every person who possesses any controlled substance specified in subdivision (c), unless upon the prescription of a physician, dentist, podiatrist, or veterinarian, licensed to practice in this state, shall be guilty of an infraction or a misdemeanor.

(c) This section shall apply to any material, compound, mixture, or preparation containing any of the following substances:

(1) Chlordiazepoxide.
(2) Clonazepam.
(3) Clorazepate.
(4) Diazepam.
(5) Flurazepam.
(6) Lorazepam.
(7) Mebutamate.
(8) Oxazepam.
(9) Prazepam.
(10) Temazepam.
(11) Halazepam.
(12) Alprazolam.
(13) Propoxyphene.
(14) Diethylpropion.
(15) Phentermine.
(16) Pemoline.
(17) Fenfluramine.
(18) Triazolam.

(AM '01)

11375. Possession for Sale of Certain Controlled Substances

(a) As to the substances specified in subdivision (c), this section, and not Sections 11377, 11378, 11379, and 11380, shall apply.

(b)(1) Every person who possesses for sale, or who sells, any substance specified in subdivision (c) shall be punished by imprisonment in the county jail for a period of not more than one year or state prison.

(2) Every person who possesses any controlled substance specified in subdivision (c), unless upon the prescription of a physician, dentist, podiatrist, or veterinarian, licensed to practice in this state, shall be guilty of an infraction or a misdemeanor.

(c) This section shall apply to any material, compound, mixture, or preparation containing any of the following substances:

(1) Chlordiazepoxide.
(2) Clonazepam.

(3) Clorazepate.

(4) Diazepam.

(5) Flurazepam.

(6) Lorazepam.

(7) Mebutamate.

(8) Oxazepam.

(9) Prazepam.

(10) Temazepam.

(11) Halazepam.

(12) Alprazolam.

(13) Propoxyphene.

(14) Diethylpropion.

(15) Phentermine.

(16) Pemoline.

(17) Triazolam.

(AM '01)

NOTE: This version shall not become operative unless fenfluramine and its salts and isomers are removed from Schedule IV of the federal Controlled Substances Act (21 U.S.C.A. Sec. 812; 21 C.F.R. 1308.14).

11377. Possession of Certain Controlled Substances

(a) Except as authorized by law and as otherwise provided in subdivision (b) or Section 11375, or in Article 7 (commencing with Section 4211) of Chapter 9 of Division 2 of the Business and Professions Code, every person who possesses any controlled substance which is (1) classified in Schedule III, IV, or V, and which is not a narcotic drug, (2) specified in subdivision (d) of Section 11054, except paragraphs (13), (14), (15), and (20) of subdivision (d), (3) specified in paragraph (11) of subdivision (c) of Section 11056, (4) specified in paragraph (2) or (3) of subdivision (f) of Section 11054, or ***(5) specified in subdivision (d), (e), or (f) of Section 11055, unless upon the prescription of a physician, dentist, podiatrist, or veterinarian, licensed to practice in this state, shall be punished by imprisonment in a county jail for a period of not more than one year or in the state prison.

(b)(1) Any person who violates subdivision (a) by unlawfully possessing a controlled substance specified in subdivision (f) of Section 11056, and who has not previously been convicted of such a violation involving a controlled substance specified in subdivision (f) of Section 11056, is guilty of a misdemeanor.

(2) Any person who violates subdivision (a) by unlawfully possessing a controlled substance specified in subdivision (g) of Section 11056 is guilty of a misdemeanor.

(c) In addition to any fine assessed under subdivision (b), the judge may assess a fine not to exceed seventy dollars ($70) against any person who violates subdivision (a), with the proceeds of this fine to be used in accordance with Section 1463.23 of the Penal Code. The court shall, however, take into consideration the defendant's ability to pay, and no defendant shall be denied probation because of his or her inability to pay the fine permitted under this subdivision. *(AM '01)*

11378. Possession for Sale

11378.

Except as otherwise provided in Article 7 (commencing with Section 4211) of Chapter 9 of Division 2 of the Business and Professions Code, every person who possesses for sale any controlled substance which is (1) classified in Schedule III, IV, or V and which is not a narcotic drug, except subdivision (g) of Section 11056, (2) specified in subdivision (d) of Section 11054, except paragraphs (13), (14), (15), (20), (21), (22), and (23) of subdivision (d), (3) specified in paragraph (11) of subdivision (c) of Section 11056, (4) specified in paragraph (2) or (3) of subdivision (f) of Section 11054, or ***(5) specified in subdivision (d), (e), or (f), except paragraph (3) of subdivision (e) and subparagraphs (A) and (B) of paragraph (2) of subdivision (f), of Section 11055, shall be punished by imprisonment in the state prison. *(AM '01)*

11378.5. Possession for Sale of Phencyclidine

Except as otherwise provided in Article 7 (commencing with Section 4211) of Chapter 9 of Division 2 of the Business and Professions Code, every person who possesses for sale phencyclidine or any analog or any precursor of phencyclidine which is specified in paragraph (21), (22), or (23) of subdivision(d) of Section 11054 or in paragraph (3) of subdivision (e) or in subdivision (f), except subparagraph (A) of paragraph (1) of subdivision (f), of Section 11055, shall be punished by imprisonment in the state prison for a period of three, four, or five years.

11379. Transporting, Importing, Selling Controlled Substance

(a) Except as otherwise provided in subdivision (b) and in Article 7 (commencing with Section 4211) of Chapter 9 of Division 2 of the Business and Professions Code, every person who transports, imports into this state, sells, furnishes, administers, or gives away, or offers to transport, import into this state, sell, furnish, administer, or give away, or attempts to import into this state or transport any controlled substance which is (1) classified in Schedule III, IV, or V and which is not a narcotic drug, except subdivision (g) of Section 11056, (2) specified in subdivision (d) of Section 11054, except paragraphs (13), (14), (15), (20), (21), (22), and (23) of subdivision (d), (3) specified in paragraph (11) of subdivision (c) of Section 11056, (4) specified in paragraph (2) or (3) of subdivision (f) of Section 11054, or ***(5) specified in subdivision (d) or (e), except paragraph (3) of subdivision (e), or specified in subparagraph (A) of paragraph (1) of subdivision (f), of Section 11055, unless upon the prescription of a physician, dentist, podiatrist, or veterinarian, licensed to practice in this state, shall be punished by imprisonment in the state prison for a period of two, three, or four years.

(b) Notwithstanding the penalty provisions of subdivision (a), any person who transports for sale any controlled substances specified in subdivision (a) within this state from one county to another noncontiguous county shall be punished by imprisonment in the state prison for three, six, or nine years. *(AM '01)*

11379.5. Transporting, Importing, Selling Phencyclidine

(a) Except as otherwise provided in subdivision (b) and in Article 7 (commencing with Section 4211) of Chapter 9 of Division 2 of the Business and Professions Code, every person who transports, imports into this state, sells, furnishes, administers, or gives away, or offers to transport, import into this state, sell, furnish, administer, or give away, or attempts to import into this state or transport phencyclidine or any of its analogs which is specified in paragraph (21), (22), or (23) of subdivision (d) of Section 11054 or in paragraph (3) of subdivision (e) of Section 11055, or its precursors as specified in subparagraph (A) or (B) of paragraph (2) of subdivision (f) of Section 11055, unless upon the prescription of a physician, dentist, podiatrist, or veterinarian licensed to practice in this state, shall be punished by imprisonment in the state prison for a period of three, four, or five years.

(b) Notwithstanding the penalty provisions of subdivision (a), any person who transports for sale any controlled substances specified in subdivision (a) within this state from one county to another noncontiguous county shall be punished by imprisonment in the state prison for three, six, or nine years.

11379.6. Manufacture of Controlled Substances - Penalties

(a) Except as otherwise provided by law, every person who manufactures, compounds, converts, produces, derives, processes, or prepares, either directly or indirectly by chemical extraction or independently by means of chemical synthesis, any controlled substance specified in Section 11054, 11055, 11056, 11057, or 11058 shall be punished by imprisonment in the state prison for three, five, or seven years and by a fine not exceeding fifty thousand dollars ($50,000).

(b) Except as otherwise provided by law, every person who offers to perform an act which is punishable under subdivision (a) shall be punished by imprisonment in the state prison for three, four, or five years.

(c) All fines collected pursuant to subdivision (a) shall be transferred to the State Treasury for deposit in the Clandestine Drug Lab Clean-up Account, as established by Section 5 of Chapter 1295 of the Statutes of 1987. The transmission to the State Treasury shall be carried out in the same manner as fines collected for the state by the county.

11380.   Adult Using, Soliciting or Intimidating Minor for Violation

(a) Every person 18 years of age or over who violates any provision of this chapter involving controlled substances which are (1) classified in Schedule III, IV, or V and which are not narcotic drugs or (2) specified in subdivision (d) of Section 11054, except paragraphs (13), (14), (15), and (20) of subdivision (d), <u>specified in paragraph (11) of subdivision (c) of Section 11056,</u> specified in paragraph (2) or (3) or subdivision (f) of Section 11054, or specified in subdivision (d), (e), or (f) of Section 11055, by the use of a minor as agent, who solicits, induces, encourages, or intimidates any minor with the intent that the minor shall violate any provision of this article involving those controlled substances or who unlawfully furnishes, offers to furnish, or attempts to furnish those controlled substances to a minor shall be punished by imprisonment in the state prison for a period of three, six, or nine years.

(b) Nothing in this section applies to a registered pharmacist furnishing controlled substances pursuant to a prescription. *(AM '01)*

11380.5.   Drug Violations in Public Park or Beach; Penalty Enhancement

(a)(1) Notwithstanding any other provision of law, any person who is convicted of the possession for sale or the sale of heroin, cocaine, cocaine base, methamphetamine, or phencyclidine (PCP), in addition to the punishment imposed for that conviction, shall be imprisoned in the state prison for an additional one year if the violation occurred upon the grounds of a public park , public library, or ocean-front beach.

(2) For the purposes of this section, a "public park or ocean-front beach"includes adjacent public parking lots and sidewalks.

(3) For the purposes of this section, "public library"means a library, or two or more libraries, operated by a single entity by one or more jurisdictions that serves the general public without distinction.

(b) The additional punishment provided in this section shall not be imposed unless the allegation is charged in the accusatory pleading and admitted by the defendant or found to be true by the trier of fact.

(c) The additional punishment provided in this section shall not be imposed in the event that any other additional punishment is imposed pursuant to Section 11353.1, 11353.5, 11353.6, 11353.7, or 11380.1.

(d) Notwithstanding any other provision of law, the court may strike the additional punishment provided for in this section if it determines that there are circumstances in mitigation of the additional punishment and states on the record its reasons for striking the additional punishment.

(e) This section shall apply to a public park , public library, or ocean-front beach only if the following conditions are satisfied:

(1) The city council , county board of supervisors, or special district board having jurisdiction over the public park , public library, or ocean-front beach adopts an ordinance designating the public park, public library, or ocean-front beach as a "drug-free zone"pursuant to this section.

(2) Notice of this law is posted at the public park , public library, or ocean-front beach.

(f) For purposes of this section, a "public park"includes a public swimming pool and a public youth center.

(g) This section shall remain in effect only until January 1, 2003, and as of that date is repealed, unless a later enacted statute, that is enacted before January 1, 2003, deletes or extends that date.

11382.   Substance Delivered in Lieu of Controlled Substance

Every person who agrees, consents, or in any manner offers to unlawfully sell, furnish, transport, administer, or give any controlled substance which is (1) classified in Schedule III, IV, or V and which is not a narcotic drug, or (2) specified in subdivision (d) of Section 11054, except paragraphs (13), (14), (15), and (20) of subdivision (d), <u>specified in paragraph (11) of subdivision (c) of Section 11056,</u> or specified in subdivision (d), (e), or (f) of Section 11055, to any person, or offers, arranges, or negotiates to have any such controlled substance unlawfully sold, delivered, transported, furnished, administered, or given to any person and then sells, delivers, furnishes, transports, administers, or gives, or offers, or arranges, or negotiates to have sold, delivered, transported, furnished, administered, or given to any person any other liquid, substance, or material in lieu of any such controlled substance shall be punished by imprisonment in the county jail for not more than one year, or in the state prison. *(AM '01)*

11383. Possession for Manufacturing Purposes

(a) Any person who possesses both methylamine and phenyl-2-propanone (phenylacetone) at the same time with the intent to manufacture methamphetamine, or who possesses both ethylamine and phenyl-2-propanone (phenylacetone) at the same time with the intent to manufacture N-ethylamphetamine, is guilty of a felony and shall be punished by imprisonment in the state prison for two, four, or six years.

(b) Any person who possesses at the same time any of the following combinations, or a combination product thereof, with intent to manufacture phencyclidine (PCP) or any of its analogs specified in paragraph (22) of subdivision (d) of Section 11054 or paragraph (3) of subdivision (e) of Section 11055 is guilty of a felony and shall be punished by imprisonment in the state prison for two, four, or six years:

(1) Piperidine and cyclohexanone.

(2) Pyrrolidine and cyclohexanone.

(3) Morpholine and cyclohexanone.

(c)(1) Any person who, with intent to manufacture methamphetamine or any of its analogs specified in subdivision (d) of Section 11055, possesses ephedrine or pseudosphedrine, or any salts, isomers, or salts of isomers of ephedrine or pseudoephedrine, or who possesses a substance containing ephedrine or pseudoephedrine, or any salts, isomers, or salts of isomers of ephedrine or pseudoephedrine, at the same time any of the following, or a combination product thereof, is guilty of a felony and shall be punished by imprisonment in the state prison for two, four, or six years:

(A) Ephedrine, pseudoephedrine, norpseudoephedrine, N-methylephedrine, N-ethylephedrine, N-methylpseudoephedrine, N-ethylpseudoephedrine, or phenylpropanolamine, plus hydriodic acid.

(B) Ephedrine, pseudoephedrine, norpseudoephedrine, N-methylephedrine, N-ethylephedrine, N-methylpseudoephedrine, N-ethylpseudoephedrine, or phenylpropanolamine, thionyl chloride and hydrogen gas.

(C) Ephedrine, pseudoephedrine, norpseudoephedrine, N-methylephedrine, N-ethylephedrine, N-methylpseudoephedrine, N-ethylpseudoephedrine, or phenylpropanolamine, plus phosphorus pentachloride and hydrogen gas.

(D) Ephedrine, pseudoephedrine, norpseudoephedrine, N-methylephedrine, N-ethylephedrine, N-methylpseudoephedrine, N-ethylpseudoephedrine, chloroephedrine and chloropseudoephedrine, or phenylpropanolaninime, plus any "reducing" agent.

(2) Any person who, with intent to manufacture methamphetamine or any of its analogs specified in subdivision (d) of Section 11055, possesses hydriodic acid or any product containing hydriodic acid is guilty of a felony and shall be punished by imprisonment in the state prison for two, four, or six years.

(d) For purposes of this section, "reducing" means a chemical reaction in which hydrogen combines with another substance or in which oxygen is removed from a substance.

(e) For purposes of this section, possession of the optical, positional, or geometric isomer of any of the compounds listed in this section shall be deemed to be possession of the derivative substance.

(f) For purposes of this section, possession of immediate precursors sufficient for the manufacture of methylamine, ethylamine, phenyl-2-propanone, piperidine, cyclohexanone, pyrrolidine, morpholine, ephedrine, pseudoephedrine, norpseudoephedrine, N-methylephedrine, N-ethylephedrine, phenylpropanolamine, hydriodic acid, thionyl chloride, or phosphorus pentachloride shall be deemed to be possession of the derivative substance. Additionally, possession of essential chemicals sufficient to manufacture hydriodic acid, with intent to manufacture methamphetamine, shall be deemed to be possession of hydriodic acid. Additionally, possession of any compound or mixture containing piperidine, cyclohexanone, pyrrolidine, or morpholine ephedrine, pseudoephedrine, norpseudoephedrine, N-methylephedrine, N-ethylephedrine, phenylpropanolamine, hydriodic acid, thionyl chloride, or phosphorus pentachloride shall be deemed to be possession of the substance.

(g) Subdivisions (a), (b), (c), (e), and (f) do not apply to drug manufacturers licensed by this state or persons authorized by regulation of the Board of Pharmacy to possess those substances or combinations of substances.

11390. Cultivation of Spores or Mycelium Capable of Producing a Controlled Substance

Except as otherwise authorized by law, every person who, with intent to produce a controlled substance specified in paragraph (18) or (19) of subdivision (d) of Section 11054, cultivates any spores or mycelium capable of producing mushrooms or other material which contains such a controlled substance shall be punished by imprisonment in the county jail for a period of not more than one year or in the state prison.

11391. Transportation, Importation, Sale or Furnishing of Spores or Mycelium Capable of Producing a Controlled Substance

Except as otherwise authorized by law, every person who transports, imports into this state, sells, furnishes, gives away, or offers to transport, import into this state, sell, furnish, or give away any spores or mycelium capable of producing mushrooms or other material which contain a controlled substance specified in paragraph (18) or (19) of subdivision (d) of Section 11054 for the purpose of facilitating a violation of Section 11390 shall be punished by imprisonment in the county jail for a period of not more than one year or in the state prison.

11488. Seizure of Items Subject to Forfeiture; Notice to Franchise Tax Board

(a) Any peace officer of this state, subsequent to making or attempting to make an arrest for a violation of Section 11351, 11351.5, 11352, 11355, 11359, 11360, 11378, 11378.5, 11379, 11379.5, 11379.6, or 11382 of this code, or Section 182 of the Penal Code insofar as the offense involves manufacture, sale, purchase for the purpose of sale, possession for sale or offer to manufacture or sell, or conspiracy to commit one of those offenses, may seize any item subject to forfeiture under subdivisions (a) to (f), inclusive, of Section 11470. The peace officer shall also notify the Franchise Tax Board of a seizure where there is reasonable cause to believe that the value of the seized property exceeds five thousand dollars ($5,000).

(b) Receipts for property seized pursuant to this section shall be delivered to any person out of whose possession such property was seized, in accordance with Section 1412 of the Penal Code. In the event property seized was not seized out of anyone's possession, receipt for the property shall be delivered to the individual in possession of the premises at which the property was seized.

(c) There shall be a presumption affecting the burden of proof that the person to whom a receipt for property was issued is the owner thereof. This presumption may, however, be rebutted at the forfeiture hearing specified in Section 11488.5.

11550. Use Prohibited

(a) No person shall use, or be under the influence of any controlled substance which is (1) specified in subdivision (b), (c), or (e), or paragraph (1) of subdivision (f) of Section 11054, specified in paragraph (14), (15), (21), (22), or (23) of subdivision (d) of Section 11054, specified in subdivision (b) or (c) of Section 11055, or specified in paragraph (1) or (2) of subdivision (d) or in paragraph (3) of subdivision (e) of Section 11055, or (2) a narcotic drug classified in Schedule III, IV, or V, except when administered by or under the direction of a person licensed by the state to dispense, prescribe, or administer controlled substances. It shall be the burden of the defense to show that it comes within the exception. Any person convicted of violating this subdivision is guilty of a misdemeanor and shall be sentenced to serve a term of not less than 90 days or more than one year in *** a county jail. The court may place a person convicted under this subdivision on probation for a period not to exceed five years and, except as provided in subdivision (c), shall in all cases in which probation is granted require, as a condition thereof, that the person be confined in *** a county jail for at least 90 days. Other than as provided by subdivision (c), in no event shall the court have the power to absolve a person who violates this subdivision from the obligation of spending at least 90 days in confinement in *** a county jail.

(b) Any person who (1) is convicted of violating subdivision (a) when the offense occurred within seven years of that person being convicted of two or more separate violations of that subdivision, and (2) refuses to complete a licensed drug rehabilitation program offered by the court pursuant to subdivision (c), shall be punished by imprisonment in *** a county jail for not less than 180 days nor more than one year. In no event does the court have the power to absolve a person convicted of a violation of subdivision (a) that is punishable under this subdivision from the obligation of spending at least 180 days in confinement in *** a county jail unless there are no licensed drug rehabilitation programs reasonably available.

For the purpose of this section, a drug rehabilitation program shall not be considered reasonably available unless the person is required to pay no more than the court determines that he or she is reasonably able to pay, in order to participate in the program.

(c) The court may, when it would be in the interest of justice, permit any person convicted of a violation of subdivision (a) punishable under subdivision (a) or (b) to complete a licensed drug rehabilitation program in lieu of part or all of the imprisonment in the county jail. As a condition of sentencing, the court may require the offender to pay all or a portion of the drug rehabilitation program.

In order to alleviate jail overcrowding and to provide recidivist offenders with a reasonable opportunity to seek rehabilitation pursuant to this subdivision, counties are encouraged to include provisions to augment licensed drug rehabilitation programs in their substance abuse proposals and applications submitted to the state for federal and state drug abuse funds.

(d) In addition to any fine assessed under this section, the judge may assess a fine not to exceed seventy dollars ($70) against any person who violates this section, with the proceeds of this fine to be used in accordance with Section 1463.23 of the Penal Code. The court shall, however, take into consideration the defendant's ability to pay, and no defendant shall be denied probation because of his or her inability to pay the fine permitted under this subdivision.

(e) Notwithstanding subdivisions (a) and (b) or any other provision of law, any person who is unlawfully under the influence of cocaine, cocaine base, heroin, methamphetamine, or phencyclidine while in the immediate personal possession of a loaded, operable firearm is guilty of a public offense punishable by imprisonment in a county jail for not exceeding one year or in state prison.

As used in this subdivision "immediate personal possession" includes, but is not limited to, the interior passenger compartment of a motor vehicle.

(f) Every person who violates subdivision (e) is punishable upon the second and each subsequent conviction by imprisonment in the state prison for two, three, or four years.

(g) Nothing in this section prevents *** deferred entry of judgment or a defendant's participation in a preguilty plea drug court program under Chapter 2.5 (commencing with Section 1000) of Title 6 of Part 2 of the Penal Code unless the person is charged with violating subdivision (b) or (c) of Section 243 of the Penal Code. A person charged with violating this section by being under the influence of any controlled substance which is specified in paragraph (21), (22), or (23) of subdivision (d) of Section 11054 or in paragraph (3) of subdivision (e) of Section 11055 and with violating either subdivision (b) or (c) of Section 243 of the Penal Code or with a violation of subdivision (e) shall be ineligible for *** deferred entry of judgment or a preguilty plea drug court program. *(AM '01)*

12671. Possession, Sale or Use of Unclassified and Unregistered Fireworks

It is unlawful for any person to sell, offer for sale, use, discharge, possess, store, or transport any type of fireworks within this state unless the State Fire Marshal has classified and registered such fireworks.

12672. Time of Sale for Safe and Sane Fireworks

It is unlawful for any person to sell, or offer for sale, safe and sane fireworks at any time outside of the period specified in Section 12599.

12677. Unlawful Possession of Dangerous Fireworks

It is unlawful for any person to possess dangerous fireworks without holding a valid permit.

12679. Storage, Sale or Discharge of Fireworks Near Flammable Liquids

It is unlawful for any person to store, sell, or discharge any type of fireworks in or within 100 feet of a location where gasoline or any other flammable liquids are stored or dispensed.

12680. Discharge of Fireworks Where Injury to Other Person Likely

(a) Except as provided in subdivision (b) or (c), it is unlawful for any person to place, throw, discharge or ignite, or fire dangerous fireworks at or near any person or group of persons where there is a likelihood of injury to that person or group of persons or when the person willfully places, throws, discharges, ignites, or fires the fireworks with the intent of creating chaos, fear, or panic.

(b) Subdivision (a) does not apply to a person described in Section 12517 who uses special effects. For purposes of this subdivision, "special effects" means articles containing any pyrotechnic composition manufactured and assembled, designed, or discharged in connection with television, theater, or motion picture productions, which may or may not be presented before live audiences, and any other articles containing any pyrotechnic composition used for commercial, industrial, educational, recreational, or entertainment purposes when authorized by the authority having jurisdiction.

(c) Subdivision (a) does not apply to a person holding a fireworks license issued pursuant to Chapter 5 (commencing with Section 12570). *(AM '00)*

12681. Sale of Safe and Sane Fireworks; Fixed Place of Business

It is unlawful for any person to sell or transfer any safe and sane fireworks to a consumer or user thereof other than at a fixed place of business of a retailer for which a license and permit has been issued.

12683. Sale or Use of Unregistered Emergency Signaling Device

It is unlawful for any person to sell, use, or discharge any emergency signaling device not registered by the State Fire Marshal.

12684. Unauthorized Use of Emergency Signaling Device

It is unlawful for any person to use or discharge any registered emergency signaling device in any manner other than that permitted by the instructions for use.

12685. Public Display of Fireworks; Permit Required

It is unlawful for any person to conduct a public display without possessing a valid permit for this purpose.

12689. Sell, Deliver Dangerous Fireworks

(a) It is unlawful for any person to sell, give, or deliver any dangerous fireworks to any person under 18 years of age.

(b) It is unlawful for any person who is a retailer to sell or transfer any safe and sane fireworks to a person who is under 16 years of age.

(c) Except as otherwise provided in subdivision (d), it is unlawful for any person who is a retailer to sell or transfer to a person under the age of 18 any rocket, rocket propelled projectile launcher, or similar device containing any explosive or incendiary material whether or not the device is designed for emergency or distance signaling purposes. It is also unlawful for a minor to possess such a device unless he or she has the written permission of, or is accompanied by, his or her parent or guardian while it is in his or her possession.

(d) Model rocket products including model rockets, launch systems, and model rocket motors designed, sold, and used for the purpose of propelling recoverable model rockets may be sold or transferred pursuant to regulations, adopted by the State Fire Marshal which the Fire Marshal determines are reasonably necessary to carry out the requirements of this part.

25189.5. Disposal, Transportation to, Treatment or Storage of Hazardous Waste at Unauthorized Facility

(a) The disposal of any hazardous waste, or the causing thereof, is prohibited when the disposal is at a facility which does not have a permit from the department issued pursuant to this chapter, or at any point which is not authorized according to this chapter.

(b) Any person who is convicted of knowingly disposing or causing the disposal of any hazardous waste, or who reasonably should have known that he or she was disposing or causing the disposal of any hazardous waste, at a facility which does not have a permit from the department issued pursuant to this chapter, or at any point which is not authorized according to this chapter shall, upon conviction, be punished by imprisonment in a county jail for not more than one year or by imprisonment in the state prison.

(c) Any person who knowingly transports or causes the transportation of hazardous waste, or who reasonably should have known that he or she was causing the transportation of any hazardous waste, to a facility which does not have a permit from the department issued pursuant to this chapter, or at any point which is not authorized according to this chapter, shall, upon conviction, be punished by imprisonment in a county jail for not more than one year or by imprisonment in the state prison.

(d) Any person who knowingly treats or stores any hazardous waste at a facility which does not have a permit from the department issued pursuant to this chapter, or at any point which is not authorized according to this chapter, shall, upon conviction, be punished by imprisonment in a county jail for not more than one year or by imprisonment in the state prison.

(e) The court also shall impose upon a person convicted of violating subdivision (b), (c), or (d), a fine of not less than five thousand dollars ($5,000) nor more than one hundred thousand dollars ($100,000) for each day of violation, except as further provided in this subdivision. If the act which violated subdivision (b), (c), or (d) caused great bodily injury, or caused a substantial probability that death could result, the person convicted of violating subdivision (b), (c), or (d) may be punished by imprisonment in the state prison for one, two, or three years, in addition and consecutive to the term specified in subdivision (b), (c), or (d), and may be fined up to two hundred fifty thousand dollars ($250,000) for each day of violation.

(f) For purposes of this section, except as otherwise provided in this subdivision, "each day of violation" means each day on which a violation continues. In any case where a person has disposed or caused the disposal of any hazardous waste in violation of this section, each day that the waste remains disposed of in violation of this section and the person has knowledge thereof is a separate additional violation, unless the person has filed a report of the disposal with the department and is complying with any order concerning the disposal issued by the department, a hearing officer, or court of competent jurisdiction. *(AM '99)*

25189.6. Hazardous Waste; Handling, etc. with Reckless Causing Unreasonable Risk

(a) Any person who knowingly, or with reckless disregard for the risk, treats, handles, transports, disposes, or stores any hazardous waste in a manner which causes any unreasonable risk of fire, explosion, serious injury, or death is guilty of a public offense and shall, upon conviction, be punished by a fine of not less than five thousand dollars ($5,000) nor more than two hundred fifty thousand dollars ($250,000) for each day of violation, or by imprisonment in a county jail for not more than one year, or by imprisonment in the state prison, or by both the fine and imprisonment.

(b) Any person who knowingly, at the time the person takes the actions specified in subdivision (a), places another person in imminent danger of death or serious bodily injury, is guilty of a public offense and shall, upon conviction, be punished by a fine of not less than five thousand dollars ($5,000) nor more than two hundred fifty thousand dollars ($250,000) for each day of violation, and by imprisonment in the state prison for 3, 6, or 9 years. *(AM '99)*

25189.7. Burning or Incineration of Hazardous Waste at Unauthorized Facility

(a) The burning or incineration of any hazardous waste, or the causing thereof, is prohibited when the burning or incineration is at a facility which does not have a permit from the department issued pursuant to this chapter, or at any point which is not authorized according to this chapter.

(b) Any person who is convicted of knowingly burning or incinerating, or causing the burning or incineration of, any hazardous waste, or who reasonably should have known that he or she was burning or incinerating, or causing the burning or incineration of, any hazardous waste, at a facility which does not have a permit from the department issued pursuant to this chapter, or at any point which is not authorized according to this chapter, shall, upon conviction, be punished by imprisonment in a county jail for not more than one year or by imprisonment in the state prison.

(c) The court also shall impose upon a person convicted of violating subdivision (b) a fine of not less than five thousand dollars ($5,000) nor more than one hundred thousand dollars ($100,000) for each day of violation, except as otherwise provided in this subdivision. If the act which violated subdivision (b) caused great bodily injury or caused a substantial probability that death could result, the person convicted of violating subdivision (b) may be punished by imprisonment in the state prison for one, two, or three years, in addition and consecutive to the term specified in subdivision (b), and may be fined up to two hundred fifty thousand dollars ($250,000) for each day of violation. *(AM '99)*

25215.2. Disposal of Lead Acid Battery; Requirements

(a) Except as provided in subdivisión (b), no person shall dispose, or attempt to dispose, of a lead acid battery at a solid waste facility, or on or in any land, surface waters, watercourses, or marine waters.

(b) A person may dispose of a lead acid battery at any of the following locations:

(1) A facility established and operated for the purpose of recycling, or providing for the eventual recycling of, lead acid batteries, including a facility located at a solid waste facility.

(2) An establishment which is a dealer pursuant to Section 25215.3.

(c) This section shall become operative on January 1, 1989.

118925. Smoking on Public Transportation Prohibited

It is unlawful for any person to smoke tobacco or any other plant product in any vehicle of a passenger stage corporation, the National Railroad Passenger Corporation (Amtrak) except to the extent permitted by federal law, in any aircraft except to the extent permitted by federal law, on a public transportation system, as defined by Section 99211 of the Public Utilities Code, or in any vehicle of an entity receiving any transit assistance from the state.

118930. Required No Smoking Notices

A notice prohibiting smoking, displayed as a symbol and in English, shall be posted in each vehicle or aircraft subject to this article.

118935. Designated Smoking Areas on Public Transportation; Signs Required

(a) Every person and public agency providing transportation services for compensation, including, but not limited to, the National Railroad Passenger Corporation (Amtrak) to the extent permitted by federal law, passenger stage corporations, and local agencies that own or operate airports, shall designate and post, by signs of sufficient number and posted in locations that may be readily seen by persons within the area, a contiguous area of not less than 75 percent of any area made available by the person or public agency as a waiting room for these passengers where the smoking of tobacco is prohibited. Not more than 25 percent of any given area may be set aside for smokers.

(b) Every person or public agency subject to subdivision (a) shall also post, by sign of sufficient number and posted in locations as to be readily seen by persons within the area of any building where tickets, tokens, or other evidences that a fare has been paid for transportation services that are provided by the person or public agency, a notice that the smoking of tobacco by persons waiting in line to purchase the tickets, tokens, or other evidences that a fare has been paid is prohibited.

(c) It is unlawful for any person to smoke in an area posted pursuant to this section.

PUBLIC RESOURCES CODE

4022. Impersonating a Ranger

(a) The titles of ranger, park ranger, and forest ranger, and derivations thereof, may only be used by persons who are peace officers under Chapter 4.5 (commencing with Section 830) of Title 3 of Part 2 of the Penal Code, employees of the Department of Forestry and Fire Protection, or employees of the Department of Parks and Recreation classified as State Park Ranger (Permanent Intermittent). Any person, other than a peace officer or employee of the Department of Parks and Recreation, as described in this section, or employee of the Department of Forestry and Fire Protection, who willfully wears, exhibits, or uses any authorized badge, insignia, emblem, device, label, title, or card of a ranger, park ranger, forest ranger, or a derivation thereof, to identify the person as a ranger, park ranger, or forest ranger, or who willfully wears, exhibits, or uses any badge, insignia, emblem, device, label, title, or card of a ranger, park ranger, or forest ranger, which so resembles the authorized version that it would deceive an ordinary, reasonable person into believing that it is authorized for the use of a ranger, park ranger, or forest ranger, is guilty of an infraction.

(b) Subdivision (a) does not apply to positions and titles of agencies of the United States government or to any local agency which is officially using any title specified in subdivision (a) as of January 1, 1990.

5008.1. Animals in Parks; Conditions for Admission

(a) When it is determined by the director to be in the public interest, and subject to the fees, rules, and regulations of the department, visitors to units of the state park system may bring animals into those units.

(b) Any animal brought into a state park system unit pursuant to subdivision (a) shall be under the immediate control of the visitor or shall be confined, and under no circumstance shall the animal be permitted to do any of the following:

(1) Pose a threat to public safety and welfare.

(2) Create a public nuisance.

(3) Pose a threat to the natural or cultural resources of the unit or to the improvements at the unit.

(c) The department may require a person bringing an animal into a state park system unit pursuant to subdivision (a) to provide proof of appropriate immunizations and valid licenses.

(d) This section does not apply to dogs used to lawfully pursue game in season at units of the state park system where hunting is allowed.

5008.2. Nuisance Animals; Peace Officer Powers

(a) Peace officers and other designated employees of the department may capture any animal

(1) which is not confined or under the immediate control of a person visiting the unit, (2) which poses a threat to public safety and welfare, to the natural or cultural resources of the unit, or to the improvements at the unit, or (3) which is a public nuisance.

(b) Peace officers may dispatch any animal which poses an immediate or continuing threat (1) to public safety and welfare or (2) to wildlife at the unit.

(c) Owners of animals with identification that have been captured or dispatched pursuant to this section shall be notified within 72 hours after capture or dispatch.

(d) This section does not apply to dogs used to lawfully pursue game in season at units of the State Park System where hunting is permitted.

(e) The authority conferred by this section on peace officers or designated employees of the department may only be exercised on or about property owned, operated, controlled, or administered by the department.

WELFARE & INSTITUTIONS CODE

207.1. Detention of Minor in Jail or Lockup

(a) No court, judge, referee, peace officer, or employee of a detention facility shall knowingly detain any minor in a jail or lockup, except as provided in subdivision (b) or (d).

(b) Any minor who is alleged to have committed an offense described in subdivision (b), paragraph (2) of subdivision (d), or subdivision (e) of Section 707 whose case is transferred to a court of criminal jurisdiction pursuant to Section 707.1 after a finding is made that he or she is not a fit and proper subject to be dealt with under the juvenile court law, or any minor who has been charged directly in or transferred to a court of criminal jurisdiction pursuant to Section 707.01, may be detained in a jail or other secure facility for the confinement of adults if all of the following conditions are met:

(1) The juvenile court or the court of criminal jurisdiction makes a finding that the minor's further detention in the juvenile hall would endanger the safety of the public or would be detrimental to the other minors in the juvenile hall.

(2) Contact between the minor and adults in the facility is restricted in accordance with Section 208.

(3) The minor is adequately supervised.

(c) A minor who is either found not to be a fit and proper subject to be dealt with under the juvenile court law or who will be transferred to a court of criminal jurisdiction pursuant to Section 707.01, at the time of transfer to a court of criminal jurisdiction or at the conclusion of the fitness hearing, as the case may be, shall be entitled to be released on bail or on his or her own recognizance upon the same circumstances, terms, and conditions as an adult who is alleged to have committed the same offense.

(d)(1) A minor 14 years of age or older who is taken into temporary custody by a peace officer on the basis of being a person described by Section 602, and who, in the reasonable belief of the peace officer, presents a serious security risk of harm to self or others, may be securely detained in a law enforcement facility that contains a lockup for adults, if all of the following conditions are met:

(A) The minor is held in temporary custody for the purpose of investigating the case, facilitating release of the minor to a parent or guardian, or arranging transfer of the minor to an appropriate juvenile facility.

(B) The minor is detained in the law enforcement facility for a period that does not exceed six hours except as provided in subdivision (g).

(C) The minor is informed at the time he or she is securely detained of the purpose of the secure detention, of the length of time the secure detention is expected to last, and of the maximum six-hour period the secure detention is authorized to last. In the event an extension is granted pursuant to subdivision (g), the minor shall be informed of the length of time the extension is expected to last.

(D) Contact between the minor and adults confined in the facility is restricted in accordance with Section 208.

(E) The minor is adequately supervised.

(F) A log or other written record is maintained by the law enforcement agency showing the offense that is the basis for the secure detention of the minor in the facility, the reasons and circumstances forming the basis for the decision to place the minor in secure detention, and the length of time the minor was securely detained.

(2) Any other minor, other than a minor to which paragraph (1) applies, who is taken into temporary custody by a peace officer on the basis that the minor is a person described by Section 602 may be taken to a law enforcement facility that contains a lockup for adults and may be held in temporary custody in the facility for the purposes of investigating the case, facilitating the release of the minor to a parent or guardian, or arranging for the transfer of the minor to an appropriate juvenile facility. While in the law enforcement facility, the minor may not be securely detained and shall be supervised in a manner so as to ensure that there will be no contact with adults in custody in the facility. If the minor is held in temporary, nonsecure custody within the facility, the peace officer shall exercise one of the dispositional options authorized by Sections 626 and 626.5 without unnecessary delay and, in every case, within six hours.

(3) "Law enforcement facility," as used in this subdivision, includes a police station or a sheriff's station, but does not include a jail, as defined in subdivision (i).

(e) The Board of Corrections shall assist law enforcement agencies, probation departments, and courts with the implementation of this section by doing all of the following:

(1) The board shall advise each law enforcement agency, probation department, and court affected by this section as to its existence and effect.

(2) The board shall make available and, upon request, shall provide, technical assistance to each governmental agency that reported the confinement of a minor in a jail or lockup in calendar year 1984 or 1985. The purpose of this technical assistance is to develop alternatives to the use of jails or lockups for the confinement of minors. These alternatives may include secure or nonsecure facilities located apart from an existing jail or lockup, improved transportation or access to juvenile halls or other juvenile facilities, and other programmatic alternatives recommended by the board. The technical assistance shall take any form the board deems appropriate for effective compliance with this section.

(f) The Board of Corrections may exempt a county that does not have a juvenile hall, or may exempt an offshore law enforcement facility, from compliance with this section for a reasonable period of time, until December 1, 1992, for the purpose of allowing the county or the facility to develop alternatives to the use of jails and lockups for the confinement of minors, if all of the following conditions are met:

(1) The county or the facility submits a written request to the board for an extension of time to comply with this section.

(2) The board agrees to make available, and the county or the facility agrees to accept, technical assistance to develop alternatives to the use of jails and lockups for the confinement of minors during the period of the extension.

(3) The county or the facility requesting the extension submits to the board a written plan for full compliance with this section by September 1, 1987.

(g)(1)(A) Under the limited conditions of inclement weather, acts of God, or natural disasters that result in the temporary unavailability of transportation, an extension of the six-hour maximum period of detention set forth in paragraph (2) of subdivision (d) may be granted to a county by the Board of Corrections. The extension may be granted only by the board, on an individual, case-by-case basis. If the extension is granted, the detention of minors under those conditions shall not exceed the duration of the special conditions, plus a period reasonably necessary to accomplish transportation of the minor to a suitable juvenile facility, not to exceed six hours after the restoration of available transportation.

(B) A county that receives an extension under this paragraph shall comply with the requirements set forth in subdivision (d). The county also shall provide a written report to the board that specifies when the inclement weather, act of God, or natural disaster ceased to exist, when transportation availability was restored, and when the minor was delivered to a suitable juvenile facility. In the event that the minor was detained in excess of 24 hours, the board shall verify the information contained in the report.

(2) Under the limited condition of temporary unavailability of transportation, an extension of the six-hour maximum period of detention set forth in paragraph (2) of subdivision (d) may be granted by the board to an offshore law enforcement facility. The extension may be granted only by the board, on an individual, case-by-case basis. If the extension is granted, the detention of minors under those conditions shall extend only until the next available mode of transportation can be arranged.

An offshore law enforcement facility that receives an extension under this paragraph shall comply with the requirements set forth in subdivision (d). The facility also shall provide a written report to the board that specifies when the next mode of transportation became available, and when the minor was delivered to a suitable juvenile facility. In the event that the minor was detained in excess of 24 hours, the board shall verify the information contained in the report.

(3) At least annually, the board shall review and report on extensions sought and granted under this subdivision. If, upon that review, the board determines that a county has sought one or more extensions resulting in the excessive confinement of minors in adult facilities, or that a county is engaged in a pattern and practice of seeking extensions, it shall require the county to submit a detailed explanation of the reasons for the extensions sought and an assessment of the need for a conveniently located and suitable juvenile facility. Upon receiving this information, the board shall make available, and the county shall accept, technical assistance for the purpose of developing suitable alternatives to the confinement of minors in adult lockups. Based upon the information provided by the county, the board also may place limits on, or refuse to grant, future extensions requested by the county under this subdivision.

(h) Any county that did not have a juvenile hall on January 1, 1987, may establish a special purpose juvenile hall, as defined by the Board of Corrections, for the detention of minors for a period not to exceed 96 hours. Any county that had a juvenile hall on January 1, 1987, also may establish, in addition to the juvenile hall, a special purpose juvenile hall. The board shall prescribe minimum standards for that type of facility.

(i)(1) "Jail," as used in this chapter, means any building that contains a locked facility administered by a law enforcement or governmental agency, the purpose of which is to detain adults who have been charged with violations of criminal law and are pending trial, or to hold convicted adult criminal offenders sentenced for less than one year.

(2) "Lockup," as used in this chapter, means any locked room or secure enclosure under the control of a sheriff or other peace officer that is primarily for the temporary confinement of adults upon arrest.

(3) "Offshore law enforcement facility," as used in this section, means a sheriff's station containing a lockup for adults that is located on an island located at least 22 miles from the California coastline.

(j) Nothing in this section shall be deemed to prevent a peace officer or employee of an adult detention facility or jail from escorting a minor into the detention facility or jail for the purpose of administering an evaluation, test, or chemical test pursuant to Section 23157 of the Vehicle Code, if all of the following conditions are met:

(1) The minor is taken into custody by a peace officer on the basis of being a person described by Section 602 and there is no equipment for the administration of the evaluation, test, or chemical test located at a juvenile facility within a reasonable distance of the point where the minor was taken into custody.

(2) The minor is not locked in a cell or room within the adult detention facility or jail, is under the continuous, personal supervision of a peace officer or employee of the detention facility or jail, and is not permitted to come in contact or remain in contact with in-custody adults.

(3) The evaluation, test, or chemical test administered pursuant to Section 23157 of the Vehicle Code is performed as expeditiously as possible, so that the minor is not delayed unnecessarily within the adult detention facility or jail. Upon completion of the evaluation, test, or chemical test, the minor shall be removed from the detention facility or jail as soon as reasonably possible. No minor shall be held in custody in an adult detention facility or jail under the authority of this paragraph in excess of two hours.

300. Jurisdiction of Juvenile Court [Repeals 1-1-2006]

Any child who comes within any of the following descriptions is within the jurisdiction of the juvenile court which may adjudge that person to be a dependent child of the court:

(a) The child has suffered, or there is a substantial risk that the child will suffer, serious physical harm inflicted nonaccidentally upon the child by the child's parent or guardian. For the purposes of this subdivision, a court may find there is a substantial risk of serious future injury based on the manner in which a less serious injury was inflicted, a history of repeated inflictions of injuries on the child or the child's siblings, or a combination of these and other actions by the parent or guardian which indicate the child is at risk of serious physical harm. For purposes of this subdivision, "serious physical harm" does not include reasonable and age-appropriate spanking to the buttocks where there is no evidence of serious physical injury.

(b) The child has suffered, or there is a substantial risk that the child will suffer, serious physical harm or illness, as a result of the failure or inability of his or her parent or guardian to adequately supervise or protect the child, or the willful or negligent failure of the child's parent or guardian to adequately supervise or protect the child from the conduct of the custodian with whom the child has been left, or by the willful or negligent failure of the parent or guardian to provide the child with adequate food, clothing, shelter, or medical treatment, or by the inability of the parent or guardian to provide regular care for the child due to the parent's or guardian's mental illness, developmental disability, or substance abuse. No child shall be found to be a person described by this subdivision solely due to the lack of an emergency shelter for the family. Whenever it is alleged that a child comes within the jurisdiction of the court on the basis of the parent's or guardian's willful failure to provide adequate medical treatment or specific decision to provide spiritual treatment through prayer, the court shall give deference to the parent's or guardian's medical treatment, nontreatment, or spiritual treatment through prayer alone in accordance with the tenets and practices of a recognized church or religious denomination, by an accredited practitioner thereof, and shall not assume jurisdiction unless necessary to protect the child from suffering serious physical harm or illness. In making its determination, the court shall consider (1) the nature of the treatment proposed by the parent or guardian, (2) the risks to the child posed by the course of treatment or nontreatment proposed by the parent or guardian, (3) the risk, if any, of the course of treatment being proposed by the petitioning agency, and (4) the likely success of the courses of treatment or nontreatment proposed by the parent or guardian and agency. The child shall continue to be a dependent child pursuant to this subdivision only so long as is necessary to protect the child from risk of suffering serious physical harm or illness.

(c) The child is suffering serious emotional damage, or is at substantial risk of suffering serious emotional damage, evidenced by severe anxiety, depression, withdrawal, or untoward aggressive behavior toward self or others, as a result of the conduct of the parent or guardian or who has no parent or guardian capable of providing appropriate care. No child shall be found to be a person described by this subdivision if the willful failure of the parent or guardian to provide adequate mental health treatment is based on a sincerely held religious belief and if a less intrusive judicial intervention is available.

(d) The child has been sexually abused, or there is a substantial risk that the child will be sexually abused, as defined in Section 11165.1 of the Penal Code, by his or her parent or guardian or a member of his or her household, or the parent or guardian has failed to adequately protect the child from sexual abuse when the parent or guardian knew or reasonably should have known that the child was in danger of sexual abuse.

(e) The child is under the age of five and has suffered severe physical abuse by a parent, or by any person known by the parent, if the parent knew or reasonably should have known that the person was physically abusing the child. For the purposes of this subdivision, "severe physical abuse" means any of the following: any single act of abuse which causes physical trauma of sufficient severity that, if left untreated, would cause permanent physical disfigurement, permanent physical disability, or death; any single act of sexual abuse which causes significant bleeding, deep bruising, or significant external or internal swelling; or more than one act of physical abuse, each of which causes bleeding, deep bruising, significant external or internal swelling, bone fracture, or unconsciousness; or the willful, prolonged failure to provide adequate food. A child may not be removed from the physical custody of his or her parent or guardian on the basis of a finding of severe physical abuse unless the social worker has made an allegation of severe physical abuse pursuant to Section 332.

(f) The child's parent or guardian caused the death of another child through abuse or neglect.

(g) The child has been left without any provision for support; physical custody of the child has been voluntarily surrendered pursuant to Section 1255.7 of the Health and Safety Code and the child has not been reclaimed within the 14-day period specified in subdivision (e) of that section; the child's parent has been incarcerated or institutionalized and cannot arrange for the care of the child; or a relative or other adult custodian with whom the child resides or has been left is unwilling or unable to provide care or support for the child, the whereabouts of the parent are unknown, and reasonable efforts to locate the parent have been unsuccessful.

(h) The child has been freed for adoption by one or both parents for 12 months by either relinquishment or termination of parental rights or an adoption petition has not been granted.

(i) The child has been subjected to an act or acts of cruelty by the parent or guardian or a member of his or her household, or the parent or guardian has failed to adequately protect the child from an act or acts of cruelty when the parent or guardian knew or reasonably should have known that the child was in danger of being subjected to an act or acts of cruelty.

(j) The child's sibling has been abused or neglected, as defined in subdivision (a), (b), (d), (e), or (i), and there is a substantial risk that the child will be abused or neglected, as defined in those subdivisions. The court shall consider the circumstances surrounding the abuse or neglect of the sibling, the age and gender of each child, the nature of the abuse or neglect of the sibling, the mental condition of the parent or guardian, and any other factors the court considers probative in determining whether there is a substantial risk to the child.

It is the intent of the Legislature that nothing in this section disrupt the family unnecessarily or intrude inappropriately into family life, prohibit the use of reasonable methods of parental discipline, or prescribe a particular method of parenting. Further, nothing in this section is intended to limit the offering of voluntary services to those families in need of assistance but who do not come within the descriptions of this section. To the extent that savings accrue to the state from child welfare services funding obtained as a result of the enactment of the act that enacted this section, those savings shall be used to promote services which support family maintenance and family reunification plans, such as client transportation, out-of-home respite care, parenting training, and the provision of temporary or emergency in-home caretakers and persons teaching and demonstrating homemaking skills. The Legislature further declares that a physical disability, such as blindness or deafness, is no bar to the raising of happy and well-adjusted children and that a court's determination pursuant to this section shall center upon whether a parent's disability prevents him or her from exercising care and control.

As used in this section "guardian" means the legal guardian of the child.

(k) This section shall be repealed on January 1, 2006, unless a later enacted statute extends or deletes that date. *(AM '98, '00)*

300. Jurisdiction of Juvenile Court [Effective 1-1-2006]

Any child who comes within any of the following descriptions is within the jurisdiction of the juvenile court which may adjudge that person to be a dependent child of the court:

(a) The child has suffered, or there is a substantial risk that the child will suffer, serious physical harm inflicted nonaccidentally upon the child by the child's parent or guardian. For the purposes of this subdivision, a court may find there is a substantial risk of serious future injury based on the manner in which a less serious injury was inflicted, a history of repeated inflictions of injuries on the child or the child's siblings, or a combination of these and other actions by the parent or guardian which indicate the child is at risk of serious physical harm. For purposes of this subdivision, "serious physical harm" does not include reasonable and age-appropriate spanking to the buttocks where there is no evidence of serious physical injury.

(b) The child has suffered, or there is a substantial risk that the child will suffer, serious physical harm or illness, as a result of the failure or inability of his or her parent or guardian to adequately supervise or protect the child, or the willful or negligent failure of the child's parent or guardian to adequately supervise or protect the child from the conduct of the custodian with whom the child has been left, or by the willful or negligent failure of the parent or guardian to provide the child with adequate food, clothing, shelter, or medical treatment, or by the inability of the parent or guardian to provide regular care for the child due to the parent's or guardian's mental illness, developmental disability, or substance abuse. No child shall be found to be a person described by this subdivision solely due to the lack of an emergency shelter for the family. Whenever it is alleged that a child comes within the jurisdiction of the court on the basis of the parent's or guardian's willful failure to provide adequate medical treatment or specific decision to provide spiritual treatment through prayer, the court shall give deference to the parent's or guardian's medical treatment, nontreatment, or spiritual treatment through prayer alone in accordance with the tenets and practices of a recognized church or religious denomination, by an accredited practitioner thereof, and shall not assume jurisdiction unless necessary to protect the child from suffering serious physical harm or illness. In making its determination, the court shall consider (1) the nature of the treatment proposed by the parent or guardian, (2) the risks to the child posed by the course of treatment or nontreatment proposed by the parent or guardian, (3) the risk, if any, of the course of treatment being proposed by the petitioning agency, and (4) the likely success of the courses of treatment or nontreatment proposed by the parent or guardian and agency. The child shall continue to be a dependent child pursuant to this subdivision only so long as is necessary to protect the child from risk of suffering serious physical harm or illness.

(c) The child is suffering serious emotional damage, or is at substantial risk of suffering serious emotional damage, evidenced by severe anxiety, depression, withdrawal, or untoward aggressive behavior toward self or others, as a result of the conduct of the parent or guardian or who has no parent or guardian capable of providing appropriate care. No child shall be found to be a person described by this subdivision if the willful failure of the parent or guardian to provide adequate mental health treatment is based on a sincerely held religious belief and if a less intrusive judicial intervention is available.

(d) The child has been sexually abused, or there is a substantial risk that the child will be sexually abused, as defined in Section 11165.1 of the Penal Code, by his or her parent or guardian or a member of his or her household, or the parent or guardian has failed to adequately protect the child from sexual abuse when the parent or guardian knew or reasonably should have known that the child was in danger of sexual abuse.

(e) The child is under the age of five and has suffered severe physical abuse by a parent, or by any person known by the parent, if the parent knew or reasonably should have known that the person was physically abusing the child. For the purposes of this subdivision, "severe physical abuse" means any of the following: any single act of abuse which causes physical trauma of sufficient severity that, if left untreated, would cause permanent physical disfigurement, permanent physical disability, or death; any single act of sexual abuse which causes significant bleeding, deep bruising, or significant external or internal swelling; or more than one act of physical abuse, each of which causes bleeding, deep bruising, significant external or internal swelling, bone fracture, or unconsciousness; or the willful, prolonged failure to provide adequate food. A child may not be removed from the physical custody of his or her parent or guardian on the basis of a finding of severe physical abuse unless the social worker has made an allegation of severe physical abuse pursuant to Section 332.

(f) The child's parent or guardian caused the death of another child through abuse or neglect.

(g) The child has been left without any provision for support; the child's parent has been incarcerated or institutionalized and cannot arrange for the care of the child; or a relative or other adult custodian with whom the child resides or has been left is unwilling or unable to provide care or support for the child, the whereabouts of the parent are unknown, and reasonable efforts to locate the parent have been unsuccessful.

(h) The child has been freed for adoption by one or both parents for 12 months by either relinquishment or termination of parental rights or an adoption petition has not been granted.

(i) The child has been subjected to an act or acts of cruelty by the parent or guardian or a member of his or her household, or the parent or guardian has failed to adequately protect the child from an act or acts of cruelty when the parent or guardian knew or reasonably should have known that the child was in danger of being subjected to an act or acts of cruelty.

(j) The child's sibling has been abused or neglected, as defined in subdivision (a), (b), (d), (e), or (i), and there is a substantial risk that the child will be abused or neglected, as defined in those subdivisions. The court shall consider the circumstances surrounding the abuse or neglect of the sibling, the age and gender of each child, the nature of the abuse or neglect of the sibling, the mental condition of the parent or guardian, and any other factors the court considers probative in determining whether there is a substantial risk to the child.

It is the intent of the Legislature that nothing in this section disrupt the family unnecessarily or intrude inappropriately into family life, prohibit the use of reasonable methods of parental discipline, or prescribe a particular method of parenting. Further, nothing in this section is intended to limit the offering of voluntary services to those families in need of assistance but who do not come within the descriptions of this section. To the extent that savings accrue to the state from child welfare services funding obtained as a result of the enactment of the act that enacted this section, those savings shall be used to promote services which support family maintenance and family reunification plans, such as client transportation, out-of-home respite care, parenting training, and the provision of temporary or emergency in-home caretakers and persons teaching and demonstrating homemaking skills. The Legislature further declares that a physical disability, such as blindness or deafness, is no bar to the raising of happy and well-adjusted children and that a court's determination pursuant to this section shall center upon whether a parent's disability prevents him or her from exercising care and control.

As used in this section, "guardian"means the legal guardian of the child. *(AD '00)*

305. Temporary Custody of Minors: Peace Officers without Warrant

Any peace officer may, without a warrant, take into temporary custody a minor:

(a) When the officer has reasonable cause for believing that the minor is a person described in Section 300, and, in addition, that the minor has an immediate need for medical care, or the minor is in immediate danger of physical or sexual abuse, or the physical environment or the fact that the child is left unattended poses an immediate threat to the child's health or safety. In cases in which the child is left unattended, the peace officer shall first attempt to contact the child's parent or guardian to determine if the parent or guardian is able to assume custody of the child. If the parent or guardian cannot be contacted, the peace officer shall notify a social worker in the county welfare department to assume custody of the child.

(b) Who is in a hospital and release of the minor to a parent poses an immediate danger to the child's health or safety.

(c) Who is a dependent child of the juvenile court, or concerning whom an order has been made under Section 319, when the officer has reasonable cause for believing that the minor has violated an order of the juvenile court or has left any placement ordered by the juvenile court.

(d) Who is found in any street or public place suffering from any sickness or injury which requires care, medical treatment, hospitalization, or other remedial care.

601.   Disobedient or Truant Minor

(a) Any person under the age of 18 years who persistently or habitually refuses to obey the reasonable and proper orders or directions of his or her parents, guardian, or custodian, or who is beyond the control of that person, or who is under the age of 18 years when he or she violated any ordinance of any city or county of this state establishing a curfew based solely on age is within the jurisdiction of the juvenile court which may adjudge the minor to be a ward of the court.

(b) If a minor has four or more truancies within one school year as defined in Section 48260 of the Education Code or a school attendance review board or probation officer determines that the available public and private services are insufficient or inappropriate to correct the habitual truancy of the minor, or to correct the minor's persistent or habitual refusal to obey the reasonable and proper orders or directions of school authorities, or if the minor fails to respond to directives of a school attendance review board or probation officer or to services provided, the minor is then within the jurisdiction of the juvenile court which may adjudge the minor to be a ward of the court. However, it is the intent of the Legislature that no minor who is adjudged a ward of the court pursuant solely to this subdivision shall be removed from the custody of the parent or guardian except during school hours.

(c) To the extent practically feasible, a minor who is adjudged a ward of the court pursuant to this section shall not be permitted to come into or remain in contact with any minor ordered to participate in a truancy program, or the equivalent thereof, pursuant to Section 602.

(d) Any peace officer or school administrator may issue a notice to appear to a minor who is within the jurisdiction of the juvenile court pursuant to this section.

602.   Minor in Violation of Law

(a) Except as provided in subdivision (b), any person who is under the age of 18 years when he or she violates any law of this state or of the United States or any ordinance of any city or county of this state defining crime other than an ordinance establishing a curfew based solely on age, is within the jurisdiction of the juvenile court, which may adjudge such person to be a ward of the court.

(b) Any person who is alleged, when he or she was 14 years of age or older, to have committed one of the following offenses shall be prosecuted under the general law in a court of criminal jurisdiction:

(1) Murder, as described in Section 187 of the Penal Code, if one of the circumstances enumerated in subdivision (a) of Section 190.2 of the Penal Code is alleged by the prosecutor, and the prosecutor alleges that the minor personally killed the victim.

(2) The following sex offenses, if the prosecutor alleges that the minor personally committed the offense, and if the prosecutor alleges one of the circumstances enumerated in the One Strike law, *** subdivision (d) or (e) of Section 667.61 of the Penal Code, *** applies:

(A) Rape, as described in paragraph (2) of subdivision (a) of Section 261 of the Penal Code.

(B) Spousal rape, as described in paragraph (1) of subdivision (a) of Section 262 of the Penal Code.

(C) Forcible sex offenses in concert with another, as described in Section 264.1 of the Penal Code.

(D) Forcible lewd and lascivious acts on a child under the age of 14 years, as described in subdivision (b) of Section 288 of the Penal Code.

(E) Forcible sexual penetration ***, as described in subdivision (a) of Section 289 of the Penal Code.

(F) Sodomy or oral copulation in violation of Section 286 or 288a of the Penal Code, by force, violence, duress, menace, or fear of immediate and unlawful bodily injury on the victim or another person.

(G) *** Lewd and lascivious acts on a child under the age of 14 years, as defined in subdivision (a) of Section 288, unless the defendant qualifies for probation under subdivision (c) of Section 1203.066 of the Penal Code.   *(AM by initiative measure 3-2000) (AM '01)*

625.   Temporary Custody of Pre-Delinquent, Delinquent, Ill or Injured Minor by Peace Officer without Warrant

A peace officer may, without a warrant, take into custody a minor:

(a) Who is under the age of 18 years when such officer has reasonable cause for believing that such minor is a person described in Section 601 or 602, or

(b) Who is a ward of the juvenile court or concerning whom an order has been made under Section 636 or 702, when such officer has reasonable cause for believing that person has violated an order of the juvenile court or has escaped from any commitment ordered by the juvenile court, or

(c) Who is under the age of 18 years and who is found in any street or public place suffering from any sickness or injury which requires care, medical treatment, hospitalization, or other remedial care.

In any case where a minor is taken into temporary custody on the ground that there is reasonable cause for believing that such minor is a person described in Section 601 or 602, or that he has violated an order of the juvenile court or escaped from any commitment ordered by the juvenile court, the officer shall advise such minor that anything he says can be used against him and shall advise him of his constitutional rights, including his right to remain silent, his right to have counsel present during any interrogation, and his right to have counsel appointed if he is unable to afford counsel.

625.1. Minor, Voluntary Chemical Test

Any minor who is taken into temporary custody pursuant to subdivision (a) of Section 625, when the peace officer has reasonable cause for believing the minor is a person described in Section 602, or pursuant to subdivision (b) or (c) of Section 625, may be requested to submit to voluntary chemical testing of his or her urine for the purpose of determining the presence of alcohol or illegal drugs. The peace officer shall inform the minor that the chemical test is voluntary. The results of this test may be considered by the court in determining the disposition of the minor pursuant to Section 706 or 777. Unless otherwise provided by law, the results of such a test shall not be the basis of a petition filed by the prosecuting attorney to declare the minor a person described in Section 602, nor shall it be the basis for such a finding by a court pursuant to Section 702.

871. Escape by Minor Under Custody or Commitment

(a) Any person under the custody of a probation officer or any peace officer in a county juvenile hall, or committed to a county juvenile home, ranch, camp, or forestry camp, or any person being transported to or from a county juvenile hall, home, ranch, camp, or forestry camp, who escapes or attempts to escape from that place or during transportation to or from that place, is guilty of a misdemeanor, punishable by imprisonment in the county jail not exceeding one year.

(b) Any person who commits any of the acts described in subdivision (a) by use of force or violence shall be punished by imprisonment in a county jail for not more than one year or by imprisonment in the state prison.

(c) The willful failure of a person under the custody of a probation officer or any peace officer in a county juvenile hall, or committed to a county juvenile home, ranch camp, or forestry camp, to return to the county juvenile hall, home, ranch, camp, or forestry camp at the prescribed time while outside or away from the county facility on furlough or temporary release constitutes an escape punishable as provided in subdivision (a). However, a willful failure to return at the prescribed time shall not be considered an escape if the failure to return was reasonable under the circumstances.

(d) A minor who, while under the supervision of a probation officer, removes his or her electronic monitor without authority and who, for more than 48 hours, violates the terms and conditions of his or her probation relating to the proper use of the electronic monitor shall be guilty of a misdemeanor. If an electronic monitor is damaged or discarded while in the possession of the minor, restitution for the cost of replacing the unit may be ordered as part of the punishment.

(e) The liability established by this section shall be limited by the financial ability of the person or persons ordered to pay restitution under this section, who shall, upon request, be entitled to an evaluation and determination of ability to pay under Section 903.45.

871.5. Bring, Send or Possess Contraband into Juvenile Facilities

(a) Except as authorized by law, or when authorized by the person in charge of any county juvenile hall, home, ranch, camp, or forestry camp, or by an officer of any such juvenile hall, home, or camp empowered by the person in charge to give such an authorization, any person who knowingly brings or sends into, or who knowingly assists in bringing into, or sending into, any county juvenile hall, home, ranch, camp, or forestry camp, or any person who while confined in such an institution possess therein, any controlled substance, the possession of which is prohibited by Division 10 (commencing with Sec. 11000) of the Health and Safety code, any firearm, weapon, or explosive of any kind, or any tear gas or tear gas weapon shall be punished by imprisonment in a county jail for not more than one year or by imprisonment in the state prison.

(b) Except as otherwise authorized in the manner provided in subdivision (a), any person who knowingly uses tear gas or uses a tear gas weapon in an institution or camp specified in subdivision (a) is guilty of a felony.

(c) A sign shall be posted at the entrance of each county juvenile hall, home, ranch, camp, or forestry camp specifying the conduct prohibited by this section and the penalties therefor.

(d) Except as otherwise authorized in the manner provided in subdivision (a), any person who knowingly brings or sends into, or who knowingly assists in bringing int, or sending into, any county juvenile hall, home, ranch, camp, or forestry camp, or any person who while confined in such an institution knowingly possesses therein, any alcoholic beverage shall be guilty of a misdemeanor.

1768.7. Escape or Attempt from Calif. Youth Authority

(a) Any person committed to the authority who escapes or attempts to escape from the institution or facility in which he or she is confined, who escapes or attempts to escape while being conveyed to or from such an institution or facility, who escapes or attempts to escape while outside or away from such an institution or facility under custody or Youth Authority officials, officers, or employees, or who, with intent to abscond from the custody of the Youth Authority, fails to return to such an institution or facility at the prescribed time while outside or away from the institution or facility on furlough or temporary release is guilty of a felony.

(b) Any offense set forth in subdivision (a) which is accomplished by force or violence is punishable by imprisonment in the state prison for a term of two, four, or six years. Any offense set forth in subdivision (a) which is accomplished without force or violence is punishable by imprisonment in the state prison for a term of 16 months, two or three years or in the county jail not exceeding one year.

(c) For purposes of this section, "committed to the authority" means a commitment to the Youth Authority pursuant to Sec. 731 or 1731.5; a remand to the custody of the Youth Authority pursuant to Sec. 707.2; a placement at the Youth Authority pursuant to Sec. 704, 1731.6, or 1753.1; or a transfer to the custody of the Youth Authority pursuant to subdivision (c) of Sec. 1731.5.

1768.8. Assault or Battery by Person Confined in Youth Authority Against a Person Not So Confined

(a) An assault or battery by any person confined in an institution under the jurisdiction of the Department of the Youth Authority upon the person of any individual who is not confined therein shall be punishable by a fine not exceeding two thousand dollars ($2,000), or by imprisonment in the county jail not exceeding one year, or by both a fine and imprisonment.

(b) An assault by any person confined in an institution under the jurisdiction of the Department of the Youth Authority upon the person of any individual who is not confined therein, with a deadly weapon or instrument, or by any means of force likely to produce great bodily injury, is a felony punishable by imprisonment in the state prison for two, four, or six years.

5150. Dangerous or Gravely Disabled Person

When any person, as a result of mental disorder, is a danger to others, or to himself or herself, or gravely disabled, a peace officer, member of the attending staff, as defined by regulation, of an evaluation facility designated by the county, designated members of a mobile crisis team provided by Section 5651.7, or other designated professional person designated by the county may, upon probable cause, take, or cause to be taken, the person into custody and place him or her in a facility designated by the county and approved by the State Department of Mental Health as a facility for 72-hour treatment and evaluation.

Such facility shall require an application in writing stating the circumstances under which the person's condition was called to the attention of the officer, member of the attending staff, or professional person has probable cause to believe that the person is, as a result of mental disorder, a danger to others, or to himself or herself, or gravely disabled. If the probable cause is based on the statement of a person other than the officer, member of the attending staff, or professional person, such person shall be liable in a civil action for intentionally giving a statement which he or she knows to be false.

5157. Required Information Given to Person Taken into Custody

(a) Each person, at the time he or she is first taken into custody under provisions of Section 5150, shall be provided, by the person who takes such other person into custody, the following information orally. The information shall be in substantially the following form:

My name is _____ .

I am a _____. (peace officer, mental health professional) with _____ (name of agency).

You are not under criminal arrest, but I am taking you for examination by mental health professionals at _____ (name of facility). You will be told your rights by the mental health staff.

If taken into custody at his or her residence, the person shall also be told the following information in substantially the following form:

You may bring a few personal items with you which I will have to approve. You can make a phone call and/or leave a note to tell your friends and/or family where you have been taken.

(b) The designated facility shall keep, for each patient evaluated, a record of the advisement given pursuant to subdivision (a) which shall include:

(1) Name of person detained for evaluation.

(2) Name and position of peace officer or mental health professional taking person into custody.

(3) Date.

(4) Whether advisement was completed.

(5) If not given or completed, the mental health professional at the facility shall either provide the information specified in subdivision (a), or include a statement of good cause, as defined by regulations of the State Department of Mental Health, which shall be kept with the patient's medical record.

(c) Each person admitted to a designated facility for 72-hour evaluation and treatment shall be given the following information by admission staff at the evaluation unit. The information shall be given orally and in writing and in a language or modality accessible to the person. The written information shall be available in the person's native language or the language which is the person's principal means of communication. The information shall be in substantially the following form:

My name is _____.

My position here is _____.

You are being placed into the psychiatric unit because it is our professional opinion that as a result of mental disorder, you are likely to:

(check applicable)

harm yourself _____

harm someone else _____

be unable to take care of your own _____

food, clothing, and housing needs _____

We feel this is true because _____

(here with a listing of the facts upon which the allegation of dangerous or gravely disabled due to mental disorder is based, including pertinent facts arising from the admission interview.)

You will be held on the ward for a period up to 72 hours.

This does not include weekends or holidays.

Your 72-hour period will begin _____ (day and time.)

During these 72 hours you will be evaluated by the hospital staff, and you may be given treatment, including medications.

It is possible for you to be released before the end of the 72 hours. But if the staff decides that you need continued treatment you can be held for a longer period of time.

If you are held longer than 72 hours you have the right to a lawyer and a qualified interpreter and a hearing before a judge.

If you are unable to pay for the lawyer, then one will be provided free.

(d) For each patient admitted for 72-hour evaluation and treatment, the facility shall keep with the patient's medical record a record of the advisement given pursuant to subdivision (c) which shall include:

(1) Name of person performing advisement.

(2) Date.

(3) Whether advisement was completed.

(4) If not completed, a statement of good cause.

If the advisement was not completed at admission, the advisement process shall be continued on the ward until completed. A record of the matters prescribed by subdivisions (a), (b), and (c) shall be kept with the patient's medical record.

8100. Possession of Firearm or Deadly Weapon by Mental Patient

(a) A person shall not have in his or her possession or under his or her custody or control, or purchase or receive, or attempt to purchase or receive, any firearms whatsoever or any other deadly weapon, if on or after January 1, 1992, he or she has been admitted to a facility and is receiving inpatient treatment and, in the opinion of the attending health professional who is primarily responsible for the patient's treatment of a mental disorder, is a danger to self or others, as specified by Sec. 5150, 5250, or 5300, even though the patient has consented to that treatment. A person is not subject to this subdivision once he or she is discharged from the facility.

(b)(1) A person shall not have in his or her possession or under his or her custody or control, or purchase or receive, or attempt to purchase or receive, any firearms whatsoever or any other deadly weapon for a period of six months whenever, on or after January 1, 1992, he or she communicates to a licensed psychotherapist, as defined in subdivisions (a) to (e), inclusive, of Sec. 1010 of the Evidence Code, a serious threat of physical violence against a reasonably identifiable victim or victims. The six-month period shall commence from the date that the licensed psychotherapist reports to the local law enforcement agency the identity of the person making the communication. The prohibition provided for in this subdivision shall not apply unless the licensed psychotherapist notifies a local law enforcement agency of the threat by that person. The person, however, may own, possess, have custody or control over, or receive pr purchase any firearm if a superior court, pursuant to paragraph (3) and upon petition of the person, has found, by a preponderance of the evidence, that the person is likely to use firearms or other deadly weapons in a safe and lawful manner.

(e) "Deadly weapon," as used in this section and Sections 8101, 8102, and 8103 means any weapon, the possession or concealed carrying of which is prohibited by Section 12020 of the Penal Code.

(f) "Danger to self" as used in subdivision (a), means a voluntary person who has made a serious threat of, or attempted, suicide with the use of a firearm or other deadly weapon.

(g) A violation of subsection (a) of, or paragraph (1) of subdivision (b) of, this section shall be a public offense, punishable by imprisonment in the state prison, or in a county jail for not more than one year, by a fine not exceeding one thousand dollars ($1,000), or by both that imprisonment and fine.

(h) The prohibitions set forth in this section shall be in addition to those set forth in Sec. 8103.

(i) A violation of this section shall be a public offense punishable by imprisonment in the state prison, or in the county jail for not more than one year or by a fine not exceeding one thousand dollars ($1,000), or by both that fine and imprisonment.

8101. Supply Deadly Weapon or Firearm To Mental Patient

(a) Any person who shall knowingly supply, sell, give, or allow possession or control of a deadly weapon to any person described in Section 8100 or 8103 shall be punishable by imprisonment in the state prison, or in a county jail for a period of not exceeding one year, by a fine of not exceeding one thousand dollars ($1,000), or by both the fine and imprisonment.

(b) Any person who shall knowingly supply, sell, give, or allow possession or control of a firearm to any person described in Section 8100 or 8103 shall be punished by imprisonment in the state prison for two, three, or four years.

(c) "Deadly weapon," as used in this section has the meaning prescribed by Section 8100.

8102. Authority to Confiscate Firearm or Deadly Weapon from Mental Patient

(a) Whenever a person, who has been detained or apprehended for examination of his or her mental condition or who is a person described in *** Section 8100 or 8103, is found to own, have in his or her possession or under his or her control, any firearm whatsoever, or any other deadly weapon, the firearm or other deadly weapon shall be confiscated by any law enforcement agency or peace officer, who shall retain custody of the firearm or other deadly weapon.

"Deadly weapon," as used in this section, has the meaning prescribed by *** Section 8100.

(b) Upon confiscation of any firearm or other deadly weapon from a person who has been detained or apprehended for examination of his or her mental condition, the peace officer or law enforcement agency shall notify the person of the procedure for the return of any firearm or other deadly weapon which has been confiscated.

Where the person is released, the professional person in charge of the facility, or his or her designee, shall notify the person of the procedure for the return of any firearm or other deadly weapon which may have been confiscated.

Health facility personnel shall notify the confiscating law enforcement agency upon release of the detained person, and shall make a notation to the effect that the facility provided the required notice to the person regarding the procedure to obtain return of any confiscated firearm.

(c) Upon the release of a person as described in subdivision (b), the confiscating law enforcement agency shall have 30 days to initiate a petition in the superior court for a hearing to determine whether the return of a firearm or other deadly weapon would be likely to result in endangering the person or others, and to send a notice advising the person of his or her right to a hearing on this issue. The law enforcement agency may make an ex parte application stating good cause for an order extending the time to file a petition. Including any extension of time granted in response to an ex parte request, a petition must be filed within 60 days of the release of the person from a health facility.

(d) If the law enforcement agency does not initiate proceedings within the 30-day period, or the period of time authorized by the court in an ex parte order *** issued pursuant to subdivision (c), it shall make the weapon available for return.

(e) The law enforcement agency shall inform the person that he or she has 30 days to respond to the court clerk to confirm his or her desire for a hearing, and that the failure to respond will result in a default order forfeiting the confiscated firearm or weapon. For the purpose of this subdivision, the person's last known address shall be the address provided to the law enforcement officer by the person at the time of the person's detention or apprehension.

(f) If the person responds and requests a hearing, the court clerk shall set a hearing, no later than 30 days from receipt of the request. The court clerk shall notify the person and the district attorney of the date, time, and place of the hearing.

(g) If the person does not respond within 30 days of the notice, the law enforcement agency may file a petition for order of default. *(AM '01)*

8103. Purchase or Control of Firearm by Mental Patient

(a)(1) No person who after October 1, 1955, has been adjudicated by a court of any state to be a danger to others as a result of a mental disorder or mental illness, or who has been adjudicated to be a mentally disordered sex offender, shall purchase or receive, or attempt to purchase or receive, or have in his or her possession, custody, or control any firearm or any other deadly weapon unless there has been issued to the person a certificate by the court of adjudication upon release from treatment or at a later date stating that the person may possess a firearm or any other deadly weapon without endangering others, and the person has not, subsequent to the issuance of the certificate, again been adjudicated by a court to be a danger to others as a result of a mental disorder or mental illness.

(2) The court shall immediately notify the Department of Justice of the court order finding the individual to be a person described in paragraph (1). The court shall also notify the Department of Justice of any certificate issued as described in paragraph (1).

(b)(1) No person who has been found, pursuant to Section 1026 of the Penal Code or the law of any other state or the United States, not guilty by reason of insanity of murder, mayhem, a violation of Section 207, 209, or 209.5 of the Penal Code in which the victim suffers intentionally inflicted great bodily injury, carjacking or robbery in which the victim suffers great bodily injury, a violation of Section 451 or 452 of the Penal Code involving a trailer coach, as defined in Section 635 of the Vehicle Code, or any dwelling house, a violation of paragraph (1) or (2) of subdivision (a) of Section 262 or paragraph (2) or (3) of subdivision (a) of Section 261 of the Penal Code, a violation of Section 459 of the Penal Code in the first degree, assault with intent to commit murder, a violation of Section 220 of the Penal Code in which the victim suffers great bodily injury, a violation of Section 12303.1, 12303.2, 12303.3, 12308, 12309, or 12310 of the Penal Code, or of a felony involving death, great bodily injury, or an act which poses a serious threat of bodily harm to another person, or a violation of the law of any other state or the United States that includes all the elements of any of the above felonies as defined under California law, shall purchase or receive, or attempt to purchase or receive, or have in his or her possession or under his or her custody or control any firearm or any other deadly weapon.

(2) The court shall immediately notify the Department of Justice of the court order finding the person to be a person described in paragraph (1).

(c)(1) No person who has been found, pursuant to Section 1026 of the Penal Code or the law of any other state or the United States, not guilty by reason of insanity of any crime other than those described in subdivision (b) shall purchase or receive, or attempt to purchase or receive, or shall have in his or her possession, custody, or control any firearm or any other deadly weapon unless the court of commitment has found the person to have recovered sanity, pursuant to Section 1026.2 of the Penal Code or the law of any other state or the United States.

(2) The court shall immediately notify the Department of Justice of the court order finding the person to be a person described in paragraph (1). The court shall also notify the Department of Justice when it finds that the person has recovered his or her sanity.

(d)(1) No person found by a court to be mentally incompetent to stand trial, pursuant to Section 1370 or 1370.1 of the Penal Code or the law of any other state or the United States, shall purchase or receive, or attempt to purchase or receive, or shall have in his or her possession, custody, or control any firearm or any other deadly weapon, unless there has been a finding with respect to the person of restoration to competence to stand trial by the committing court, pursuant to Section 1372 of the Penal Code or the law of any other state or the United States.

(2) The court shall immediately notify the Department of Justice of the court order finding the person to be mentally incompetent as described in paragraph (1). The court shall also notify the Department of Justice when it finds that the person has recovered his or her competence.

(e)(1) No person who has been placed under conservatorship by a court, pursuant to Section 5350 or the law of any other state or the United States, because the person is gravely disabled as a result of a mental disorder or impairment by chronic alcoholism shall purchase or receive, or attempt to purchase or receive, or shall have in his or her possession, custody, or control any firearm or any other deadly weapon while under the conservatorship if, at the time the conservatorship was ordered or thereafter, the court which imposed the conservatorship found that possession of a firearm or any other deadly weapon by the person would present a danger to the safety of the person or to others. Upon placing any person under conservatorship, and prohibiting firearm or any other deadly weapon possession by the person, the court shall notify the person of this prohibition.

(2) The court shall immediately notify the Department of Justice of the court order placing the person under conservatorship and prohibiting firearm or any other deadly weapon possession by the person as described in paragraph (1). The notice shall include the date the conservatorship was imposed and the date the conservatorship is to be terminated. If the conservatorship is subsequently terminated before the date

listed in the notice to the Department of Justice or the court subsequently finds that possession of a firearm or any other deadly weapon by the person would no longer present a danger to the safety of the person or others, the court shall immediately notify the Department of Justice.

(3) All information provided to the Department of Justice pursuant to paragraph (2) shall be kept confidential, separate, and apart from all other records maintained by the Department of Justice, and shall be used only to determine eligibility to purchase or possess firearms or other deadly weapons. Any person who knowingly furnishes that information for any other purpose is guilty of a misdemeanor. All the information concerning any person shall be destroyed upon receipt by the Department of Justice of notice of the termination of conservatorship as to that person pursuant to paragraph (2).

(f)(1) No person who has been (A) taken into custody as provided in Section 5150 because that person is a danger to himself, herself, or to others, (B) assessed within the meaning of Section 5151, and (C) admitted to a designated facility within the meaning of Sections 5151 and 5152 because that person is a danger to himself, herself, or others, shall own, possess, control, receive, or purchase, or attempt to own, possess, control, receive, or purchase any firearm for a period of five years after the person is released from the facility. A person described in the preceding sentence, however, may own, possess, control, receive, or purchase, or attempt to own, possess, control, receive, or purchase any firearm if the superior court has, pursuant to paragraph (5), found that the People of the State of California have not met their burden pursuant to paragraph (6).

(2) For each person subject to this subdivision, the facility shall immediately, on the date of admission, submit a report to the Department of Justice, on a form prescribed by the Department of Justice, containing information that includes, but is not limited to, the identity of the person and the legal grounds upon which the person was admitted to the facility.

Any report prescribed by this subdivision shall be confidential, except for purposes of the court proceedings described in this subdivision and for determining the eligibility of the person to own, possess, control, receive, or purchase a firearm.

(3) Prior to, or concurrent with, the discharge, the facility shall inform a person subject to this subdivision that he or she is prohibited from owning, possessing, controlling, receiving, or purchasing any firearm for a period of five years. Simultaneously, the facility shall inform the person that he or she may request a hearing from a court, as provided in this subdivision, for an order permitting the person to own, possess, control, receive, or purchase a firearm. The facility shall provide the person with a form for a request for a hearing. The Department of Justice shall prescribe the form. Where the person requests a hearing at the time of discharge, the facility shall forward the form to the superior court unless the person states that he or she will submit the form to the superior court.

(4) The Department of Justice shall provide the form upon request to any person described in paragraph (1). The Department of Justice shall also provide the form to the superior court in each county. A person described in paragraph (1) may make a single request for a hearing at any time during the five-year period. The request for hearing shall be made on the form prescribed by the department or in a document that includes equivalent language.

(5) Any person who is subject to paragraph (1) who has requested a hearing from the superior court of his or her county of residence for an order that he or she may own, possess, control, receive, or purchase firearms shall be given a hearing. The clerk of the court shall set a hearing date and notify the person, the Department of Justice, and the district attorney. The People of the State of California shall be the plaintiff in the proceeding and shall be represented by the district attorney. Upon motion of the district attorney, or on its own motion, the superior court may transfer the hearing to the county in which the person resided at the time of his or her detention, the county in which the person was detained, or the county in which the person was evaluated or treated. Within seven days after the request for a hearing, the Department of Justice shall file copies of the reports described in this section with the superior court. The reports shall be disclosed upon request to the person and to the district attorney. The court shall set the hearing within 30 days of receipt of the request for a hearing. Upon showing good cause, the district attorney shall be entitled to a continuance not to exceed 14 days after the district attorney was notified of the hearing date by the clerk of

the court. If additional continuances are granted, the total length of time for continuances shall not exceed 60 days. The district attorney may notify the county mental health director of the hearing who shall provide information about the detention of the person that may be relevant to the court and shall file that information with the superior court. That information shall be disclosed to the person and to the district attorney. The court, upon motion of the person subject to paragraph (1) establishing that confidential information is likely to be discussed during the hearing that would cause harm to the person, shall conduct the hearing in camera with only the relevant parties present, unless the court finds that the public interest would be better served by conducting the hearing in public. Notwithstanding any other law, declarations, police reports, including criminal history information, and any other material and relevant evidence that is not excluded under Section 352 of the Evidence Code, shall be admissible at the hearing under this section.

(6) The people shall bear the burden of showing by a preponderance of the evidence that the person would not be likely to use firearms in a safe and lawful manner.

(7) If the court finds at the hearing set forth in paragraph (5) that the people have not met their burden as set forth in paragraph (6), the court shall order that the person shall not be subject to the five-year prohibition in this section on the ownership, control, receipt, possession or purchase of firearms. A copy of the order shall be submitted to the Department of Justice. Upon receipt of the order, the Department of Justice shall delete any reference to the prohibition against firearms from the person's state mental health firearms prohibition system information.

(8) Where the district attorney declines or fails to go forward in the hearing, the court shall order that the person shall not be subject to the five-year prohibition required by this subdivision on the ownership, control, receipt, possession, or purchase of firearms. A copy of the order shall be submitted to the Department of Justice. Upon receipt of the order, the Department of Justice shall, within 15 days, delete any reference to the prohibition against firearms from the person's state mental health firearms prohibition system information.

(9) Nothing in this subdivision shall prohibit the use of reports filed pursuant to this section to determine the eligibility of persons to own, possess, control, receive, or purchase a firearm if the person is the subject of a criminal investigation, a part of which involves the ownership, possession, control, receipt, or purchase of a firearm.

(g)(1) No person who has been certified for intensive treatment under Section 5250, 5260, or 5270.15 shall own, possess, control, receive, or purchase, or attempt to own, possess, control, receive, or purchase any firearm for a period of five years.

Any person who meets the criteria contained in subdivision (e) or (f) who is released from intensive treatment shall nevertheless, if applicable, remain subject to the prohibition contained in subdivision (e) or (f).

(2) For each person certified for intensive treatment under paragraph (1), the facility shall immediately submit a report to the Department of Justice, on a form prescribed by the department, containing information regarding the person, including, but not limited to, the legal identity of the person and the legal grounds upon which the person was certified. Any report submitted pursuant to this paragraph shall only be used for the purposes specified in paragraph (2) of subdivision (f).

(3) Prior to, or concurrent with, the discharge of each person certified for intensive treatment under paragraph (1), the facility shall inform the person of that information specified in paragraph (3) of subdivision (f).

(4) Any person who is subject to paragraph (1) may petition the superior court of his or her county of residence for an order that he or she may own, possess, control, receive, or purchase firearms. At the time the petition is filed, the clerk of the court shall set a hearing date and notify the person, the Department of Justice, and the district attorney. The People of the State of California shall be the respondent in the proceeding and shall be represented by the district attorney. Upon motion of the district attorney, or on its own motion, the superior court may transfer the petition to the county in which the person resided at the time of his or her detention, the county in which the person was detained, or the county in which the person was evaluated or treated. Within seven days after receiving notice of the petition, the Department of Justice shall file copies of the reports described in this section with the superior court. The reports shall be dis-

closed upon request to the person and to the district attorney. The district attorney shall be entitled to a continuance of the hearing to a date of not less than 14 days after the district attorney was notified of the hearing date by the clerk of the court. The district attorney may notify the county mental health director of the petition, and the county mental health director shall provide information about the detention of the person that may be relevant to the court and shall file that information with the superior court. That information shall be disclosed to the person and to the district attorney. The court, upon motion of the person subject to paragraph (1) establishing that confidential information is likely to be discussed during the hearing that would cause harm to the person, shall conduct the hearing in camera with only the relevant parties present, unless the court finds that the public interest would be better served by conducting the hearing in public. Notwithstanding any other provision of law, any declaration, police reports, including criminal history information, and any other material and relevant evidence that is not excluded under Section 352 of the Evidence Code, shall be admissible at the hearing under this section. If the court finds by a preponderance of the evidence that the person would be likely to use firearms in a safe and lawful manner, the court may order that the person may own, control, receive, possess, or purchase firearms. A copy of the order shall be submitted to the Department of Justice. Upon receipt of the order, the Department of Justice shall delete any reference to the prohibition against firearms from the person's state mental health firearms prohibition system information.

(h) For all persons identified in subdivisions (f) and (g), facilities shall report to the Department of Justice as specified in those subdivisions, except facilities shall not report persons under subdivision (g) if the same persons previously have been reported under subdivision (f).

Additionally, all facilities shall report to the Department of Justice upon the discharge of persons from whom reports have been submitted pursuant to subdivision (f) or (g). However, a report shall not be filed for persons who are discharged within 31 days after the date of admission.

(i) Every person who owns or possesses or has under his or her custody or control, or purchases or receives, or attempts to purchase or receive, any firearm or any other deadly weapon in violation of this section shall be punished by imprisonment in the state prison or in a county jail for not more than one year.

(j) "Deadly weapon," as used in this section, has the meaning prescribed by Section 8100. *(AM '99)*

10980.　Aid or Public Assistance; Unlawful Acts; Punishments

(a) Any person who, willfully and knowingly, with the intent to deceive, makes a false statement or representation or knowingly fails to disclose a material fact in order to obtain aid under the provisions of this division or who, knowing he or she is not entitled thereto, attempts to obtain aid or to continue to receive aid to which he or she is not entitled, or to receive a larger amount than that to which he or she is legally entitled, is guilty of a misdemeanor, punishable by imprisonment in the county jail for a period of not more than six months, a fine of not more than five hundred dollars ($500), or by both such imprisonment and fine.

(b) Any person who knowingly makes more than one application for aid under the provisions of this division with the intent of establishing multiple entitlements for any person for the same period or who makes an application for such aid for a fictitious or nonexistent person or by claiming a false identity for any person is guilty of a felony, punishable by imprisonment in the state prison for a period of 16 months, two years, or three years, a fine of not more than five thousand dollars ($5,000), or by both such imprisonment and fine, or by imprisonment in the county jail for a period of not more than one year, or a fine of not more than one thousand dollars ($1,000), or by both such imprisonment and fine.

(c) Whenever any person has, by means of false statement or representation or by impersonation or other fraudulent device, obtained or retained aid under the provisions of this division for himself or herself or for a child not in fact entitled thereto, the person obtaining such aid shall be punished as follows:

(1) If the total amount of such aid obtained or retained is four hundred dollars ($400) or less, by imprisonment in the county jail for a period of not more than six months, a fine of not more than five hundred dollars ($500), or by both such imprisonment and fine.

(2) If the total amount of such aid obtained or retained is more than four hundred dollars ($400), by imprisonment in the state prison for a period of 16 months, two years, or three years, a fine of not more

than five thousand dollars ($5,000), or by both such imprisonment and fine; or by imprisonment in the county jail for a period of not more than one year, or a fine of not more than one thousand dollars ($1,000), or by both such imprisonment and fine.

(d) Any person who knowingly uses, transfers, acquires, or possesses blank authorizations to participate in the federal Food Stamp Program in any manner not authorized by Chapter 10 (commencing with Section 18900) of Part 6 with the intent to defraud is guilty of a felony, punishable by imprisonment in the state prison for a period of 16 months, two years, or three years, a fine of not more than five thousand dollars ($5,000), or by both such imprisonment and fine.

(e) Any person who counterfeits or alters or knowingly uses, transfers, acquires, or possesses counterfeited or altered authorizations to participate in the federal Food Stamp Program or food stamps in any manner not authorized by the Food Stamp Act of 1964 (Public Law 88-525 and all amendments made thereto) or the federal regulations pursuant to the act is guilty of forgery.

(f) Any person who fraudulently appropriates food stamps or authorizations to participate in the federal Food Stamp Program with which he or she has been entrusted pursuant to his or her duties as a public employee is guilty of embezzlement of public funds.

(g) Whoever knowingly uses, transfers, sells, purchases, or possesses food stamps or authorizations to participate in the federal Food Stamp Program in any manner not authorized by Chapter 10 (commencing with Section 18900), of Part 6, or by the federal Food Stamp Act of 1977 (Public Law 95-113 and all amendments made thereto) is; (1) guilty of a misdemeanor if the face value of the food stamps or the authorizations to participate is four hundred dollars ($400) or less, and shall be punished by imprisonment in the county jail for a period of not more than six months, a fine of not more than five hundred dollars ($500), or by both such imprisonment and fine, or (2) guilty of a felony if the face value of the food stamps or the authorizations to participate exceeds four hundred dollars ($400), and shall be punished by imprisonment in the state prison for a period of 16 months, two years, or three years, a fine of not more than five thousand dollars ($5,000), or by both such imprisonment and fine or by imprisonment in the county jail for a period of not more than one year, or a fine of not more than one thousand dollars ($1,000), or by both such imprisonment and fine.

11482. False Representation to Obtain, or Unlawful Receipt or Attempt to Receive Aid

Any person other than a needy child, who willfully and knowingly, with the intent to deceive, makes a false statement or representation or knowingly fails to disclose a material fact to obtain aid, or who, knowing he or she is not entitled thereto, attempts to obtain aid or to continue to receive aid to which he or she is not entitled, or a larger amount than that to which he or she is legally entitled, is guilty of a misdemeanor, except as specified in Section 11482.5 and shall be subject to prosecution under the provisions of Chapter 9 (commencing with Section 10980) of Part 2.

14014. Fraud to Obtain Health Care Services

(a) Any person receiving health care for which he or she was not eligible on the basis of false declarations as to his or her eligibility or any person making false declarations as to eligibility on behalf of any other person receiving health care for which that other person was not eligible shall be liable for repayment and shall be guilty of a misdemeanor or felony depending on the amount paid on his or her behalf for which he or she was not eligible, as specified in Section 487 of the Penal Code.

(b)(1) Any person who willfully and knowingly counsels or encourages any individual to make false statements or otherwise causes false statements to be made on an application, in order to receive health care services to which the applicant is not entitled, shall be liable to the Medi-Cal program for damages incurred for the cost of services rendered to the applicant.

(2) Paragraph (1) shall be implemented to the extent permitted by federal law and to the extent that implementation of paragraph (1) does not affect the availability of federal financial participation.

15630.   When Reports of Adult Abuse Are Mandatory

(a) Any person who has assumed full or intermittent responsibility for care or custody of an elder or dependent adult, whether or not that person receives compensation, including administrators, supervisors, and any licensed staff of a public or private facility that provides care or services for elder or dependent adults, or any elder or dependent adult care custodian, health practitioner, or employee of a county adult protective services agency or a local law enforcement agency is a mandated reporter.

(b)(1) Any mandated reporter, who, in his or her professional capacity, or within the scope of his or her employment, has observed or has knowledge of an incident that reasonably appears to be physical abuse, abandonment, isolation, financial abuse, or neglect, or is told by an elder or dependent adult that he or she has experienced behavior constituting physical abuse, abandonment, isolation, financial abuse, or neglect, or reasonably suspects that abuse shall report the known or suspected instance of abuse by telephone immediately or as soon as practically possible, and by written report sent within two working days, as follows:

(A) If the abuse has occurred in a long-term care facility, except a state mental health hospital or a state developmental center, the report shall be made to the local ombudsman or the local law enforcement agency.

Except in an emergency, the local ombudsman and the local law enforcement agency shall report any case of known or suspected abuse to the State Department of Health Services and any case of known or suspected criminal activity to the Bureau of Medi-Cal Fraud, as soon as is practical.

(B) If the suspected or alleged abuse occurred in a state mental health hospital or a state developmental center, the report shall be made to designated investigators of the State Department of Mental Health or the State Department of Developmental Services or to the local law enforcement agency.

Except in an emergency, the local law enforcement agency shall report any case of known or suspected criminal activity to the Bureau of Medi-Cal Fraud, as soon as is practical.

(C) If the abuse has occurred any place other than one described in subparagraph (A), the report shall be made to the adult protective services agency or the local law enforcement agency.

(2)(A) A mandated reporter who is a physician and surgeon, a registered nurse, or a psychotherapist, as defined in Section 1010 of the Evidence Code, shall not be required to report, pursuant to paragraph (1), an incident where all of the following conditions exist:

(i) The mandated reporter has been told by an elder or dependent adult that he or she has experienced behavior constituting physical abuse, abandonment, isolation, financial abuse, or neglect.

(ii) The mandated reporter is not aware of any independent evidence that corroborates the statement that the abuse has occurred.

(iii) The elder or dependent adult has been diagnosed with a mental illness or dementia, or is the subject of a court-ordered conservatorship because of a mental illness or dementia.

(iv) In the exercise of clinical judgment, the physician and surgeon, the registered nurse, or the psychotherapist, as defined in Section 1010 of the Evidence Code, reasonably believes that the abuse did not occur.

(B) This paragraph shall not be construed to impose upon mandated reporters a duty to investigate a known or suspected incident of abuse and shall not be construed to lessen or restrict any existing duty of mandated reporters.

(3)(A) In a long-term care facility, a mandated reporter shall not be required to report as a suspected incident of abuse, as defined in Section 15610.07, an incident where all of the following conditions exist:

(i) The mandated reporter is aware that there is a proper plan of care.

(ii) The mandated reporter is aware that the plan of care was properly provided or executed.

(iii) A physical, mental, or medical injury occurred as a result of care provided pursuant to clause (i) or (ii).

(iv) The mandated reporter reasonably believes that the injury was not the result of abuse.

(B) This paragraph shall not be construed to require a mandated reporter to seek, nor to preclude a mandated reporter from seeking, information regarding a known or suspected incident of abuse prior to reporting. This paragraph shall apply only to those categories of mandated reporters that the State Department of Health Services determines, upon approval by the Bureau of Medi-Cal Fraud and the state long-term care ombudsman, have access to plans of care and have the training and experience necessary to determine whether the conditions specified in this section have been met.

(c)(1) Any mandated reporter who has knowledge of, or reasonably suspects that, types of elder or dependent adult abuse for which reports are not mandated have been inflicted upon an elder or dependent adult or that his or her emotional well-being is endangered in any other way, may report the known or suspected instance of abuse.

(2) If the suspected or alleged abuse occurred in a long-term care facility other than a state mental health hospital or a state developmental center, the report may be made to the long-term care ombudsman program. Except in an emergency, the local ombudsman shall report any case of known or suspected abuse to the State Department of Health Services and any case of known or suspected criminal activity to the Bureau of Medi-Cal Fraud, as soon as is practical.

(3) If the suspected or alleged abuse occurred in a state mental health hospital or a state developmental center, the report may be made to the designated investigator of the State Department of Mental Health or the State Department of Developmental Services, or to a local law enforcement agency or to the local ombudsman. Except in an emergency, the local ombudsman and the local law enforcement agency shall report any case of known or suspected criminal activity to the Bureau of Medi-Cal Fraud, as soon as is practical.

(4) If the suspected or alleged abuse occurred in a place other than a place described in paragraph (2) or (3), the report may be made to the county adult protective services agency.

(5) If the conduct involves criminal activity not covered in subdivision (b), it may be immediately reported to the appropriate law enforcement agency.

(d) When two or more mandated reporters are present and jointly have knowledge or reasonably suspect that types of abuse of an elder or a dependent adult for which a report is or is not mandated have occurred, and when there is agreement among them, the telephone report may be made by a member of the team selected by mutual agreement, and a single report may be made and signed by the selected member of the reporting team. Any member who has knowledge that the member designated to report has failed to do so shall thereafter make the report.

(e) A telephone report of a known or suspected instance of elder or dependent adult abuse shall include the name of the person making the report, the name and age of the elder or dependent adult, the present location of the elder or dependent adult, the names and addresses of family members or any other person responsible for the elder or dependent adult's care, if known, the nature and extent of the elder or dependent adult's condition, the date of the incident, and any other information, including information that led that person to suspect elder or dependent adult abuse, requested by the agency receiving the report.

(f) The reporting duties under this section are individual, and no supervisor or administrator shall impede or inhibit the reporting duties, and no person making the report shall be subject to any sanction for making the report. However, internal procedures to facilitate reporting, ensure confidentiality, and apprise supervisors and administrators of reports may be established, provided they are not inconsistent with this chapter.

(g)(1) Whenever this section requires a county adult protective services agency to report to a law enforcement agency, the law enforcement agency shall, immediately upon request, provide a copy of its investigative report concerning the reported matter to that county adult protective services agency.

(2) Whenever this section requires a law enforcement agency to report to a county adult protective services agency, the county adult protective services agency shall, immediately upon request, provide a copy of its investigative report concerning the reported matter to that law enforcement agency.

(3) The requirement to disclose investigative reports pursuant to this subdivision shall not include the disclosure of social services records or case files that are confidential, nor shall this subdivision be construed to allow disclosure of any reports or records if the disclosure would be prohibited by any other provision of state or federal law.

(h) >Failure to report physical abuse, abandonment, isolation, financial abuse, or neglect of an elder or dependent adult, in violation of this section, is a misdemeanor, punishable by not more that six months in the county jail or by a fine of not more than one thousand dollars ($1,000), or by both that fine and imprisonment. Any mandated reporter who willfully fails to report physical abuse, abandonment, isolation, financial abuse, or neglect of an elder or dependent adult, in violation of this section, where that abuse results in death or great bodily injury, is punishable by not more than one year in a county jail or by a fine of not more than five thousand dollars ($5,000) or by both that fine and imprisonment. *(AM '99)*

15633.   Report Confidentiality; Dependent Adult Abuse

(a) The reports made pursuant to Sections 15630 and 15631 shall be confidential and may be disclosed only as provided in subdivision (b). Any violation of the confidentiality required by this chapter is a misdemeanor punishable by not more than six months in the county jail, by a fine of five hundred dollars ($500), or by both that fine and imprisonment.

(b) Reports of suspected elder or dependent adult abuse and information contained therein may be disclosed only to the following:

(1) Persons or agencies to whom disclosure of information or the identity of the reporting party is permitted under Section 15633.5.

(2)(A) Persons who are trained and qualified to serve on multidisciplinary personnel teams may disclose to one another information and records that are relevant to the prevention, identification, or treatment of abuse of elderly or dependent persons.

(B) Except as provided in subparagraph (A), any personnel of the multidisciplinary team that receives information pursuant to this chapter, shall be under the same obligations and subject to the same confidentiality penalties as the person disclosing or providing that information. The information obtained shall be maintained in a manner that ensures the maximum protection of privacy and confidentiality rights.

(c) This section shall not be construed to allow disclosure of any reports or records relevant to the reports of elder or dependent adult abuse if the disclosure would be prohibited by any other provisions of state or federal law applicable to the reports or records relevant to the reports of the abuse.

15634.   Suspected Elder or Dependent Adult Abuse Reporting; Civil or Criminal Liability of Reporting Person

(a) No care custodian, health practitioner or employee of an adult protective service agency or a local law enforcement agency who reports a known or suspected instance of elder or dependent adult abuse shall be civilly or criminally liable for any report required or authorized by this article. Any other person reporting a known or suspected instance of elder or dependent adult abuse shall not incur civil or criminal liability as a result of any report authorized by this article, unless it can be proven that a false report was made and the person knew that the report was false. No person required to make a report pursuant to this article, or any person taking photographs at his or her discretion, shall incur any civil or criminal liability for taking photographs of a suspected victim of elder or dependent adult abuse or causing photographs to be taken of such a suspected victim or for disseminating the photographs with the reports required by this article. However, this section shall not be construed to grant immunity from this liability with respect to any other use of the photographs.

(b) Any care custodian, health practitioner, or employee of an adult protective services agency or a local law enforcement agency who, pursuant to a request from an adult protective services agency or a local law enforcement agency, provides the requesting agency with access to the victim of a known or suspected instance of elder or dependent adult abuse shall not incur civil or criminal liability as a result of providing that access.

(c) The Legislature finds that, even though it has provided immunity from liability to persons required to report elder or dependent adult abuse, that immunity does not eliminate the possibility that actions may be brought against those persons based upon required reports of abuse. In order to further limit the financial hardship that those persons may incur as a result of fulfilling their legal responsibilities, it is necessary that they not be unfairly burdened by legal fees incurred in defending those actions. Therefore, a care custodian, health practitioner, or an employee of an adult protective services agency or a local law enforcement agency may present a claim to the State Board of Control for reasonable attorneys'fees incurred in any action against that person on the basis of making a report required or authorized by this article if the court has dismissed the action upon a demurrer or motion for summary judgment made by that person, or if he or she prevails in the action. The State Board of Control shall allow that claim if the requirements of this subdivision are met, and the claim shall be paid from an appropriation to be made for that purpose. Attorneys' fees awarded pursuant to this section shall not exceed an hourly rate greater than the rate charged by the Attorney General at the time the award is made and shall not exceed an aggregate amount of fifty thousand dollars ($50,000). This subdivision shall not apply if a public entity has provided for the defense of the action pursuant to Section 995 of the Government Code.

(d) Any person who fails to report an instance of elder or dependent adult abuse, as required by this article, is guilty of a misdemeanor and shall be punished by imprisonment in the county jail not exceeding six months, by a fine of not exceeding one thousand dollars ($1,000), or by both that fine and imprisonment.

15636. Withdrawal of Consent to Investigate Abuse; Dependent Adult

(a) Any victim of elder or dependent adult abuse may refuse or withdraw consent at any time to an investigation or the provision of protective services by an adult protective services agency or long-term care ombudsman program. The adult protective services agency shall act only with the consent of the victim unless a violation of the Penal Code has been alleged. A local long-term care ombudsman shall act only with the consent of the victim and shall disclose confidential information only after consent to disclose is given by the victim or pursuant to court order.

(b) If the elder or dependent adult abuse victim is so incapacitated that he or she cannot legally give or deny consent to protective services, a petition for temporary conservatorship or guardianship may be initiated in accordance with Section 2250 of the Probate Code.

15656. Injure Elder or Dependent Adult

(a) Any person who, under circumstances or conditions likely to produce great bodily harm or death, willfully causes or permits any elder or dependent adult, with knowledge that he or she is an elder or a dependent adult, to suffer, or inflicts unjustifiable physical pain or mental suffering upon him or her, or having the care or custody of any elder or dependent adult, willfully causes or permits the person or health of the elder or dependent adult to be injured, or willfully causes or permits the elder or dependent adult to be placed in a situation such that his or her person or health is endangered, is punishable by imprisonment in the county jail not exceeding one year, or in the state prison for two, three, or four years.

(b) Any person who, under circumstances or conditions other than those likely to produce great bodily harm or death, willfully causes or permits any elder or dependent adult, with knowledge that he or she is an elder or a dependent adult, to suffer, or inflicts unjustifiable physical pain or mental suffering on him or her, or having the care or custody of any elder or dependent adult, willfully causes or permits the person or health of the elder or dependent adult to be injured or willfully causes or permits the elder or dependent adult to be placed in a situation such that his or her person or health may be endangered, is guilty of a misdemeanor.

(c) Any caretaker of an elder or a dependent adult who violates any provision of law prescribing theft or embezzlement, with respect to the property of that elder or dependent adult, is punishable by imprisonment in the county jail not exceeding one year, or in the state prison for two, three, or four years when the money, labor, or real or personal property taken is of a value exceeding four hundred dollars ($400), and by a fine not exceeding one thousand dollars ($1,000), or by imprisonment in the county jail not exceeding one year, or by both that imprisonment and fine, when the money, labor, or real or personal property taken is of a value not exceeding four hundred dollars ($400).

(d) As used in this section, "caretaker" means any person who has the care, custody, or control of or who stands in a position of trust with, an elder or a dependent adult.

(e) Conduct covered in subdivision (b) of Section 15610.57 shall not be subject to this section.

R